CLAIRE PETULENGRO

HEALTH SIGNS

CLAIRE PETULENGRO

HEALTH SIGNS

Maximize Your Body's Potential
Through Your Stars

PAN BOOKS

First published 2000 by Pan Books
an imprint of Macmillan Publishers Ltd
25 Eccleston Place, London SW1W 9NF
Basingstoke and Oxford
Associated companies throughout the world
www.macmillan.co.uk

ISBN 0 330 37404 4

1 3 5 7 9 8 6 4 2

A CIP catalogue record for this book is available from
the British Library.

Typeset by SX Composing DTP, Rayleigh, Essex
Printed and bound in Great Britain by
Mackays of Chatham plc, Chatham, Kent

To my husband, Rob, for without his love and support this book would not have been written. To my mother and father, who gave me the courage to believe that anything is possible. To Bradley, for his patience.

You can do it, Louie!

And last but not least to my Take Three Guardian Angels, Vikki McIvor and Melanie Cantor, and to the wonderful Gordon Wise.

Acknowledgements

Thank you to all the staff at Parkhill Medical Practice in Torquay and to Jackie Young for their time and help in clarifying points and supplying information for this book. Eva and Leo Petulengro also went to great lengths to dig out the correct recipes for herbal potions and lotions; thank you to them for their patience, and to Bradley Tullett, who worked tirelessly to modernize so many of the recipes, and helped me keep track of my writing when I could no longer tell the difference between a hundred and a thousand words.

Contents

What's Astrology Got to do with your Health?

CHANCES ARE THAT we have all from time to time glanced at our horoscope in the newspaper, whether out of curiosity or belief. Many a person who has met a new partner has read the loved one's sign along with their own to see if the stars think they are destined to be together. Some of you will read your stars on a daily basis and pick out the bits you like, ignoring the forecast if it doesn't sound good enough. But just what is astrology, and how much deeper does it go than the predictions you read in the papers?

Astrology has been described as 'the mirror image of life upon this earth, using the patterning of the planets in our solar system'. By studying the trends of the planets, it is possible to set a pattern for our own lives, and although this pattern should not be rigidly lived by, it makes an excellent guide to how to make the most of our lives and the opportunities we have.

I'm well known as an astrologer, and I'm often stopped by strangers who say, 'Go on then, guess what sign I am.' I might look at their features to see if they have the moon face and curvy figure of the Cancer sun sign, or I might listen to their voice to see if they have the tone of the Taurus, or look for the penetrating gaze of the Scorpio. But what's important here is the reason that people stop me and ask me these questions. We can't resist a peek at our stars. We all want to know more about ourselves and the people we live with. Are we making the best of our lives and are we with the right person? Should we go for the solo career we dream of or the new house? But there's one thing we may be failing to take notice of – the link between astrology and health, and how astrology can help us feel better on the inside so that we project a better image on the outside.

My hope is that you will draw from *Health Signs* what you need to make your life a better and more productive one. You'll also discover the amazing links between your sign and the different herbs that can provide you with more energy than any modern-day drug. Herbs and plants, and even weeds, are more powerful than you realize. The common aspirin we take when we have a headache is derived from the bark of a tree. Dandelions, which most of us want to rid our gardens of, have a high content of vitamin A, four times more vitamin C than lettuce, more iron than spinach and are extremely rich in potassium. This unappreciated plant also has the amazing ability to grow almost anywhere – as gardeners know only too well! I've probably got as much to tell you on the subject of herbs as I do about the stars, as you will see when you look through the book.

My Background in Astrology

I was lucky enough to have as a mother a Romany gypsy and as a father a 'Gorger', which in our language means a non-Romany. I have seen both sides of the coin. I went to school, but there was too much going on in the family home for me to want to stay there (though I mostly did). My family are clairvoyants, more commonly called fortune-tellers. They predict the future, and I was brought up learning the arts of astrology and palmistry, and tarot-card and crystal-ball reading. This can have different effects on your social life. I have vivid memories of the children at primary school telling me that they could not come round to play with me because I was a dirty gypsy or that my mother was a witch. When I got to high school it was a different story. Everybody would crowd round at lunch times asking me to read their palms and draw up their charts to see if the boys they fancied would ever ask them out.

My grandmother, Eva Petulengro Senior, was the most fascinating person you could ever hope to meet. Born under the sign of Taurus the bull, she had four children and was a force to be reckoned with if anyone tried to interfere with her raising her family. My mother, who is also called Eva, was born in a vardo, a Romany caravan, in Spalding, Lincolnshire. It was not until my mother was twenty-two that her family first moved into bricks and mortar. They had gone to Brighton and fallen in love with the sea, especially my mother. She is a Piscean through and through and it was probably her love of water that persuaded my grandmother to make the change.

But my family never quite got used to leaving their vardos. You will often find that if a Romany has moved into a house the rest of the family will have their vardos parked closed by, even in the driveways. The need to keep the close-knit community still remains.

The Romanies are a disappearing race, and no longer travel the roads as they once did. More and more Romanies are marrying Gorgers because they do not mix enough with other Romany families. Not everyone knows that Romanies were one of Hitler's targets: he had hundreds of thousands of them killed. He, however, had astrologers on his staff – though he was not afraid to have them killed, too, if they made a prediction that was not to his liking. Winston Churchill hired his own astrologer, called Louis de Wohl, to work out Hitler's chart so that he could see on which dates Hitler would be advised to invade. Clever move, and it looks like it proved to be to the advantage of us all.

Throughout the ages astrology has gone in and out of fashion. There were times when it was thought to be the only way to live life. Henry VIII made many of his marriages and indeed decisions for the country based on the advice of astrologers. To save themselves from torture, however, his astrologers had to predict a coming child would be a boy. There have been times, too, when it has been illegal to practise astrology. Even the great Nostradamus faced charges for bringing his beliefs to the people.

The first newspaper horoscope appeared in 1899 and it certainly caught on. Modern-day astrologers are now free to practise without the restrictions and threats put on them in the past. (Except for Jersey in the Channel

Islands! Here it is illegal to give a palm or clairvoyant reading thanks to an ancient witchcraft law that has never been changed. If you take money for a reading you could be thrown into jail.)

My family came from India centuries ago and travelled over time to Britain, landing on the coast of Scotland. It is very hard to trace back a Romany family because for so long many of them could not read or write, thanks to the lack of schooling. They were also on the move a great deal. They were taught by their families the skills necessary to carry on their lifestyle, which meant only basic reading and writing. Many of the men were skilled blacksmiths and all were taught palmistry and astrology. One of the reasons why Romanies are more psychic than Gorgers is because they were not taught to believe in boundaries. The sky was the limit and you could become whatever you dreamed.

My favourite childhood memories are of all of us sleeping in one room, getting under our bedcovers and talking late into the night about tales of the past and the fascinating art of astrology. My mother brought me up to be aware of what I was feeling about myself and the people I met and I believe this is an important part of a healthy mind. If you cannot have faith in yourself and your feelings, then what or who can you trust? How many times have you thought that something was going to happen and it did? Maybe you knew you'd see your friend in town and, lo and behold, you bump into her. Maybe you knew that the shortage of cash wouldn't last long. Some say it's an angel on your shoulder looking after you. That may be so, but don't deny your own powers of intuition and sixth sense either.

My uncle Leo Petulengro is a famous palmist. When I was a little girl he used to bet me money that I could not tell him what the different lines on the hands meant. Well, this I can tell you is an excellent way to get any child to learn, although probably not the correct way as I stayed up many a night practising the names of the lines and the mounts on the hands to get the pennies from my uncle. I must say he always paid, which as you can imagine became expensive as I got older.

Herbs, Health and the Stars

Just what does all of this have to do with health and herbs? Well, Romanies travelled, and they also chose to live off the land. Herbs are the mainstay of any Romany life because without them it would be impossible to have a well-balanced diet. And the best way to use them is to link them with your star sign. For example, if you are a Taurus, you may suffer with throat problems, as Taurus rules the throat. You must be sure to avoid mucus-producing foods such as dairy produce and wheat-based foods like bread. Sodium sulphate is what the bull needs, so if you were born 21 April to 21 May, stock up on spinach and lettuce. These should ward off any looming problems. As you'll discover, there is similar advice for each sign of the zodiac.

As we move on in life and bigger and better discoveries are made, we seem also to go back more and more to ancient beliefs and alternative medicines for answers to our health and beauty problems. In recent years it has become 'trendy' to look to herbal remedies, but the Romanies have sworn by them for centuries. The rich and famous swear by their remedies made with 'real herbal extracts' but they may not realize it is far more of a luxury and a treat to make them yourself. They're also not really that exclusive – anyone can get hold of the ingredients. Skin-care recipes can take very little time to make and can give so much pleasure. You can even eat some of the face creams and masks I shall be telling you about, so give it a go!

Most of my family have lived to a very old age. Romanies tend to put this down to the herbs that they live on. If ever I had an ailment as a child, a trip to the doctor's was never first on my mother's mind. She would look at my nails and the colour of my hands. She would check my eyes and tongue and look at the colour of my skin. I never had a major illness during my childhood and, although I cannot say that my family's beliefs are the sole reason for this, I do believe that the Romany way of life is a healthy one. They have remedies for self-inflicted illnesses, such as hangovers, too!

Certain parts of the body are ruled by certain star signs. Migraine sufferers are often Aries, as Aries rules the head. People with kidney problems are usually Libra, as Libra rules the kidneys. Taurus, as we saw, often has throat problems because Taurus rules the throat. This doesn't mean that every Libra will go into hospital for a kidney operation, or that every Taurus will have throat problems – or be an excellent singer (although most of them are secret performers and are sure to be caught singing into a hairbrush!). But it does mean that a basic pattern has been established over the years and that by following certain guidelines you can become more aware of your own health disposition. This way you can improve your general health and you won't have to visit the doctor every time you feel off-colour. Of course you must go to the doctor if you think something is seriously wrong, but if you know that you are having the common cold again or your allergy to a food has brought you out in a rash, then follow the guidelines before you have to spend an hour in your local surgery.

The main part of this book is divided into the twelve signs of the zodiac, and each sign is divided into the different stages of life. If you have a baby you can see what foods are likely to improve his or her sleep; if you have teenagers, what will mellow their moods; or if you or your partner are going through the menopause, what you need to get beyond it. Certain star signs are more prone to particular problems than others. Read up who gets what and learn how to prevent it.

Understanding the Cusp and Cross-over Dates by using the Ephemerides

Most of us know what sign we were born under. However, those of us born on the cusp, the cross-over dates, are not always sure. Different literature can give different answers. I get letters from clients wanting to know which sign they are: are they Aries or Taurus, or Scorpio or Sagittarius, or whatever. For some people it's an identity crisis. Why the discrepancy? In different years the sun comes into the signs at slightly different times. If you were born on 23 September 1967, for example, you would be a Virgo. If you were born eighteen years later on the same date you would be a Libra, as that year the sun left Virgo earlier. It would take a newspaper too many of its pages to list all of the cross-over dates for all of the signs over the last hundred years. At the back of this book you will find an ephemerides, a chart which does exactly that. This will show you what sign you really are if you were born on the cusp.

Here is the general guide that you will see in most newspapers and magazines. If you are within a couple of days of the cross-over dates then check your birthdate and year in the chart at the back of the book, just to be sure.

ARIES	21 March – 20 April
TAURUS	21 April – 21 May
GEMINI	22 May – 21 June
CANCER	22 June – 23 July
LEO	24 July – 23 August
VIRGO	24 August – 23 September
LIBRA	24 September – 23 October
SCORPIO	24 October – 22 November
SAGITTARIUS	23 November – 21 December
CAPRICORN	22 December – 20 January
AQUARIUS	21 January – 19 February
PISCES	20 February – 20 March

Having Fun and your Health

Leading a healthy life doesn't mean that you can't have fun. It's all about balance. It's about what is the right diet for your time of life and your sign. If you are a Gemini who at 55 is still going out every night of the week and working the next day, you are going to feel the stresses and strains more than a 25-year-old. You will, however, take it better than most, and indeed better than a 25-year-old Pisces. You must work out your own health charts to find what your body needs. If you want to blow off a little steam every now and then, you need only to learn the word moderation. A little of what you fancy does you good, but certain star signs like to take those words to the extreme. Gemini, Scorpio, Cancer and Pisces are all very good at throwing themselves in at the deep end of life.

The word 'diet' is today always associated with losing weight, but really your diet is just what you eat. And if you are eating the right food you won't even need to think about how much you weigh, only about how you feel inside – which will, amazingly, end up showing up your dream weight on the scales as well. The majority of people who lose or gain weight do so when they are at a low ebb. How many times do you think about your weight when life is going well? Virgos are known to be the best at taking care of their health and when they do suffer from problems it is usually because they have been too busy playing Florence Nightingale to others to look after themselves.

The following list shows you which signs rule which parts of the body in astrological terms, and also how each of us looks, according to our star signs. Who knows, you could start guessing the star signs of your friends and work colleagues and end up doing a spot of predicting yourself!

Who Rules What

ARIES rules the head. You will often notice that women, in particular, of this sign go through a stage of dying their hair at some point in their life, as this is a very important part of the body to them.

TAURUS rules the throat and you can sometimes tell people born under this sign by their bull neck and their stocky posture. They also have very individual voices and are the ones that you will hear singing in the shower.

GEMINI rules the chest and shoulders. These people are known as the Peter Pans of the zodiac, looking younger and more youthful the older they get. The 30-year-old really does still look 18. They also have sparkling eyes.

CANCER rules the breasts and stomach and women who are typical of this sign will have a curvy and probably voluptuous figure – that's not to say that the men won't be curvy, too! You will also often notice a round or moon-shaped face.

LEO rules the back, spine and heart, and Leo is known as the ruler of the kingdom too. Leo's hair is very lion's mane-like, and they are proud of it.

VIRGO rules the intestines. People born under Virgo like to make sure they keep everything in good order. They are perfectionist dressers with slender, fine features.

LIBRA rules the kidneys. Those born under Libra have symmetrical yet gentle features. They are approachable, and have a warm glow about them that is sure to give them away as real softies.

SCORPIO rules the reproductive organs. Those born under Scorpio can often be found with a bump on their nose, and are most commonly recognized for their penetrating gaze that is so hard to break away from.

SAGITTARIUS rules the thighs, buttocks and pelvis. These people look like athletes, even if they're not. They also tend to do a bit of a gallop when they walk. Both men and women have something of the youthful Adonis about them.

CAPRICORN rules the bones. Those born under this sign tend to have very close-set eyes. These, like Geminis, also tend to look younger the older they get. Watch out for a slow but sure walk.

AQUARIUS rules the circulation. These people are usually very tall. Blue eyes are common in this sign and very crisp facial features.

PISCES rules the feet. Piscean eyes are usually widely spaced and watery. They have an inexplicable air about them and always turn heads when they enter a room.

Have a look around and see if friends and colleagues follow these traits. Does your Piscean boss give you an uncertain feeling because of her Piscean aura? Does your stocky-necked male Taurean friend always manage to ward off problems for you in a club? It can be great fun to guess the star signs of friends. Who knows, you may just turn out to be an expert star-sign spotter!

A Note on the Signs

At the start of each Health Sign chapter I describe the attributes of each sign of the zodiac. So that you are not confused by any astrological jargon, I should explain a few terms.

A sign's *triplicity* means the element – fire, earth, air and water – it is associated with. 'Tri', because the signs are linked in groups of three to each element. Triplicity comes into play when the spiritual and material aspects have been taken care of. It is an indicator of the level and nature of creativity we each possess.

The *fire signs*, Aries, Leo and Sagittarius, are certainly the fireworks of the zodiac. Initiators, full of enthusiasm, they live life to the full, encouraging and giving energy to others.

The *earth signs*, Taurus, Virgo and Capricorn, are the grounded elements, practical and sometimes slow-moving. They need to know all the facts before they'll make a decision to embark on something.

The *air signs*, Gemini, Libra and Aquarius, are the communicators of the zodiac, with the ability to take the fire and earth signs' ideas and put them into effect.

The *water signs*, Cancer, Scorpio and Pisces, act on their emotions and bring feeling and intuition to bear on things. They trust less in what they see and more in what they feel.

The twelve signs of the zodiac are also further defined through being grouped into three sets of four; each constituting a *quadruplicity*. Each quadruplicity has a name: *cardinal*, *fixed* and *mutable*. The quadruplicity a sign belongs to is an indicator of its qualities, the quality of our lives, and how we confront events on this earth.

The *cardinal* signs are Aries, Cancer, Libra and Capricorn. They take the lead in a situation and are brilliant at organizing other people and living life to the full, although they may not always be that organized themselves.

The *fixed* signs are Taurus, Leo, Scorpio and Aquarius. They tend to be stubborn and need a lot of emotional reassurance. Once they've made up their minds or have a set way of doing things, it's hard to get them to change!

The *mutable* signs, Gemini, Virgo, Sagittarius and Pisces, are ever versatile. Always on the lookout for the meaning of life, they also often use up more energy than they have.

Understanding Romany Health Sign Lore

The Traditions

THE ROMANIES ARE a funny old race. We try extremely hard to hold on to our lifestyle and although we have nothing against 'Gorgers' (non-Romanies) you will not normally find us mixing with them.

The reason for this is that Romanies don't want the race to die. The more Romanies mix with Gorgers the more likely it is that the race will be watered down and will eventually vanish for ever. I married out myself. I will raise our children as Romanies and will make sure that they are aware of their history, but I also know that my family line will never be what it was.

When I was a little girl I remember being introduced to the boys of my age and noticing the funny looks on the parents' faces. I was to find out in later years that they were examining me, making a judgement about my looks, character, intellect and even parenting skills, to see if I may be a suitable match in years to come for their sons. Luckily my mother did not support this tradition (she married out of our race, as I did). None the less, it is important to try to keep the race going. (I'm not talking about marrying your cousin, need I say!)

My husband's name is Rob and many of my family say that he is more like a Romany than I am. To say it was love at first sight would be an understatement. The moment we met something inexplicable clicked. I felt that I had found my place in life just by looking into his eyes, although I hadn't known before I met him that I was looking.

Of course I asked him what star sign he was. He told me he was Sagittarius. I was very surprised. Besides, I'm a Scorpio, and I did not see how I could ever feel romantically about mixing fire and water together. I asked him if I could draw up his chart and was extremely happy, ecstatic even, to find out that he was actually a fellow Scorpio. You see, my husband was born on the cusp, and had spent twenty-six years of his life believing he was a Sagittarius! I often wonder how many people go through life believing they are a sign they are not, and wondering why their character does not seem to match the one they read about. How awful to go through life with a mistaken identity.

When we got married we had two wedding ceremonies: a Church of England service and, more important to me, a Romany wedding ceremony. This was performed by my uncle Leo, and part of it involves the mixing together of a pinprick of blood. Herbs were bound around our hands and we drank for health, fertility and good luck.

Without this service, I don't think I could have really felt married. My friends commented afterwards about how romantic it was to watch a couple not only promising to be together for life but eating food from each other's hands and drinking from each other's cup. Please note: we only shared a tiny amount of blood. The idea is that it enables a true Romany's non-Romany partner to enter the race. It was *champagne* we drank from each other's cup – I don't want anyone thinking we're vampires! Herbs, you may note, also played a vital part in the ceremony of marriage. Their luck and symbolism are a vital part of the blessing for the bride and groom. They're not just good for your health!

Romany parents have always taught their children about the stars and the lines on the hands and how to live off the land. Remember, they have always been a race of people with no fixed home. It was essential to be able to look to the stars for guidance and to the land for food.

Astrology is something I have had a passion for all of my life. It's partly because all the best stories my grandmother told me when I was a child were linked to the planets and the characters who lived in the sky. This certainly made a change from Snow White and the Seven Dwarfs! One of the stories was about Aries the ram. My grandmother used to tell me how Phrixus sacrificed the golden ram on which he had escaped the evil designs of his stepmother. The place where the sacrifice was carried out and the golden fleece hung was the grove of Ares. The sacred ram had been sent by Hermes to fly Phrixus and his sister Helle to sanctuary in the city of Colchis. Helle fell off into a river en route (called as a result Hellespont). I could lie in bed for hours and listen to these tales, which were a lot more interesting than the tales my friends were hearing.

There's another fairy tale I often heard when I was young about the Romanies being blacksmiths who would not give the soldiers the third nail for the cross of Jesus when they found out what the nails were being used for. For this they were cursed to wander the land and never settle. That is why many Romanies wear a necklace with a nail in it. I cannot vouch for this story. All I know is that I heard it quite a few times when I was growing up.

When my ancestors wanted to set up home in a new place they would pick somewhere for the land around and what it could produce. My mother often used to go to bed not knowing where she would wake up and was most shocked once to be woken up by a cow with its head stuck in the vardo window licking her face! When they moved on again they would always leave the land in a good state so the herbs could carry on growing. In fact many a landowner who allowed my family to stay on his land commented that we left the land in a better state than it was before we arrived. We would care for the land and sometimes plant herbs in case another family came by.

Today we often hear of travellers causing havoc and leaving the places where they stay in a bad state, and it upsets me that this is what some people think Romanies do. But Romanies and travellers are not the same. Romanies are an age-old race who have certain traditions and beliefs and who abide by very important unwritten laws. Travellers are usually not gypsies, but people who choose to pack up and live off the land. They could be from any race and of any religion. When you see the filth some travellers live in, believe me that this could not be further from what a real Romany's home would look like.

You will never step into a cleaner place than a vardo. It is a Romany's pride and joy. All Romanies are taught that when you live in a small space it is essential to keep it spotless. It is a showpiece. When you travel from place to place you need meeting points at certain times of the year, where you know you will find other families. On these occasions it is a bit of competition to see who has done the most with their homes. Appleby Fair, which still takes place in Cumbria every June, used to be one of the main meeting places for catching up on news and showing off what you had done to your vardo. You could often tell which family were in residence simply by the colour of their wagons because each family had its own colour scheme. But year after year you see less and less pure-bred Romanies there. The Fair has been protected since the granting of a Royal Charter by James II in 1685.

The vardo where my mother was born is now on National Trust land on Farthey Island in Essex and is looked after very well by the people who live there. It is not painted in her family colours any longer but it still has a magical feel about it whenever I visit it. You can imagine the family taking to the road and living out of what is a surprisingly small space. Maybe this is why Romanies are so close. They don't have room for any secrets. You certainly couldn't sneak someone home, even for a cup of tea, without waking up your parents. I actually did a cookery programme in the vardo five years ago to show people how you could prepare and cook food while on the road. The 'belly box' at the back of the vardo is used to store food, and is large enough to store more than my larder can!

At the end of the filming I actually found it hard to leave behind what had been a part of my mother's childhood. It was only with the knowledge that it was on protected ground with a loving family to care for it that I could walk away that day.

When many people think of a Romany they think of hooped gold earrings. The reason Romanies wear lots of gold is because when they used to travel, they didn't use banks. They would put their money into gold so that if hard times came along they could simply sell some of it, and what better place to keep it than in your ears and round your neck? Although with time they did use banks, you will still see Romanies with gold sovereigns and hooped gold earrings. Newborn children are given gold sovereigns. I was given mine by my Aunt Adeline when I was born and when I was sixteen my mother and father had it put on a gold chain for me. You will also find that Romanies collect valuable plates like Crown Derby. They like to display them in their vardos. For our wedding Rob and I were given beautiful Mason's Ironstone dinnerware by all of my relations. As the gifts continue the tradition lives on, the reason for them as practical as they are symbolic.

Travelling the road is very different to how it used to be, of course. A lot of Romanies couldn't read or write, so they didn't go by the road signs that we would now look for. If you were going to a horse fair or even to a funeral you would know which way the other families had gone by a symbol placed on the road, such as clumps of grass piled in a certain position. I often wonder if to be true to my roots I should set off with my husband and take to the road like my mother, grandmother, great-grandmother – indeed all of my ancestors. But the truth is that the world is not the same as it was fifty years ago. Even twenty years ago people in houses would leave their back doors open or the key under the mat, but most people wouldn't dream of doing that now. The world has changed and with it our notions of security, and travelling around the country in a vardo is unlikely to be as friendly as it once was. Certainly the way you would be received has changed; I blame this partly on the ever-growing number of travellers, who can behave like squatters.

In their own right, astrologers haven't always been popular. In the 1600s William Lilly became famous . . . for getting all of his predictions completely wrong. He did, however, successfully predict both the Great Plague and the Fire of London. The only problem was that, because his past predictions had not been accurate, he was arrested and accused of starting the fire to make his prediction come true! He was later freed, but it must have been tough trying to prove your science in those days if that was the sort of attitude you faced.

Understanding What your Body Needs

Each of our signs is governed by our ruling planet and also whether we are an earth, air, fire or water sign dictates how certain things help and even hinder us in our lives. For example, the water signs of the zodiac, Cancer, Scorpio and Pisces, oddly enough are lousy drinkers. When you get to know your sign you can start to feed your body what it needs to be at its best. To help you, I've included recipes that my family have used for centuries, those for specific signs of the zodiac and those which anyone can use. If followed properly these recipes should make you feel stronger both mentally and physically. However, I ought to preface these with a story handed down from my great-great-grandmother.

Being an expert in herbs and potions my great uncle Alga (whose nickname was 'the fish' because he could drink so much) was always being called upon to give advice for people's ailments. One day he had been to the public house in the town they were staying and was, as my grandmother used to say, too *motte* (drunk!). His cheeky sense of humour got the better of him when a local man with receding hair asked him if the Romanies had a cure for baldness. By way of a joke, Uncle Alga told him that he must go to the local farmer's cow field, take some cow dung – it had to be steaming – and place it on his head. This, he said, would surely cure the man's problem. Well, the man did it, and the strangest thing was that he actually began to grow hair! Pretty soon the other men of the village were *paying* the farmer for his steaming cow dung. My great-great-grandfather insisted on leaving the town the following year because he was so embarrassed at what Alga had done to this poor man. Who knows – it could have been the herbs the cows had eaten from the fields that stimulated the man's hair growth. But it didn't work on anybody else who tried it, and I most definitely don't recommend you try that one at home.

Stress and Sleeplessness: A Practical Application of Herbal Medicine

The first step to a better life is listening to what your body is telling you. These days stress is an everyday part of life and many of us find it impossible to make time in our busy schedules for relaxing, what with jobs, homes and families to juggle. It is enough to drive the sanest insane. For some of us relaxing is also work, because looking after the family and enjoying a meal with friends means that you are once again putting others first.

Often, stress manifests itself in sleeplessness. We've all been there, when your bed is soft, you're warm, but it's four in the morning and you're wide awake and staring at the ceiling. Many people who tell their doctor that they have trouble sleeping are immediately put on sleeping tablets, but there are far better and less addictive ways of getting a good night's sleep. If you use sleeping pills you may be asking for more trouble than you realize, because you will wake up feeling drowsy and cloudy-minded.

Sleep should come in stages. When a person begins to fall asleep, their body experiences a slight decrease in temperature, blood pressure and heart rate. The mind relaxes and this is the first stage of sleep. As the bodily processes slow down even more, the sleeping pattern passes through more stages until the final, heavenly, deep-sleep stage is reached. This is what is known as orthodox sleep. After deep sleep the body starts to become more active. While you are still sleeping the heart rate increases, sexual organs are aroused and the eyeballs dart backward and forward behind closed lids. This rapid eye movement (REM) occurs when you are dreaming. Throughout the night deep sleep alternates with REM sleep, with deep sleep gradually becoming less frequent. Many scientists believe that both forms of sleep are essential to good health.

Herbal teas can encourage an excellent night's sleep. The soporific effects of herbs have been known and used for thousands of years in China, Greece and Egypt. Herbal teas are made from infusions of the dried roots, leaves or flowers of herbs. Use them just like ordinary tea leaves but without adding milk or sugar. The taste may take some time to get used to after your normal teabags but after a while you will become hooked and can work your way through the flavours, discovering the different blends. If you find them too unpalatable at first, add a touch of honey.

Valerian (which was called 'all-heal' in medieval times) is an excellent herb to aid relaxation and sleep. The root provides one of the best herbal sedatives. It is at its most effective when drunk as a cold tea. Melissa, or lemon balm, is one of the earliest known medicinal herbs. A relaxing tea can be made using its dried leaves. Camomile tea is also very popular and if you want to try making it yourself from the herb, use dried flower heads. It has exceptionally soothing effects, especially on the digestion. A pillow filled with hops is also a good way to encourage sleep. It has a very distinct smell. If you have a child who cannot sleep, try giving them orange-flower water to drink. Cowslip is very good too (especially if you are in pain or have arthritis) – turn to page 57 for my recipe for making your own cowslip tea.

Here are some others you can try: California poppy, kava, sweet woodruff, wild passionflower, lavender, Scotch pine, lime blossom, fennel and peppermint. Health food shops will sell most of these in teabag form, or you can make an infusion from fresh or dried herbs. One teaspoon of the herb will do per cup of hot water.

If you decide to consult a homeopath you may even be sent away with a measure of coffee-bean extract, which contains caffeine – according to homeopathy what can cause sleeplessness can also cure it. No, don't go reaching for the wine. That leads to snoring, and will not give you a properly rested sleep.

If you are also able to finish your evening off with a herbal bath containing camomile, lavender or orange blossom, you should wake up ready to take on the world – or even a day with the family.

Of these herbs that help set up a better sleeping pattern, all are suitable for every star sign. You will find that certain herbs suit you better than others and if you read the chapter on your sign you can see what your lucky herb is. If you keep a clipping or even plant a bush of your lucky herbs and plants you should find life starts to take on a more tranquil feeling. Don't be afraid of trusting and learning to listen to your body. If you cannot sleep well at night then it is hard to get anything done, as a tired mind and body can trigger off many other problems including depression and mood swings.

You will find lots of recipes in this book for age-old herbal preparations, and I discuss the Romany use of herbs in more detail at the end of the book. If you decide to make up some of these preparations, bear in mind that they won't last for ever! Don't make up too big a batch, take them regularly as instructed, and make up a fresh batch if they have gone at all stale.

I believe that taking pharmaceutical drugs is rarely the right answer. Did you know the word 'drug' comes from the Saxon 'dregen' which means to dry? Drugs originally were dried herbs, which was what a medical person centuries ago would prescribe for someone who was ill. The word means something rather different now. I am not against modern drugs: I am grateful that ailments can now be cured which years ago would have meant a shortened life for the sufferer. But I do think it's important to recognize and use the old methods that have been tried and tested for centuries, especially to help us in our day-to-day living when we just need to cope.

Health Signs Research

As I've said, the Romany people believe that for most natural complaints there are remedies and antidotes supplied by nature. This belief is derived from experience. For centuries our people have wandered across Europe and when someone fell ill there was no doctor on hand to tend them. Consequently we had to devise our own cures for many ailments, and we used materials nearest to nature – herbs.

Herbs of course are the basis of many modern medicines, and herbal cures are still widely stocked and sold by herbalists, chemists and even supermarkets. Our own cures are the result of a mixture of years of experience and scraps of knowledge gleaned from other people as we travelled.

Eventually from our experiments successful herbal cures emerged and were passed down from generation to generation. In recent years people seem to have become much more health conscious, and since there is a definite link between health and astrology there are also different herbs which apply to each sign's particular weaknesses. I will tell you later in this book where they can be found and how to apply them. My people have used these recipes for centuries and they have definitely proved their worth. Nowadays, however, my people take their herbs and vitamins alongside each other as they recognize that both are valuable.

Vitamins were first identified in 1906. The two most important facts to know about vitamins are, firstly, that they are not capable of being produced by the body itself and, secondly, that they are essential for the body's metabolism. Their use today is widespread and vitamins are recognized as an important part of modern-day health.

The Queen and the Queen Mother have been taking herbs and vitamins for years. It was actually a heroine of the Romanies, Dame Barbara Cartland, who encouraged many of the Royals to try the remedies that my family swear by. (Barbara Cartland lobbied to have the law changed in 1964 with regard to sites for Gypsies so that their children could go to school. She also founded the Cartland Onslow Romany Trust with a private site in Hatfield for families of Romany Gypsies and is the founder and president of the national association for health. This is someone who respected the Romanies and their knowledge and folklore. She has worked to bring to people's attention the good that my people can do and I hope she has been recognized for this.)

There are many other celebrities who swear by vitamins and herbs. Mel Gibson attributes his good health to vitamins and in 1993 forked out $250,000 to defend consumers' rights against US threats to ban over-the-counter vitamins. There's one celebrity who certainly believed they were worth their claims. Even Baroness Thatcher the ex-prime minister thanks vitamins for her stamina and strength.

To supplement my other research, before I sat down to write this book I carried out a survey to see just what it was that people are suffering from and if I could prove a link between certain star signs and certain conditions or problems. In order to get a good cross section I canvassed people who worked in high-street shops, housewives, schoolteachers, builders, television companies, producers, pop singers, actors, retired couples and other groups of the population. Please bear in mind that my research is based on the health problems people had and I did not take into account the many star signs that were fit and well when I questioned them. This is what I found.

People born under the sign of Aries seemed to suffer mostly from eczema, irritable bowel syndrome, strokes, heart attacks, angina and asthma. This sign is very prone to stress and if they allow problems to get the better of them then various ailments can arise. But you cannot live a perfect life eating the right thing day and night, we all have our vices and slip up from time to time, so do not be too hard on yourself. I was surprised that this sign suffered from as much asthma as they did; usually the ram is prone to migraines rather than having problems associated with breathing. The people that did suffer from headaches also listed a large chocolate and caffeine intake, so if you are prone to headaches it may be worth cutting down on both to see if this eases any problems. Clumsiness was common and it's likely you will see more of the Aries child in the emergency room suffering from cuts and sprained ankles than any other sign. I also found that the Aries who filled in their forms had more hurried writing than most of the other signs, which could be because they are always in a rush.

People born under the sign of Taurus appeared to suffer from a lot of stress, which is not usually a major problem for the bull. The reason behind this seemed to be to do with their figures and sudden weight loss or gain. My feeling is that by following these rapid weight-loss programmes this food-loving sign is likely to have tried diets that they cannot stick to. Diets are about a lifestyle and not about a week of crash dieting, especially if you are sun sign Taurus. You love your food too much. Throat problems were common and usually the Taureans that smoked were all making an effort to give up. Asthma was present with around 20 per cent of the people questioned and it generally seemed to get worse when under pressure or in stressful situations.

People born under the sign of Gemini found that their busy lives dictated most of the problems and many complained that there were 'not enough hours in the day'. Dermatitis was another problem mentioned and could well link to the high stress levels and busy schedules. Thirty per cent said that they had eyestrain but had not been to the opticians in over a year, so that may be due to poor eyesight. Don't forget to give Gemini children plenty of vitamin A, which helps with the eyes, skin and growth.

People born under the sign of Cancer suffered from quite a few thrush-related problems, especially those in their late teens and early twenties. Cancerians love to look good and it may be that they are tempted to squeeze into tight outfits which exacerbate this problem. Back problems, hayfever, sinusitis, IBS and arthritis were also common. It may well be the emotional nature of this sign that led many of the people questioned to have problems that do not always fall under the rulership of their sign. If you are a Cancerian try to make sure that you keep a check between real and imaginary problems. Liver problems that Cancerians were prone to occurred mainly in the over eighties.

People born under the sign of Leo did list heart problems as the most common ailment, and, although they were not always major problems, it did show that this is their weakest point. Try to watch out for high blood pressure and guard against fatty foods. You can read up on which foods are best for you under your sun sign chapter. Asthma was another problem and I put this down to the fact that many of us are just living in the wrong climate for our elements. On the whole Leos did seem to have the best health with the least number of allergies. Their ruling planet the sun makes stresses and pressures more likely to come out instead of being locked up as some of the other signs do. This, along with the fact that they cannot hide the way they are feeling for too long, probably helps their health.

People born under the sign of Virgo found that hypertension, osteoarthritis, hayfever and paladrumic rheumatism were the biggest problems. This was overall the healthiest of all the signs questioned and, as they are known as the sign most likely to 'cry wolf', I was quite surprised to find that they were so honest with their answers as they are known to be hypochondriacs. Throat problems were not as frequent as I expected and this may well be because more Virgos now are aware of the dangers of smoking and seem to be well informed. In fact, some Virgoans I spoke to were more informative about health than a group of trainee nurses I talked to. Part of the reason that Virgos get problems treated quicker is that they are the first to run to the doctor or to tell friends if they are not feeling well.

People born under the sign of Libra listed anaemia, cancer, skin and food allergies. The people that had listed problems with cancer were mostly in their eighties. Kidney problems were also present in the older generations which surprised me, although the under thirties did admit that they drank too much and suffered from pains around the stomach and abdomen which could be the kidneys crying out for water (although there are other diagnoses). Just try to make sure that you don't overindulge and that you don't punish a body that has to last you for many years to come.

People born under the sign of Scorpio had had more hysterectomy operations than any other sign. They also listed gall bladder problems and IBS. On the lower scale we also saw a greater number of chicken pox sufferers below the age of ten. This is a sign that is likely to be prone to thrush and problems around the generative organs, but perhaps because we are so much better informed and aware of our bodies, this sign is obviously taking heed more than any of the zodiac signs and knows what to guard against. Indeed, it was Cancerians who were more prone to thrush, perhaps because they least expect it and don't take steps to prevent it, e.g. over-perfumed soaps, etc. Other surveys have shown Scorpios and Cancerians to be very thrifty, and fewer money worries can mean less stress.

People born under the sign of Sagittarius found varicose veins, IBS, heart attacks and cancer to have been the most common cause of problems. The archer has always been known to have an athletic-looking figure so I was surprised to see that they were so worried about their legs. The number that had treatment was very few and I can't help thinking that it was vanity speaking and that their legs were likely to be in better shape than Tina Turner's, who incidentally is a Sagittarian.

People born under the sign of Capricorn found hayfever, asthma, bowel cancer, blocked arteries and a small percentage found problems with losing weight. This sign is known to love their food and many Capricorns listed bad eating habits, some even eating three main large meals a day. Fry-ups were a favourite for breakfast and some rethinking on dietary needs is definitely needed for the majority. Fifteen per cent had received cosmetic surgery on their teeth and as teeth problems are common in Capricorns it was difficult to work out whether it was through vanity or necessity.

People born under the sign of Aquarius found strokes, gynaecological problems, ulcerative colitis, angina, heart and blood problems, prickly heat and heartburn to be their main health complaints. This may sound quite serious but it was in actual fact the prickly heat and heartburn that came out as the biggest complaint. Just make sure that you watch circulation and what types of shoes you wear – a small percentage of Aquarians found problems had developed through wearing ill-fitting shoes over a period of years.

People born under the sign of Pisces had heart problems, circulatory problems and asthma. The circulatory problems were not clear whether they related to the feet or not, which come under the rulership of Pisces. Rheumatism was only in the over fifties and in general the main worry was that they drunk too much, which knowing the sign of the fish they probably did. Interestingly, Pisceans are evidently prone to higher credit card expenditure than any other sign of the zodiac (according to a national newspaper survey). This can of course lead to stress-related problems if the debts mount up. I expected to see more extremes for this sign and I can't help suspecting that there were quite a few Pisceans who left out a few too many of the questions!

I wish you *kooshti sante*, which is Romany for good health, and hope that you can find the time to start to listen to what your body needs and what works for you and your star sign.

Healthy Eating for your Star Sign

IT IS IMPORTANT that we all try to follow a balanced lifestyle and diet throughout our lives no matter what age or stage we may be at. But with the pressures that modern life can bring it is very easy to forget what we should be eating and drinking. But there are things we can all include in our diet to improve our energy levels and make our lives better, as well as the recommendations you'll find listed in your star sign chapter.

Lots of other books will guide you towards what is healthy for your diet, so I'm not going to repeat all their advice here. It's important to understand what certain sorts of food do to and for your system. But certainly the most important steps to a healthy mind and body are regular exercise and a healthy diet. A little bit of what you fancy can do you good from time to time, but the real key is not to overindulge. Try to eat plenty of fruit and vegetables – and organic, where possible. Include them at every meal. Bread, rice, pasta and potatoes are staple foods, which are all naturally low in fat. They contain carbohydrate, which has less than half the calories of the same weight of fat but fills you up just as well. These foods will satisfy your hunger for longer than a quick chocolate bar. Use staple foods as the basis of your meal and have small portions of meat, fish and cheese. Meals made up of mostly cheese or meat will only give you indigestion.

Cereals are also great for the morning for all the signs as they hold the key to having healthy bowels. They are also fortified with vitamins and minerals, to supplement those you take in through other healthy foods (although ideally you want to choose foods where these are occurring naturally), and are high in fibre. Watch out for the chocolate-covered cereals though: if you get stuck into these you are really missing the point. They should only be used as a teaser to get young children into the idea of cereals. Watch out for the sugar content.

Fat is quite a frightening word but we all need a certain amount of it in our diet, especially the essential fatty acids found in evening primrose, borage and olive oils, and fish oils. The problem is that most people tend to eat too much and of the wrong sort. Try to use cooking fats and oils sparingly and don't feel that you have to soak your food in it. Put foods into hot oil if you are going to fry; if you don't you'll end up marinating your food in the oil and then ingesting too much fat. Experiment with boiling, grilling, steaming and baking too. You'll be able to taste the flavour of the foods much more, instead of disguising everything with oils. If you eat meat that is high in its own natural fats and then you cook it in oil, you're heading for overkill. Try to spread breads with only a modest amount of butter. Most books on healthy eating will explain the 'good' and 'bad' fats to you.

Certain star signs are more likely to indulge in

overeating than others. Taureans and Librans see food as art and cannot resist an appetizing dish, even if they have already eaten. It is not good for a Pisces to overindulge as they put on weight in strange places. One too many chocolate eclairs can end up looking like ten. Pisces likes to snack and my advice for them is to avoid going to the supermarket hungry, and always take a list. After all, if it's not in your cupboard you cannot eat it. Aries are quite lucky as they tend to burn off most of their fat, but they do have problems with eating foods that can cause headaches. They also suffer a weakness for chocolate . . .

In today's Western world the availability (or over availability) of foods can turn all of us into gluttons. Treating food as a delicacy can be much more fun and is certain to leave you with more energy to enjoy the other aspects of life. You will never feel full after a packet of crisps but you'll always feel guilty!

Red meat is an important source of iron and other nutrients but it can also be very rich in fat, so trim excess fat from your meat before you cook it. Pulses are a good alternative to meat and are extremely popular with Virgos and Scorpios. Add pulses to your casseroles, or use soya (but avoid anything that is known to be genetically modified!), which is fairly widely available in supermarkets. This reduces the fat level and makes the meat go a lot further. Housewives of years ago used to use soya without telling their husbands when they needed to make a meal go further than their budgets would allow. Many men spent the 1960s eating shepherd's pie with both mince and soya in and never even knew it. Pulses are fun to cook with and also provide fibre, which helps reduce the amount of cholesterol in the blood.

Oily fish provides the essential fatty acids that can help protect you from heart disease so try to discover the pleasures of fish like herring and mackerel, or try vegetarian sources such as linseeds sprinkled on to your food. Fish is especially good for subjects born under the signs of Leo and Scorpio. It really is all about experimenting and making the effort to put the foods that you need into dishes that you find appealing. When my brother Bradley was younger he refused to eat potatoes. I remember asking him when I was about eight why he ate mashed potatoes if he didn't like potatoes and he said to me, 'Don't be silly, they're not potatoes, they're mash, that's different.' Like a fool I told him the truth and he stopped eating them. But my point is that if you don't like the idea of something, turn it into something you *do* like.

White fish, chicken and turkey can be low in fat too. With poultry, go for the most naturally reared possible. The key though really is to eat in moderation, and if you are cooking for one, learn the art of freezing. It is all too easy to stuff yourself with seconds and thirds for fear of wastage.

Dairy produce, fish, vegetables, soya, pulses and sesame seeds are all good sources of calcium and are vital for healthy bones and teeth. It is especially important that Taureans and Capricorns get enough calcium. All children need a good intake of calcium and magnesium to build healthy teeth and bones. If you are worried about having too much fat in your diet, then use low-fat milks instead. They contain similar amounts of calcium as the full-cream versions. Again, opt for organic if possible.

Regular teeth-brushing is vital if you want to be able to enjoy the taste of your food until a ripe old age. Capricorn children are the worst at cleaning their teeth. Sugars in food supply our mouths with bacteria, which produce the acid that attacks the tooth enamel. Saliva promotes the repair process that prevents cavities from forming in your mouth. Flossing is something that too many of us are embarrassed to do but could save us from the embarrassment of having to have those lovely pearly whites taken out!

Alcohol and your Sign

Water signs – Cancer, Scorpio and Pisces – are the worst drinkers of the zodiac, I'm afraid, because it hits them like a train, though they will deny that they are drunk even when unable to stand up.

Health authorities say that if you are a woman you should drink no more than 14 units per week and if a man no more than 21. (One unit is half a pint of beer or lager, and that does not include the extra-strong varieties. One glass of wine or measure of spirit is equal to one unit also.) However, not all men are the same shape and size and neither are all women. After all, give a Libran woman a pint of lager and a Cancerian man the same and I can assure you that it will be the woman who will still be standing and able to drink another. What the guidelines offer is a general rule of thumb for the average person.

You can tell an Aries as he's the one shouting, 'One for the road,' and believe me it's a very long road by the time he's ready to go. Geminis will turn into the life and soul of the party, and Leos will look exactly the same no matter how much they've had. The only way you'll be able to tell that they've had a drink is that they'll start telling you their life story, which can mean you won't get away until daybreak.

It's up to you to know how drink affects you individually. It's not just about what is good for your body, it's about how alcohol affects you mentally. If you get aggressive or depressed, then don't bother with it. Alcohol can be a depressant. If you are not feeling on top form or if you have had an illness, you must avoid alcohol until you feel you can cope with its effects. You must learn your own limit. If you are honest with yourself you will know when you have had your limit and when you are acting in a way that you are not really proud of. But don't forget to look up my star sign drink recipes and hangover cures, just in case.

Stress and your Sign

Stress is a modern-day killer. High blood pressure, heart trouble, stomach ulcers, headaches, insomnia and so forth are believed to be at least partly due to an impaired nervous system caused by the stress and tension of today's demands. The signs most prone to stress and nervous tension are Aries, Gemini and Aquarius. Many medical people believe that a harmonious functioning of the nervous system and a well-balanced emotional disposition are essential to good health, so if you are Aries, Gemini or Aquarius, make sure that you are eating the right foods and deflecting any stress you may be facing. Dealing with problems on your own is not the way forward, as you must have learnt by now, so try to share your difficulties.

Yin and Yang

We've probably all heard of these terms but not all of us know what they mean. Yin and Yang are all about the combining of energies and the creation of the equal balance that we need for the world to work. Yin is female and is sensitive, intuitive and feeling. It creates through fusion and preserves and builds. Yang is masculine and is vibrant and self-assured. On their own they are nothing. Together they allow life to work. The yang force allows the solid yin to work. Something that is solid such as the heart is a yin organ but its yang quality is what allows a human to function. Solid things are often yin with yang its working part. Each star sign is also either yin or yang. Here is your guide to compatibility:

Aries	Yin
Taurus	Yang
Gemini	Yin
Cancer	Yang
Leo	Yin
Virgo	Yang
Libra	Yin
Scorpio	Yang

Sagittarius	Yin
Capricorn	Yang
Aquarius	Yin
Pisces	Yang

Foods also differ in their emotional, spiritual, mental and physical effects: yin foods expand energy; yang contracts it. Certain foods are specifically associated with particular yin and yang qualities. If you want to explore yin/yang healthy eating further – what to boost and what to counterbalance – you can take my Health Sign information and combine it with the ancient Chinese wisdom which explores it more fully. You will find books on this in many health food shops, or in a good bookstore.

The Right Health Signs Remedy for the Right Time of Life

Pregnancy and Childcare

HOW CAN YOU know exactly what is and isn't right for a new baby? Certain star signs take to pregnancy and childbirth better than others but I feel that every star sign has enough special qualities to enable them to fulfil the role of mother or father to perfection. Librans, it is said, make the best fathers, but Geminis will always talk to their children as an equal no matter what age they are. It is up to you to use the qualities of your star sign to be the best you can – read on to find these out!

Just as each adult is individual, so is each child. A mother of four children is sure to tell you that each child was a very different experience and required a different sort of care. You can read about how your child will grow up in the chapter for their sign.

But first things first! What should you be putting into your body before you have conceived, whatever your sign?

Folic acid is now commonly known to be essential. A daily intake of 400 microgrammes is advised preconceptually and up to the twelfth week of pregnancy for healthy development of the baby's nervous system. It is available in tablet form but can also be found in brewer's yeast (Marmite), green vegetables, potatoes, liver, nuts and seeds. Have a test from your health care practitioner to see if you are lacking anything and to make sure that your rubella inoculation is up to date.

In the womb your baby has only one source of nutrients to rely on: you! So eat as well as you can. Try to reduce your intake of sugary and salty foods. This can be particularly hard for Taurus, Virgo and Capricorn, who are tempted to use pregnancy as an excuse to eat what they want, and not what their baby needs.

Try to avoid convenience foods that have been highly processed. (For the Gemini in a hurry this may prove rather difficult!) If you don't have time or simply don't enjoy cooking fresh foods, find a family member or friend who is willing to prepare them for you. I cannot stress enough how important this is, perhaps more than you could ever imagine. That fresh carrot has so many more vitamins than the frozen version, even after cooking. If you have saved time by one-stop shopping at a supermarket, you can find time to prepare fresh vegetables. Don't forget, by the way, to pick up some fruit while you're there. You can find out what are the best fruits for your sign in your individual chapter. Your senses will be heightened during pregnancy and you should find that the taste of fresh fruit and vegetables will tantalize your tastebuds.

Cooked meats from supermarkets should also be avoided. They may contain bacteria that can reach your baby. If you fancy some cold chicken then you are going to have to plan ahead and cook it the day before. No matter what sign you are, you are sure to enjoy your own food more than something a stranger has prepared. Have a look at what I've said in The Romany Use of Herbs, and see if any of the ideas there appeal to your tastebuds. These recipes could seduce you into cooking! Once you taste the aroma and smells of home-made food you'll never go back to convenience or take-away fast foods.

Calcium is important for the healthy development of your baby's bones and teeth. You will probably need twice as much as normal. Great sources of this are yoghurt, leafy green vegetables and some dairy products, including milk and cheese (but not in excess to prevent digestive upset), although you should avoid soft cheese or cheese made from unpasteurized milk as these may carry bacteria to your unborn child. (See also page 37.)

However, protein is vital, and your needs will increase with each month of pregnancy. Eat a variety of protein-rich food: fish, meat, nuts, pulses and most dairy foods. Animal fats are not so good for you, though, so eat only lean cuts of your favourite meats.

Iron is another essential mineral during pregnancy and your baby will need to build up a store of it too. The extra blood your body produces during this time needs the extra iron so that it can carry oxygen. We have all heard about pregnant women craving strange foods. This is almost invariably for a good reason, and it may, for example, be about getting enough iron. When a pregnant woman craves a delicious piece of dark chocolate it is not just because of its sweet taste – dark chocolate is also a fantastic source of iron. Iron can also be found in leafy green vegetables, but let's face it, that's not half as much fun as reaching for the bar of dark chocolate. If you are anaemic, though, please visit your doctor and have him or her run some tests and prescribe for you exactly what your body needs. Liquid iron tonics are available, and a good intake of vitamins B12 and C are essential for iron absorption.

We all fancy what we can't have and the key to avoiding alcohol during pregnancy is to give yourself other treats instead. My friend who is a keen wine-drinker chose to drink her soft drinks out of her best cut-crystal wine glasses to make them into something special. And buy good soft drinks. Admire the colour and smell just as you would with a good bottle of wine. Some soft drinks that you buy in health food shops can cost almost as much as a bottle of wine anyway!

A juicing machine is also a good investment. An expectant mother can juice the hours away discovering different concoctions. There are plenty of juicing recipes throughout this book but the best for you are those in your sun sign chapter. If you know the exact date that your baby is due to be born then why not try making the appropriate fruit cocktail for him or her to drink on their behalf? This is also an excellent way of seducing a late baby from the womb.

Caffeine should be avoided or at least limited to less than four cups of tea or coffee a day. As a stimulant, it is thought it can make your baby's heart beat faster. It also has a very bad effect on the digestive system. You could try changing over to herbal teas (but not acidic fruit teas), which don't contain caffeine. Raspberry-leaf tea is actually known for easing labour pains but it can precipitate labour, so beware. It's an excellent post-pregnancy tonic.

Health Signs

If you can eat a balanced diet with plenty of fresh food, avoiding processed convenience foods, you probably won't need to take extra supplements. However, many of us find it impossible to make enough time to invest in our bodies and health, so we turn to the convenience of easily available vitamin supplements. If you're on any sort of income support you should be able to get your vitamins and folic acid free from your doctor.

Listen to your body. It will often tell you what it needs. So if you have conceived a child and fancy a pizza with bananas and chocolate on top, go ahead and order it!

Teenagers

We all remember the emotional teenage years. It seems silly now that we could have worried so much about such inconsequential things. Would he call? Does he like me? Do I look too fat? Do I look too thin? But the truth is that, when a teenager, problems are serious and emotions are strong. It is vital that parents respect the bad mood or down spell their teenager is going through. If you laugh at them the first time they burst into tears because a friend has let them down, then you are unlikely to be confided in again. Virgo, Cancer, Scorpio and Pisces are wise old souls who spend most of their teen years wishing they were older and most of their forties wishing they were sixteen again. Every age should be valued, and every age should be catered for with the correct food.

Here is a health drink that is fantastic for the teenager and very good for clearing up acne. It does not taste as good as the fizzy drinks they'll want to reach for but if they can get used to it they are sure to see improvements within a fortnight. I still take this as a pick-me-up when I have been working in London for long stretches of time or bashing away on my computer, and I always feel better after doing so. I also used it religiously as a teenager and all I can say is that I was never teased about spots and never had to worry about them. In fact I remember feeling left out because I was the only one in my class who didn't have any spots to squeeze! On that note I shall give you the recipe.

Kooshti Sante Drink

My mother named this 'good health' in Romany. Use a mug or teacup to measure out the ingredients. (If you use a teacup rather than a mug, you'll get the same result, just less of it. Maybe that's the way to start off.)

2 cups chopped dark green spinach leaves
1/4 cup chopped parsley
3 cups fresh orange juice (preferably freshly squeezed)

Blend the ingredients in a liquidizer, and then sieve the result. It's ready to drink!

This is very rich in both iron and vitamin C, essential for a clear complexion. If you can drink a glass of this a day you will find the improvement to your skin is incredible.

For teenagers, as for everyone else, it is once again a question of a little of what you fancy . . . If teenagers want a fry-up, then let them have it, but make sure that you give them something healthy the following day. Who knows, their bodies may have needed that bit of fat or grease, but if they want the same later in the day, you know it is time to draw the line. Many doctors are now saying that you cannot get spots from a fry-up. Spots are due to the oils your body produces, and are more a hormonal thing than a chip thing, or are to do with how your liver handles oils. The main reason to limit fried food, in my book anyway, is for the sake of your heart and to keep you healthy, whatever your age.

Many people ask me what their children's weight should be, but there is no strictly correct answer. It depends on many factors. We have all seen chubby children grow into gorgeous teenagers. However, once your child's a teenager you should look at their whole lifestyle and eating pattern. The overweight 13-year-old almost certainly does not need a weight-loss diet, but rather needs you to interest them in a new sport, or in eating more healthy foods. Make sure you look at the whole picture, not just at what friends may be saying.

Later on in the book you'll find lots more Romany beauty recipes. But here are a few I think are essential for surviving the teenage years! The cleansers and toners that will be beneficial to any teenager's skin-care regime – and with the money saved on the store-bought varieties, will leave some spare cash for the latest clothes to go with the new and improved looks that should result. As with all recipes to improve the skin or general health, for maximum benefits you should keep up what you've started. The application is as important as the cream or lotion itself! Since these are home-made from natural ingredients, they won't last for ever. You only want to use the best on your skin, so start afresh if the preparation starts to go at all stale.

Teenager's Shampoo

This is an excellent shampoo that you can make for greasy teenage hair. Once they see the effect, the Arians, Sagittarians and Leos will be marketing it in the schoolyard!

2 teaspoons fresh thyme, sage, camomile or yarrow
1 cup hot water

Simply add the herb to the hot water to make an infusion. Leave for 24 hours, then strain and use as a final rinse after you shampoo normally.

Cucumber Cleanser

People still swear by soap and water but I have always believed you cannot beat a good cleansing cream. This is the one my great-grandma Eva Alice used to make. It is especially good for Virgo, Taurus and Capricorn.

First you must learn how to melt down the oils and wax. If you are going to give this recipe to a young or clumsy teenager I recommend you do it with them the first time. It seems a bit like a cookery recipe and may even be the first step to getting them into the kitchen. Besides, what better way to discover the delights of food then through the beauty secrets of the skin? The oils and waxes should be available in your local chemist. If not, ask them to order it for you. (If they won't, take my advice and change your chemist.)

3 teaspoons beeswax
4 teaspoons coconut oil
4 teaspoons olive oil
4 teaspoons cucumber juice (from a grated and squeezed cucumber)
¾ teaspoon glycerine
a pinch of borax
a drop of natural green colouring, optional

Fill a large saucepan with water and heat it to simmering point. Have ready a bowl that will fit over the pan and will not crack in the hot water, preferably a Pyrex one. Melt the beeswax with the coconut oil and olive oil in the bowl over the simmering water, mixing well all the time. Do not leave this unattended or it will clot.

With a separate small saucepan and bowl construct the same appliance as above and heat the cucumber juice with the glycerine, borax and colouring (if you want it, for presentation) until the borax dissolves completely. When the contents of both bowls are melted, remove from the heat. Slowly add the oil mixture to the borax mixture, stirring until well mixed. Allow to cool completely. Transfer to a spotlessly clean airtight container and store in the refrigerator. This way it keeps for longer, and is also at a refreshing temperature every time you use it.

Massage into your skin in upward stroking motions – the massage is as important as the cream itself.

Bom Bom's Toner

My brother used this toner whenever he suffered from acne (in his words, 'the odd spot'). It refreshed him and also made sure that any spots he had attacked did not get infected. (I have three brothers and I shall not name the user of this toner! Let's just say he knows who he is. I'm sure he would recommend this to the spotty teenager, if he dared reveal his identity.) I especially recommend this to Aries, Leo and Sagittarius.

handful of dark, scented rose petals
600 ml/1 pint boiling water
225 g/8 oz sugar
4 tablespoons distilled witch hazel

Take a large, spotlessly clean screw-top jar and put all the ingredients in it. Screw the lid on firmly and wrap the jar in a clean tea towel. Shake the mixture so that the ingredients are mixed together. Leave to steep for 4 hours. Strain into another spotlessly clean jar, add the witch hazel and store in the refrigerator. Fantastic against spots.

Gaggie's Miracle Moisturizer

This is great for combination or oily skin and I call it Gaggie's Miracle Moisturizer because my grandmother taught me the secret benefits of jasmine. This is a favourite with Taureans in particular, although it will benefit all of the twelve signs and should leave you feeling richly pampered. Your friendly chemist should be able to supply the ingredients.

2 tablespoons emulsifying wax
2 tablespoons sunflower oil
1 teaspoon lanolin
½ teaspoon borax
9 tablespoons water
1½ teaspoons glycerine
1 teaspoon distilled witch hazel
3 drops jasmine oil

Melt the emulsifying wax, sunflower oil and lanolin in the way described on page 49 for Cucumber Cleanser. In the same way, in a separate bowl heat the borax in the water with the glycerine and witch hazel. Remove both bowls from the heat and slowly add the glycerine mixture to the oil mixture, stirring constantly. Allow to cool, then add the jasmine oil and stir well.

You'll go crazy for this cream once you see how your skin laps it up. Remember, as with all home-made creams, keep this in a spotlessly clean airtight jar in the refrigerator. (It makes them nice and cool to use so you will probably start storing your shop-bought moisturizers in the same way.) Use them regularly, as they won't keep for ever, and make up a fresh batch rather than let an old one sit around and go stale.

Lavender Heaven Moisturizer

This is great for dry skin. Lavender is a favourite among the Romany people. It is often used to stuff pillows for restful sleep. Why not make this lotion as a birthday or Christmas present? Once your friends and family have tried it you'll be well in, because they'll want to use it for the rest of their life! Even though lavender is often associated with old age, it's also perfect for young skins.

2 teaspoons beeswax
1 teaspoon emulsifying wax
4 teaspoons almond oil
4 tablespoons hot water
3–5 drops lavender oil

Melt the beeswax and emulsifying wax as described on page 49 for Cucumber Cleanser. Remove from the heat and slowly add the almond oil. Mix in well then add the water. Allow to cool before adding the lavender oil.

Mid-life Crisis

Is this a figment of the forty-something's mind or is it a real and scary thing to go through? It depends on the person. Geminis, Virgos, Sagittarians and Capricorns are the Peter Pans of the zodiac but, contrariwise, they are the ones who worry about ageing the most. The forty-something may feel that his or her looks are fading and that it is all downhill from here. But the truth is that at this age you have not only more knowledge than you ever did before but you're also experienced enough to know how to make the most of your looks. Here are a few recipes to help you find your confidence again.

Uncle Leo's Pep Drink

This is an alcoholic drink my uncle Leo used to make when I was a child. It is probably the only thing that got him through a baby-sitting session with me and my brothers. It wasn't until much later that I got to try it myself. Watch out, though. Just take a little to get you in the party mood. Too much and it will relax you to the extent that you sleep through all the fun. And do not take it to the party with you. YOU HAVE BEEN WARNED!

50 g/2 oz fresh burdock leaves
25 g/1 oz fresh yarrow
25 g/1 oz dandelion herb (flowers)
300 g/10 oz malt
40 g/1½ oz hops
6 litres/10 pints water
50 g/2 oz sugar
25 g/1 oz yeast

Place all the ingredients except the sugar and the yeast in a large saucepan. Bring it to the boil, then reduce the heat to low and simmer for 2 hours. Strain off into an earthenware pot or an enamelled pan.

Stir together the sugar and yeast, adding a little of the liquor to make a paste. While the liquor is still warm, stir in the sugar and yeast paste. Cover with a cloth and allow to stand in a warm place for 24 hours. Skim off the yeast that has risen to the top and bottle the liquor in spotless screw-top bottles. Avoiding all temptation, another, and if the reading is high your doctor or nurse might suggest you come back for another test to be sure). This is the best way to protect yourself, especially once you reach middle age – but don't forget to put the advice you're given about reducing your blood pressure into action.

Another complaint I hear from the middle-aged is about sleeping. This is usually because of the amount of worry they have on their minds.

Here is a great recipe to help you sleep easier. It is one I give to insomniacs whatever their age. Cowslip is fantastic for encouraging sleep, especially if you cannot sleep because of pain. Many rheumatism and arthritis sufferers use cowslip tea.

Cowslip Tea

You can use greater quantities of the herb if you want to but start off slow and add more as you go. As my father John used to say: 'You can always add to a recipe, but it is much more difficult to take away.' Don't forget to give this to older relations too.

1 teaspoon dried cowslip flowers
1 mug hot water

Steep the cowslip in the hot water for a few minutes, strain, then drink the infusion. Add sugar and milk if you wish, but once you get used to the taste and see the effect it can have on your insomnia, you won't need it.

Old Age

We know what we fear as we approach old age: rheumatism, arthritis, insomnia and Alzheimer's. When we were young we looked for things to help us grow but what we need now is something to preserve what we have!

Listen to what your body is trying to tell you – as we should all have been doing right from the beginning. We only get one body – if you respect it, it will respect you! So if you are out shopping and your feet are killing you, don't carry on just to please friends and family. Stop, find a place to sit down and have a refreshment. Virgos, listen hard. I know you are good at dishing out advice, but you find it hard to take it yourself. You must look after yourself as well as everyone else.

Dandelion Potion

The dandelion root is a fantastic herb to help with rheumatism. (Sagittarians and Pisceans are susceptible to rheumatism.) It is also good for liver disorders. As with all my recipes you might think it simpler to go to a shop and buy a ready-made remedy, but let me tell you mine are better for you. Give it a try and you'll be glad you did.

25 g/1 oz dandelion root
1.2 litres/2 pints water

Put dandelion root and water in a saucepan, bring to the boil, then reduce the heat and simmer for 10 minutes.

Strain. Drink a wineglassful first thing in the morning and again at tea-time. Store in the refrigerator in a clean screw-top bottle.

Parsnip Remedy for Chilblains

Chilblains are unpleasant to have at any age, but especially as we get older. Here is something to try. Romanies have been using this recipe for many years and although some have tried adding other ingredients I would say that this simple and original way really is the best.

2 or 3 parsnips
1½ tablespoons powdered alum

Cover the parsnips with water and boil until tender. Remove and discard (or eat!) the parsnips and stir the alum into the cooking water. Allow to cool to body temperature. Stir well then bathe your hands and feet in the solution until you start to feel relief. Let this solution dry and do not rinse. Keep repeating daily until the chilblains are gone.

For insomnia, mostly suffered by Aries, Gemini and Aquarius, just follow the recipe for cowslip tea on page 57.

Nervous stress can increase as we get older if family pressures grow out of control. Well, take My Family's De-stresser and all you will be able to think about is relaxing. Are your worries really worth getting so stressed about? It's not good for you, you know. Think about it – can you afford to fret about when your granddaughter will get rid of the fool she's chosen to go out with, and do you have to sort out everyone's finances? Maybe if you stop worrying about everyone they'll start taking responsibility for their own decisions – and you can start taking responsibility for your health.

My Family's De-stresser

Potassic tartrate of iron has been used by my family for years to stop stress. It is not a herb, but is a great and successful remedy to help you relax, whatever sign you were born under. A rogue friend of my uncle's used to sell this for a fortune as a miracle potion, but it really is cheap to make and very effective, so give it a go. You can't afford not to.

15 g/½ oz potassic tartrate of iron
600 ml/1 pint boiling water

Mix the ingredients together and place in a sterilized screw-top container. Take just 1 teaspoon, 2 or 3 times a day. Use for as long as is needed and then discard.

Money

What are we like with money? How we handle money, whatever our age, can have a lot to do with our wellbeing. A recent survey showed that Pisceans spend more on their credit cards than any other sign of the zodiac, so they need to watch they don't overdo the spending and leave themselves broke or in debt. Scorpios and Cancer, according to the survey, are the most thrifty. Cancerians spend the most on clothes and eating out, while Aquarians spend more on their holidays. Pisceans and Librans spend most on motoring. Librans spend the least on food and dining out. Scorpios are most likely to hide credit-card bills from partners – and I for one can vouch for that. Taureans love food but tend not to spend a lot of money eating out. They seem to prefer the joys of home cooking – or others paying for them!

Dealing with Problems in Life

Emotional difficulties can and do arise at any time of life. A death in the family, a break-up from a loved one – we don't handle this any better when we are 80 than when we were 20, or vice versa. It still hurts. Cancer, Leo, Virgo and Sagittarius take problems to heart for the longest length of time, while Scorpio, Cancer and Pisces jump in at the deep end but can recover a little quicker so long as they don't wallow. What can we do to move on from the stage we feel has devastated our lives and how can we learn to live again?

Fire signs – Aries, Leo and Sagittarius – tend to bottle up their feelings and all too often when they do break down will reveal to close ones that it is nothing to do with a recent problem, but was something that happened months ago. The secret to being a successful fire sign is to talk about your problems when you have them. If you live with or have a close one who is a fire sign, check often how their life is going. Don't just say, 'How are you?' Try to refer to the specific areas of this person's life that you know are likely to cause worry.

Earth signs – Taurus, Virgo and Capricorn – get stressed when their security is threatened. Moving house is a nightmare for them because without their base they are nothing. If you want to make life happy for one of these signs then provide a happy base. A pregnant earth sign is often an ecstatic one, so long as she is really and truly happy with her partner. I would advise these signs not to make changes until they are really sure or their fear alone will spell failure.

Air signs – Gemini, Libra and Aquarius – need to watch that they don't get hurt by their own openness. These are the people who wear their hearts on their sleeves and say I love you before the other person has had a chance to ask their name. They are great networkers, however, so can generally get over stress more quickly than most because they have always got something new going on. A little more forethought and these signs could save themselves a lot of stress.

Water signs – Cancer, Scorpio and Pisces – tend to get a little too emotionally involved in everything that's going on in their lives and in the lives of their friends, family and sometimes even their neighbours. If you see a water sign crying don't get out the hankies too quickly. Some of them enjoy the waterworks, and you could be mistaking tears of joy for tears of sorrow. The secret to being a successful water sign is to look at life's dilemmas for what they really are and not to make problems where you really don't have to.

Now you can start to set up your own ground rules for life.

Working Out your Own Health Chart

EACH OF THE following chapters will help you to understand your star sign's health needs, what to look out for, and that prevention is better than cure. However, the first thing is to work out how healthy you are:

- Do you get out of breath when you walk upstairs?
- Do you wake up feeling groggy and lethargic with no energy?
- Are you taking medication, or do you have a medical condition?

If the answer to any of the above is yes, then consult your doctor before taking up any of my recommendations.

It is essential to any human body to get exercise and oxygen. It is not enough just to eat well. But don't forget what we learned from the previous chapter. Your body tells you things for a reason and if you feel tired or ill your body is telling you to slow down and not push yourself so hard. If your body aches after exercise because it is the first you have done in years, it is telling you to try to build up your fitness slowly.

If you are overweight and find it difficult even to think of exercise, then simply try to walk a little extra each day. Try to walk instead of getting the bus or into the car if it is just a short distance. Rome wasn't built in a day! Our bodies need constant assessment if they are to be used to the best of their abilities. You will all find your own ways of balancing your lifestyle depending on your star sign. Learn your own limitations and set a pace that suits you, your lifestyle, your age, and also your partner. It is no fun going out on a romantic date and then munching your way through lettuce leaves while your partner looks aghast. Compromise is a key word.

Before you enter a keep-fit regime make sure you are doing it for yourself and not for anyone else. If you are happy with yourself then your close ones will be happy with you too, because they will be able to sense your wellbeing and sense of fulfilment. Many of us, if we are confident that we look good, will feel better on the inside. Our physical appearance can count for how we feel about ourselves and our lives. We have all gone through the experience of getting ready to go out for an important date, having a crisis of confidence about how we look and thinking we'd feel happier staying in. (I hope you didn't give in to that feeling.)

How about losing weight for a special occasion, be it a wedding, a birthday, a summer holiday or a new person in our lives? How often have we tried it and how often have we failed? It is no good trying to lose weight quickly. All that will happen is that the body will store more fat for the future because it thinks there's a famine on. It starts to think survival. Over time your body weight creeps up instead of going down. Instead you have to think of a change that works for you which you can make on a permanent basis. Information is what we lack, and I'm here to help.

When you read the chapter for your sign you will find out what vitamins and minerals your body needs and what you can do to prevent problems from occurring. Certain signs will need a back-up of particular vitamins more than other signs, and it will be up to you to read, digest and use the information that I have gathered for you. Don't forget that there are also times in our lives when we need extra help with nutrients, such as pregnancy, the teenage years or whenever we are facing change. Look after your body like you do your car. You wouldn't expect your car to run without petrol, or even for very long without being serviced, would you? It's the same for your body. Look after it and it will give you good service.

Did you know that many of us don't even breathe in enough oxygen? I am sure if it cost a fortune and the government decided to give it out free for a month we would grab as much as we could. But as long as something is in front of our noses and isn't difficult to get we don't value it. Breathe in through your nose, allow your lungs to fill up, then let it out through your mouth. It's the first step to a healthier life.

Ask yourself some important basic questions:

- Do you have any injuries that prevent you from exercising normally?
- Do you have a job that demands overtime on a regular basis so that you are left with no time for your personal life?

- Do you find that you shudder at even the thought of light exercise?
- Have you not managed to find the time or motivation to do any form of exercise in the last year?

If you answered yes to even one of the above questions, then you must go slow to begin with. The best way to do this is to find something that isn't normally classed as 'exercise': such as walking to the shops. If you rush your body it will go on strike. (You've already been to the doctor's surgery and had your blood pressure taken, haven't you?) Take heed, Aries, Leo and Sagittarius. You often start with so much enthusiasm that you are exhausted and discouraged before you've achieved anything.

Different forms of exercise suit different signs. In the list that follows I have put the exercises in reverse order of challenge. Mind you, knowing Virgo, Capricorn and Aries, they will try the hardest ones first!

ARIES

If you have not exercised before or for a long time try walking, and then eventually speed-walking, which is gentler on the joints than jogging.

If you are generally fit and healthy and want to try something new, go for squash or badminton.

If you are looking for a challenge, try properly supervised bungee jumping – a fast thrill for an exciting fire sign like you!

TAURUS

If you have not exercised before or for a long time try light gardening, a simple exercise to increase your mobility and one that any bull will enjoy. Nature walks are also great for this earth sign who loves all things natural.

If you are generally fit and healthy and want to try something new, then long-distance running should be right up your street.

If you are looking for a challenge, try triathlon – the perfect challenge as you have the persistence and endurance to succeed through all conditions. You could also team up with a Leo to do this, as it's a sport that also suits them.

GEMINI

If you have not exercised before or for a long time try light rowing – that should start to get the air back in your lungs.

If you are generally fit and healthy and want to try something new, outdoor aerobics will get you full of energy and life.

If you are looking for a challenge, hang-gliding couldn't be better.

CANCER

If you have not exercised before or for a long time try beginner's dancing lessons: good for the stylish crab and enough exercise to get you motivated to the next stage.

If you are generally fit and healthy and want to try something new, try a more advanced watersport like aquarobics, waterskiing, snorkelling or diving. After a class, follow up with a beauty treatment as a reward for your hard work.

If you are looking for a challenge, you'll look good speedboat driving and it will provide you with the exhilaration you are seeking.

LEO

If you have not exercised before or for a long time try gentle step exercises at home. You'll find your own pace for exercise without wearing yourself out to impress those watching.

If you are generally fit and healthy and want to try something new, circuit training will build up both confidence and muscles.

If you are looking for a challenge, try triathlon. Or try competing against a Taurus. It'll be a close call which one of you will win. Dare you try?

VIRGO

If you have not exercised before or for a long time try line dancing. Someone as sociable and caring as you will love this fun and energetic activity.

If you are generally fit and healthy and want to try something new, horse-riding is the ideal exercise for an animal-lover like you.

If you are looking for a challenge, try paragliding. You'll love the views of the countryside and you will feel like you're on top of the world.

LIBRA

If you have not exercised before or for a long time try the step machine at a slow pace before moving on to the next challenge.

If you are generally fit and healthy and want to try

something new, hand weights at the gym should improve the parts of your body you want to tone or shape up.

If you are looking for a challenge, take flying lessons. You'll love the excitement.

SCORPIO

If you have not exercised before or for a long time try a treasure hunt. Your natural curiosity will make you a leader and you won't even notice you're using your legs while you hunt for the mystery prize.

If you are generally fit and healthy and want to try something new, jet-skiing or water-skiing should provide the thrill you seek.

If you are looking for a challenge, paragliding or powerboat racing are just the ticket for you.

SAGITTARIUS

If you have not exercised before or for a long time try beginner's ballet lessons – great exercises even if you don't want to pursue the dance side of the study.

If you are generally fit and healthy and want to try something new, boxercise is perfect for punching away the stresses of the day.

If you are looking for a challenge, you'll find you are naturally good at a precision sport like the firing range.

CAPRICORN

If you have not exercised before or for a long time, walking is a great exercise and this sign loves to look at the sights around them while they go along. Try to get a little distance going slowly to build up your endurance.

If you are generally fit and healthy and want to try something new, bike riding will get the air into your lungs and have you feeling and looking good.

If you are looking for a challenge, dirt-track racing will be a great experience for you.

AQUARIUS

If you have not exercised before or for a long time, try bowling. Very sociable for talkative you.

If you are generally fit and healthy and want to try something new, hurdles is the answer. Some of the best hurdlers are Aquarians.

If you are looking for a challenge, take flying lessons. There is no better feeling for you than flying high in the air.

PISCES

If you have not exercised before or for a long time try walking in beautiful scenery. Combine it with painting; you are known for your artistic abilities. Remember that you have to walk to find your destination!

If you are generally fit and healthy and want to try something new, swimming or water aerobics are perfect for you with your water affinity.

If you are looking for a challenge, try diving courses and even a diving holiday. With a breathing apparatus and all those fabulous sights you'll discover that you feel more at home under the water than above it.

YOUR HEALTH SIGNS

ARIES

THE RAM

Ruling Planet: Mars, the Roman god of war

Triplicity or Element: Fire

Quadruplicity or Mode: Cardinal

Key words: Headstrong, opinionated, action initiator, leader, loyal to a cause, egotistical, passionate

The Origin of Aries

A winged golden ram was sent by Hermes to fly Phrixus and his sister Helle away from the evil designs of their stepmother to sanctuary in the city of Colchis. Helle fell off into a river en route, at a place that became Hellespont, and Phrixus sacrificed the golden ram in the Grove of Ares, hanging the golden fleece there. This, in Greek mythology, is the story of Aries.

What Aries is Like

This is a sign that appears at first glance to know where it is going. Aries are initiators, and loyal to the causes they feel are important. Sometimes opinionated, they are none the less a great addition to anybody's life. With an Aries around life will never be boring. They are always re-inventing themselves and finding new ways to encourage their friends and family into new undertakings. The only let-down is that they put so much energy into motivating themselves and those around them that they run out of steam before things are completed.

Don't be fooled into thinking that you know what an Aries wants. What may be their dream today will have changed by tomorrow. Their ruling planet Mars is the planet of change and unpredictability. An Aries cannot say at 15 what life will be like when they are 25, and if you ask them when they reach 25 what they think about their past, they will be too busy planning the future to be able to remember.

Action is the key word. They are always on the go and planning the next move. This is the first sign of the zodiac and the need to plan or start new things is always on their mind. The sun enters Aries on or around 21 March. This is the springtime of life and the beginning of the astrological new year, so no wonder Aries like new starts. They need to prove to themselves that they are truly alive and without new beginnings they can feel suffocated. Change is an essential part of their lives. Lucky for those of us who marry one, life itself is so full of changes, what with puberty, marriage, children and career, that there is usually enough to keep an Aries occupied without them wanting to change partner.

Try to make sure you listen when they talk, no matter how boring some of their precious information may seem. To them the latest goings on in a soap opera may seem crucial. Listen with interest until as always they run out of steam. Aries children in particular are great fun to have around. They get so excited about things that they cannot get the words out fast enough.

Aries is the first of the fire signs and is cardinal in its quality – which is why it is good at starting new things and initiating action. Cardinal signs are eager and impatient of delays, so woe betide you if you keep them waiting, especially concerning matters of the heart. They like to forge ahead with things and to be in charge, even if they don't really know what they are doing. Continuity can sometimes be a problem. They may not sustain the enthusiasm they start out with. There are ways around this, of course. One is for Aries to be an initiator at work, handing over projects to a more conscientious sign for completion.

If you've ever worked with an Aries you will know they can bring inspiration to the dullest of days. They also know how to make someone laugh. They often get into trouble in their schooldays for talking too much and it is more often than not a Scorpio they will team up with for mischief in the classroom – they have the same ruling planet and know just how to cause a riot.

Red is their colour, and you will often see them don red when they are planning to go to war, or even when they are setting out to seduce someone. They love to be noticed and can go to great lengths to get attention. They are not, however, sly. They are very straight-forward, and they will not lie to you – unless they feel it is absolutely necessary. They have the ability to set their mind on something and to go for it with all the energy of a superjet on its way to war. Their ruling planet Mars is the Roman god of war. Which should explain why many people simply step out of the way and let them through when they see them coming. There are not many signs that would mess with a determined or angry Aries.

If you have a young Aries around you might want to make sure they wear extra head protection during sports. They are clumsy and have a tendency to knock their heads. But it won't hurt them. They can take rough-and-tumble better than most – probably because by the time they're ten they're quite used to it.

Fire signs are hot and explosive and sometimes like a bomb waiting to go off. You can upset them and not even know they are angry with you. It builds up and builds up until all of a sudden they explode in a shocking way. Don't worry. They don't have a split personality and once they have shouted and let the pressure out they will be right back to normal.

If Aries were an object it would be a rocket waiting to take off, and astounding everyone by its abilities once it does. These people would be great as sprinters but are never long-distance runners.

Aries can make it or break it. They have to make sure they put their energies into the right things and don't get led astray. The ram symbolizes physical courage but they also have belligerent instincts (from the planet Mars) and if you see the male sheep leading his flock you'll see the characteristic Aries boss complex. Aries can do much good for the world because they are energy personified but they don't have much invested in complete peace because then it gets boring for them. They can be incredibly tactless at times.

They fall in love hard and fast and have been known to marry on impulse. They can't imagine life without that special person – unless of course you ask them a week later when the love drug has worn off! Aries shouldn't marry young. This is one sign that really shouldn't be given the key of the door until they are 21.

Aries are accident-prone. Many of them have high motor insurance because of their common accidental knocks. The safest game for them to play is probably chess; although knowing them they could well end up throwing the pieces around.

The biggest problem for Aries is nerves, especially in high-power jobs. You will think they are doing fine but underneath their cool smile they are agonizing that they could be doing better. You may find it hard to get an Aries to talk about their problems, but be patient. Deep down they are longing to tell you what is on their mind. They just need a little coaxing to do so. They are often accused of being selfish, and indeed they believe they must put themselves first if they are ever to be of help to others. It is the ram's logic, and it makes perfect sense to them. They are forceful, feeling and full of bright ideas and strong ambitions. For the ram to be the best they can, they must find someone who can keep them going and support them in their ideas and dreams.

How to Spot an Aries

You can sometimes tell an Aries by the way they walk with their head sticking out. Sometimes they have a rather prominent nose!

The Devil and the Angel

The DEVIL ARIES is power mad, totally irresponsible and a reckless leader. Butch Cassidy was an Aries! The actor Robert Downey Jnr and blues legend Billie Holiday are two other unpredictable Aries. Robert Downey Jnr starred in the film *Chaplin*, but I wonder if he knew the star he was portraying also shared his sign?

The ANGEL ARIES is virtuous, strong and benevolent. Sir Elton John, who is always raising money for charity and trying to make the world a better place, is a wonderful example. Another great Aries is Andrew Lloyd Webber, whose talent and love of the arts led him to fame and fortune, from which lucky place he has aided many charities. He doesn't do anything by halves but puts his heart and soul in to everything he ventures into. He has staying power and is sure to be around for years to come. Another side of Aries shows up in his changing private life. He needs someone who can keep up with his ever-changing moods.

Aries Health and Development from Child to Adult

Most Aries babies love noise and if you are having problems getting them to sleep then try putting on some loud music – I am not talking about ballads here. They don't like to be left alone and will scream the place down if you attempt to ignore them. (As the adult, so too the child). If you can get an Aries child to express his or her emotions and to talk about problems you might save yourself and other people explosive showdowns later on. You'll be doing everyone a favour. In appearance Aries children are often delicate but don't be fooled: this is one of the more robust signs of the zodiac.

At five years of age they are likely to start developing bad habits and to rebel against cleanliness and good manners. Don't worry – this is simply a test to see how far they can go. The best way to deal with them at this age is not to be amused at their antics. Without an audience, it is pointless for them to continue in any mischief. Tantrums won't last long. They give it their best and then flake out from all the effort. At this age they need a very firm hand. This is the make or break stage. Watch out, too, for your Aries child's clumsiness. A little knock can result in a big bruise.

At eleven years of age they start to show the artistic and sensitive side of their nature. Many Aries children decide to take up theatrical studies or drama lessons. They get involved in all of their friends' problems and end up getting hurt as they are accused of being a gossip when they were only trying to help. This is the start of the 'agony aunt' role that continues for the rest of their lives. These are the people you can talk to easily. They are quick to learn at this age and their active brain generally gets them to the top of their class. They are not usually a loner. They are more likely to be the leader of the pack, quite often class captain or organizer of discussions.

At this age they suffer from common colds and flu. When the bugs circulate in school the Aries child always manages to catch them.

At 16 the arts are likely to exert an ever stronger pull and the Aries teenager may want to take up an artistic profession. Those that pursue this desire do well at this age. Teen stars are often Aries. They just need to make sure they keep their feet on the ground. Too much energy and success too soon can fire off the rocket but doesn't make for an easy landing. They need someone to keep consistency in their life or they will only experience overnight success. If you want to support them, however, be persistent. They don't always listen to advice straight away.

Their relationship with the opposite sex is a fulfilling one and they have a great understanding of partners. Childhood sweethearts often turn out to be their marriage partners. They have a great gift of charming the opposite sex. Family ties become stronger at this age and you may find the 11-year-old who couldn't wait to go on school trips now wants to come home after a Saturday night out instead of staying at a friend's.

The teenage years are when they could go either way and you need to make sure that you keep a check on their health during this time as they are unlikely to be able to find the time to do so themselves. You see their personal life is more than likely to be at full flare at this stage.

At 21 they are likely to already have had three or four relationships they thought they would never get over. It is now that they will be ready for a long-lasting relationship. They like to mould their partners and provided that partners are willing to be guided by them a fruitful and lasting association will result. They adore children and will spend time with them and take great pains to make them happy, but Arians don't like changing nappies. They usually manage to hold a secure position in life and their clever ideas mean that some twenty-somethings have made themselves into young millionaires.

In their forties they love to impress people and throw parties for any reason they can think up. They don't always succeed with their in-laws because of a tendency to say what they shouldn't. They always know when they've said something wrong but by then it is probably too late. Where health is concerned they are over-cautious and fearful, and make terrible patients. A small ailment will last them for ages. It is actually the thought of being helpless that worries them. They suffer from a bit of an insecurity complex too. However, they never seem to look their age and you could not possibly accuse them of being conformers.

In their seventies they seem finally to slow down and to deal with things as they should have done in their twenties. They will spend a lot of their old age trying to make up the friendships they lost through their temper fifty years ago. They are quite mellow now but can still shock. This is the character you meet and think delightfully sweet but who can cut you down with a single sentence if they want to. Don't be fooled, this sign can never be what you would call old, it is just a statement of their years of experience and that is all that this figure really means to them.

Aries Careers . . .

Sports commentator. You'd just love all that fast-moving action.

Lecturer. Telling people what they need to know and being admired for it – ideal.

Motor mechanic, especially at Formula 1. You'd always be behind a winner.

Social worker or air hostess. You are good at looking after people, and you like to be needed.

Inventor. Right up your street. You are an original.

. . . not so Aries Careers

Secretary. You cannot take orders and you are likely to end up smashing the keyboard over your boss's head.

Understudy in the theatre. How could anyone ever think of putting you second?

Night-security guard. Forget it. You would go crazy with no one to talk to. You'd end up talking to the wall and getting carried away in a straitjacket.

Famous Aries

Composer Andrew Lloyd Webber, singers Diana Ross, Elton John and Aretha Franklin, actors Alec Guinness, Richard Chamberlain, Dennis Quaid and James Caan, ex-prime minister John Major, sprinter Linford Christie, fashion designer Vivienne Westwood.

Health Sore Points

Aries rules the head, brain and face. This simply means that if you are born under this sign you are prone to stress in these parts of your body. When you feel low, these are the areas that suffer. Eyestrain, for example, is a potential problem, as is weak eyesight. Aries should try to avoid undue stress because you are subject to nervous strain.

A typical Aries with problems, whether business or emotional, is likely to have trouble sleeping. You lie in bed turning over all the possibilities: 'Will I get that promotion?' 'Is this the right person for me?'

Some Aries also have trouble with their stomach and kidneys. I'm afraid alcohol is not very good for you: you can't handle it!

Your ruling planet Mars is a fighter and so you can pull yourself out of the worst of illnesses by sheer willpower. The other side of that coin is that some of your illnesses are caused by being always on the go, never stopping. You run on pure nervous energy and sometimes have to be reminded to eat. (Not a problem a Virgo will suffer from, I can assure you!) At work you ask someone to do a job and, impatient for action, you interfere and end up doing it yourself.

Cures and Counsel

The main key to your good health is to make sure you don't bottle up your feelings. The more you bottle up, the bigger the bang. Learn to let off steam.

Get regular eye tests. If you don't catch it early, you may end up with pebble glasses. You have been warned!

Eat regularly. Have a proper breakfast before you go to work, and have a good lunch. Don't overindulge at dinner and try not to eat too late at night. Aries often have food intolerance. Be honest with yourself. If there are certain foods you know make you ill then don't eat them. You may love chocolate but the red blotches it brings out on your face are unlikely to win you any new admirers.

If you suffer from headaches try to get fresh air rather than reach for the pill bottle every time. The Aries headache is often a sign of stress, whether physical or psychological. Relaxation exercises, massage or even a few drops of camomile or lavender oil in your bath water can help relieve tension headaches. They will relax the blood vessels and alleviate tension. Or drink an infusion of lime flower, valerian or vervain made from a teabag or otherwise one teaspoon of each herb per cup of hot water. Or gently massage your temples with five drops of juniper essential oil diluted with two tablespoons of olive oil.

Headaches due to stress or tiredness really are best cured by rest. We can never find time to rest but it is the quickest way to cure a problem – so make the time! Migraine sufferers should try to avoid alcohol, cheese, chocolate, cocoa, cream, oranges and coffee. Make sure that you cut down on them one at a time so that you can work out which one of them is upsetting your body.

If headaches are continuous seek advice from a doctor.

If sleeplessness is a problem avoid tea and coffee before bed as these stimulate your brain and make it harder for you to relax. The best way to induce sleep is to take a relaxing herbal bath before you retire each evening. This winds you down from your day and stops you thinking about your problems when you get into bed. Not winding down before bed is why many of us toss and turn once we are in it. Soak up and inhale relaxing herbs while you bathe, such as camomile, lavender, meadowsweet or valerian. If you want to relax aching muscles then try bergamot, hyssop and rosemary.

To make your own herbal oils put crushed leaves into a clean bottle or jar and pour olive oil over the top. Screw on the lid or place a cork in the top. Leave on your kitchen or bathroom window for a fortnight, turning it frequently, then strain it into a clean bottle and use as you wish. Add this to your bath and you will feel the difference, not only in your senses, but also in the softness of your skin.

An Aries needs regular exercise. Without the lungs working well you won't be running on full steam. This applies to your body as well as your brain. The best exercise for the ram would be something that uses up a lot of energy fast such as squash or boxing. When life has become stressful there is nothing better for an Aries than to take out the stress on an object such as a squash ball or a punch bag. It should save you from bottling up your anxieties and you and your loved ones will be better off for that.

Juniper for Jumpy Aries

Romanies recommend juniper berries for all kinds of Aries afflictions: nervous strain, eyestrain and stomach ailments. In southern Europe juniper grows wild but elsewhere their berries and sprigs can be obtained from most good herbalists and health food stores. The berries may be chewed neat if preferred.

1 dozen juniper berries
900 ml/1½ pints boiling water
honey

Crush the berries, put into a pot and cover with the boiling water. Allow to steep for 10 minutes, then strain and drink, with honey to taste.

Mint Tea

Another excellent remedy for upset stomachs.

handful of fresh mint
mugful of milk

Boil the mint in the milk and drink hot.

Aries Aniseed

This is a great booster for Aries health.

1.2 litres/2 pints orange juice
1 tablespoon ground aniseed
squeeze of fresh lemon juice

Mix them together and drink. Then sit back and wait for the energy surge!

Good Aries Food

Aries can be deficient in the cell salt kali phosphoricum, also known as potassium phosphate. A deficiency causes nervous problems, and as you are vulnerable to stress you need to keep an eye on your intake. The best source is tomatoes. Tomatoes also contain vitamins A, B and C and they are so versatile in the kitchen that you won't have any difficulty including them in your diet. Kali phosphoricum will cleanse your system and enable you to operate on a more centred basis. Of course your health depends on your lifestyle and what else you are eating but if you can stock up on kali phosphoricum you should see an improvement.

Dandelions are rich in potassium so try the recipe for

dandelion coffee on page 187. That should help you relax and relieve any tension. Try using dandelion leaf in salads, too. Lemons and celery are two other good Aries foods. Lemons are cleansing and healing and good for brain operation, making you feel more alert and alive. They contain phosphorus, which is nourishment for brain and nerve cells. Celery is rich in potassium and a fantastic system cleanser. It is good against gout and rheumatism. Give it to an Aries in their seventies and you should see an improvement in their mobility within days. Grapefruit, parsnips and apples are other good Aries foods.

Aries tend to regard food as simple fuel and go for instant foods to banish hunger. Asking an Aries to wait for their food is generally considered unacceptable! These are the guests who hang around the kitchen asking you if they can test the dish just to make sure it's OK. When you wonder where the cheese has gone to that you need to make the sauce, just look down their top for the crumbs – you are sure to find the evidence there!

This sign knows exactly what it does and does not want to eat. If an Aries child tells you she doesn't like cauliflower then don't force it on her, she means it.

The good news is that Aries tend to burn off the food they gobble down very quickly and that is the beauty of being a fire sign: their metabolic rate is high. They will, however, need extra protein to keep their energy high and to help build up muscles. There are not many Aries vegetarians. They love their meat too much.

Aries must choose food that will sustain them and keep their brain on good form. Try the recipes on pages

93–6. I have an Aries friend who insists on eating beef bourguignonne before any important project! Find what's good for you and resist the lure of fast, convenience 'fuel'.

Plants for Star Therapy

Honeysuckle is your plant and to have it around is great therapy. It is easily grown against a wall or a trellis for support. This plant doesn't take too kindly to being transplanted but once it feels at home, the hardy types grow well.

Health Checklist

- For headaches take feverfew, magnesium, B complex especially B2 and B3, and evening primrose oil.
- For nervous problems take vitamins B1 (thiamin) and B6 (pyroxidine) or better still B-complex to prevent imbalance or overdose.
- For stomach problems try peppermint oil rubbed on the stomach or taken internally, according to your pharmacist's advice.
- And if you suffer from neuralgia vitamin B1 (thiamin) should help.
- B1 can be found in brown rice; peas, beans, breakfast cereals and Marmite and should aid your nervous system by releasing the energy you are in need of. B6 can be found in wholemeal bread and

wholegrains, liver, fish, bananas, wheatbran, yeast extract and brewer's yeast, and will promote healthy skin and nerves and help hormone production and the production of antibodies.

Are You a True Aries?

Be honest! When you have finished, count up your A's and Bs, then turn to the advice below.

1 Do you often run on no energy and agree to go out when you know you have had enough?
2 If the answer to question 1 is yes is it more than twice a week that you push yourself to the limit?
3 Do you eat any of the following foods on a regular basis: lemons, celery, tomatoes, grapefruit, parsnips, apples?
4 Do you often get headaches?
5 Do you find you cannot talk about a problem when it happens but wait until you can contain it no longer?
6 When you attend a party or a night out with friends do you indulge more than you know you should?
7 Do you drink more than four cups of tea or coffee a day?
8 Do you suffer from muscle tension?
9 Do you play a sport at least once a week?
10 Do you often fail to talk to your partner or loved one about your daily stresses?
11 Do you find that you automatically take the lead in situations?

12 Have you gone through more styles of dress and hair than you can remember?
13 Is red your favourite colour?
14 Underneath the cool face you show in the workplace are you really terrified when under pressure?
15 Have you knocked your head more than twice, that you can remember, while rushing around and playing games as a child, or indeed rushing around as an adult?
16 Is it some time (more than two years) since you went for an eye test?
17 Do you find it difficult to sleep when you are having problems at work or in your personal life?
18 Do you rarely set aside time in your busy day to eat a good breakfast, lunch and dinner?
19 Would you reach for a hamburger rather than a healthy option?
20 Do you drink more than you know you should?

If you answered 'yes' to most questions, you are a typical ram. You are headstrong and a born leader and achiever. You will often wonder if it was really you that made the shocking decision you seem to have just announced. Be careful – you may not be being good to yourself. You need to stop and listen and learn about your star sign and what it needs to allow you to be at your best – before you run yourself into the ground. Maybe it is time for a lifestyle reassessment. Try to get some support from friends and family in the process. Boost your vitamin intake and listen to your body's needs too.

I hope that you answered yes to question 3. That

means you are eating the correct foods for your star sign. You have the ability to do so much with your life and if you do suffer from headaches or have any problems with sleep then don't delay, get them sorted out. Your life will be what you make it, so make it the best.

If you answered no to question 3, then try to make sure that you make the fruit and vegetables listed a part of your regular diet.

You can never do enough for your body and it is important that you reassess yourself each month to see how you can improve the quality of your life. Exercise is essential and if you don't enjoy sport (though most Aries do) then try walking to your destination once a week to start off with. I can promise you that you will soon start both to see and feel a difference within yourself if you do.

If you answered 'no' to most questions, you do not appear to be a typical Aries, and maybe a Cancer, Leo or Pisces is holding you back emotionally from doing what you really want. No one can stop an Aries for long, however. You will always strike out for your dreams in the end.

Read the moon signs chapter towards the end of the book to find out more about yourself.

Redo the questionnaire if the status of your life changes. Try to find out whether you behave differently when you are on top form and flying through life to when you are simply paddling. I hope that you make an effort to find out more about the potential that lies within your sign. You could uncover a fun and exciting character.

The Drinker's Guide to the Zodiac

Aries cannot tolerate alcohol well but sometimes they just insist. Aries' ruling planet is Mars, the planet of change and unpredictability, and you just never know how drink is going to affect them. Never try to keep up drink for drink with an Aries. They can drink someone under the table if they put their mind to it, so they may end up with the hangover from hell but they won't even remember where they spent the evening! On the other hand, they may get legless after just a glass.

Pink Bacardi

Here's a good drink for an Aries, but only if you really must!

4 or 5 ice cubes
juice of 1 lemon
4 or 5 drops grenadine
3 parts light golden rum
1 teaspoon sugar or syrup

Put the ice cubes into a cocktail shaker. Pour the lemon juice, sugar, grenadine and rum over the ice. Shake until a frost forms. Strain and pour into a chilled martini glass.

Star Menu

Drunken Salmon

Now don't be fooled by the name of this recipe. It is meant to inebriate the fish not you. It also contains just enough wine to satisfy an Aries without giving them a headache the next day. This is enough for 2.

75 g/3 oz butter
1 medium-sized onion, diced
2 x 225 g/8 oz salmon steaks
salt and freshly ground black pepper
350 ml/12 fl oz red wine
a bouquet garni
2 sprigs of parsley
1 bay leaf
2 cloves garlic, chopped
2 teaspoons flour

Preheat the oven to 180°C/325°F/gas 4.

Melt 50 g/2 oz of the butter in a flameproof shallow casserole dish, add the onion and cook until nicely browned. Add the salmon, sprinkle with salt and pepper, and pour in the red wine. It should cover the salmon completely. Add the bouquet garni, parsley, bay leaf and garlic. Cover the casserole and cook for 15–20 minutes, depending on the thickness of the salmon steaks. When the salmon is cooked remove it to a very hot serving dish. Discard the bouquet and bind the sauce by mixing the remaining butter with the flour and adding it little by little to the cooking juices, blending all together well. Check the seasoning, pour the sauce over the salmon and serve at once.

You can vary this dish by frying mushrooms with the onions. Or use dry white wine instead of red.

Top Tomatoes

This dish is suitable for the most difficult of guests! It is also a great dish for children, and uses the tomatoes that are so vital in the diet of an Aries. It goes well with the Drunken Salmon, and has to be one of the quickest and simplest main course dishes you can make. I always turn to this when unexpected guests turn up ravenous. It is also a very compatible dish for people born under the sign of Virgo. Good for 4 people.

4 large tomatoes, skinned and chopped
150 g/6 oz button mushrooms, chopped
75 g/3 oz Cheddar or Edam cheese, finely grated
75 g/3 oz fresh granary breadcrumbs
salt and freshly ground black pepper
a good pinch of mixed herbs
40 g/1½ oz butter or margarine, plus extra for greasing

To skin tomatoes simply drop them in a pan of boiling water for a minute and then take out carefully with a slotted spoon. Place under running cold water and the skin should come off easily.

Preheat the oven to 220°C/425°F/gas 7.

Grease an ovenproof dish with butter or margarine. Layer the tomatoes, mushrooms, cheese and breadcrumbs until all of the ingredients are used up, finishing off with a layer of breadcrumbs, remembering to season as you go. Dot with butter or margarine and bake in the hot oven until crisp and golden: about 25 minutes.

If you are a garlic lover, add some to your breadcrumbs, but not if you are going out on the town on a first date as this dish tends to hold garlic very well. Great to give your partner if he's going out with friends though: he'll never get chatted up.

Marsala Peaches

Aries will love this. Serves 6.

4 tablespoons marsala wine
25 g/1 oz caster sugar
2 eggs, beaten
3 ripe peaches, halved and stoned
fresh mint sprigs, to decorate

Place a heatproof bowl such as Pyrex over a pan of gently simmering water, pour in the marsala and add the sugar, and stir gently until the sugar has dissolved. Add the eggs, whisking well with a whisk or hand-held electric beater. When the mixture looks thick and frothy, serve it immediately over ripe peaches and decorate with mint sprigs.

Star Beauty

Overly perfumed cosmetics and skin-care products can bring Aries skin out in a rash. Natural ingredients are the only route for a safe skin-care regime, I'm afraid. Wear a good perfume or aftershave if you want a strong scent. Mind you, natural ingredients can smell fantastic. Don't be fooled by strong-smelling chemicals, which can often smell sour later.

Berry Beautiful Mask for Men

Here is a beauty mask that works amazingly well on men, and many of the women in my family make it for their partners. They may be wary of trying it, but once they have had a go it will become a regular part of their beauty regime. It is good for sensitive skin because it does not contain any of the harsh chemicals that many store-bought masks do. As with any treatment, however, if you do feel any irritation or discomfort, simply rinse off immediately.

This mask not only smells fantastic but is a brilliant cleanser for problem or spot-prone skin. Raspberries contain vitamin C, essential for rapid healing and growth of healthy tissue. This treatment feeds the skin and rids you of nasty blemishes. Even if you don't suffer from bad skin, one try of my berry beautiful mask is guaranteed to leave you feeling like royalty.

2 tablespoons raspberries, well mashed
1 teaspoon natural yoghurt
1 teaspoon oatmeal

Combine all the ingredients into a smooth paste. Apply to the face, making sure to avoid the eye area, and rinse off after twenty minutes.

Head massage is an excellent beauty treatment for an Aries. Aries, buy your partner a course on how to give good massages! They can learn, too, about the best area to massage to cure various ailments. Bear in mind, though, that the head of an Aries can be sensitive, and soft massage is what's called for, not a Swedish pummel! Leave that kind of treatment for Gemini . . .

Your Ideal Health Sign Holiday

You need excitement and fast-paced action. Snow sports are ideal for you. Skiing in Austria is my tip for the ram. If you haven't tried it yet, then get on the piste. You'll have a ball.

TAURUS

THE BULL

Ruling Planet: Venus, the planet of love

Triplicity or Element: Earth

Quadruplicity or Mode: Fixed

Key words: Stubborn, sensual, loyal, affectionate and materialistic, craves stability and security

The Origin of Taurus

The god Zeus was in love with a beautiful princess called Europa. Zeus could change himself into anything he wanted, so he turned himself into a beautiful white bull and mingled with the rest of Europa's herd. Europa was immediately attracted to this beautiful beast and became very friendly with it. One day she went for a ride on its back and the bull swam away over the seas with her, where he revealed himself as the handsome god Zeus. This form of Zeus was placed in the skies as a constellation, now known as Taurus – the bull.

What Taurus is Like

Almost everyone knows that the key word for Taurus is stubborn. They are also patient and reliable. If they make you a promise they are highly unlikely to break it. They are methodical. Lovers of the home, they often marry too young. They want to experience everything before everyone else. Lovers of food, they have to watch their waistline – they can't resist a beautiful-looking dish. They also love money and can at times be materialistic.

Stability is essential to Taurus and without a good partner to guide them they can get themselves into a lot of trouble. If their loved ones look after them, they will return the favour tenfold. Both emotional and material security is essential. Sometimes they need to learn to be a little more flexible, but there is always thought behind their actions.

Taurus rules the throat and many people of this sign have soft gentle voices. Some of the best singers in the world are born under this sign. Barbra Streisand, James Brown and Tammy Wynette were all born under the sign of Taurus the bull.

If you employ someone of this sun sign do not expect them to be fast workers. They will not cut corners. They will go the proper route and will not allow you to see what they have done until they are proud of their efforts.

They will always be there for their true friends, sometimes paying a high personal price to do so. They are capable of giving intelligent and practical advice.

Their ruling planet is Venus the planet of love. The heart will always rule the head of a Taurus. Relationships are extremely important to them and a single Taurus is not usually a very happy one. They need a partner to be best friend and lover all rolled into one.

They like to flirt but will not allow their partners to do so. A partner who flirts will see the possessive and jealous side of a Taurus surface – not a pleasant sight. A Taurus with an unreciprocated crush on someone can become a little obsessive. Never lead a Taurus on if you don't mean it because you'll never get rid of them.

They are the first of the fixed quality signs in the zodiac, which is where they get their stubbornness from. Don't take advantage of their good nature. When they want to be stubborn they will dig their heels in and will not forgive you no matter how much begging and grovelling you do.

Their element is earth and they are often likened to a house, solid and dependable. Earth signs are dependable and ambitious but they also hate admitting they're wrong. Long marriages are what they crave and the home and family are terribly important to them. They are likely to return to the same shops time after time.

The three most important things to a Taurus are food, sex and money, and sometimes all three mixed together!

Their colours are pastel shades, so you usually see them in pale blues, greens and pinks. Don't be fooled by these subtle shades. They don't need to wear bright colours to let you know they're around. Their mere presence is enough.

Almost all Taureans are prone to laziness, I'm afraid, although not in a slobbish way. It just takes them a while to get themselves together. Take them for a night on the town and you will not have a pretty sight the morning after. In fact you'll be lucky if they get up before lunch.

They will get the tasks that life presents to them completed, but in their own time, and if you tell them to hurry up then they will take even longer just to make a point. (Exactly what the point is I'm really not sure!)

They are willing to wait for what they want in life. When I was a child I had a Taurean friend. She desperately wanted a doll she had seen. Well, I also wanted this same doll, which as I remember was very expensive. I begged my parents non-stop in my crafty Scorpio way to buy me the doll. She, on the other hand, waited and saved up her pocket money and did odd jobs for her family for six weeks so that she could buy it herself. She did buy her doll and got much enjoyment from it. Her gift of patience is what made it possible.

Because of the hard work they put into things Taureans make excellent employees. If you treat them well they will stay with you until retirement beckons.

Just make sure that you buy them a cake instead of a watch. Or just give them the cash. The feeling of money in their pockets will do more for them than any bunch of flowers you could present.

We all have to struggle from time to time to make our bodies what we'd like. But even more so in the case of the bull. Because of their tendency to overindulge in food they can put on weight around the waist and neck. However, they are also naturally athletic, and if they commit to it should have no problem working out at the gym or doing regular exercise.

The biggest problem for them is looking after their voices. Funny, really, considering a lot of them crave to be singers. A little honey in hot water is always excellent for the throat.

How to Spot a Taurus

You can often tell Taureans by their unusual voices. They can also be spotted by their bull-like neck – mostly the men – and occasionally by their soft, sensual, even features. The men are usually stocky. Jack Nicholson looks a typical Taurean and you can tell just by the broad neck and the way he walks that he is proud to be this sign and isn't afraid who knows it.

The Devil and the Angel

Jack Nicholson is regarded by many as a bit of a DEVIL TAURUS. He's often seen with a consecutive string of beauties on his arm, and a glint in his eye!

The ANGEL TAURUS is patient, loving, dependable and solid. Pope John Paul II would be an Angel Taurus, always there for his church, religion and beliefs and deeply committed to the love of his life, God. Another prime example, of course, is Her Majesty Queen Elizabeth.

Taurus Health and Development from Child to Adult

Taurean babies can be demanding and have irregular sleep patterns, and seem at first to need a lot more attention than other babies. Amazingly, at about three months they surprise us all and turn into little angels. Don't be fooled though. Once they learn the useful art of walking they will get their noses into anything they can and you will have to move those valuables out of reach. Darkness, noise and dogs, which usually terrify small children, hold no fear for little Taureans. Their fascination for the scary may get them into trouble so you'll have to watch their daring moods.

At five years of age their traits are likely to be impulsiveness, initiative, intuition and definitely stubbornness. You will be surprised at the way they develop and make achievements at school. Their reports from their teachers will show them to be full of character. However, if they don't like their teacher they may refuse to learn, so it is important you sort out character clashes as soon as they occur. Some parents, ambitious about their child's career, may even go to the extremes of moving schools. Taurean children need to be able to relate to their peers, too, or they will rebel against them, and you know how long that stubbornness can last! At this age it is essential they learn the basics of reading and writing or they will be left behind when the hard work really begins. They will, however, have an unconventional way in which to achieve their aims.

At 11 their personality develops even stronger and the independent nature becomes more evident. Their worst subjects are usually sport and mathematics. They love music, in which they should definitely be encouraged. Indeed, if only parents encouraged the closet hair-brush-singing Taureans better we might have a few more vocalists to choose from in our record collections. They have a natural ear for music and if possible should be encouraged to take after-school music lessons. In appearance these are most striking children, not afraid to strut their stuff around the classroom should their parents' budgets allow them to dress to their expensive and with-it tastes.

At 16 they will have a magnetic appeal to the opposite sex. These are the teenagers who will be caught reading love notes their classmates have passed to them. At this age, however, they will not have a very high opinion of the opposite sex in general, so beware, this is the love-them-and-leave-them age. They can be callous in the extreme but they will attract admirers like moths to a flame. Education could go either way as their social life tends to dictate their time. Encourage them fully in anything they are good at. For the 16-year-old Taurus who starts to study the career they wish to be in will usually be the director or owner of the company by 30. That steadfast determination will see them plod on no matter how boring it may seem to others. That is why a lot of entertainers who make it late are born under this sign. They don't give up until they have reached their goal, no matter how long it takes. As they say, better late than never.

At 21 this is a very practical person indeed. They should never be hurried, or rather, won't be hurried. They will be generous to those they love but if they don't like you watch out because they'll walk all over you. They get bored with small talk so if you're trying to chat them up then cut to the chase and don't bother with the small talk. They can get on quite easily in their chosen profession unless forced to do a job they don't like or feel they don't look good in. Then they will be indignant. They usually marry in a hurry as they like to prove they can do it before anyone else, so if you have the right effect on them you could find yourself talking baby names before the first date is over. If they are not besotted by you, then marriage talk is definitely a no-no. Between 20 and 25 they usually make their mark and are established in their chosen job or profession. They like the good life and to have nice things around them. Taurean tastes, though, can vary widely.

At 40 they start to make provisions for their old age. This is when they start to throw extra money into their pension plan and make arrangements for a comfortable retirement. They are at their peak now both mentally and physically. In fact they usually look better now than they did at 18. Regardless of their station in life, whatever level they are in their profession, they carry with them an air of authority and wisdom. Men at this age can experience some digestive problems, probably from over-indulgence, and the reason they suffer from it more than women is because they don't like to seek help.

In their seventies they can annoy people very easily with their opinions on things. They refuse to be wrong and disapprove of situations they know nothing about. Few end up living with their siblings. They wouldn't last two minutes together with the Taurean's biased views on modern-day living. If they can learn to listen when others talk then they stand a chance. Watch out for rheumatism at this age. Exercise on a regular basis is terribly important. Always ready to shock with a flirty comment, they are addictive even at grand old 70.

Taurean Careers . . .

Singer or dancer. You are naturally light on your feet.

Restaurant owner. A good choice with all that food and lovely cash to count.

Banker. Even more lovely cash to count.

. . . not so Taurean Careers

Hairdresser. Too clumsy, I'm afraid.

Judge. You would fall too hard for a sob story and let everybody off.

Speed typist. Too slow, I'm afraid.

Wine taster. You'd forget to spit it out and swallow it instead.

Famous Taureans

Actors Jack Nicholson, Shirley MacLaine, Al Pacino, child star Shirley Temple, singers Barbra Streisand, Mica Paris, Engelbert Humperdinck, Mark Morrison, James Brown, Tammy Wynette and Stevie Wonder, prime minister Tony Blair.

Health Sore Points

Taurus rules the throat and if any ailment is going to affect you it's likely to show up first as a sore throat or a husky voice. Even if it is only a visit to a nightclub you are unlikely to find yourself in top voice the following morning. Smoky atmospheres take their toll on you and although you are unlikely to feel bad you will sound as if you have been up all week.

The way a Taurus eats is a talent all of its own. You are so sensual about food that you could make somebody fall in love with you just by watching you eat. So of course overindulgence and indigestion also come into play. The first thing that needs to be learned is moderation. If Taureans could just learn when they have had enough they wouldn't get bloated or have acid indigestion. A little and often is the way most older bulls like to eat as they have learned through the years the consequences of not listening to their bodies.

If you ask Taureans if they are tired or if they want to have a rest they will probably become more energetic just to prove you wrong. Never – and this is important – never challenge a Taurus to a drinking competition. Not only will they drink you under the table, they'll still carry on after you've dropped. And if you want to impress them when you buy them a drink, buy only the best wine because they are sure to take note of the price.

Because of the influence of the ruling planet Venus Taureans will often find they can't eat when they are in love. That is why they call it being lovesick! Some go to the other extreme and cannot stop eating when they are in love.

Cures and Counsel

Regular exercise is really good for Taurus. If it is possible to walk to work then you will have found the first step to good health. If you can get into walking at an early stage you will probably keep to it. There may be a few bulls around with a rounded stomach from too much late-night munching but a big stomach on a Taurus does not look like it belongs. It is rather like a spare part. You will never look comfortable with the excess weight because you know it is not supposed to be there. And don't go shopping on an empty stomach – you'll buy too much food!

It is important, if you use your voice for your job, that you take regular drinks to help with dryness of the throat. If you have to give a talk or a lecture then mucus-producing foods must be avoided. So it is out with the chocolate and milk, as well as other dairy products and bread. Many singers are advised not to eat chocolate before they perform, this is because it produces mucus in the throat and prevents the voice performing at its best.

Some simple exercises, from the comfort of an armchair, are very good for the Taurean neck. Gently drop the head forward on to the chest and roll it round from right to left, opening the mouth as your head goes back and then bringing it round to the front again. Do this twice, then start with the head forward resting on your chest and move it back until you are looking at the ceiling (remember to open your mouth as the head goes back, it's important for correct breathing). Then with your head in its normal position let your left ear drop to your left shoulder and then your right ear to the right shoulder. Go through this routine twice. Take five minutes out of each day for this and stiffness should start to become a rarity.

Funny how we can all find half an hour to sit down and watch our favourite soap opera and yet we can never find five minutes for a bit of real self-indulgence. Believe me, you will get far more de-stressing from doing exercises like these than from watching one of the soaps. After the drama of a soap you probably have to lie down and rest! The key is to make the time and there is no time like the present. In fact, put this book down and try it now. No excuses. If you don't find time for yourself then no one else will. Put yourself at the top of your priorities.

Trust your instincts and learn what is good for you and what is making you feel ill. We've all seen that friend who insists on having another glass of red wine at the party even though they have obviously had their fill. This is probably the Taurus – they don't always know when to stop.

Inhalation Potion

Here's an inhalation to relieve Taurean catarrh.

leaves from the horse chestnut tree, dried
150 ml/5 fl oz warm water
25 g/1 oz saltpetre

Soak the dried leaves in the water with the saltpetre for 1 hour. Remove the leaves and allow them to dry. When completely dry, crumble them into a powder. Burn on a tin or spoon and inhale the fumes. (Children must be supervised.)

Blackcurrant Cure for Sore Throats

Romanies have been using the leaves as well as the currants for many years to cure sore throats.

50 g/2 oz blackcurrants
25 g/1 oz blackcurrant leaves
300 ml/½ pint water

Bring the currants and leaves to the boil in the water then reduce the heat and simmer for 15 minutes. Strain and drink as required.

Thyme Tea for the Throat

My grandmother always insisted this tea be made in a china teapot. I think it was just about the pleasure she took in her crockery but I'm going to insist you do the same. I've never made it any other way and I don't intend to start now.

2 teaspoons fresh wild thyme leaves (or ½ teaspoon dried thyme)
900 ml/1½ pints boiling water

Put the herb in a china teapot, cover with the freshly boiled water and leave for 1 hour. Strain and drink as required.

Two Indigestion Remedies

Quassia chips should be available from your local health food shop. By the way, don't be afraid to request items that aren't currently stocked. After all, the shopkeepers will never know you want it if you don't ask, and you could be doing a lot of people a favour if you get in a successful herb or remedy.

Take only the amount recommended in the recipes. Avoid your Taurean tendency to overindulge. It won't harm you, but it could cancel out what you are trying to achieve.

10 g/½ oz quassia chips
600 ml/1 pint water

Boil the quassia chips in the water for 15 minutes. Strain and take 1 tablespoon of the liquid 3 times daily after meals.

7 g/¼ oz fresh camomile
15 g/½ oz fresh catmint
15 g/½ oz fresh dandelion
15 g/½ oz agrimony
900 ml/1½ pints water

Bring the herbs to the boil in the water and then simmer for 15 minutes. Take 2 tablespoons 3 times daily after meals.

Good Taurus Food

Taureans have a tendency to be deficient in the cell salt natrum sulphuricum, otherwise known as sulphate of soda or sodium sulphate. As a result of this the most common ailments for this stubborn and sensual sign are rheumatism, arthritis, and some pancreas, liver and kidney problems. Don't forget that exercise is as important as diet and mobility of the joints must be maintained. Sitting in one position for too long can cause stiffness so you need to make sure you take regular breaks and exercise the neck muscles in particular.

There are many ways you can take care of deficiencies. Natrum sulphuricum is found in apples, celery, spinach, radishes, cos lettuce, strawberries and pomegranates. Variety is the spice of life and Taurus certainly has a variety to choose from here.

Strawberry Strengthener

Here is a delicious way to get sodium sulphate in the diet. It is especially good for teenagers.

1 pear, peeled and cored
a handful of strawberries, hulled
150 ml/5 fl oz water

It is easier to make if you have a juicing machine, but if not just mash the fruit together, whisk in the water and drink it.

Apples are particularly good for Taurus, with their high sodium content. 'An apple a day keeps the doctor away' could never be more true than for you. Apples are great for the blood and can also help ward off rheumatism, gout, gall stones and bladder difficulties. Taurus should learn to experiment with the pleasures of apple sauce, apple pie or apple juice to do themselves a favour for years to come.

The main key is regularity and making a conscious effort to eat breakfast, lunch and dinner. Eat as much fruit as possible. Prevention is better than any cure.

We've all been there in a restaurant with friends and in a party spirit, wanting to order what we know our stomachs cannot handle. Taurus, with love so often on your mind, don't miss your chance by overindulging in the food and drink beforehand! I always watch people whenever I'm out and when I see a poor chap trying to find the strength to put another forkful of food into his mouth, I know he is a Taurean. They have this look on their face which says, 'I can't help myself.' Never tell a Taurus when they've had enough or they will continue out of spite. You must seduce the food away from them. Remember this is a very sexy sign and they need to be flirted with at every available moment if you want them to follow your whims and desires.

Many Taureans in their teenage years battle with eating disorders and it needs a strong family background and good support to prevent this progressing into a serious problem. Fluctuating weight can lead you to seek extreme measures and I am here to tell you: don't even think about it. Extreme measures don't work. If you are unhappy with your weight then look at your lifestyle and seek a permanent change, not a temporary one, which is what crash dieting is. At the back of my book you will find a list of numbers and helplines. If you need any help then you can talk in person to an expert.

Believe me, I have learnt over the past twelve years of giving readings that eating disorders are never your friend, they are always the enemy. I have seen the best relationships break down because the person (man or woman) with the problem doesn't share it with their partner. The partner criticizes the loved one for ignoring their difficulty, forgetting of course the great lengths they have gone to in order to hide their problem.

Earth signs, strangely enough, do need to make sure that they get enough fat in their diets, so don't go all extremely-low-fat on me.

Learn what is in your food. And watch your taste for luxury. It is no good putting a little bit of expensive fuel into a car that has to go on a long journey. Cheap fuel will not do either. This sign must have good quality and lasting foods in order to be able to think straight and to operate in the best possible way.

Steer away from products that are rich and fattening. A lean diet (but not totally fat-free) is best for a Taurean.

Choose the lean cuts of meat and reach for the fruit instead of the chocolate bar. Chocolate can depress you and is the worst thing to turn to for comfort.

A hungry Taurean will never be satisfied by a hamburger but will always crave good quality food. Convenience food doesn't usually agree with you and you end up complaining, so I need hardly advise against such foods here.

Plants for Star Therapy

The lucky plant for Taurus is the periwinkle, a pretty and colourful flower. This grows best on rocky ground and is great to use as ground cover. If you want to plant some in your garden to bring luck then sow it in the spring.

Health Checklist

- For that vulnerable Taurus throat, baptisia or lachesis are fantastic and are what many of the top homeopaths recommend. They are also good for toxic intestinal conditions. And stock up on zinc lozenges, which contain vitamin C.
- The best drink for a Taurus is water and plenty of it. This is the simplest, best and most effective health measure – and the cheapest too. There is no excuse for not drinking lots of water, so give it a go. You will end up feeling and looking 100 per cent better.
- To reduce catarrh turn to zinc, which can be found in seafood, beef, pork, dairy products, green

vegetables and cereals. Or take supplements, if you must. Recommended daily intake is 15 mg.

- Vitamin C, which helps the body fight infections, can be found in blackcurrants, kiwi fruit, peas, potatoes, Brussels sprouts, broccoli and oranges. Or take supplements, if you must. Recommended daily intake is 60 mg.
- Sniff tea tree and eucalyptus oils and take garlic supplements to ward off colds, if you can spot the symptoms in time.
- For digestion difficulties try peppermint oil and marsh mallow (the herb, not the sweet!) taken internally or rubbed on externally. If you've overeaten, try the herb centaury. But remember, Taurus, you don't have to eat something just because it looks nice.
- Do the neck exercises I gave you on page 110 to avoid stiffness.

Are You a True Taurus?

Be honest! Write down 'yes' or 'no', then read the advice below.

1. Do you continue eating your food, even when you know you are full?
2. If the answer to number 1 is yes, do you do this to annoy a loved one when you know they think you are being a pig?
3. Do you eat any of the following on a regular basis: strawberries, apples, spinach and celery?

4 Do you suffer often from sore throats?
5 Do you find that your heart rules your head in love?
6 Do you flirt with friends' partners?
7 Do you jump into relationships too quickly?
8 Do you suffer from neck problems?
9 Do you secretly enjoy a good argument?
10 Do you lie about the cost of things to impress friends?
11 Are you greedy about money?
12 Are you or have you been a closet pop star in your time?
13 Do you think it is OK for you to flirt but not for your partner?
14 Do you tend to go for pastel shades?
15 Have you ever been in love to the point of not being able to think of anything but the person who has stolen your heart? Have you ever been obsessed?
16 Do you find you lose your voice after a night on the tiles, even if you don't smoke?
17 Have you been known to lie in after midday on your day off?
18 Do you drink water on a regular basis?
19 Do you turn to chocolate when someone has upset you or you are worried?
20 Do you usually order too much food so that you have to leave some behind (or force it down!)?

If you answered mostly 'yes' then you are a very honest Taurean indeed. You are a fun-loving, home-loving entertainer and a good supporter of friends and family. Everyone should have a Taurean to look after them! Just make sure that you have someone to look after you as well. You deserve something back for all that you give others.

If you answered yes to questions 1, 2 and 4 then you may have an allergy to certain foods and you should think about finding out what it is that doesn't agree with you.

If you answered yes to question number 3 then you are on the right path to good health because these foods are essential to you.

If you answered yes to question number 7 then well done. You are over the first hurdle when you can admit that your heart rules your head. Just try to let your head tell your heart what to do from time to time.

If you answered no to question 6 then watch out because if the flirt in you hasn't come out yet you may be building up to something that could shock all around. Just remember, it's OK to flirt, but don't take it any further. You're too emotional for that scene, Taurus.

If you answered mostly 'no' then you don't seem to be a typical Taurean and you could be missing out on a great deal of fun. If you answered no to question 9 then you don't know what you're missing, Taurus. That's where your talent lies. You have so much inside you. It's time to let it all out!

I hope question 3 wasn't one you answered no to. Taureans love food and I am sure you will be able to devise some recipes into which to incorporate these foods.

Learn more about your moon sign by reading the chapter later on in this book. It may explain some of those outbursts that take you by surprise. And maybe you should get a family member to go through the survey again with you. You know that stubbornness is one of your main traits and you may be too stubborn to admit what deep down you know to be true. Enjoy learning about yourself and keep this book to hand for future reference. Try the questionnaire again in six months to see if there's any change. If you can be honest with yourself, you'll be on the right track.

The Drinker's Guide to the Zodiac

Gin and Scotch are taboo for this sign, I'm afraid. If you are looking for an alternative drink, you'll probably be safest with brandy or sherry. Wine can give Taureans acid indigestion.

Lord Chamberlain

Here's how to tantalize a Taurus. Watch out, though, because the results could be too much for you to handle. Perhaps you'd better make up your drink too so that you can party together with the fuel that your individual signs require.

4–5 ice cubes
1 part port
1 part dry French vermouth
3 drops angostura bitters
2 parts brandy
1 thin slice of lemon

Put the ice cubes into a glass jug. Pour the port and vermouth over the ice, shake the bitters over and add the brandy. Stir vigorously, strain and pour into a chilled Martini glass. Squeeze the lemon over the mixture and drop it in.

Star Menu

One way to a Taurean heart is definitely through the stomach!

Oyster Passion

Taureans love beautiful and seductive food. Oysters are a winner though they may not be filling enough for the greedy bull. All the same, try this romantic dish on a Taurean. They might be so impressed that you don't make it to dessert! This really should be just for 2 people.

20 oysters, scrubbed and opened
225 g/8 oz coarse salt
60 g/generous 2 oz butter
3 rashers bacon
2 tablespoons dried breadcrumbs
a dash of Tabasco
½ teaspoon of salt
1 tablespoon chopped spring onions
100 g/4 oz cooked spinach
chopped fresh parsley

Arrange the oysters on a bed of the coarse salt in a shallow pan and set aside. Preheat the grill to hot. In a frying pan melt the butter, add the rest of the ingredients and cook over a gentle heat for 10 minutes or until you have a lightly cooked stuffing. Divide the stuffing between the oysters and place under the hot grill until bubbling and browning to your approval.

Stuffed Baked Apples

Although this recipe contains sugar it is not as fattening as the cakes Taurus can be known to head for. But it is just as tasty, and apples, as we know, are a very good food for the bull. This serves 4.

4 even-sized cooking apples
75 g/3 oz mixed dried fruit
2 tablespoons demerara sugar
25 g/1 oz butter
1½ tablespoons water

Preheat the oven to hot (230°F/450°C/gas 8). Core the apples (you'll need to use a corer for a neat result) and make a cut in the skin around the middle. Place in an ovenproof dish. Mix together the dried fruit and sugar and use to fill the apples. Put a little butter on each apple and sprinkle the water over them. Bake until the apples soften: about 1 hour.

Star Beauty

Making your own beauty products will take the pressure off that abused Taurean purse! And they are wonderfully good for you too.

Neck Cream

Older Taureans worry that their neck will sag and some will buy creams and lotions at any price to try to prevent it. Here is a cream you can make for the Taurean neck. Lend it to the other signs if you can spare it – I'm sure they'll appreciate it!

2 egg yolks
2 tablespoons cider vinegar
120 ml/4 fl oz olive oil
mayonnaise

Mix the egg yolks, cider vinegar and olive oil together and then add enough mayonnaise so that you have a paste. Apply in upward motions to the neck. Put a towel underneath your head and neck and lie down for 10 minutes with your eyes closed. You should start to feel the difference in your skin as soon as you take it off.

Eye Mask

Here is a great beauty secret that is certain to become a firm favourite. It is fantastic for reducing puffiness or swelling around the eyes. Taureans often suffer from this because you are too conscientious (and stubborn) to take off the time you need. Test this for coolness on your wrist before you put it on your eyes. It moisturizes, nourishes and feeds the delicate area around the eyes.

The lecithin prevents the cream from going off. Do not add any perfume as it could cause irritation. Get the lanolin from your chemist. There are two types:

anhydrous, which has no added water, and hydrous, which has a high water content. Use the anhydrous type in this recipe.

1 tablespoon lanolin (see note above)
1½ tablespoons almond oil
1 tablespoon powdered lecithin
2 teaspoons cold water

Fill a pan with water and place on the heat. Fit a heat-proof bowl over the pan and put the lanolin in it. Stir as the water heats up and the lanolin melts. Remove the melted lanolin from the heat and slowly add the almond oil and the lecithin, beating carefully to avoid lumps. Add the cold water and beat it all together well using an electric hand-held beater or a wooden spoon.

You will have made about 25 g/1 oz rich cream in about 5 minutes. It really is very simple. Although rich the cream will be runny and will not drag your skin. Transfer to a clean, screw-top jar and keep in the refrigerator.

Your Ideal Health Sign Holiday

France is the place for the bull. With all that great food and wine you won't want to leave. Make sure you do plenty of walking and sightseeing to work off those extra calories. Nowhere could be more romantic than France for the sign ruled by Venus, the goddess of love.

GEMINI

THE TWINS

Ruling Planet: Mercury, the planet of communication

Triplicity or Element: Air

Quadruplicity or Mode: Mutable

Key words: Generous, restless, adaptable, excitable, fickle, two-sided

The Origin of Gemini

Gemini represents, according to Greek mythology, the twin gods Castor and Pollux, sons of the great god Zeus. They were the friends and protectors of all seamen. Because of all the work they did to protect men of the sea they were immortalized as a constellation.

What Gemini is Like

This is the first dual sign in the zodiac and if you know one then you will agree that they are hard to miss. This sign represents communication, the need to talk and to live. Don't even bother getting involved in a debate with someone born under this sign because they have the ability to talk about everything with authority – even things they know nothing about. And they will outlast you. If you say black they say white just to be different. Even if they were to agree with you about a matter they may decide to disagree just to liven things up. They love to play devil's advocate. But they will always try to help the lesser soul.

Adaptable and versatile, they are the Peter Pan of the zodiac, looking more youthful the older they get. The funny thing is that when life is stressful and there is lots going on, they feel quite normal. As soon as things start to calm down they worry.

You can guarantee that Gemini will have a full social calendar. When they say they have to check their diary, they mean it. Always busy, they're likely to get someone else to handle everyday chores. They need to plan ahead when shopping, otherwise they'll buy all the wrong things.

They are often jacks of all trades, but masters of none. They suffer from a short attention span and have a low boredom threshold. They cannot concentrate on one thing, and they are never thinking about what they are currently doing, but about what they will be doing tomorrow. They will look for fun elsewhere should you be unable to supply it.

My mother used to say that special television programmes that last ten minutes should be made for Geminis. Their attention span may be short but don't get me wrong – they will debate the programme for at least two hours afterwards.

Watch out if you are dating somebody of this sign. They can send out more signals than Clapham Junction. Sizzling-hot one minute and icy-cold the next. They won't be afraid to flirt with your friends either. To them it is plain old fun and if you make a point of it they will think you're strange.

They get on better with the opposite sex. They are in their prime position when able to talk from an experienced stance about how unknowledgeable others are about their own sex. Being a modern man or woman will do you no good as they have already decided that you don't know what it means.

If you invite them to a party you will never look back. They can entertain and make even the grumpiest of signs laugh. Being the first mutable sign of the zodiac and with air as their element they are the party people. But give them advance warning if you want to invite them anywhere, because they are likely to be booked up months in advance. They will also say they are free when they're not. They make ten arrangements and then attend the one they're in the mood for on the day.

The colour that brings luck for this sign is yellow and you will often see them donning it when after a new conquest.

Many people born under the sign of Gemini work in the media. They can handle stress and they thrive on gossip. Air signs – Gemini, Libra and Aquarius – can also take other people's ideas and make them happen, and are especially good at making a success out of fire signs' ideas – Aries, Leo and Sagittarius. (Think about it: fire needs air. An air sign can make a fire sign's idea happen in a way the fire sign could not do on its own, yet the air sign probably couldn't have thought up the idea in the first place. It's team work.) Media is ideal for Gemini because they find it hard to learn any one subject fully and if they can keep learning titbits quickly enough they never get bored. New projects cannot come quickly enough for them, so they are ideal for this fast-changing world.

Gemini have a tendency to get attracted to bad relationships. They want to heal the world and they think it is their job to make everyone better. Don't get angry if you hear them say 'I know' when you tell them about your problems. They really do think they know.

Be kind to this sign. At first they can seem like know-it-alls who think they have been everywhere and done everything, but this is just a cover-up for a very vulnerable and beautiful personality.

What I love about this sign is its versatility. If you say let's go to the moon tomorrow they may well say yes. Their ruling planet Mercury is the planet of travel and communication and many young Geminis get themselves mixed up in foreign love affairs. If you ask a middle-aged Gemini who their first love was their eyes are likely to mist over as they try to remember a name that is too foreign to recall. But don't be fooled. They will remember all they got up to. Their memories retain all of the fun points of their lives.

These characters are logical, rational and intelligent, but because of the influence of Mercury need to move on to new heights and new places. Many Geminis find themselves trying to move abroad at some point in their lives. It is that old story of the grass always being greener.

Unlike many of us Geminis can do two things at once, and many are ambidextrous. They must be careful not to break too many promises or they could earn themselves a most unsavoury reputation. But, believe me, with one of these around you will not need to turn on the television. A Gemini is entertainment enough, and more addictive than any soap, that's for sure!

How to Spot a Gemini

Sparkling eyes are a giveaway, probably because they are brimming over with all the latest gossip they have been able to glean.

The Devil and the Angel

The DEVIL GEMINI is the character who is cynical and selfish and lives purely for his or her own pleasure.

Numerous relationships aren't unusual for Geminis and they probably haven't even bothered to tell half of their lovers that that particular romance is over. (They didn't have the time!)

Marilyn Monroe was a bit of a devil Gemini. She loved the media and she also had her share of lovers, moving on when she had learned all she could from them. The depressive side of her was also typical. Geminis can make out they want fun and then get upset when they're not offered a serious relationship. She was one of my idols when I was younger because she made so much from her life after starting out with nothing. Her non-stop existence and the typical way she would start a film but have problems finishing it also intrigued me.

Then there is the ANGEL GEMINI, always happy and in a party spirit, full of love and making time for anyone that needs their good yet not 100 per cent researched advice. A prime example is Prince William, who put his own feelings to one side when people were grieving over his mother's death, without fully understanding what was happening himself. Here is a man who is sure to link charity and media together in the future to help his country. Let's watch and see.

Gemini Health and Development from Child to Adult

The Gemini baby is a most individual one. Some mothers get worried at this time when the baby boy Gemini prefers a doll to a bear. Don't worry. They get on better with the opposite sex even at this age and can play as happily with their brother's or sister's toys as with their own. They will also enjoy ripping up paper and books so don't leave your favourite book in their pram, and definitely don't let them handle photo albums yet. They are daydreamers and their eyes are usually their most distinctive feature. Even before they can talk their eyes will sparkle a knowing look to you. As a tiny baby they should not really be any trouble and you shouldn't have to face too many sleepless nights with this one.

At five years of age you are likely to see a quiet and obedient child who is a pleasure to be with and not too demanding. Conversations with them will be as good as with your friends, and their wit and humour is likely to match even the funniest of your companions. They will be neat, tidy and well mannered. You should be able to take them to most adult functions without worrying that they will misbehave and show you up. They may not yet show signs of any particular talent but they will want to know about everything. They often have an aloof air and are very fond of daydreaming. Do not expect their educational reports to be fantastic. There is some way to go yet before teachers realize just what an individual they are dealing with.

At 11 they start to show a love of the arts and will probably want to go and see shows for their birthday rather than get a toy. They are starting to learn more and more from people now instead of from things and whether you pick up tickets for a ballet or a wrestling match your Gemini is sure to appreciate it – unless of course they've seen it before. It has to be a new experience. If the Gemini's friends talk about liking a band then the Gemini will explain that he or she liked them before they were famous. Geminis are not liars, but they do like to expand the truth at times. The way they see it is that if they know they're telling a tall story, then so should you. This is also a child that's happy to play alone, but beware, they do have a tendency for wandering off and can even forget where they live. Sewing their names and addresses in their clothes is highly recommended.

At 16 they will be more independent than ever and won't like being told what time to come home. Staying out late at night or even overnight is not uncommon. But don't be concerned: the chances of them being cosied up with one person and getting up to no good are few. They're just too busy partying and talking to lots of friends. They have far too much to say right now to waste it on just one other. They will not necessarily show a great interest in the opposite sex now. It is more characters and personalities that will draw them in. Friends are likely to be very varied and of many different styles as they try to decide which bits to take from each person. They are very popular and have a terrific sense of humour. In fact they probably won't be afraid to throw a party while you're home and may even spend most of the evening talking to the older generation and ignoring their friends. Watch out next year, though. At 17 they fall in love hard and fast. They'd better not marry yet, however, because they haven't finished cocooning and changing.

At 21 they are lazy but lucky. Many Geminis at this age decide to study something that deep down they know they will never pursue. Their personality gets them places but they don't yet have the desire to reach the top. They are perfectly happy to potter about and may even attempt some world travel, although funds will probably get them only as far as the train station. Their pleasures right now are simple: alcohol, relationships and possibly an obscure sport left over from their schooldays. They can at times be terrible scroungers, a little backward about coming forward when it's time to pay for things, even if they've got the money. If there's a serious relationship around then problems are likely to be money-based or down to that roving eye. They haven't yet got an awful lot of time for children.

The two ages when they are most likely to be unfaithful are 19 and 26. If they marry between 26 and 29 it is usually for the right reasons and their tight-fisted attitude and selfish streak vanish immediately.

At 40 they are mentally 21 and their hobbies and interests will be pretty similar to those of the years before. They will be wearing similar styles to when they were younger and can usually get away with it. However, the unfaithful traits have definitely gone by now and they are quite happy to settle down with one person only. It is unlikely that they have stayed in the same profession without at least trying another one as they always think they should be doing something else.

In their seventies they are still partying with people of all ages and are not afraid to strut their stuff. Swelling of the joints can become a problem but as long as they take something to calm it down it should not become a major worry. You will see them catnapping and then waking up to see what they have missed. You are unlikely to believe any of the stories they tell you about their past and yet they are probably telling the truth. Well, mostly.

Gemini Careers . . .

Air stewardess. Links both travel and people together, so ideal for you.

Socialite with a string of lovers. Just perfect.

Editor of a tabloid newspaper. Just think of all that gossip, with more constantly on the way.

Any job involving sales skills.

. . . not so Gemini Careers

Nun or priest. My goodness, all that time on your own? You must be joking! (Although I'm sure you'd like to hear the confessions.)

Pub landlord. What, listening to people's problems instead of talking about them?

Butcher. You are a real animal lover.

Anything that involves being perfectly on time. You'll get there when you get there.

Famous Geminis

Comedian Bob Monkhouse, actors Joan Collins, Priscilla Presley, newspaper magnate Lord Beaverbrook, model Naomi Campbell, presenter Anthea Turner, singers Noel Gallagher and Kylie Minogue, ad man Charles Saatchi.

Health Sore Points

Gemini rules the chest, shoulders, nervous system and lungs. Any Gemini who smokes can be spotted a mile away: it doesn't suit you! You probably don't even bother to puff, just hold the cigarette for effect. You know it doesn't really agree with you. You are probably only smoking because someone told you years ago not to.

You are so busy having a good time you don't remember to pay attention to health problems until it is too late to easily do something about them. Gemini is the schoolchild with the rash who is too busy asking Mum for permission to go to a party to tell her about the itching, and by the time the child does report the problem, half the school has chicken pox. Nervous exhaustion and mental strain are often a problem for Gemini. You are too busy thinking of new things to wonder if your brain can cope with the overload. You want to know everything about everyone and quite often your health problems are of your own making.

Geminis eat at midnight, thinking the meal is a teatime one. You are such great party-goers that partners can never drag you home. Even when the sun comes up you are still claiming, 'It's early!' But a healthy mind and body go hand in hand so Geminis must make sure to get the correct amount of sleep. Each person finds his or her own level but you need to make sure you really are getting the amount you need and that you are not just conning yourself into thinking you look good with black rings under your eyes.

A broken arm or strained shoulder is likely to occur

at some point during your teens. Hands and arms are a problem because you use your hands until they are ready to drop off. You shake the hand of every new person you meet, and you have a strong handshake. You are likely to be tapping away on a keyboard or ringing up sales on a till and then going home, where you won't sit still for longer than ten minutes, always finding something to do or to clean.

Most of Gemini's problems stem from mental stress. You need a strong character to balance you so you don't burn yourself out.

Cures and Counsel

Just because Geminis thrive on stress doesn't mean it's always good for you. It is vital that if you have a hard day you reward your body by doing something relaxing, something to help you wind down. A good hobby for you would be yoga: it is peaceful and should help calm both mind and body. But I'm afraid it's unlikely a Gemini will stop at the yoga. The madman jogging past your house at ten p.m. is likely to be John the Gemini working off the last of the day's energy.

A lot of Geminis wear clothes that look good but do nothing for comfort, and they don't dress for the weather either. Runny noses can be a problem for Geminis so it may be a good idea to think about what makes you sneeze. Do you blow up around the eyes and nose every time you visit your friend and her cat? Wise up and either get some antihistamines or ask your friend to visit you instead (and leave her cat behind).

Eyestrain is another problem and most Geminis end up needing glasses for driving or watching television. Whether they wear them or not is another thing though. Have you known someone for years who is starting to look at you funny? It is really a Gemini who is too embarrassed to wear their specs.

Nervous strain is more often than not in residence. My Juniper for Jumpy Aries on page 86 is ideal for nervy Gemini too.

The vulnerable Gemini lungs can be improved with fresh air but I advise walking rather than running for this gorgeous and communicative sign.

One of the best ways for you to avoid or cure any ailment is to create a new pace. You can't just take things the way they are. You need to make life interesting and to keep adding things to it. Everyone will want to know all about your past and who has been involved in making you the person you are, yet they are unlikely to reveal the same information to you.

So avoid boredom, but don't overdo the activity. Find a happy medium in life. You can party, which I know you will, but also know when it is time to come home. Staying out on a work night can only be done for so long before it starts to show on both your physical appearance and your ability to do the job. Take care of your nervous system. Listen to friends advising you to rest. (I know your mind is on something else but try to listen!) And get as much nourishment as you can for when you are on the run. Here is a health drink that includes the vitamins that a Gemini needs to get through their hectic and exciting lifestyle.

Lung Ease

This won't cure lung problems but it will relieve congestion and is also good for smokers.

50 g/2 oz chestnut tree leaves (Castana vesco) (*not* horse chestnut)
1.2 litres/2 pints water

Boil the leaves in the water for 5 minutes. Strain then cool. Take a small wineglassful twice daily with honey or brown sugar to your taste. Store in the refrigerator in a screw-top bottle or jar.

Dandelion Root for Rheumatism

Gemini are at risk of rheumatic-type illnesses and dandelion is a good thing to take for these. The root brings with it all the goodness of the earth. This is also excellent for detoxifying the liver.

25 g/1 oz dandelion root, scrubbed
water

Dry the root in the oven for an hour at 150°C/300°F/gas mark 2. When brittle but not burned, grind to a powder. Store in an airtight container – ideally a stone jar. When required, simmer for 10–15 minutes in 1 cup of water per teaspoon of dandelion root. Take 2 tablespoons morning and evening.

Gemini Power Juice

This promotes both clear thinking and confidence. Drink this before you embark on a busy day and you should find you can tackle the most difficult of projects (or people).

1 parsnip
½ cucumber
½ carrot
good pinch of fresh parsley

Juice them and drink!

My *Kooshti Sante* health drink for teenagers on page 47 is also good to boost the energy levels of Gemini.

Here's another piece of health advice. This sign can have two relationships at the same time when they're young and it is the danger element and the duality of their sign that can lead them to do it. So, Gemini, watch out that you don't get caught or you could find yourself in for a verbal or physical assault!

With the hustle and bustle of a busy Gemini lifestyle it is important to tune in to what the body tells us. If arms and shoulders ache it is because they are trying to warn us that they need attention and probably a rest. It is a foolish man who does not listen to his body. Your body can only give you so many alarm calls before the factory packs up and goes on strike. Listen when your associates suggest that you rest. They are trying to help.

Good Gemini Food

Geminis have a tendency to lack the cell salt kali muriaticum, otherwise known as potassium chloride. This deficiency can make you feel run down and can result in swollen glands, asthma, eczema, runny noses and allergic reactions. These are all nature's ways of trying to slow you down and make you rest. Kali mur can be found in many herbs including comfrey, marigold root, tansy, red clover and liquorice. Let me guess which one we'd all go for. Well, it's OK, go ahead. Liquorice is actually good for you. There are also some great recipes using herbs at the start of this book. Once tried, they are certain to become favourites, even for Geminis, who don't like to follow recipes in books. Perhaps not even mine!

Kali mur can also be found in watercress, cauliflower, turnips, goat's milk, green beans, Brussels sprouts and lettuce. Why not try asking your local pharmacist or health food store for some fun fruit and vegetable drinks, or make up your own? And try the recipes at the end of this chapter in your Star Menu. No, you don't have to become a vegetarian, just add these dishes to your diet.

Just as Taurus should be avoiding mucus-producing foods, you should actually be stocking up on them. Make sure that you get plenty of milk. Goat's cheese in particular should provide you with extra energy.

We all know when we have eaten too much bad food or drunk more than we should have. It takes a strong star sign to know when enough is enough. If you feel that you are eating more than you should and are worried about it then try piling lots of extra vegetables on your plate alongside a modest amount of your favourite fatty food. Most of us eat too fast, especially speedy Gemini. If we slowed down we would realize in time when we were full, rather than ten minutes later when the weight hits our stomachs and we feel sick.

Don't go for too many fatty foods, Gemini. You put on weight in unusual places. It could be the breasts or even the ankles that start to show the signs of the chocolate or the booze and it will not look natural on a Gemini so a healthy diet is essential if you are to hold your head up and look your best – which I must add is very important to you. You don't have brilliant digestive powers so go easy on raw foods.

Watch out for foods that raise your blood pressure. There are enough pressures in life without eating foods that add to the strain! Salt is a prime culprit, so avoid it in cooking.

Snacking is not for you. Skipping meals and then eating too much in one day can play havoc with your body. Geminis burn off a lot of energy but uneven eating will have an impact on that delicate nervous system. Team up with your body and make your lifestyle and eating habits work for you.

Plants for Star Therapy

Myrtle is a shrub which attracts good luck for this twin sign. It is both long-living and evergreen. Rather like you – always youthful and good-looking! Also like you, it needs a lot of space to grow to its full size. Most varieties have a lovely scent and right back to Roman times it has been regarded as a symbol of happiness. You can buy myrtle from any good nursery and plant it in the spring.

Health Checklist

- You are one of the signs that can really benefit from taking vitamin supplements on a regular basis because no matter how much you try, you don't eat when you should. You are always in too much of a rush. Eating is more of a social than a health thing. Many great chefs, however, are born under your sign. Gemini cooks are inventive: they make up their own recipes as they go along.
- For eyestrain try bilberry extract and vitamin B complex.
- Thiamin (vitamin B1) is good for nervous problems. It releases energy and aids the nervous system. Take a supplement or turn to foods such as brown rice, peas, beans, breakfast cereals and Marmite.
- All the water-soluble vitamins, the B complex and C, are good to take on a regular basis. The body doesn't store these and they need constant replacement; something burn-up Geminis need to bear in mind. There really is no excuse for not giving your body what it needs. Who would have thought, hundreds of years ago, that you could swallow a tablet that could help prevent health problems and ensure good eyesight, skin and nails?

Are You a True Gemini?

Be honest! Write down 'yes' or 'no', add up your score, then read the advice below.

1 Do you find that you cope with life better when it is stressful than when it is quiet?
2 Do you find that you enjoy food better when it is linked to social or romantic occasions?
3 Have you ever two-timed a lover?
4 Have you broken or strained an ankle or wrist through rushing?
5 Do you eat cauliflower, turnips, green beans or Brussels sprouts on a regular basis?
6 Do you drink a glass of milk at least once a week?
7 Do you find that you are always thinking of tomorrow instead of today?
8 Do you find yourself cold in the winter because you have not put on enough sensible clothing?
9 Do you have to strain your eyes when watching television or reading?
10 Do you find that you never have enough hours in the day to do what is on your agenda?
11 Do people comment that you look younger the older you get?
12 Do you find yourself saying things just to be different or to cause a debate?
13 Do you have a short attention span?
14 Do you blow hot and cold with your close ones, leaving them dazed and confused?

15 Do you get on better with the opposite sex than your own?
16 Do you find yourself drawn to yellows?
17 Do you find it impossible to say no to a party?
18 Do you have naturally sparkling eyes, even when you haven't had a drink?
19 Have you at some point in your life thought of emigrating or making a major move of towns, or indeed done so?
20 Do you find yourself wearing summer clothes in winter and vice versa, just because they look good?

If you answered mostly 'yes' you are a prime example of a Gemini. You live life at a hundred miles an hour with your eye on tomorrow instead of today. You are a typical Gemini in both good and bad habits. If you answered yes to question 1 then you truly are a typical Gemini as they thrive on stress. Fast-paced jobs are for you, especially if you answered yes to question 13. The more pressure and the more quickly you have to complete a job, the better you will do it. You need a partner who can keep up with your fast-paced life but who can also slow you down a little so you don't burn yourself out too soon.

If you answered yes to question 9, get yourself some glasses! Squinting does not look attractive and the longer you leave it the worse it will get.

Well done if you answered yes to questions 5 and 6, but don't forget to keep making a conscious effort to get the food your sign needs. You need more energy than most to cope with all that is going on in your life.

*

If you have answered mostly 'no' then you do not appear to be a typical Gemini. The chances are you have a partner who is able to stop you in your tracks. Air signs need people in their lives in order to feel alive and they often attract characters who are too strong. This may not be a bad thing but it does mean that you must take care not to allow your true self to be constricted. Make sure you are not missing out on all the fun you could be having. After all, we're all allowed to be a little crazy sometimes. The other great thing about your sign is that you often look younger the older you get, so it is never too late to fulfil your dreams or to start something new.

If you answered no to question 5 then start to incorporate those foods into your diet as soon as possible. They will not only benefit your health but they will have you thinking more clearly too.

Don't forget to read up about your moon sign in the chapter towards the end of the book.

The Drinker's Guide to the Zodiac

The Gemini will always accept a drink but not always finish it because they are bound to have somewhere else they are expected to be or someone else they want to see. However, if you serve this, you may just find them staying for another!

Fresh Wind

If you are feeling adventurous, then go for it. All I can say is the events that follow will prove interesting.

4 or 5 ice cubes
1 part dry French vermouth
juice of ½ fresh grapefruit
½ teaspoon Cointreau
3 parts vodka

Put the ice cubes into a glass jug. Pour the vermouth, grapefruit juice, Cointreau and vodka over the ice. Stir gently, and strain into a chilled Martini glass.

Star Menu

Heavenly Potato Dauphinoise

Although the best foods for a Gemini really are the mucus-producing ones, that doesn't mean you can reach for the chocolate cake with a clear conscience. Try this dairy recipe, which you can serve with your main course. Serves 4.

1 kg/2 lb sweet potatoes, peeled and thinly sliced
1 clove garlic, crushed
salt and freshly ground pepper
freshly grated nutmeg
chopped fresh parsley, plus sprigs to garnish
350 ml/12 fl oz double cream whisked with 6 tablespoons of milk
60 ml/4 fl oz double cream, for the top layer

Preheat the oven to 180°C/350°F/gas 4. Grease an ovenproof dish with butter and layer your potatoes on the bottom, seasoning as you go with the garlic, salt, pepper, nutmeg and parsley. Pour the cream and milk over the potato layers and shake the dish so the liquid goes all the way through the potatoes. Pour just cream over the top and garnish with sprigs of parsley. Bake for about 2 hours, until tender all through and golden on top.

Nathan's Party Piece

Anything that's energy-making is good for a Gemini. Here is a dish that is sure to make them want to party all night. Serves 2 as a main course or 4 as a starter.

200 g/8 oz egg tagliatelle pasta
salt
1 tablespoon olive oil
1 clove garlic, crushed
1 onion, chopped
6 mushrooms, chopped
½ red, ½ green and ½ yellow pepper, cut into strips
10 slices thin honey-roast ham, cut into strips
small tin sweetcorn, drained
cayenne pepper
mixed dried herbs
half a glass dry white wine
75 ml/5 fl oz single cream or crème fraîche
grated Cheddar cheese, to taste

Put a large pan of water on to boil for the pasta. When it reaches a rolling boil, add some salt and the pasta.

Heat the oil in a frying pan, add the garlic and onion and gently fry until the onion starts to soften. Add the mushrooms, peppers, ham, sweetcorn and a pinch each of cayenne pepper and mixed herbs. Stir well. Slowly add the dry white wine and reduce so the mixture starts to bubble and the alcohol boils away, then add the cream or crème fraîche, but do not allow it to cook for too long or to burn.

When the pasta is tender but *al dente* (firm to the bite), drain it into a pasta dish and toss with the sauce. Add the grated cheese and another sprinkle of cayenne pepper. Place under grill until brown and bubbling, then serve at once.

Perfect Pizza

This is slightly naughty but contains that all-important goat's cheese, so good for Gemini. It is also perfect to dish out to the many friends that this sign always has popping round.

If you want to, you can use ready-made pizza bases, but why not make your own? They're so much tastier.

For the pizza base:
1 packet (7 g/¼ oz) active dry yeast
1 teaspoon sugar
250 g/9 oz plain flour
2 tablespoons olive oil, plus extra for brushing
150 ml/5 fl oz water
½ teaspoon salt

For the topping:
2 tablespoons polenta
4 fresh tomatoes, sliced

1 tablespoon olive oil
½ onion, chopped
2 closed-cap mushrooms, sliced
small tin sweetcorn, drained
8 cherry tomatoes
tin tuna fish in sunflower oil
150 g/5 oz goat's cheese, cut into pieces
25 g/1 oz freshly grated Parmesan cheese

To make the dough, mix together the yeast, sugar and a third of the flour. Pour in the oil and most of the water and mix together, preferably in a food processor. When well combined, add the remaining flour and the salt and mix into a dough. Add a little more water if necessary to get a dough of the right consistency. It should feel like a soft ball that is not falling apart. Brush some oil around the dough and place in an oiled bowl covered with a clean tea towel. Leave for 1 hour to rise.

Preheat the oven to the highest setting and oil a medium-sized pizza pan. Sprinkle with polenta.

Skin the fresh tomatoes (see page 95) and chop them. Cook in the olive oil until they take on a sauce consistency. Set aside.

Knead the dough on a floured board, using enough flour to prevent it sticking. Roll it out large enough to fit into your pizza pan and gently press it down so that it reaches the edges. Spread the tomato sauce evenly over the base and arrange the onion, mushrooms, sweetcorn, cherry tomatoes, chunks of tuna fish, goat's cheese and Parmesan on top. Bake in the preheated oven until the cheese is bubbling and starting to brown. You should be able to see that the base is done as it will puff and brown with the cheese. Cooking time is approximately 15 minutes but do check after 10.

Star Beauty

Gemini's main beauty secret is fresh air and sunshine. They need to make sure that they can fill their lungs with the oxygen their sign needs so much. Put a Gemini in a room for a week and you will open the door to a crazy person. Geminis do not like being on their own, either. Even just to know someone else is in the house will do. This has applied to Geminis since the beginning of time.

Adeline's Skin Softener

A good cream is essential for Gemini skin. This one was handed down to me by my aunt Adeline Lee, who used to refuse to share this with Gorgers (non-Romanies). Now she has given it to me to share with you. She swears it is the secret behind her soft skin, which no one she meets fails to comment on.

The best time to apply this, Adeline says, is in the mornings while you are doing housework. It is absolutely brilliant for nourishing the skin, keeping wrinkles at bay and getting rid of spots (because it heals infections).

1 teaspoon virgin olive oil
1 teaspoon clear runny honey
juice of 1/4 lemon

Mix the olive oil and honey together well in a clean jar with a lid (a jam jar would do). Add the lemon juice – it does not mix in easily but is essential if you are to get the best results – close the lid and shake the jar really well. Place in the refrigerator. When you are ready to use it, shake it again and work it into your face, shoulders, hands and arms in circular movements.

Now you have a choice. You can either rinse cotton wool in lukewarm water and take the cream off in upward movements, or you can get an Aries, a Libra or a Gemini to lick it off – that is Adeline's recommendation for a romantic conclusion.

Your Ideal Health Sign Holiday

A train around Europe is the answer for this gypsy of the zodiac. With your short attention span you need to be able to get up and go whenever you feel like it. So many different languages in such a short distance will fascinate you too. Watch out you don't leave a string of broken hearts behind.

CANCER

THE CRAB

Ruling Planet: The Moon

Triplicity or Element: Water

Quadruplicity or Mode: Cardinal

Key words: Changeable, protective, loving, shrewd, caring

The Origin of Cancer

This sign originates from a crab who nipped the foot of the great Hercules who at the time was fighting a snake in the marshes. Hercules crushed the crab under his foot but Hera picked it up and placed it amid the stars.

What Cancerians are Like

Cancer is ruled by the moon and those born under this sign have features, such as a rounded, 'moon-shaped' face, that link to it. They will change their minds about things just as the moon changes. Partners of a Cancerian run for cover when there's a full moon! But they are extremely protective of their loved ones and go to great lengths to take care of their family. They are emotional, so if you are going to the cinema on a first date with a Cancerian I advise you to skip the tearjerkers.

Be careful of arguing with them as you are likely to lose. They have a cunning skill with words and can shock and hurt you when they want to. This should be a dual, or twin, sign as their personality is so changeable. You may think that they will never speak to you again after an argument but they will shock you by inviting you over for an intimate dinner for two. Unlike fire signs this character does not bottle its feelings up. If they are unhappy with you they will not hesitate to let you know.

People may call Cancerians selfish but the truth is that they will look after themselves before they look after anyone else. When you think about it, that's the sensible way to do it. They are especially self-protective when young, and become nurturing when grown up.

They are capable of making any space into a home and when people visit them they are immediately made to feel welcome. They have a tendency to be defensive and if you ask them where they have been you may as well openly accuse them of having an affair. It is not paranoia, it is just that they like to have a bit of privacy and they don't like it to be invaded. If you have a private life with a Cancerian don't give anyone else the details. They like to keep business and pleasure totally separate too.

They make great travellers because they can make any place into their home. They are a pleasure to be around because they make their friends and loved ones feel wanted, needed and loved. Great parents, they can make a child feel guilty without having to raise a hand. Just one look from a Cancerian parent is enough to stop any teenager in its path. Moodiness is their main fault. If you took this away you'd have someone who was perfect! Of all the signs, surveys have shown them to spend the most on clothes and eating out.

Their instincts lead them well and if they don't like someone they're usually right not to. Do believe them if they tell you not to trust someone. Their sense of perception is unlikely to have let them down in the past and should be trusted.

Their sense of thrift and shrewd negotiating abilities leads them well in business. Don't be fooled by their friendly nature when doing business with them. They will not do you any favours. Their business sense will not allow them to. None the less, born worriers, they often fret about things that haven't happened and probably never will happen. This is a result of their overactive imagination, which makes them a bit of a storyteller when the mood is right.

This is the second cardinal sign of the zodiac and because it is a water sign Cancerians are better off when they live near water. Moon-like smoky-grey and silvery-blue colours are lucky for them.

The hidden depths within Cancerians are enough to shock anyone, especially themselves. If they fall in love then they are stuck because there will be nothing they can do to get out of it. Because this sign is so influenced by its emotions, its state of health is a mirror image of its emotional state. Problems in Cancerians' personal lives will show in their health. This is something they need to learn to take control of. Many a heartbroken Cancerian has been unable to work or carry on with a normal life until they have managed to get over their ex.

I have never met a nasty Cancerian and that is probably because their emotions wouldn't allow them to do anything bad. If you have ever had your heart broken by a Cancerian, believe me, they will be feeling guilty for years to come, even if they don't let you know about it.

Every twenty years the moon will return to the birth position in the Cancer horoscope. For these shrewd and emotional souls it means that at 20, 40, 60 and so on they reach a major turning point, a milestone in their lives.

The crab doesn't forget what it has learned. It always applies past experiences, especially emotional ones, to present situations. It is also able to understand the emotions of others. If a Cancerian's partner is under par then the Cancerian is likely to feel under the weather too. They tend to imitate, subconsciously, the feelings of others. A depressed Cancerian is not a good person to have around. In this state they are unpredictable and capable of saying things they do not really mean.

Because Cancerians are so sensitive, people think they are not strong. On the contrary, they are very strong indeed. They do have a weakness, however. They are extremely insecure and they don't handle this trait very well. Cancerians need to trust in their partner's love a little more. This option is a lot less hard work than the position of insecurity, which in itself can break up relationships unnecessarily.

How to Spot a Cancerian

This is the first of the water signs and you can sometimes tell them by their rounded and rather moon-shaped face. Their figure is usually quite a curvy one and their forehead can be quite large. However, you are unlikely to notice someone is a Cancerian at first glance because it is not necessarily the way they look that is obvious, but rather the way they talk, hold themselves and express their emotions.

The Devil and the Angel

The DEVIL CANCERIAN is crazy for the limelight, out to make as much money as possible and just can't stop themselves from getting a reputation. A prime example is actor Sylvester Stallone, whose life is always in the tabloids and whose business ventures are always huge. And yet you still can't help but admire him.

The ANGEL CANCERIAN is loving, caring, feels it is their job to take care of the world and is extremely protective of those less capable. The late Princess Diana, whose reputation and work speak for themselves, was an Angel Cancerian.

Cancer Health and Development from Child to Adult

The Cancerian baby is a beautiful but fussy child, although well behaved with it. That is, until the age of three, when they gain a bit more confidence and adopt a somewhat cheeky and pushy attitude. Do not turn your back on this child for long. This is the type that could escape the clutches of armed guards, and if you look away for a second they are certain to have wandered off to coo at something pretty or interesting they've seen. Do not waste your money on expensive toys, either. They will get thrown into a corner and never seen again. This is the infant that will have more fun playing with a tin of soup than with a baby toy.

At five years of age this child cannot be conned about anything. You will think they must have been here before, they are so wise and clever. Maybe too much for their own good. If you tell them to drink their milk, they will want to know the scientific facts and see the proof to confirm it's worth their while. That shrewd business sense has already kicked in, believe me. Do not push them into developing their talents either. This is one sign that must be left to progress naturally. When they are ready to learn the currency of real money instead of trying to pay with Monopoly money, they will let you know.

At eleven years of age they will surprise you with how self-sufficient they are. Even if they get stuck with their homework they are unlikely to tell you but will muddle on until they find a solution. OK, the naughty Cancerian may be paying a classmate to do their work, but at least they are finding a solution to their problem! At this age their friends are usually younger than them. While never a bully at school, they do not run away from a fight. Their emotions and sense of pride will not allow them to. If they return home with a bloody nose, ask for an explanation before you ground them, as it is likely to be quite valid. The chances are, if they get into a fight, it is because they were sticking up for a friend.

At 16 you see the kind of teenager that any parent would love to have. When they go to a friend's for tea they converse just as easily with the parent as with the friend. They are polite, kind and very faithful. It is during these years that they learn a lot from life, as they take everything and everyone extremely seriously. They admit their true feelings too quickly, which can turn them into a broken-hearted or an over-confident character, depending on the response of the object of their affections. They have a terrific memory and are extremely imaginative. They also develop a strong urge to travel, and they realize that they have to work their way up from the bottom of the ladder to get to the top. They do not believe in shortcuts.

At 21 they have encountered the Cancerian milestone at 20 (remember the moon returns to its birth position in the Cancer horoscope every twenty years) and are usually well prepared for what lies ahead, especially workwise. In emotional matters they may still have a lot to learn. If they marry at 20 then 21 can be a very trying year. They are not usually promiscuous before marriage but they can be after! They often marry between 20 and 25 years of age, and they need someone who can fit in with their hectic lifestyles, ideally someone with as hectic a schedule as theirs. If they are in love with you they will settle down and work at their home life, making a generous partner and an excellent parent. Cancer and Libra are the two top parenting signs.

At 40 the urge for them to uproot is usually very strong, however well organized and comfortable their life may be. The 20-year cycle is kicking in again. If the urge to move on is not satisfied they may look for changes elsewhere. The changes are usually major. The good employee may break away and set up their own business; the self-employed businessman may decide to become a homebody. If the Cancerian hasn't married the right person then frustration is taken out in work or even in drinking. Healthwise, they don't usually eat what they should and so can face much nagging from loved ones. All the same, at this age Cancerians are no mugs.

At 70 Cancerians are making their decisions based on what has happened in the past. If they like you, they will give you almost anything. If, however, you have done them a wrong or upset someone close to them then you'd be better off trying to get blood out of a stone. Watch out for the sneaky eating and drinking they will get up to. Check behind books for stashes of chocolate and the odd bottle: you're likely to find it. Be careful not to get on the wrong side of them or they will cause everyone around to know just how wrong you have been and you may become embarrassed by the attention they focus on you. You couldn't get a more loving grand-parent, though, and as long as you surround them with children they should be fine.

Cancerian Careers . . .

Doctor or nurse. Taking care of people is part of your nature.

Pool attendant. Just looking at all that lovely water would be great and you could dream the day away, your favourite occupation.

Teaching. Especially young children.

Mother and multi-business entrepreneur. You could make money and raise your children, two of your favourite things.

Founder of a major charity. You are able to make money and to make a difference.

. . . not so Cancerian careers

Miner. No looking at the moon and no water nearby – definitely not!

Voluntary charity worker. Not unless you own the charity. You don't understand the concept of working for free.

Anything that involves low pay. You like lots of money and big business.

Milkman or postman. You could never get up that early, please.

Famous Cancerians

Author Dame Barbara Cartland, singer Lena Horne, actors Bryan Brown, Pamela Anderson and Kathy Bates, the late Princess Diana, President Nelson Mandela, the Sultan of Brunei, tycoon Richard Branson.

Health Sore Points

Cancer governs the stomach, digestive system and liver. The stomach is often the first area to be affected by stress, especially for Cancerians.

Nervous exhaustion is a leading problem in Cancerians. You are always thinking about what you have done, what you are currently doing and what you are going to do next. You forget to eat when you have a crisis on so when you finally sit down you overindulge. Indigestion often results. Nervous exhaustion can also bring on migraine.

Allergies often prove to be a problem for you, especially when life is not going too well.

Emotional stress can affect you too. If I give a reading to a Cancerian who is unhappy in a relationship I have to tell them to get out of the relationship quick. A bad relationship can do you more harm than ten packets of cigarettes.

Cures and Counsel

Exercise for Cancerians should be anything to do with water. Although not always great swimmers, the majority of you have a fascination with the sea. Not necessarily swimming in it – just to be able to look at it is relaxing.

Why not try a flotation tank? This would be an ideal way of understanding your element a little better, and you may even like it.

If you can learn not to be so ruled by your emotions and so open to emotional blackmail you will be on the path to a much longer, happier and healthier life. We all have the power to say yes or no to situations.

A good rule is to watch out for changes in the moon. Do you feel different when the moon is in different states? Does a full moon leave you full of energy or ready for bed by lunchtime? If you can learn how the different phases of the moon make you feel, then you should be able to prepare yourself in advance. Some Cancerians refuse to cook when there is a new moon and go out for dinner instead. The rules are yours to decide. Just work out what feels best.

Don't allow yourself to get overly stressed. Try a luxurious bath with your favourite drink: only one glass of wine though, please, or even better for you, a glass of milk. Sensual smelling bubbles and foam are better for your character than bath oils.

To guard against migraine, take regular light meals to prevent your blood-sugar levels from dropping. Use ginger in your cooking or take it with boiling water as a tea. All you have to do is grate a little and steep it in hot water. Try to eat a little more oily fish such as salmon or mackerel. Feverfew is a herbal remedy for migraine which, although it cannot stop an attack once it has started, can reduce the frequency with which attacks occur. You can get feverfew in tablet form or tincture but I prefer the fresh leaves. You can grow it on your windowsill very easily. A couple of leaves each day is what the experts recommend: stick them in a piece of bread and wash it down with a little milk. Don't eat feverfew straight because it does not taste very pleasant. You can also soak a cloth in an infusion of feverfew which can be placed across the forehead to relieve headaches. As with any health worry, however, if it persists call your doctor and get some further advice.

As I believe is the case with all signs, if you can listen to your body and read the warning signs, you should be able to solve any problem. Prevention is better than cure, so for you, Cancerians, listen to your emotions. If someone doesn't make you feel good, don't stick around them. A little more self-confidence wouldn't go amiss, too, and there really is no reason why you shouldn't have it.

Mandrake Indigestion Remedy

If you suffer from indigestion from time to time I recommend a tea made from the mandrake root. This is obtainable from herbalists and good health food stores, and should bring the relief you are looking for.

25 g/1 oz mandrake root
600 ml/1 pint water

Boil the root in the water for 10 minutes. Strain and take one teaspoon five times daily. Keep in a clean bottle in the refrigerator.

To keep your liver in good order you should include citrus fruits, particularly grapefruit, in your diet, along with prunes, tomatoes and apples. Here are two liver-cleansing recipes to use for detoxing after a period of over-indulgence, or once a month for regular maintenance.

Barberry Liver Cleanser

My people have for centuries used the shrub barberry to cleanse and tone the liver. This wild shrub with its pretty yellow flowers may be well known to you but it is the red berries left when the yellow petals have fallen that we need for this remedy.

30 ml/1 fl oz barberry juice
10 g/½ oz sugar
600 ml/1 pint water

Boil together for 10 minutes and drink when cool.

Sage Liver Tonic

Sage is a pretty and useful herb to grow and is also a liver tonic.

handful of fresh sage, well washed,
or 1 teaspoon dried sage
600 ml/1 pint hot, not boiling, water

Place the herb in a jug, add the water, cover and leave for 24 hours. Take a wineglassful each morning. (Do not strain, leave the sage in the water.) Keep in the refrigerator.

Cancerian Juice Booster

Take this regularly to ensure your body is getting what it needs. Within five days you will see an improvement in your skin.

4 large carrots
2 handfuls watercress
a sprig of coriander
1 stick of celery

Juice these together and drink a wineglassful every day.

Good Cancerian Food

Cancerians tend to lack cell salt calcium fluoride, commonly known as fluoride of lime. Fifty per cent of our bones are made up of calcium so you can imagine how important it is. While teeth and bones incorporate 99 per cent of the body's total calcium, the other 1 per cent is involved in cell structure and function as well as in the blood, where it aids clotting. Calcium is also needed for healthy nerves and muscles. Without it the body will not operate as it should and varicose veins, haemorrhoids and bad eyesight can set in. Don't worry. You simply have to eat foods that supply you with a good amount of the cell salt that the crab needs. There is no reason not to make yourself aware of your body's needs. I have too often heard the man or woman over fifty who says, 'I wish I had eaten differently,' or 'If only I had done so and so.' Well, you now have the information that you need for your sign, so there is no excuse.

Milk is the obvious source. As a child you probably wouldn't drink it unless on your own initiative. You often hear the parents of Cancerians saying, please, drink it for me, because they have learnt that the emotional way will work. (Don't ever try force-feeding a Cancerian; you'll be fighting a losing battle! Gentle persuasion is the answer.)

Cabbage (Savoy and red), watercress, kale, prunes, cottage cheese, sardines and parsley are other sources high in calcium that you should be including in your diet (see also page 37). Parsley can be used daily in almost any dish you are preparing. Even chocolate contains calcium, but make sure it doesn't give you headaches.

There should be no reason not to go out and buy fresh produce. Supermarkets are open 24 hours a day now, which really does leave no excuse, although tracking down healthy organic produce should be a priority.

Undercooked foods can often cause a problem so sushi is out for you I'm afraid. It is important that everything is cooked through properly to make sure that no bacteria can harm you.

Some signs in the zodiac have to make a careful plan of what they eat but with the crab it is more a case of when you eat and the quality of the food. You refuse rump steak and insist on fillet, and friends might think you a snob for it, but unless you eat the best cuts of meat you'll be unable to digest them. It is partly a psychological thing, but believe me, if you don't eat the best quality food, you'll wish you had. Beware of a Cancer's sweet tooth, though, or that fabulous figure could get out of control.

Plants for Star Therapy

Privet attracts good luck to Cancerians. If you don't like the conventional hedge, find an odd corner for a single bush. It takes readily from a cutting but needs a lot of moisture. White flowers are also lucky for you and roses, lilies and water lilies should all be placed nearby when you are celebrating a special occasion.

Health Checklist

- Honeysuckle is great to help a Cancerian who is having sleeping problems. Fill a pillow with fresh honeysuckle and you can guarantee that your dreams will be sweet ones.
- For stomach problems, try taking digestive enzymes (extracted from pineapple and papaya) or peppermint oil. B2 detoxes the liver.
- For liver problems or just to keep them in check, get Bio-light liquid from your health food store. It's a great de-tox, and comes in several flavours.
- Nervous exhaustion can be tackled with vitamin B complex and vitamin E. The nervous system

depends upon an adequate intake of those vitamins.

- Thiamin (B1), between 50 and 100 mg daily, helps with muscle co-ordination and the nerves. It also acts as a general pick-me-up when energy is flagging or in times of stress, which can produce symptoms such as irritability, headaches, loss of appetite and indigestion.
- For the blues, 50–100 mg vitamin B6 on its own can help (but *not* if pregnant).
- Buy vitamins in tablet form if you are not able to get enough of what you need from your food.

Are You a True Cancerian?

Be honest! Write down 'yes' or 'no', then read the advice below.

1 Are you at times overly defensive, even when you know you are in the wrong?
2 Is moodiness probably your biggest fault?
3 Do you follow your instincts in business and personal matters?
4 Do you suffer more from health problems when you have personal problems to cope with?
5 Do you eat or drink any of the following on a regular basis: milk, cabbage, watercress, kale, prunes, cottage cheese, parsley?
6 Do you like your food undercooked rather than overcooked?
7 Do you drink more than seven units of alcohol a week?

8 Do you work more hours than your close ones would like you to?
9 Do you suffer from any allergies?
10 Do you choose the cheaper cuts of meats and produce when you are shopping?
11 Do you have what others would describe as a voluptuous figure?
12 Do you find that you need to get out of the house when there is a full moon?
13 Do you follow your instincts in life?
14 Do you feel calmer when you are able to look at the sea or be near water in general?
15 Do you find yourself going for smoky-greys and silvery-blue colours?
16 Do you find that your health is a mirror image of your emotional state?
17 Do you find that you can feel the effect of even one alcoholic drink?
18 Do you suffer from digestive problems?
19 Do you find yourself getting overemotional at sad films and songs?
20 Have you been known to change your mind quicker than the wind?

If you answered 'yes' to most questions then you are a typical Cancer. You are sensitive, loving and caring and have been known to wear your heart on your sleeve. Your sign has so many fantastic points that you are certain never to be lonely. Just make sure that you do not waste your time in a situation you do not want to be in. You are too special to be with someone you do not really love and it is a trap you must avoid.

You may want to observe when there is a full moon to see if you do act differently. That way you can prepare yourself for any outbursts you may have.

I hope you answered yes to question 5 as the fruit and vegetables listed really are what your body needs to be healthy. Try not to drink too much alcohol. You don't need much to get drunk and it may make you over-emotional. Make sure that you always pick the best cuts of meat even if it means buying a smaller piece. Your digestion requires the best cuts I'm afraid, so no supermarket savings for a Cancerian.

If you answered 'no' to most questions then you are not a typical Cancerian, or maybe you have learned to overrule the sensitive situations in your life. Or perhaps you are doing this survey on a sensitive day. Is it the time of the full moon? Are your defences up? I hope that you take some time to learn more about the typical traits of a Cancerian and let yourself go to learn a little about the real you. You could be opening the gates to a new and exciting period of your life.

If you answered no to question 5 then you must try to make a conscious effort to add the right fruit and vegetables to your shopping basket.

Did you answer no to question 13? You should start to trust your instincts, as I can promise you they will lead you well. Don't be afraid to listen to your feelings, and don't be afraid to realize your dreams. Now why not look up your moon sign and learn about some strengths you maybe never knew you had?

The Drinker's Guide to the Zodiac

Water signs are not great drinkers. With Cancer it is a bit of a mental thing. If they know they have had alcohol they feel drunk before it has even begun to take effect.

A very mean trick my mother once played on her Cancerian secretary was to fill a bottle of vodka with water and to pour her large drinks from it. Other friends were around and my mother didn't get the chance to explain the joke to her secretary. Some time later my mother found the poor woman had crept off home to bed. The following morning she looked terrible and yet no alcohol had passed her lips. The hangover had well and truly set in for the day and my mother's explanations cut no ice!

Cancerians, if they do drink, prefer long to short drinks. If you ply one with shorts (and succeed in getting through their self-discipline), you'll get what you deserve. You'll be hearing a few home truths as pent-up feelings come rushing out! But here's a drink that's well worth making for a Cancerian: in moderation, of course.

Old-Fashioned

How to captivate a Cancer!

1 sugar cube
2 drops angostura bitters
2 or 3 ice cubes
1 part whisky
1 slice lemon
1 maraschino cherry

Put the sugar cube into the bottom of an old-fashioned glass. Shake the bitters over the sugar and mix them together, spreading the mixture around the glass. Add the ice cubes, pour the whisky over, twist the lemon over the drink and drop it in, garnish with the cherry, and serve.

Star Menu

Cancerians like food that stimulates the emotions and tantalizes the tastebuds.

Pasta and Vegetables in Lemon and Cream Sauce

The parsley is for presentation and for good digestion (so don't forget to eat it). You can also serve Parmesan cheese with this dish, if you like. Serves 6.

2 unwaxed lemons
240 ml/8 fl oz double cream (it's OK, you're Cancerian, you're allowed it!)
3 tablespoons olive oil
2 cloves garlic, crushed
1 large or 2 small courgettes, cut into short, thin strips
2 large red peppers, seeded and cut into short, thin strips
salt and freshly ground black pepper
500 g/1 lb fresh linguini pasta (or dried, if you wish, but fresh tastes better)
parsley sprigs, to garnish

Put a large pot of water on to boil for the pasta.

Finely grate the skin of the lemons (use a zester, if you have one, or the finest teeth on the box grater) and squeeze 2 tablespoons of juice from one of them. Combine the lemon zest, lemon juice and double cream in a small saucepan and heat gently until it thickens enough to coat the back of a spoon: about 6 minutes.

Meanwhile, heat the olive oil in a large frying pan over a medium-high heat. Add the garlic and cook, stirring frequently, until pale golden: about 5 minutes. Stir in the courgettes and peppers and cook until tender. Season to taste with salt and pepper.

Then salt your boiling water and add the pasta, cooking until tender but *al dente* (firm to the bite). Fresh pasta takes no time at all to cook. Drain well and transfer to a pasta bowl. Add the lemon cream and the vegetables and toss well. Garnish with parsley.

Citrus Sorbet

This recipe will work wonders on a Cancerian. You need an ice-cream maker. If you don't have one, ask a friend. You'll be surprised how many people have one going to waste in their wedding-present cupboard. If not, then think about investing in one. They are worth every penny.

This sorbet will lift the spirits of any Cancerian who feels blue. Serves 6–8.

125 g/4 oz sugar
120 ml/4 fl oz water
500 ml/2 pints freshly squeezed orange juice, strained
150 ml/5 fl oz freshly squeezed grapefruit juice, strained
5 tablespoons freshly squeezed lemon juice, strained

Dissolve the sugar in the water in a small heavy saucepan over a low heat. Increase the heat, bring to the boil, then simmer for 5 minutes or until you are left with a syrup. Allow to cool completely. Blend with the fruit juices, cover and refrigerate overnight. Transfer to ice-cream maker and process according to directions. Freeze for at least 2 hours. Serve to a disgruntled Cancerian and watch the change.

Star Beauty

This sign has the face shape most of us are dying to have. (Ignore them if you hear them complaining their face is too fat.)

Egg and Lemon Face Pack

This will leave you looking (and feeling) as if you've spent a week at a health farm. It's good for teenage skin as well and helps spots to heal. (You can get fuller's earth from a health food store or chemist's.)

1 egg white
juice of 1 lemon
fuller's earth

Combine the egg white and lemon juice and add enough fuller's earth to make a thick paste. Pat the mask on to your face and leave for 20 minutes.

Rinse off with warm water or distilled witch hazel.

Your Ideal Health Sign Holiday

Paris and Rome are both the answer for the crab. Rich in feeling, and plenty of shops to spend your dosh in. Indeed, you've probably already visited them. Married crabs in particular should ditch the beach holiday and try the capitals. I guarantee it will spark off passion.

LEO

THE LION

Ruling Planet: The Sun

Triplicity or Element: Fire

Quadruplicity or Mode: Fixed

Key words: Generous, warm-hearted, proud, fun-loving, dignified

The Origin of Leo

Leo the lion derived its name when Hercules fought a lion that haunted the forests. Hercules killed the lion and then the great god Zeus placed its body amid the stars for all to see. The lion of course has a great link with royalty. The royal standard bears the lion, and many members of the royal family are born under the sign of Leo, including Princess Anne and Princess Margaret.

What Leo is Like

The face Leos show to the outside world says they can do absolutely anything they want to, yet inside they are trying to find the courage to be what they want to be. They love to live life to the full and can often be seen dragging friends out to yet another party. They refuse to let the time of the day dictate when they can or cannot have fun. Ruled by the sun, they are happy-natured and experience some great highs, but when they feel low they feel very low. On low days nothing that anyone says can make them feel different. Generous, warm-hearted and oh so proud Leo is a mystery even to itself.

Leo is faithful and loving. You will not go wrong if you pick this sign for a partner. Just look out for that temper. They are the second of the fixed signs and are also the second of the fire elements. When they blow, they really blow. I don't advise you hang around if you see them about to go off. As the second of the fixed signs, they are as stubborn as a Taurus but more unpredictable.

They have a creative side which they must try to use. If they don't the world could be missing out on a gifted and talented individual. A Leo that doesn't use his or her artistic talents in some form or other will always regret it. Whether it's a musical instrument, even one that is never played to an audience, or creativity in the kitchen, the talents are there and must be explored. It is quite a feat for the lion to sit down and learn something – they are too busy socializing – but it would be a great shame if they let a real talent go to waste by not working on it.

Luxury, glamour and – surprisingly – organization are three of the main things they require in their lives. They need to find a job that can connect them with people and success. A boring, mundane job is as good as a jail sentence to them. Organization and planning are important. They have to know all of the facts first and without a proper schedule are unlikely to go ahead with what you may ask of them. But put this character in charge of people and you'll find a born leader with a courageous heart. Out shopping they will be attracted by good packaging, and they are likely to return home with champagne and caviar – and a new date, too – if you're not careful!

At times you might think they are showing off. Their extravagant natures can make it look like they are trying to be something they are not. You just have to give Leo the Glamourpuss a little space. They turn heads wherever they go. They like the world to revolve around them. From a very young age they were popular and they just don't know any different. They are great hosts and great guests. Invite them to a party and they'll add their special touch to the gathering. Leo's real bad point is arrogance, but they don't even know they have it.

Their worst fear in life is losing their dignity. They do not want people to think badly of them. If you ever want to get rid of a Leo, just embarrass him. He's sure to run a mile and never return.

Reds, yellows and oranges are associated with the sun and are lucky for the lion to wear. They also get the lion noticed. Leo will don red to seduce someone.

This is a great boss to have. Leos take an interest in other people and will never intentionally let you down. (Everyone should have a Leo as a friend in their lives.) If they achieve success in life then it does not usually vanish. A Leo that has made it usually stays at the top. However, they are easily taken advantage of, which is precisely why many of them work for other people earning them money rather than owning their own business. The ones that have made it to the top have usually got the right partner to balance them out.

You have to stick around if you want to get to know a Leo. This isn't the sort of character you can get to know in a day. There are many different depths and sides to them. If they invite you for dinner make sure you accept. They are usually great cooks and their homes are worth looking around.

They need to find a partner who can see them for the person they are and who can bring this rocket-like character back down to earth where they belong. Just don't ever tell them they don't look good in an outfit. They'll burn it before you can change your mind.

Once upon a time there was a little girl who was born under the sign of Leo. She had a problem with understanding the subject of maths. She missed two weeks of class because of the flu, and so missed the beginning of a new topic. Why didn't she ask for help, you may think. Oh no. The teacher would probably laugh at her. The whole class would probably laugh at her. So, she struggled on. When it came to choosing a career, she really wanted to go into her own business but she didn't think she could ever manage the books. So she started work at a fashion house, where she ended up being manager. But it wasn't the same as being her own boss, so she decided to pay a tutor and learn maths again but this time on her own. She did and pretty soon she had passed all of the exams that she had failed at school. The little girl in the story is a friend of mine who now runs a top designer store in London and the profits are in her own pocket instead of her boss's. Once someone sat down and explained the simplicity of figures, she found it really easy. The hard bit was finding the courage to ask. Point taken, Leos? I hope so.

How to Spot a Leo

Their hair is usually thick and curly. Hairdressers love it.

The Devil and the Angel

The DEVIL LEO is arrogant, showy and vain. These people know all about their own popularity and exactly what to do with those glamorous features. A good example would be J. D. Rockefeller, the millionaire philanthropist, whose money earned him the popularity and fame he desired.

Then there is the ANGEL LEO, who is determined, passionate, ambitious and a born leader. If Louise Brown, the world's first test-tube baby, is not a born leader and an angel Leo then I don't know who is.

Leo Health and Development from Child to Adult

The Leo baby should not be pushed to do things before its time. Don't be disappointed if at first they don't seem to be as active as other babies. This clever sign is a late developer, biding their time and waiting for their moment. Be content to help them with their favourite occupation at this age: eating. They tend to look good as babies. Their ruling planet, the sun, helps them to shine in a way that many other parents will envy.

At five years of age they will suddenly shake off this idle manner and become vital and full of fun and energy. Watch out for them – they don't have any sense of danger yet. They believe that anything is possible and the world is their oyster. This is great, but just don't let them go wandering off. This is the child that pulls down the baked-bean display in the supermarket while trying to find out what happens when they move the bottom tin. At this age the legs and feet are vulnerable to knocks and bruises and shin pads are advisable when playing any sports.

At eleven years of age their reputation as a madcap is almost in full bloom. While other children talk of being pop stars, the Leo child is dreaming of becoming an explorer, a steeplejack or a racing driver. Not for them the desk or the factory floor. They have a thirst for danger – and the means to satisfy it. But mothers, in particular, will detect another, quieter side to their Leo children. Beneath that brash exterior they have a great deal of self-control. They have a talent for gentler pursuits, too, such as literature and the arts. The young Leo the lion is a very loyal person, and will remain so. In future years their partner is sure to bless this trait.

At 16 they go off the rails, but not too badly. They tend to believe anything that anybody tells them and with their misplaced loyalty they always seem to be covering up for their friends' misdeeds. Then they fall in love with the very worst person their parents could imagine, often because they believe there is good in everyone and want to demonstrate it. They will often go out with more than one person, just to prove what a grown-up they are. Adolescence is an unattractive age for this birth sign and Leo men in particular tend to become rather big-headed. If there is any difficult work to be done they are quick to go missing. If their better feelings are called upon the pleas fall on stony ground. Thank goodness they grow out of this stage.

At 21 they finally come into their own and start to feel mature enough about relationships to settle with just one person. They are hard workers and handle money very well, which is rare in any star sign. Lucky is the partner they choose because Leo usually mates for life – no matter how attractive their workmates may be. They may make advances at the office party but they will flee at the slightest sign of response. You just have to contend with their arrogance. To impress the Joneses or the people at the club they will have to be seen in the latest fashion, even though they are unlikely to have got round to buying a new cooker yet. They are too proud to talk about their problems but all partners of Leos will come to recognize the long brooding silences that mean they have troubles.

Forty is a crisis time for the Leo, I'm afraid, and can be an extremely trying time for those around them. They begin to feel that life is passing them by and that they have been cheated of some of its rewards. They feel they should have a bigger house and a better bank balance. As always they mask their forebodings, which makes things worse. It takes a patient partner to see through the Leo's brooding stage. But the stage does pass, and throughout this time the Leo will be loyal, so don't be tempted to find someone new if you really love them.

At 70 Leos may be subject to circulatory troubles, heart problems and back ailments. They are generally, I must quickly add, healthy, if not always wealthy and wise. You should see them develop into old age gracefully. They are still fun to be around and spread sunshine wherever they go. Still proud, they will not always talk about their health problems, so you should make sure they go for their regular check-ups.

Leo Careers . . .

Judge or police officer. Just think of all those people waiting to see what your ruling will be.

Animal trainer. King-of-the-jungle instincts coming out there.

Managing director of a company. Just the name, not the job, of course.

Model. All of those people standing around admiring you and you don't even have to speak.

. . . not so Leo Careers

Understudy actor. Second best? Not on your life.

Waitress. People telling you what to do – forget it.

Arctic explorer. As a child of the sun, you'd freeze.

Quiz show host. You'd tell them all the answers were right even if they weren't.

Famous Leos

Ex-spice Girl Geri Halliwell, boxer Chris Eubank, Princess Beatrice, composer Lionel Bart, singer Whitney Houston, Jacqueline Kennedy Onassis, Princess Anne, Princess Margaret and the Queen Mother, actors Sean Penn, Patrick Swayze, Antonio Banderas, Robert Redford and Christian Slater, moon walker Neil Armstrong, presenter Ulrika Jonsson and Madonna.

Health Sore Points

Leo rules the back, spine and heart and when you are working too hard or under stress you often experience lower back pain. The reason the back affects Leos may be because you should be walking on all fours, like the lion you really are. Surprisingly for a four-legged animal, you have good upright posture, and you'll only see a Leo slouch in worrying or stressful times.

The heart is the main thing that needs to be watched, so salt consumption should be restricted. Weak circulation is another possible problem. Good diet and regular exercise are vital for a long Leo life and, as with all fire signs, anything that gets that energy out and stops it from being bottled up is good.

Overexertion is common for busy, sociable, gossipy Leo. You'll go crazy if you are not out doing something. I hear stories about Leos who go missing for days on end seeking out new company and parties. They don't intend to do it, it just happens. It's part of their nature. There is no better way for Leos to unwind than to come home and put their feet up on a cushion, but of course they'll be straight on the phone organizing a party or where to go that night.

Lions get high on caffeine. Those of you who drink a lot of tea, coffee or Coca-Cola look like you are on some high-powered, illegal drug. You handle alcohol better than you handle caffeine. Leo children are often overactive and giving them Coca-Cola doesn't help. But don't snatch it off them. They become hooked. Many a middle-aged Leo can be caught in the broom cupboard at work nursing their can of coke against the possible onslaught of their mother.

Cures and Counsel

You are full of vitality and can easily absorb the energy-giving power of the sun. Good weather sees a happy lion but don't bother trying to make one laugh if it's raining. You need to see sunshine to feel alive. A happy Leo is a slightly tanned one. (Using the proper suntan cream, of course.)

Leos live long, and you often feel better as you grow older. All that wisdom you've gathered makes you feel powerful.

You need to make sure that you are breathing correctly. (Not everyone does, you know.) Breathe in through the nose, let those lungs fill up, and then out through the mouth.

Don't work too early or too late. Leos need to get up at the right hour and go to sleep when it gets dark to present their best possible face to the world.

Learn to slow down a little. Try not to overexert yourself. It's a good idea to have one day a week on a fruit-only diet to clear those toxins out. Put your feet up on that day and relax.

As with all fire signs, it's vital that you learn to let out your anger and your stresses as you experience them. Don't suffer in silence. The sooner you talk about your problems the sooner you can move on and start living again.

Valerian Tea

Tea made from the valerian root can do wonders for the circulation. Valerian is cultivated in many gardens and grows wild in marshy forests, but for herbal remedies the root is used and it is easiest to buy this from a health store. Besides improving circulation, this calms frayed nerves and alleviates tension. I thoroughly recommend it. Romanies believe that nature knows best and this really is the best remedy I know.

1 piece valerian root
600 ml/1 pint boiling water

Cover the root with boiling water and leave to infuse for an hour. Strain and drink a wineglassful daily. Store in the refrigerator.

Dandelion Coffee

Dandelion is great for a Leo because it contains substances they need (potassium) and at the same time provides a cost-effective caffeine kick. (It can't just be coincidence that the plant is named after the lion: it's called in French 'lion's teeth' which to English ears sounds like 'dandelion'.) This lovely drink, made from a recipe handed down by my great-grandmother, will do you ten times more good than regular coffee. It has a terrific effect on the nervous system, is good for the liver, and Romanies often take it as a tonic.

When the dandelion is in flower, dig it up by the roots, wash it thoroughly and dry it in the sun. When the root is thoroughly dried, cut it up into small pieces. Put the pieces in a tin and place them in the oven at 150°C/300°F/gas 2 for an hour or until brittle. Remove from the oven, tip into a mortar or on to a board, and pound into a fine powder. Sieve and store in a jar until needed. Use as any instant coffee. Start off with 1 teaspoonful per cup and increase the amount as you develop your taste for it.

Cissy's Tonic

Here is a health drink that is good for anyone born under the sign of Leo. It's a vitamin boost and is good for the bowels too. It's named after my great aunt.

1 pineapple, peeled
1 mango, peeled and stone removed

Blend in a juicing machine and drink half a cup a day for a week each month.

The Leo Shoulder Stand

Here is an exercise for Leo's achy back. (But remember that it's up to you to stand tall when you are walking and to sit correctly when you are seated. Good posture has a magic effect on your confidence too.) This is based on a yoga exercise. Since I discovered it I have passed it on to several Leo friends, who swear by it and have noticed a major difference in the way their back feels.

Instead of a headstand, which can be a little too strenuous, this is a shoulder stand. It is really relaxing and should stretch muscles you never knew you had without causing any pain or problems. It can even, if you do it often enough, slim down the hips, ankles, calves and abdomen.

Lie on your back, inhale and lift up your legs and body so that they are pointing directly upwards and your weight is resting on your shoulders. Use your arms to support the small of your back. Maintain a stable position. Now lower your legs backwards on an exhalation until your feet are resting behind your head and you look rather like a triangle. Just lower the feet as far as comfortable. Do not strain. Breathe freely then, on an exhalation, uncurl the spine slowly and, with control, slowly lift the feet back over the head and then lower the legs back to the starting position. This might make your shoulders feel stiff at first but it will wear off really quickly if you do it regularly. Next time you are aching and feel like lying down and going to sleep, don't. Revitalize your body and your life with the Leo shoulder stand.

A massage every six weeks or so is also good for posture, not to mention a bit of sheer self-indulgence. If you don't spoil yourself, no one else will, as my mother always said to me. When I was a little girl I was anxious for every beauty remedy my mother and her family could tell me about. I'd lie on my parents' bed with potato peelings over my eyes one week, cucumber the next and cold teabags the week after. All of the older generation of my family look ten to fifteen years younger than they are and I put this down to the few minutes a day they take out of life for themselves. I remember going to my auntie's house one day and seeing a mixture in the kitchen that looked so delicious I wanted to put my finger in it and lick it off. I asked my auntie first. 'Goodness me, Claire, no,' she said. 'That's my mayonnaise and lemon hair mask for bedtime!'

Walking is really good for a Leo, but they are sometimes reluctant to do it. The older they get the more they become set in their ways. So start now and make sure that you get those Leos you love out of the armchair and into regular walks. It will be more beneficial than you realize for the less they exercise the sooner the rheumatism starts to set in. If you cannot walk locally, find a nice scenic view that you can even drive to, breathe in that air and get those muscles moving.

Good Leo Food

You need to make sure you get enough of the cell salt magnesia phosphorica, otherwise known as magnesium phosphate. The lungs, brain, nerves and muscles all need this if they are to function optimally.

Magnesium phosphate promotes cell building in nerve and lung tissue and helps maintain good blood pressure. It also assists in promoting the alkaline balance of body fluids, which gives greater elasticity to tissues and flexibility to joints. The cell salt is also good for blood condition, vital for the heart, which Leo rules.

Plums, wheat bran, peas, cocoa, oranges, lemons and lettuce should all provide you with what you need. And listen to what your body is telling you. If you need a vitamin, your body starts to crave a food that supplies it. When you want chocolate it may well be iron that your body is after, though it's worth remembering that green leafy vegetables will give you the iron and a lot more besides.

A Leo in a restaurant rarely chooses her meal from

the menu. She's more tempted to look around and see who has the most appetizing dish. Leos love beauty and beautiful food is the order of the day for them.

Leos must beware of overindulgence. They need a partner who can recognize that look on their face and say, 'You've had enough, haven't you?' If you let them, they will eat for England. If Leo is out on a date, however, there'll be some effort to be elegant, unless keenness for the food overtakes them. My brother Bradley, who is an Aries, once had a date with a Leo. They went to a spaghetti house where Bradley's date went at her spaghetti with so much enthusiasm that she ended up looking like she'd been in a fight. There was no second date. Pacing your eating is hard for a fire sign, but if you can manage to do it you are sure to make your life (and that of your nearest and dearest) much more pleasant.

Plants for Star Therapy

The pretty little evergreen shrub St John's Wort, also known as the Rose of Sharon, is your luck from mother nature. One of the oldest of British native plants this thrives practically anywhere and spreads rapidly, making an attractive splash of colour with its deep yellow flowers.

Health Checklist

- If you suffer from strain on the heart try co-enzyme Q10. This vitamin-like substance is found in all cells of the body, particularly in heart muscles, nerve tissue and blood. It aids the transfer of oxygen and energy between the blood and body cells and between components of those cells. If you are deficient in Q10, and this is often an affliction of athletes and the elderly, take a supplement of 10–30 mg daily, widely available in health food shops and chemists. It occurs naturally in peanuts, spinach, bran, beef, sardines and mackerel.

- Antioxidants, for example, vitamins A, C and E, beta-carotene and lecithin, and found in parsley, garlic and fish oils, should help combat against free radicals, which are thought to damage body cells – making you prone to disease and the effects of ageing. Eat more fresh tuna, salmon, pilchards, sardines, herring and mackerel – they are all good for you, as of course are fresh fruit and vegetables.
- Avoid strain on the back by working to develop good posture. Make sure you have a firm bed and, if you work sitting down, that your chair is correct for you.
- For overexertion, rest! Restore your energy reserves with iron, Q10 and good nutrition.
- Weak circulation can be treated with vitamin E or ginkgo biloba, which are especially good for those with cold hands and feet or poor memory and concentration.
- You should always try to get the vitamins and minerals you need from the foods you eat, but if your busy schedule prevents that then try the supplements from the health food store or chemist. They could save you from problems later on in life.
- Any foods that put strain on the heart are not good

for you. Make sure you eat meat in moderation, and the best cuts only, and watch against overindulgence once you have hit 50. Excess weight on a Leo is a lot harder to shift as you get older and yet that is precisely when we have more time to overindulge.

- Ease up on the schedule. Leos are all or nothing people and while it is great to give everything you decide to do 100 per cent, sometimes you need to ease up and say no to things.

Are You a True Leo?

Be honest! Write down 'yes' or 'no', then read the advice below.

1 Do you find that you bend forward when you walk without meaning to?
2 Does pride stop you from saying what you really mean to those you love?
3 Do you find it difficult to talk about your problems when they happen, holding in your anger and hurt until you can hold it in no longer?
4 When you walk past a mirror or a reflective surface do you always glance at yourself in it?
5 Does it take you longer than 5 minutes to decide what to wear on a Saturday morning?
6 Do you eat any of the following on a regular basis: plums, wheat bran, peas, oranges, lemon, lettuce or cocoa?
7 Do you put more salt than you know you should on your food?

8 Do you find yourself unusually happy and more relaxed when the sun is out?
9 Do you suffer from weak circulation?
10 Does one cup of coffee send you spinning off into hyper-space?
11 Do you usually drink more than one variety of drink when you're out for the evening?
12 Do you party until you're ready to drop?
13 Do you find your back aching at the end of a working day?
14 Even though you are described by friends as happy-natured, would you say you are also prone to depression?
15 When you eat out at a restaurant do you choose from the menu or by looking at what other people are eating?
16 Do you find yourself coming home with the milkman more than once a month?
17 Can you handle your drink better than most?
18 If you don't get a good night's sleep are you a lion with a sore head the next day?
19 Do you survive a lot of the time on pure nervous energy?
20 Were you an overactive child?

If you answered 'yes' to most questions then you are a typical Leo. Proud and strong, although lacking confidence on the inside. A born leader who needs to feel admired to feel loved. Just make sure that you answered yes to question 6 as the fruit and vegetables listed there are essential for your good health. You must also learn when to take the lead and when to step back, for you have a tendency to lead in things you know nothing about. If you answered yes to questions 2 and 3, try to make an effort to communicate your feelings as they happen. The more quickly you learn to do this, the more quickly you'll get rid of stress you've been carrying about.

Enjoy your life, because there's much for you to enjoy. Just remember to rest every now and then. You don't always have the energy to do everything you want.

If you answered mostly 'no' then you are not a typical Leo, but look again at questions 4, 5 and 8. Did you answer yes to these, or think about answering yes? If so, then you are a real Leo underneath the cool exterior you are trying to present. Nobody wants to be thought a show-off but one of Leo's main characteristics is that they are able to do so in a way that is both adorable and acceptable. Look up your moon sign and see if any of your moon sign traits fit.

If you answered no to question 6 then try to start eating some of the foods I have listed. You should be able to find something there that you can add to your regular menu. Look at the recipes I have given for your sign and try to experiment with the dishes. You may find yourself becoming more of a Leo as you start to eat the foods that match your sign.

If you answered no to questions 11, 12 and 16 then you are indeed a grown-up Leo. There are not many Leos who can resist a party or an offer of a good drink and a good night out. You've obviously learned when to say no.

The Drinker's Guide to the Zodiac

Leos can drink, and they love strange concoctions. Outwardly they look sober, however much they've had, but the fact that you are getting their life story might give the game away. They like to mix their drinks (something to do with their need to experience everything). But they rarely have an alcohol problem. It's more likely to be Coca-Cola they are hiding in their bags.

We all know that drinking alcohol in excess is no good for anyone, and Leos certainly need to know about moderation. They hate to leave a half-empty glass, especially if it's Scotch or Bourbon. Oh yes, especially Bourbon. Champagne leaves Leos cold, but they will love a Glasgow. If you know where to buy Alka Seltzer trade price, better tell your Leo friends.

Glasgow

4 or 5 ice cubes
3 drops angostura bitters
3 drops Pernod
1 part dry French vermouth
3 parts whisky

Put the ice cubes into a glass jug. Shake the bitters and the Pernod over the ice. Pour in the vermouth and whisky. Stir vigorously, strain and pour into a chilled Martini glass.

Star Menu

The best foods for a Leo are hot and spicy. Fire signs need something that can match their mood.

Hot Tomato Salsa

This spicy salsa dish should kick you into life.

200 g/7 oz tin chopped tomatoes
1/4 teaspoon crushed dried chillies
1 onion, chopped
2 cloves garlic, crushed
1/4 teaspoon caster sugar
1 tablespoon olive oil
1 tablespoon red wine vinegar
a good pinch of salt and freshly ground pepper
a bunch of fresh parsley, chopped

Put the tomatoes, chillies, onion, garlic and sugar into a food processor. Blend together until you have a purée.

Heat the oil in a medium-sized saucepan, add the puréed tomato and cook over a medium heat until it thickens to a sauce-like consistency: about 10 minutes. Remove from the heat and stir in the vinegar, salt and pepper. Serve hot or cold with parsley stirred in at the last minute.

Chicken Fajita

Here's an explosion of tastes set to delight even the most experienced of eaters. Serves 6.

finely grated rind and juice of 2 limes
a good pinch of salt and freshly ground black pepper
a handful of fresh coriander, chopped
300 g/10 oz boneless and skinless chicken breasts
1 'family size' packet tortillas, to serve
salad leaves, to serve
hot tomato salsa (see page 197)
topping made from a pot of fromage frais, combined with freshly chopped coriander and freshly ground black pepper

Put the lime zest and juice, salt and pepper into a large bowl and stir. Add the chicken breasts to your newly made lime marinade and turn until evenly coated. Place a plate or lid over the bowl and leave to marinate for 2 or 3 hours, preferably in the refrigerator.

Lightly oil a frying pan and heat until the oil is really hot. Place the marinated chicken in the frying pan and sear, turning as it starts to change colour. Remove the chicken from the pan and cut into thin strips, being careful not to burn your hands. A knife and fork comes in handy here.

Wrap in a tortilla and serve with salad, tomato salsa and fromage frais topping.

Chocolate Crème Brûlée To Die For

Cocoa is good for Leos and this chocolate dessert should leave you in heaven. Remember to save a slice for your friends. Don't let your eyes be bigger than your belly.

15 g/½ oz cocoa powder
300 ml/½ pint double cream
50 g/2 oz caster sugar
2 egg yolks
½ teaspoon vanilla extract

Preheat the oven to 150°C/300°F/gas 2.

In a small saucepan combine the cocoa powder, cream and half of the caster sugar and heat until you can see bubbles appearing. In a bowl beat the egg yolks and stir in the vanilla extract. Pour the cream and cocoa powder in and mix well. Pour into small white heat-proof cups.

Place the cups in a baking dish and pour enough boiling water into the pan to come halfway up the sides of the cups. Bake for half an hour, then allow to cool. Refrigerate overnight. When you are ready to serve them, sprinkle the remaining sugar over and grill until you get a golden crust, watching them all the time so they don't burn.

Star Beauty

Egg Mask for Leo's Shining Glory

The hair is Leo's main concern so here's a fantastic recipe to stimulate hair growth and promote its strength and vitality. Eggs are full of protein and have long been used in many countries around the world as a beauty treatment for hair (and skin too). This will restore thickness and strength to your hair.

2 eggs (for long hair) or 1 egg plus a little water (for short hair)

Beat the eggs and water if using and work into clean wet hair. Massage with your fingertips and then wrap a towel around the hair. Leave for 10 minutes. While you are waiting, why not get a little egg on your face? Separate an egg, beat up the white and smooth it over your face. Two minutes before your hair is ready, beat up the egg yolk and add it to your face mask. Wash it off well and then rinse your hair using warm (not hot!) water, not once but twice.

A Leo friend of mine mixes a little brandy with the eggs before using the mixture in exactly the same way. And she drinks a little while she's waiting!

Gaggie's Growth Tonic

Here is another beauty recipe that should make the hair of the Leo shine beautifully and promote new hair growth.

50 g/2 oz fresh or 10 g/¼ oz dried rosemary
50 g/2 oz southernwood
50 g/2 oz sage
25 g/1 oz bay leaves
fresh lemon juice

Put all the herbs in a bowl with a squeeze of fresh lemon juice and cover with boiling water. Allow to cool then dip your fingers in and massage into the scalp with strong circular motions. As with any shampoo or hair treatment, the massage applied to the scalp is as important as the ingredients themselves. Strain the herbs before use.

Your Ideal Health Sign Holiday

Las Vegas, the city of gambling and showgirls, is the perfect place for the lion to be the king of the jungle. This fantasy land is a great experience for such a fun-loving sign as you. You'll love the bright lights and excitement of this dream spot in Nevada.

VIRGO

THE VIRGIN

Ruling Planet: Mercury, the planet of communication

Triplicity or Element: Earth

Quadruplicity or Mode: Mutable

Key words: Modest, shy, practical, intelligent, overcritical, perfectionist

The Origin of Virgo

Virgo was named after the virgin goddess Astraea and is associated with purity. She found earth so imperfect that she fled to the heavens to live.

What Virgo is Like

This is a sign that is often underestimated. These are the healers and helpers of the world and the perfectionists of the zodiac. It is the second of the mutable signs. They have the ability to look at people and know what is wrong with their lives, and the annoying thing is they are usually right. If they think someone's boyfriend is the unfaithful sort then he probably is. He may not have done anything yet but they can tell – he's got that look. Virgos like to look after people but they sometimes become interfering. And although they know what everyone else should be doing with their lives, they don't always know what to do with their own.

Virgos have a certain confidence about them that people turn to in times of trouble. You can count on them to be there when needed and to say the right thing. They have a tendency to be a bit too truthful, however, and sometimes people find them just plain rude.

Greens and dark browns represent the earthy nature of this sign. You will find Virgos at their most confident and comfortable when they wear these colours.

They like a good drama, and you mustn't be fooled by the sob stories they tell you about their personal lives.

They also tend to read more deeply into what people say than they should. Don't tell them you are having a problem with your partner or before you know it everyone's heard you are about to be divorced. Be careful what you say to a Virgo; you may regret it later. It's hard to resist, though. Virgos inspire such confidence.

Ruled by the communicative planet Mercury they are often at home in foreign lands. What is important to them is how they arrange their domestic environment. Their element is earth and that makes Virgo home-loving. Young Virgos usually have a well-equipped bedroom that's like a mini-apartment with all the latest stereo and computer equipment.

Virgos show the world their cool side but if you can get beneath the mystery their ruling planet Mercury confers on them you'll see a born worrier and something of a hypochondriac.

Being a mutable sign means they can get on with people of all ages and from all walks of life. But not everyone else agrees they can get on with a Virgo. You may be stinging after that argument but your Virgo friend can carry on the next day as if nothing happened, thinking you enjoyed the drama as much as she did. Unless of course she is still in drama mode, in which case your problem is bigger than any issue currently affecting the world.

I once had a good Virgo friend who used to say to me: 'Hi, how are you, because I've had a really bad day and this is what happened to me . . .' I couldn't get a word in edgeways, although I'm sure she thought she knew everything that was going on in my life. She once went to a lot of trouble to track me down to tell me a friend of hers had broken up with her boyfriend. Now I like gossip as much as the next person but by this I was not amused. Especially when I found out that they had not split up, merely had a disagreement. I loved this friend dearly but found it hard to cope with her constant need to make a drama out of every little thing in life.

Virgos can't help being critical, and most of the time they are right in their judgements, but they do go overboard from time to time because of that little drama queen that lurks within. And they are better at dishing out criticism than receiving it. If you misbehave your Virgo friends will dissect it and discuss it for months. But if they misbehave – well, that's OK. Don't think them unprincipled. They are highly principled and work well in positions of responsibility.

Many Virgos work in the health industry and do extremely well in it. They are capable of great precision work and can become brilliant surgeons. They are capable of running a tight ship but they can also bend the rules when they feel it necessary. Here they are rather similar to a Leo, though perhaps not quite as generous with their finances. If a Virgo pays for your dinner he or she is unlikely to forget it, even when you return the favour twofold.

Work has to be what a Virgo wants to make it. They can be self-important but are so confidence-inspiring that you'll probably go along with it. They get on well in life because they are so convincing.

Virgos take their health very seriously. And if a friend is ill, they like to know all about it. They can talk with authority on many different subjects and if they don't know the facts they will go and look them up.

There was once a ballet dancer who used to tour the towns with different shows. Her colleagues used to talk about the ballet injuries they were suffering from, and so did she. Very often, when one of them would moan about a bruise or a sprain, she would join in with, 'I know, I know.' These rather colourful performances began to get on everyone's nerves. One day one of the dancers said, taking the name from the curry she'd had the night before, 'Oh I've got a rogan josh sprain. It's very rare but it's named because of its heat and it is so painful.' Sarah, our Virgo, said, 'I had that years ago. I know. It does hurt, doesn't it?' Everyone laughed and Sarah didn't find it at all amusing to have had a joke played on her. She swore she really had suffered from a rogan josh sprain, or something sounding just like it, although I am told that she has since gone off curries because they remind her of her embarrassment.

If they plan ahead, Virgos are excellent shoppers. And if you want to go round the world with someone, you could do much worse than resourceful, adaptable, loving but cool-headed Virgo, who, what's more, will look after you if you pick up a bug. The only problem is that on your return there will be endless discussions of things that went wrong and how it could all have been done better.

Put two Virgos in a room together and leave them there. No matter how late you get back they will still be there discussing life and how they would heal the world. Argumentative, yes, but analytical and methodical. Talk about anything and this sign will have something to say about it. They are a mine of information, useless or otherwise.

How to Spot a Virgo

You can usually tell a Virgo by the way they dress. A lot of thought will have gone into the outfit and even if it is casual you can bet they planned it the night before right down to the colour of the underwear. They often have slender and fine features, although this is not always the rule.

The Devil and the Angel

The DEVIL VIRGO is opinionated, doesn't think twice about speaking his mind and tends to be overcritical. A good example is Oasis singer Liam Gallagher, whose outspoken opinions on drugs and life in general have got him into many a scrape with the press.

Then there is the ANGEL VIRGO, who is patient, animal-loving and caring. A perfect example is the late Mother Theresa, whose work was tireless and whose opinions sometimes shocked but were always stated with the aim of improving the world.

Virgo Health and Development from Child to Adult

The Virgo baby usually starts out in life looking very much like its father but in temperament and personality being much like its mother. This is not the most patient of babies, especially for the first four months, but after that the crying and tantrums should stop and you will be left with a child who is weighing up your every move. They are now very serene, and often remain so for the rest of their lives. Keep them occupied or they will catnap during the day and then you'll be up most of the night, watching them watch you to see what you're up to.

At five years of age you should be able to detect the first signs of real determination. If you don't learn their ways quickly they will soon be able to get anything they want out of you, and still convince you you're not giving them enough. A trip to the zoo or the park will be gratefully accepted but quickly followed with: 'Where are we going next?' The young Virgo has a larger than average appetite and their tastes will run more to savoury dishes than sweet. If you throw a dinner party you can guarantee that the Virgo child will pop up to taste the food that they think is really in their honour, but be careful as they may just eat the lot. They can converse quite easily with adults but may appear a little arrogant as their views are pretty strong even at this age. They will probably go down with minor childhood illnesses but they lead a charmed life where more serious illnesses are concerned. They will be capable of sustaining an interest for many years and will not flit from hobby to hobby as some children do. They are also likely to keep the same close friends in their life for some time to come.

At eleven years this child will make it clear that they do not want to be a leader and that they are one of nature's reliable second-in-command. They are the sort of child a teacher likes to make a pet of as they are steadfast, honest and hardworking. The Virgo earns the respect of their schoolmates, just as they will their workmates later on. They are very mature for their age, both with friends and romantically too. They will usually have a beau or their eye firmly stuck on someone, and you might as well listen to what they have to say about this because they'll carry on regardless anyway. The young Virgo makes friends with the opposite sex early on in life compared to other signs. They may even start to develop physically a little before the other children. When other kids are playing cowboys and Indians this child has already moved on to kiss chase.

At 16 they are still the golden child and may even stay behind after classes to talk to the teacher, just because they feel like it or for a friendly debate. They are a steadying influence on the friends around them, talking about what their friends are experiencing as if they'd already done it all years ago. The newly adolescent Virgo is a sensible sort of person, until, of course, romance gets them into trouble. For a sign with so many opinions and views on life, they can be very naive in the love sector. They will fall for the wrong sort time and time again at this age, and they just don't seem to learn their lesson. Vanity and self-indulgence are their downfall and you can bet that by now they have more than one mirror in their bedroom.

At 21 they usually feel ripe for marriage and settling down. Their earth quality is urging them to do so. They lapse comfortably into a domestic, easy-going life but are also something of a go-getter, especially if their partner encourages them. They tend to be attracted to domineering partners. Left to their own devices the Virgo is a little too soft to play to success. There is a feeling of mischief when they near 30 and they may feel the temptation to stray. A very short leash would be required.

At 40 they begin to slip into middle age with more grace than any other sign. There is sometimes a bit of stress around here and maybe trouble with the stomach or throat, but manageable if they are getting the right nutrients from their food. Romance and mischief often go hand in hand around this time. If they can't find gossip in other people's lives they'll be tempted to start some in their own. They dress well for their age and look younger than they are. Friends are mostly of the opposite sex and work will start to feel less important than it used to for them.

At 70 they are looking and feeling good but need to eat at regular times to avoid bowel and stomach problems. They can live for many many years beyond this and usually decide to give up on life when they can no longer find anything interesting to gossip about. Fall-outs with family can cause problems because the bored 70-year-old Virgo has decided to be difficult. Look out for older Virgo men and the younger-woman syndrome. If they can afford it they will have a gorgeous 21-year-old on their arm for all to see and they will love every minute of it. In fact, they will claim it is what keeps them young at heart.

Virgo Careers . . .

Organizer of anything at all. Virgos love this.

Secretary. But you will, of course, tell your boss what he or she should be doing.

Film producer. Deciding on all those great storylines and shots: ideal.

Scientist. You don't give up easily in your quest for answers.

Pioneer in medical science. You have a natural affinity with health and hospitals.

. . . not so Virgo Careers

Astronaut. Earth signs shouldn't leave the planet.

Waitress. Don't they know who you think you are?

Any seafaring job. Earth signs need to keep their feet out of water and on solid ground.

Famous Virgos

Singers Michael Jackson and Harry Connick Jr, actors Hugh Grant and Richard Gere, athlete Michael Johnson, boxers Billy Hardy and Lennox Lewis, musician Charlie 'Bird' Parker, Sir Richard Attenborough.

Health Sore Points

Virgo rules the intestines so you need to keep the digestive system in good working order. It also rules the stomach, nervous system and throat.

Virgos enjoy good health, but you worry about problems that aren't there. Yes, you're a little bit of a hypochondriac, Virgo. Look in the bathroom cabinet. Isn't there an array of bottles and medicines there?

Your biggest problem is crying wolf. When something really does go wrong you may not be believed. Your voice goes very quiet when you are ill, and for those who know you this can be a good indicator of something wrong. No more will you dissect people's lives and dramas – at least until your health improves.

Your work often affects your health. A stressful job can give you stomach pains and bowel problems. You are good at working funny hours because your brain does not change with the hours of the sun or moon. You can function just as easily at midnight or midday. But the stress of your job may have you on a roller-coaster ride that upsets your stomach. If your job is not stressful, then you'll be inventing drama in your personal life, in which case a sore throat is usually the first problem to occur.

Most ailments you get are there to hide an emotional problem. You don't like it when life doesn't go your way, but rather than talk about a problem you disguise it. It is much better that you talk about what's bothering you rather than make yourself ill. You really can become ill when you fall in love because it takes you over body and soul. You'll never admit this, of course. You will be telling your friends you are dewy-eyed because you've got a cold coming, and you are so convincing they will probably believe you.

Headaches and migraines are the perfect clue that something is not agreeing with you, although if it is a chocolate or cheese allergy you'd probably rather have the headache than not have the cheese or chocolate.

Cures and Counsel

Virgos usually enjoy very good health, but you are given to worrying, which can bring on nervous exhaustion. One of the main things for Virgos to take care of is not to overdo things, especially your social lives. Instead of changing at work to go straight to a party or to meet friends, try to make time to slow down. Take a break before rushing into your next mode for the evening.

A lot of Virgos do not get enough fresh air. You have an affinity with nature and all things earthy and you should make sure you get regular walks. If you have a problem you will probably find yourself just walking and thinking and breathing, returning home with more ideas and energy than when you left. So make sure you get a regular walk, especially on your day off. There is no excuse! Even the high-flying businessmen I give readings to take breaks. (The successful ones, that is!) If you don't, you are going to explode. All you need is to find a route that's pretty and scenic and take 10 or 15 minutes out of your morning to get the fresh air into your lungs.

Walking is a perfect form of exercise for an earth sign, more so than for the other elements. A Virgo househusband I know makes the effort every day to walk to his local postbox or to the shop to buy some milk or whatever he feels they may be running out of. Then he doesn't feel so bad about being stuck indoors all day. He told me that when he first decided to do this he didn't want to tell his wife, also a Virgo, in case she made him stick to it. You see a Virgo is very good at telling others what they should do, but they don't like to have the pressure put on themselves. So he used to say, 'I'm just going to buy some butter.' Eventually she began to get suspicious about him buying things in ones and twos instead of all at once, especially when they didn't need what he bought. Finally, at eight o'clock one morning full of energy, he told his wife he was popping out to get some washing powder. What normal person goes to the shop at eight in the morning? They didn't even need any washing powder! She accused him of having an affair. He came clean and told her he was only going round the block to get some air into his lungs. Well, being a Virgo herself, and probably to get him back for acting so strangely, she had him jogging round the block that night and even bought him a membership card for the gym for Christmas.

You need to find the exercise you like and stick to it. Join a club or group if you want to further your abilities. There is no point in being an earth sign and not using what the gods have given you. Outdoor sports really are the best, although not necessarily swimming or flying. You need to keep to the earth-bound activities your sign craves. Running is good for you and you should find that you are left with more energy than you started with.

Virgos are more likely to be vegetarians than any other sign. You are very aware of what you put into your bodies – indeed, you can be annoyingly fussy about it. As the intestines are your main health weakness, it is vital you keep regular bowel movement. Constipation is an early sign of a stressed Virgo.

The remedies here should serve you well, but don't forget to eat well too, and try the Virgo Stress Buster on a regular basis. Don't be a hypochondriac if you can help it! A positive attitude is essential if you are to make the most of your life. Learn to listen to your body, to trust it and to do what it requires. Put the right oil in the machine and it will serve you well.

Balm for Nerves

Balm will relieve your nervous tension. This mint grows wild from July to September in mountainous areas and in some hilly districts, but is probably easiest to buy in dried form.

25 g/1 oz fresh balm or 1 teaspoon of dried
600 ml/1 pint boiling water

Cover the balm with boiling water and leave to infuse for 10 minutes. Take one teaspoon when it's cool for a calming effect, but not more than twice a day. Keep refrigerated.

Horseradish Throat Remedy

For your throat I recommend horseradish. Only the fresh article will do. Scoop half a teacupful from the horseradish and soak it well in vinegar. Leave it to stand for 24 hours, making sure the horseradish is covered by the vinegar. Add 1 tablespoon glycerine, mix well together, and take half a teaspoon in a wineglass of hot water when necessary. Sip very slowly.

Oak Bark Remedy

For stomach upsets.

15 g/½ oz bark from an oak tree
600 ml/1 pint water

Boil the bark in the water for 5 minutes. Strain, cool and take 1 tablespoon daily. Keep in the refrigerator.

Virgo Stress Buster

Here is a juice drink that contains the ingredients a Virgo needs to battle through any stressful times in life.

1 apple
5 large strawberries
10 raspberries
10 blackberries
the juice of 1 lemon

Juice the apple first in a juicer and then pour into a blender. Add the strawberries, raspberries, blackberries and lemon and drink to drain away the stresses of the day.

If you don't own a juicer you can mash up the apple with a potato masher, but let me tell you they're worth every penny.

Good Virgo Food

Virgos tend to have a deficiency in the cell salt kali sulphuricum, also known as potassium sulphate. A lack of this cell salt can lead to clogged pores because of the thickening of the oils of the skin. This impedes the elimination of the body's impurities through the pores, which results in them being thrown back on the internal organs. The internal organs become overworked, which leads to colds, coughs, catarrh, pleurisy, pneumonia and such like. These conditions are nature's way of throwing out the impurities which the overworked body cannot expel.

All you need is to include these foods in your diet (they are very similar to those for Aries): tomatoes, lemons, celery, grapefruit, apples and the herb valerian.

I don't advise a Virgo to try too many different kinds of new foods. Things unknown throw you into a quandary. You may tell friends who've invited you to dinner that you eat anything and everything, but that's because you want to be thought of as cultured and adventurous. Those of you out there who want to invite a Virgo round for dinner: let me suggest that you do something fairly simple with plenty of vegetables and remember that the majority of vegetarians are Virgos!

Virgos in their teens should drink plenty of water and shouldn't clog up their skin with make-up. The pores of the skin, particularly when young, should be kept clean. Recent studies show no link between eating fried food and getting spots, but I'm still not convinced, especially not for Virgos. Then again, a little of what you fancy . . . If you stop children, or anyone for that matter, from eating what they want then at some point they will only want it more, and when they do eat what they crave you can be sure that it will be to excess. If you are in charge of what a Virgo is eating, never tell them no, because they will only eat it in private when you are out of the way.

Fatty foods are not good for you. You do need fat but you get enough from ordinary foods. Go easy on the cooking oils and think about grilling foods instead of frying them. You can read more about fat intake in the chapter on healthy eating if you are concerned, but really it is up to you to listen to your body and its needs and not to be greedy or overindulge. You like to give yourself sweet foods as a reward, especially when you're feeling blue. Resist the temptation to reach for the chocolate cake, and try to sort out this habit before it sets in permanently.

Plants for Star Therapy

Lavender is your lucky plant and requires a sunny spot in your garden where it will give pleasure both with its lovely perfume and its appearance. Dry its flowers and use them to gently perfume your linen. This is your plant and should bring you good luck and good fortune.

Or make yourself a lavender pillow for your bedroom. (I'm talking to you men, too, you know! Once you have had a good night's sleep with one of these in your room you won't care what people think.) Take an old pillowcase (ideally a small one or you'll need a lot of lavender; or cut it down to size) and stuff it with fresh lavender from your garden. Sleep with it under your normal pillow and the next morning you'll feel refreshed and relaxed.

Health Checklist

- Virgo, spend some of that time you spend on others on yourself!
- You don't have many health problems but when you do feel ill the whole world gets to know about it. Herbal remedies work well for Virgos and should always be tried first.
- If you're not eating the diet you know you should, take a one-a-day multivitamin and mineral tablet.
- Zinc lozenges are good for Virgo throat problems. Or try the Horseradish Throat Remedy on page 215, or the Taurus remedies on pages 111 and 112.
- For stomach problems, look to the pro-biotics, acidophillus and bifidus. Try, too, the Oak Bark Remedy on page 216.
- Your most important key to health is to find a way to avoid colds and flu. Virgos catch colds more easily than the other signs. First thing is to dress for the weather. You can still look good in a scarf you know! If you think you've already picked something up, follow these steps:

1 Go to bed (yes, no matter how gorgeous the date you're being offered).

2 Drink plenty of liquids to avoid fluid loss caused by sweating and to flush out those toxins.
3 Ask your local chemist (or, better, send someone out to ask for you) for advice on medications, especially herbal ones, to help relieve symptoms.
4 Hug a hot-water bottle if you feel shivery.
5 Call your doctor for advice if your symptoms persist for more than a few days.
6 A bout of flu means you may have to forget about work for at least a week, and if you suffer regularly you may want to think about having a flu vaccination as a precaution, or perhaps better, take echinacea, zinc and vitamin C.

The Drinker's Guide to the Zodiac

Virgos are good listeners – until, that is, they have had a few and then they can't stop talking. You won't get a word in edgeways between the gin and tonics, but when they start talking, they've usually got something worth hearing, so hang about. After two drinks they're good at telling jokes, even though they can never remember the end. Unlucky for the rest of us they aren't big drinkers! A lot of Virgos find alcohol gives them kidney problems and they choose to alternate their drinks with water when they are out.

Greybeard

Give your Virgo a Greybeard, then get ready to listen to the stories.

4 or 5 ice cubes
3 drops angostura bitters
1 teaspoon cherry brandy
1 part sweet Italian vermouth
2 parts dry French vermouth
4 parts vodka
1 slice of fresh lemon

Put the ice cubes into a cocktail shaker and shake the bitters over them. Pour in the cherry brandy, vermouths and vodka, shake lightly and strain. Pour into a glass and twist the lemon over the mixture and drop it in.

Are You a True Virgo?

Be honest! Write down 'yes' or 'no', then read the advice below.

1 Do you find yourself constantly giving friends and family advice about their lives, although you are unwilling to accept any advice on your own?
2 Do you feel happier and more confident in your own home than in those of your friends?
3 Do you find it hard to tell a story as it is? Be honest, do you like to exaggerate the details to make it sound better?
4 On a weekly basis do you eat any of the following: tomatoes, lemons, celery, grapefruit or apples?
5 Do you find yourself always running late for the next place you are supposed to be?
6 Do you exercise or get out in the fresh air on a weekly basis?

7 Are you or have you ever been a vegetarian?
8 Do you find it almost impossible to keep a juicy secret?
9 If there is a cold going around, do you usually catch it?
10 Do you suffer from digestive problems?
11 If someone is not feeling well do you go out of your way to play nursemaid?
12 Do you always put a great deal of thought into what you are wearing?
13 Do you find yourself giving advice that some would say is too truthful and honest?
14 Have you ever thought about working in the health environment?
15 If you think you have a cold or flu do you run to the doctor before you really need to?
16 Do you find yourself discussing people's lives as if they were the latest soap opera to all and sundry?
17 Do friends accuse you of having verbal diarrhoea?
18 Do you find that herbal remedies work better for you than pharmaceutical drugs?
19 Do you find yourself overbooking your day just so as not to miss out on what friends and family might be doing?
20 Have you ever taken up an exercise or sport just so that you can tell people you are doing one?

If you answered 'yes' to most questions then you are a typical Virgo, always there for friends and always knowing the right thing to do in a situation. Just make sure that question 4 was one you answered yes to. It is essential that you get the correct foods into your diet. You are one of the healthiest signs of the zodiac and if you complain about something it is usually because you are in need of attention rather than serious medical help. Do be careful of crying wolf. Better stick to other stories!

Try to get yourself a better routine instead of arranging things around your social life. If you could put half as much energy into your career as you do your social status you would have reached the top of the career ladder by now.

If you answered yes to question 1 then be careful that you are not putting your nose where it is not wanted. You could find yourself in for a dressing down. You are a great addition to anyone's life but do remember to stop and listen to what close ones are trying to say to you. You may just be missing a compliment.

If you answered 'no' to most questions then you are not a typical Virgo at all. Mind you, a lot of true Virgos answer questions with what they would like to be the truth, rather than what actually is. Why not try answering the questions again, based on past experiences? It can be hard for a true Virgo to say what they are really feeling as they worry too much about what others think of them. Who knows, you could actually be a truer Virgo than those who answered mostly 'yes'. Look up your moon sign too and read more about how that will affect you.

Try to make sure that you eat the foods your sign needs. You should be able to think a lot clearer once you have the correct nutrition.

If you answered no to question 14 you could be missing out on a profession that was made for you. I advise you to read the beginning of this chapter again, to see if you recognize any qualities that have been lying dormant. Yours is a truly wonderful character and it is up to you to make the most of what your sign has to offer.

Star Menu

Earth signs love food and they love the home, and Virgos often cook up a storm for friends and family. You prefer to eat at home than in a restaurant because you like to be in your own surroundings. Not on your own though. There are always a few friends sitting around Virgo's kitchen table.

Two-colour Soup

This soup is perfect for the sign of Virgo. It looks great in the bowl and gives the impression of perfection even before you get to taste it. Once you've tried my two-colour soup you will never go back to the stuff in tins. This makes enough soup for 4.

3 or 4 leeks, white part only, sliced
450 g/1 lb carrots, chopped
1 onion, chopped
1 kg/2 lb potatoes, chopped
1.2 litres/2 pints water
50 g/2 oz butter
2 tablespoons double cream
salt and freshly ground black pepper
4 sprigs of mint

Put the leeks into one large saucepan and the carrots into another. Divide the onion, potato and water between the saucepans, cover and simmer until tender. Allow to cool then purée each mixture separately in a liquidizer or food processor. Divide the butter between the purées, and add the cream to the leek mixture only. Season both soups. Put each into a separate container and place in the refrigerator to chill.

Serve the soup in chilled bowls, slowly pouring from both containers at the same time so that there is one colour in each half of the bowl. Garnish each bowl with a mint sprig.

Warren Surprise

Tomatoes, lemons and celery are good for Virgos. This vegetarian chili contains all of these and more. It's wonderfully delicious. The recipe was originally given to me by a Virgo friend. It was her favourite dish. Funny that she was instinctively eating all the things her body needed to be fit and well. The recipe has been adjusted over the years by my brother, who used to cook it for me. We used to call it 'surprise' because we never knew what he was going to put in, but now the dish has settled into the form given here.

Don't be put off by this long list of ingredients. Once everything has been chopped up it is a quick dish to prepare.

6 tablespoons olive oil
3 onions, finely chopped

1 tablespoon crushed garlic
3 sticks celery, chopped
1 green pepper
2 carrots, chopped
8 mushrooms, chopped
1 tablespoon ground cumin
¾ teaspoon dried basil
¾ teaspoon oregano
1 teaspoon crushed dried chillies
2 tablespoons chilli powder (this isn't pure chilli!)
1 teaspoon salt
½ teaspoon pepper
2 x 400 g/14 oz cans chopped tomatoes (or equivalent, fresh)
500 ml/18 fl oz tomato juice
3 tablespoons tomato purée
400 g/14 oz can red kidney beans, undrained
½ teaspoon Tabasco
1 tablespoon Worcestershire sauce
2 tablespoons lemon juice
125 g/4 oz bulgur wheat
4 tablespoons dry red or white wine
2 tablespoons chopped green chillies, or to taste
2 tablespoons chopped fresh parsley, or to taste

Heat the olive oil in a large saucepan and fry the onions and garlic in it until the onion begins to soften. Then add the celery, green pepper, carrots, mushrooms, cumin, basil, oregano, dried chillies, chilli powder, salt and pepper. Cook over a low heat for about 5 minutes, stirring. Then add the tomatoes, tomato juice, tomato purée, red kidney beans and their liquid, Tabasco,

Worcestershire sauce and lemon juice. Stir and cook for another 5 minutes until boiling. Then add the bulgur wheat and wine, reduce to a simmer and cook for a further 25 minutes, uncovered. Thin with more tomato juice if too thick.

Garnish with fresh green chillies and parsley and serve over rice. This dish tastes even better the next day and it freezes very well too.

Deep-fried Potato Skins with Herby Cheese Dip

Potato skins are a good source of potassium and they are tasty too. To prepare the potatoes, bake potatoes as you ordinarily would (that is, up to 1½ hours in a hot oven). Cut in half, scoop out the potato flesh (eat it or set aside for another dish) and cut the skins into segments. Deep-fry them in hot oil, ideally in a deep-fat fryer. Drain on kitchen paper and serve immediately with the dip. Obviously, deep-fried foods aren't the best things for you, so make this as a treat rather than an everyday part of your diet! You could use the dip as a baked potato garnish, too.

90 g/3 oz softened butter
6 tablespoons milk
125 g/4 oz Cheddar cheese, grated
4 drops Tabasco
salt and freshly ground black pepper
chopped fresh chives and parsley, to taste
a sprig of chervil, to garnish

Cream the butter in a bowl and slowly add the milk and grated cheese. Beat until smooth (blend in a food processor if you like). Add the Tabasco and season to taste with salt and pepper. Stir in the fresh herbs and mix together well. Transfer into a serving bowl, smooth the top with the back of a spoon and garnish with a sprig of chervil. Serve with hot fried potato skins.

Blue Cheese Dip

This is another great dip for potato skins, but is also good to dip celery into, another crucial ingredient in the Virgo diet. It's also great with a chunk of French bread.

125 g/4 oz Danish blue or Roquefort cheese
90 g/3 oz full-fat soft cheese, at room temperature
1 tablespoon lemon juice
salt to taste

Blend all the ingredients together until smooth and creamy. Go easy on the salt; the cheese is already salty. And since this is rich, make a little go a long way.

Orange Fruit Sorbet

This dessert is good enough to pass any Virgo's test.

125 g/4 oz caster sugar
300 ml/½ pint water
1 tablespoon lemon juice
finely grated rind of 1 orange and 1 lemon
300 ml/½ pint freshly squeezed orange and lemon juice (about 3 oranges and 1 lemon)
2 egg whites

Dissolve the sugar in the water in a small heavy saucepan over a low heat. Increase the heat, bring to the boil, then simmer for 5 minutes or until you are left with a syrup. Put the lemon juice and orange and lemon rinds into a bowl and pour the hot syrup over. Allow to cool completely. Add the mixed fruit juices, strain into a freezing tray and place in the freezing compartment of the refrigerator. Leave until half-frozen then turn the mixture into a bowl. Whisk the egg whites until stiff, fold into the frozen mixture, return to the tray and freeze until solid. Take out of the freezer at least 10 minutes before serving.

Star Beauty

For all Virgos I recommend that each evening before you do anything you take a bath. Not too hot and not too cold. Too cold will not relax you and too hot will make you sleepy. This will give you time to review your day and will also stop you from going into the evening with too much energy and burning yourself out. Add a handful of Epsom salts to the bath. There's nothing better to see you from the day pleasantly into the evening.

Root Mask

The root mask has been used in my family for generations. All you have to do is to mash up some boiled carrots and turnips, allow to cool and place on a clean face. Lie down for 10 minutes and relax, preferably with cold camomile teabags on your eyelids. Rinse off with warm water. It contains vitamin A, which is great for irritated skin. A certain auntie of mine has been known to prepare this dish for dinner on a Sunday with enough to use on her face afterwards. The perfect Sunday afternoon treat after cooking for the family.

Mayonnaise Mask

Another great beauty secret for Virgos is mayonnaise – ideally home-made with fresh, organic eggs. Yes, that's it. You simply put it on your face and on your hair and leave for 15 minutes. Just make sure that you rinse it thoroughly or you'll smell odd. It will nourish the skin and hair and leave it feeling soft. You can also add some mayonnaise to the beauty creams in the chapter on Outer Health. Don't dismiss the idea – mayonnaise really does wonders for you.

Your Ideal Health Sign Holiday

Switzerland is the answer for the perfectionist of the zodiac. There is very little that can go wrong on a holiday there. Even if the weather is bad you can cuddle up with your lover in front of a fire with a delicious fondue and discuss what you want to do with your life – and that of your friends, family, colleagues . . .

LIBRA

THE SCALES

Ruling Planet: Venus, the planet of love

Triplicity or Element: Air

Quadruplicity or Mode: Cardinal

Key words: Balance, justice, harmony, partnership, sociability, refinement

The Origin of Libra

Libra holds in her hands the scales of justice. She represents for eternity the virtues of Themis, goddess of justice, who was also the mother of Astraea, who became Virgo. Side by side they represent equity in the heavens.

What Libra is Like

Libra represents balance and harmony, as its astrological symbol, the holder of the scales of justice, shows. Librans always try to do what is right, and are capable of seeing both sides of an argument. The scales also symbolize that the Libran feels incomplete, out of balance, without a partner.

Venus, Libra's ruling planet, is the planet of love, and like the sign of Taurus, which is also ruled by Venus, the heart will always rule the head. One of the most natural (and paternal) signs in the zodiac, along with Cancer, they make the best parents, especially as fathers. Quite often the men of this sign choose fatherhood late in life. Having lived and learned, they have a lot of knowledge to pass on to their children. Librans have a great empathy with the younger generation. These are the parents who get down on their hands and knees and join in with the children's games at parties.

Librans work out ideas by talking them through with other people. They need to talk and to discover other people's views before they can make a decision. This is an air sign, and like Gemini, another air sign, it needs to communicate. We all interconnect, you see, which is how the world is able to work. Librans get on well with people and should not be left to work on their own, when they won't be at their best.

Great socializers, Librans are the last to leave a party. They love to flirt, too, though they usually don't mean anything by it. Yes, this is the sign people are always whispering about, positive they are having an affair. Believe me, it's when they stop flirting that you should worry.

They adore beautiful things and the Libran home is a lovely place, revealing all the care Librans put into choosing each item or furniture or decoration. It's not always tidy, though. They are also known for their laziness. They love beautiful food too, again like Taurus, although Taureans don't just love it, they also eat a lot of it. Librans can be irritating shoppers, as they deliberate over everything. Of all the signs, surveys have shown them to spend the least on buying food and dining out.

Libra is a cardinal sign and they have been likened to a fast bird, flitting from place to place and stopping when they see something beautiful. They are, however, shrewd shoppers, and will go back to look at something two or three times before they decide to buy it. I remember going shopping with my dad when I was 11. I was desperate for a pair of shoes with a tiny heel on them, and I knew my mother would not buy them for me. I cleverly arranged for just me and my Libran dad to go shopping. I am ashamed to say that I had my dad wrapped around my little finger. What I hadn't bargained for, however, was the way the Libran scales of justice would come into play. We went back to the shop three times during the course of the afternoon while my father made me look at other options and deliberated over what my mother would say and the consequences of our actions. Needless to say, I am a Scorpio, and I got my shoes on our third visit at quarter past five after convincing my father I would get plenty of wear out of them. He also managed to talk my mother round. What a champion. The end of the story must be told, however. I outgrew them within the month and was by then anyway only wearing roller boots!

Libra seems composed at first glance, but if you look beneath the charm you will at times glimpse a depressive character. No one is happy when their life is not going as they'd like it to, but Librans also get upset about things they shouldn't. In particular, they let other people's woes get to them. They feel it is their job to make sure that no one is unloved.

Balance in life is key for Librans. They need to work, rest and play. Without the combination of these three they will not feel fulfilled.

How to Spot a Libra

Librans wear good fabrics and attractive colours. They choose clothes not by the price or even the look but the quality of the fabric. They also look approachable, and have gentle features, often perfectly symmetrical.

The Devil and the Angel

The DEVIL LIBRAN is lazy, moody, philandering, unreliable and calculatingly charming. Tommy Lee, the rock star whose womanizing has got him into plenty of trouble, has been seen to have demonstrated some of these traits.

The ANGEL LIBRAN is sensitive, a lover of animals and beautiful food, romantic, charming and a real family person. The late Linda McCartney is a perfect example. She spent her life caring for animals by creating beautiful and healthy vegetarian food and also managed to raise a harmonious family.

All Librans are good at heart. Even the naughty Libran is an angel underneath. They have just gone a step too far. All people born under this sign need balance and when they don't get it is when things start to go wrong. They always regret their actions, and an unforgiven Libra is a heavily burdened one.

Libra Health and Development from Child to Adult

The Libran baby is one any mother would be proud of. They very quickly show all of the qualities she could possibly hope for. Alertness, quick wit and intelligence often reveal themselves within weeks of birth. This is quite a musical child as well. Some parents swear their Libran baby is not just cooing but cleverly singing along to their favourite song. As they start to get older they can play for hours on their own and are very willing to amuse themselves. Their downfall is their lack of self-confidence. It is important that you encourage them as much as possible to try. If they fall over, help them to their feet and encourage them again to walk.

At five years of age they are not quite so easy to please and have joined what can only be described as the awkward squad. They become self-willed and moody. But don't be concerned. That flair so early promised is still there and will remain with them despite ups and downs. They start to develop an opinion on things at this age and if they tell you they are not going to eat their peas then you must believe them because they really won't. If you try force-feeding there will be such tears that you will feel like a monster. They have a way with words and use them to get round their parents, especially their mother. Beware of this causing resentment among the rest of the family.

At 11 they will prove to you just how clever they are by excelling in at least one subject at school. Art often catches their eye, although you cannot guarantee they will do what the teacher has asked. They are likely to go off at a tangent. They are saved from being called a swot at school by their sense of fun, through which they manage to make even the toughest of class bullies laugh. This is indeed a popular child who is quick to pick up on new ideas. They notice the opposite sex quite early, and this discovery can land them in hot water.

At 16 they are being spoilt rotten by their loved ones and, once again, their mother. It is hard to stop this one talking now and the gift of the gab that you encouraged in the child may turn out to be less of a gift than you thought! They are not afraid of hard work and are good with figures, although being a fully fledged accountant would be too extreme for the Libran. Figures could be part of a job but not the whole of it. Music is a passion now and many Librans pick up their first guitar or tackle their first drum set at 16. They have a tendency to marry too young, even as young as 18. As they mature their tastes grow and develop and they often outgrow their partner.

At 21 they might be ready, or getting ready, to settle down for real. They improve as partners the older they get, so they are good marriage material so long as you understand each other well at the outset. Don't think your Libran partner won't flirt, though. It is in their nature to do so and they won't stop no matter how much they love you. Be suspicious if they *stop* flirting. A young Libran is very clever with money so long as only small amounts are involved: a classic case of penny-wise, pound-foolish. This doesn't necessarily improve with experience, and, if in love, they may let the object of their affections spend their last penny: the heart may talk the head into pleasing others. However, they don't believe in taking gambles. As parents they can be one minute too easy-going, priding themselves on their liberal outlook, the next minute the martinet, stifling their children. They really do get better and better with age, however, and later become the wonderful parents their sign can make them. Younger siblings tend to have an easier life than first-borns with Libran parents.

At 40 Librans hate the thought of growing old but to give them their due they do stay younger than many. The middle-aged Libran will seek out younger friends of both sexes. At 40 their friends will be in their twenties and at 50 their friends will be in their thirties. They are oversensitive about their age now, and Mr Libra in particular needs to watch out he doesn't overindulge in alcohol and give himself kidney problems. This character is clever, likeable and doesn't go off the rails as easily as others can. Librans are hardly ever argumentative, unless you give them good reason. They learn very quickly, and never allow anyone to walk over them more than once.

At 70 this character really has been everywhere and seen everything. Not a minute of the day will go by when they haven't got something humorous to say. A flirt now more than ever, and with the young generations drawn like a magnet, they need to be careful not to get themselves a reputation as a cradle-snatcher. They need to avoid eating rich foods. Simple, traditional dishes are best for avoiding problems. Oh, and look under the bed. They always stash money away for a rainy day, only by now they may have forgotten where they put it!

Libran Careers . . .

Dress designer. All those lovely fabrics and colours to touch every day.

Poet. Just like fellow Libran T. S. Eliot, you'd be a natural.

Romantic novelist. You really do make good writers.

Actor. Especially in love scenes.

Politician. On second thoughts, you might be a little too honest for this.

. . . not so Libran Careers

Student or lecturer at a single-sex college. No one to flirt with!

Nun or monk. Still no one to flirt with.

Any job that means wearing unattractive clothes.

Debt collector. You'd come back empty-handed when you heard a sob story.

Dentist or surgeon. You hate inflicting pain on others.

Maths teacher. You couldn't cope with all those figures.

Accountant. Even worse.

Famous Librans

Singers Olivia Newton John, Julie Andrews, Meatloaf and Bob Geldof, actors Gwyneth Paltrow, Brigitte Bardot and Charlton Heston, Body Shop founder Anita Roddick, writer Michael Crichton, footballer Matt Le Tissier.

Health Sore Points

Libra governs the kidneys, lumbar region and also the skin. I remember the day my Libran father went into hospital for a kidney operation. 'Typical Libra,' my mother said. This doesn't necessarily mean that *you* are going to have a kidney operation. But it's an example that is close to home for me. It does mean, however, that you should look after your kidneys, and I will suggest how further on in the chapter. In short, go easy on alcohol and drink lots of water. (And apart from that operation, my father never had a day's illness in his life!)

Librans have a very sweet tooth. You often have a stash of sweets or chocolates hidden somewhere just in case. For younger Librans in particular, this means possible tooth decay. Librans just cannot help over-indulging in sweets. My father, as a boy, used to run errands for the soldiers staying locally during World War II because they would pay him in the sweets that were so difficult to get hold of at the time. He didn't care what danger he got in so long as he got his sugar fix.

Backache occurs when a Libran is in the wrong job. The only solution is to change jobs. With the talents you possess it shouldn't be difficult to find another post.

Diabetes is not uncommon although it is not clear why this affects this sign.

Fresh air is vital for air signs and Librans that do not get enough oxygen cannot function properly. If you work long hours indoors make sure you get out into the fresh air regularly.

As with other signs Librans can suffer from stress and the key here is not to get involved in problems that are not yours to solve.

Watch out for the snoring Libran. Nine times out of ten this is caused by alcohol. Cheese is also bad for Librans to eat before bedtime. Librans are the ones who get those cheese-induced nightmares so famous in old wives' tales.

Cures and Counsel

Generally speaking Libra is a strong sign with few ailments. The main thing is to look after the kidneys and to constantly flush out the system by drinking lots of water, as much as you can in a day.

It is vital that Librans get enough exercise. For some reason, this is a sign that seems to think it doesn't need it. Believe me, Libra, you do! Why not join a health club? You will like the social aspect too. If you like someone you often want to join in with whatever their interests are, so why not get friendly with some keen exercisers!

Be careful in the alcohol department. Librans get worse hangovers than most, although they may not admit it. You smile and say you feel fine, but actually you are dying to get away to the nearest toilet bowl. Librans who have learnt what excessive drinking can do to them are cautious drinkers and particular about their choice of drinks. Once bitten, twice shy: this applies to Libra. You are not easily persuaded to change your drink or to experiment if it has led to trouble in the past. Beer or lager are usually your favourites but brandy is the drink you can really enjoy. Wine sends you to sleep unless it's expensive champagne, ideally mixed with brandy into a glamorous cocktail. You are great company to drink with but ask your friends to remember what you say and do, because you won't.

The best way for a Libran to keep in general good health is to deal carefully with matters of the heart. When you're in love you appear helpless. It's never easy to know straight away if a relationship is right or wrong, but trust your instincts and look for the warning signs. Keep your standards high, Libra. Don't stay in a bad relationship because it is easier than getting out of it. If something isn't working, stand up and say so. Life is what you make it, so don't accept anything but the best for yourself. My lovely Libran father always listened to his body and his emotions and made them work for him. You can do it too.

Broom Herb Tea

Romanies are great believers in the therapeutic properties of the broom herb, whether to cleanse the kidneys or for the treatment of a small stone. Incidentally this attractive bush is so called because its branches were once used for sweeping.

2 tablespoons broom tops (collected while the broom is young)
425 ml/¾ pint water

Brew the broom tops in the water as if making tea. Strain and allow to cool. Take a tablespoon both morning and night. It's best to make it fresh each time.

Periwinkle for Diabetes

When a Romany suffers from diabetes they take the herb periwinkle, which can be found in most British gardens. There are three types of periwinkle: great, lesser and red. They are all equally effective.

25 g/1 oz fresh periwinkle
900 ml/1½ pints water

Boil the herb in the water for 10 minutes. Drink a wineglassful three times a day.

Libra Juice Sluice

Once a week try this health drink, especially if you have been overindulging in the alcohol department. This will get your body back on the right track. I know a Libran who makes supplies of this for her Saturday job at a nursing home. Yes, she's in a typical caring Libran job, but she always goes out partying on a Friday night. She makes this up before she goes out so that she can drink it the following morning. It's that ancient Libran proverb of having to work, rest and play, you see. Of course, it's best when drunk straight away.

1 bunch seedless grapes
1 nectarine, stone removed

Juice in a juicing machine or mash and sieve. Then drink it up.

Good Libra Food

Librans often lack the cell salt natrum phosphoricum, also known as phosphate of soda. This salt helps to maintain the balance in the fluids of the body and it is very important that the diet always includes a good amount of it.

The foods you need are similar to those I recommend for Taureans: spinach, lettuce, apples and strawberries, but the Librans I know also love cabbages, which are very healthy.

There are also herbs that can help the kidneys and are sources of phosphate of soda: meadow sweet, dandelion, celery tops, couchgrass, juniper and uva ursi. All of these will be available from a good herbalist.

A Libran really does have a sixth sense about what to eat. You thrive better on vegetables that grow above the ground rather than beneath it. Mushrooms, bamboo shoots and cabbage leaves are great for you, which means you are often lovers of Chinese foods. Stir-fries are a great treat for Libra. They are satisfying visually as well as nutritionally.

Experiment with mint in your cooking, because this herb falls under your sign. Even a little mint on cooked new potatoes turns a boring dish into a tantalizing one.

If you want to convince a Libran to eat his or her food then make the table and the food look good and they won't care if it's not chocolate. When I think of Librans at mealtimes I think of a dinner table set with beautiful flowers, a nice bottle of wine, plenty of loving family and friends and mouthwatering dishes. If more Librans take time to create this scene they will be leading happier lives.

Your sign is all about balance and that extends of course to food. Balance means the right amount of the right sorts of food, and eating in comfortable, harmonious surroundings.

You have a sweet tooth but sweets and sugary foods won't give you the long-lasting energy you need. Cut down on sugar in tea and coffee and look to sweet foods that contain natural sugars. The high you get from chocolate can bring you down as fast, so look for other ways of finding energy. A piece of fruit will give you a lot more goodness and energy than a chocolate bar, and will please your aesthetic eye. Keep a beautiful, well-stocked fruit bowl at home all the time and replenish it regularly.

Sweet and sugary foods don't do your waistline any good either. The easiest way to avoid them is not to put them in your basket while you are shopping. If it's not in the house, you can't eat it. How about making yourself some Coronation Turkey (see page 250)? A dish of this instead of a slice of cake will give you so much more nourishment and pleasure.

Plants for Star Therapy

The holly is lucky for you. You can buy large or small strains. If you particularly want to have berries on your holly, ask your supplier whether you should take a pair of bushes for pollination purposes.

Health Checklist

- The best thing for a Libra is to drink plenty of water to cleanse the kidneys and flush out any impurities.
- Cranberry is good for cystitis and kidney infections and comes in such enjoyable forms. Why not include it in your shopping trolley? Make sure it's low in added sugar and additives.
- Consider consulting a homeopath about kidney problems. Cantharis is a good remedy for problems such as certain cases of cystitis.
- Make sure you get the vitamins your sign needs. Vitamins and minerals are found in everyday foods

and if you eat a varied and well-balanced diet you'll get what you need. If you eat something you know isn't good for you, follow it up with a healthy meal.

- If you are having problems with your skin, you need vitamins A and E. You can find vitamin A in cod liver oil, liver, butter, cheese and eggs, and vitamin E in vegetable oils, peanuts, eggs, wholemeal bread, wheatgerm and green leafy vegetables. Eat plenty of these and if your problem is still there then consider supplements. Also good for the skin are zinc, evening primrose oil and antioxidants such as vitamins A, C and E and beta-carotene. Aloe vera lotion or gel is good to apply to the skin. Seek advice from your pharmacist or doctor if the problem persists.
- If you suffer from diabetes, ask your doctor about taking chromium.
- If you do take pills such as headache tablets, go for the lowest dose. Medicines affect Librans quicker than most. You might find your headache is cured with just one tablet.

Are You a True Libra?

Be honest! Write down 'yes' or 'no', then read the advice below.

1 Does your heart rule your head?
2 Are you usually one of the last people to leave a party?
3 Do you find you cannot help but flirt?

4 Do you have a passion for beautiful objects?
5 Are you attracted to pale blues and pinks?
6 Do you eat spinach, lettuce and apples on a regular basis?
7 Have you ever had any kidney complaints?
8 Do you have a weakness for sweet foods?
9 Are you attracted by looks rather than personality?
10 Do you dislike your own company?
11 Do you find yourself mothering the younger generation?
12 Do a couple of drinks make you sloppy and silly?
13 Are you a sucker for a designer label?
14 Have you ever taken up an exercise just because it looked or sounded good to friends?
15 Do you get depressed when you are on your own? Do you need company?
16 Do you find yourself rearranging friends' houses and wardrobes for them?
17 Do you sometimes argue just for the sake of it?
18 Do you worry more than you know you should about your looks and about getting older?
19 Have you ever lied about your age?
20 Are you an incurable romantic?

If you answered 'yes' to most questions, then you are a typical Libran, and you are often in two minds about the things you do. If you answered yes to question 1 you already know what a broken heart feels like. But make sure, if you didn't answer yes to question 6, that you start to put the right foods in your shopping basket. If you don't have a healthy body you cannot operate at your best and a Libran always has something going on.

You are one of the signs of the zodiac that is always a pleasure to be with: you are fair and you always do your best to see the other person's point of view (sometimes to the point of being manipulated). Your ruling planet Venus makes you a sucker for a sob story and a pretty face, so be careful not to be played for a fool. Watch out that number 3 does not become a habit for you, and that you don't take what you know to be fun too far. If you answered yes to question 12 then you must also set boundaries for yourself and know where to draw the line.

If you answered 'no' to most questions, perhaps a broken heart or a hard experience early on has made you put up a protective barrier. You are stronger willed than most Librans and that should give you the strength to be the best that you possibly can.

Still, make sure that you are eating the correct foods. If you answered no to question 6 then diet is the first thing you need to work on.

Look up what your moon is in to find out if that is having a stronger influence on you than your sun sign. Your moon sign may dictate your first reaction to things. You may have answered the questions with what you would like to do rather than what you really do.

There are so many good qualities in a Libran. It is up to you to read about yourself and find out what talents and attributes are lying dormant. Try doing this questionnaire at a different time of day. Your answers in the morning might be different to those in the evening. Chances are, if most of your answers were 'no', that there's a colourful Libran inside you just dying to get out. Give them a go, you don't know what you're missing.

The Drinker's Guide to the Zodiac

Alcohol and Libra don't go together well. Those Libran kidneys don't like it. Men of this sign should drink lager or beer rather than spirits, while bearing in mind their fattening potential. Drunken Libran becomes extremely sloppy and romantic but it's nothing to get excited about: they follow this up very quickly by falling asleep.

For special occasions, however, and in small doses, there's nothing like a Champagne Cocktail for a Libran.

Champagne Cocktail

Impress a Libran with this.

1 sugar cube
1 drop angostura bitters
a dash of orange Curaçao
½ measure brandy (2 fl oz)
champagne (the more expensive, the better, for a Libran)

Put the sugar cube into a champagne glass and put a drop of angostura bitters on it. Add a dash of orange Curaçao and the brandy and top up to the brim with champagne. Enjoy with strawberries, that very Libran fruit.

Star Menu

Librans like food to look beautiful, and enjoy a harmonious, well-laid table.

Coronation Turkey

The beauty of this dish is that you eat it cold, so it will fit into any Libran's busy social whirl. Serves 8.

25 g/1 oz butter
1 medium onion, chopped
1 clove of garlic, crushed
2 tablespoons tomato purée
2 tablespoons curry powder
4 tablespoons apricot jam
4 tablespoons lemon juice
425 ml/¾ pint mayonnaise
1 kg/2 lb cooked turkey (or chicken if you prefer), diced
salt and freshly ground black pepper
500 g/1 lb seedless green and black grapes
90 g/3 oz flaked almonds, toasted briefly under a hot grill or in a dry frying pan
cooked rice
a few sprigs of watercress

Melt the butter in a frying pan and gently fry the onions and garlic until soft. Add the tomato purée, curry powder, apricot jam and 2 tablespoons of the lemon juice and then stir until the jam has melted. Blend in a liquidizer or food processor, then transfer to a bowl and leave to cool. When cold, stir into the mayonnaise in a large bowl. Fold in the chopped turkey. Season to taste with salt and pepper, cover and chill overnight in the refrigerator.

Toss the washed grapes in the remaining lemon juice and stir into the turkey mayonnaise. Taste and check seasoning. Pile into a large serving dish and sprinkle with browned flaked almonds. Put the cooked rice around the edges and garnish with watercress.

Crazy Cabbage

A great way to get a Libran child to eat the foods you know are good for them is to make the dish look fun and interesting and pretty. Your children will be positively keen to eat this cabbage, and you can relax in the knowledge that they are getting the nutrients they need. Serves 4.

1 medium cabbage, halved
50 g/2 oz oatmeal
1 onion, chopped
a good pinch of dried mixed herbs
75 g/3 oz mushrooms
25 g/1 oz Parmesan cheese
50 g/2 oz butter, melted
2 egg yolks, beaten
1 tomato, sliced
25 g/1 oz dried breadcrumbs
75 g/3 oz Cheddar cheese, grated
a sprig of fresh parsley

For the sauce:
25 g/1 oz butter
2 tablespoons flour
300 ml/½ pint milk
¼ teaspoon English mustard
salt and freshly ground black pepper

First, make the sauce. Melt the butter in a saucepan, add the flour, stir well and then start adding the milk a little at a time. Stir the mixture constantly so it doesn't go lumpy or catch on the bottom of the pan. Add the mustard and season with salt and pepper. Set aside.

Preheat the oven to 180°C/350°F/gas 5.

Parboil half of the cabbage for about 5 minutes, then drain and leave to cool. In a bowl, mix together the oatmeal, onion, mixed herbs, mushrooms and Parmesan. Stir in the melted butter. Add the egg yolks and mix thoroughly.

Shred the remaining cabbage finely. Mix with about 150 ml/5 fl oz of the sauce and spread over the bottom of a well-greased ovenproof dish. Separate the leaves of the parboiled cabbage. Place spoonfuls of the oatmeal mixture on the larger cabbage leaves and roll up into parcels. Place cabbage parcels (with the join underneath) on top of the shredded cabbage, alternating with the tomato slices. Cover with the remaining sauce. Mix the dried breadcrumbs with the Cheddar cheese and sprinkle over the top. Bake until the cabbage is cooked through and the cheese on top is golden: about 20 minutes.

Apple Crumble

This is fun to make, tastes great and is good for you.

500 g/1 lb apples
125 ml/4 fl oz water
125 g/4 oz brown sugar

finely grated lemon rind
90 g/3 oz butter
150 g/5 oz plain flour
60 g/2 oz caster sugar
¼ teaspoon ground ginger

Preheat the oven to 200°C/400°F/gas 6.

Peel, core and slice the apples into a saucepan. Add the water, brown sugar and lemon rind. Cook gently with the lid on until soft. Transfer to a pie dish.

In a bowl rub the butter and flour together until they resemble breadcrumbs. Mix in the caster sugar and ground ginger. Sprinkle the crumble over the apple and press down lightly. Bake until the crumble is nicely browned: about 40 minutes.

Star Beauty

When you are happy you have an inner glow that means you don't need to do a lot for the outside. But you have a weakness for beautiful things and so spend more than average on beauty products. You love expensive bottles and exquisite smells. You like to look good but more important to you is how much of a pleasure the products are to use.

I always buy Libran friends and family things I know they will get pleasure from, which means scented bubble baths and aftershave. I know they love to smell good, and to pose, though never in an arrogant way: they simply enjoy themselves. The Libran child will dress up in parents' clothes and shoes but evening wear and glittery jewellery is what will draw their attention. Lock up your make-up from a Libran daughter, who will otherwise 'borrow' the latest lipstick just to be able to get the case out in front of her friends.

To enhance that inner beauty, there is nothing better than a good massage. This will make Libra feel like a million dollars.

To keep eyes shining beautifully, don't throw away camomile teabags after you've made tea but cool them in the refrigerator and place over eyelids.

Libran Face Mask

A super face mask that is compatible to your star sign. You'll feel radiant after this.

2 tablespoons fuller's earth
1 tablespoon witch hazel
1 teaspoon honey
pinch of ground cloves

Mix the ingredients together well then smooth on to a clean face (ideal is just before you get into your bath). Relax for 20 minutes then rinse off with warm water.

Your Ideal Health Sign Holiday

Rome, the city of love and opera, is the place for you. There's nothing a Libran loves more than beautiful things and this is one place where you can be sure of finding them. Just be careful with the spending. You'll want to buy everything in sight. The museums and the history here have made many a Libran pack up their home elsewhere and stay.

SCORPIO

THE SCORPION

Ruling Planet: Mars, the planet of war, and Pluto, the god of the underworld

Triplicity or Element: Water

Quadruplicity or Mode: Fixed

Key words: Intensity, depth, determination, jealousy

The Origin of Scorpio

A scorpion stung and killed the great Orion, the mighty hunter, as a result of a plot hatched by Apollo, who was jealous of Orion's friendship with his sister Artemis, as well as Orion's good looks. Both now immortalized in the heavens, Orion now flees Scorpio for eternity, dipping below the horizon when Scorpio rises.

What Scorpio is Like

You have only to mention the word 'Scorpio' and people let out a knowing sigh. Oh yes, the sting of the Scorpion. That nasty way they have of being vindictive and scheming. Well, stop and think for a moment. The only time that a scorpion will attack is out of self-defence. When they sting, they also sting themselves. Can't be that scheming, can they? Don't hurt a Scorpio, and they won't hurt you.

This is the second most psychic sign in the zodiac (Pisces being the first). Scorpios can tell from a mile off if someone is no good, which may be a problem, because if they don't like someone it will show. It may not be anything you've done. It's what you are capable of doing or what their senses tell them about you that counts. This is the man who tells his wife, 'I don't like your new friend.' No, she may not have done anything wrong, but the husband can sense that this new friend will lead his wife astray.

Scorpios are passionate, secretive, jealous, obsessive,

loyal, determined and overemotional. Life with them can be both heaven and hell at the same time. Look deep into your Scorpio's eyes to find out what's going on: the poker face will not be giving anything away. Scorpio colours are deep reds and maroons, which match the dramatic undertones of this character. You can meet a Scorpio and think you must have met him or her somewhere before. It's the lasting effect a Scorpio has.

Scorpios find it easy to get involved in things that seem dangerous or exciting. The man or woman you know would be no good for you wants to go out on a date. You think it's OK to say yes just for the experience, but before you know it this person has moved into your home and frightened away all your friends. On the other hand, Scorpios can be so successful that their names go down in the history books. They find the gold at the end of the rainbow. Think of this as a choice. You could be an extremist who either makes it in the world and is 100 per cent successful or who loses everything trying (though the ride will be fun). If you want to go for the gamble, then you are clearly a Scorpio, as this is the basis of what appeals to you.

Similar to their polar-opposite, Taurus, Scorpios also love food, sex and money. Unlike the sceptical bull, however, they are deeply interested in astrology and religion. The ten-year-old who asks, 'What happens when you die?' is probably a Scorpio. Scorpios are not morbid. They just want the answers to the mysteries of life. Not a lot to ask, really, is it?

This is a water sign whose feelings and emotions run deep. Scorpios need to take care not to be sucked into the tidal wave of their own feelings. They are sometimes attracted to bad relationships because they want to see what bad feels like, rather like a young child who wants to touch the hot tap to see what hot is. And people are drawn to them, because of the secretiveness of their nature. Behind that mysterious surface, something big must be going on. In my own experience, this can mean hiding credit card bills from my partner!

Scorpio is ruled by Mars, which brings change and unpredictability, and Pluto, who guards souls in the afterlife. At 16 no Scorpio can predict what life will be at 26. Expect the unexpected and you will be on the right track. The 16-year-old shopworker could be a multi-millionaire with a chain of shops by 26. You just never know.

This is a fixed sign. They are not afraid of being stubborn and will dig their heels in while they wait for what they want. They know they will get it in the end. They don't mean to be vindictive, they just want what they want. However, fate always throws in some interesting twists and turns, just for the ride.

Those born under Scorpio are often involved in the theatre or media, but never at the lower end of the scale. They need to go where the money is so they start at the bottom and then take the lift to the top. They are not what you would call materialists, however, because although they enjoy earning money they have no qualms about spending it either, especially on their nearest and dearest.

Many famous actors are Scorpios (Demi Moore, Meg Ryan, Leonardo di Caprio, for a start) and they are all known for researching their roles as deeply as possible.

The same goes for Scorpios in real life. Everything they do becomes a drama and they sometimes go into things too deeply. In order to be a healthy and happy Scorpio you need to avoid things that could lead to trouble or unhappiness, instead of embracing them.

People find Scorpios overpowering and inhibiting because they are so full of energy. If they can focus this energy, they become extremely successful. If not, they go to the other extreme, which is not a pretty sight. A desire to experiment with drink and drugs can be dangerous. The reason they're not frightened to dice with death is because death intrigues them. A strong partner and the right influences are what's needed for this sign. When cooking or entertaining, they are likely to make more of the shopping and preparation than they do of eating the dish. And they are likely to be extravagant.

If let down in love, Scorpios become extremely resentful of the opposite sex. Whether they fall into or out of love, they always fall hard. Jealousy is their worst trait – they will not always admit to it – and is the downfall of many a Scorpio relationship. Scorpios can become scarily obsessive and need a major jolt to pull out of it. Jealousy is also rife in the workplace for them. They may say they are pleased at a colleague's promotion but underneath they are working out how to beat them in the rat race to get to the top of the ladder. Sexy is another word for them. They have this way of walking and acting that others interpret as a come-on. Don't be scared of making a wrong conclusion about a Scorpio's desires, however. You'll soon know about them, in no uncertain terms.

Scorpios are subject to emotional turmoil of their own making. Their jealousy can lead them to suspect their partner, however undeserving of this their partner is. Addiction is a possible problem, whether to a person or to a substance. It is the water element that makes them vulnerable. Strangely Scorpios can often calm themselves just by looking at water or by stepping into a bath, to be engulfed and relaxed by their element.

The main thing to know about Scorpios is that if you are good to them they will be good to you. Take advantage of them and break their hearts and they will either seek revenge or forget that you were ever born.

Life with this sign will always be unpredictable and you will never know what they are thinking until you see the explosion of their latest plan or fad. And by then it's too late to stop it!

How to Spot a Scorpio

Look for the penetrating gaze. Whereas some signs are nervous to look you in the eye, a Scorpio will look straight into your soul. There is also sometimes a small bump on the nose. Beautiful Scorpios Vivien Leigh and Bette Davis both had such a nose.

The Devil and the Angel

The DEVIL SCORPIO is jealous, crafty, aggressive, ruthless and dangerous. Ike Turner, certainly from what we hear in the press, has pushed his luck and his life to the limit, and is to many people an example of a Scorpio who's gone too far.

The ANGEL SCORPIO has the gift of spiritual healing and often rises to great scientific heights in the medical world. These Scorpios are ardent, emotional and brilliant. An example of this would be Madame Curie. Scorpio is also a sign for great actors, including Meg Ryan, Jodie Foster and Demi Moore.

Scorpio Health and Development from Child to Adult

The Scorpio baby is an endearing yet restless child who will not understand the word 'no'. This baby loves to feel in charge and to show dominance from an early age. This bossy attitude can needle parents, who need a lot of self-control to stop themselves getting annoyed. This baby does not think it was born with a silver spoon in its mouth – it knows it was. No matter what age the brothers and sisters, this baby has all and sundry eating out of its hands, and knows just when to coo: that is, when you have been pushed right to the edge. They are not lazy, though, and their constant energy can be exhausting for those who have to cope with their needs.

At five years of age they will be driving their teachers crazy as well as their parents and their somewhat mysterious behaviour keeps people on their toes. At seven or eight these children become a little light-fingered and you may find them going home with your friend's house keys after you dropped in for tea. This phase does not last, and is really just for mischief and fun. Their quick temper can land them in fights, especially as they stick up for the weaker soul. They also go through a phase of disappearing, although they are more likely to be playing up the road than trying to leave the country. Anyone who kidnapped this child would let them go within the hour, after being psychoanalysed by them and talked half to death.

At 11, this child has the whole class under a spell and is capable of leading a revolution. Teachers should take this child's warning seriously. If this child does not get on with you it is you that has to change, not the child. This child does nothing by halves and excels at some subjects while bombing at others. Like Taurus, Scorpio children are closet singers, but they act out their roles as well. They don't just sing the song but have the costume that goes with it. They usually hate the opposite sex at this age because they despise all that they do not understand. They feel they should know everything without having to learn it. If they don't already know the subject they feel as if their psychic abilities have failed them.

At 16 they have a flair for acting and will probably be involved in some sort of drama class. If this teenager has a problem, they are not upset, they are devastated. Nothing is ever merely funny, it is hilarious. They dislike no one, but hate some. Their strong sexual drive is now surfacing and there is a lot of romantic misbehaviour at this age. They are also developing an appetite for work and will tackle the most difficult tasks with gusto. They want to be number one, and they will walk over anyone who gets in their way. They have no regard for authority, and no respect for their elders.

At 21 many Scorpios have a big fall-out with their father. They boast they are happy to be single when they are not, and a certain overconfidence can mean those in relationships get rejected or two-timed. They need a very clever partner with whom to reach an understanding. They are not the easiest of people to live with. Possessive both before and after marriage, their own experience and strong imagination causes arguments and mistrust. Their abrupt manner is not understood by everyone. There are often misunderstandings with in-laws who may not like this seemingly self-assured person. It's all right for the Scorpio to go for a night out with friends but not for their partner to. Their children have to watch out too that they don't get a dressing down.

At 40 they don't have masses of close friends. They choose one or two who understand them and are able to tolerate their manner. They are great company, however, and a younger audience in particular is usually in awe of this captivating Scorpio. Scorpios, in turn, find themselves drawn to younger partners and this can lead to marriage break-up – a tight leash at this time is called for! If their finances permit, they might lead a double life. Those having an affair with a Scorpio and waiting for divorce to free their lover up will be waiting for a long time. To keep this emotional, dramatic and oh so sexy sign at your side, you need to keep them constantly entertained and, of course, on that pedestal where they placed themselves. If you admire them, they will admire you.

At 70 they have an air of royalty about them. You'd think they must have been famous at some point. They think that too, even if they haven't. Forgetfulness can be a problem and their grip on the concept of time becomes a bit loose. If you invite them to dinner they are likely to turn up the night before or the night after.

Their five-year-old's capacity for getting lost now returns, and you may want to give them a piece of jewellery with their name and address on it. Other aspects of the five-year-old return too. If they like you they may be nasty to you just for effect.

Scorpio Careers . . .

Journalist. You could get to the bottom of any story.

Foreign correspondent. Even better. You'd like assignments with a spot of danger.

Dramatic actress. You will win awards for great performances.

Spiritualist or astrologer. You have an insatiable appetite for the world of clairvoyance and prediction.

. . . not so Scorpio Careers

Mistress or bit on the side. You'd end up killing the spouse.

Understudy. Only if you thought you'd get the role.

One of a sheikh's many wives. A Scorpio could never be part of a harem. You are enough for ten men on your own.

Famous Scorpios

Actors Demi Moore, Jodie Foster, Julia Roberts, Sally Fields, Whoopi Goldberg, Meg Ryan, Winona Ryder,

Leonardo di Caprio and Roseanne Barr, footballers Diego Maradona and Ian Wright, singers k.d. lang, Art Garfunkel, Joni Mitchell and Neil Young, songwriter Tim Rice, hypnotist Paul McKenna, First Lady Hillary Rodham Clinton.

Health Sore Points

Scorpio rules the reproductive organs and in particular the womb. Typical problems are menstrual pains for women and urinary infections for men. These can be avoided by careful diet and tuning of the body.

If a Scorpio woman wants to conceive a child she must put aside all stressful thoughts and concentrate on relaxing. If she lets her woes dominate her mind her body will be upset too. A client of my mother's many years ago was having problems conceiving a child. She and her husband longed for a child. As soon as she walked into the room my mother could tell she was too stressed even to think straight and also that she was a Scorpio. My mother did something that some people would not approve of. She asked the woman if she drank, and when her client replied no, my mother suggested she tried relaxing with a drink that very evening with her husband. 'Do I need red or white wine in order to conceive?' she asked. 'Why not get a bottle of each?' my mother replied! My mother was just trying to get her to relax and hang loose a little. This woman, who did have her longed for child, is still a client of my mother's. What's important about this story is that Scorpios can get so wrapped up in their problems that they make things more difficult than they need to be.

Extremists, Scorpios smoke or drink, if at all, to excess. You fall victim to fiendish hangovers (and should perhaps put two and two together!).

Scorpio ruling planet Mars makes you strong-willed and resolute. Your personal magnetism is so strong you are likely to have an exhausting social life, but your recuperative abilities are amazing.

Cures and Counsel

Scorpio (along with Pisces) is the most dramatic sign of the zodiac. You can get into situations that are bad for you, such as destructive relationships, sometimes just to find out what they are like. You may come out stronger but you would be better trying to find strength from other areas of your life instead. Try not to get too wrapped up in yourself, and try not to stay in emotional set-ups that are bad for you. Learn to judge honestly whether a situation is healthy for you or not. If you cannot leave a bad relationship straight away, at least see it as a process you are going through but one which you will come out of.

Good advice for anyone is to avoid stressful situations, and this is certainly true for Scorpio. Geminis, for example, can thrive on stress, but Scorpios most certainly do not.

Make time for yourself. Half an hour out of anybody's day really is a possibility. Scorpios should use this to wind down and discover the joys of relaxation.

Aromatherapy oils in the bathwater are wonderful for you. Tell your concerned lover or housemates that you are not drowning in there, just dreaming.

Recreational drugs, it goes without saying, should not be taken. Some may have become acceptable socially but that doesn't make them right or good for you. Scorpios get addicted more easily than most, because they never do anything by halves. (There are more Scorpios and Pisces in drugs clinics than any other sign!) Scorpios get addicted to people, too, especially unsuitable ones. Your instincts tell you if someone might be bad for you. Then you must resist the temptation to go for the danger. Don't even go on the first date, and you won't get the chance to become addicted. (I know it's easily said!)

Thrush can be a problem for Scorpio women. Wear cotton clothing next to the skin and avoid clothing that is too tight. Follow the instructions for treatment from your local pharmacist or doctor should thrush occur. Perfumed soaps and bath unguents can also cause problems. This sign of the zodiac likes strong smells, but should resist using highly perfumed products in the bath. Another good reason for using aromatherapy oils instead.

Water retention can be a problem for this water sign. Eat foods high in potassium, such as potatoes, asparagus, bananas, melon, strawberries and tuna fish. (You will find a great tuna fish recipe on page 278.)

Scorpios are often affected by nasal catarrh. Include plenty of radishes, celery and tomatoes in the diet, and try soapwort tea (page 269) from time to time.

Regular check-ups are important for any sign of the zodiac but Scorpios in particular need to avoid sleeping on worries or letting problems go by unexamined. This is a sign that can think it has something wrong for a year before doing anything about it. Regular check-ups should ensure peace of mind both for Scorpios and their loved ones.

Some Scorpios are wrongly thought of as asthmatic when all they need are a few simple breathing lessons. Try this exercise to help you breathe better. You will find that your whole body starts to take on a new shape and you should feel more confident each time you try it. Stand normally and take in a normal breath through your nose. Breathe out through your mouth and repeat. Don't breathe too deeply. This will do more harm than good. It is a mistake to think that the bigger the breaths you take, the better. This is not true. Short and medium breaths are just as important. Take in as much breath as you feel you need before speaking. This has the added advantage of making you think about what you are going to say for once!

You can begin to learn about your breathing by lying down on the floor and breathing deeply in and out for a few seconds. Now breathe in gently through your nose again and breathe out to a prolonged hum. Now try breathing in gently for three counts and humming out (with your mouth closed) for three counts.

Taking exercise is good both for your breathing and for your all-round fitness. If a class sparks you into taking up a fitness routine, you won't look back. Indeed, a year on and you'll probably be teaching it!

Soapwort Tea

A centuries-old natural cure for catarrh is soapwort, which you can buy in dried form from a herbalist. It has a juice that lathers like soap in hot water, hence its name. A tea made from the herb should clear the head and nose and bring relief.

1 large pinch of dried soapwort
600 ml/1 pint water

Boil the herb in the water for 10 minutes, when it should be lathering, then strain and bottle. Take a small glassful morning and night.

Shepherd's Purse Tea

To keep the uterus in good order, try the common garden herb shepherd's purse. My people, the Romanies, believe this herb to be a strengthener for the uterus, and therefore particularly important for Scorpio women. Either chew a handful of well-washed leaves and swallow them, or make tea from the leaves and pods.

1 teaspoon leaves and pods of fresh shepherd's purse
mug or teacup water

Brew the leaves in the water. Strain. Take a glassful daily.

Scorpio Juice Booster

Here's a health drink to help promote good heart, muscles and nervous system. You need a juicing machine to get a good result. Knowing Scorpios, who don't do anything half-heartedly, you'll soon be investing in one.

1 orange, peeled
1 pineapple, peeled
1 plum, stoned
1 tangerine, peeled

Juice and drink. If you don't have a juicer, mash by hand and sieve.

Chinese Strengthening Remedy

Here is a Chinese remedy to strengthen and improve the libido and ovaries of a Scorpio. You can get the ingredients from a Chinese store.

sesame or other oil to stir-fry
50 g/2 oz black sesame seeds
50 g/2 oz walnuts, soaked and chopped
50 g/2 oz longan, stoned and chopped (this comes tinned, like lychee)
50 g/2 oz black dates, stoned and chopped

Heat the oil and stir-fry. You can use this as a sauce.

Good Scorpio Food

Scorpios tend to lack the cell salt calcarea sulphurica, otherwise known as calcium sulphate, or plaster of Paris. A deficiency can lead to catarrh, lung troubles, boils, ulcers, carbuncles, abscesses and disorders of the liver and kidneys. If you get enough it helps eliminate corroding organic matter, preventing it from lying dormant in the system and injuring the surrounding tissue.

To get enough of this cell salt you need regular intake of cabbage, kale, watercress, milk, prunes, cottage cheese and onions.

Some Scorpios in their teens either love or hate foods, and, with their tendency towards obsession, this can develop into a problem. Bulimia is not uncommon in this sign. It is, however, something Scorpios usually grow out of as curiosity and imagination take them elsewhere.

All of the vitamins and minerals you need can be found in your diet if you eat well enough. If you are too busy to eat well, or eat too many ready-prepared foods, are getting over an illness, are a new vegetarian, pregnant or just growing older, you might consider taking supplements. A recent report on children's diets showed they are not getting enough vitamin C. They are getting *less* than they did during World War II when food was short. The popularity of junk foods and convenience meals has children eating too much fat and sugar and not enough fruit and vegetables. For vitamin C look in particular to blackcurrants, kiwi fruit, guava, peppers, peas, potatoes, Brussels sprouts, broccoli and oranges. As your sign benefits greatly from vitamin C, why not make your own convenience food for when you are too busy to cook? Make your own dishes in advance and freeze them. Of course, this is not so good from a nutrition point of view as freshly prepared food, since the vitamin C and other values will diminish with storage or freezing, but you will get the benefit of knowing what is in your meal and not having to consume the additives and artificial flavourings that are in so many manufactured convenience meals.

Your taste in food changes from day to day, and it is not always a good idea to book a restaurant far in advance. You probably won't have the same enthusiasm when you get there. You want what you want when you want it. If you crave a dish there is no waiting around for it. Pregnant Scorpios will have their partners out and about in the middle of the night trying to source obscure foods.

Pluto, one of your two ruling planets, is the god of the underworld, and is largely where you get that extremism from. You are also the sign that is not afraid to try the weird and wonderful. You are the traveller who stands on the streets of a far-away city eating fried insects, while unable to stomach the gherkin in your burger at home. The good side of this is that you are unlikely to eat an unvaried, stodgy and unwholesome diet.

Gassy drinks aren't good for you, and a Scorpio feeling bloated and uncomfortable is not fun to be with. Then you may find yourself short on people to give you sympathy.

Plants for Star Therapy

In some quarters the hawthorn tree or bush has a reputation for being unlucky, but this is not so for Scorpio. If you have space, do grow some for yourself to attract luck. The pink- or red-flowered varieties are particularly lucky for Scorpios, and these are hardy little trees, requiring very little attention. Just stake the young tree firmly in a place with plenty of light and air. Shepherd's purse will bring good luck, and when drunk as a tea, good health.

Health Checklist

- If you suffer from heart problems, or just want to ensure a healthy heart, take essential fatty acids from either oily fish (fresh tuna, salmon, pilchards, sardines, herring and mackerel) or plant oils such as flaxseed (by sprinkling linseeds on your food).
- Also for the heart, 10–30 mg co-enzyme Q10 is valuable. It can be absorbed by the body from peanuts, spinach, beans, bran, beef, sardines and mackerel. It helps to release the energy in food for use by the body's cells. Pregnant women should *not* take it as a supplement.
- For generative organ problems, make zinc a regular part of your diet. This is found in seafood, beef, pork, dairy products, green vegetables, seeds, nuts, pulses and cereals. It is particularly easy to add green vegetables to a dish or a meal and there are so many different varieties around that you need never eat the same vegetable twice in a month let alone a week.
- For nasal catarrh take zinc, vitamin C and garlic supplements. For relief, sniff tea tree or eucalyptus oil.

Are You a True Scorpio?

Be honest! Write down 'yes' or 'no', then read the advice below.

1 Do you become addicted to certain situations to the extent that they rule your life?
2 Do you make the love of your life the centre of your universe?
3 Do you eat any of the following foods on a regular basis: watercress, kale, milk, prunes, cottage cheese, onions?
4 Do you weigh people up and cast an opinion as soon as you meet them?
5 Do people often comment on your eyes?
6 Do you go for extreme situations in life?
7 Does drink affect you more than you admit?
8 Do you love dark reds and maroons?
9 Has your life taken twists and turns that you never dreamed it could?
10 If you didn't like someone you worked with, would it show?
11 Would you describe yourself as an all-or-nothing person?
12 Do you feel happy when you are near the sea or in the bath?
13 Are you very secretive about your private life?
14 Are you an impulsive shopper?
15 Are you intensely loyal to friends who you know care for you?
16 Have you ever wanted to be involved in the theatre or the media?
17 Do you gossip about secrets that friends have told you in confidence?
18 If you smoke or drink, is it to an extreme?
19 Do you plan more social events than you know you have time to complete?

20 Have you ever found yourself jealous of someone or something to a point that you know is a little extreme?

If you answered 'yes' to most questions then you truly are a dramatic, intense and typical Scorpio. People are in awe of you and your dramatic decisions and opinions. You never do anything by halves. Be careful not to get involved in any bad situations. Your co-ruler Pluto is the god of the underworld and loves nothing more than to see you do something inadvisable. Combine Pluto with your other ruler, Mars, the planet of war and unpredictability, and you'll see that you are ready to take on the world. You are not troublesome exactly, but you get involved in major events instead of minor ones. This can mean a lot of fun and success but also a lot of hard work.

Make sure, if you did not answer yes to question 3, that you can do so by next month. If you do not get the foods your body craves you will not be able to deal with the drama-packed life that a Scorpio leads. You need energy foods and plenty of liquid. Eat plenty of fibre to keep your bowels working well and if you are a woman make sure that you are not taking a form of contraception that disagrees with you. Drugs affect Scorpios more than other signs.

If you answered mostly 'no' then you are perhaps experiencing the calm before the storm. A Scorpio cannot go through life without some fireworks. Perhaps the reason you are not a typical Scorpio is that you have a partner who is overshadowing you, especially if you are involved with a fellow water sign. You don't always realize what is going on in your own life when all your attention is focused on close ones. If you answered no to question 9, then hold tight. No Scorpio can go through life without at least two major dramatic changes. Don't worry, they are usually good ones. Check your moon sign and read the advice that goes with it. You may feel this applies to you more. On the other hand, you could be such a true Scorpio that you feel the questions I have asked, such as 19 and 20, are just a part of normal life. Why not ask a loved one to fill in the questionnaire for you, and compare your results? You may be surprised by their answers.

The Drinker's Guide to the Zodiac

The only way to describe a Scorpio and drink is in terms of a game of Russian roulette. You won't know what your Scorpio is going to do until the drink has decided which way it is going to affect them. This unpredictable drinker can get high one night on two small Scotches, and another night might need six for the same effect. And you won't know how to take them, either way. (I'm not recommending anyone drinks this much, by the way. Just making a point.) Scorpios can go to extremes, often to impress friends and lovers. Go easy. You are much more fun when you are just being yourself.

If you want to make a Scorpio a drink, you couldn't do better than a Whisky and French.

Whisky and French

This will put a Scorpio in a very happy mood. If, Scorpio, you are making this yourself, go easy on the measures. This is supposed to be an enjoyable drink, not a knock-out. If you overdo it you may find yourself running off with the milkman (or milkwoman) before you know where you are.

1 part dry French vermouth
2 parts whisky

Pour the French vermouth into a sherry glass, add the whisky, stir lightly and serve.

Star Menu

Oriental Supper

The best foods for a Scorpio are foods high in potassium, such as tuna fish and asparagus in this Oriental supper. Serves 4.

bunch of fresh asparagus
½ teaspoon freshly grated ginger
2 spring onions, chopped and sliced
2 tablespoons chopped chives
grated rind and juice from 1 lemon
2 tablespoons dry sherry
2 tablespoons dark soy sauce
3 tablespoons olive oil
4 tuna steaks

salt and freshly ground black pepper
½ red onion, chopped
½ courgette, diced
½ red pepper, cut into strips
butter, salt and freshly ground pepper, to serve

Cut the tough ends off the asparagus stems and then make a cut in the bottom of each stem. Cook in boiling water until tender, or *al dente* if you prefer.

Make a dressing by combining the ginger, spring onions, chives, lemon rind and juice, sherry, soy sauce and 2 tablespoons of the olive oil. Set aside.

Fry the tuna steaks on both sides in the remaining olive oil in a hot frying pan. Transfer to a hot plate and add the onion, courgette and red peppers to the hot pan. As they quickly brown, add the dressing. Pour over the tuna and serve immediately with the asparagus. Serve with butter and salt and pepper.

My Mother's Onion Rings

As a side dish to a main course or even as a starter, maybe with a dip, try my mother's onion rings. They've made her the toast of many a gathering at our house. Make as many as you think you'll need, or maybe a little more, to be on the safe side. They will be very popular.

onions, sliced into rings
full-cream milk
salt and freshly ground black pepper
flour

Put the onion rings in a bowl, cover with full-cream milk and season with salt and pepper. Leave for 15 minutes. Put a little flour into a plastic bag, preferably a zip-lock bag or even just a carrier bag. Using a slotted spoon, transfer the onions to the bag, close it, and shake it well. If you are making a lot of onion rings, then do a few at a time to ensure they get evenly coated. For best results deep-fry in a deep-fat fryer. If you don't have one, fry in a frying pan in batches. Put on kitchen paper to drain when done and then serve.

Scorpio's Tiramisu

This is a sure-fire way to get Scorpio's attention. They'll never turn down a dessert with alcohol in it! It's worth the effort of making, so give it a go. Make it the day before you want to serve it. Serves 6–8.

250 g/9 oz mascarpone cheese
40 g/1½ oz caster sugar
3 eggs, separated
240 ml/8 fl oz Kahlua liqueur
480 ml/14 fl oz very strong black coffee
24 Italian sponge fingers
cocoa powder

Put the mascarpone, sugar and egg yolks into a bowl and whisk with a hand-held electric mixer (or a whisk), until well blended. Whisk the egg whites until they are stiff and fold into the mascarpone mixture. Fold in until evenly blended and then spoon a quarter into the base of a large dessert bowl.

Combine the liqueur and coffee and dip 8 of the sponge fingers into it, allowing them to absorb the mixture. Place in a single layer on top of the mascarpone in the bowl. Cover the sponge fingers with another quarter of the mascarpone mixture. Dip another 8 sponge fingers into the coffee and liqueur mixture again, and repeat the process, finishing with a layer of mascarpone. Use the back of a spoon to smooth the top and then sift cocoa powder over it. Don't be shy, use plenty. Cover and chill in the refrigerator for 24 hours.

Star Beauty

The eyes are very important to a Scorpio and many people say that you can see the souls of a Scorpio through his or her eyes. Apply Vaseline to the eyelashes at night-time (careful not to get it into the eyes). It nourishes the lashes and stops them from becoming dry and drab.

Romany Eye Lotion

Here is an extremely simple beauty treatment that Scorpio women in my family have been using for years. It will reduce any puffiness or swelling.

2 large thin slices of potato

Place on the eyes. Relax. That's it.

Scorpio Sensuous Bath Oil

To keep the reproductive system healthy, and in particular for women to avoid common ailments such as thrush, don't use highly perfumed bath products. Try this bath oil instead. It is easy and inexpensive to make, and is a present for Scorpio friends, especially if you put it in a pretty coloured bottle. It's made from olive oil (from your kitchen) and almond oil (from your chemist's or health food store); both better than baby oil, which rests on the surface of the skin and isn't absorbed. The oil keeps for two weeks in the refrigerator.

2–3 tablespoons fresh herbs such as rosemary and lavender, or rose petals or jasmine, or a combination
2 eggs
4 tablespoons olive oil
4 tablespoons almond oil
4 tablespoons vodka (yes, vodka)
125 ml/4 fl oz milk, whisked
2 teaspoons runny honey

Crush the chosen herbs and petals using a mortar and pestle. Put into a spotlessly clean 300 ml/½ pint jar. In a bowl, beat together the eggs, olive oil and almond oil. Add the vodka – it allows the oil to disperse – and then the milk. Pour into the jar, add the honey and shake well (with the lid screwed on, need I say!). Use some of this in your next bath. Start with a tablespoon. Your skin will feel like silk.

After-bath Cream

This is an excellent cream for when you step out of the bath. To prepare the peel, grate the fruits' skins and dry in the airing cupboard or other warm place. Grind with a mortar and pestle.

1 tablespoon dried, ground and sieved orange peel
1 tablespoon dried, ground and sieved lemon peel
2 tablespoons ground almonds
a pinch of salt
4 tablespoons wheatgerm flour
1 tablespoon dried thyme, ground and sieved
2 drops almond oil or jasmine oil

Mix together all of the ingredients except the oil. Then add the oil drop by drop until you have a workable paste. Store in a stoppered jar, and apply to washed skin.

Your Ideal Health Sign Holiday

Egypt and New York are two places that will fascinate the scorpion. You love both danger and excitement. You also love the unknown and are attracted to anything that is different or unusual, especially people. These are two places where you are guaranteed a thrilling, fascinating time.

SAGITTARIUS

THE ARCHER

Ruling Planet: Jupiter, the planet of self-expansion

Triplicity or Element: Fire

Quadruplicity or Mode: Mutable

Key words: Optimistic, freedom-loving, philosophical, expansive, honest

The Origin of Sagittarius

The horse-man, or centaur, Chiron, was in Greek mythology the tutor to many heroes and the friend of Hercules. He was also famous for his knowledge of medicine, music and archery – and he is usually shown bearing a bow and arrow. The gods immortalized him as a constellation, known to us as Sagittarius, Latin for 'the archer'.

What Sagittarius is Like

Just looking at the picture of the archer will tell you some of their major character traits. They are always looking for new targets in life. When they don't know what they want they can be unreliable and messy but, like their picture shows, when they take aim and fire they can reach the sky and nothing can stop them. They need to trust their own instincts. Outside influences can cause them to lose faith in their abilities. Optimistic and freedom-loving, they are great company to be around and are always in the mood for a party. Honest by nature they won't mind telling you if you look awful in what you are wearing, though in their characteristic jovial and good-humoured way. Their tendency to be over-optimistic causes them a few broken hearts, especially in their teens. Don't be fooled, though. They love a challenge. They can do brilliantly in their careers, very often setting themselves up for life at an early age.

Ask Sagittarians what they want to achieve and they

will tell you their ambitions, and these will sound like their life and soul's dream. Stick around and watch them achieve these ambitions, and you'll see them then set new goals. Ask about the old ambitions and they'll be brushed aside as unimportant. Sagittarians have a constant supply of new goals.

They sometimes take risks they shouldn't, fuelled by their ardent enthusiasm for life and the need to live it to the full. One of the dual, or mutable, signs of the zodiac, they are extremely versatile, which is probably why they move so quickly from one idea to another. If they ever slowed down and looked at what they'd done with their lives so far they'd probably realize how exhausted they should be.

The archer symbolizes liberation, the freeing of mankind from the material into the spiritual. The archer's arrow aims towards the heavens. Jupiter, the largest planet in the solar system, is Sagittarius's ruling planet, and symbolizes the need to grow and expand. Just as Jupiter is large so are the plans of this fascinating and complex sign.

Spend just one hour in Sagittarius's company and you will see that this sign is happy-go-lucky, determined, considerate and a general delight to be around. You will also see that it is anxious, flighty, unconventional and changeable. This is a fire sign which lives up to its element perfectly. The fervent feelings contained within Sagittarius mean you'll never know what they are going to do next. Don't ever think Sagittarians won't shock and surprise you. The young woman leaving school who wants to be a secretary could tomorrow be running her own company. If Sagittarians are serious in their careers there is no way they will not reach the top.

The colours for this sign are rich purples and dark blues, rich being the operative word. See this sign walking into a bank in these colours and you can bet they will get the loan they're after. Who in their right mind would refuse a fire sign on a mission?

Sagittarians are extremely intellectual and although they may make silly mistakes in their younger years the older people of this sign rarely do anything without having checked out all the details first. If they engage their super-planning skills, they are very effective shoppers.

Those born under this sign like practical jokes, and they have been known to let their jokes get out of hand. But they are good workers, capable of completing their work quickly and efficiently. Do check the very small details, though, as they obviously won't have time for the unimportant bits. This is the great party-goer and party-giver, who throws a party with every imaginable kind of alcohol but forgets to provide you with any food to soak it up.

Life will never be boring with a Sagittarius, and if your archer loves you then it will be completely and intensely and you need have no fears.

Do beware their stories, however. These can become extremely tall. And if they think you're impressed, they will try to make it an even bigger and better story for your enjoyment.

The golden rule with people of this sign is to give them space to act in their own individual way. They also need plenty of physical space to move about in. Putting them in a small flat or house is a sure-fire way to see them decline. Restless Sagittarians often feel more at home outdoors than in. They don't like to feel trapped and confined, and many of their relationships flourish or founder depending upon the environment they begin in. Constrict them physically or mentally and they will up and leave quicker than you can say 'I'm sorry'.

How to Spot a Sagittarius

Sagittarians are usually marked by their athletic appearance. You might even notice them galloping when they are in a hurry! However, despite their athletic appearance, they may not actually be that fit.

The Devil and the Angel

The DEVIL ARCHER is changeable, a gambler, does what he or she wants and likes to break the mould. Frank Sinatra, who lived life in the fast lane and was known for his love of fast people, was a bit of a devil archer. But this sign of the zodiac really cannot help being good. Even the devils are angels in disguise.

The ANGEL ARCHER is ambitious, animal-loving, kind, gentle and out to do all he or she can for the good of the world. Nostradamus the prophet was an angel archer. He went so far in his mission to help people that he paid the price of losing his nearest and dearest. The world turned against him even when his predictions started to become true.

Sagittarius Health and Development from Child to Adult

The Sagittarian baby is very easy to look after and doesn't give its parents much trouble. Placid by nature, there is, however, a strong sense of independence, which comes through even at this tender age. Baby archers learn things a lot quicker if left to their own devices. This is the child that will be walking when you're not looking, and as soon as you look falls down.

At five years of age, whether girl or boy they are the apple of their daddy's eye, and vice versa. The child makes a conscious effort to be like Dad and does anything to please him. At this age they can be undemonstrative but need a lot of reassurance and plenty of displays of affection. If not given reassurance they can withdraw and stay independent. It is crucial that you show them plenty of affection now because this is where the ground rules are laid. They will excel in certain areas that surprise you but will feel as relaxed in their achievements as they do in their failures.

At 11 they are bright at school and have friends that hang on to their every word. They are intellectual in their tastes and one step ahead of their classmates in clothes and fashions. They are avid collectors, and have a strong pride in their possessions and belongings. They are clean and neat without being pushed into it. This is one child you don't have to tell to clean their room. Their relationship with both parents is good. You should be able to take them to more places than you could most children, and they will mix well with all ages and know how to behave.

At 16 they might start to experience the pangs of their first love. Being a slow starter, they won't have had much experience with the opposite sex until now. They take relationships at this age much too seriously and you need to be careful that she doesn't come home with an engagement ring on her finger, or he with the ring in a box ready to propose to his loved one. They need the reins of their relationships pulling in at this age. If you can stop them from marrying too young they will probably wait until quite a bit later.

At 21 this is a great partner for anyone. Sagittarians provide well for those they love, including their parents. They are happiest in a career with plenty of activity and variety, and cope surprisingly well under stress. They are not the type to indulge in two relationships at a time because if they do fall for someone else, everyone will know about it. They handle problems in life rather well and it is the strength and love of their families that keeps them so together and centred. If they find themselves alone and without a love in their lives they can become destructive and may turn to gambling or drink. This is to get the attention they are lacking. A single Sagittarian at this age is not a happy one.

By 40 they have built up a reputation for being there for their friends and family, and many people rely on them. People will often rope a Sagittarian into lying for them to cover up for something but I don't recommend it because they don't make great liars. This is the age when they try to take a step up in life and make their mark. Personal life has taken precedence until now but it's about to take a back seat. They will uproot and change job and may act out of character. Don't be alarmed. They have every intention of taking their loved ones with them, indeed are probably making these changes for their family. Nine times out of ten they are successful at making these changes, so support them. They simply haven't had the chance before to do what they wanted. Life is busy for this sign and it is only in their forties that they see any space in which to do the things they've dreamt about. Now all they have to do is take aim and be determined and the sky really is the limit. Some even emigrate at this age, finding it easier than they would have done at 21.

At 70 they are likely to think they have more wrong with them than they do. They are probably just bored. They stick to friends of their own sex (in contrast to their late teens) and may spend their days sitting around and criticizing members of the opposite sex. Don't take them too seriously though. This is just another stage in the life of the archer. If they want to do anything they will do it, but they have to want it, not you. Convince them that days out are their idea not yours to get them to do what you want.

Sagittarian Careers . . .

Top footballer. All those people adoring you in a sport you're naturally good at.

Barman. All that free drink and all those people to talk to. A nightclub would be even better because it stays open later.

Astronaut. Ideally on a journey to discover a new planet.

Comedian. You are a natural at making people laugh.

. . . not so Sagittarian Careers

Bar owner. You'd go bust because you'd sup all the profits and give all your friends free drinks.

Librarian. You couldn't bear all that silence.

Usher. Once again, the silence would be too much for you, and there'd be no one for you to party with.

Famous Sagittarians

Cricketer Imran Khan, singers Frank Sinatra, Tina Turner and Little Richard, footballer Ryan Giggs, tennis ace Monica Seles, designer Gianni Versace, ski-jumper Eddie Edwards, actors Daryl Hannah, Teri Hatcher and Kim Basinger.

Health Sore Points

Sagittarius rules the hips, thighs, nerves and arteries. You need to be careful not to underexercise or to overexercise. Moderation is what's needed. Because the archer is restless and adventurous, there is a likelihood of pulled muscles resulting from trying new exercises and diving in (not literally) at the deep end. Sporty Sagittarians must make sure they wear the correct protective gear and do all the warm-up and 'warm-down' exercises a sport requires. Otherwise you will be subject to pulled muscles, especially hamstrings.

The commonest accidents you suffer are those affecting the lower limbs, such as sprains, dislocation of the hip and fracture of the thigh. Being so restless and so constantly on the move doesn't help matters.

Sagittarius needs to keep the blood in good condition, taking precautions against anaemia and other such disorders. Talk to your doctor if in doubt.

Being very vulnerable to colds, Sagittarians should wrap up well and watch out for others' germs in the winter months. Echinacea, available from health food shops, is a useful herb for keeping colds at bay.

Rheumatism is another problem for Sagittarians. Some of you suffer from it in your teens. This is your body warning you to look after yourself, in particular to wrap up in the cold winter months and to wear good, comfortable shoes. Sagittarians don't suit high and narrow heels. The archer is not made to totter. Those hooves must always be ready for a gallop.

The liver also comes under the ruling of this sign and it doesn't do any harm to take liver salts from time to time to help keep the liver in good condition. Overindulgence is generally to be avoided, too, especially in alcohol. You can hold your drink well but you quickly become bloated on it. If a Sagittarian makes it as far as being an alcoholic, you can bet it has been a real accomplishment to get there.

Sagittarians love food but don't always find the time to learn to cook to the standards they require. If you do get involved in the pleasures of cooking, you turn it into a career and either become a chef or buy a restaurant. If you gain weight it is usually around the hips, especially in women. However, you are naturally fit and burn off a lot of energy.

Cures and Counsel

The best way for a Sagittarian to stay fit and healthy is to think about your physical and mental health in conjunction. Walking, for example, is good for the body and mind, and you love walking, but you don't always bother to do it. Think of a Sagittarian as a horse with blinkers on. Put something right in front of their eyes and they won't notice it. Don't get me wrong, you are intelligent. You just need a bit of guidance sometimes.

Swimming is another excellent form of exercise for the athletic Sagittarian. It is also a great form of exercise for helping pulled muscles and ligaments get back into shape. Swimming is often recommended to Sagittarians who have muscular problems.

If your job is physically demanding, be careful how much sport you take on in your spare time. Gentle swimming and walking are fine, but burning the candle at both ends with hard work and vigorous games of squash and football, for example, will not do you any favours. This is the 90-year-old you have to stop from running for the bus – Sagittarius always thinks it has the body of a 16-year-old.

It is never nice when you feel off colour and cannot find the energy in your body to do what your mind wants to. If you are the parent of an archer, look after them in the early years and make sure they cover up in cold weather. Adult Sagittarius, coats can look just as sexy as skimpy clothes, and a lot more mysterious. So if it's image you are worried about, invest in a few new clothes, stylish but warm, to fend off the colds and rheumatism you are prone to.

Try herbal teas to help you relax. Camomile and valerian are particularly good for helping ease away the stresses of the day. A potential problem for Sagittarians is that they never keep the same pace. Close ones often don't know how to keep up with them because their plans change all the time. Listen to your body from time to time. Let me give you an idea of a typical Sagittarius. They will agree to go out with friends for the morning, and the day, and for supper and for the evening after. They don't know how to resist the lure of the social scene, especially if single.

Fresh air is the cheapest and probably the most effective preventative measure you can take. Put archers in a room full of smoke or a crowded environment and if there's a cold about, they will get it. However, it is not quite enough just to get fresh air when you can. How you breathe is also important. You should breathe in through the nose and out through the mouth. A good exercise for the morning is to lie in bed with eyes closed and to breathe in gently, counting slowly to three, allowing your lungs to fill up with air. Then slowly breathe out, controlling your breath as you go, until you have expelled all the air from your lungs. If you do this for a couple of minutes before getting out of bed, you should start to notice the way you breathe as you go about your day. You will want to feel the air going into your lungs and the oxygen enriching your body. Think about it, oxygen is free, and it's probably one of the only things in life that is. So use it and enjoy it. Who knows, they may decide to charge for it in years to come.

It goes without saying, but I'll say it anyway. You should be eating a balanced diet. The chances are that if you're born under this sign you eat on the hoof. Typical lunchtime food for Sagittarius would be a burger on the run. But seeing as your mind is alert at 6 a.m., you could easily create a healthy packed lunch for yourself. And you can do better than an apple and a ham sandwich. Why not make your own gorgeous pasta salads, quiches and pizza to nibble at during the day? If you make the food yourself you know what's in it. You can also get good take-away lunches from supermarkets now; the sort I could only dream of as a child. Resist the fast-food options, whose energy surge will send you back down to earth quicker than a brick off the Empire State Building.

We never feel happy when life isn't going our way. Relationship problems, career setbacks, financial worries: the list is endless. Sagittarians can guard against nervous exhaustion by making sure they stay in control of their lives. As one of the three fire signs (the others are Aries and Leo), you have a tendency to allow your problems to build up and get out of hand. Sometimes someone else has to step in before it becomes ridiculous. Learn to admit when something is not going your way. You will feel so much better when you talk about things. Partners of Sagittarians must learn to recognize as early as possible the warning signals that things are skittering out of control: you will save yourself and your archer partner a lot of unnecessary bother if you do. Try the herbal teas I recommend on page 24. These should leave you with more energy and a more positive mind. But remember, if you are genuinely unhappy with something in your life, the solution may be to change it. And don't feel you always have to be the one to do the changing. Any good relationship with a partner, even a good job, is about compromise.

Burdock Root Remedy

The Romanies swear by burdock roots to keep the blood in good order. This is easily gathered if you live near any open country; you may even have some in your garden, your local supermarket or oriental food store. The seeds can be used in the same way to make a tea: substitute a handful for the root. We Romanies also believe that burdock seeds in a little muslin bag, hanging around the neck, are helpful for rheumatism.

a burdock root, freshly pulled
1.2 litres/2 pints water

Scrub the root clean, chop it up, then boil it in the water for 15 minutes. Cool, strain and drink a wineglassful three times a day. Make up a new batch as necessary.

Sagittarius Juice Booster

Here is a health drink that comes under the ruling of your star sign. Take it by way of preparation, from before an important day or event to the morning after one to complete your recovery! (Especially if over-indulgence was involved.)

1 fresh ruby grapefruit
1 orange
150 g/5 oz strawberries

Either use a juicing machine, or squeeze the citrus fruit, mash the strawberries and press the mixture through a sieve. You should find this drink has an immediate effect, and replaces any vitamins you are lacking.

Raspberry Cold Cure

Here is a great home-made remedy to prevent colds. If you find that you're struck down for a few days each winter with a streaming nose and bulging eyes, try the following. It takes time to prepare, so think ahead and start making it up before the cold season sets in. Pick the raspberries in season for later use; dry them by slicing them, blanching them with 2 tablespoons ascorbic acid (or 5 × l g vitamin C tablets) in 1 litre/2 pints water, then dry on an absorbent cloth in a very low oven with the door ajar to allow the steam to escape for 10 hours. Store in an airtight container in a cool, dry place until needed.

dried raspberries
sugar lumps

Fill a jar (such as a pasta jar, or anything with a lid) half full with dried raspberries and then fill to the top with sugar lumps. (Sounds crazy, but stick with me.) Leave the fruit and sugar to macerate for 4 weeks. When the sugar has dissolved completely, add another layer of sugar lumps to refill the jar. When this layer has dissolved as well, your potion is ready. If you think you have a cold coming on, put a little of this raspberry juice into a glass of hot water. It tastes wonderful and has the power to stop any cold dead in its tracks. This juice stays fresh for more than a year. Simply make up a fresh batch every year at the beginning of October and you'll have your own magic – and cheap – remedy at hand.

Good Sagittarius Food

The cell salt Sagittarians need is silica, which is quartz or flint. In the body it is found in hair, nails and skin and also in the membrane covering the bones. A deficiency results in weak nails and poor hair and skin condition. You need to include these foods in your diet to ensure you get enough silica: parsnips, asparagus and cucumber. Also good for Sagittarius, especially against winter colds, are unpolished rice, horseradish, onions, barley, red cabbage and cherries. I am sure you can find plenty there that you like and can add to your diet on a regular basis.

Foods that strengthen the bones are also good, so that means eating plenty of foods containing calcium and magnesium (see page 37).

Celery is a valuable root for rheumatism sufferers. Cooked gently in milk and then eaten with the milk, this neutralizes the excess acids in the body that underlie this complaint. You can also eat it uncooked. Celery doesn't make you fat and it has a distinct flavour. Give it a go. Your aching limbs, hips and thighs will thank you.

It is so much better to get the nutrients you need

from food than from supplements, but if you haven't the time to do the shopping you'd like, or if you just can't resist the chocolate bars and hate the fruit and vegetables, then go for the tablets. (And think about developing a taste for some fruit and vegetables, too. Why not? You don't have to like them all.) Calcium and vitamin D will help keep your bones strong, and vitamin E will help keep your tissues supple and will look after your ligaments. The oils on page 274 are also essential, especially if you're not taking any of the food that I have recommended. It's your body, so make sure you look after it. It's got to last you!

Plants for Star Therapy

The maple is Sagittarius's luck from mother nature. If you want to grow this pretty tree, remember that it appreciates plenty of sunshine and reasonable protection from frost. In its original form it is too large for the average garden, but bush varieties are available. A particularly attractive one is the Japanese maple.

Health Checklist

- For stress, don't forget the burdock root recipe on page 297. If you're in a hurry, turn to the quick teas your local supermarket or health food shop is sure to carry. They're good to keep in the cupboard for when you've had that phone call you've been dreading or a day with the kids has taken its toll. All

those that follow here are good for stress headaches. (If you are pregnant, stick to camomile, lemon and lime or peppermint to be on the safe side.)
* Elderflower tea: if you are recovering from a cough or a cold or feeling a little run down.
* Fennel tea relieves indigestion, especially that caused by stressful mealtimes. Its lovely aniseed taste helps food go down more easily and it takes away that bloated feeling.
* Peppermint tea: if you have overindulged in alcohol or just feel sickly, it will bring you nicely back down to earth.
* Camomile tea helps relieve anxiety attacks and should help you sleep more easily. For lack of sleep due to pain stick to cowslip tea (page 57), which is fantastic.
* Rosehip tea contains vitamin C and has a pleasant taste.

- If you suffer from nervous exhaustion, improve your intake of the B vitamins. Good sources are brown rice, seeds, beans, breakfast cereals and Marmite.
- For blood disorders or anaemia, you need iron and vitamin B12. Iron can be found in beef, pork, offal, liver and kidney, canned pilchards, sardines, eggs, fortified cereals, spinach, cocoa powder, tomato paste, apricots and green leafy vegetables. B12 can be found in meat, poultry, fish, eggs, cheese, milk, molasses and breakfast cereals.
- Rheumatism can be treated and prevented with evening primrose oil and starflower (also known as borage) oil.
- A good walk is the way to clear a cloudy head. If you

had too much to drink the night before then make the effort to walk round the block. Once you've managed to conquer the front door you'll be past the worst. It's a case of getting air into your lungs and getting everything to work properly again.

Are You a True Sagittarius?

Be honest! Write down 'yes' or 'no', then read the advice below.

1 Do you find that once you've made up your mind, nothing can stop you from getting what you want?
2 Do you eat any of the following foods on a regular basis: parsnips, cucumbers, asparagus, strawberries, cherries, red cabbage?
3 Are you attracted to dark blues and rich purples?
4 Are you an impatient cook?
5 When you make a mistake is it usually a very silly one?
6 Have you ever had any problems with your hips or thighs?
7 Do you allow stresses to build up before you deal with them?
8 Do you have a temper that gets the better of you?
9 Can you tell a story without exaggerating?
10 Are you a stickler for details?
11 Are you always striving for success, no matter how much you already have?
12 Would you describe yourself as an optimist?

13 When you have made up your mind, are you relentless in your mission?
14 Do you often change moods without warning?
15 Do you get anxious to the point of being overstressed when you are going somewhere important?
16 Do you have a mischievous sense of humour?
17 Do you dive into new situations at the deep end?
18 In relationships, are you an all-or-nothing person?
19 Would you describe yourself as restless?
20 Do you sprain an ankle or a joint at least every year?

If you answered 'yes' to most questions, you are a Sagittarian through and through, striving and running through life to get what you want. Make sure that you are eating the correct foods for your sign. If you answered yes to question 2 then you will not only be a typical Sagittarian, but one that is living life at its best too. Deal with any health complaints as soon as they arise and avoid the tendency of your sign to leave things until they become unbearable.

You may at some point in your life have to learn the art of counting to ten before you speak, especially if you answered yes to questions 7 and 8. Try to honour friends' trust in you by not telling their secrets to all and sundry. If you answered yes to question 19 you may have to look for a more fulfilling career. Unless a Sagittarian is doing more than they are physically able to they will always have energy to burn, and if that is not put into something productive it can turn into pure mischief. Your life will always be interesting, and peopled with interesting characters. If you have an ambition you haven't yet fulfilled, go for it now. With the power of a fire sign behind you, the sky's the limit.

If you answered 'no' to most questions you do not sound like a typical Sagittarian. However, I bet you answered the questions in under three minutes. I'd really like you to go through them again and spend a whole minute on each one, to see if the score comes out differently. My bet is that if you take your time with each question your answers will be a little more accurate.

If you answered no to question 2, you need to make a conscious effort to eat more of the fruit and vegetables your sign needs. Even if you feel healthy, you can always do more to ensure you stay that way. Health is the most important thing to look after and should always be your first priority. Take a good look at your eating patterns, and also check your moon sign in the back of the book to see if you find that relevant to your health as well. Sagittarians remind me of a champagne cork waiting to go off, and the chances are that the dynamic and unmissable Sagittarian is bubbling up waiting to be released. Are you hiding the real you?

The Drinker's Guide to the Zodiac

I don't want to encourage anyone to drink too much, as you know. This is a health book. However, if it is a special occasion, go ahead, and wait for the fireworks. Remember this is a cocktail – you're not supposed to drink the bottle! I've made sure none of my drinks will set the signs off in a negative way, but of course over-indulgence will make anyone ill.

Why not throw an astrological cocktail party? The results are sure to be fun.

Zombie Voodoo

Sagittarians, it must be said, can hold their drink, although this one is unlikely to be what the archer is used to. This should send the archer into another solar system. (Remember, no drinking and driving. No, not even after a sip.)

4 or 5 ice cubes
juice of 1 lime or lemon
juice of ½ orange (or 2 tablespoons unsweetened canned or carton juice)
3 drops angostura bitters
1 teaspoon sugar or sugar syrup
1 egg white
1 part white rum
1 part golden rum
a maraschino cherry
1 slice of orange
a sprig of mint
½ part dark rum

Put the ice cubes into a cocktail shaker. Pour the fruit juices and shake the bitters over the ice. Add the sugar, egg white, and white and golden rum. Shake until a frost forms. Pour without straining into a Collins glass.

Garnish with the fruit and pour the dark rum over. Stir once and serve.

Star Menu

Sagittarians love good food and drink, they just don't always want to prepare it. Here are some dishes to prepare for a Sagittarius you love.

Stuffed Fillet Steak Parcels

This would tantalize the tastebuds of any sign, but it is especially good for Sagittarius. Serves 2.

4 small fillet steaks
50 g/2 oz butter
1 tablespoon olive oil
1 clove garlic, chopped
250 g/10 oz fresh or frozen prawns, cooked and shelled
5 mushrooms, chopped
mixed herbs (fresh coriander and parsley, or dried bouquet garni)
4 sheets filo pastry, fresh and frozen, thawed
150 ml/¼ pint dry white wine
50 g/2 oz Cheddar cheese, grated
140 ml/5 fl oz single cream
salt and pepper

Preheat the oven to 170°C/325°F/gas mark 3.

Grill the fillet steak for about 4 minutes on each side under a high heat. Set aside.

Melt half the butter and olive oil in a frying pan, add the garlic and stir until golden. Don't allow the garlic to burn. Then add the prawns and mushrooms with a pinch of herbs and cook for 3 minutes. Then pour in the white wine and cook until it bubbles and is absorbed. Continue to cook until everything browns to your approval. Then stir in the cheese slowly and let it melt into a creamy sauce. Do not let it burn. Season to taste.

Melt the remaining butter in a small pan. Take a piece of the steak and brush it with a little of the melted butter. Place it in the centre of a square of buttered filo pastry big enough to form an envelope around the steak. Spread the steak with half of the prawn and cheese mixture. Place another piece of steak on top to form a sandwich. Fold the pastry around the steak into a neat bundle, and brush with more butter. Make another bundle in exactly the same way. Bake for 15 minutes or until the pastry is golden brown.

Fiery Creamed Carrots and Parsnips

This is a great accompaniment to the fillet steak parcels, and the horseradish gives it the kick that Sagittarius likes to experience with food. Serves 6–8.

500 g/1 lb 2 oz carrots, sliced
250 g/9 oz parsnips, sliced
12–16 crumbled wheat crackers
2 tablespoons melted butter
240 ml/8 fl oz mayonnaise
2 tablespoons chopped fresh parsley
2 tablespoons freshly grated horseradish

salt and freshly ground black pepper
2 tablespoons almonds

Preheat the oven to 200°C/400°F/gas 6.

Boil the carrots and parsnips for 10 minutes in boiling water. Drain and then mash them. Mix with the crackers and butter. Set aside. Combine the mayonnaise, parsley and horseradish, and season to taste with salt and pepper. Toss with the vegetables and almonds and transfer to a buttered ovenproof dish. Top with a few remaining crackers and bake, uncovered, for about 30 minutes until the top has browned.

Marion's Coffee Cake

This is delicious served with ice cream, and was discovered by my mother-in-law, who I sent out to find the best possible recipe to satisfy the tastes of a Sagittarius.

1 teaspoon Camp coffee (or chicory coffee essence)
1 dessertspoon hot water
100 g/4 oz self-raising flour
100 g/4 oz caster sugar
1 level teaspoon baking powder
100 g/4 oz soft margarine (or butter)
2 large eggs
50 g/2 oz chopped walnuts
To ice:
100 g/4 oz unsalted butter, softened
50 g/2 oz icing sugar
1 tablespoon instant coffee or essence
1 dessertspoon hot water

Preheat the oven to 170°C/325°F/gas 3.

Dissolve the coffee in hot water and allow to cool. Sieve the flour and sugar with the baking powder into a bowl, then add the margarine and eggs. Cream until smooth, then add the coffee. Blend, then fold in the walnuts. Bake in a lined tin for half an hour, and ice the top when cool with the other ingredients, combined. Decorate with walnuts (optional).

Star Beauty

For athletic Sagittarius, exercise is as good a beauty regime as anything. For hips and thighs these simple exercises produce results.

Lie on the floor on your back with your arms outstretched. Pull your feet up to your body, with the soles flat on the floor, so your knees point up to the ceiling. Then steadily swing your knees from side to side until your thighs hit the floor. Repeat 10 times.

Still lying on the floor but with the legs outstretched and your arms stretched out in line with your hips, bend your left leg so that your knee touches your chest. Lift the leg high into the air and over so that your knee touches your elbow in a controlled roll, then back to your chest, then down again. Repeat with the other leg. Do this on each leg at least 12 times.

Now stand with your legs wide apart, imagining a line down the centre of your body to keep yourself straight. Keeping your back straight sway your hips from side to side, making sure you are in control of the movement the whole time, ten times. You should be able to feel your inner thigh working. If you can do this every morning, or even just once a week to start with, you should start to feel at your best and you will even start to stand differently.

Almond oil makes a good body cream, for face as well as arms and legs. Rub it into the skin to stop it from drying out. For rough skin on elbows try this Romany recipe. Cut a raw potato in half and rub the juice on the elbows. This most basic recipe has excellent results.

Your Ideal Health Sign Holiday

Adventure holidays and backpacking are ideal for the archer. You love adventure and sport. Climbing holidays would suit you too, giving you the chance to prove that you can survive in the natural world as well as in the business world. You will be excellent at taking care of yourself and others on holiday.

CAPRICORN

THE GOAT

Ruling Planet: Saturn, the planet of structure

Triplicity or Element: Earth

Quadruplicity or Mode: Cardinal

Key words: cautious, reserved, prudent, ambitious, constructive, disciplined

The Origin of Capricorn

Capricorn the goat is the god Pan in another disguise. He was once attacked by a giant, and turned himself into a goat in order to escape. This is how he has been immortalized in the heavens.

What Capricorn is Like

The more you get to know a Capricorn, the more there is to find out. Those born under this sign are cautious and serious and extremely ambitious. Yet there is a wicked sense of humour there just dying to get out. They are planners, and can annoy partners by giving them a schedule of what they are going to do and when. They plan well in business too, and make good bosses. They are steadfast, and love to be in control of situations. They would give up a love affair simply because it did not fit in with what they had planned. Sad, really, but they can't break away from the path to success they have chosen.

Dependable yet ambitious, many top media people are Capricorns, successful yet grounded, and a positive influence on those around them. Practical and self-sufficient, they are unlikely to ask for help, but offer it and they'll thank you for the favour. However, they hate admitting they are wrong.

Tell them your secrets and your secrets will be safe. Don't tell them what to do, though. They like to be boss. Their ruling planet, Saturn, is the planet of self-control and discipline. It gives them the urge to build for security and for the family, and it also throws up great challenges throughout life. People ruled by Saturn are figures of authority. Dastardly attractive, they look powerful even if they are not.

They like to be seen doing the right thing. They also like the rather conservative colours associated with their sign and often wear them. These are dark greens, greys, browns and black.

Their sense of humour is like no other. They can be overwhelming at times. If you have a lot of Capricorn friends you might think you have a few too many! This sign is self-contradictory. They are ambitious but at the same time pessimistic, always believing that something will go wrong and everything will fail. These loyal friends will put themselves out for you but just make sure you're prepared to return the favour because they will ask for one back.

What I love about earth signs is that they are dependable and good in a crisis, and this is particularly true in the case of Capricorn. Marry a Capricorn and you marry for life, though you'll have to wait until they've got the success they want from their career before they tie the knot.

The annoying thing about Capricorns is their tendency to grumble. They've always got a bigger problem than yours. And if there's something they want they will walk over whoever's in the way to get it. They won't see this as a fault. It's just part of doing their job. They can be opportunists. They can also be plodders. But not often. Usually they are strong-willed, determined and hard-working. If your Capricorn boss asks you in a nice and friendly tone of voice to do something, don't think that means, 'Whenever you're ready.' It means, 'I'm being nice but do it right away or else.'

Watch out for their bad temper but remember that their bark is worse than their bite.

Capricorns flourish best in the countryside and it is unlikely you will see a genuinely happy goat living in a city. If they have a flat in the city instead of a house in the country, you can bet it is filled with greenery. And they may not even know why they are doing it.

You won't find a Capricorn without a pension plan of some sort as Saturn also governs old age and the need for security later in life is always at the front of the thrifty goat's mind. Family responsibilities are also important to them. They go out of their way to look after their elders.

Capricorns will love you for ever if you grant them respect. They will always be good to you, though you may like to keep an eye on what they are doing when you are not around. No Christmas is ever complete without a Capricorn around to make the home feel like a home. Just don't overcook the turkey or you'll be in for an earbashing.

As they get older many Capricorns become keen gardeners, spending hours pottering around thinking of all the people they have met and all the things they have done with their lives.

How to Spot a Capricorn

Their noses may look almost broken, like a boxer's, going vertically down before sticking out. They can have close-set eyes and are sometimes big and stocky, although this is not always the rule.

The Devil and the Angel.

The DEVIL CAPRICORN is ruthless about getting to the top and has a temper so bad you'd think he had a split personality. The irresistible Elvis Presley exemplifies fervent struggle to get to the top, but let's not forget how much he loved his mum. He wasn't a complete devil! Al Capone was a power-hungry Capricorn whose love for money and notoriety was well known.

The ANGEL CAPRICORN strives to make a difference in the world, pursuing a career and breaking the barrier of discovery at the same time. Isaac Newton, whose discoveries informed and improved our lives, was an Angel Capricorn.

Capricorn Health and Development from Child to Adult

The Capricorn infant is extremely perceptive. These babies seem even to know when their parents need a little peace and quiet. They suffer more teething problems than most. They fit into family life very well and should sleep with few problems. This baby is very little trouble and a delight to have around. Only be careful of that sensitive skin. They may have allergies to certain foods so you should look out for rashes and remember what they had to eat. They need to wear lots of protection in the sun.

At five years of age the placid Capricorn child may be taken advantage of by older brothers and sisters. This child is obedient and does what it's told. They won't risk a telling-off for anything trivial. If they do get into trouble it's for something worthwhile. At school they are no dunce but not particularly brilliant either. They are usually somewhere in the middle of the class, and won't show where their true talents lie until they get older. They are observers, waiting patiently and watching what everyone else is doing. The truth is they are planning their move very carefully. These master planners are just beginning to develop their planning muscles.

At 11 they start to come into their own and to develop a flair for things. They can surprise their family with how skilled they are. They are still taking things slowly but usually end up at the top. They do their homework slowly and to parents this may look like laziness but it is not. It's thoroughness. Wait for those glowing reports and you'll see. To Capricorns, if a thing is worth doing, it is worth doing well. Conflict with fathers can occur at this age but it is only a phase and is sure to pass. It is simply that they are trying to work out who they are and they tend to do this from a critical point of view rather than a constructive one.

At 16 they are keen and willing students of life, but they listen and learn rather than push themselves forward. They like mechanical things. The boys also like football, and the girls analyse the opposite sex as a fulltime occupation. A shy streak can often stop them from having relationships yet, but nevertheless they go to great lengths to find out everything they can about the object of their affections. If they do have a partner, they will stick with them. A good-looking Capricorn is a sitting duck for partner-hunting singles.

At 21, if they have managed to stay single, they will be experiencing a life full of adventure, trouble and excitement. If they have married too young they will still be growing and will need their partner to grow with them. To marry at 23 or 24 is lucky for them. By then they will be ready to accept the responsibility. They are a fair-minded marriage partner who sticks to obligations. Meanwhile they like to work to a pattern in all things and are struggling day and night to make their plans and dreams come true.

At 40 they are in their prime and usually in a position of power in the workplace. Many will have their own business. If by chance they have a minor position at work then they act like they own the company. They have an air about them that cannot be ignored. Their arrogance may serve them well at work but it will also make them as many enemies as friends. They may well embark on parenthood at 40. Because of their ability to stay young, they make fantastic parents. They are able to see things through young eyes. Like other signs Capricorns can be flirts too, and they need to be careful they don't take what is only meant as fun too far. They also need to be careful at this age that they don't have any lazy habits, like smoking or indolence, although serious Capricorn rarely does.

At 70 they still want to do the things they did at 21. They might dress a little too young for their age. They can enjoy activities and sports but should know when their body has had enough. Their critical nature is strongly in evidence at this age. They've seen and done everything, don't you know!

Capricorn Careers . . .

Filmstar. Being adored like that – how perfect!

Stockbroker. Just imagine being paid to make all that lovely money all day long.

Politician. The power would attract you. Nixon was a Capricorn.

Veterinary surgeon. You have a natural love and affinity for animals.

Mountaineer. All that lovely fresh air and exercise: ideal.

. . . not so Capricorn Careers

Driving examiner. No one would be perfect enough to pass your test.

Bank cashier. You'd never be able to stomach handing out all that cash – you'd be in danger of wanting to take it home yourself.

Sailor. Not enough land for this earth sign.

Any career where you can't get to the top by butting all your rivals out of the way.

Famous Capricorns

Singers Vanessa Paradis and Annie Lennox, actors Gerard Depardieu, Denzel Washington, Ted Danson,

Anthony Hopkins and Mel Gibson, footballer Vinnie Jones, King Juan Carlos of Spain, photographer David Bailey, boxer Muhammed Ali.

Health Sore Points

The knees, skeleton, bones and skin are ruled by Capricorn. This means calcium levels need to be watched and children of this sign must make sure they get enough. Capricorns have the power to reach a very ripe old age indeed, but you must take care of your lungs. Capricorn, don't smoke. It really doesn't suit you and it is especially bad for you of all signs.

Capricorns are prone to knocking their knees and many athletes of this sign end up wearing bandages on their knees to protect them. You need to take particular care of knees as you get older.

You have an amazing ability to look younger as you get older. The 60-year-old man with a gorgeous young blonde on his arm is probably a Capricorn. They won't look out of place either. Goats are sensible about what they eat and drink and do not generally overindulge in anything, so often have the body to go with the youthful face.

You need to watch out for skin disorders, chills and rheumatism. Take regular walks and get lots of fresh air. Wrap up well in cold weather. You often see a Capricorn in skimpy clothing in a cold snap, and it's not a good idea.

Keep moving! Any job that means sitting down all day in a cramped position is no good for you. Your joints easily stiffen and you need to guard against this.

A Capricorn child will swear blind they have cleaned their teeth when they haven't. I advise all parents of Capricorn children to check the toothbrush: you are sure to find it dry as a bone by the sink. Capricorns need to guard against teeth problems later in life by taking care of teeth when young.

Sunburn can be a problem for sensitive Capricorn skin. Always use good quality sunscreens made for sensitive skins, and don't overdo sun exposure.

Capricorn's vulnerability to rheumatism and chills has a lot to do with lifestyle. Goats don't know when to stop, and a minor ailment will be ignored as inconvenient until it turns into a bigger ailment. A Capricorn in love is the worst of the lot when it comes to caring for health. The lovelorn goat trips and knocks itself until it is covered in little bruises. That sensitive skin will break out in spots too.

Capricorn teenagers should be encouraged to be active. How they are in their teens is often how they will stay. But don't tell them what to do. You have to make it look like their idea. Praise is a good way to encourage them into anything.

Many Capricorns have faulty breathing, often as a result of poor posture. Examine your posture right now, before you've had a chance to straighten up. Is your back curved? Are you breathing shallowly in quick little breaths? You need to straighten your back (not ram-rod, just comfortably straight) and breathe well. Good deep breaths will get everything circulating around your body and will fend off lethargy. Improve your breathing and your posture now and you'll thank me later, I promise you.

Cures and Counsel

Do all you can to ensure an enjoyable old age because you are going to be around for a long time. Treat your body well and respect it and it will last a lifetime. In your favour is that you are one of the signs I worry about least because you generally look after yourselves so well. Just avoid that earth-sign tendency towards laziness.

In the right company, Capricorn blooms like a flower in spring. If your Capricorn friend is ill then rally round and visit and lift those flagging spirits because your friend will get better much more quickly if you do. Don't think you can give Capricorns health advice, though. This is one sign with its own ideas about the right diet and lifestyle (even if it actually got them from me! – but then I will only have confirmed what the goat already knew).

You are not too good in hot weather. If you love the bronzed look you'd better fake it. The suntan from a bottle looks just as good as any a holiday can give you, and I won't tell anybody, I promise. And you won't be encouraging wrinkles.

Take gentle exercise. Some signs need harsh, fast exercise, but gentle movements are the answer for you, you'll be glad to hear.

Like anybody else, if you are unhappy with a relationship or a situation in your life, then don't stay in it but make a change. Life moves on and gets better if you let it. Earth-sign Capricorn loves the home more than most and doesn't like to rock the boat. I once had as a client a Capricorn housewife who hated her husband

and found her kids hard to handle but stayed put because she loved her house! I don't recommend this. Life's too short not to be made the most of. You've made the first step by picking up this book. The next step is to make sure that what you are doing is really making you happy.

You must also take care not to be too harsh on yourself about what you can or cannot do. Eat a little bit of what you fancy from time to time and don't get a guilt complex about it. Once you know what your sign needs you'll know where you can be indulgent without doing harm. You can safely indulge yourself with the chocolate recipe on page 333, for example. And let your hair down occasionally. Learn to compromise, and to allow yourself a little pleasure.

If you suffer from bad knees, as many Capricorns do, stock up on parsley and devil's claw, an African herb that is available as a supplement and which besides being good for aches and rheumatic pain can help gastro-intestinal problems. You can chop parsley over many dishes and parsley sauce is great with fish and new potatoes.

Capricorn lungs are not as strong as those of other signs and it is something of a disaster for Capricorns to smoke. They'll have one of those coughs that make you feel sick, but they will stubbornly carry on just to prove to you they can do what they want when they like.

Lungwort Tea

To keep lungs working well, the aptly named lungwort is excellent. This grows in shady nooks in wooded country and blooms from March until May. The spotted leaves resemble a lung. Gather some to prepare this remedy. The ribwort can be got from a good herbalist and is inexpensive.

½ teaspoon dried lungwort or 250 g/8 oz leaves
½ teaspoon dried ribwort or 250 g/8 oz leaves
500 ml/1 pint water

Make the two herbs into a tea by simmering in the water for 5–10 minutes, to taste. Strain. Drink a wineglassful every morning, with a little honey if it makes it more palatable for you. Use regularly and make a new batch as required; refrigerate.

Coltsfoot and Cleavers for Teeth

These two herbs help keep teeth strong. Coltsfoot blooms in the springtime and is a pretty addition to any garden. Cleavers, perhaps better known as goose grass, is an attractive climbing plant. In each case, you need the leaves.

250 g/8 oz coltsfoot leaves
500 ml/1 pint water

Simmer the leaves in the water for 10 minutes to make a tea, then strain. Take a wineglassful three times daily. Make up a new batch as necessary.

250 g/8 oz cleaver leaves, finely chopped
500 ml/1 pint milk

Steep the leaves in hot milk for 3 to 4 minutes. Strain and take a tablespoonful before meals. Make up a new batch as necessary.

Capricorn Juice Booster

A wineglassful of this every morning will do you the power of good. It is delicious and healthy, and – a bonus – wards off constipation too.

½ watermelon, seeds removed
125 ml/4 fl oz still water
squeeze of fresh lemon juice

Juice the ingredients together in a juicing machine, or mash and sieve the watermelon and add the water and lemon juice.

Good Capricorn Food

Capricorn often lacks the cell salt calcarea phosphorica, or calcium phosphate. This cell salt has an affinity for albumen, which it uses as a cement to build up the bony structure. It's the master builder of the body, important in creating new blood vessels and digestive fluids, for example.

Foods that contain this cell salt include cabbage, watercress, kale, milk and prunes. Add some of these into your diet and you will be on the right track. Other foods that are good for you are cottage cheese and onions. If you live with a Cancerian or a Scorpio you'll be laughing, because you all need similar foods. And by the way, prunes are delicious! Try one and see.

Capricorns are careful eaters. You have a pretty good instinct for what you should and shouldn't be eating, and are proud of your knowledge of food. You know where the organic food section of the supermarket is. And you know to avoid the cake section! You savour flavours and can stop eating when you want to, something many of the other signs cannot. You can identify individual ingredients in a dish more easily than most people can. Don't try tricking the Capricorn into eating foods he or she doesn't like by disguising them. You'll be wasting your time. That mashed-up carrot and swede will never be the coloured potato you're trying to make it out to be.

Capricorns are proud of their bodies. You notice an extra pound very quickly and act even more quickly to get rid of it. This doesn't mean that every Capricorn owns a gym membership or even a pair of trainers, it just means that Capricorns are more aware than many other signs of how their body feels and how it may change as each year goes by. Their awareness of their diet contributes to their good body care. But beware that 40-year-old Capricorn still trying to get into the jeans he or she wore twenty years ago. Put the jeans out of their way and save them the torment.

Capricorns pick their drinks as carefully as their food. Keith Floyd, the television cook and wine expert, is a typical Capricorn, who treats his food as a masterpiece he must create to perfection.

Plants for Star Therapy

Solomon's seal is lucky for you. You need to find the darkest, dampest spot in your garden for this plant. It is easily satisfied and thrives where little else will grow. It's of the lily family with spikes of bell-shaped flowers and you'll find it an asset to any flower arrangement. But watch out for slugs and snails around it: it seems to be good for them too!

Herbs that are great for a Capricorn include Solomon's seal, comfrey, black hellebore, plantain, shepherd's purse, mullein, cinchona, elder and knapweed. Look at the packaging in a health food shop to see what each treats, or consult a herbalist.

Health Checklist

- For skin disorders try zinc, which can be found in seafood, beef, pork, dairy products, green vegetables, seeds, nuts, pulses and cereal, and vitamin A, which can be found in cod liver oil, liver, butter, cheese and eggs. The B vitamins, vitamin E, antioxidants and evening primrose oil are also important for the skin.
- For chills, take ginkgo biloba.
- For rheumatism, ask your health food store for devil's claw, evening primrose oil and starflower (borage) oil.
- Treat liver problems with Bio-light detox liquid.
- For teeth, make sure you get enough calcium,

magnesium, vitamin C (blackcurrants, kiwi fruit, peas, potatoes, Brussels sprouts, broccoli, guava, peppers and oranges) and vitamin D (kippers, mackerel, eggs, milk and some fortified margarines).

- As always, if you are not eating well enough, for whatever reason, take the supplements you need. But it is always better to get what you need from your food. Try the recipes in the chapter on pages 331–4.

Are You a True Capricorn?

Be honest! Write down 'yes' or 'no', then read the advice below.

1 Would you describe yourself as stubborn?
2 Do many people comment that you look younger the older you get?
3 Do you eat any of the following on a regular basis: cabbage, watercress, kale, milk, prunes, cottage cheese, onions?
4 Do you feel happier in the countryside than in the city?
5 Do you prefer dark greens, greys, browns and blacks?
6 Have you planned ahead for your old age and security?
7 Is your bark worse than your bite in disputes?
8 Do you have a love of nature?
9 Have you ever suffered from weak knees?
10 As a child would you do anything to avoid cleaning your teeth?

11 Do you dress for fashion rather than for the weather?
12 Have you ever suffered from skin disorders?
13 Would you say you have a dry sense of humour?
14 Do you keep secrets fairly well?
15 Are you rather arrogant with people less able than you?
16 Are you materialistic?
17 Do you put your work before your friends' problems?
18 Were you a wise old child?
19 Are you impatient?
20 Are you a stickler for order?

If you answered 'yes' to most questions then you are a typical Capricorn. I hope you answered yes to question 3, because those are the foods you should be eating. If not, how about making a start? They really are essential to Capricorn good health. If you answered yes to impatience, in question 19, then do try to slow down a little. Mind you, while I have never met a patient Capricorn, I must also admit they use their impatience to their advantage. They get to the top of their careers by not taking no for an answer.

You are one of the Peter Pans of the zodiac, looking younger the older you get, and never short of attention from admirers. The surprising thing is that many Capricorns think that nobody loves them while they in fact have hordes of secret admirers who are just too afraid to tell this overwhelming sign the extent of their feelings. Slow but sure is the best way for the goat to proceed in life. You should find you are able to make the most of any situation because you look at it from a grounded position, rather than getting overexcited (like you fire signs out there!). If you have suffered from any health problems, in particular weak knees, start taking preventative measures now. Good health is important for a Capricorn: you need to be fit in body to feel fit in mind and to be able to manage your successful life.

If you answered 'no' to most questions, then I am surprised, because a goat is usually a typical goat through and through. Get a friend who knows you well to do the survey on your behalf. They may disagree with some of the answers that you gave. Check your moon sign, too. Perhaps that is eclipsing your sun sign.

If you answered no to question 1 then you are obviously being stubborn, so change your answer – only kidding! Seriously, stubbornness can be a good trait at times – don't be afraid of using it. If you answered no to question 8 you don't know what you're missing. You should get to grips with nature. You goats love to roam, but not too far or to too foreign a place.

I hope you learn more about your sign and the good points that you are hiding. We all keep certain traits covered up as a result of our upbringing and the signs that have influenced us, but if you can learn a little more about who you are and what your talents are you could uncover a great deal of fun that you never knew existed, and you could even make a few of your dreams come true. Why not start by cooking up some of your star recipes? You could also try your zodiac cocktail to get you feeling like your sign: then just leave the rest to the planets.

The Drinker's Guide to the Zodiac

A Capricorn is quite happy on lager, so long as there is plenty of it. Southern Comfort gets one in the party spirit. Wine, however, is not usually a Capricorn's cup of tea.

Watch the eyes; this is where a Capricorn's drink counter is. Here is my rule of thumb: three drinks and they're bright, five and they're pink, and when the eyes are red they have had enough! On a serious note: because the knees, liver and teeth are sensitive areas, Capricorns need to be particularly careful not to drink too much alcohol and to get enough calcium.

Surf Rider Cocktail

This is how to make Capricorn's zodiac drink.

4 or 5 ice cubes
juice of ½ lemon
juice of 1 orange (or 4 tablespoons of unsweetened canned or carton juice)
½ teaspoon grenadine
1 part sweet Italian vermouth
3 parts vodka

Put the ice cubes in a cocktail shaker. Pour over the fruit juices, grenadine, vermouth and vodka. Shake until a frost forms, then strain and pour into a glass.

Star Menu

Here are recipes both health-conscious and delicious, two things particularly important to a Capricorn.

Avocado, Mozzarella Cheese and Tomato Starter

It is said that an avocado contains everything you need and that you could live on nothing else. Avocados are indeed delicious and nutritious but don't forget they are also fattening. I don't recommend you live on them alone. What about all the other delicious foods you can eat them in conjunction with? Here is a delicious starter. Serves 2.

2 bags buffalo mozzarella (half-fat is just as tasty!), drained and rinsed
2 beef tomatoes
1 avocado
olive oil
vinegar
salt and freshly ground black pepper
fresh basil

Slice the mozzarella cheese and divide it between 2 plates. Slice the tomatoes and arrange on the plates with the mozzarella. Cut the avocado in half lengthways, cutting around the central stone. Holding the avocado in both hands, twist the two cut halves in opposite directions to separate them. Ease out the stone using either your fingers or a knife point. Take the skin off with a sharp knife. Sometimes the skin comes off easily and sometimes you have to peel it thinly. Slice the avocado either lengthways or widthways and arrange alongside the tomatoes and mozzarella.

Sprinkle a little olive oil and vinegar to taste over the salad and season. Add basil leaves to garnish and for their exquisite flavour.

Spaghetti Pie

This dish is another favourite in my household and is especially good for introducing children to the delights of cheese. Serves 6 to 8 accompanied by salad and good crusty bread.

125 g/4 oz spaghetti
1 egg, beaten
5–6 tablespoons Parmesan cheese, grated
15 g/½ oz butter or margarine
240 ml/8 fl oz ricotta cheese
240 ml/8 fl oz bottled tomato or meat sauce for pasta
125 g/4 oz mozzarella cheese, shredded

Preheat the oven to 180°C/350°F/gas 4.

Cook the spaghetti until *al dente* in boiling water and drain it.

Combine the egg, Parmesan and butter in a large bowl and stir in the hot spaghetti. Press the mixture evenly into the bottom and up the sides of a 22 cm/9 inch pie dish. Spread the ricotta over the crust. Spoon the tomato sauce over the ricotta. Bake for 20 minutes, then remove from the oven and sprinkle with the mozzarella. Bake for another 5 minutes or so, until the cheese melts and the crust sets. Remove from the oven, allow to stand for 5 minutes and cut into wedges.

Chocolate Soufflé

This is a dessert to have any Capricorn falling into the arms of its maker. Try it and rich rewards will follow. Serves 6.

2 fresh organic free range eggs, separated
50 g/2 oz sugar
12 tablespoons evaporated milk
50 g/2 oz milk chocolate
15 g/½ oz gelatine
4 tablespoons warm water
whipped cream and cherries to decorate, optional

Whisk the egg yolks with the sugar until thick and creamy. Whip the evaporated milk and add to the eggs and sugar. Put the chocolate into a heatproof bowl over a saucepan of simmering water and melt slowly. Add the chocolate to the milk, egg and sugar mixture. Put the gelatine in a small bowl, add the warm water and stir until dissolved. Add to the chocolate mixture.

Beat the egg whites until stiff and stir into the chocolate mixture. Distribute among 6 small pots (or teacups). Add some whipped cream and a cherry for decoration if you desire. NB This recipe contains uncooked eggs. Use only the freshest organic free range eggs, and don't store this any longer than 24 hours. If you are concerned about raw eggs, this can be baked at 150°C/300°F/gas 4 for half an hour, until set.

Star Beauty

It is vital that Capricorns take good care of their teeth, and those who don't when young may find themselves paying a lot for dental treatment when older. Why not make your own toothpaste to keep your teeth in the best possible condition? Here is one that has been used in my family for generations, especially by those who pride themselves on still having their own pearly whites well into old age. And it's much cheaper than the stuff you can buy.

Health and Beauty for Teeth

Many of the smokers in my family swear by this toothpaste because it is great for removing nicotine stains. Plain salt can be used on its own if you like, or you can add dried crushed lemon or orange peel to really whiten the teeth. During the war members of my family used to use the ashes of burnt bread flavoured with peppermint, charcoal or even burnt rosemary when they couldn't get hold of anything else, and these were equally effective. Did you know, by the way, that some people use crushed strawberries to clean their teeth? Strawberries act as an excellent polisher, and of course also taste fantastic.

3 tablespoons bicarbonate of soda
2 tablespoons salt

Mix together and keep it in a pot with a lid. Use as you would any other toothpaste, but not for sensitive teeth. The Romanies used to apply this with their fingers!

Your Ideal Health Sign Holiday

Cruises are perfect for you. This goat loves to see places but prefers not to have to walk too far. As you cruise from island to island, enjoying the beautiful view, you can stretch your legs on deck. There's plenty to see, and you can also retire to the safety of your cabin when you want to.

For the Capricorns who prefer to keep dry land beneath their feet, how about a luxury camper van with all the earthly comforts you desire? Then you can just pull up to your destination of choice and still have your own bed to retire to at night!

AQUARIUS

THE WATER BEARER

Ruling Planet: Saturn, the planet of structure, and Uranus, the planet of disruption

Triplicity or Element: Air

Quadruplicity or Mode: Fixed

Key words: Independent, intellectual, distant, idealistic

The Origin of Aquarius

Greek mythology has it that Aquarius was the water bearer to the deity Zeus. In life he was the beautiful Ganymede; he now lives on in the heavens as cup bearer to the gods.

What Aquarius is Like

Air sign Aquarius is great at talking but possesses this trait somewhat erratically. Since they can also be aloof, you may think they are quiet, but once they start talking they just don't stop. Their opinion is always honest and you always know where you stand with them. If angry with you, they do not bottle it up as fire signs do. They are also unpredictable. You never know what they are going to say or do next.

This is an individual and inventive mind, and Aquarians are able to make great progress in improving the quality of other people's lives. They are friendly and humanitarian by nature and make a wonderful best friend, but you can never bank 100 per cent on them in a crisis. They are more interested in good times. If you are looking for a party partner, this is it.

Aquarians have an original personality in a way that no other sign does. You might think their independent nature would make them loners but they make friends wherever they go. Saturn and Uranus are their ruling planets. Saturn symbolizes the past and Uranus the future. The present doesn't mean a thing to Aquarius.

This is a poised, calm, fascinating and clever sign, witty, charming and courageous, and with a pioneering nature that opens up many opportunities for mankind. Their element air represents the need for personal space. None the less, they work best in groups, and indeed their sign represents friendship. You often find them working in the social services, where their friendly nature puts people at ease instantly. They are positive thinkers, even when things are at their bleakest. This sign would make a wonderful political leader, but it's something an Aquarian rarely wants to do.

The beauty of this sign is that while they say yes to everything you ask and smile sweetly, and then go and do exactly what they want, you feel that they did what you asked. They are great parents, giving their children the love they need but also understanding a teenager's need for privacy. They aren't too hot at housework. I remember a man who thought his Aquarian wife a perfect homemaker until he returned home early one day to find that a hired cleaner actually did all the work.

The Aquarian colours are significant to the water that they bear: electric blue and turquoise. These colours suit them well.

Young Aquarians need to be in a school that allows them to grow and develop. A strict environment will restrict their potential. And don't force them to do things they don't want to or to eat foods they don't like. Let them be who they are and they will grow and flourish beyond your wildest dreams.

Aquarians get on best with the opposite sex. Their admirers often think they can read them like a book but they should watch out. Clever Aquarius leads many an admirer up the garden path. You won't always know what's going on in their lives and you probably shouldn't ask, for they need space and time for themselves. They reveal only what they want to. Pry, and they'll disappear before you can say 'second chance'. Their weakness is that they often stay in relationships or jobs they have outgrown. For some reason, this sign, which can change the course of mankind with its discoveries, doesn't know how to get out of a bad personal situation.

Don't expect any amazing presents off your Aquarius lover. They are not the most generous of signs with their money. They are so courteous you will feel like royalty, but don't wait to be showered with gifts. Out shopping they are likely to be distracted as they strike up conversations. But they do seem to spend a lot on holidays.

Aquarians have a highly developed sense of duty and a deep understanding of human nature. They can be dedicated and single-minded in the pursuit of a goal they have set themselves. Work can be an Aquarian's life, and they do not fear long hours. They will take on the world if they can.

This is a character that is an asset to anybody's life. They have something to add to every conversation, and if you need help they have enough generosity of spirit to give it. You will never feel lonely with an Aquarius as a friend.

How to Spot an Aquarius

Many people born under this sign have startlingly blue eyes and crisp angular features. They can also be tall and loose limbed.

The Devil and the Angel

The DEVIL AQUARIAN listens to no advice and does exactly what he or she wants. This is not necessarily bad. Elvis's daughter Lisa Marie Presley, for example, has not allowed her public status to stop her doing anything that she needed to do in order to grow.

The ANGEL AQUARIAN is continuously growing on the inside and on the outside is determined to make the world a better place. The Angel Aquarian commits to a relationship with humanity (though they may not commit to a personal one, in case it stops their growth). Oprah Winfrey, who is always growing and developing and whose love for people and need to help has made a real change in the world, is an Angel Aquarian. Aquarian Charles Darwin's profession is typical of this sign too.

Aquarius Health and Development from Child to Adult

The Aquarius baby can be destructive in nature, and is likely to reject cuddly toys for an old slipper or blanket. None the less, this baby is forward and happy, and sure to bring joy into the life of any new parents. Don't leave this communicative sign alone for long. Aquarians demand your attention and need your approval of the new things they learn. They make more cooing noises than most babies and learn to talk quickly. They mimic all they can. They don't believe they have time to waste.

At five years of age they still love having an

audience. These are the five-year-olds that put on a show in the front room and charge neighbours and relations to see it. They have a keen business sense even at this tender age. Some people say they have an old head on young shoulders. But there will be many times when you are unable to get through to them. They are absolutely and resolutely individual, with an unusual and charming disposition. They get into trouble when you least expect it, and they do this to keep your attention. With five-year-olds, this can mean some awkward situations, so watch the tablecloths and ornaments.

At 11 they are popular with people of all ages, and although they probably have a best friend they will be members of numerous clubs and participate in many after-school activities. Their relationship with their special friend lasts through thick and thin. They are brilliant in many subjects at school but dunces in those they find dull, no matter how vital these subjects are. They reject routine and do things in their own time or not at all, including, I'm afraid, homework. But don't push them. They'll do it when they are ready and if they say they haven't it could be just a tease. There's no point in getting angry with an 11-year-old Aquarian. They will just laugh at you.

At 16 they have developed a keen business instinct and a capacity for hard work. They should be able to work for extremely long hours without feeling tired or fatigued. They are not very good at attending to detail, however, and prefer to leave this to others. This sign frequently suffers periods of nervous tension which can affect the digestion, particularly around exam times. Aquarians don't mollycoddle themselves and often abuse their health by sheer overindulgence. Any serious problems or worries usually occur for this sign around the ages of 19, 28 and 50.

At 21 they are often ready to get married and they make a fair-minded marriage partner and a good provider. Their home will be their castle. In many cases the marriage is affected not by extra-marital affairs but by their easy-going attitudes in financial matters. Their individuality has asserted itself over their capacity for hard work and they'd as soon be in the garden (or in the pub) as in the office. They live for today and feel sure that everything will come right in the end. Aquarians take a long time to mature. If you are married to one, hang around. You don't want to give up early and then miss out on the best bit.

At 40 they develop a much stronger personality and start to realize that life is what you make it. Many Aquarians only now start to climb the steep ladder towards security. They usually succeed, but you won't find them in a job that is routine. They may bite off more than they can chew and they won't be told wrong from right by others. A tiny number of Aquarians are always on the make, taking shortcuts and never going by the book, bordering on the dishonest if not downright criminal. But there are very few of those.

At 70 they can talk to people of all ages and backgrounds. But they've also developed a few unchangeable habits, like breakfast and lunch at rigidly set times and of precisely dictated dimensions. They never completely lose their marbles. No matter how whacky they may seem, they are probably humouring you. Don't lie to them. They'll catch you out. They will have plenty of hobbies and interests to keep them amused and alert. Even if it's just keeping an eye on a small investment they won't forget about it or get it wrong. This is what keeps an Aquarian going into a ripe old age.

Aquarian Careers . . .

Flight attendant. Your two loves joined together: meeting people and being in your element, the air.

Detective. You can get secrets out of anyone, and find out anything.

Spy. You give nothing away.

Comedian. Your sense of humour is second to none, but I can't guarantee everyone will get the joke.

. . . not so Aquarian Careers

Mortician. You'd go stir crazy without someone to talk to. You need to feel fully alive at all times (so you won't enjoy the company of the dead).

Strip artist. You couldn't reveal yourself to anybody like that. You need a little privacy, please.

Disco dancer. You hate too much noise and attention. You like to be quietly noticed.

Famous Aquarians

Princess Caroline of Monaco, singers Phil Collins, Natalie Imbruglia and Neil Diamond, actors Paul

Newman, Bridget Fonda, Mia Farrow and Jennifer Aniston, Harrods boss Mohammed Al Fayed, ballet dancer/actor Mikhail Baryshnikov, TV host Oprah Winfrey, Elvis's daughter Lisa Marie Presley, boxing champ Prince Naseem Hamed.

Health Sore Points

Aquarius rules the circulation and the ankles. You need to be careful you don't sprain your ankles. They are not as strong as they should be. (But then telling an Aquarian to slow down and think about what they are doing is like talking to a brick wall.) Legs can be prone to problems too.

You feel the cold more than most signs, thanks to your often poor circulation, and like Capricorn you have a tendency not to dress for the weather. So don't shiver in that slinky dress thinking you look great!

Aquarians are sensitive people and subject to periods of nervous tension. Nervousness often affects the digestion, and it is a particularly bad idea for a lovelorn Aquarius on a date with their beloved to be adventurous in their menu choices.

Aquarian women are more likely than other signs to suffer cramps during their period. Drink plenty of water and avoid alcohol at this time. (Alcoholic drinks dehydrate you and make you feel much worse.)

Your character is individual and so are your ailments. Many of your ailments are self-inflicted. With luck you'll have a strong partner keeping an eye on you.

Cures and Counsel

Don't let trivial emotional problems get the better of you. Aquarians attract more friends (and hangers-on) than most but make sure you are not doing without sleep trying to answer everyone's demands. It wouldn't be good for an Aquarius to try to exist on some silly amount of sleep like five hours a night. Without the correct amount of sleep you will not be able to think straight or make the correct decisions about important issues. Those are the times when trivial problems will grow out of proportion.

See pages 23–6 for general advice about sleeping. Remember an hour before bedtime not to do anything that will make it hard for you to sleep. Drinking wine will probably make you snore and will certainly prevent you from getting the depth of sleep your body requires. If you don't sleep deeply enough you won't feel refreshed when you wake up. End your evening with a relaxing bath and a cup of your favourite herbal tea. Valerian is the best one for your sign. It can be drunk hot or cold and is good with a slice of lemon. If you want to spoil yourself then drink it in the bath while you soak away the worries of the day. You should then find yourself drifting into peaceful sleep without any problem.

You must also make sure your lifestyle has the right amount of work and play in it. There is no point in working hard to keep a home you don't spend any time in, for example. Make time for relaxation and a little pampering and that way you'll ward off many health problems.

Wear comfortable shoes for your vulnerable legs and ankles. If your feet are hurting and your ankles are swollen then adjust your footwear. I know I'd rather have great legs in nice shoes at 50 than swollen ankles in high-heeled shoes at 30. (But you are not the worst sign for wearing bad shoes. That's Pisces! They are willing to limp for a month so long as they looked good for a night.) If you stand for long hours during the day and get pain down your legs you may even have to rethink your job. This is your body's early-warning system. You should pay it some attention.

Exercise is one of the best things you can do for your ankles and legs, and you cannot beat the power of water, in particular water aerobics. Join a class, or make up your own. Even just swimming a length a week will gradually build up stamina and strength and make your legs sleeker. Better still for Aquarius the air sign is a regular swimming class or exercise routine where you can settle down for a good old gossip afterwards. Anyway, some sort of exercise has got to be factored in to your social life. You'd stay at a party until you got kicked out, wouldn't you? Don't be scared that exercise will turn you into a mass of muscle. It took Arnold Schwarzenegger a lot of work to look like that you know! Get some advice from the instructors at your local swimming pool or gym if you are really worried about getting too muscly.

If you ski, consider getting extra ankle support to prevent injuries and stop you having your fun ruined.

Exercise will get the circulation going too. Children of this sign should be encouraged in school sports because at a young age they keep up even the hardest of sports just for the social aspect and could end up becoming experts. When Aquarians get older they work out that you can pretend to do some sports while sitting at the bar or in the restaurant of a sports centre looking good. Unfortunately for the rest of us, they probably do. We're the ones going red as beetroots working out every week and looking as flabby as ever. The Aquarian is still sitting there, unopened gym bag by the feet, looking perfectly trim. Life isn't fair and Aquarians have got it made in this area.

Aquarians always seek their own remedies before listening to advice from others. You've probably got home remedies lurking in the back of your cupboard somewhere. Uranus and Saturn, your ruling planets, do give you an interest in the health industry so your diet is usually pretty good. Like all air signs you are better sticking to a light and nourishing diet. Stodgy foods make you feel heavy. Crisps are out, I'm afraid. You could eat ten packets and still not be full, so try to reach for something more satisfying to munch on next time.

Just remember to keep the summer outfits for the summer and to get the winter scarves out when the snow starts falling. And if you give yourself half the time you give others you'll have a fantastic quality of life. The last person you think about is yourself and that needs to change.

Angelica Tea

Angelica helps relieve cold symptoms. It also stimulates the circulation, which is good for Aquarius, and it can ease indigestion. You should not take it, however, if you suffer from diabetes. If in doubt, consult your doctor.

Harvest the leaves for drying before the plant flowers. Cut the stems back only after the plant has flowered and you've collected the seeds. Make a tea from the dried leaves and sweeten with a little honey.

Cramp Remedy

Cramp seems to be prevalent in Aquarians and this is an old Romany cure. You can get all the ingredients from a good herbalist. This is not an immediate cure, but if you persevere with it you should find it a great reliever.

25 g/1 oz prickly ash bark
25 g/1 oz vervain
25 g/1 oz black cohosh root
1 tablespoon composition essence

Mix the herbs together well and divide into three portions. Boil one portion in 600 ml/1 pint water for 20 minutes, then cool and strain. Add 1 tablespoon composition essence (this is a hot peppery mixture). Take one wineglassful three times a day between meals. It's best when freshly made, so keep a stock of the ingredients to brew up more when this batch is finished.

Aquarius Power Juice

Some Aquarians say this has more effect on them than a stiff gin. Sit back and wait for it to kick in.

equal amounts of: apricot, blackcurrants, cherries, grapes, greengage, guava, kiwi fruit, melon, papaya, passion fruit, peach and raspberries

Start off with equal amounts of each fruit and then adjust the quantities to suit your own taste next time. Juice the fruit in a juicing machine or liquidizer. Chill before drinking or serve it over ice.

Good Aquarius Food

Aquarians need to be sure to get a good portion of sodium foods, and are susceptible to a deficiency in natrum muriaticum (a.k.a. sodium chloride), which could mean that the water in your body is not being controlled properly. This does not mean that you should reach for the salt shaker, though! You need to eat apples, spinach, Swiss chard, radishes and cos lettuce. These all come under the rulership of Aquarius (and of sun sign Taurus).

If you feel lethargic or you lack energy, the first thing is to cut out heavy foods. An Aquarian doesn't like to feel weighed down or bloated. That jacket potato is fine, but don't cover it with cheese. A little soured cream with chives would be good instead. Trade in the steak and kidney pie for the chicken pie, or better still for lightly poached chicken with a salad. Or try my heavenly Pasta Pacifico on page 354. Wholegrain rice is also a good food for you. It supplies energy-giving carbohydrate, B vitamins, iron, zinc and calcium, and should keep you feeling light enough to do all that's on your busy agenda.

Plants for Star Therapy

Foxglove is lucky for you. It grows wild in hedgerows and on the fringes of woods, but you can also get garden varieties in a wide range of beautiful colours from white to magenta. It blooms all summer and its tall spikes of bell-shaped flowers are strong, graceful and decorative. Why not try having some foxglove around the house or in your garden? Just the sight of it will calm you down and help you relax.

Health Checklist

- If you suffer from bad nerves, try ginseng, a plant that has long been used as a nerve tonic – but it is also a *stimulant.*
- The vitamin B complex is also good for nerves.
- For bad circulation try ginkgo biloba (from your health food store) or fish oil supplements. Add ginger to your cooking and eat plenty of tuna, salmon, pilchards, sardines, herring and mackerel.
- Vitamin E, in vegetable oils, eggs, peanuts, wholemeal bread, wheatgerm and green leafy vegetables, is also good for the circulation.
- For cramps look to magnesium supplements, and eat more seafood, pasta, peas, soya beans, nuts and wholemeal bread. Try brewer's yeast too.
- For nervous indigestion try peppermint tea.

Are You a True Aquarius?

Be honest! Write down 'yes' or 'no', then read the advice below.

1 Do you hate your own company?
2 Do you eat any of the following on a regular basis: apples, spinach, Swiss chard, radishes, lettuce, strawberries, pomegranates?
3 Have you ever had any problems with your nerves, legs or ankles?
4 Are you a very sensitive person?
5 Do you get talked into doing things you don't really want to do?
6 Have you stayed in a job you didn't like for longer than you know you should have?
7 Do you always try your own remedies before calling up the doctor or visiting the chemist?
8 Are you often told that you underdress for the weather?
9 Are you comfortably messy in your home?
10 Do you love electric blue and turquoise?
11 Do you have a private side a lot of friends don't really know about?
12 Have you ever sprained your ankle?
13 Would you say you were forgetful?
14 Do you get on more through your personality than your skills in the workplace?
15 Do you have your own style of doing everyday jobs?
16 Are your best friends fellow air signs (Libra and Gemini as well as Aquarius)?

17 Have you ever been told you live in a dream world?
18 Were you told off at school for not concentrating and having a 'faraway look' in your eyes?
19 Are you always able to see the funny side of a problem?
20 Do friends confide their deepest secrets to you?

If you answered 'yes' to most questions then you are a typical Aquarian. You need to be around people to feel alive and you want to be involved in everything. I hope that question 2 was among those you answered yes to. If not, do make an effort to eat more of these foods, all of which contain the vitamins you need.

Not always the tidiest of signs you probably live in what you would call 'an organized mess'. You like to analyse all the situations in your life, and besides your sociable side have a very private nature. If you are mixing a lot with other air signs then you are sure to be having an enjoyable social life. Just make sure you don't give away too many of your friends' secrets or you may start to find yourself short of invitations! You are sensitive and need to be constantly praised. You like to please others and so are quite easily bullied into doing things you don't want to. Being liked is a necessity for you. But make sure you're not letting others dictate your life to you.

If you answered 'no' to most questions you're not a typical Aquarian. Perhaps you don't feel as confident as you'd like to around new faces. The chances are you are holding back. Let all your good points show! An Aquarian need never have a boring time. Look at your moon sign, too, for more information about yourself. And maybe get a friend to go through this questionnaire with you. It can be hard to be completely honest about yourself. If you answered no to question 16, then try to get to know some other air signs. You may find you've been missing out on a good thing. Who knows, maybe a romance will blossom for the unattached. Above all, follow the health tips for your sign and look after yourself well.

The Drinker's Guide to the Zodiac

Just in case I need to remind you: go easy on the alcohol. Talkative Aquarians can drink and chat at great speed, and may be drinking more than they realize. Steer clear of shorts if you know it's going to be a long night. You'll last the pace and may be able to lift your head off the pillow the following morning.

Between the Sheets

The quietest of Aquarians will become daring after this. Don't drink it too often!

4 or 5 ice cubes
3 drops angostura bitters
1 teaspoon sugar or sugar syrup
1 part crème de cacao
1 part thin cream
2 parts brandy
1 slice of lemon

Put the ice cubes into a cocktail shaker. Pour the bitters, sugar, crème de cacao, cream and brandy over the ice. Shake until a frost forms, then strain and pour into a glass. Twist the lemon over the drink, drop it in and serve.

Star Menu

The best foods for an Aquarian are filling but light. The following recipes fulfil this slightly tricky order, so why not try them out.

Pasta Pacifico

This healthy dish has fish, whose essential vitamins combat stress and strengthen cells, and carbohydrate energy-booster tagliatelle. Serve with a tossed green salad for extra flavour and nutrients. Serves 4.

1 teaspoon butter
2 teaspoons olive oil
1 clove garlic, chopped
1 onion, chopped
50 g/2 oz button mushrooms, chopped
150 g/6 oz prawns, fresh or frozen, shelled
500 g/1 lb 4 oz fillet cod, in chunks
500 g/1 lb 4 oz fillet haddock, in chunks
120 ml/4 fl oz dry white wine
freshly ground black pepper
mixed herbs
cayenne pepper

salt
tagliatelle (egg pasta ribbons) (see packet instructions)
50 g/2 oz Cheddar cheese, grated
250 ml/10 fl oz crème fraîche
1 tomato, sliced
chopped fresh parsley, to garnish

Set a pot of water on to boil for the pasta.

Melt the butter in the olive oil in a frying pan and add the garlic, onion, mushrooms and prawns. Cook until the onions start to soften. Now add the cod and haddock and pour in the white wine. The fish will start to cook in the wine and juices. Season with black pepper, mixed herbs and a pinch of cayenne pepper.

Meanwhile, salt the boiling water, add the tagliatelle and cook until *al dente*. Drain the pasta.

Preheat the grill to hot.

When the fish is cooked (it will have lost its translucency), add the pasta to the sauce and toss well. Stir in the crème fraîche and transfer to a heatproof dish. Arrange slices of tomato on top and scatter with the grated cheese. Place under the hot grill until the cheese is brown and bubbling. Scatter with parsley and serve.

Carrot and Orange Soup

This is delicious and warming and capable of giving an Aquarian that kick-start they are always searching for. Serve with buttered fresh French bread.

50 g/2 oz butter
1 onion, chopped

450 g/1 lb carrots, sliced
salt and freshly ground black pepper
chopped fresh oregano
chopped fresh coriander
juice (or mashed flesh) of 1 large, juicy orange, such as a Florida orange
600 ml/1 pint vegetable stock, either home-made or store-bought

Melt the butter in a saucepan and add the onions and carrots. Cook slowly, making sure they do not burn. As the onion starts to soften, add the orange juice and stock, and salt, pepper, oregano and coriander to taste. Cook until the carrots are tender. Serve as it is or purée it in a blender. Either way, serve with a sprinkle of coriander on top.

Vanilla Walnuts

This recipe is also good with pecan nuts, and is a favourite with at least three Aquarians I know. A word of warning: these are so delicious you'll be tempted to finish them all up by yourself in the kitchen. Alert your friends and family to this possibility so they can save you from yourself.

125 g/4 oz sugar
2½ tablespoons corn oil
1 tablespoon vanilla extract
450 g/1 lb walnut halves
¼ teaspoon salt
¼ teaspoon ground coriander

¼ teaspoon ground cinnamon
¼ teaspoon nutmeg, preferably freshly grated
¼ teaspoon ground allspice

Preheat the oven to 230°C/450°F/gas 8.

In a mixing bowl combine the sugar, oil and vanilla. Blanch the walnuts for 1 minute in boiling water. Drain well and while still hot add to the sugar and oil mixture in the bowl. Toss well then leave to stand for 10 minutes.

Arrange the walnuts in a layer on a baking tray. Bake for 30 minutes until light brown and crispy, taking the tray out of the oven every 10 minutes or so to move the nuts around. Combine all the remaining ingredients in a bowl and toss the hot nuts in the mixture until they are evenly coated. Serve at once or store in an airtight container. They should keep a week – or 2 days in a Pisces household!

Star Beauty

Fresh air and exercise are a vital part of your beauty regime so make sure you do an outdoor activity at least once a week, even if it's just walking to a friend's or relative's house (preferably a friend or relative who lives a good leg-stretch away).

See page 281 for Scorpio's treatment for tired eyes: this would be good for you too.

Avoid heavily perfumed beauty and bath products. Your skin is too sensitive for them. Lovage is excellent to use in your bath instead of manufactured products and it acts as a purifier and a deodorant. Put some lovage leaves into a muslin bag and place in your bath water. You may also want to try the Scorpio bath oils (see page 282). They are subtle enough for your gentle skin too.

Strawberry Moisturizer

Your sensitive skin can react to even the faintest of perfumes in a moisturizer. Try this home-made one. It is perfect for your skin: rich in vitamins and enzymes and perfume free (except for the wonderful natural fragrance of strawberries, that is).

1 punnet of strawberries, hulled
1 teaspoon sugar for every 4 strawberries
2 teaspoons emulsifying wax
2 teaspoons almond oil
1 teaspoon distilled witch hazel
4 teaspoons mucilage of tragacanth, from a herbalist

Cook the strawberries and sugar together over a gentle heat, mashing them well, until you have a lovely strawberry sludge. Sieve the strawberries so that you are only left with the juice.

Melt the emulsifying wax in a heatproof bowl set in a saucepan of simmering water. Then add the almond oil, witch hazel and mucilage of tragacanth and stir well. Set aside to cool, then place in a spotlessly clean screw-top jar. Keep in the refrigerator and use it cold to moisturize your skin. It should last you a month: put the date you made it on the label.

Turmeric Face Mask

Stress often brings you out in spots. A great mask can be made up of ingredients in the kitchen cupboard.

1 teaspoon sea salt
2 teaspoons clear honey
1 teaspoon turmeric

Combine the sea salt, honey and turmeric, spread on your face, avoiding the eye area, and relax for 25 minutes. Then wash off with warm water and a sponge.

Your Ideal Health Sign Holiday

A club holiday is the answer for you. You need to talk to as many people as possible when you're on holiday and so it suits you to be part of a group. You'll get to know everyone in five minutes flat, and will love having people to share your experiences and laughter with.

PISCES

THE FISHES

Ruling Planet: Jupiter, the planet of self-expansion, and Neptune, the planet of confusion

Triplicity or Element: Water

Quadruplicity or Mode: Mutable

Key words: Emotional, sensitive, moody, imaginative, impressionable, changeable

The Origin of Pisces

The two fishes were at one time Venus and Cupid. They turned themselves into fishes to escape Typhon the giant, and were placed in the heavens, their constellation becoming part of the zodiac.

What Pisces is Like

What an individual sign this is. The two fishes swimming in opposite directions represent the dual nature of Pisceans. They want to do everything and go everywhere at once. If only they realized that by swimming in both directions at once they are not getting anywhere!

This is the most psychic sign of the zodiac. If they have a feeling about something or someone, they are right 99 per cent of the time. You can trust their hunches. If they dislike someone for no apparent reason, then that person is certain to do something in the future that will prove the Piscean right.

The Pisces element is water and all Pisces should live near water if they can. If not, they should have a bowl of water in their room. It may sound crazy but I know enough Pisceans to know that it works. Soft shades of green remind them of the sea and empower them.

This character appears strong and unstoppable but is in reality incredibly sensitive. Pisceans are likely to be suffering silently if you have hurt them. They are compassionate and kind, selfless and sympathetic. There is nothing they would not do for those they love. They are, however, easily led and can be secretive. Their biggest downfall is their susceptibility to addiction. I'm afraid there are a lot of Pisceans in drug and alcohol rehabilitation clinics. This means Pisces need to take extra care. If you think something might become addictive, please don't try it, even if you are really curious about the effect.

Because they spend so much time helping others, the fishes often neglect their own lives. They help other people's dreams become reality but don't give enough time to their own. There is also a lazy streak that can kick in every now and then. And yet Pisceans are versatile enough for almost any career, and in particular make great musicians, gifted at whichever instrument they choose. Indeed they should be sure to go into a profession that is artistic. Not to exploit their main talent would be a crime. If they don't go into the arts you can be sure they will do something artistic in their spare time. They also often go into the caring professions, and plough a lot of money into charities. But don't be fooled into thinking they are a pushover: there are many layers to their dramatic and loving personalities.

Don't believe everything Pisceans say. Their hearts may be in the right place but they have a tendency to stretch the truth and make their stories more colourful. It is the entertainer in them that makes them tell a story in all its glory plus a little bit more. They don't always face reality, and this can make living with them difficult for the more practical and pragmatic among us. You have to keep telling them what is going on in 'the real world'. On the other hand, they give off sexual vibes hotter than anyone, so that can't be bad.

The ruling planets are Jupiter and Neptune. Jupiter

represents self-expansion and the need to keep on moving through life. Pisces can get through bad experiences. They learn from them and can even enjoy the challenge. Sometimes they create bad experiences for themselves, rather like Scorpio does, just to see what it feels like. They just need to make sure they can get out of these situations they create, and without wasting a lot of time.

Their dual rulers can give Pisceans split personalities and make them difficult to understand. It's not just you who cannot understand Pisceans. They often cannot understand themselves.

If a Pisces loves you it will be with all of his or her heart. Pisceans need love in order to live, and they also need a good partner to balance them and stop them going off the rails. This is the young woman who would work to put her husband through college and wouldn't even think about the sacrifice that she was making. However, I'm sure that years later she would make it into a colourful tale of bread crusts and woe.

This, along with Cancer, is a sign of the zodiac that really shouldn't drink. Drink affects fishes badly and even seems to change them into different people. Mind you, they will deny they are drunk, even when they are falling over in the process.

Pisceans stay in the mind. If you meet them just once, you won't forget them. They mix well with people of all ages, and talk to kings just as easily as to paupers. The famous or rich of this sign usually take their lives right to the limit.

Just try not to hurt a Pisces. They put themselves up for it, and have masses of love to give, but need protecting in return. This is a sign that is as deep as the sea, and if they have any secrets they will take them to the grave.

How to Spot a Pisces

Their eyes are widely spaced, intense and also rather watery. Some people call these eyes 'bug' or 'almond' eyes.

The Devil and the Angel

The DEVIL PISCEAN is a dramatist and likes to dice with drink, drugs and the extreme side of life. Drew Barrymore, who starred in *ET*, was on cocaine and alcohol before she even reached her teens. She now talks openly about it and tells a few colourful stories, and has also shown how a Piscean can turn their life around with determination. The fact that she is an actor is also typical of her sign.

The ANGEL PISCEAN is a pure artist and loves nothing more than painting, drawing and sharing his or her talents with the world. Michelangelo was a perfect Angel Piscean, and his artwork in the Sistine Chapel speaks for itself.

Pisces Health and Development from Child to Adult

The Pisces baby will show its true self as soon as it emerges from the womb. Indeed, this is the only time you will see Pisceans without all the dramatics they soon start to display. They are attention-seekers. Day by day this baby will prove how noisy and impatient it really is and I doubt the parents will get a whole night's sleep in the first year. Their faces are full of personality and their eyes will tell you what they are thinking long before they discover the wonderful world of speech.

At five years of age a selfish streak develops, and it is important to suppress this before it gets too well developed. Sharing toys will be unheard of, and the small fishes will even make up an imaginary friend who is all theirs and no one else's. Remember, Mum, you can take away a toy but you can't take away an imaginary friend. They are becoming very sensitive now and you may think they've been bullied and beaten up when they come home in floods of tears, but more likely they've been called a name, as that is all it takes. They feel misunderstood at school, and at home they moan and groan until their parents give in and make concessions, which are usually a lot more generous than the situation warranted. The beleaguered parents are thinking: 'Anything for a quiet life!'

It will become obvious that the Pisces child at 11 years of age is both a bookworm and a born leader. Parents would be wise to watch for faults that could become ingrained if not checked. Idleness, arrogance and a tendency to bully can emerge and stand out in school reports. But they are extremely popular. If they decide to have a party on the same day as a schoolmate, then the schoolmate might as well give in, because popularity is in the fishes' favour. They are already aware of the opposite sex and they enjoy the power that their evergrowing sexuality grants them. No, not behind the bike sheds – they are too dramatic and important for all that.

At 16 the classic pattern for this birth sign will be emerging. Their moods and tastes change like the wind and they flirt like there's no tomorrow. Don't buy them expensive clothes. They will have moved on to a new style before you've paid off the credit-card bill. When young Pisces starts to work, they feel they should be the boss straight away, and they risk being sacked again and again for insolence and laziness. But watch out at 16 for the birth of a flair for business. This is a sign that can make money, and it will be spent on loved ones. Parents will be repaid for the fashions they had to splash out on. But it's easy come, easy go. They'd blow every last penny on a party for all their friends if the mood took them. This is also the age to start watching over Pisceans where drink and drugs are concerned. This is an addictive personality. Pisceans can get so deep into something there's no turning back.

At 21 their friends are thinking about settling down with one person. Not the fishes though. They rarely fall into that tender trap until at least 23. Their roving eye costs them many a relationship. They discover that if they give someone enough attention that person will fall for them, and it's all just too tempting. Clever talking usually gets them out of serious trouble. If they let you down for a date it will not be because the car broke down, but because they were caught in a shoot-out and had to give mouth-to-mouth to an injured policeman. They go through life with a swagger, but don't be deceived. This is often a disguise for their lack of confidence.

By 40 they will have married in fact if not in spirit.

They still fancy every attractive face or cute body they see (or cute legs, in the case of the Piscean). They spend their money freely but want their partner to account for every penny – yes, they even want to see receipts. As far as making a home is concerned, they are Mr or Mrs Permanent-Temporary. They leave their homes half-finished, never really regarding one fixed place as home. One of their more lovable traits begins to show at this age: they often pick up lame dogs, but this doesn't always go down well with their partner.

At 70 it's a case of look out, here comes another Peter Pan. About this time the fishes become bored with the same old routine, and go missing on secret day-trips of exploration. They are secret gamblers and may even decide to run a poker circle – all with people of the opposite sex, of course! They may be getting a bit long in the tooth but they still see themselves as a bit of a stunner. The trouble is Piscean health hazards are making themselves felt, especially bad feet and occasionally chest problems. Hardly romantic, is it! The liver may play up a little too, probably through overindulging in drink in their forties. Years of eating irregularly, drinking to excess and generally abusing their health will start to take their toll. However, there is no real worry. Piscean health, although not quite 100 per cent, never really takes as big a knock as it deserves.

Piscean Careers . . .

Clairvoyant or astrologer. You are a natural psychic.

Champion swimmer. You feel more at home in water than out of it.

Writer. You could write for ever and never run out of ideas.

Estate agent. You'd convince your clients that a semi was really a castle.

. . . not so Piscean Careers

Fish and chip shop, or fish restaurant owner. My god, you couldn't kill your own kind.

Waitress. No one would ever get their food. You'd be too busy talking and telling tales.

Marathon runner. Your feet couldn't take it.

Any job that entails telling the whole truth.

Famous Pisceans

Singers Nat King Cole, Nina Simone, Michael Bolton and Fats Domino, ex-Beatle George Harrison, jailed Barings dealer Nick Leeson, Impressionist artist Pierre Auguste Renoir, composer George Frederick Handel, actors Elizabeth Taylor, Rex Harrison and Sharon Stone, physicist Albert Einstein.

Health Sore Points

Pisces rules the feet. The fishes must watch out for swollen ankles and water retention. Because you are ruled by Jupiter and Neptune, you are affected by chills, gout and sluggishness of the liver. Your planets also make you extremely empathetic and if a close one is feeling ill you are likely to get the same illness.

Your most common fault is buying, out of vanity, shoes that do not fit and are not good for your feet. You are born under such a sexy sign that you always want to look good, and you believe in suffering for beauty.

Then there's that addictive personality, which can lead to dependence on drink, nicotine or drugs.

Cures and Counsel

Pisceans must look after their feet. Promise yourself to go for regular checks at the chiropodist. You don't have to have a problem to go for a check-up. If the chiropodist sees something developing, he or she can prevent it.

Ideally all Pisceans would have partners who can stop them losing track of life and getting too involved in bad situations. It wouldn't occur to a Pisces to get out of a bad situation unless someone else pointed it out. A Piscean can get into a bad habit and stay with it for years because it so quickly felt like normality. Pisces, listen to good advice – your instinct will tell you what's good – and listen to what your body tells you too. You may kid yourself that seven days in a row on the town is not harming your health but you must remember your tendency to succumb to addiction. You, even more than fellow water signs Cancer and Scorpio, need to keep a close watch over what you are doing with your life.

You are more likely than many others to have an out-of-the-ordinary job, which makes it all the more important to work on your lifestyle, whether you are a secretary or a movie star, a caretaker or a pilot of a 747. You must work out if you are eating the right foods, getting enough sleep and that you feel as you should. We all know the times when we feel at our best and it is up to us to create the situations that make us feel good as often as possible.

Regular mealtimes are one answer. These are periods when you know you must sit down, relax and eat well, letting stress fade away. Don't allow yourself to make excuses not to eat comfortably and well. Snacking is a habit of people born under this sign and varied eating patterns can give you digestive problems as well as contributing to that knot of anxiety. A regular eating pattern will enable you to work out more quickly which foods disagree with you, too. It's too easy to forget that snack on the run, or to pretend you never had it. Watch out for following the bad habits of friends, too. They may have them better in control. You are not so good at drawing the line, and one drink for your friend will end up as five for you.

Pisceans are not the best dieters in the world. You are too tempted by the latest food fads and too good at convincing yourself that you didn't really eat that whatever it was two hours earlier. Or that because that chocolate bar is low-calorie you can eat five of them. You're a snacker, and you're also inclined to get hooked on particular foods. Like many people you sometimes turn to food and drink to make your problems go away. You'll eat a whole plateful of food as a between-meals snack, not out of piggishness but because you are on an emotional roller-coaster. We all know food doesn't solve emotional problems (especially when your ex gets to see you waddling up the road). If you want to moderate or reduce your intake, better get a good friend or partner to help you, ideally one who can cook and prepare food for you.

If you overindulge in drink you'll know what a sluggish liver can feel like. It's something Pisces are prone to, so it will be up to you to set your own pace and not try to set a record. Dandelions are excellent for the liver, and what's more are your lucky plant. Try the dandelion coffee on page 187.

One of the individual things about a Pisces is that they must have a vice in life. Whether it is cigarettes or chocolate cake, they need to let a little of the devil come through. It's largely for effect, so they may only do it in front of their loved ones, but it is a key part of the Pisces character. Acknowledge it, but keep it on a tight rein if you can.

Your artistic and creative nature can get you into situations that are bad for your health. You, more than other signs of the zodiac, create your own ailments by living life to the extreme. You don't have the word moderation in your vocabulary. You can get so wrapped up in your emotions that you eat when you are sad, or bored, or in love, instead of when you are hungry. Try not to eat for the sake of it. If a Piscean puts on weight he or she often tells friends, 'I don't know how I put it on, I hardly eat a thing.' Lucky for you you don't usually finish everything on the plate. Like Libra, you like the look of a dish first, and are more interested in savouring taste than in consuming quantity.

You'll probably find you simply cannot eat food quickly. All the more reason for ensuring you have relaxed mealtimes. If you take your time over a meal you should be able to avoid indigestion. Make sure you include the foods recommended for you below to ward off rheumatism, chest or feet problems. If you really can't find time to cook or eat well because of your busy and dramatic lifestyle, then take supplements to keep you as fighting fit as you need to be.

It's no good my telling you to get lots of exercise. You probably hate exercise, don't you? Well swimming is ideal for you. To you it doesn't even feel like exercise, just being in your element.

Fancy Footwork

- Think about investing in a foot spa, or else make your own footbath from a washing-up bowl. Add a few drops of mint, yarrow, rosemary, camomile or lavender essential oil to the water. Lavender is especially good as a pick-you-up before a night out. Salt is another good ingredient for a footbath. After the bath sprinkle alum powder on tired or sore feet. It's a good healer and hardener.

  If you can't be bothered with the bowl of water and you are too tired to think straight, then simply relax and elevate your feet on some pillows. If you suffer from aching veins this will allow the pressure to subside and the circulation to go back to normal.
- Foot massage is an important part of a Pisces routine. Do it after your bath or footbath, when your feet are relaxed and warm. Dry feet first. Rub each toe with small circular movements and then pull it

gently. Then, using both hands and again in circular movements, stroke and knead the sole of the foot and then the top of the foot. It may feel strange massaging your own feet but it is probably the best way. A partner's attempts usually last about 30 seconds. Many of my Piscean clients say, 'If you want the job done properly, then do it yourself'!

Foot massage can even help relieve monthly cramps and pains. The best place to apply pressure is around the Achilles tendon, just behind the ankle.

- Get in the habit of doing foot exercises. This is one my Piscean mother used to do. Sit down and simply roll a jar or milk bottle backwards and forwards under the feet. My mother did this with a glass milk bottle, but not everyone gets these now. A jar of mayonnaise will do. (You won't be opening it!) Use it cool from the refrigerator and it will soothe aching or swollen feet at the same time.

Try picking up pencils with your toes. This strengthens the muscles.

If your feet feel tense or you've been wearing unsuitable shoes, then kick off your shoes and stand with your feet apart and your hands at the top of your legs. Bend your left knee and now put all of the weight on the ball of the right foot. Bounce three times and then repeat with your right leg. This exercise will loosen up cramped feet.

If you are sitting on the settee at home or even at a desk at work, kick off your shoes. Curl your toes as tightly as you can and then release them, stretching out as far as you can. This helps relax tense feet too.

Remedy for Chilblains

Don't let your feet suffer! This remedy is soothing if you have chilblains.

rough kitchen salt
half a lemon or onion

Soak your feet in hot water into which you've put a handful of rough salt. When you've had enough, dry them and rub them with lemon or onion.

Elderberry Cold Remedy

To keep colds at bay.

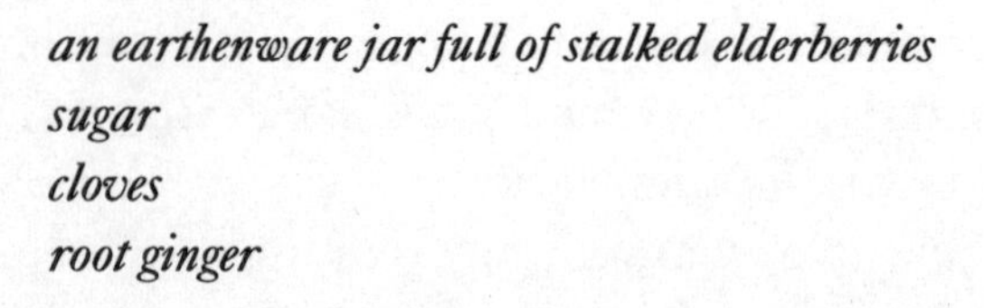

an earthenware jar full of stalked elderberries
sugar
cloves
root ginger

Cover the jar with a tight-fitting lid. Put into a low oven and leave until the juice starts to flow. Pour this off into a pan. Squeeze the berries through muslin to get the last drops. To every 600 ml/1 pint of juice add 250 g/8 oz of loaf sugar, half a dozen cloves and a small piece of bruised root ginger. Put the pan over a low heat and gradually bring to the boil. Simmer for 25 to 30 minutes, then strain and leave to cool. When completely cool, pour into bottles and cork securely. Dilute to taste with hot water if you feel a cold coming on.

Pisces Juice Booster

This is the best health drink for a Pisces.

2 pineapple slices
1 mango, skinned, flesh cut from around stone

Juice it and drink it. If you don't have a juicing machine, you have to mash and sieve the flesh. I recommend investing in a juicing machine and juicing to your heart's content.

Good Pisces Food

Pisceans often lack the cell salt ferrum phosphoricum, or phosphate of iron. This helps keep the blood red and makes sure that the circulation is what it should be. This is especially important for the fishes, who need good circulation to keep their feet warm and healthy. Iron is also essential for preventing low blood pressure, anaemia, inflammation, gastritis and rheumatism.

Phosphate of iron has a great affinity for oxygen and is the means by which oxygen enters the bloodstream. If you are getting enough you should both look and feel healthier. Green leafy vegetables are an essential source. You can also get iron from dark chocolate, but I advise you to go for the vegetable much more often than the sweet. There are some fantastic recipes for you later in this chapter.

Don't overcook leafy vegetables or you will lose the essential iron ingredient.

There are many foods that will give you the range of nutrients you need and the ones that fall under the rulership of your sign include dried peas, beans, spinach, lettuce, raisins, prunes, dates, figs, nuts, cereals, root vegetables and fresh fruit. There's plenty there for you to choose from. Don't forget about variety. With your intense nature you are likely to spend three months eating just one of these foods. There will also be certain foods that you cannot abide and will always say no to.

You enjoy your food but you really do find it hard to stick to regular eating times. Growing up with a Piscean mother, I never knew when lunch or dinner was going to be ready. It was my Libran father who always made sure we ate at the right times and that dinner was on the go when I came home. But then again I fondly remember my mother cooking for ten if I came home at two in the morning with an array of friends for a party. She could cook up a storm at any time of the day or night and she always enjoyed it. After a night out at a nightclub my friends would always say, 'Let's go back to Claire's for some food, I'm sure Eva will be up.' And she always was and boy did she cook!

It's hard to tell the children of this sign what they should eat. They know fairly early in life what they will and won't put in their mouths and it is no use trying to convince them otherwise.

Although you don't have an awful lot of discipline where food is concerned, you are good at helping others. Pisceans make great parents and always ensure their children get the best food. Go for dinner at their house and you will see the five thousand fed but there is unlikely to be enough for them to have a plateful themselves. It is all or nothing depending on their mood. Pisceans need to learn to give themselves some of the same care they give to others.

I know one Pisces who has the figure of a skeleton. She won't eat any fried food or any meat, but if you put a box of chocolates in front of her it will be gone within half an hour. This is a typical Pisces. Find their weakness and you've got them. So find yours and know it. Then all you have to do is find some support and determination to learn how your body works and what it really needs. You must also learn that it is not your job to take care of the whole wide world!

Plants for Star Therapy

The dandelion is your lucky flower and although you may spurn it as a weed I can tell you that in Arctic regions large expanses of this flower are considered one of the most beautiful sights of their short summer. The young leaves are used in many countries in salads and are fantastic against rheumatism.

Health Checklist

- Pisces, like all water signs, need to watch their capacity for addiction, whether to people, situation, food, drugs or drink.
- For rheumatism try evening primrose oil, devil's claw or starflower (borage) oil from your health food store.
- For any chest problems Omega 3 oil, which can be

found in fresh tuna, salmon, pilchards, sardines, herring, mackerel and linseeds. Evening primrose oil is also good, as is antioxidant vitamin A which is in cod liver oil, butter, cheese and eggs. An extremely important thing to avoid if you suffer chest pain is caffeine.

- For chills or feet problems, ginkgo biloba should do the trick. It helps to maintain healthy blood circulation.
- For gout, try zinc, vitamin B6 (found in wholemeal bread, liver, fish, bananas, wheatbran, yeast extract and brewer's yeast) or calcium and magnesium.
- If you suffer any sluggishness of the liver, try de-toxing for a fortnight. There are a number of well-researched books available on de-toxing; make sure you de-tox safely, and follow their advice carefully.

Are You a True Pisces?

Be honest! Write down 'yes' or 'no', then read the advice below.

1 When you are in a relationship does your loved one become the centre of your universe?
2 Do you eat any of the following foods on a regular basis: green leafy vegetables, raisins, dates, nuts, cereals?
3 Have you ever had any problems with your feet?
4 Do you do things to an extreme?
5 Do you rarely stop drinking when you've had enough?

6 Do you have intense friendships and then move on when the friendship has run its course?
7 Do you do the opposite of what a close one says just to prove a point?
8 Have you ever gone into a situation you knew was bad just to see what it felt like?
9 Do you feel happier when you are near water, such as in the bath or near the sea?
10 Do you dramatize your life?
11 Do you buy shoes for the look rather than comfort?
12 Are you of a jealous nature?
13 Are you lazy?
14 Do your tastes outweigh your income?
15 Are you naturally artistic?
16 Can you judge people well, even after only one meeting?
17 Do friends describe you as dreamy?
18 Are you unable to understand the word 'no' when friends say it to you?
19 Were you a 'wise old child'?
20 When life is at its best do you forget little things like eating?

If you answered 'yes' to most questions you truly are a typical Pisces. Try not to be too dramatic, or get too involved in things that aren't good for you, or you may find yourself in a situation you cannot get out of. Use water therapy to relax, and try to make some time each week to consider if what you are doing is what you really want. If you answered yes to question 11 then it's time to get some comfortable footwear. Keep the fancy stuff for special occasions. Go barefoot at home.

Consult a chiropodist if you have real problems with your feet. If you answered yes to question 14, make sure you don't hide your expenses from your partner, or you could be putting your relationship in jeopardy. Honesty is always the key to Piscean problems. Tell the truth and don't talk yourself out of a good relationship, which if you are a typical Pisces you will have done at some point in the past. Be careful of your tendency to make more out of a situation than is necessary. I'm sure you know the difference between what's daring and what's stupid!

I hope you answered yes to question 2. Take special note of the vitamins you can take if your lifestyle is a busy one. Give yourself the respect you deserve.

If you answered 'no' to most questions perhaps you need to relax into your sign a little more. It's one thing to resist the lure of extremes but it is quite something else to deny the dramatic side of your nature completely. Let your hair down a little and try to enjoy yourself. Who knows, you may have fun.

If you answered no to question 2, I recommend you do some work on your diet. Make sure these foods are going on to your table regularly. Try the recipes that follow and those in the chapter at the end of this book, The Romany Use of Herbs.

If you answered no to question 1, then well done. You've avoided the typical Pisces trap of throwing yourself hook, line and sinker into a relationship. Or maybe it just hasn't happened to you yet. In that case, be aware of the possibility and watch out it doesn't creep up on you.

Have a look at your moon sign. If it is in a fire sign – Aries, Leo or Sagittarius – you'll be more of a go-getter than many a Pisces. Then again, why not get a friend to go through the questionnaire again with you. They might uncover some little white lies, or remind you of a few times in your life when you did the very things you are denying!

The Drinker's Guide to the Zodiac

I cannot stress too strongly that Pisces are very weak in the alcohol department. The expression 'to drink like a fish' was probably invented for you. But I can't leave you out of my drinker's guide to the zodiac. Just remember the word 'moderation'.

Red Lady

I invented this Red Lady to bring colour to Piscean cheeks. The only trouble is, the colour may still be there the following day! Drink stirs the Pisces imagination. Not only do they see double, but everything they say will have a double meaning too.

3 ice cubes
3 parts red wine (burgundy, claret or vino tinto)
1 part vodka

Put the ice cubes in a glass jug. Pour the wine and vodka over the ice and stir vigorously. Strain and pour into a chilled Martini glass.

Star Menu

The best foods for a Pisces have a seductive quality. This soulful sign will look for meaning behind the dish you are about to serve them, so think about what you'd like to convey. Try serving oysters. Your Pisces lover is sure to get your drift.

French Onion Soup

This has the depth of flavour and sophisticated style the Piscean is always looking for.

1 kg/2 lb onions, thinly sliced
2 tablespoons vegetable oil
4 teaspoons sugar
salt and freshly ground black pepper
600 ml/1 pint vegetable stock
2 cloves garlic, crushed
a few drops of lemon juice
French bread
4 tablespoons grated Gruyère cheese
chopped fresh parsley

Sauté the onions in the oil in a large frying pan for 10 minutes or until soft. Add the sugar, season with salt and pepper and cook for another 15 to 20 minutes over a low heat, allowing the onions to brown but not burn. Stir from time to time. Add the stock, garlic and lemon juice, bring to the boil and then simmer for 10 minutes.

Preheat the grill to hot. Check and adjust the

seasoning of the soup and ladle it into bowls that you can put under the grill. Top each bowl with a slice of French bread sprinkled with Gruyère cheese and parsley, and place under the hot grill until bubbling and brown. Serve at once.

Hamburger Steaks Baked with Cream

This is an out-of-the-ordinary hamburger, which will impress visitors, especially if they have dropped by – although it's so delicious the Pisces may eat it all themselves!

750 g/1½ lb minced beef
125 g/4 oz dried breadcrumbs
4 tablespoons chopped onion
1 egg
1½ tablespoons Worcestershire sauce
salt and freshly ground black pepper
25 g/1 oz butter
2 carrots, chopped
2 sticks celery, chopped
1 tablespoon flour
240 ml/8 fl oz single cream
1 can cream of celery soup

Combine the beef, breadcrumbs, onion, egg, Worcestershire sauce and salt and pepper to taste. Form into 8 patties.

Preheat the oven to 200°C/400°F/gas 6.

Melt the butter in a frying pan and fry the burgers on both sides until well browned. Transfer to a baking dish large enough to take them in one layer. Sauté the carrot and celery in the fats remaining in the pan. Add the flour and stir well. Combine the cream and soup and add to the vegetables. Simmer and allow to blend well and thicken. Pour over the patties and cover tightly with tin foil. Bake for 1 hour and then serve immediately on hamburger buns.

Top Secret Steak Sauce

Guests are sure to think you've slaved for hours to make this fabulous sauce. A friend of mine goes so far as to serve it up with chips during the week when she is feeling daring!

1 bottle Heinz chilli sauce
1 bottle mango chutney
1 bottle Worcestershire sauce
¼ tablespoon cognac or brandy
1 tablespoon Dijon mustard
1 teaspoon sugar
2 drops red or green food colouring (optional)

Combine the ingredients in a blender until smooth. If you put this in a fancy bottle it makes an excellent present.

Rock Cakes

Delicious and super-easy to make.

200 g/7 oz self-raising flour
½ teaspoon mixed spice
125 g/4 oz butter, softened
7 tablespoons unrefined light brown sugar
125 g/4 oz mixed dried fruit
1 egg, beaten with 1 tablespoon milk
a little extra butter for greasing

Preheat the oven to 200°C/400°F/gas 6.

Sift the flour into a mixing bowl and add in the butter. Lightly rub together with your fingers, then sift in the spice with two-thirds of the sugar, the dried fruit and the egg and milk mixture. Mix lightly so that the mixture just holds together. Spoon heaped tablespoons of the mixture on to a greased baking tray, leaving room for spreading, then sprinkle with the rest of the sugar. Bake for about 15 minutes, or until lightly browned. Transfer the rock cakes using a wide spatula (they are quite fragile) to a wire rack to cool down a little. Eat while still warm.

Star Beauty

Look after your feet and the rest of your body will follow. Neglect them and you'll feel the effects all over. Squash your feet into ill-fitting shoes and the discomfort will show on your face. Wearing high heels all the time will give you a bad back, besides possible corns, bunions and calluses. Feet work harder than any other part of your body. Did you know that a quarter of all your bones are in your feet? You cannot do anything unless your feet feel good.

Pisces Skin Lotion

This old Romany secret for good skin came to me from my mother, herself a Pisces. She started using this recipe just before she read the palms of the Beatles in the Sixties and she swears her beautiful skin was her ticket backstage.

We use this lotion under make-up. It sets foundation and powder beautifully.

25 g/1 oz red dock root, chopped up
50 g/2 oz elder flowers
50 g/2 oz pure lard or substitute
1 teaspoon pure lemon juice
50 g/2 oz plain cold cream

Put the dock root, elder flowers, lard and lemon in a heatproof glass dish and heat slowly in a medium pre-heated oven for 1 hour. Then strain, allow to cool and mix in with the cold cream. Keep in the fridge in an airtight container.

Cabbage Cleanser (for the insides!)

I must tell you the secret of cabbage water. Keep the water you've cooked your cabbage in, and drink it, hot or cold. It purifies and cleanses the blood and gets rid of pimples. It's also got plenty of iron. Once you see the good it can do you, you'll start to enjoy the taste of it. 'A good skin comes from within,' as my mother always told me.

Your Ideal Health Sign Holiday

Paris is the perfect holiday destination for you. You can enjoy the beauty of the capital and have a watery walk by the river Seine. You soak up the experience and go home with memories you'll never forget.

Moon Signs

AT THE BACK of this book you will find an ephemerides, which will tell you not only which sign your sun is in, but also which sign your moon is in. Just look up the entry for the date, day and time of your birth. Some people find that their moon is in their mother's sun sign. Curious but true. But why bother with your moon sign? Isn't it enough just to get to know your sun sign?

Think about the times when you said something and then wished you hadn't. Or when you revealed a secret you know you shouldn't have, and you don't understand what made you say it. It's not you, it's the stars. If you learn about how they control you, then you will learn more about yourself.

Your sun sign reveals your true self but it does not always tell you how other people see you. Your moon sign reveals how you will intuitively and instinctively react and respond. It governs your first reactions, and it reveals how other people will see you. Knowing more about your moon sign can add to your understanding of yourself, and save you from many a blunder.

Your moon sign may also explain why you suffer

from ailments or health problems you didn't think were associated with your sign. Someone with their moon in Pisces may go for the dramatic shoe styles that sun in Pisces prefers, and develop typical Piscean foot problems as a result.

Moon in Aries

You are very positive about life and great at giving others confidence in themselves. You are also quick to jump to conclusions about people, and find it hard to keep your emotions in check. You can be bold, rebellious, impudent and physical. You rush in where angels fear to tread, and find yourself in inadvisable situations. You often make decisions too quickly for the liking of your close ones, who might be trying to slow down your impatient impulses. 'More haste less speed' is something you are likely to have been advised, although you are unlikely to have been able to heed it.

You do not always think about the consequences of your actions and later may regret them. You are often the mouthpiece for others, saying what everyone else is thinking, and this probably landed you in trouble at school. I'll bet you were no stranger to detention. You will achieve a lot in life because you have the edge over many others. You are not afraid to ask for promotion or a pay rise. Your gut instinct can be relied on. You lack patience, of course, and you need a partner who can keep up with your fast-paced lifestyle. Just be careful that you do not allow this assertiveness to turn into aggression or you could find yourself in unnecessary physical disputes.

You need action and excitement and have a quick temper. You tend to put yourself first and some friends may regard you as selfish. Passionate and fervent, your love life is often spontaneous and most definitely at its best when unplanned.

You are prone to some of the Aries ailments, namely problems linked to the head, such as migraines and headaches. Clumsy and prone to knocks and bruises, you are too busy 'doing' to remember about 'thinking'. Turn to the Aries chapter and read the health advice there. Try to think a little more before you speak. People with their moon in Aries have a head like a pressure cooker, so full of gossip held in under stress that thoughtless words always leak out!

Moon in Taurus

You need stability, reliability and constant loving support. A secure group of people around you is vital. However, you handle difficulties in life better than most signs. You are a cautious and deliberate soul. Development is slow, unlike the moon in Aries people, and you can sometimes think so long and hard about what you should be doing that you miss the boat. Everything you do will be considered and reconsidered just to make sure that nothing can go wrong. You love luxury and need to feel comfortable with your surroundings in order to operate successfully. Beautiful objects and possessions give you confidence.

You are honest and hardworking and you don't like to take shortcuts. You like to feel you are doing everything thoroughly and well. You would never intentionally hurt anyone. Indeed, you go out of your way to help those you love or those who cannot help themselves. You offer help so often that you may sometimes regret it. You have a life of your own to lead too, you know. Deliberate though you are, even some of your promises are unintentionally made.

Your need for both mental and physical stability can make you look insecure to new partners and friends in your life. You can give the impression that you are not competent, but as soon as anyone gets to know you they will discover how untrue this is. Your professionalism always eventually shines through. Be careful of impulse spending, and especially of spending more than you can afford to. If the money is in your pocket and you see something nice, it will be in a bag two seconds later and you will arrive home wondering what on earth possessed you to spend money you couldn't afford to.

You may be prone to some of the ailments Taureans suffer from, in particular throat problems. Turn to the chapter for Taurus and read up on the precautions you should be taking. Learning not to waste money on things you don't need or even really want will also do you a lot of good.

Moon in Gemini

You have an answer for everything, and an opinion on everything. At school you thought you could do your teachers' jobs better than they could. You told them so too, which caused some problems. You're versatile and capable of doing more than one thing at once. Your friends know you to be a chatterbox, always having to get your word in and say what you think or feel about other people's business. The annoying thing is you usually do know what you're talking about.

You need always to communicate, but you can also find it hard to face certain things, and may run away from stressful situations. Where your sun is will dictate whether you come back and deal with a problem once you have run from the room. To talk about one thing instead of ten is hard for a person with their moon in Gemini. Some stressful situations are of your own making. You have a tendency to look at some things too deeply and to dramatize small events. Mind you, behind that stressed-looking face is a person probably enjoying the minor tiff you are having with a colleague or lover.

You may have Gemini's vulnerability to nervous stress and to eyestrain. Turn to the chapter for sun sign Gemini and read up on the appropriate remedies you should be taking.

Aries, Cancerians, Virgos, Sagittarians and Aquarians also suffer from nerve-related problems, so if your sun sign is one of these, it is particularly important to take precautionary remedies against stress and anxiety. If you are a sun sign Gemini as well as a moon sign Gemini, then take a visit to the optician's. It is possible that your eyes are under strain.

Moon in Cancer

Your first reaction is usually defensive. You don't like to expose what you are really feeling and thinking. Your instincts are sound and should be trusted but sometimes you let your emotions get the better of your judgement. You are very caring and sensitive. Your outlook is rather pessimistic and you need an optimist to balance you up.

You are a hoarder, and never want to throw anything out. You've probably got old medicines in the back of the bathroom cabinet. I'm sure you'd never dream of actually using them, but you really should dispose of them anyway. Think of the space you'll make. One thing worth keeping in your medicine cabinet is liver salts. This will help you to keep everything in good working order. Something else that's good for you is a little outburst every now and then at a loved one. They will know you well enough not to take it too seriously.

Your digestive system is delicate. Acid indigestion is not uncommon for people with their moon in Cancer, especially when dealing with people they are not comfortable with. A tip: never go to dinner with someone you dislike. You're sure to end up with indigestion. Indeed, any problems that agitate you will end up upsetting your stomach and digestive system. Turn to the chapter on sun sign Cancer for more information and advice.

Intolerance to dairy products is quite common with those with this moon sign. If your child has moon in Cancer, they need careful introduction to foods. Be persistent too. If they don't try foods when they are young they may never try them.

If your sun sign is Virgo or Aries, try to make sure you eat at a regular time each day. That way you should be able to get your body into a comfortable routine and should avoid digestive problems.

Moon in Leo

You're great to have around in an emergency. You take control of situations immediately and you always know exactly what to do. Every adventure holiday should have a moon-in-Leo in their team. You are happy and enthusiastic, but bossy when the mood takes you. You give inspiration to all you meet and always have a good word for people. You are popular and make friends and receive smiles wherever you go. Don't be surprised if people offer you their phone numbers within five minutes of meeting you.

You are a natural performer and when out with friends will stand up and hold court to those around. Your determination and ambition will see you go far in life. You are not afraid to take chances. Just like the sun sign of Leo you are loyal, loving, proud and a born leader. Your sun sign will dictate whether this first impression is lasting or not. With moon in Leo you certainly get off to a good start.

Be aware of circulation and lower back problems and read the Leo chapter to see what preventative measures you can take. Long car journeys are not good for you. Always break up long journeys, if only by getting out of the car to walk around a bit and take in some air. This is, indeed, a good idea for anyone on a long journey so don't let any of your passengers tell you differently.

If you are a sun sign Scorpio make sure you take regular breaks from work. You work much better in short time-chunks rather than for long stretches. You function best self-employed or in a flexi-time job, so that you can go with your energy flow. You complete a lot more if you go with your energy surges. Listen to your body and learn about what feels right. Be good to your body and it will be good to you.

Moon in Virgo

You are a real chatterbox, especially when nervous or caught in a corner. You walk into a party or gathering and know immediately if you are welcome or not. You've been known to walk in one door and straight out the other! You can talk yourself into things that you don't want to do and need to learn the art of thinking before speaking. You are always full of new ideas and are a great source of inspiration to co-workers.

Your reflexes are excellent, and you are certain to have an answer to any dilemma a friend is suffering from. You question everything that everyone says and often end up in arguments that you swear you didn't start. You have an answer and an opinion on everything, but can unwittingly hurt friends' feelings because you don't always think before you speak. Later you realize you put your foot in it, and have to do the repair work.

You are a worrier, and can develop stress-related stomach problems. With the knowledge you appear to exude you land yourself in high-powered jobs that you are not always up to. Your superiors are unlikely to have seen through the apparent authority with which you always talk. If you do end up out of your depth, and are suffering stomach problems as a result, turn to the chapter for sun sign Virgo and read up on how you should treat the problem. And don't worry. You'll always pull through in that stressful situation in the end.

Moon sign Virgos can suffer from throat problems, usually from staying out too late and talking in smoky atmospheres. Read the sun sign Taurus chapter for ideas on how to deal with this. In addition, the chapter for sun sign Sagittarius will advise you on treating nervous exhaustion. If you are sun sign Virgo or Sagittarius, then make a conscious effort to take half an hour out of your day, every day, to do something relaxing. A quiet break to lie down with your eyes closed, taking in all that has happened to you that day, is a good and simple idea. Mind you, I know many Sagittarians and Virgos who get rid of stress or worries much more easily by boxing a punching bag. Give them all a try if you cannot decide which will work best for you!

Moon in Libra

You know how every situation should be handled. You can calm difficult situations and placate angry people. Everyone should have a friend with the moon in Libra. You see things from other people's points of view and are excellent at understanding others' problems.

You need to be loved by everybody and your craving for affection can sometimes see you going out of your way to win friends. Try to ensure you do things because you really want to and not because you think it will impress others. Life is good for you; you have the ability to bring everything back into focus. Just like someone who is sun sign Libra, you can bring balance into life.

You could be both judge and jury. You refuse to be pushed into decisions but make up your own mind in as fair and honest a way as possible.

However, you are poor at arguments in which you are directly or emotionally involved. You need to make a conscious effort not to let emotional problems affect your health. Your health really is a mirror image of your emotional state. We all feel down when something has not gone our way but you are capable of letting it rule your life. 'Stop the world,' you say. 'There's no way I can carry on as normal now.' This doesn't last, of course, but it is very annoying for others who are relying on you.

If you suffer from kidney complaints or any other typical Libra ailments turn to the remedies in that sun sign chapter. It is particularly important to take care of your diet because you may be prone to diabetes.

Water is a vital part of the Libra diet, both sun and moon sign. It has the magical ability to keep everything flowing properly. Always drink plenty, and especially if you have drunk too much alcohol! A pint of water before bedtime will go a long way towards improving your morning state. If you don't, you'll feel dehydrated and depressed come the morning.

Moon in Scorpio

This is a strong moon sign. Your reactions can be powerful, sometimes too much so. This can be both positive and negative. You can help and inspire many weaker signs, giving constant love, support and advice. Do watch out, though, for unprovoked outbursts caused by the strength of your emotions. And beware of the power of what you say. If someone asks you to go round the world with them and you say yes, they will certainly take that as a commitment.

Your emotions are so strong that you can be overpowering to others. You have the most incredible willpower. You go after what you want with a fervour and a determination that may shock those around you.

Jealousy is your main problem. You fail to see the innocence in any situation, and you easily adopt an accusatory tone. Deep, intense, secretive and mysterious is how you first appear to new people in your life. It may take some time before they are able to warm to you. If you don't like someone you meet I'm afraid it will show on your face. You may be right not to like them, but you will come across as hard work, and as judgemental. Sometimes this trait will do you favours, but not always.

Keep the reproductive system in good order by following the remedies in the chapter for sun sign Scorpio. You can also follow the remedies for catarrh, a likely ailment, in the chapter for sun sign Taurus. Take account of some of Leo's herbal remedies for stressful days. Leo rules the heart, which also affects Scorpios, so be sure to look after your heart with a healthy lifestyle. Then you'll glide through the many exciting opportunities that will always be put before anyone with their moon in Scorpio.

Moon in Sagittarius

You always look on the bright, positive side. You love a big challenge, and often choose the hard route over the easy route in life, but you don't always pay attention to details. You get quite restless and need to be kept constantly entertained if you are to stick around. Your impatient nature means you refuse to wait for answers, but your good humour should keep you on the straight and narrow.

You have a volatile temper, and act before you think. You need to curb your tendency to get too angry too quickly. Many people with their moon in Sagittarius get involved in an argument without even thinking and halfway through, when the other person thinks it's World War III, back off unexpectedly because their anger has cooled.

You are versatile and unpredictable. You may even come across as a little crazy. But you're not. You're just living up to your stars.

To avoid rheumatism and blood disorders turn to the chapter for sun sign Sagittarius and read up on the advice there. Also consider the vitamins recommended for Aries, Cancer and Virgo. Many of the recipes for these signs can combat nervous stress for you too.

Because you are quick-moving and sometimes careless, you may find yourself bumping into things and getting sprains and bruises. You are just going to have to learn the gift of patience, which could take someone with their moon in Sagittarius many years. The age-old trick of counting to ten before speaking could also save a lot of the friendships and relationships in your life. If you stop and think you'll realize when your impulsive response is the wrong response. It's a long process but a rewarding one. It's all part of making the most of what you are.

Moon in Capricorn

You seem at first to be detached, on the outside looking in at life. This cool exterior is hiding a great, very dry, sense of humour. You are ambitious and have a flair which many others find irresistible. You do not easily show your emotions, and prefer to bide your time before giving any clues to your real feelings. There's a mean and moody side to you that can scare people off and it is only those who've known you for a long time who know the real you.

You are practical and down to earth and create a secure life for yourself. It is not often that someone with their moon in Capricorn makes a silly, impulsive decision. Careful thought goes into your decisions and you think of the future instead of living for the moment. If you are a water sun sign (Cancer, Scorpio or Pisces), this thoughtful attitude can lead to fretting and you must take firm steps to ensure that you relax and don't brood. Promise yourself a cut-off point where you will either make a decision or centre on something else. The remedies in the Cancer, Scorpio and Pisces chapters will be great for you. You see, we are all in some way connected to each other and can help each other.

You may be prone to skin disorders, as many sun sign Capricorns are. Turn to the chapter for Capricorn and follow the advice there. The Cancerian remedies for the liver are also good for you.

If you need a little space, take some, just as you must give others the room they need from time to time. You can lack confidence, which may make relationships slow to get off the ground. People with their moon in Capricorn are often attracted to partners who are older. Don't forget to smile next time you meet a new face. It'll break the ice a lot quicker.

Moon in Aquarius

Many people are drawn to you. You seem distant and yet exude magnetic appeal. You appear untouchable, but you'll help out anyone in trouble and do your utmost for those you love. Indeed, you might be so busy helping out your many friends that your loved ones feel neglected. Your reactions are unpredictable; even you don't know what you'll do in any given situation. You love your freedom, and emotional commitment can stifle you. When you meet the right person this will change, although you'll still keep certain hobbies and interests private.

Your humanitarian nature can get you involved in many worthy causes. Your hand goes to your pocket for a donation before you even realize it. You may offer your services to charities or good causes, but watch out that your thousand and one other commitments don't render these new ones impossible to fulfil.

Try to be less detached and aloof. You don't have to cope alone. Let other people help you.

Nerves, legs and ankles must be taken care of. Turn to the chapter for sun sign Aquarius to see what remedies you can take. Follow some of the advice in sun sign chapters Aries, Virgo and Sagittarius too. These are all sun signs that take on too much. Try to set life at an easier pace for yourself. If you don't start now, you never will, because you love to put things off. Make yourself the gift of some of your own precious time.

Moon in Pisces

You are an emotional cocktail. It is hard for you to deal with anything unemotionally. You can cry at a memory and can laugh as easily too. Stress can lead you to addictions and you need a strong partner to keep you on the straight and narrow.

Your psychic abilities allow you to weigh up people very quickly. You are compassionate, sensitive and creative. You have good instincts, as do moon sign Scorpios, about who is good for you. You should trust your own instincts, because your psychic and intuitive nature is spot on, but go easy when sharing them with others. You need to wait until other people are ready and open to you. A husband or wife, or long-term partner, will be used to your psychic side, but others may accuse you of being quick to judge until they get to know you better.

This intuitive ability works excellently in business and if you can choose a career that demands quick decision-making you'll be on the right track.

Your emotions are not always your ally, I'm afraid. Self-deception is a problem, and you can convince yourself that something that has drawn your attention is right for you, just because you want to experience it. You're very sensitive too, and need to be careful not to be too hurt by what others say.

Watch out for feet problems and also for rheumatism. Look up the remedies you can take in the chapter for sun sign Pisces. Read the chapter for sun sign Sagittarius too, because they suffer similar problems to Pisces. Take particular care to get enough vitamins. Take advantage of the herbal remedies and vitamin supplements that are available. If you are positive about life, then life will prove positive for you.

Discovering the Age of Aquarius

For the next two thousand years we will be in the Age of Aquarius. It sounds like such a long time! However, at the turn of the millennium we left the Age of Pisces, which we were also in for approximately two thousand years. In the Age of Pisces Jesus was born, who as we all know ministered first to the fishermen. Christianity has a preoccupation with the symbol of the fish. Pisces was the age the Christians were born into.

In astrological terms 'the Age of Aquarius' means that the vernal equinox has left the sign of Pisces and has entered the sign of Aquarius, an air sign. The Age of Aquarius opens up a whole new world of exciting events but is also set to make all of us more aware of our abilities and our senses, in particular our sixth sense. People often ask me what your sixth sense is. You know the smell of freshly brewed coffee. But try to explain to a person who has never smelt it what the aroma of coffee is like. Your sixth sense is a bit like that. Hard to explain, but you know what it is. We all know our five senses: smell, touch, taste, sight and hearing. The sixth sense is your ability to sense things about life. It is like intuition but on a much bigger scale. It is time that we learned to trust it more. Our senses will not let us down and are ready to lead us well. Strange to think that we are all influenced not only by our sun sign, our ascendant, our moon sign, and so on, but also by the age we are in.

We have all met people that we did not like at first sight. How did we know that we did not like them or that they would not be a good influence on our lives? Was it their smell, or the look of them? It is our sixth sense that tells us whether someone is good or bad for us in life. Having this sixth sense at our fingertips doesn't mean that we always follow it though. Sometimes we see something that doesn't feel right, and then go into one of our other senses for more information. None the less, many people rely on their instincts to get on in their jobs, be they a detective, a gambler, a good lawyer at the bar or a broker on the stock market.

If you remember the musical *Hair* you will remember the song 'The Dawning of the Age of Aquarius'. 'When the moon is in the seventh house and Jupiter aligns with Mars, then peace will guide the planets and love will steer the stars. This is the dawning of the Age of Aquarius.' The musical, famous in its time, was referring to the astrological fact that we are approaching a time of free-thinking and understanding: an altogether more psychic age.

Let me give you some examples of earlier ages, all of which lasted approximately two thousand years. The Age of Gemini, about six to eight thousand years ago, was the time of Adam and Eve. The sign of the twins is sometimes referred to as Adam and Eve in ancient astrology. Moses threw out the golden calf, which ended the Age of Taurus and took the world into the Age of Aries. This was followed by the Age of Pisces, where we have been for the last two thousand years. I don't think there is anyone who is not secretly waiting to see if they really feel the spiritual and magical effects of the dawning of this next and very important age. Just make sure that you make the most of it, by learning to trust your instincts.

Many people also believe that Karma is strongly related to this new age and that people will no longer be able to get away with mistreating others. Let's make the Age of Aquarius one to benefit us and our grandchildren, so that we can be proud of what we have made the world into. We all make a difference in whatever we do. Think about it. If you get shouted at at work for something you haven't done, you leave feeling upset and angry. You'll be angry and sour with all the people you come into contact with. You'll cut people up in your car, or give the person next to you on the train too little room. Those people you have come in contact with will then have their moods turned sour, which they'll take home with them. When you get home you shout at your partner just to relieve the anger you are still feeling and so trouble begins to brew.

However, if we can all make the effort to be nice to one another and go out of our way to let that person in the car go ahead of us, to make room for that other person on the crowded train and to be happy to see our partners, who were hoping that we were in a good mood and might have prepared something extra nice for us, then we should find that we can kick-start this new and exciting time now, instead of later. Remember life is very often what you make it, and we should be able to make the future one that previous generations had only ever dreamed of.

It's what is called a chain reaction, and the effect over the coming two thousand years is certain to be a dramatic one. Changes start with ourselves, so if you really want to know exactly when the Age of Aquarius begins, then this is the answer: as soon as you are ready to allow it!

MORE ROMANY RECIPES

The Romany Use of Herbs

IT'S FUNNY TO think that we are now willing to pay a fortune for herbs that Romanies have plucked from the hedgerows for centuries. We Romanies have always known that herbs, besides adding flavour to food, are essential to good health. We used them to stay fit and well and to take the place of expensive ingredients we could not afford.

I remember going shopping with my grandmother when I was a teenager and how disgusted she was to see the price that supermarkets were charging for simple herbs such as parsley and tarragon. Even now they are quite expensive, and 'trendy' too. Many people have a pot of parsley on their kitchen windowsill. But parsley is not just to put on your potatoes. If you can learn the many different ways to use herbs you can open up for yourself a whole new world of tastes and flavours.

Watch the cows in the fields. They know exactly which herbs they should eat and which they shouldn't. Sick animals usually know which herb to chew on to cure a bad stomach or a sickness. I believe that years ago, when we didn't have the technology or the readily available information of today, we trusted our instincts. Our ancestors knew what was good and what was bad for them. A lot of what they knew had been learned over centuries and passed down. There was no chemist's to run to for a cure for an upset stomach or headache, but there would have been family recipes, remedies and herbs. I am not saying that we should go sniffing the hedgerows and tasting the plants but I do feel that perhaps we should trust what our own senses are telling us a little more. After all, we can all smell bad milk, or tell if meat is a funny colour or doesn't smell right. And we Romanies, more than most, have not forgotten our ancestral lore.

You can save yourself a bit of money, and increase the pleasure of cooking and eating, if you grow your own herbs. It might sound like a responsibility but it is really more of an enjoyable hobby. Herbs don't need much room to flourish. All you need to start off is two or three pots by a window or in a window box. The hardest part is deciding which herbs to grow. My favourites are parsley, oregano, mint, sage, rosemary and basil.

You will need to keep the pots as near to the light as possible and every now and then put them out in the rain, though not when it is windy. Allow some room in the pots for the roots of the herbs to spread. If you are trying this for the first time, you may be better off with individual pots of herbs. Some herbs have bossy roots that can smother the others. You can use many different kinds of pots, whatever you like. Strawberry pots, with their pockets for herbs to grow out of, are my mother's favourites. She's put them outside the back door.

Before planting, cover the holes of the pot with broken bits of cups or plates, leaving space for the water to seep through. Then get the compost and plant the herb some 5 cm/2 inches deep. Press the soil around it so that it is well secured and water it immediately. Water your herbs as often as you feel they need it but never allow them to stand in water. Overwatering will kill them.

Joey Grey's Potatoes

This is a dish my grandmother used to make for me when I was a child, and I now make it for my family. The man who invented the dish was Joey Grey. According to my grandmother, this was a man who knew how to cook the most tasty dishes. His namesake dish was made in my grandmother's day when they had no money to buy anything else.

I wish Joey knew that his dish is more delicious to me than any expensive cut of meat. I do hope none of you throws away the juice from the Sunday roast, it would be a crime. Keep it for a day or two (no more) and use it for this dish. Serves 4–6

2 slices of back bacon, chopped
oil for frying
3 large onions, thinly sliced
5 large white potatoes, thinly sliced
the fat and juices from a roast joint
salt and freshly ground pepper
1 teaspoon chopped fresh rosemary

Fry the bacon briefly in a little oil in a deep frying pan or large saucepan. Add the onions and cook until soft and golden. Then add the potatoes and the fat and juices from a joint, and stir the potatoes until coated with fat and juices. Cover with hot water, season with salt and pepper, and add the rosemary. Cover the pan and simmer until the potatoes are tender: about 25 minutes, stirring occasionally to prevent browning. Serve at once.

Angel Surprise

This angelica and mint dip has long been a favourite for the pregnant women in my family.

a handful of fresh young angelica leaves
a handful of fresh mint leaves
mayonnaise
your choice of fresh vegetables, cleaned and chopped into sticks

Chop the leaves very finely, mix them into the mayonnaise, and then dip in the vegetables to your heart's content.

Vegetable Soup with Bay

For good health you should be eating fresh vegetables every day. Here's a delicious way to do so. Serves 4

1 large onion, chopped
a little butter, olive oil or vegetable spray for frying

turnips, carrots, swede and potatoes, or other root vegetables of your choice, chopped into bite-size pieces
900 ml/1½ pints vegetable stock (use a stock cube or save the water you cook vegetables in)
2 bay leaves

Fry the onion in the butter or oil in a large saucepan until soft. Add the vegetables and brown them a little, keeping them moving about so they don't burn. Add the stock and bay leaves, bring to the boil and then simmer until the vegetables are tender. Serve at once.

Home-made Tomato Sauce

Much better than anything you can buy.

450 g/1 lb tomatoes
1 onion, chopped
a little oil for frying
1 flowering head of dill, chopped
salt and freshly ground black pepper

Plunge the tomatoes into boiling water, leave them for 1 minute and then plunge them into cold water. This will make it possible for you to peel off the skin without any trouble. Then chop them and set aside.

Gently fry the onion in a little oil until soft. Add the dill, chopped tomatoes and stock, and season with salt and pepper. Pour into a jar or bottle when cool, shake and chill. Use as required.

Clunky's Dressing

This one's named after me. When I was learning to cook I was nicknamed Clara Clunk because I was so heavy-handed!

1 clove garlic, finely chopped
1 tablespoon Dijon mustard
1 tablespoon mixed herbs
4 tablespoons white wine vinegar
4 tablespoons dry white wine
120 ml/4 fl oz olive oil

Put the ingredients in a screwtop jar and shake well to combine.

Maddison's Mint Chutney

This is excellent with lamb dishes. It's named after my niece, who added the mustard to my mother's traditional recipe.

900 ml/1½ pints wine vinegar
450 g/1 lb brown sugar
350 g/12 oz seedless raisins
1 dried red chilli pepper
2 teaspoons dry mustard powder
2 teaspoons salt
225 g/8 oz tomatoes, chopped
450 g/1 lb apples, cored and chopped
6 small onions, chopped
1 mugful of chopped fresh mint
3 peppercorns, crushed

Put the vinegar in a saucepan and bring almost to the boil. Add the brown sugar, raisins, chilli, mustard and salt, and stir well until the sugar has dissolved. Take off the heat. Add the tomatoes, apples, onions, mint and peppercorns and mix together. Put into clean jars and seal at once. Label and date them, and store in a cool dark place or in the refrigerator. The chutney is ready to use after 1 month. Do not heat it any further.

The chutney improves and matures with age. This recipe will make a large jar's worth. It should last up to three months.

Parsley Mayonnaise

Quicker and easier to make than you might imagine.

3 large egg yolks
½ teaspoon mild mustard
300 ml/½ pint olive oil
1 teaspoon fresh lemon juice
1½ tablespoons chopped fresh parsley

Whisk the egg yolks and mustard together. Then the olive oil, drop by drop, whisking continuously until your mixture is thick and all the oil has gone in. Add the lemon juice and parsley, and serve at once with jacket potatoes or toasted sandwiches.

Romany Beauty Secrets

THESE RECIPES ARE for both men and women, young and old, and have been passed down to me by my mother and grandmother, and their mothers and grandmothers before them. In the chapter The Right Health Signs Remedy for the Right Time of Life, you'll have discovered beauty and health secrets appropriate to people of specific ages and stages in life. These ones are universal – although some signs will enjoy making them up much more than others! As I've said before, you only want to use the best on your skin, so make up a fresh batch if anything starts to go at all stale.

Face Massage

It is not just what you use, it is the way you apply it. The age-old art of massage can relieve stress and prevent lines appearing on the face (although it won't get rid of existing ones, whatever manufacturers tell you). It doesn't take long to do this and if you do it regularly you'll find it an excellent wind-down, draining away the stresses of the day. Think about it: pure self-indulgence. So, when you apply lotions, start at the base of the throat and apply the lotion with both hands, stroking upwards towards the edge of the jaw bone. Use a deep swift stroking motion. You may find it easier to use the back of your hand, performing a swift rolling motion of one finger after another.

Now, at the edge of your jaw bone, just below the ear, use thumb and forefinger to pinch the skin, working your way to the centre of the chin. Do this six times. This is great for preventing a double chin and my mother has had me doing it since I was 14. I now do it in the car at traffic lights (you don't have to be applying lotion) when I think no one is looking. It stimulates and improves the circulation, pumping the cells up and improving the skin.

Now massage your lotion into your face, always using an upward motion. If you use a downward motion you'll drag the skin down too.

We work out our bodies but we forget our faces, the most exposed part. Here are some more face exercises. Pinch your eyebrows to release the tension from straining your eyes, if you've been sitting at a computer all day for example. When I have finished writing, I always take a bag of frozen vegetables from the freezer and use the bag as a home-made ice pack on my eyes for 5 or 10 minutes to wind down and give the muscles a chance to relax. You can also buy special eye packs that you keep in the refrigerator which are excellent for a quick pick-me-up. They should put these in the minibars of hotel rooms instead of alcohol.

If you suffer from migraines do not try to pummel

them away. Soft feathery strokes and very little pressure are the answer. A migraine is something that needs coaxing away. If you are aggressive towards it, it will get aggressive back.

Storage

To store the recipes here and in your own sun sign chapters, you need screw-top jars and pots. Get into the habit of saving ones you come across. Small jam jars are excellent. You can also buy empty bottles from chemists and herbalists and they are good and cheap. Make sure they are spotlessly clean and sterilized, and label them with the cream you've put inside and the date you made it. Store them in the refrigerator. Most home-made creams keep for 6 weeks. Then it's time to move on to a new one!

Cleanser

Home-made cleansers are wonderfully refreshing. You know exactly what's gone in them, and they haven't been sitting in the chemist's or in a warehouse for months. The ones you buy will never be as good as the ones you make yourself. You simply have to make the time for this! Don't be put off by the long list of ingredients (you can get them from a chemist's or herbalist's). This takes me 8½ minutes to make.

You cannot have good skin if you do not keep it clean and a good cleanser is essential to men, women and children alike.

½ tablespoon beeswax
1 tablespoon emulsifying wax
5 tablespoons baby oil
2½ tablespoons coconut oil
2 tablespoons water
¼ teaspoon borax
1 tablespoon distilled witch hazel
a few drops of the essential oil of your choice (I like lemon verbena)

Measure the waxes and oils into an enamel bowl and melt them slowly over a pan of simmering water. In a separate bowl, over another saucepan of simmering water, heat the water and borax until the borax is thoroughly dissolved. Add the witch hazel and remove from the heat (or it will evaporate). When the waxes are melted, remove from the heat and stir in the contents of the other bowl, stirring all the time. When the cream begins to cool, add the perfume of your choice. Transfer to a screw-top jaw and label it. Use it straight from the refrigerator for an extra refreshing experience.

Root Mask

Carrots are rich in vitamin A, which is great for irritated skin. The turnip is a great cleanser for all the signs but particularly suits Virgo's earthy nature.

2 carrots, peeled and chopped
2 turnips, peeled and chopped

Boil the carrots and turnips together, then drain and mash them to a paste. When cool enough to apply to the face, smooth all over and relax for 10 minutes. Rinse off with milk, then with water.

Tomato Mask

Tomatoes are excellent for getting rid of blackheads. Peel and mash a tomato and strain it through a sieve. Stir in some oatmeal, and use as you would any face mask.

Citrus Toner

This is excellent for all skin types and all star signs.

peel of 1 orange, sliced
peel of ½ lemon, sliced
240 ml/8 fl oz milk
1 tablespoon caster sugar

Put the orange and lemon peel in a pan, add the milk and sugar and bring to the boil. Take off the heat and leave to cool. Strain, pour into a bottle and keep in the refrigerator. Use as you would any toner. It will keep, if refrigerated, 3–4 weeks.

Rose's Moisturizer

My sister-in-law is a beautician. She makes this up for her clients as a pre-wedding pampering treatment. I have named it after her as she is the one who remembered how my grandmother made it and has kept it going.

This is pure luxury. It may seem costly but it will last you and you'll feel like royalty. It's quick to make, and lovely and rich. These oils are similar to our body oils.

3 teaspoons beeswax
3 teaspoons emulsifying wax
120 ml/4 fl oz almond oil
120 ml/4 fl oz avocado oil
4 tablespoons rosewater
a few drops of your favourite perfume

Melt the waxes in an enamel bowl over a pan of simmering water, then add the avocado and almond oils. Stir well, then slowly add the rosewater, stirring constantly. Transfer to a spotless screw-top jar.

Mouth Freshener

To battle bad breath, chew a clove, or even add it to a mouthwash. A great mouthwash is rosewater. Buy it from a chemist's and add nothing to it. It's cheaper and a lot more effective than shop-bought ones.

Herbal Tonic

This is a great pick-me-up and is good if you've got a stressful week on.

3 teacupfuls sarsaparilla chips
2 sticks Spanish liquorice (must be Spanish)
2 teaspoons Epsom salts
2.5 litres/4 pints water

Put all the ingredients into a large saucepan, bring to the boil, then simmer until the liquorice has melted. Stand to cool overnight, then mix so that all the sediment comes to the top, strain through a muslin cloth and store in screw-top bottles. You should end up with 900 ml/1½ pints of tonic.

Take a wineglassful each morning before breakfast.

Food for Healthy Skin

For beautiful, healthy skin you must eat well. The main foods that Romanies swear by for beautiful skin are onions, watercress, celery and radishes. Turnip tops and potatoes are good too.

Onions contain free uncrystallized sugar, starch, alkaline salts and sulphur, and provide our bodies with a great deal of goodness. I throw some whole onions into my Sunday roast and my guests always find them mouthwatering.

Watercress contains iron and sulphur, which cleanse the inside of your body. Eat it raw in salads and you will be amazed at what this simple food can do for you.

Celery falls under the essential foods list of many of the signs, including Aries, Taurus, Gemini, Virgo, Libra and Aquarius. With its organic sulphur and essential salts it is brilliant for treating rheumatism. Steamed celery is easy to make. Serve with a little condensation still clinging to it and you'll soon end up craving this dish to go with the other flavours on your dinner table. You cannot beat raw celery and cheese at the end of a meal, either. Cheese is full of calcium for strong bones and teeth.

Radishes purify the blood and improve the complexion. Boil and eat them as a vegetable or add them raw to salads. Many Romanies who have bad digestion eat radishes alongside the foods that cause them difficulty (but which they still want to eat) and find that the radishes solve the digestion problems.

Boiled turnip tops do wonders for your complexion and cleanse the blood too, so include them in your diet from time to time. Some people find that turnips give them wind, but turnip tops are different and well worth adding to your diet, so make sure that you give them a try.

The humble potato is very good for you too, especially if you scrub the skin instead of peeling it. There are minerals and vitamins directly under the skin and by peeling you are taking away the very thing you need. People still omit potatoes from their diet when they want to lose weight, but you really shouldn't. Potatoes are a great source of goodness. Their citric content, together with their salts of potash and sulphur, help to keep the skin and hair in prime condition. Indeed, it was the introduction of the potato in the 16th century that helped win the battle against skin diseases like leprosy and scurvy. It's only the butter and sauces we add to potatoes that make them fattening.

Romany Herbal Dandruff Treatment

This worked long before the brands in the chemist's were invented, and will probably be around a lot longer too.

Wash your hair with your usual shampoo and dry with a towel in circular movements to massage the scalp and stimulate hair growth. Dampen a hairbrush with rosewater and eau de Cologne, using equal amounts of each. Then put a little lemon on to the hairbrush and brush through.

Dandelion Wine

This will finish off your beauty treatments by adding a little colour to your complexion.

2 litres/3½ pints dandelion petals, picked fresh in season
2 litres/3½ pints boiling water
thinly peeled rind of 1 orange
1 lemon, thinly sliced
900 g/2 lb sugar
a piece of whole ginger
½ tablespoon brewer's yeast

Put the dandelion petals in a large pot and cover with the boiling water. Cover the pot with a cloth and leave to stew for 72 hours. Stir twice daily.

Strain the liquor into a saucepan and add the orange rind, lemon slices, sugar and ginger. Bring to the boil and allow to boil for 25 minutes. Remove from the heat and set aside to cool. Spread the brewer's yeast on a piece of toast and add this to the dandelion mixture. Leave for 1½ days. Then pour into a bottle with a secure lid.

After 2 months decant the wine into a wine bottle and keep for at least another month before drinking. The bread should have dissolved into the mixture. I always make this about August time so that it is ready for Christmas.

Useful Addresses

IF YOU HAVE a problem in life, no matter what it is, there is always someone, somewhere, who can help you. Life is full of challenges and at times we all need a bit of guidance and support, or even just an ear into which to pour our problems. Astrology is all about finding out more about yourself, who you are, where you are going and what you can make of your life and your destiny. For those times when you have a specific problem or need some particular advice, here are some sources of special support. And I hope that this book has enabled you to learn more about you and your health and how you can make astrology work for you.

BEREAVEMENT
(020) 7247 1080 (10 a.m. to 4 p.m. Monday-Friday; answerphone at other times)
Area served: UK
Service offered: Helpline for bereaved people, those supporting them and professionals. Offers advice, information, listening, counselling and referrals to the nearest or most appropriate service.
Address: 20 Norton Folgate, London E1 6DB

CHILDLINE

0800 1111 (freephone)
Area served: UK
Service offered: 24-hour helpline for children and young people in danger and/or distress. Offers counselling, support and advice for any child with any problem. Refers children in danger to appropriate helping agencies. Other lines:
Childline for children in care: 0800 88 44 44 (6 p.m. to 10 p.m. daily; freephone)
Textphone: 0800 400222 (2 p.m. to 9 p.m. daily; freephone)
Address: Freepost 1111, London N1 0BR

NATIONAL DRUGS HELPLINE

0800 77 66 00 (freephone)
Area served: UK
Service offered: Helpline for anyone concerned about drug misuse, including drug users, their families, friends and carers. Information, advice and counselling about all aspects of drug misuse. Referrals to local and national agencies. Can send out written information in a range of languages.
Address: PO Box 5000, Glasgow G12 8BR

BREAST CANCER CARE HELPLINE

0808 800 6000
Area served: UK
Service offered: Helpline for women with breast cancer or other breast-related problems, and for their families and friends. Provides support and information. Deals with emotional well-being as well as information about

medical treatments, side effects and problems. Referrals to other agencies and support groups. Staff include breast-care nurses. Produces a range of information booklets on all aspects of breast cancer.
Address: Kiln House, 210 New Kings Road, London SW6 4NZ

CANCERLINK
0800 132 095 (freephone); 01527 871051
Area served: UK
Service offered: Advice and support for people affected by cancer, themselves, carers, families and friends. Provides information on types of cancer, risk reduction, screening, physical and emotional effects, treatment, counselling, referrals.
Address: 11–21 Northdown Street, London N1 9BN

AGE CONCERN ENGLAND
0800 731 4931 (freephone)
Area served: England and Wales
Service offered: Telephone service for older people, their families and people working with them. Offers information, advice, support and referrals. Issues dealt with include residential care, income and benefits, housing, health, consumer, legal and community care. Local referrals.
Address: 1268 London Road, London SW16 4ER

LONDON RAPE CRISIS CENTRE
(020) 7837 1600
Area served: UK
Service offered: Helpline for women and girls who

have been raped or sexually abused, their friends, families and partners. Offers advice, information, counselling and listening. Deals with legal, medical, pregnancy, STD and abortion issues. Also provides information about local self-help groups and face-to-face counselling services.
Address: PO Box 69, London WC1X 9NJ

SAMARITANS
0345 909090 (local rate)
Area served: UK
Service offered: 24-hour confidential, emotional support for anyone in crisis. Also confidential e-mail service: send a message to samaritans@anon?twwells.com and your name and address will be deleted before it is transmitted to the Samaritans.

Sun Sign and Moon Sign Tables

If your birthday falls on the cusp – or 'changeover' date between two signs – then you will need to use the Sun Sign Tables that follow starting on page 433 to check exactly when the signs changed over in the year of your birth, to find out your dominant sign.

If you find no listing for your date of birth, the entry relating to the nearest date before yours applies.

Earlier in the book I discussed moon signs – the sign the moon is in at the time of your birth, which can dictate certain dominant traits in your personality and your health. To find out your moon sign simply look up the year and month of your birth in the Moon Sign Tables starting on page 440. If you find no listing for your actual date of birth, then the sign the moon is in on the date shown in the list preceding your birthday prevails.

These tables are based on Greenwich Mean Time and take into account British Summer Time year by year where appropriate. They are based on the Geocentric Tropical Zodiac. If you were born elsewhere, work out the British equivalent to your time of birth by adding or subtracting the appropriate number of hours for a rough indication of your moon sign, or indeed your sun sign if you were born on the cusp. However, the positioning of the stars does vary according to geographical location, so you would be best advised to consult a full ephemeris with information relevant to your birthplace for more accurate information, or to consult an astrologer personally. There are also several ephemerides and astrological advice sites on the internet. MSP-Online.com will be able to tailor a chart for you.

SUN SIGNS

1920–31

Aqu	21 Jan 1920
Pis	19 Feb 1920
Ari	20 Mar 1920
Tau	20 Apr 1920
Gem	21 May 1920
Can	21 Jun 1920
Leo	23 Jul 1920
Vir	23 Aug 1920
Lib	23 Sep 1920
Sco	23 Oct 1920
Sag	22 Nov 1920
Cap	22 Dec 1920

Aqu	20 Jan 1921
Pis	19 Feb 1921
Ari	21 Mar 1921
Tau	20 Apr 1921
Gem	21 May 1921
Can	21 Jun 1921
Leo	23 Jul 1921
Vir	23 Aug 1921
Lib	23 Sep 1921
Sco	23 Oct 1921
Sag	22 Nov 1921
Cap	22 Dec 1921

Aqu	20 Jan 1922
Pis	19 Feb 1922
Ari	21 Mar 1922
Tau	20 Apr 1922
Gem	21 May 1922
Can	22 Jun 1922
Leo	23 Jul 1922
Vir	23 Aug 1922
Lib	23 Sep 1922
Sco	24 Oct 1922
Sag	23 Nov 1922
Cap	22 Dec 1922

Aqu	21 Jan 1923
Pis	19 Feb 1923
Ari	21 Mar 1923
Tau	21 Apr 1923
Gem	22 May 1923
Can	22 Jun 1923
Leo	23 Jul 1923
Vir	24 Aug 1923
Lib	24 Sep 1923
Sco	24 Oct 1923
Sag	23 Nov 1923
Cap	22 Dec 1923

Aqu	21 Jan 1924
Pis	19 Feb 1924
Ari	20 Mar 1924
Tau	20 Apr 1924
Gem	21 May 1924
Can	21 Jun 1924
Leo	23 Jul 1924
Vir	23 Aug 1924
Lib	23 Sep 1924
Sco	23 Oct 1924
Sag	22 Nov 1924
Cap	22 Dec 1924

Aqu	20 Jan 1925
Pis	19 Feb 1925
Ari	21 Mar 1925
Tau	20 Apr 1925
Gem	21 May 1925
Can	21 Jun 1925
Leo	23 Jul 1925
Vir	23 Aug 1925
Lib	23 Sep 1925
Sco	23 Oct 1925
Sag	22 Nov 1925
Cap	22 Dec 1925

Aqu	20 Jan 1926
Pis	19 Feb 1926
Ari	21 Mar 1926
Tau	20 Apr 1926
Gem	21 May 1926
Can	22 Jun 1926
Leo	23 Jul 1926
Vir	23 Aug 1926
Lib	23 Sep 1926
Sco	24 Oct 1926
Sag	23 Nov 1926
Cap	22 Dec 1926

Aqu	21 Jan 1927
Pis	19 Feb 1927
Ari	21 Mar 1927
Tau	21 Apr 1927
Gem	22 May 1927
Can	22 Jun 1927
Leo	23 Jul 1927
Vir	24 Aug 1927
Lib	24 Sep 1927
Sco	24 Oct 1927
Sag	23 Nov 1927
Cap	22 Dec 1927

Aqu	21 Jan 1928
Pis	19 Feb 1928
Ari	20 Mar 1928
Tau	20 Apr 1928
Gem	21 May 1928
Can	21 Jun 1928
Leo	23 Jul 1928
Vir	23 Aug 1928
Lib	23 Sep 1928
Sco	23 Oct 1928
Sag	22 Nov 1928
Cap	22 Dec 1928

Aqu	20 Jan 1929
Pis	19 Feb 1929
Ari	21 Mar 1929
Tau	20 Apr 1929
Gem	21 May 1929
Can	21 Jun 1929
Leo	23 Jul 1929
Vir	23 Aug 1929
Lib	23 Sep 1929
Sco	23 Oct 1929
Sag	22 Nov 1929
Cap	22 Dec 1929

Aqu	20 Jan 1930
Pis	19 Feb 1930
Ari	21 Mar 1930
Tau	20 Apr 1930
Gem	21 May 1930
Can	22 Jun 1930
Leo	23 Jul 1930
Vir	23 Aug 1930
Lib	23 Sep 1930
Sco	24 Oct 1930
Sag	23 Nov 1930
Cap	22 Dec 1930

Aqu	21 Jan 1931
Pis	19 Feb 1931
Ari	21 Mar 1931
Tau	21 Apr 1931
Gem	22 May 1931
Can	22 Jun 1931
Leo	23 Jul 1931
Vir	24 Aug 1931
Lib	24 Sep 1931
Sco	24 Oct 1931
Sag	23 Nov 1931
Cap	22 Dec 1931

1932–43

Aqu 21 Jan 1932
Pis 19 Feb 1932
Ari 20 Mar 1932
Tau 20 Apr 1932
Gem 21 May 1932
Can 21 Jun 1932
Leo 23 Jul 1932
Vir 23 Aug 1932
Lib 23 Sep 1932
Sco 23 Oct 1932
Sag 22 Nov 1932
Cap 22 Dec 1932

Aqu 20 Jan 1933
Pis 19 Feb 1933
Ari 21 Mar 1933
Tau 20 Apr 1933
Gem 21 May 1933
Can 21 Jun 1933
Leo 23 Jul 1933
Vir 23 Aug 1933
Lib 23 Sep 1933
Sco 23 Oct 1933
Sag 22 Nov 1933
Cap 22 Dec 1933

Aqu 20 Jan 1934
Pis 19 Feb 1934
Ari 21 Mar 1934
Tau 20 Apr 1934
Gem 21 May 1934
Can 22 Jun 1934
Leo 23 Jul 1934
Vir 23 Aug 1934
Lib 23 Sep 1934
Sco 24 Oct 1934
Sag 22 Nov 1934
Cap 22 Dec 1934

Aqu 20 Jan 1935
Pis 19 Feb 1935
Ari 21 Mar 1935
Tau 21 Apr 1935
Gem 22 May 1935
Can 22 Jun 1935
Leo 23 Jul 1935
Vir 24 Aug 1935
Lib 23 Sep 1935
Sco 24 Oct 1935
Sag 23 Nov 1935
Cap 22 Dec 1935

Aqu 21 Jan 1936
Pis 19 Feb 1936
Ari 20 Mar 1936
Tau 20 Apr 1936
Gem 21 May 1936
Can 21 Jun 1936
Leo 23 Jul 1936
Vir 23 Aug 1936
Lib 23 Sep 1936
Sco 23 Oct 1936
Sag 22 Nov 1936
Cap 22 Dec 1936

Aqu 20 Jan 1937
Pis 19 Feb 1937
Ari 21 Mar 1937
Tau 20 Apr 1937
Gem 21 May 1937
Can 21 Jun 1937
Leo 23 Jul 1937
Vir 23 Aug 1937
Lib 23 Sep 1937
Sco 23 Oct 1937
Sag 22 Nov 1937
Cap 22 Dec 1937

Aqu 20 Jan 1938
Pis 19 Feb 1938
Ari 21 Mar 1938
Tau 20 Apr 1938
Gem 21 May 1938
Can 22 Jun 1938
Leo 23 Jul 1938
Vir 23 Aug 1938
Lib 23 Sep 1938
Sco 24 Oct 1938
Sag 22 Nov 1938
Cap 22 Dec 1938

Aqu 20 Jan 1939
Pis 19 Feb 1939
Ari 21 Mar 1939
Tau 21 Apr 1939
Gem 21 May 1939
Can 22 Jun 1939
Leo 23 Jul 1939
Vir 24 Aug 1939
Lib 23 Sep 1939
Sco 24 Oct 1939
Sag 23 Nov 1939
Cap 22 Dec 1939

Aqu 21 Jan 1940
Pis 19 Feb 1940
Ari 20 Mar 1940
Tau 20 Apr 1940
Gem 21 May 1940
Can 21 Jun 1940
Leo 23 Jul 1940
Vir 23 Aug 1940
Lib 23 Sep 1940
Sco 23 Oct 1940
Sag 22 Nov 1940
Cap 21 Dec 1940

Aqu 20 Jan 1941
Pis 19 Feb 1941
Ari 21 Mar 1941
Tau 20 Apr 1941
Gem 21 May 1941
Can 21 Jun 1941
Leo 23 Jul 1941
Vir 23 Aug 1941
Lib 23 Sep 1941
Sco 23 Oct 1941
Sag 22 Nov 1941
Cap 22 Dec 1941

Aqu 20 Jan 1942
Pis 19 Feb 1942
Ari 21 Mar 1942
Tau 20 Apr 1942
Gem 21 May 1942
Can 22 Jun 1942
Leo 23 Jul 1942
Vir 23 Aug 1942
Lib 23 Sep 1942
Sco 24 Oct 1942
Sag 22 Nov 1942
Cap 22 Dec 1942

Aqu 20 Jan 1943
Pis 19 Feb 1943
Ari 21 Mar 1943
Tau 20 Apr 1943
Gem 21 May 1943
Can 22 Jun 1943
Leo 23 Jul 1943
Vir 24 Aug 1943
Lib 23 Sep 1943
Sco 24 Oct 1943
Sag 23 Nov 1943
Cap 22 Dec 1943

Sun Signs

1944–55

Aqu 21 Jan 1944
Pis 19 Feb 1944
Ari 20 Mar 1944
Tau 20 Apr 1944
Gem 21 May 1944
Can 21 Jun 1944
Leo 22 Jul 1944
Vir 23 Aug 1944
Lib 23 Sep 1944
Sco 23 Oct 1944
Sag 22 Nov 1944
Cap 21 Dec 1944

Aqu 20 Jan 1945
Pis 19 Feb 1945
Ari 20 Mar 1945
Tau 20 Apr 1945
Gem 21 May 1945
Can 21 Jun 1945
Leo 23 Jul 1945
Vir 23 Aug 1945
Lib 23 Sep 1945
Sco 23 Oct 1945
Sag 22 Nov 1945
Cap 22 Dec 1945

Aqu 20 Jan 1946
Pis 19 Feb 1946
Ari 21 Mar 1946
Tau 20 Apr 1946
Gem 21 May 1946
Can 22 Jun 1946
Leo 23 Jul 1946
Vir 23 Aug 1946
Lib 23 Sep 1946
Sco 24 Oct 1946
Sag 22 Nov 1946
Cap 22 Dec 1946

Aqu 20 Jan 1947
Pis 19 Feb 1947
Ari 21 Mar 1947
Tau 20 Apr 1947
Gem 21 May 1947
Can 22 Jun 1947
Leo 23 Jul 1947
Vir 24 Aug 1947
Lib 23 Sep 1947
Sco 24 Oct 1947
Sag 23 Nov 1947
Cap 22 Dec 1947

Aqu 21 Jan 1948
Pis 19 Feb 1948
Ari 20 Mar 1948
Tau 20 Apr 1948
Gem 21 May 1948
Can 21 Jun 1948
Leo 22 Jul 1948
Vir 23 Aug 1948
Lib 23 Sep 1948
Sco 23 Oct 1948
Sag 22 Nov 1948
Cap 21 Dec 1948

Aqu 20 Jan 1949
Pis 18 Feb 1949
Ari 20 Mar 1949
Tau 20 Apr 1949
Gem 21 May 1949
Can 21 Jun 1949
Leo 23 Jul 1949
Vir 23 Aug 1949
Lib 23 Sep 1949
Sco 23 Oct 1949
Sag 22 Nov 1949
Cap 22 Dec 1949

Aqu 20 Jan 1950
Pis 19 Feb 1950
Ari 21 Mar 1950
Tau 20 Apr 1950
Gem 21 May 1950
Can 21 Jun 1950
Leo 23 Jul 1950
Vir 23 Aug 1950
Lib 23 Sep 1950
Sco 23 Oct 1950
Sag 22 Nov 1950
Cap 22 Dec 1950

Aqu 20 Jan 1951
Pis 19 Feb 1951
Ari 21 Mar 1951
Tau 20 Apr 1951
Gem 21 May 1951
Can 22 Jun 1951
Leo 23 Jul 1951
Vir 23 Aug 1951
Lib 23 Sep 1951
Sco 24 Oct 1951
Sag 23 Nov 1951
Cap 22 Dec 1951

Aqu 21 Jan 1952
Pis 19 Feb 1952
Ari 20 Mar 1952
Tau 20 Apr 1952
Gem 21 May 1952
Can 21 Jun 1952
Leo 22 Jul 1952
Vir 23 Aug 1952
Lib 23 Sep 1952
Sco 23 Oct 1952
Sag 22 Nov 1952
Cap 21 Dec 1952

Aqu 20 Jan 1953
Pis 18 Feb 1953
Ari 20 Mar 1953
Tau 20 Apr 1953
Gem 21 May 1953
Can 21 Jun 1953
Leo 23 Jul 1953
Vir 23 Aug 1953
Lib 23 Sep 1953
Sco 23 Oct 1953
Sag 22 Nov 1953
Cap 22 Dec 1953

Aqu 20 Jan 1954
Pis 19 Feb 1954
Ari 21 Mar 1954
Tau 20 Apr 1954
Gem 21 May 1954
Can 21 Jun 1954
Leo 23 Jul 1954
Vir 23 Aug 1954
Lib 23 Sep 1954
Sco 23 Oct 1954
Sag 22 Nov 1954
Cap 22 Dec 1954

Aqu 20 Jan 1955
Pis 19 Feb 1955
Ari 21 Mar 1955
Tau 20 Apr 1955
Gem 21 May 1955
Can 22 Jun 1955
Leo 23 Jul 1955
Vir 23 Aug 1955
Lib 23 Sep 1955
Sco 24 Oct 1955
Sag 23 Nov 1955
Cap 22 Dec 1955

Sun Signs

1956–67

Aqu 21 Jan 1956
Pis 19 Feb 1956
Ari 20 Mar 1956
Tau 20 Apr 1956
Gem 21 May 1956
Can 21 Jun 1956
Leo 22 Jul 1956
Vir 23 Aug 1956
Lib 23 Sep 1956
Sco 23 Oct 1956
Sag 22 Nov 1956
Cap 21 Dec 1956

Aqu 20 Jan 1957
Pis 18 Feb 1957
Ari 20 Mar 1957
Tau 20 Apr 1957
Gem 21 May 1957
Can 21 Jun 1957
Leo 23 Jul 1957
Vir 23 Aug 1957
Lib 23 Sep 1957
Sco 23 Oct 1957
Sag 22 Nov 1957
Cap 22 Dec 1957

Aqu 20 Jan 1958
Pis 19 Feb 1958
Ari 21 Mar 1958
Tau 20 Apr 1958
Gem 21 May 1958
Can 21 Jun 1958
Leo 23 Jul 1958
Vir 23 Aug 1958
Lib 23 Sep 1958
Sco 23 Oct 1958
Sag 22 Nov 1958
Cap 22 Dec 1958

Aqu 20 Jan 1959
Pis 19 Feb 1959
Ari 21 Mar 1959
Tau 20 Apr 1959
Gem 21 May 1959
Can 22 Jun 1959
Leo 23 Jul 1959
Vir 23 Aug 1959
Lib 23 Sep 1959
Sco 24 Oct 1959
Sag 23 Nov 1959
Cap 22 Dec 1959

Aqu 21 Jan 1960
Pis 19 Feb 1960
Ari 20 Mar 1960
Tau 20 Apr 1960
Gem 21 May 1960
Can 21 Jun 1960
Leo 22 Jul 1960
Vir 23 Aug 1960
Lib 23 Sep 1960
Sco 23 Oct 1960
Sag 22 Nov 1960
Cap 21 Dec 1960

Aqu 20 Jan 1961
Pis 18 Feb 1961
Ari 20 Mar 1961
Tau 20 Apr 1961
Gem 21 May 1961
Can 21 Jun 1961
Leo 23 Jul 1961
Vir 23 Aug 1961
Lib 23 Sep 1961
Sco 23 Oct 1961
Sag 22 Nov 1961
Cap 22 Dec 1961

Aqu 20 Jan 1962
Pis 19 Feb 1962
Ari 21 Mar 1962
Tau 20 Apr 1962
Gem 21 May 1962
Can 21 Jun 1962
Leo 23 Jul 1962
Vir 23 Aug 1962
Lib 23 Sep 1962
Sco 23 Oct 1962
Sag 22 Nov 1962
Cap 22 Dec 1962

Aqu 20 Jan 1963
Pis 19 Feb 1963
Ari 21 Mar 1963
Tau 20 Apr 1963
Gem 21 May 1963
Can 22 Jun 1963
Leo 23 Jul 1963
Vir 23 Aug 1963
Lib 23 Sep 1963
Sco 24 Oct 1963
Sag 23 Nov 1963
Cap 22 Dec 1963

Aqu 21 Jan 1964
Pis 19 Feb 1964
Ari 20 Mar 1964
Tau 20 Apr 1964
Gem 21 May 1964
Can 21 Jun 1964
Leo 22 Jul 1964
Vir 23 Aug 1964
Lib 23 Sep 1964
Sco 23 Oct 1964
Sag 22 Nov 1964
Cap 21 Dec 1964

Aqu 20 Jan 1965
Pis 18 Feb 1965
Ari 20 Mar 1965
Tau 20 Apr 1965
Gem 21 May 1965
Can 21 Jun 1965
Leo 23 Jul 1965
Vir 23 Aug 1965
Lib 23 Sep 1965
Sco 23 Oct 1965
Sag 22 Nov 1965
Cap 22 Dec 1965

Aqu 20 Jan 1966
Pis 19 Feb 1966
Ari 21 Mar 1966
Tau 20 Apr 1966
Gem 21 May 1966
Can 21 Jun 1966
Leo 23 Jul 1966
Vir 23 Aug 1966
Lib 23 Sep 1966
Sco 23 Oct 1966
Sag 22 Nov 1966
Cap 22 Dec 1966

Aqu 20 Jan 1967
Pis 19 Feb 1967
Ari 21 Mar 1967
Tau 20 Apr 1967
Gem 21 May 1967
Can 22 Jun 1967
Leo 23 Jul 1967
Vir 23 Aug 1967
Lib 23 Sep 1967
Sco 24 Oct 1967
Sag 22 Nov 1967
Cap 22 Dec 1967

Sun Signs

1968–79

Aqu	20 Jan 1968
Pis	19 Feb 1968
Ari	20 Mar 1968
Tau	20 Apr 1968
Gem	21 May 1968
Can	21 Jun 1968
Leo	22 Jul 1968
Vir	23 Aug 1968
Lib	22 Sep 1968
Sco	23 Oct 1968
Sag	22 Nov 1968
Cap	21 Dec 1968

Aqu	20 Jan 1969
Pis	18 Feb 1969
Ari	20 Mar 1969
Tau	20 Apr 1969
Gem	21 May 1969
Can	21 Jun 1969
Leo	23 Jul 1969
Vir	23 Aug 1969
Lib	23 Sep 1969
Sco	23 Oct 1969
Sag	22 Nov 1969
Cap	22 Dec 1969

Aqu	20 Jan 1970
Pis	19 Feb 1970
Ari	21 Mar 1970
Tau	20 Apr 1970
Gem	21 May 1970
Can	21 Jun 1970
Leo	23 Jul 1970
Vir	23 Aug 1970
Lib	23 Sep 1970
Sco	23 Oct 1970
Sag	22 Nov 1970
Cap	22 Dec 1970

Aqu	20 Jan 1971
Pis	19 Feb 1971
Ari	21 Mar 1971
Tau	20 Apr 1971
Gem	21 May 1971
Can	22 Jun 1971
Leo	23 Jul 1971
Vir	23 Aug 1971
Lib	23 Sep 1971
Sco	24 Oct 1971
Sag	22 Nov 1971
Cap	22 Dec 1971

Aqu	20 Jan 1972
Pis	19 Feb 1972
Ari	20 Mar 1972
Tau	19 Apr 1972
Gem	20 May 1972
Can	21 Jun 1972
Leo	22 Jul 1972
Vir	23 Aug 1972
Lib	22 Sep 1972
Sco	23 Oct 1972
Sag	22 Nov 1972
Cap	21 Dec 1972

Aqu	20 Jan 1973
Pis	18 Feb 1973
Ari	20 Mar 1973
Tau	20 Apr 1973
Gem	21 May 1973
Can	21 Jun 1973
Leo	22 Jul 1973
Vir	23 Aug 1973
Lib	23 Sep 1973
Sco	23 Oct 1973
Sag	22 Nov 1973
Cap	22 Dec 1973

Aqu	20 Jan 1974
Pis	19 Feb 1974
Ari	21 Mar 1974
Tau	20 Apr 1974
Gem	21 May 1974
Can	21 Jun 1974
Leo	23 Jul 1974
Vir	23 Aug 1974
Lib	23 Sep 1974
Sco	23 Oct 1974
Sag	22 Nov 1974
Cap	22 Dec 1974

Aqu	20 Jan 1975
Pis	19 Feb 1975
Ari	21 Mar 1975
Tau	20 Apr 1975
Gem	21 May 1975
Can	22 Jun 1975
Leo	23 Jul 1975
Vir	23 Aug 1975
Lib	23 Sep 1975
Sco	24 Oct 1975
Sag	22 Nov 1975
Cap	22 Dec 1975

Aqu	20 Jan 1976
Pis	19 Feb 1976
Ari	20 Mar 1976
Tau	19 Apr 1976
Gem	20 May 1976
Can	21 Jun 1976
Leo	22 Jul 1976
Vir	23 Aug 1976
Lib	22 Sep 1976
Sco	23 Oct 1976
Sag	22 Nov 1976
Cap	21 Dec 1976

Aqu	20 Jan 1977
Pis	18 Feb 1977
Ari	20 Mar 1977
Tau	20 Apr 1977
Gem	21 May 1977
Can	21 Jun 1977
Leo	22 Jul 1977
Vir	23 Aug 1977
Lib	23 Sep 1977
Sco	23 Oct 1977
Sag	22 Nov 1977
Cap	21 Dec 1977

Aqu	20 Jan 1978
Pis	19 Feb 1978
Ari	20 Mar 1978
Tau	20 Apr 1978
Gem	21 May 1978
Can	21 Jun 1978
Leo	23 Jul 1978
Vir	23 Aug 1978
Lib	23 Sep 1978
Sco	23 Oct 1978
Sag	22 Nov 1978
Cap	22 Dec 1978

Aqu	20 Jan 1979
Pis	19 Feb 1979
Ari	21 Mar 1979
Tau	20 Apr 1979
Gem	21 May 1979
Can	21 Jun 1979
Leo	23 Jul 1979
Vir	23 Aug 1979
Lib	23 Sep 1979
Sco	24 Oct 1979
Sag	22 Nov 1979
Cap	22 Dec 1979

Sun Signs

1980-91

Aqu	20 Jan 1980
Pis	19 Feb 1980
Ari	20 Mar 1980
Tau	19 Apr 1980
Gem	20 May 1980
Can	21 Jun 1980
Leo	22 Jul 1980
Vir	22 Aug 1980
Lib	22 Sep 1980
Sco	23 Oct 1980
Sag	22 Nov 1980
Cap	21 Dec 1980
Aqu	20 Jan 1981
Pis	18 Feb 1981
Ari	20 Mar 1981
Tau	20 Apr 1981
Gem	21 May 1981
Can	21 Jun 1981
Leo	22 Jul 1981
Vir	23 Aug 1981
Lib	23 Sep 1981
Sco	23 Oct 1981
Sag	22 Nov 1981
Cap	21 Dec 1981
Aqu	20 Jan 1982
Pis	18 Feb 1982
Ari	20 Mar 1982
Tau	20 Apr 1982
Gem	21 May 1982
Can	21 Jun 1982
Leo	23 Jul 1982
Vir	23 Aug 1982
Lib	23 Sep 1982
Sco	23 Oct 1982
Sag	22 Nov 1982
Cap	22 Dec 1982
Aqu	20 Jan 1983
Pis	19 Feb 1983
Ari	21 Mar 1983
Tau	20 Apr 1983
Gem	21 May 1983
Can	21 Jun 1983
Leo	23 Jul 1983
Vir	23 Aug 1983
Lib	23 Sep 1983
Sco	23 Oct 1983
Sag	22 Nov 1983
Cap	22 Dec 1983

Aqu	20 Jan 1984
Pis	19 Feb 1984
Ari	20 Mar 1984
Tau	19 Apr 1984
Gem	20 May 1984
Can	21 Jun 1984
Leo	22 Jul 1984
Vir	22 Aug 1984
Lib	22 Sep 1984
Sco	23 Oct 1984
Sag	22 Nov 1984
Cap	21 Dec 1984
Aqu	20 Jan 1985
Pis	18 Feb 1985
Ari	20 Mar 1985
Tau	20 Apr 1985
Gem	21 May 1985
Can	21 Jun 1985
Leo	22 Jul 1985
Vir	23 Aug 1985
Lib	23 Sep 1985
Sco	23 Oct 1985
Sag	22 Nov 1985
Cap	21 Dec 1985
Aqu	20 Jan 1986
Pis	18 Feb 1986
Ari	20 Mar 1986
Tau	20 Apr 1986
Gem	21 May 1986
Can	21 Jun 1986
Leo	23 Jul 1986
Vir	23 Aug 1986
Lib	23 Sep 1986
Sco	23 Oct 1986
Sag	22 Nov 1986
Cap	22 Dec 1986
Aqu	20 Jan 1987
Pis	19 Feb 1987
Ari	21 Mar 1987
Tau	20 Apr 1987
Gem	21 May 1987
Can	21 Jun 1987
Leo	23 Jul 1987
Vir	23 Aug 1987
Lib	23 Sep 1987
Sco	23 Oct 1987
Sag	22 Nov 1987
Cap	22 Dec 1987

Aqu	20 Jan 1988
Pis	19 Feb 1988
Ari	20 Mar 1988
Tau	19 Apr 1988
Gem	20 May 1988
Can	21 Jun 1988
Leo	22 Jul 1988
Vir	22 Aug 1988
Lib	22 Sep 1988
Sco	23 Oct 1988
Sag	22 Nov 1988
Cap	21 Dec 1988
Aqu	20 Jan 1989
Pis	18 Feb 1989
Ari	20 Mar 1989
Tau	20 Apr 1989
Gem	21 May 1989
Can	21 Jun 1989
Leo	22 Jul 1989
Vir	23 Aug 1989
Lib	23 Sep 1989
Sco	23 Oct 1989
Sag	22 Nov 1989
Cap	21 Dec 1989
Aqu	20 Jan 1990
Pis	18 Feb 1990
Ari	20 Mar 1990
Tau	20 Apr 1990
Gem	21 May 1990
Can	21 Jun 1990
Leo	23 Jul 1990
Vir	23 Aug 1990
Lib	23 Sep 1990
Sco	23 Oct 1990
Sag	22 Nov 1990
Cap	22 Dec 1990
Aqu	20 Jan 1991
Pis	19 Feb 1991
Ari	21 Mar 1991
Tau	20 Apr 1991
Gem	21 May 1991
Can	21 Jun 1991
Leo	23 Jul 1991
Vir	23 Aug 1991
Lib	23 Sep 1991
Sco	23 Oct 1991
Sag	22 Nov 1991
Cap	22 Dec 1991

Sun Signs

1992–2000

Sign	Date
Aqu	20 Jan 1992
Pis	19 Feb 1992
Ari	20 Mar 1992
Tau	19 Apr 1992
Gem	20 May 1992
Can	21 Jun 1992
Leo	22 Jul 1992
Vir	22 Aug 1992
Lib	22 Sep 1992
Sco	23 Oct 1992
Sag	22 Nov 1992
Cap	21 Dec 1992
Aqu	20 Jan 1993
Pis	18 Feb 1993
Ari	20 Mar 1993
Tau	20 Apr 1993
Gem	21 May 1993
Can	21 Jun 1993
Leo	22 Jul 1993
Vir	23 Aug 1993
Lib	23 Sep 1993
Sco	23 Oct 1993
Sag	22 Nov 1993
Cap	21 Dec 1993
Aqu	20 Jan 1994
Pis	18 Feb 1994
Ari	20 Mar 1994
Tau	20 Apr 1994
Gem	21 May 1994
Can	21 Jun 1994
Leo	23 Jul 1994
Vir	23 Aug 1994
Lib	23 Sep 1994
Sco	23 Oct 1994
Sag	22 Nov 1994
Cap	22 Dec 1994
Aqu	20 Jan 1995
Pis	19 Feb 1995
Ari	21 Mar 1995
Tau	20 Apr 1995
Gem	21 May 1995
Can	21 Jun 1995
Leo	23 Jul 1995
Vir	23 Aug 1995
Lib	23 Sep 1995
Sco	23 Oct 1995
Sag	22 Nov 1995
Cap	22 Dec 1995
Aqu	20 Jan 1996
Pis	19 Feb 1996
Ari	20 Mar 1996
Tau	19 Apr 1996
Gem	20 May 1996
Can	21 Jun 1996
Leo	22 Jul 1996
Vir	22 Aug 1996
Lib	22 Sep 1996
Sco	23 Oct 1996
Sag	22 Nov 1996
Cap	21 Dec 1996
Aqu	20 Jan 1997
Pis	18 Feb 1997
Ari	20 Mar 1997
Tau	20 Apr 1997
Gem	21 May 1997
Can	21 Jun 1997
Leo	22 Jul 1997
Vir	23 Aug 1997
Lib	22 Sep 1997
Sco	23 Oct 1997
Sag	22 Nov 1997
Cap	21 Dec 1997
Aqu	20 Jan 1998
Pis	18 Feb 1998
Ari	20 Mar 1998
Tau	20 Apr 1998
Gem	21 May 1998
Can	21 Jun 1998
Leo	23 Jul 1998
Vir	23 Aug 1998
Lib	23 Sep 1998
Sco	23 Oct 1998
Sag	22 Nov 1998
Cap	22 Dec 1998
Aqu	20 Jan 1999
Pis	19 Feb 1999
Ari	21 Mar 1999
Tau	20 Apr 1999
Gem	21 May 1999
Can	21 Jun 1999
Leo	23 Jul 1999
Vir	23 Aug 1999
Lib	23 Sep 1999
Sco	23 Oct 1999
Sag	22 Nov 1999
Cap	22 Dec 1999
Aqu	20 Jan 2000
Pis	19 Feb 2000
Ari	20 Mar 2000
Tau	19 Apr 2000
Gem	20 May 2000
Can	21 Jun 2000
Leo	22 Jul 2000
Vir	22 Aug 2000
Lib	22 Sep 2000
Sco	23 Oct 2000
Sag	22 Nov 2000
Cap	21 Dec 2000

MOON SIGNS

1920

Gem	2 Jan 1920	22:12
Can	4 Jan 1920	22:19
Leo	6 Jan 1920	22:31
Vir	9 Jan 1920	00:47
Lib	11 Jan 1920	06:48
Sco	13 Jan 1920	16:58
Sag	16 Jan 1920	05:44
Cap	18 Jan 1920	18:34
Aqu	21 Jan 1920	05:40
Pis	23 Jan 1920	14:34
Ari	25 Jan 1920	21:32
Tau	28 Jan 1920	02:43
Gem	30 Jan 1920	06:05

Can	1 Feb 1920	07:54
Leo	3 Feb 1920	09:06
Vir	5 Feb 1920	11:19
Lib	7 Feb 1920	16:20
Sco	10 Feb 1920	01:15
Sag	12 Feb 1920	13:21
Cap	15 Feb 1920	02:13
Aqu	17 Feb 1920	13:19
Pis	19 Feb 1920	21:38
Ari	22 Feb 1920	03:36
Tau	24 Feb 1920	08:05
Gem	26 Feb 1920	11:42
Can	28 Feb 1920	14:40

Leo	1 Mar 1920	17:23
Vir	3 Mar 1920	20:41
Lib	6 Mar 1920	01:54
Sco	8 Mar 1920	10:11
Sag	10 Mar 1920	21:36
Cap	13 Mar 1920	10:25
Aqu	15 Mar 1920	21:57
Pis	18 Mar 1920	06:24
Ari	20 Mar 1920	11:42
Tau	22 Mar 1920	14:58
Gem	24 Mar 1920	17:25
Can	26 Mar 1920	20:02
Leo	28 Mar 1920	23:21
Vir	31 Mar 1920	03:48

Lib	2 Apr 1920	10:00
Sco	4 Apr 1920	18:34
Sag	7 Apr 1920	05:42
Cap	9 Apr 1920	18:25
Aqu	12 Apr 1920	06:31
Pis	14 Apr 1920	15:49
Ari	16 Apr 1920	21:28
Tau	19 Apr 1920	00:07
Gem	21 Apr 1920	01:14
Can	23 Apr 1920	02:23
Leo	25 Apr 1920	04:49
Vir	27 Apr 1920	09:22
Lib	29 Apr 1920	16:19

Sco	2 May 1920	01:38
Sag	4 May 1920	12:59
Cap	7 May 1920	01:39
Aqu	9 May 1920	14:08
Pis	12 May 1920	00:31
Ari	14 May 1920	07:23
Tau	16 May 1920	10:34
Gem	18 May 1920	11:13
Can	20 May 1920	11:01
Leo	22 May 1920	11:50
Vir	24 May 1920	15:11
Lib	26 May 1920	21:51
Sco	29 May 1920	07:33
Sag	31 May 1920	19:20

Cap	3 Jun 1920	08:04
Aqu	5 Jun 1920	20:38
Pis	8 Jun 1920	07:42
Ari	10 Jun 1920	15:56
Tau	12 Jun 1920	20:34
Gem	14 Jun 1920	21:56
Can	16 Jun 1920	21:26
Leo	18 Jun 1920	21:02
Vir	20 Jun 1920	22:46
Lib	23 Jun 1920	04:06
Sco	25 Jun 1920	13:20
Sag	28 Jun 1920	01:15
Cap	30 Jun 1920	14:06

Aqu	3 Jul 1920	02:30
Pis	5 Jul 1920	13:36
Ari	7 Jul 1920	22:37
Tau	10 Jul 1920	04:45
Gem	12 Jul 1920	07:40
Can	14 Jul 1920	08:03
Leo	16 Jul 1920	07:32
Vir	18 Jul 1920	08:13
Lib	20 Jul 1920	12:04
Sco	22 Jul 1920	20:03
Sag	25 Jul 1920	07:31
Cap	27 Jul 1920	20:22
Aqu	30 Jul 1920	08:36

Pis	1 Aug 1920	19:18
Ari	4 Aug 1920	04:09
Tau	6 Aug 1920	10:55
Gem	8 Aug 1920	15:14
Can	10 Aug 1920	17:11
Leo	12 Aug 1920	17:41
Vir	14 Aug 1920	18:27
Lib	16 Aug 1920	21:29
Sco	19 Aug 1920	04:13
Sag	21 Aug 1920	14:45
Cap	24 Aug 1920	03:22
Aqu	26 Aug 1920	15:36
Pis	29 Aug 1920	01:54
Ari	31 Aug 1920	10:02

Tau	2 Sep 1920	16:19
Gem	4 Sep 1920	20:57
Can	7 Sep 1920	00:03
Leo	9 Sep 1920	02:02
Vir	11 Sep 1920	03:55
Lib	13 Sep 1920	07:11
Sco	15 Sep 1920	13:20
Sag	17 Sep 1920	22:59
Cap	20 Sep 1920	11:09
Aqu	22 Sep 1920	23:32
Pis	25 Sep 1920	09:57
Ari	27 Sep 1920	17:34
Tau	29 Sep 1920	22:48

Gem	2 Oct 1920	02:32
Can	4 Oct 1920	05:29
Leo	6 Oct 1920	08:14
Vir	8 Oct 1920	11:23
Lib	10 Oct 1920	15:45
Sco	12 Oct 1920	22:14
Sag	15 Oct 1920	07:31
Cap	17 Oct 1920	19:16
Aqu	20 Oct 1920	07:52
Pis	22 Oct 1920	18:56
Ari	25 Oct 1920	02:51
Tau	27 Oct 1920	07:33
Gem	29 Oct 1920	09:59
Can	31 Oct 1920	11:35

Leo	2 Nov 1920	13:38
Vir	4 Nov 1920	17:03
Lib	6 Nov 1920	22:24
Sco	9 Nov 1920	05:49
Sag	11 Nov 1920	15:27
Cap	14 Nov 1920	03:03
Aqu	16 Nov 1920	15:44
Pis	19 Nov 1920	03:39
Ari	21 Nov 1920	12:44
Tau	23 Nov 1920	18:02
Gem	25 Nov 1920	19:59
Can	27 Nov 1920	20:12
Leo	29 Nov 1920	20:33

Vir	1 Dec 1920	22:46
Lib	4 Dec 1920	03:50
Sco	6 Dec 1920	11:52
Sag	8 Dec 1920	22:10
Cap	11 Dec 1920	09:59
Aqu	13 Dec 1920	22:38
Pis	16 Dec 1920	11:02
Ari	18 Dec 1920	21:28
Tau	21 Dec 1920	04:21
Gem	23 Dec 1920	07:14
Can	25 Dec 1920	07:13
Leo	27 Dec 1920	06:16
Vir	29 Dec 1920	06:37
Lib	31 Dec 1920	10:07

1921

Sign	Date	Time
Sco	2 Jan 1921	17:27
Sag	5 Jan 1921	03:58
Cap	7 Jan 1921	16:10
Aqu	10 Jan 1921	04:49
Pis	12 Jan 1921	17:10
Ari	15 Jan 1921	04:14
Tau	17 Jan 1921	12:39
Gem	19 Jan 1921	17:23
Can	21 Jan 1921	18:35
Leo	23 Jan 1921	17:45
Vir	25 Jan 1921	17:04
Lib	27 Jan 1921	18:46
Sco	30 Jan 1921	00:26
Sag	1 Feb 1921	10:04
Cap	3 Feb 1921	22:14
Aqu	6 Feb 1921	10:59
Pis	8 Feb 1921	23:03
Ari	11 Feb 1921	09:51
Tau	13 Feb 1921	18:44
Gem	16 Feb 1921	00:53
Can	18 Feb 1921	03:57
Leo	20 Feb 1921	04:33
Vir	22 Feb 1921	04:20
Lib	24 Feb 1921	05:21
Sco	26 Feb 1921	09:29
Sag	28 Feb 1921	17:37
Cap	3 Mar 1921	05:03
Aqu	5 Mar 1921	17:45
Pis	8 Mar 1921	05:43
Ari	10 Mar 1921	15:58
Tau	13 Mar 1921	00:14
Gem	15 Mar 1921	06:28
Can	17 Mar 1921	10:35
Leo	19 Mar 1921	12:51
Vir	21 Mar 1921	14:08
Lib	23 Mar 1921	15:50
Sco	25 Mar 1921	19:34
Sag	28 Mar 1921	02:35
Cap	30 Mar 1921	12:58
Aqu	2 Apr 1921	01:21
Pis	4 Apr 1921	13:27
Ari	6 Apr 1921	23:30
Tau	9 Apr 1921	06:59
Gem	11 Apr 1921	12:15
Can	13 Apr 1921	15:58
Leo	15 Apr 1921	18:47
Vir	17 Apr 1921	21:21
Lib	20 Apr 1921	00:25
Sco	22 Apr 1921	04:54
Sag	24 Apr 1921	11:46
Cap	26 Apr 1921	21:28
Aqu	29 Apr 1921	09:25
Pis	1 May 1921	21:45
Ari	4 May 1921	08:12
Tau	6 May 1921	15:31
Gem	8 May 1921	19:50
Can	10 May 1921	22:18
Leo	13 May 1921	00:16
Vir	15 May 1921	02:52
Lib	17 May 1921	06:46
Sco	19 May 1921	12:22
Sag	21 May 1921	19:53
Cap	24 May 1921	05:34
Aqu	26 May 1921	17:17
Pis	29 May 1921	05:50
Ari	31 May 1921	17:04
Tau	3 Jun 1921	01:02
Gem	5 Jun 1921	05:17
Can	7 Jun 1921	06:46
Leo	9 Jun 1921	07:18
Vir	11 Jun 1921	08:41
Lib	13 Jun 1921	12:10
Sco	15 Jun 1921	18:10
Sag	18 Jun 1921	02:28
Cap	20 Jun 1921	12:39
Aqu	23 Jun 1921	00:24
Pis	25 Jun 1921	13:03
Ari	28 Jun 1921	01:01
Tau	30 Jun 1921	10:12
Gem	2 Jul 1921	15:22
Can	4 Jul 1921	16:55
Leo	6 Jul 1921	16:33
Vir	8 Jul 1921	16:26
Lib	10 Jul 1921	18:28
Sco	12 Jul 1921	23:43
Sag	15 Jul 1921	08:05
Cap	17 Jul 1921	18:43
Aqu	20 Jul 1921	06:43
Pis	22 Jul 1921	19:23
Ari	25 Jul 1921	07:41
Tau	27 Jul 1921	17:58
Gem	30 Jul 1921	00:35
Can	1 Aug 1921	03:17
Leo	3 Aug 1921	03:10
Vir	5 Aug 1921	02:19
Lib	7 Aug 1921	02:52
Sco	9 Aug 1921	06:33
Sag	11 Aug 1921	14:00
Cap	14 Aug 1921	00:30
Aqu	16 Aug 1921	12:42
Pis	19 Aug 1921	01:20
Ari	21 Aug 1921	13:29
Tau	24 Aug 1921	00:06
Gem	26 Aug 1921	07:57
Can	28 Aug 1921	12:16
Leo	30 Aug 1921	13:29
Vir	1 Sep 1921	13:06
Lib	3 Sep 1921	13:06
Sco	5 Sep 1921	15:24
Sag	7 Sep 1921	21:21
Cap	10 Sep 1921	06:58
Aqu	12 Sep 1921	19:00
Pis	15 Sep 1921	07:39
Ari	17 Sep 1921	19:28
Tau	20 Sep 1921	05:41
Gem	22 Sep 1921	13:40
Can	24 Sep 1921	19:05
Leo	26 Sep 1921	21:56
Vir	28 Sep 1921	23:01
Lib	30 Sep 1921	23:41
Sco	3 Oct 1921	01:37
Sag	5 Oct 1921	06:22
Cap	7 Oct 1921	14:46
Aqu	10 Oct 1921	02:12
Pis	12 Oct 1921	14:50
Ari	15 Oct 1921	02:33
Tau	17 Oct 1921	12:07
Gem	19 Oct 1921	19:20
Can	22 Oct 1921	00:31
Leo	24 Oct 1921	04:07
Vir	26 Oct 1921	06:39
Lib	28 Oct 1921	08:48
Sco	30 Oct 1921	11:34
Sag	1 Nov 1921	16:08
Cap	3 Nov 1921	23:38
Aqu	6 Nov 1921	10:18
Pis	8 Nov 1921	22:50
Ari	11 Nov 1921	10:51
Tau	13 Nov 1921	20:18
Gem	16 Nov 1921	02:39
Can	18 Nov 1921	06:40
Leo	20 Nov 1921	09:32
Vir	22 Nov 1921	12:17
Lib	24 Nov 1921	15:31
Sco	26 Nov 1921	19:37
Sag	29 Nov 1921	01:03
Cap	1 Dec 1921	08:32
Aqu	3 Dec 1921	18:41
Pis	6 Dec 1921	07:03
Ari	8 Dec 1921	19:36
Tau	11 Dec 1921	05:45
Gem	13 Dec 1921	12:06
Can	15 Dec 1921	15:11
Leo	17 Dec 1921	16:34
Vir	19 Dec 1921	18:02
Lib	21 Dec 1921	20:52
Sco	24 Dec 1921	01:33
Sag	26 Dec 1921	08:01
Cap	28 Dec 1921	16:16
Aqu	31 Dec 1921	02:32

Moon Signs

1922

Sign	Date	Time
Pis	2 Jan 1922	14:44
Ari	5 Jan 1922	03:41
Tau	7 Jan 1922	14:57
Gem	9 Jan 1922	22:25
Can	12 Jan 1922	01:46
Leo	14 Jan 1922	02:20
Vir	16 Jan 1922	02:13
Lib	18 Jan 1922	03:21
Sco	20 Jan 1922	07:02
Sag	22 Jan 1922	13:33
Cap	24 Jan 1922	22:28
Aqu	27 Jan 1922	09:16
Pis	29 Jan 1922	21:33
Ari	1 Feb 1922	10:35
Tau	3 Feb 1922	22:39
Gem	6 Feb 1922	07:41
Can	8 Feb 1922	12:28
Leo	10 Feb 1922	13:38
Vir	12 Feb 1922	12:58
Lib	14 Feb 1922	12:35
Sco	16 Feb 1922	14:23
Sag	18 Feb 1922	19:32
Cap	21 Feb 1922	04:05
Aqu	23 Feb 1922	15:12
Pis	26 Feb 1922	03:44
Ari	28 Feb 1922	16:41
Tau	3 Mar 1922	04:51
Gem	5 Mar 1922	14:47
Can	7 Mar 1922	21:17
Leo	10 Mar 1922	00:08
Vir	12 Mar 1922	00:21
Lib	13 Mar 1922	23:44
Sco	16 Mar 1922	00:14
Sag	18 Mar 1922	03:34
Cap	20 Mar 1922	10:42
Aqu	22 Mar 1922	21:18
Pis	25 Mar 1922	09:55
Ari	27 Mar 1922	22:48
Tau	30 Mar 1922	10:37
Gem	1 Apr 1922	20:28
Can	4 Apr 1922	03:45
Leo	6 Apr 1922	08:12
Vir	8 Apr 1922	10:08
Lib	10 Apr 1922	10:36
Sco	12 Apr 1922	11:07
Sag	14 Apr 1922	13:26
Cap	16 Apr 1922	19:01
Aqu	19 Apr 1922	04:28
Pis	21 Apr 1922	16:43
Ari	24 Apr 1922	05:37
Tau	26 Apr 1922	17:07
Gem	29 Apr 1922	02:18

Sign	Date	Time
Can	1 May 1922	09:11
Leo	3 May 1922	14:04
Vir	5 May 1922	17:18
Lib	7 May 1922	19:21
Sco	9 May 1922	21:00
Sag	11 May 1922	23:32
Cap	14 May 1922	04:25
Aqu	16 May 1922	12:46
Pis	19 May 1922	00:20
Ari	21 May 1922	13:12
Tau	24 May 1922	00:44
Gem	26 May 1922	09:28
Can	28 May 1922	15:25
Leo	30 May 1922	19:33
Vir	1 Jun 1922	22:47
Lib	4 Jun 1922	01:43
Sco	6 Jun 1922	04:42
Sag	8 Jun 1922	08:18
Cap	10 Jun 1922	13:31
Aqu	12 Jun 1922	21:25
Pis	15 Jun 1922	08:24
Ari	17 Jun 1922	21:12
Tau	20 Jun 1922	09:08
Gem	22 Jun 1922	18:02
Can	24 Jun 1922	23:26
Leo	27 Jun 1922	02:27
Vir	29 Jun 1922	04:36
Lib	1 Jul 1922	07:04
Sco	3 Jul 1922	10:29
Sag	5 Jul 1922	15:05
Cap	7 Jul 1922	21:12
Aqu	10 Jul 1922	05:27
Pis	12 Jul 1922	16:16
Ari	15 Jul 1922	04:59
Tau	17 Jul 1922	17:27
Gem	20 Jul 1922	03:09
Can	22 Jul 1922	08:55
Leo	24 Jul 1922	11:25
Vir	26 Jul 1922	12:21
Lib	28 Jul 1922	13:26
Sco	30 Jul 1922	15:59
Sag	1 Aug 1922	20:35
Cap	4 Aug 1922	03:22
Aqu	6 Aug 1922	12:19
Pis	8 Aug 1922	23:23
Ari	11 Aug 1922	12:05
Tau	14 Aug 1922	00:56
Gem	16 Aug 1922	11:41
Can	18 Aug 1922	18:39
Leo	20 Aug 1922	21:44
Vir	22 Aug 1922	22:15
Lib	24 Aug 1922	22:05
Sco	26 Aug 1922	23:02
Sag	29 Aug 1922	02:27
Cap	31 Aug 1922	08:54

Sign	Date	Time
Aqu	2 Sep 1922	18:12
Pis	5 Sep 1922	05:41
Ari	7 Sep 1922	18:29
Tau	10 Sep 1922	07:23
Gem	12 Sep 1922	18:50
Can	15 Sep 1922	03:11
Leo	17 Sep 1922	07:47
Vir	19 Sep 1922	09:07
Lib	21 Sep 1922	08:43
Sco	23 Sep 1922	08:27
Sag	25 Sep 1922	10:11
Cap	27 Sep 1922	15:16
Aqu	30 Sep 1922	00:03
Pis	2 Oct 1922	11:40
Ari	5 Oct 1922	00:35
Tau	7 Oct 1922	13:19
Gem	10 Oct 1922	00:43
Can	12 Oct 1922	09:51
Leo	14 Oct 1922	16:00
Vir	16 Oct 1922	19:03
Lib	18 Oct 1922	19:42
Sco	20 Oct 1922	19:26
Sag	22 Oct 1922	20:06
Cap	24 Oct 1922	23:34
Aqu	27 Oct 1922	07:00
Pis	29 Oct 1922	18:06
Ari	1 Nov 1922	07:03
Tau	3 Nov 1922	19:39
Gem	6 Nov 1922	06:33
Can	8 Nov 1922	15:22
Leo	10 Nov 1922	22:04
Vir	13 Nov 1922	02:35
Lib	15 Nov 1922	05:00
Sco	17 Nov 1922	05:58
Sag	19 Nov 1922	06:52
Cap	21 Nov 1922	09:32
Aqu	23 Nov 1922	15:36
Pis	26 Nov 1922	01:39
Ari	28 Nov 1922	14:20
Tau	1 Dec 1922	02:59
Gem	3 Dec 1922	13:32
Can	5 Dec 1922	21:32
Leo	8 Dec 1922	03:32
Vir	10 Dec 1922	08:08
Lib	12 Dec 1922	11:38
Sco	14 Dec 1922	14:13
Sag	16 Dec 1922	16:27
Cap	18 Dec 1922	19:34
Aqu	21 Dec 1922	01:09
Pis	23 Dec 1922	10:14
Ari	25 Dec 1922	22:22
Tau	28 Dec 1922	11:11
Gem	30 Dec 1922	22:01

Moon Signs

1923

Can	2 Jan 1923	05:39
Leo	4 Jan 1923	10:33
Vir	6 Jan 1923	13:59
Lib	8 Jan 1923	16:58
Sco	10 Jan 1923	20:04
Sag	12 Jan 1923	23:33
Cap	15 Jan 1923	03:56
Aqu	17 Jan 1923	10:06
Pis	19 Jan 1923	18:57
Ari	22 Jan 1923	06:36
Tau	24 Jan 1923	19:33
Gem	27 Jan 1923	07:07
Can	29 Jan 1923	15:18
Leo	31 Jan 1923	19:56

Vir	2 Feb 1923	22:11
Lib	4 Feb 1923	23:38
Sco	7 Feb 1923	01:37
Sag	9 Feb 1923	04:58
Cap	11 Feb 1923	10:08
Aqu	13 Feb 1923	17:18
Pis	16 Feb 1923	02:43
Ari	18 Feb 1923	14:20
Tau	21 Feb 1923	03:14
Gem	23 Feb 1923	15:30
Can	26 Feb 1923	00:55
Leo	28 Feb 1923	06:30

Vir	2 Mar 1923	08:40
Lib	4 Mar 1923	09:00
Sco	6 Mar 1923	09:16
Sag	8 Mar 1923	11:06
Cap	10 Mar 1923	15:34
Aqu	12 Mar 1923	23:02
Pis	15 Mar 1923	09:07
Ari	17 Mar 1923	21:05
Tau	20 Mar 1923	09:59
Gem	22 Mar 1923	22:31
Can	25 Mar 1923	09:04
Leo	27 Mar 1923	16:12
Vir	29 Mar 1923	19:35
Lib	31 Mar 1923	20:06

Sco	2 Apr 1923	19:25
Sag	4 Apr 1923	19:33
Cap	6 Apr 1923	22:20
Aqu	9 Apr 1923	04:48
Pis	11 Apr 1923	14:51
Ari	14 Apr 1923	03:08
Tau	16 Apr 1923	16:06
Gem	19 Apr 1923	04:32
Can	21 Apr 1923	15:27
Leo	23 Apr 1923	23:49
Vir	26 Apr 1923	04:55
Lib	28 Apr 1923	06:47
Sco	30 Apr 1923	06:32

Sag	2 May 1923	05:58
Cap	4 May 1923	07:14
Aqu	6 May 1923	12:06
Pis	8 May 1923	21:07
Ari	11 May 1923	09:12
Tau	13 May 1923	22:13
Gem	16 May 1923	10:26
Can	18 May 1923	21:02
Leo	21 May 1923	05:40
Vir	23 May 1923	11:52
Lib	25 May 1923	15:24
Sco	27 May 1923	16:34
Sag	29 May 1923	16:37
Cap	31 May 1923	17:27

Aqu	2 Jun 1923	21:04
Pis	5 Jun 1923	04:43
Ari	7 Jun 1923	16:02
Tau	10 Jun 1923	04:56
Gem	12 Jun 1923	17:02
Can	15 Jun 1923	03:09
Leo	17 Jun 1923	11:11
Vir	19 Jun 1923	17:22
Lib	21 Jun 1923	21:43
Sco	24 Jun 1923	00:19
Sag	26 Jun 1923	01:46
Cap	28 Jun 1923	03:20
Aqu	30 Jun 1923	06:43

Pis	2 Jul 1923	13:28
Ari	4 Jul 1923	23:51
Tau	7 Jul 1923	12:24
Gem	10 Jul 1923	00:35
Can	12 Jul 1923	10:32
Leo	14 Jul 1923	17:53
Vir	16 Jul 1923	23:09
Lib	19 Jul 1923	03:05
Sco	21 Jul 1923	06:08
Sag	23 Jul 1923	08:43
Cap	25 Jul 1923	11:33
Aqu	27 Jul 1923	15:42
Pis	29 Jul 1923	22:23

Ari	1 Aug 1923	08:11
Tau	3 Aug 1923	20:21
Gem	6 Aug 1923	08:46
Can	8 Aug 1923	19:07
Leo	11 Aug 1923	02:18
Vir	13 Aug 1923	06:43
Lib	15 Aug 1923	09:26
Sco	17 Aug 1923	11:38
Sag	19 Aug 1923	14:12
Cap	21 Aug 1923	17:49
Aqu	23 Aug 1923	23:03
Pis	26 Aug 1923	06:25
Ari	28 Aug 1923	16:15
Tau	31 Aug 1923	04:11

Gem	2 Sep 1923	16:50
Can	5 Sep 1923	03:58
Leo	7 Sep 1923	11:52
Vir	9 Sep 1923	16:15
Lib	11 Sep 1923	18:02
Sco	13 Sep 1923	18:46
Sag	15 Sep 1923	20:05
Cap	17 Sep 1923	23:14
Aqu	20 Sep 1923	04:52
Pis	22 Sep 1923	13:03
Ari	24 Sep 1923	23:23
Tau	27 Sep 1923	11:22
Gem	30 Sep 1923	00:05

Can	2 Oct 1923	11:59
Leo	4 Oct 1923	21:13
Vir	7 Oct 1923	02:39
Lib	9 Oct 1923	04:34
Sco	11 Oct 1923	04:24
Sag	13 Oct 1923	04:08
Cap	15 Oct 1923	05:42
Aqu	17 Oct 1923	10:30
Pis	19 Oct 1923	18:42
Ari	22 Oct 1923	05:32
Tau	24 Oct 1923	17:47
Gem	27 Oct 1923	06:28
Can	29 Oct 1923	18:38

Leo	1 Nov 1923	04:59
Vir	3 Nov 1923	12:05
Lib	5 Nov 1923	15:22
Sco	7 Nov 1923	15:36
Sag	9 Nov 1923	14:37
Cap	11 Nov 1923	14:38
Aqu	13 Nov 1923	17:39
Pis	16 Nov 1923	00:47
Ari	18 Nov 1923	11:25
Tau	20 Nov 1923	23:52
Gem	23 Nov 1923	12:31
Can	26 Nov 1923	00:27
Leo	28 Nov 1923	11:00
Vir	30 Nov 1923	19:18

Lib	3 Dec 1923	00:22
Sco	5 Dec 1923	02:13
Sag	7 Dec 1923	01:56
Cap	9 Dec 1923	01:31
Aqu	11 Dec 1923	03:10
Pis	13 Dec 1923	08:35
Ari	15 Dec 1923	18:07
Tau	18 Dec 1923	06:20
Gem	20 Dec 1923	19:02
Can	23 Dec 1923	06:39
Leo	25 Dec 1923	16:39
Vir	28 Dec 1923	00:50
Lib	30 Dec 1923	06:50

1924

Sign	Date	Time
Sco	1 Jan 1924	10:21
Sag	3 Jan 1924	11:47
Cap	5 Jan 1924	12:21
Aqu	7 Jan 1924	13:54
Pis	9 Jan 1924	18:13
Ari	12 Jan 1924	02:22
Tau	14 Jan 1924	13:48
Gem	17 Jan 1924	02:27
Can	19 Jan 1924	14:04
Leo	21 Jan 1924	23:32
Vir	24 Jan 1924	06:48
Lib	26 Jan 1924	12:13
Sco	28 Jan 1924	16:08
Sag	30 Jan 1924	18:52
Cap	1 Feb 1924	21:02
Aqu	3 Feb 1924	23:43
Pis	6 Feb 1924	04:12
Ari	8 Feb 1924	11:37
Tau	10 Feb 1924	22:09
Gem	13 Feb 1924	10:34
Can	15 Feb 1924	22:32
Leo	18 Feb 1924	08:08
Vir	20 Feb 1924	14:44
Lib	22 Feb 1924	18:56
Sco	24 Feb 1924	21:46
Sag	27 Feb 1924	00:16
Cap	29 Feb 1924	03:12
Aqu	2 Mar 1924	07:11
Pis	4 Mar 1924	12:44
Ari	6 Mar 1924	20:26
Tau	9 Mar 1924	06:35
Gem	11 Mar 1924	18:43
Can	14 Mar 1924	07:07
Leo	16 Mar 1924	17:30
Vir	19 Mar 1924	00:25
Lib	21 Mar 1924	03:59
Sco	23 Mar 1924	05:26
Sag	25 Mar 1924	06:28
Cap	27 Mar 1924	08:37
Aqu	29 Mar 1924	12:47
Pis	31 Mar 1924	19:12
Ari	3 Apr 1924	03:45
Tau	5 Apr 1924	14:11
Gem	8 Apr 1924	02:12
Can	10 Apr 1924	14:52
Leo	13 Apr 1924	02:13
Vir	15 Apr 1924	10:19
Lib	17 Apr 1924	14:25
Sco	19 Apr 1924	15:23
Sag	21 Apr 1924	15:04
Cap	23 Apr 1924	15:33
Aqu	25 Apr 1924	18:29
Pis	28 Apr 1924	00:39
Ari	30 Apr 1924	09:39

Sign	Date	Time
Tau	2 May 1924	20:36
Gem	5 May 1924	08:47
Can	7 May 1924	21:30
Leo	10 May 1924	09:29
Vir	12 May 1924	18:55
Lib	15 May 1924	00:26
Sco	17 May 1924	02:09
Sag	19 May 1924	01:33
Cap	21 May 1924	00:49
Aqu	23 May 1924	02:05
Pis	25 May 1924	06:49
Ari	27 May 1924	15:16
Tau	30 May 1924	02:22
Gem	1 Jun 1924	14:47
Can	4 Jun 1924	03:26
Leo	6 Jun 1924	15:28
Vir	9 Jun 1924	01:39
Lib	11 Jun 1924	08:39
Sco	13 Jun 1924	11:55
Sag	15 Jun 1924	12:15
Cap	17 Jun 1924	11:28
Aqu	19 Jun 1924	11:43
Pis	21 Jun 1924	14:52
Ari	23 Jun 1924	21:56
Tau	26 Jun 1924	08:27
Gem	28 Jun 1924	20:50
Can	1 Jul 1924	09:27
Leo	3 Jul 1924	21:10
Vir	6 Jul 1924	07:14
Lib	8 Jul 1924	14:53
Sco	10 Jul 1924	19:35
Sag	12 Jul 1924	21:30
Cap	14 Jul 1924	21:48
Aqu	16 Jul 1924	22:11
Pis	19 Jul 1924	00:31
Ari	21 Jul 1924	06:11
Tau	23 Jul 1924	15:36
Gem	26 Jul 1924	03:36
Can	28 Jul 1924	16:10
Leo	31 Jul 1924	03:37
Vir	2 Aug 1924	13:04
Lib	4 Aug 1924	20:19
Sco	7 Aug 1924	01:22
Sag	9 Aug 1924	04:31
Cap	11 Aug 1924	06:20
Aqu	13 Aug 1924	07:51
Pis	15 Aug 1924	10:28
Ari	17 Aug 1924	15:32
Tau	19 Aug 1924	23:54
Gem	22 Aug 1924	11:14
Can	24 Aug 1924	23:47
Leo	27 Aug 1924	11:17
Vir	29 Aug 1924	20:17

Sign	Date	Time
Lib	1 Sep 1924	02:36
Sco	3 Sep 1924	06:53
Sag	5 Sep 1924	09:59
Cap	7 Sep 1924	12:40
Aqu	9 Sep 1924	15:32
Pis	11 Sep 1924	19:16
Ari	14 Sep 1924	00:42
Tau	16 Sep 1924	08:39
Gem	18 Sep 1924	19:23
Can	21 Sep 1924	07:54
Leo	23 Sep 1924	19:51
Vir	26 Sep 1924	05:05
Lib	28 Sep 1924	10:51
Sco	30 Sep 1924	13:58
Sag	2 Oct 1924	15:53
Cap	4 Oct 1924	18:02
Aqu	6 Oct 1924	21:19
Pis	9 Oct 1924	02:06
Ari	11 Oct 1924	08:30
Tau	13 Oct 1924	16:49
Gem	16 Oct 1924	03:22
Can	18 Oct 1924	15:47
Leo	21 Oct 1924	04:20
Vir	23 Oct 1924	14:31
Lib	25 Oct 1924	20:47
Sco	27 Oct 1924	23:25
Sag	30 Oct 1924	00:02
Cap	1 Nov 1924	00:39
Aqu	3 Nov 1924	02:53
Pis	5 Nov 1924	07:34
Ari	7 Nov 1924	14:39
Tau	9 Nov 1924	23:43
Gem	12 Nov 1924	10:34
Can	14 Nov 1924	22:56
Leo	17 Nov 1924	11:49
Vir	19 Nov 1924	23:09
Lib	22 Nov 1924	06:50
Sco	24 Nov 1924	10:15
Sag	26 Nov 1924	10:37
Cap	28 Nov 1924	09:57
Aqu	30 Nov 1924	10:26
Pis	2 Dec 1924	13:39
Ari	4 Dec 1924	20:10
Tau	7 Dec 1924	05:32
Gem	9 Dec 1924	16:51
Can	12 Dec 1924	05:20
Leo	14 Dec 1924	18:12
Vir	17 Dec 1924	06:06
Lib	19 Dec 1924	15:13
Sco	21 Dec 1924	20:24
Sag	23 Dec 1924	21:54
Cap	25 Dec 1924	21:17
Aqu	27 Dec 1924	20:41
Pis	29 Dec 1924	22:06

1925

Ari 1 Jan 1925 02:57
Tau 3 Jan 1925 11:31
Gem 5 Jan 1925 22:52
Can 8 Jan 1925 11:31
Leo 11 Jan 1925 00:13
Vir 13 Jan 1925 11:53
Lib 15 Jan 1925 21:31
Sco 18 Jan 1925 04:10
Sag 20 Jan 1925 07:32
Cap 22 Jan 1925 08:21
Aqu 24 Jan 1925 08:08
Pis 26 Jan 1925 08:45
Ari 28 Jan 1925 12:00
Tau 30 Jan 1925 18:57

Gem 2 Feb 1925 05:31
Can 4 Feb 1925 18:10
Leo 7 Feb 1925 06:49
Vir 9 Feb 1925 18:00
Lib 12 Feb 1925 03:05
Sco 14 Feb 1925 09:53
Sag 16 Feb 1925 14:26
Cap 18 Feb 1925 17:01
Aqu 20 Feb 1925 18:20
Pis 22 Feb 1925 19:36
Ari 24 Feb 1925 22:21
Tau 27 Feb 1925 04:03

Gem 1 Mar 1925 13:26
Can 4 Mar 1925 01:37
Leo 6 Mar 1925 14:21
Vir 9 Mar 1925 01:22
Lib 11 Mar 1925 09:42
Sco 13 Mar 1925 15:36
Sag 15 Mar 1925 19:50
Cap 17 Mar 1925 23:06
Aqu 20 Mar 1925 01:50
Pis 22 Mar 1925 04:33
Ari 24 Mar 1925 08:04
Tau 26 Mar 1925 13:34
Gem 28 Mar 1925 22:08
Can 31 Mar 1925 09:42

Leo 2 Apr 1925 22:31
Vir 5 Apr 1925 09:53
Lib 7 Apr 1925 18:04
Sco 9 Apr 1925 23:02
Sag 12 Apr 1925 02:04
Cap 14 Apr 1925 04:31
Aqu 16 Apr 1925 07:22
Pis 18 Apr 1925 11:02
Ari 20 Apr 1925 15:44
Tau 22 Apr 1925 21:59
Gem 25 Apr 1925 06:32
Can 27 Apr 1925 17:44
Leo 30 Apr 1925 06:36

Vir 2 May 1925 18:37
Lib 5 May 1925 03:24
Sco 7 May 1925 08:20
Sag 9 May 1925 10:26
Cap 11 May 1925 11:30
Aqu 13 May 1925 13:08
Pis 15 May 1925 16:23
Ari 17 May 1925 21:34
Tau 20 May 1925 04:40
Gem 22 May 1925 13:50
Can 25 May 1925 01:07
Leo 27 May 1925 13:58
Vir 30 May 1925 02:34

Lib 1 Jun 1925 12:28
Sco 3 Jun 1925 18:21
Sag 5 Jun 1925 20:32
Cap 7 Jun 1925 20:44
Aqu 9 Jun 1925 20:53
Pis 11 Jun 1925 22:40
Ari 14 Jun 1925 03:03
Tau 16 Jun 1925 10:15
Gem 18 Jun 1925 19:56
Can 21 Jun 1925 07:35
Leo 23 Jun 1925 20:29
Vir 26 Jun 1925 09:20
Lib 28 Jun 1925 20:13

Sco 1 Jul 1925 03:31
Sag 3 Jul 1925 06:54
Cap 5 Jul 1925 07:23
Aqu 7 Jul 1925 06:48
Pis 9 Jul 1925 07:06
Ari 11 Jul 1925 09:53
Tau 13 Jul 1925 16:05
Gem 16 Jul 1925 01:37
Can 18 Jul 1925 13:32
Leo 21 Jul 1925 02:31
Vir 23 Jul 1925 15:16
Lib 26 Jul 1925 02:28
Sco 28 Jul 1925 10:54
Sag 30 Jul 1925 15:54

Cap 1 Aug 1925 17:45
Aqu 3 Aug 1925 17:40
Pis 5 Aug 1925 17:22
Ari 7 Aug 1925 18:45
Tau 9 Aug 1925 23:25
Gem 12 Aug 1925 07:56
Can 14 Aug 1925 19:38
Leo 17 Aug 1925 08:40
Vir 19 Aug 1925 21:12
Lib 22 Aug 1925 08:04
Sco 24 Aug 1925 16:43
Sag 26 Aug 1925 22:48
Cap 29 Aug 1925 02:17
Aqu 31 Aug 1925 03:40

Pis 2 Sep 1925 04:02
Ari 4 Sep 1925 05:01
Tau 6 Sep 1925 08:27
Gem 8 Sep 1925 15:39
Can 11 Sep 1925 02:34
Leo 13 Sep 1925 15:29
Vir 16 Sep 1925 03:55
Lib 18 Sep 1925 14:16
Sco 20 Sep 1925 22:16
Sag 23 Sep 1925 04:16
Cap 25 Sep 1925 08:35
Aqu 27 Sep 1925 11:28
Pis 29 Sep 1925 13:18

Ari 1 Oct 1925 15:05
Tau 3 Oct 1925 18:19
Gem 6 Oct 1925 00:35
Can 8 Oct 1925 10:33
Leo 10 Oct 1925 23:08
Vir 13 Oct 1925 11:42
Lib 15 Oct 1925 21:56
Sco 18 Oct 1925 05:11
Sag 20 Oct 1925 10:10
Cap 22 Oct 1925 13:56
Aqu 24 Oct 1925 17:11
Pis 26 Oct 1925 20:13
Ari 28 Oct 1925 23:23
Tau 31 Oct 1925 03:29

Gem 2 Nov 1925 09:44
Can 4 Nov 1925 19:05
Leo 7 Nov 1925 07:15
Vir 9 Nov 1925 20:05
Lib 12 Nov 1925 06:51
Sco 14 Nov 1925 14:03
Sag 16 Nov 1925 18:12
Cap 18 Nov 1925 20:37
Aqu 20 Nov 1925 22:47
Pis 23 Nov 1925 01:37
Ari 25 Nov 1925 05:31
Tau 27 Nov 1925 10:46
Gem 29 Nov 1925 17:49

Can 2 Dec 1925 03:18
Leo 4 Dec 1925 15:12
Vir 7 Dec 1925 04:12
Lib 9 Dec 1925 15:51
Sco 12 Dec 1925 00:01
Sag 14 Dec 1925 04:22
Cap 16 Dec 1925 05:58
Aqu 18 Dec 1925 06:35
Pis 20 Dec 1925 07:51
Ari 22 Dec 1925 10:57
Tau 24 Dec 1925 16:25
Gem 27 Dec 1925 00:18
Can 29 Dec 1925 10:26
Leo 31 Dec 1925 22:26

Moon Signs

1926

Sign	Date	Time
Vir	3 Jan 1926	11:25
Lib	5 Jan 1926	23:42
Sco	8 Jan 1926	09:17
Sag	10 Jan 1926	15:00
Cap	12 Jan 1926	17:08
Aqu	14 Jan 1926	17:06
Pis	16 Jan 1926	16:47
Ari	18 Jan 1926	18:02
Tau	20 Jan 1926	22:16
Gem	23 Jan 1926	05:54
Can	25 Jan 1926	16:29
Leo	28 Jan 1926	04:51
Vir	30 Jan 1926	17:48
Lib	2 Feb 1926	06:10
Sco	4 Feb 1926	16:38
Sag	7 Feb 1926	00:00
Cap	9 Feb 1926	03:48
Aqu	11 Feb 1926	04:36
Pis	13 Feb 1926	03:56
Ari	15 Feb 1926	03:47
Tau	17 Feb 1926	06:08
Gem	19 Feb 1926	12:22
Can	21 Feb 1926	22:28
Leo	24 Feb 1926	10:59
Vir	26 Feb 1926	23:58
Lib	1 Mar 1926	12:02
Sco	3 Mar 1926	22:26
Sag	6 Mar 1926	06:39
Cap	8 Mar 1926	12:05
Aqu	10 Mar 1926	14:38
Pis	12 Mar 1926	15:02
Ari	14 Mar 1926	14:51
Tau	16 Mar 1926	16:06
Gem	18 Mar 1926	20:42
Can	21 Mar 1926	05:29
Leo	23 Mar 1926	17:35
Vir	26 Mar 1926	06:35
Lib	28 Mar 1926	18:26
Sco	31 Mar 1926	04:16
Sag	2 Apr 1926	12:06
Cap	4 Apr 1926	18:03
Aqu	6 Apr 1926	21:59
Pis	9 Apr 1926	00:02
Ari	11 Apr 1926	01:02
Tau	13 Apr 1926	02:31
Gem	15 Apr 1926	06:20
Can	17 Apr 1926	13:55
Leo	20 Apr 1926	01:07
Vir	22 Apr 1926	13:57
Lib	25 Apr 1926	01:50
Sco	27 Apr 1926	11:17
Sag	29 Apr 1926	18:18
Cap	1 May 1926	23:31
Aqu	4 May 1926	03:30
Pis	6 May 1926	06:31
Ari	8 May 1926	08:54
Tau	10 May 1926	11:33
Gem	12 May 1926	15:46
Can	14 May 1926	22:53
Leo	17 May 1926	09:20
Vir	19 May 1926	21:53
Lib	22 May 1926	10:02
Sco	24 May 1926	19:40
Sag	27 May 1926	02:12
Cap	29 May 1926	06:23
Aqu	31 May 1926	09:18
Pis	2 Jun 1926	11:52
Ari	4 Jun 1926	14:45
Tau	6 Jun 1926	18:27
Gem	8 Jun 1926	23:42
Can	11 Jun 1926	07:14
Leo	13 Jun 1926	17:28
Vir	16 Jun 1926	05:48
Lib	18 Jun 1926	18:18
Sco	21 Jun 1926	04:39
Sag	23 Jun 1926	11:33
Cap	25 Jun 1926	15:16
Aqu	27 Jun 1926	17:00
Pis	29 Jun 1926	18:12
Ari	1 Jul 1926	20:13
Tau	3 Jul 1926	23:59
Gem	6 Jul 1926	05:56
Can	8 Jul 1926	14:16
Leo	11 Jul 1926	00:50
Vir	13 Jul 1926	13:07
Lib	16 Jul 1926	01:51
Sco	18 Jul 1926	13:06
Sag	20 Jul 1926	21:08
Cap	23 Jul 1926	01:26
Aqu	25 Jul 1926	02:47
Pis	27 Jul 1926	02:45
Ari	29 Jul 1926	03:13
Tau	31 Jul 1926	05:46
Gem	2 Aug 1926	11:25
Can	4 Aug 1926	20:07
Leo	7 Aug 1926	07:12
Vir	9 Aug 1926	19:38
Lib	12 Aug 1926	08:25
Sco	14 Aug 1926	20:16
Sag	17 Aug 1926	05:38
Cap	19 Aug 1926	11:21
Aqu	21 Aug 1926	13:29
Pis	23 Aug 1926	13:13
Ari	25 Aug 1926	12:30
Tau	27 Aug 1926	13:25
Gem	29 Aug 1926	17:38
Can	1 Sep 1926	01:48
Leo	3 Sep 1926	13:01
Vir	6 Sep 1926	01:39
Lib	8 Sep 1926	14:22
Sco	11 Sep 1926	02:14
Sag	13 Sep 1926	12:20
Cap	15 Sep 1926	19:35
Aqu	17 Sep 1926	23:21
Pis	20 Sep 1926	00:05
Ari	21 Sep 1926	23:20
Tau	23 Sep 1926	23:12
Gem	26 Sep 1926	01:51
Can	28 Sep 1926	08:35
Leo	30 Sep 1926	19:09
Vir	3 Oct 1926	07:48
Lib	5 Oct 1926	20:27
Sco	8 Oct 1926	07:57
Sag	10 Oct 1926	17:53
Cap	13 Oct 1926	01:45
Aqu	15 Oct 1926	07:01
Pis	17 Oct 1926	09:28
Ari	19 Oct 1926	09:55
Tau	21 Oct 1926	10:01
Gem	23 Oct 1926	11:50
Can	25 Oct 1926	17:07
Leo	28 Oct 1926	02:30
Vir	30 Oct 1926	14:42
Lib	2 Nov 1926	03:21
Sco	4 Nov 1926	14:36
Sag	6 Nov 1926	23:50
Cap	9 Nov 1926	07:10
Aqu	11 Nov 1926	12:40
Pis	13 Nov 1926	16:21
Ari	15 Nov 1926	18:27
Tau	17 Nov 1926	19:53
Gem	19 Nov 1926	22:10
Can	22 Nov 1926	02:54
Leo	24 Nov 1926	11:10
Vir	26 Nov 1926	22:35
Lib	29 Nov 1926	11:12
Sco	1 Dec 1926	22:37
Sag	4 Dec 1926	07:31
Cap	6 Dec 1926	13:51
Aqu	8 Dec 1926	18:21
Pis	10 Dec 1926	21:43
Ari	13 Dec 1926	00:32
Tau	15 Dec 1926	03:22
Gem	17 Dec 1926	06:59
Can	19 Dec 1926	12:20
Leo	21 Dec 1926	20:16
Vir	24 Dec 1926	07:01
Lib	26 Dec 1926	19:30
Sco	29 Dec 1926	07:27
Sag	31 Dec 1926	16:49

1927

Sign	Date	Time
Cap	2 Jan 1927	22:49
Aqu	5 Jan 1927	02:09
Pis	7 Jan 1927	04:05
Ari	9 Jan 1927	05:59
Tau	11 Jan 1927	08:55
Gem	13 Jan 1927	13:30
Can	15 Jan 1927	19:58
Leo	18 Jan 1927	04:30
Vir	20 Jan 1927	15:09
Lib	23 Jan 1927	03:26
Sco	25 Jan 1927	15:53
Sag	28 Jan 1927	02:19
Cap	30 Jan 1927	09:10
Aqu	1 Feb 1927	12:20
Pis	3 Feb 1927	13:05
Ari	5 Feb 1927	13:19
Tau	7 Feb 1927	14:50
Gem	9 Feb 1927	18:54
Can	12 Feb 1927	01:50
Leo	14 Feb 1927	11:11
Vir	16 Feb 1927	22:15
Lib	19 Feb 1927	10:30
Sco	21 Feb 1927	23:07
Sag	24 Feb 1927	10:33
Cap	26 Feb 1927	18:54
Aqu	28 Feb 1927	23:12
Pis	3 Mar 1927	00:04
Ari	4 Mar 1927	23:18
Tau	6 Mar 1927	23:07
Gem	9 Mar 1927	01:29
Can	11 Mar 1927	07:29
Leo	13 Mar 1927	16:51
Vir	16 Mar 1927	04:21
Lib	18 Mar 1927	16:47
Sco	21 Mar 1927	05:20
Sag	23 Mar 1927	17:05
Cap	26 Mar 1927	02:37
Aqu	28 Mar 1927	08:37
Pis	30 Mar 1927	10:51
Ari	1 Apr 1927	10:29
Tau	3 Apr 1927	09:36
Gem	5 Apr 1927	10:25
Can	7 Apr 1927	14:42
Leo	9 Apr 1927	23:00
Vir	12 Apr 1927	10:18
Lib	14 Apr 1927	22:52
Sco	17 Apr 1927	11:18
Sag	19 Apr 1927	22:47
Cap	22 Apr 1927	08:34
Aqu	24 Apr 1927	15:41
Pis	26 Apr 1927	19:36
Ari	28 Apr 1927	20:42
Tau	30 Apr 1927	20:28
Gem	2 May 1927	20:52
Can	4 May 1927	23:52
Leo	7 May 1927	06:38
Vir	9 May 1927	17:02
Lib	12 May 1927	05:26
Sco	14 May 1927	17:50
Sag	17 May 1927	04:56
Cap	19 May 1927	14:09
Aqu	21 May 1927	21:14
Pis	24 May 1927	02:00
Ari	26 May 1927	04:36
Tau	28 May 1927	05:49
Gem	30 May 1927	07:01
Can	1 Jun 1927	09:50
Leo	3 Jun 1927	15:37
Vir	6 Jun 1927	00:55
Lib	8 Jun 1927	12:48
Sco	11 Jun 1927	01:14
Sag	13 Jun 1927	12:14
Cap	15 Jun 1927	20:50
Aqu	18 Jun 1927	03:03
Pis	20 Jun 1927	07:24
Ari	22 Jun 1927	10:28
Tau	24 Jun 1927	12:53
Gem	26 Jun 1927	15:25
Can	28 Jun 1927	19:02
Leo	1 Jul 1927	00:48
Vir	3 Jul 1927	09:26
Lib	5 Jul 1927	20:46
Sco	8 Jul 1927	09:16
Sag	10 Jul 1927	20:35
Cap	13 Jul 1927	05:05
Aqu	15 Jul 1927	10:29
Pis	17 Jul 1927	13:41
Ari	19 Jul 1927	15:57
Tau	21 Jul 1927	18:23
Gem	23 Jul 1927	21:45
Can	26 Jul 1927	02:30
Leo	28 Jul 1927	09:00
Vir	30 Jul 1927	17:41
Lib	2 Aug 1927	04:43
Sco	4 Aug 1927	17:15
Sag	7 Aug 1927	05:13
Cap	9 Aug 1927	14:21
Aqu	11 Aug 1927	19:44
Pis	13 Aug 1927	22:03
Ari	15 Aug 1927	22:56
Tau	18 Aug 1927	00:12
Gem	20 Aug 1927	03:08
Can	22 Aug 1927	08:18
Leo	24 Aug 1927	15:38
Vir	27 Aug 1927	00:55
Lib	29 Aug 1927	12:02
Sco	1 Sep 1927	00:35
Sag	3 Sep 1927	13:08
Cap	5 Sep 1927	23:26
Aqu	8 Sep 1927	05:48
Pis	10 Sep 1927	08:14
Ari	12 Sep 1927	08:17
Tau	14 Sep 1927	08:02
Gem	16 Sep 1927	09:28
Can	18 Sep 1927	13:49
Leo	20 Sep 1927	21:13
Vir	23 Sep 1927	07:00
Lib	25 Sep 1927	18:29
Sco	28 Sep 1927	07:04
Sag	30 Sep 1927	19:52
Cap	3 Oct 1927	07:11
Aqu	5 Oct 1927	15:05
Pis	7 Oct 1927	18:49
Ari	9 Oct 1927	19:13
Tau	11 Oct 1927	18:17
Gem	13 Oct 1927	18:11
Can	15 Oct 1927	20:50
Leo	18 Oct 1927	03:07
Vir	20 Oct 1927	12:43
Lib	23 Oct 1927	00:27
Sco	25 Oct 1927	13:07
Sag	28 Oct 1927	01:47
Cap	30 Oct 1927	13:20
Aqu	1 Nov 1927	22:24
Pis	4 Nov 1927	03:54
Ari	6 Nov 1927	05:52
Tau	8 Nov 1927	05:36
Gem	10 Nov 1927	05:02
Can	12 Nov 1927	06:14
Leo	14 Nov 1927	10:49
Vir	16 Nov 1927	19:13
Lib	19 Nov 1927	06:40
Sco	21 Nov 1927	19:25
Sag	24 Nov 1927	07:52
Cap	26 Nov 1927	18:59
Aqu	29 Nov 1927	04:05
Pis	1 Dec 1927	10:35
Ari	3 Dec 1927	14:18
Tau	5 Dec 1927	15:45
Gem	7 Dec 1927	16:09
Can	9 Dec 1927	17:10
Leo	11 Dec 1927	20:31
Vir	14 Dec 1927	03:25
Lib	16 Dec 1927	13:54
Sco	19 Dec 1927	02:30
Sag	21 Dec 1927	14:57
Cap	24 Dec 1927	01:36
Aqu	26 Dec 1927	09:53
Pis	28 Dec 1927	15:59
Ari	30 Dec 1927	20:17

Moon Signs

1928

Tau	1 Jan 1928	23:13
Gem	4 Jan 1928	01:19
Can	6 Jan 1928	03:27
Leo	8 Jan 1928	06:51
Vir	10 Jan 1928	12:53
Lib	12 Jan 1928	22:17
Sco	15 Jan 1928	10:26
Sag	17 Jan 1928	23:05
Cap	20 Jan 1928	09:47
Aqu	22 Jan 1928	17:26
Pis	24 Jan 1928	22:23
Ari	27 Jan 1928	01:47
Tau	29 Jan 1928	04:41
Gem	31 Jan 1928	07:46

Can	2 Feb 1928	11:21
Leo	4 Feb 1928	15:52
Vir	6 Feb 1928	22:09
Lib	9 Feb 1928	07:03
Sco	11 Feb 1928	18:40
Sag	14 Feb 1928	07:31
Cap	16 Feb 1928	18:52
Aqu	19 Feb 1928	02:45
Pis	21 Feb 1928	07:04
Ari	23 Feb 1928	09:08
Tau	25 Feb 1928	10:41
Gem	27 Feb 1928	13:07
Can	29 Feb 1928	17:04

Leo	2 Mar 1928	22:38
Vir	5 Mar 1928	05:50
Lib	7 Mar 1928	15:04
Sco	10 Mar 1928	02:30
Sag	12 Mar 1928	15:23
Cap	15 Mar 1928	03:32
Aqu	17 Mar 1928	12:28
Pis	19 Mar 1928	17:19
Ari	21 Mar 1928	18:53
Tau	23 Mar 1928	19:05
Gem	25 Mar 1928	19:53
Can	27 Mar 1928	22:41
Leo	30 Mar 1928	04:04

Vir	1 Apr 1928	11:53
Lib	3 Apr 1928	21:46
Sco	6 Apr 1928	09:27
Sag	8 Apr 1928	22:19
Cap	11 Apr 1928	10:54
Aqu	13 Apr 1928	21:04
Pis	16 Apr 1928	03:17
Ari	18 Apr 1928	05:39
Tau	20 Apr 1928	05:35
Gem	22 Apr 1928	05:08
Can	24 Apr 1928	06:13
Leo	26 Apr 1928	10:12
Vir	28 Apr 1928	17:27

Lib	1 May 1928	03:35
Sco	3 May 1928	15:37
Sag	6 May 1928	04:31
Cap	8 May 1928	17:07
Aqu	11 May 1928	03:56
Pis	13 May 1928	11:32
Ari	15 May 1928	15:28
Tau	17 May 1928	16:24
Gem	19 May 1928	15:55
Can	21 May 1928	15:57
Leo	23 May 1928	18:16
Vir	26 May 1928	00:07
Lib	28 May 1928	09:36
Sco	30 May 1928	21:39

Sag	2 Jun 1928	10:37
Cap	4 Jun 1928	22:58
Aqu	7 Jun 1928	09:39
Pis	9 Jun 1928	17:53
Ari	11 Jun 1928	23:11
Tau	14 Jun 1928	01:44
Gem	16 Jun 1928	02:23
Can	18 Jun 1928	02:34
Leo	20 Jun 1928	04:02
Vir	22 Jun 1928	08:27
Lib	24 Jun 1928	16:42
Sco	27 Jun 1928	04:16
Sag	29 Jun 1928	17:12

Cap	2 Jul 1928	05:22
Aqu	4 Jul 1928	15:30
Pis	6 Jul 1928	23:21
Ari	9 Jul 1928	05:03
Tau	11 Jul 1928	08:48
Gem	13 Jul 1928	10:58
Can	15 Jul 1928	12:19
Leo	17 Jul 1928	14:05
Vir	19 Jul 1928	17:52
Lib	22 Jul 1928	01:02
Sco	24 Jul 1928	11:47
Sag	27 Jul 1928	00:33
Cap	29 Jul 1928	12:45
Aqu	31 Jul 1928	22:31

Pis	3 Aug 1928	05:33
Ari	5 Aug 1928	10:32
Tau	7 Aug 1928	14:17
Gem	9 Aug 1928	17:21
Can	11 Aug 1928	20:02
Leo	13 Aug 1928	22:56
Vir	16 Aug 1928	03:07
Lib	18 Aug 1928	09:53
Sco	20 Aug 1928	19:56
Sag	23 Aug 1928	08:28
Cap	25 Aug 1928	20:57
Aqu	28 Aug 1928	06:56
Pis	30 Aug 1928	13:29

Ari	1 Sep 1928	17:25
Tau	3 Sep 1928	20:06
Gem	5 Sep 1928	22:42
Can	8 Sep 1928	01:51
Leo	10 Sep 1928	05:48
Vir	12 Sep 1928	11:01
Lib	14 Sep 1928	18:11
Sco	17 Sep 1928	04:04
Sag	19 Sep 1928	16:22
Cap	22 Sep 1928	05:15
Aqu	24 Sep 1928	16:00
Pis	26 Sep 1928	22:59
Ari	29 Sep 1928	02:29

Tau	1 Oct 1928	03:58
Gem	3 Oct 1928	05:08
Can	5 Oct 1928	07:20
Leo	7 Oct 1928	11:18
Vir	9 Oct 1928	17:13
Lib	12 Oct 1928	01:14
Sco	14 Oct 1928	11:28
Sag	16 Oct 1928	23:43
Cap	19 Oct 1928	12:49
Aqu	22 Oct 1928	00:31
Pis	24 Oct 1928	08:48
Ari	26 Oct 1928	13:02
Tau	28 Oct 1928	14:15
Gem	30 Oct 1928	14:10

Can	1 Nov 1928	14:40
Leo	3 Nov 1928	17:13
Vir	5 Nov 1928	22:41
Lib	8 Nov 1928	07:04
Sco	10 Nov 1928	17:52
Sag	13 Nov 1928	06:19
Cap	15 Nov 1928	19:24
Aqu	18 Nov 1928	07:38
Pis	20 Nov 1928	17:18
Ari	22 Nov 1928	23:12
Tau	25 Nov 1928	01:29
Gem	27 Nov 1928	01:22
Can	29 Nov 1928	00:43

Leo	1 Dec 1928	01:29
Vir	3 Dec 1928	05:16
Lib	5 Dec 1928	12:53
Sco	7 Dec 1928	23:46
Sag	10 Dec 1928	12:28
Cap	13 Dec 1928	01:28
Aqu	15 Dec 1928	13:34
Pis	17 Dec 1928	23:47
Ari	20 Dec 1928	07:14
Tau	22 Dec 1928	11:23
Gem	24 Dec 1928	12:38
Can	26 Dec 1928	12:16
Leo	28 Dec 1928	12:07
Vir	30 Dec 1928	14:13

1929

Lib	1 Jan 1929	20:08
Sco	4 Jan 1929	06:09
Sag	6 Jan 1929	18:49
Cap	9 Jan 1929	07:50
Aqu	11 Jan 1929	19:32
Pis	14 Jan 1929	05:20
Ari	16 Jan 1929	13:05
Tau	18 Jan 1929	18:36
Gem	20 Jan 1929	21:42
Can	22 Jan 1929	22:51
Leo	24 Jan 1929	23:16
Vir	27 Jan 1929	00:48
Lib	29 Jan 1929	05:18
Sco	31 Jan 1929	13:57

Sag	3 Feb 1929	01:59
Cap	5 Feb 1929	14:59
Aqu	8 Feb 1929	02:33
Pis	10 Feb 1929	11:41
Ari	12 Feb 1929	18:40
Tau	15 Feb 1929	00:01
Gem	17 Feb 1929	04:00
Can	19 Feb 1929	06:44
Leo	21 Feb 1929	08:40
Vir	23 Feb 1929	10:58
Lib	25 Feb 1929	15:15
Sco	27 Feb 1929	22:54

Sag	2 Mar 1929	10:03
Cap	4 Mar 1929	22:54
Aqu	7 Mar 1929	10:42
Pis	9 Mar 1929	19:42
Ari	12 Mar 1929	01:50
Tau	14 Mar 1929	06:04
Gem	16 Mar 1929	09:22
Can	18 Mar 1929	12:23
Leo	20 Mar 1929	15:26
Vir	22 Mar 1929	19:04
Lib	25 Mar 1929	00:12
Sco	27 Mar 1929	07:49
Sag	29 Mar 1929	18:25

Cap	1 Apr 1929	07:02
Aqu	3 Apr 1929	19:16
Pis	6 Apr 1929	04:51
Ari	8 Apr 1929	10:56
Tau	10 Apr 1929	14:15
Gem	12 Apr 1929	16:12
Can	14 Apr 1929	18:03
Leo	16 Apr 1929	20:50
Vir	19 Apr 1929	01:05
Lib	21 Apr 1929	07:13
Sco	23 Apr 1929	15:34
Sag	26 Apr 1929	02:15
Cap	28 Apr 1929	14:42

Aqu	1 May 1929	03:17
Pis	3 May 1929	13:49
Ari	5 May 1929	20:49
Tau	8 May 1929	00:16
Gem	10 May 1929	01:21
Can	12 May 1929	01:44
Leo	14 May 1929	03:03
Vir	16 May 1929	06:33
Lib	18 May 1929	12:52
Sco	20 May 1929	21:53
Sag	23 May 1929	09:03
Cap	25 May 1929	21:33
Aqu	28 May 1929	10:16
Pis	30 May 1929	21:35

Ari	2 Jun 1929	05:57
Tau	4 Jun 1929	10:32
Gem	6 Jun 1929	11:55
Can	8 Jun 1929	11:34
Leo	10 Jun 1929	11:25
Vir	12 Jun 1929	13:20
Lib	14 Jun 1929	18:38
Sco	17 Jun 1929	03:32
Sag	19 Jun 1929	15:02
Cap	22 Jun 1929	03:44
Aqu	24 Jun 1929	16:23
Pis	27 Jun 1929	03:58
Ari	29 Jun 1929	13:19

Tau	1 Jul 1929	19:30
Gem	3 Jul 1929	22:12
Can	5 Jul 1929	22:19
Leo	7 Jul 1929	21:36
Vir	9 Jul 1929	22:10
Lib	12 Jul 1929	01:54
Sco	14 Jul 1929	09:44
Sag	16 Jul 1929	20:59
Cap	19 Jul 1929	09:47
Aqu	21 Jul 1929	22:19
Pis	24 Jul 1929	09:38
Ari	26 Jul 1929	19:12
Tau	29 Jul 1929	02:23
Gem	31 Jul 1929	06:42

Can	2 Aug 1929	08:14
Leo	4 Aug 1929	08:10
Vir	6 Aug 1929	08:22
Lib	8 Aug 1929	10:56
Sco	10 Aug 1929	17:21
Sag	13 Aug 1929	03:44
Cap	15 Aug 1929	16:20
Aqu	18 Aug 1929	04:49
Pis	20 Aug 1929	15:44
Ari	23 Aug 1929	00:45
Tau	25 Aug 1929	07:54
Gem	27 Aug 1929	13:01
Can	29 Aug 1929	16:02
Leo	31 Aug 1929	17:26

Vir	2 Sep 1929	18:26
Lib	4 Sep 1929	20:51
Sco	7 Sep 1929	02:21
Sag	9 Sep 1929	11:39
Cap	11 Sep 1929	23:44
Aqu	14 Sep 1929	12:15
Pis	16 Sep 1929	23:05
Ari	19 Sep 1929	07:29
Tau	21 Sep 1929	13:44
Gem	23 Sep 1929	18:24
Can	25 Sep 1929	21:51
Leo	28 Sep 1929	00:27
Vir	30 Sep 1929	02:51

Lib	2 Oct 1929	06:09
Sco	4 Oct 1929	11:40
Sag	6 Oct 1929	20:18
Cap	9 Oct 1929	07:49
Aqu	11 Oct 1929	20:24
Pis	14 Oct 1929	07:39
Ari	16 Oct 1929	16:01
Tau	18 Oct 1929	21:27
Gem	21 Oct 1929	00:53
Can	23 Oct 1929	03:23
Leo	25 Oct 1929	05:54
Vir	27 Oct 1929	09:08
Lib	29 Oct 1929	13:39
Sco	31 Oct 1929	20:01

Sag	3 Nov 1929	04:46
Cap	5 Nov 1929	15:56
Aqu	8 Nov 1929	04:32
Pis	10 Nov 1929	16:29
Ari	13 Nov 1929	01:41
Tau	15 Nov 1929	07:17
Gem	17 Nov 1929	09:52
Can	19 Nov 1929	10:52
Leo	21 Nov 1929	11:58
Vir	23 Nov 1929	14:31
Lib	25 Nov 1929	19:22
Sco	28 Nov 1929	02:40
Sag	30 Nov 1929	12:07

Cap	2 Dec 1929	23:25
Aqu	5 Dec 1929	11:56
Pis	8 Dec 1929	00:26
Ari	10 Dec 1929	10:55
Tau	12 Dec 1929	17:49
Gem	14 Dec 1929	20:47
Can	16 Dec 1929	21:04
Leo	18 Dec 1929	20:34
Vir	20 Dec 1929	21:22
Lib	23 Dec 1929	01:03
Sco	25 Dec 1929	08:11
Sag	27 Dec 1929	18:11
Cap	30 Dec 1929	05:55

Moon Signs

1930

Aqu	1 Jan 1930	18:28
Pis	4 Jan 1930	07:03
Ari	6 Jan 1930	18:26
Tau	9 Jan 1930	02:57
Gem	11 Jan 1930	07:33
Can	13 Jan 1930	08:33
Leo	15 Jan 1930	07:36
Vir	17 Jan 1930	06:56
Lib	19 Jan 1930	08:44
Sco	21 Jan 1930	14:25
Sag	23 Jan 1930	23:56
Cap	26 Jan 1930	11:53
Aqu	29 Jan 1930	00:34
Pis	31 Jan 1930	12:58
Ari	3 Feb 1930	00:21
Tau	5 Feb 1930	09:47
Gem	7 Feb 1930	16:07
Can	9 Feb 1930	18:54
Leo	11 Feb 1930	18:59
Vir	13 Feb 1930	18:13
Lib	15 Feb 1930	18:50
Sco	17 Feb 1930	22:45
Sag	20 Feb 1930	06:48
Cap	22 Feb 1930	18:12
Aqu	25 Feb 1930	06:56
Pis	27 Feb 1930	19:12
Ari	2 Mar 1930	06:08
Tau	4 Mar 1930	15:17
Gem	6 Mar 1930	22:14
Can	9 Mar 1930	02:33
Leo	11 Mar 1930	04:24
Vir	13 Mar 1930	04:53
Lib	15 Mar 1930	05:42
Sco	17 Mar 1930	08:46
Sag	19 Mar 1930	15:24
Cap	22 Mar 1930	01:40
Aqu	24 Mar 1930	14:04
Pis	27 Mar 1930	02:22
Ari	29 Mar 1930	12:58
Tau	31 Mar 1930	21:22
Gem	3 Apr 1930	03:41
Can	5 Apr 1930	08:10
Leo	7 Apr 1930	11:07
Vir	9 Apr 1930	13:10
Lib	11 Apr 1930	15:16
Sco	13 Apr 1930	18:44
Sag	16 Apr 1930	00:50
Cap	18 Apr 1930	10:07
Aqu	20 Apr 1930	21:58
Pis	23 Apr 1930	10:22
Ari	25 Apr 1930	21:08
Tau	28 Apr 1930	05:07
Gem	30 Apr 1930	10:24

Can	2 May 1930	13:53
Leo	4 May 1930	16:31
Vir	6 May 1930	19:10
Lib	8 May 1930	22:30
Sco	11 May 1930	03:06
Sag	13 May 1930	09:39
Cap	15 May 1930	18:39
Aqu	18 May 1930	06:03
Pis	20 May 1930	18:33
Ari	23 May 1930	05:54
Tau	25 May 1930	14:13
Gem	27 May 1930	19:06
Can	29 May 1930	21:24
Leo	31 May 1930	22:44
Vir	3 Jun 1930	00:37
Lib	5 Jun 1930	04:03
Sco	7 Jun 1930	09:30
Sag	9 Jun 1930	16:55
Cap	12 Jun 1930	02:20
Aqu	14 Jun 1930	13:38
Pis	17 Jun 1930	02:11
Ari	19 Jun 1930	14:13
Tau	21 Jun 1930	23:33
Gem	24 Jun 1930	04:59
Can	26 Jun 1930	06:56
Leo	28 Jun 1930	07:05
Vir	30 Jun 1930	07:28
Lib	2 Jul 1930	09:47
Sco	4 Jul 1930	14:56
Sag	6 Jul 1930	22:49
Cap	9 Jul 1930	08:49
Aqu	11 Jul 1930	20:22
Pis	14 Jul 1930	08:56
Ari	16 Jul 1930	21:25
Tau	19 Jul 1930	07:53
Gem	21 Jul 1930	14:37
Can	23 Jul 1930	17:21
Leo	25 Jul 1930	17:18
Vir	27 Jul 1930	16:34
Lib	29 Jul 1930	17:17
Sco	31 Jul 1930	21:05
Sag	3 Aug 1930	04:24
Cap	5 Aug 1930	14:34
Aqu	8 Aug 1930	02:26
Pis	10 Aug 1930	15:02
Ari	13 Aug 1930	03:31
Tau	15 Aug 1930	14:36
Gem	17 Aug 1930	22:44
Can	20 Aug 1930	03:00
Leo	22 Aug 1930	03:56
Vir	24 Aug 1930	03:13
Lib	26 Aug 1930	02:58
Sco	28 Aug 1930	05:10
Sag	30 Aug 1930	11:05

Cap	1 Sep 1930	20:35
Aqu	4 Sep 1930	08:27
Pis	6 Sep 1930	21:05
Ari	9 Sep 1930	09:20
Tau	11 Sep 1930	20:17
Gem	14 Sep 1930	05:00
Can	16 Sep 1930	10:40
Leo	18 Sep 1930	13:16
Vir	20 Sep 1930	13:44
Lib	22 Sep 1930	13:43
Sco	24 Sep 1930	15:07
Sag	26 Sep 1930	19:34
Cap	29 Sep 1930	03:48
Aqu	1 Oct 1930	15:09
Pis	4 Oct 1930	03:47
Ari	6 Oct 1930	15:51
Tau	9 Oct 1930	02:13
Gem	11 Oct 1930	10:28
Can	13 Oct 1930	16:28
Leo	15 Oct 1930	20:18
Vir	17 Oct 1930	22:24
Lib	19 Oct 1930	23:43
Sco	22 Oct 1930	01:32
Sag	24 Oct 1930	05:23
Cap	26 Oct 1930	12:27
Aqu	28 Oct 1930	22:53
Pis	31 Oct 1930	11:22
Ari	2 Nov 1930	23:33
Tau	5 Nov 1930	09:36
Gem	7 Nov 1930	16:57
Can	9 Nov 1930	22:03
Leo	12 Nov 1930	01:44
Vir	14 Nov 1930	04:41
Lib	16 Nov 1930	07:26
Sco	18 Nov 1930	10:36
Sag	20 Nov 1930	15:00
Cap	22 Nov 1930	21:42
Aqu	25 Nov 1930	07:22
Pis	27 Nov 1930	19:32
Ari	30 Nov 1930	08:05
Tau	2 Dec 1930	18:31
Gem	5 Dec 1930	01:30
Can	7 Dec 1930	05:30
Leo	9 Dec 1930	07:52
Vir	11 Dec 1930	10:04
Lib	13 Dec 1930	13:05
Sco	15 Dec 1930	17:18
Sag	17 Dec 1930	22:54
Cap	20 Dec 1930	06:11
Aqu	22 Dec 1930	15:43
Pis	25 Dec 1930	03:35
Ari	27 Dec 1930	16:28
Tau	30 Dec 1930	03:50

1931

Sign	Date	Time
Gem	1 Jan 1931	11:32
Can	3 Jan 1931	15:19
Leo	5 Jan 1931	16:31
Vir	7 Jan 1931	17:05
Lib	9 Jan 1931	18:48
Sco	11 Jan 1931	22:40
Sag	14 Jan 1931	04:50
Cap	16 Jan 1931	13:01
Aqu	18 Jan 1931	23:04
Pis	21 Jan 1931	10:54
Ari	23 Jan 1931	23:54
Tau	26 Jan 1931	12:08
Gem	28 Jan 1931	21:16
Can	31 Jan 1931	02:07

Sign	Date	Time
Leo	2 Feb 1931	03:23
Vir	4 Feb 1931	02:56
Lib	6 Feb 1931	02:54
Sco	8 Feb 1931	05:04
Sag	10 Feb 1931	10:22
Cap	12 Feb 1931	18:38
Aqu	15 Feb 1931	05:14
Pis	17 Feb 1931	17:22
Ari	20 Feb 1931	06:20
Tau	22 Feb 1931	18:53
Gem	25 Feb 1931	05:12
Can	27 Feb 1931	11:45

Sign	Date	Time
Leo	1 Mar 1931	14:23
Vir	3 Mar 1931	14:19
Lib	5 Mar 1931	13:32
Sco	7 Mar 1931	14:03
Sag	9 Mar 1931	17:30
Cap	12 Mar 1931	00:39
Aqu	14 Mar 1931	11:03
Pis	16 Mar 1931	23:26
Ari	19 Mar 1931	12:23
Tau	22 Mar 1931	00:43
Gem	24 Mar 1931	11:17
Can	26 Mar 1931	19:03
Leo	28 Mar 1931	23:27
Vir	31 Mar 1931	00:56

Sign	Date	Time
Lib	2 Apr 1931	00:48
Sco	4 Apr 1931	00:50
Sag	6 Apr 1931	02:52
Cap	8 Apr 1931	08:20
Aqu	10 Apr 1931	17:39
Pis	13 Apr 1931	05:48
Ari	15 Apr 1931	18:47
Tau	18 Apr 1931	06:49
Gem	20 Apr 1931	16:55
Can	23 Apr 1931	00:41
Leo	25 Apr 1931	06:03
Vir	27 Apr 1931	09:08
Lib	29 Apr 1931	10:34

Sign	Date	Time
Sco	1 May 1931	11:26
Sag	3 May 1931	13:14
Cap	5 May 1931	17:35
Aqu	8 May 1931	01:37
Pis	10 May 1931	13:01
Ari	13 May 1931	01:55
Tau	15 May 1931	13:53
Gem	17 May 1931	23:25
Can	20 May 1931	06:25
Leo	22 May 1931	11:26
Vir	24 May 1931	15:06
Lib	26 May 1931	17:50
Sco	28 May 1931	20:07
Sag	30 May 1931	22:48

Sign	Date	Time
Cap	2 Jun 1931	03:07
Aqu	4 Jun 1931	10:23
Pis	6 Jun 1931	21:00
Ari	9 Jun 1931	09:43
Tau	11 Jun 1931	21:53
Gem	14 Jun 1931	07:20
Can	16 Jun 1931	13:36
Leo	18 Jun 1931	17:35
Vir	20 Jun 1931	20:32
Lib	22 Jun 1931	23:22
Sco	25 Jun 1931	02:34
Sag	27 Jun 1931	06:26
Cap	29 Jun 1931	11:35

Sign	Date	Time
Aqu	1 Jul 1931	18:56
Pis	4 Jul 1931	05:09
Ari	6 Jul 1931	17:39
Tau	9 Jul 1931	06:13
Gem	11 Jul 1931	16:13
Can	13 Jul 1931	22:28
Leo	16 Jul 1931	01:40
Vir	18 Jul 1931	03:21
Lib	20 Jul 1931	05:05
Sco	22 Jul 1931	07:56
Sag	24 Jul 1931	12:18
Cap	26 Jul 1931	18:22
Aqu	29 Jul 1931	02:24
Pis	31 Jul 1931	12:46

Sign	Date	Time
Ari	3 Aug 1931	01:10
Tau	5 Aug 1931	14:04
Gem	8 Aug 1931	00:59
Can	10 Aug 1931	08:09
Leo	12 Aug 1931	11:29
Vir	14 Aug 1931	12:24
Lib	16 Aug 1931	12:45
Sco	18 Aug 1931	14:10
Sag	20 Aug 1931	17:46
Cap	22 Aug 1931	23:59
Aqu	25 Aug 1931	08:38
Pis	27 Aug 1931	19:27
Ari	30 Aug 1931	07:56

Sign	Date	Time
Tau	1 Sep 1931	20:58
Gem	4 Sep 1931	08:42
Can	6 Sep 1931	17:14
Leo	8 Sep 1931	21:45
Vir	10 Sep 1931	23:02
Lib	12 Sep 1931	22:42
Sco	14 Sep 1931	22:40
Sag	17 Sep 1931	00:40
Cap	19 Sep 1931	05:47
Aqu	21 Sep 1931	14:18
Pis	24 Sep 1931	01:28
Ari	26 Sep 1931	14:09
Tau	29 Sep 1931	03:06

Sign	Date	Time
Gem	1 Oct 1931	15:02
Can	4 Oct 1931	00:36
Leo	6 Oct 1931	06:48
Vir	8 Oct 1931	09:33
Lib	10 Oct 1931	09:49
Sco	12 Oct 1931	09:17
Sag	14 Oct 1931	09:51
Cap	16 Oct 1931	13:19
Aqu	18 Oct 1931	20:39
Pis	21 Oct 1931	07:32
Ari	23 Oct 1931	20:20
Tau	26 Oct 1931	09:11
Gem	28 Oct 1931	20:46
Can	31 Oct 1931	06:26

Sign	Date	Time
Leo	2 Nov 1931	13:38
Vir	4 Nov 1931	18:07
Lib	6 Nov 1931	20:02
Sco	8 Nov 1931	20:20
Sag	10 Nov 1931	20:39
Cap	12 Nov 1931	22:53
Aqu	15 Nov 1931	04:40
Pis	17 Nov 1931	14:33
Ari	20 Nov 1931	03:08
Tau	22 Nov 1931	15:59
Gem	25 Nov 1931	03:10
Can	27 Nov 1931	12:08
Leo	29 Nov 1931	19:05

Sign	Date	Time
Vir	2 Dec 1931	00:15
Lib	4 Dec 1931	03:43
Sco	6 Dec 1931	05:43
Sag	8 Dec 1931	07:04
Cap	10 Dec 1931	09:18
Aqu	12 Dec 1931	14:10
Pis	14 Dec 1931	22:51
Ari	17 Dec 1931	10:49
Tau	19 Dec 1931	23:44
Gem	22 Dec 1931	10:58
Can	24 Dec 1931	19:21
Leo	27 Dec 1931	01:15
Vir	29 Dec 1931	05:40
Lib	31 Dec 1931	09:17

Moon Signs

1932

Sco	2 Jan 1932	12:23
Sag	4 Jan 1932	15:15
Cap	6 Jan 1932	18:37
Aqu	8 Jan 1932	23:44
Pis	11 Jan 1932	07:49
Ari	13 Jan 1932	19:07
Tau	16 Jan 1932	08:02
Gem	18 Jan 1932	19:46
Can	21 Jan 1932	04:21
Leo	23 Jan 1932	09:38
Vir	25 Jan 1932	12:46
Lib	27 Jan 1932	15:07
Sco	29 Jan 1932	17:43
Sag	31 Jan 1932	21:06
Cap	3 Feb 1932	01:39
Aqu	5 Feb 1932	07:48
Pis	7 Feb 1932	16:15
Ari	10 Feb 1932	03:17
Tau	12 Feb 1932	16:04
Gem	15 Feb 1932	04:27
Can	17 Feb 1932	14:01
Leo	19 Feb 1932	19:48
Vir	21 Feb 1932	22:23
Lib	23 Feb 1932	23:21
Sco	26 Feb 1932	00:20
Sag	28 Feb 1932	02:39
Cap	1 Mar 1932	07:06
Aqu	3 Mar 1932	14:00
Pis	5 Mar 1932	23:15
Ari	8 Mar 1932	10:35
Tau	10 Mar 1932	23:19
Gem	13 Mar 1932	12:01
Can	15 Mar 1932	22:44
Leo	18 Mar 1932	05:55
Vir	20 Mar 1932	09:17
Lib	22 Mar 1932	09:55
Sco	24 Mar 1932	09:35
Sag	26 Mar 1932	10:07
Cap	28 Mar 1932	13:09
Aqu	30 Mar 1932	19:30
Pis	2 Apr 1932	05:04
Ari	4 Apr 1932	16:53
Tau	7 Apr 1932	05:43
Gem	9 Apr 1932	18:26
Can	12 Apr 1932	05:46
Leo	14 Apr 1932	14:20
Vir	16 Apr 1932	19:20
Lib	18 Apr 1932	20:58
Sco	20 Apr 1932	20:33
Sag	22 Apr 1932	19:57
Cap	24 Apr 1932	21:15
Aqu	27 Apr 1932	02:05
Pis	29 Apr 1932	10:56
Ari	1 May 1932	22:46
Tau	4 May 1932	11:45
Gem	7 May 1932	00:19
Can	9 May 1932	11:33
Leo	11 May 1932	20:45
Vir	14 May 1932	03:12
Lib	16 May 1932	06:32
Sco	18 May 1932	07:14
Sag	20 May 1932	06:47
Cap	22 May 1932	07:12
Aqu	24 May 1932	10:32
Pis	26 May 1932	17:57
Ari	29 May 1932	05:08
Tau	31 May 1932	18:04
Gem	3 Jun 1932	06:31
Can	5 Jun 1932	17:20
Leo	8 Jun 1932	02:13
Vir	10 Jun 1932	09:05
Lib	12 Jun 1932	13:40
Sco	14 Jun 1932	15:59
Sag	16 Jun 1932	16:45
Cap	18 Jun 1932	17:31
Aqu	20 Jun 1932	20:12
Pis	23 Jun 1932	02:26
Ari	25 Jun 1932	12:34
Tau	28 Jun 1932	01:07
Gem	30 Jun 1932	13:34
Can	3 Jul 1932	00:05
Leo	5 Jul 1932	08:18
Vir	7 Jul 1932	14:32
Lib	9 Jul 1932	19:12
Sco	11 Jul 1932	22:27
Sag	14 Jul 1932	00:37
Cap	16 Jul 1932	02:36
Aqu	18 Jul 1932	05:44
Pis	20 Jul 1932	11:35
Ari	22 Jul 1932	20:52
Tau	25 Jul 1932	08:54
Gem	27 Jul 1932	21:25
Can	30 Jul 1932	08:06
Leo	1 Aug 1932	15:56
Vir	3 Aug 1932	21:14
Lib	6 Aug 1932	00:55
Sco	8 Aug 1932	03:49
Sag	10 Aug 1932	06:31
Cap	12 Aug 1932	09:38
Aqu	14 Aug 1932	13:54
Pis	16 Aug 1932	20:14
Ari	19 Aug 1932	05:18
Tau	21 Aug 1932	16:55
Gem	24 Aug 1932	05:33
Can	26 Aug 1932	16:49
Leo	29 Aug 1932	01:01
Vir	31 Aug 1932	05:58
Lib	2 Sep 1932	08:31
Sco	4 Sep 1932	10:06
Sag	6 Sep 1932	12:00
Cap	8 Sep 1932	15:11
Aqu	10 Sep 1932	20:16
Pis	13 Sep 1932	03:31
Ari	15 Sep 1932	13:01
Tau	18 Sep 1932	00:34
Gem	20 Sep 1932	13:13
Can	23 Sep 1932	01:12
Leo	25 Sep 1932	10:30
Vir	27 Sep 1932	16:05
Lib	29 Sep 1932	18:21
Sco	1 Oct 1932	18:43
Sag	3 Oct 1932	19:02
Cap	5 Oct 1932	21:00
Aqu	8 Oct 1932	01:44
Pis	10 Oct 1932	09:27
Ari	12 Oct 1932	19:35
Tau	15 Oct 1932	07:23
Gem	17 Oct 1932	20:02
Can	20 Oct 1932	08:25
Leo	22 Oct 1932	18:56
Vir	25 Oct 1932	02:01
Lib	27 Oct 1932	05:15
Sco	29 Oct 1932	05:30
Sag	31 Oct 1932	04:40
Cap	2 Nov 1932	04:54
Aqu	4 Nov 1932	08:06
Pis	6 Nov 1932	15:07
Ari	9 Nov 1932	01:25
Tau	11 Nov 1932	13:33
Gem	14 Nov 1932	02:13
Can	16 Nov 1932	14:31
Leo	19 Nov 1932	01:34
Vir	21 Nov 1932	10:07
Lib	23 Nov 1932	15:07
Sco	25 Nov 1932	16:37
Sag	27 Nov 1932	15:58
Cap	29 Nov 1932	15:16
Aqu	1 Dec 1932	16:46
Pis	3 Dec 1932	22:09
Ari	6 Dec 1932	07:35
Tau	8 Dec 1932	19:41
Gem	11 Dec 1932	08:25
Can	13 Dec 1932	20:27
Leo	16 Dec 1932	07:12
Vir	18 Dec 1932	16:08
Lib	20 Dec 1932	22:30
Sco	23 Dec 1932	01:51
Sag	25 Dec 1932	02:41
Cap	27 Dec 1932	02:31
Aqu	29 Dec 1932	03:23
Pis	31 Dec 1932	07:16

Moon Signs

1933

Sign	Date	Time
Ari	2 Jan 1933	15:14
Tau	5 Jan 1933	02:36
Gem	7 Jan 1933	15:19
Can	10 Jan 1933	03:16
Leo	12 Jan 1933	13:26
Vir	14 Jan 1933	21:41
Lib	17 Jan 1933	04:02
Sco	19 Jan 1933	08:24
Sag	21 Jan 1933	10:53
Cap	23 Jan 1933	12:17
Aqu	25 Jan 1933	13:57
Pis	27 Jan 1933	17:31
Ari	30 Jan 1933	00:22
Tau	1 Feb 1933	10:40
Gem	3 Feb 1933	23:04
Can	6 Feb 1933	11:12
Leo	8 Feb 1933	21:15
Vir	11 Feb 1933	04:42
Lib	13 Feb 1933	09:58
Sco	15 Feb 1933	13:45
Sag	17 Feb 1933	16:42
Cap	19 Feb 1933	19:22
Aqu	21 Feb 1933	22:29
Pis	24 Feb 1933	02:56
Ari	26 Feb 1933	09:43
Tau	28 Feb 1933	19:20
Gem	3 Mar 1933	07:17
Can	5 Mar 1933	19:42
Leo	8 Mar 1933	06:17
Vir	10 Mar 1933	13:40
Lib	12 Mar 1933	18:02
Sco	14 Mar 1933	20:27
Sag	16 Mar 1933	22:18
Cap	19 Mar 1933	00:47
Aqu	21 Mar 1933	04:39
Pis	23 Mar 1933	10:16
Ari	25 Mar 1933	17:49
Tau	28 Mar 1933	03:32
Gem	30 Mar 1933	15:13
Can	2 Apr 1933	03:49
Leo	4 Apr 1933	15:15
Vir	6 Apr 1933	23:31
Lib	9 Apr 1933	03:59
Sco	11 Apr 1933	05:31
Sag	13 Apr 1933	05:51
Cap	15 Apr 1933	06:53
Aqu	17 Apr 1933	10:03
Pis	19 Apr 1933	15:54
Ari	22 Apr 1933	00:14
Tau	24 Apr 1933	10:31
Gem	26 Apr 1933	22:18
Can	29 Apr 1933	10:58
Leo	1 May 1933	23:05
Vir	4 May 1933	08:39
Lib	6 May 1933	14:15
Sco	8 May 1933	16:06
Sag	10 May 1933	15:42
Cap	12 May 1933	15:15
Aqu	14 May 1933	16:46
Pis	16 May 1933	21:34
Ari	19 May 1933	05:45
Tau	21 May 1933	16:26
Gem	24 May 1933	04:31
Can	26 May 1933	17:11
Leo	29 May 1933	05:33
Vir	31 May 1933	16:05
Lib	2 Jun 1933	23:13
Sco	5 Jun 1933	02:23
Sag	7 Jun 1933	02:31
Cap	9 Jun 1933	01:33
Aqu	11 Jun 1933	01:42
Pis	13 Jun 1933	04:50
Ari	15 Jun 1933	11:51
Tau	17 Jun 1933	22:12
Gem	20 Jun 1933	10:25
Can	22 Jun 1933	23:06
Leo	25 Jun 1933	11:16
Vir	27 Jun 1933	22:00
Lib	30 Jun 1933	06:10
Sco	2 Jul 1933	10:55
Sag	4 Jul 1933	12:30
Cap	6 Jul 1933	12:15
Aqu	8 Jul 1933	12:06
Pis	10 Jul 1933	14:02
Ari	12 Jul 1933	19:31
Tau	15 Jul 1933	04:49
Gem	17 Jul 1933	16:44
Can	20 Jul 1933	05:24
Leo	22 Jul 1933	17:18
Vir	25 Jul 1933	03:35
Lib	27 Jul 1933	11:43
Sco	29 Jul 1933	17:21
Sag	31 Jul 1933	20:26
Cap	2 Aug 1933	21:40
Aqu	4 Aug 1933	22:22
Pis	7 Aug 1933	00:11
Ari	9 Aug 1933	04:41
Tau	11 Aug 1933	12:45
Gem	13 Aug 1933	23:57
Can	16 Aug 1933	12:32
Leo	19 Aug 1933	00:22
Vir	21 Aug 1933	10:07
Lib	23 Aug 1933	17:29
Sco	25 Aug 1933	22:44
Sag	28 Aug 1933	02:20
Cap	30 Aug 1933	04:51
Aqu	1 Sep 1933	06:59
Pis	3 Sep 1933	09:44
Ari	5 Sep 1933	14:15
Tau	7 Sep 1933	21:35
Gem	10 Sep 1933	08:01
Can	12 Sep 1933	20:25
Leo	15 Sep 1933	08:30
Vir	17 Sep 1933	18:13
Lib	20 Sep 1933	00:50
Sco	22 Sep 1933	04:59
Sag	24 Sep 1933	07:48
Cap	26 Sep 1933	10:23
Aqu	28 Sep 1933	13:27
Pis	30 Sep 1933	17:27
Ari	2 Oct 1933	22:51
Tau	5 Oct 1933	06:17
Gem	7 Oct 1933	16:18
Can	10 Oct 1933	04:29
Leo	12 Oct 1933	17:01
Vir	15 Oct 1933	03:23
Lib	17 Oct 1933	10:06
Sco	19 Oct 1933	13:26
Sag	21 Oct 1933	14:54
Cap	23 Oct 1933	16:13
Aqu	25 Oct 1933	18:48
Pis	27 Oct 1933	23:18
Ari	30 Oct 1933	05:40
Tau	1 Nov 1933	13:53
Gem	4 Nov 1933	00:02
Can	6 Nov 1933	12:05
Leo	9 Nov 1933	00:57
Vir	11 Nov 1933	12:22
Lib	13 Nov 1933	20:11
Sco	15 Nov 1933	23:50
Sag	18 Nov 1933	00:34
Cap	20 Nov 1933	00:24
Aqu	22 Nov 1933	01:21
Pis	24 Nov 1933	04:50
Ari	26 Nov 1933	11:13
Tau	28 Nov 1933	20:03
Gem	1 Dec 1933	06:44
Can	3 Dec 1933	18:52
Leo	6 Dec 1933	07:48
Vir	8 Dec 1933	19:59
Lib	11 Dec 1933	05:18
Sco	13 Dec 1933	10:25
Sag	15 Dec 1933	11:47
Cap	17 Dec 1933	11:08
Aqu	19 Dec 1933	10:38
Pis	21 Dec 1933	12:16
Ari	23 Dec 1933	17:15
Tau	26 Dec 1933	01:43
Gem	28 Dec 1933	12:43
Can	31 Dec 1933	01:06

Moon Signs

1934

Leo	2 Jan 1934	13:56
Vir	5 Jan 1934	02:08
Lib	7 Jan 1934	12:19
Sco	9 Jan 1934	19:10
Sag	11 Jan 1934	22:16
Cap	13 Jan 1934	22:36
Aqu	15 Jan 1934	21:56
Pis	17 Jan 1934	22:18
Ari	20 Jan 1934	01:29
Tau	22 Jan 1934	08:27
Gem	24 Jan 1934	18:54
Can	27 Jan 1934	07:24
Leo	29 Jan 1934	20:11

Vir	1 Feb 1934	08:00
Lib	3 Feb 1934	17:59
Sco	6 Feb 1934	01:30
Sag	8 Feb 1934	06:14
Cap	10 Feb 1934	08:22
Aqu	12 Feb 1934	08:57
Pis	14 Feb 1934	09:28
Ari	16 Feb 1934	11:40
Tau	18 Feb 1934	17:03
Gem	21 Feb 1934	02:17
Can	23 Feb 1934	14:22
Leo	26 Feb 1934	03:13
Vir	28 Feb 1934	14:45

Lib	3 Mar 1934	00:01
Sco	5 Mar 1934	06:58
Sag	7 Mar 1934	11:57
Cap	9 Mar 1934	15:21
Aqu	11 Mar 1934	17:36
Pis	13 Mar 1934	19:25
Ari	15 Mar 1934	22:01
Tau	18 Mar 1934	02:47
Gem	20 Mar 1934	10:52
Can	22 Mar 1934	22:13
Leo	25 Mar 1934	11:02
Vir	27 Mar 1934	22:43
Lib	30 Mar 1934	07:36

Sco	1 Apr 1934	13:34
Sag	3 Apr 1934	17:36
Cap	5 Apr 1934	20:45
Aqu	7 Apr 1934	23:42
Pis	10 Apr 1934	02:52
Ari	12 Apr 1934	06:40
Tau	14 Apr 1934	11:56
Gem	16 Apr 1934	19:41
Can	19 Apr 1934	06:26
Leo	21 Apr 1934	19:10
Vir	24 Apr 1934	07:19
Lib	26 Apr 1934	16:31
Sco	28 Apr 1934	22:06

Sag	1 May 1934	01:01
Cap	3 May 1934	02:53
Aqu	5 May 1934	05:06
Pis	7 May 1934	08:26
Ari	9 May 1934	13:09
Tau	11 May 1934	19:24
Gem	14 May 1934	03:38
Can	16 May 1934	14:17
Leo	19 May 1934	02:55
Vir	21 May 1934	15:35
Lib	24 May 1934	01:42
Sco	26 May 1934	07:51
Sag	28 May 1934	10:28
Cap	30 May 1934	11:12

Aqu	1 Jun 1934	11:55
Pis	3 Jun 1934	14:07
Ari	5 Jun 1934	18:31
Tau	8 Jun 1934	01:17
Gem	10 Jun 1934	10:14
Can	12 Jun 1934	21:14
Leo	15 Jun 1934	09:52
Vir	17 Jun 1934	22:51
Lib	20 Jun 1934	09:58
Sco	22 Jun 1934	17:24
Sag	24 Jun 1934	20:48
Cap	26 Jun 1934	21:24
Aqu	28 Jun 1934	21:02
Pis	30 Jun 1934	21:39

Ari	3 Jul 1934	00:40
Tau	5 Jul 1934	06:47
Gem	7 Jul 1934	15:56
Can	10 Jul 1934	03:21
Leo	12 Jul 1934	16:07
Vir	15 Jul 1934	05:07
Lib	17 Jul 1934	16:47
Sco	20 Jul 1934	01:29
Sag	22 Jul 1934	06:27
Cap	24 Jul 1934	08:03
Aqu	26 Jul 1934	07:43
Pis	28 Jul 1934	07:20
Ari	30 Jul 1934	08:46

Tau	1 Aug 1934	13:26
Gem	3 Aug 1934	21:49
Can	6 Aug 1934	09:13
Leo	8 Aug 1934	22:08
Vir	11 Aug 1934	10:58
Lib	13 Aug 1934	22:32
Sco	16 Aug 1934	07:50
Sag	18 Aug 1934	14:10
Cap	20 Aug 1934	17:27
Aqu	22 Aug 1934	18:18
Pis	24 Aug 1934	18:08
Ari	26 Aug 1934	18:44
Tau	28 Aug 1934	21:56
Gem	31 Aug 1934	04:55

Can	2 Sep 1934	15:41
Leo	5 Sep 1934	04:32
Vir	7 Sep 1934	17:16
Lib	10 Sep 1934	04:22
Sco	12 Sep 1934	13:19
Sag	14 Sep 1934	20:03
Cap	17 Sep 1934	00:35
Aqu	19 Sep 1934	03:06
Pis	21 Sep 1934	04:13
Ari	23 Sep 1934	05:13
Tau	25 Sep 1934	07:47
Gem	27 Sep 1934	13:34
Can	29 Sep 1934	23:15

Leo	2 Oct 1934	11:44
Vir	5 Oct 1934	00:30
Lib	7 Oct 1934	11:19
Sco	9 Oct 1934	19:31
Sag	12 Oct 1934	01:31
Cap	14 Oct 1934	06:04
Aqu	16 Oct 1934	09:31
Pis	18 Oct 1934	12:09
Ari	20 Oct 1934	14:28
Tau	22 Oct 1934	17:34
Gem	24 Oct 1934	22:59
Can	27 Oct 1934	07:46
Leo	29 Oct 1934	19:42

Vir	1 Nov 1934	08:35
Lib	3 Nov 1934	19:40
Sco	6 Nov 1934	03:31
Sag	8 Nov 1934	08:32
Cap	10 Nov 1934	11:56
Aqu	12 Nov 1934	14:52
Pis	14 Nov 1934	17:56
Ari	16 Nov 1934	21:26
Tau	19 Nov 1934	01:47
Gem	21 Nov 1934	07:47
Can	23 Nov 1934	16:25
Leo	26 Nov 1934	03:54
Vir	28 Nov 1934	16:52

Lib	1 Dec 1934	04:38
Sco	3 Dec 1934	13:04
Sag	5 Dec 1934	17:52
Cap	7 Dec 1934	20:08
Aqu	9 Dec 1934	21:34
Pis	11 Dec 1934	23:31
Ari	14 Dec 1934	02:51
Tau	16 Dec 1934	07:57
Gem	18 Dec 1934	14:59
Can	21 Dec 1934	00:11
Leo	23 Dec 1934	11:38
Vir	26 Dec 1934	00:32
Lib	28 Dec 1934	12:58
Sco	30 Dec 1934	22:40

Moon Signs

1935

Sag	2 Jan 1935	04:26
Cap	4 Jan 1935	06:43
Aqu	6 Jan 1935	07:04
Pis	8 Jan 1935	07:18
Ari	10 Jan 1935	09:03
Tau	12 Jan 1935	13:25
Gem	14 Jan 1935	20:43
Can	17 Jan 1935	06:37
Leo	19 Jan 1935	18:27
Vir	22 Jan 1935	07:19
Lib	24 Jan 1935	19:59
Sco	27 Jan 1935	06:46
Sag	29 Jan 1935	14:09
Cap	31 Jan 1935	17:47

Aqu	2 Feb 1935	18:26
Pis	4 Feb 1935	17:47
Ari	6 Feb 1935	17:49
Tau	8 Feb 1935	20:23
Gem	11 Feb 1935	02:36
Can	13 Feb 1935	12:25
Leo	16 Feb 1935	00:35
Vir	18 Feb 1935	13:33
Lib	21 Feb 1935	02:02
Sco	23 Feb 1935	13:03
Sag	25 Feb 1935	21:39
Cap	28 Feb 1935	03:04

Pis	4 Mar 1935	05:13
Ari	6 Mar 1935	04:41
Tau	8 Mar 1935	05:43
Gem	10 Mar 1935	10:13
Can	12 Mar 1935	18:52
Leo	15 Mar 1935	06:48
Vir	17 Mar 1935	19:51
Lib	20 Mar 1935	08:08
Sco	22 Mar 1935	18:44
Sag	25 Mar 1935	03:23
Cap	27 Mar 1935	09:48
Aqu	29 Mar 1935	13:41
Pis	31 Mar 1935	15:14

Ari	2 Apr 1935	15:31
Tau	4 Apr 1935	16:19
Gem	6 Apr 1935	19:36
Can	9 Apr 1935	02:50
Leo	11 Apr 1935	13:53
Vir	14 Apr 1935	02:46
Lib	16 Apr 1935	15:00
Sco	19 Apr 1935	01:09
Sag	21 Apr 1935	09:05
Cap	23 Apr 1935	15:13
Aqu	25 Apr 1935	19:43
Pis	27 Apr 1935	22:39
Ari	30 Apr 1935	00:26

Tau	2 May 1935	02:10
Gem	4 May 1935	05:26
Can	6 May 1935	11:51
Leo	8 May 1935	21:55
Vir	11 May 1935	10:26
Lib	13 May 1935	22:47
Sco	16 May 1935	08:53
Sag	18 May 1935	16:12
Cap	20 May 1935	21:20
Aqu	23 May 1935	01:08
Pis	25 May 1935	04:13
Ari	27 May 1935	06:59
Tau	29 May 1935	09:59
Gem	31 May 1935	14:12

Can	2 Jun 1935	20:44
Leo	5 Jun 1935	06:19
Vir	7 Jun 1935	18:26
Lib	10 Jun 1935	06:59
Sco	12 Jun 1935	17:35
Sag	15 Jun 1935	00:56
Cap	17 Jun 1935	05:21
Aqu	19 Jun 1935	07:55
Pis	21 Jun 1935	09:56
Ari	23 Jun 1935	12:21
Tau	25 Jun 1935	15:54
Gem	27 Jun 1935	21:07
Can	30 Jun 1935	04:26

Leo	2 Jul 1935	14:13
Vir	5 Jul 1935	02:09
Lib	7 Jul 1935	14:52
Sco	10 Jul 1935	02:14
Sag	12 Jul 1935	10:26
Cap	14 Jul 1935	15:02
Aqu	16 Jul 1935	16:53
Pis	18 Jul 1935	17:30
Ari	20 Jul 1935	18:33
Tau	22 Jul 1935	21:21
Gem	25 Jul 1935	02:42
Can	27 Jul 1935	10:44
Leo	29 Jul 1935	21:04

Vir	1 Aug 1935	09:07
Lib	3 Aug 1935	21:54
Sco	6 Aug 1935	09:56
Sag	8 Aug 1935	19:24
Cap	11 Aug 1935	01:08
Aqu	13 Aug 1935	03:21
Pis	15 Aug 1935	03:19
Ari	17 Aug 1935	02:55
Tau	19 Aug 1935	04:08
Gem	21 Aug 1935	08:26
Can	23 Aug 1935	16:17
Leo	26 Aug 1935	03:01
Vir	28 Aug 1935	15:21
Lib	31 Aug 1935	04:08

Sco	2 Sep 1935	16:22
Sag	5 Sep 1935	02:47
Cap	7 Sep 1935	10:06
Aqu	9 Sep 1935	13:43
Pis	11 Sep 1935	14:14
Ari	13 Sep 1935	13:21
Tau	15 Sep 1935	13:11
Gem	17 Sep 1935	15:49
Can	19 Sep 1935	22:28
Leo	22 Sep 1935	08:50
Vir	24 Sep 1935	21:19
Lib	27 Sep 1935	10:05
Sco	29 Sep 1935	22:05

Sag	2 Oct 1935	08:40
Cap	4 Oct 1935	17:02
Aqu	6 Oct 1935	22:19
Pis	9 Oct 1935	00:25
Ari	11 Oct 1935	00:20
Tau	12 Oct 1935	23:54
Gem	15 Oct 1935	01:19
Can	17 Oct 1935	06:21
Leo	19 Oct 1935	15:36
Vir	22 Oct 1935	03:44
Lib	24 Oct 1935	16:31
Sco	27 Oct 1935	04:14
Sag	29 Oct 1935	14:17
Cap	31 Oct 1935	22:30

Aqu	3 Nov 1935	04:38
Pis	5 Nov 1935	08:19
Ari	7 Nov 1935	09:53
Tau	9 Nov 1935	10:29
Gem	11 Nov 1935	11:53
Can	13 Nov 1935	15:57
Leo	15 Nov 1935	23:52
Vir	18 Nov 1935	11:10
Lib	20 Nov 1935	23:52
Sco	23 Nov 1935	11:35
Sag	25 Nov 1935	21:08
Cap	28 Nov 1935	04:28
Aqu	30 Nov 1935	09:59

Pis	2 Dec 1935	14:02
Ari	4 Dec 1935	16:52
Tau	6 Dec 1935	19:03
Gem	8 Dec 1935	21:37
Can	11 Dec 1935	01:55
Leo	13 Dec 1935	09:07
Vir	15 Dec 1935	19:33
Lib	18 Dec 1935	07:58
Sco	20 Dec 1935	20:02
Sag	23 Dec 1935	05:44
Cap	25 Dec 1935	12:26
Aqu	27 Dec 1935	16:45
Pis	29 Dec 1935	19:42
Ari	31 Dec 1935	22:15

1936

Sign	Date	Time
Tau	3 Jan 1936	01:11
Gem	5 Jan 1936	05:04
Can	7 Jan 1936	10:29
Leo	9 Jan 1936	18:02
Vir	12 Jan 1936	04:05
Lib	14 Jan 1936	16:11
Sco	17 Jan 1936	04:38
Sag	19 Jan 1936	15:10
Cap	21 Jan 1936	22:17
Aqu	24 Jan 1936	02:01
Pis	26 Jan 1936	03:34
Ari	28 Jan 1936	04:36
Tau	30 Jan 1936	06:37
Gem	1 Feb 1936	10:39
Can	3 Feb 1936	16:58
Leo	6 Feb 1936	01:26
Vir	8 Feb 1936	11:49
Lib	10 Feb 1936	23:46
Sco	13 Feb 1936	12:24
Sag	15 Feb 1936	23:55
Cap	18 Feb 1936	08:20
Aqu	20 Feb 1936	12:45
Pis	22 Feb 1936	13:55
Ari	24 Feb 1936	13:35
Tau	26 Feb 1936	13:52
Gem	28 Feb 1936	16:30
Can	1 Mar 1936	22:26
Leo	4 Mar 1936	07:20
Vir	6 Mar 1936	18:18
Lib	9 Mar 1936	06:26
Sco	11 Mar 1936	19:03
Sag	14 Mar 1936	07:05
Cap	16 Mar 1936	16:51
Aqu	18 Mar 1936	22:51
Pis	21 Mar 1936	00:58
Ari	23 Mar 1936	00:31
Tau	24 Mar 1936	23:38
Gem	27 Mar 1936	00:33
Can	29 Mar 1936	04:52
Leo	31 Mar 1936	13:04
Vir	3 Apr 1936	00:08
Lib	5 Apr 1936	12:31
Sco	8 Apr 1936	01:05
Sag	10 Apr 1936	13:02
Cap	12 Apr 1936	23:22
Aqu	15 Apr 1936	06:49
Pis	17 Apr 1936	10:36
Ari	19 Apr 1936	11:20
Tau	21 Apr 1936	10:37
Gem	23 Apr 1936	10:38
Can	25 Apr 1936	13:24
Leo	27 Apr 1936	20:04
Vir	30 Apr 1936	06:22
Lib	2 May 1936	18:43
Sco	5 May 1936	07:16
Sag	7 May 1936	18:54
Cap	10 May 1936	04:56
Aqu	12 May 1936	12:46
Pis	14 May 1936	17:52
Ari	16 May 1936	20:13
Tau	18 May 1936	20:47
Gem	20 May 1936	21:12
Can	22 May 1936	23:21
Leo	25 May 1936	04:42
Vir	27 May 1936	13:48
Lib	30 May 1936	01:38
Sco	1 Jun 1936	14:11
Sag	4 Jun 1936	01:36
Cap	6 Jun 1936	11:02
Aqu	8 Jun 1936	18:17
Pis	10 Jun 1936	23:26
Ari	13 Jun 1936	02:46
Tau	15 Jun 1936	04:48
Gem	17 Jun 1936	06:30
Can	19 Jun 1936	09:09
Leo	21 Jun 1936	14:07
Vir	23 Jun 1936	22:16
Lib	26 Jun 1936	09:24
Sco	28 Jun 1936	21:52
Sag	1 Jul 1936	09:26
Cap	3 Jul 1936	18:34
Aqu	6 Jul 1936	00:55
Pis	8 Jul 1936	05:10
Ari	10 Jul 1936	08:10
Tau	12 Jul 1936	10:46
Gem	14 Jul 1936	13:39
Can	16 Jul 1936	17:28
Leo	18 Jul 1936	22:58
Vir	21 Jul 1936	06:54
Lib	23 Jul 1936	17:31
Sco	26 Jul 1936	05:54
Sag	28 Jul 1936	17:56
Cap	31 Jul 1936	03:23
Aqu	2 Aug 1936	09:24
Pis	4 Aug 1936	12:35
Ari	6 Aug 1936	14:21
Tau	8 Aug 1936	16:12
Gem	10 Aug 1936	19:12
Can	12 Aug 1936	23:52
Leo	15 Aug 1936	06:20
Vir	17 Aug 1936	14:45
Lib	20 Aug 1936	01:18
Sco	22 Aug 1936	13:36
Sag	25 Aug 1936	02:09
Cap	27 Aug 1936	12:34
Aqu	29 Aug 1936	19:12
Pis	31 Aug 1936	22:05
Ari	2 Sep 1936	22:43
Tau	4 Sep 1936	23:05
Gem	7 Sep 1936	00:55
Can	9 Sep 1936	05:16
Leo	11 Sep 1936	12:14
Vir	13 Sep 1936	21:20
Lib	16 Sep 1936	08:13
Sco	18 Sep 1936	20:32
Sag	21 Sep 1936	09:24
Cap	23 Sep 1936	20:52
Aqu	26 Sep 1936	04:52
Pis	28 Sep 1936	08:38
Ari	30 Sep 1936	09:09
Tau	2 Oct 1936	08:26
Gem	4 Oct 1936	08:37
Can	6 Oct 1936	11:30
Leo	8 Oct 1936	17:45
Vir	11 Oct 1936	03:02
Lib	13 Oct 1936	14:19
Sco	16 Oct 1936	02:47
Sag	18 Oct 1936	15:37
Cap	21 Oct 1936	03:37
Aqu	23 Oct 1936	12:58
Pis	25 Oct 1936	18:27
Ari	27 Oct 1936	20:09
Tau	29 Oct 1936	19:34
Gem	31 Oct 1936	18:49
Can	2 Nov 1936	20:01
Leo	5 Nov 1936	00:38
Vir	7 Nov 1936	09:01
Lib	9 Nov 1936	20:15
Sco	12 Nov 1936	08:52
Sag	14 Nov 1936	21:33
Cap	17 Nov 1936	09:20
Aqu	19 Nov 1936	19:10
Pis	22 Nov 1936	02:03
Ari	24 Nov 1936	05:36
Tau	26 Nov 1936	06:28
Gem	28 Nov 1936	06:11
Can	30 Nov 1936	06:40
Leo	2 Dec 1936	09:44
Vir	4 Dec 1936	16:31
Lib	7 Dec 1936	02:56
Sco	9 Dec 1936	15:28
Sag	12 Dec 1936	04:07
Cap	14 Dec 1936	15:25
Aqu	17 Dec 1936	00:41
Pis	19 Dec 1936	07:43
Ari	21 Dec 1936	12:25
Tau	23 Dec 1936	15:05
Gem	25 Dec 1936	16:24
Can	27 Dec 1936	17:36
Leo	29 Dec 1936	20:14

1937

Sign	Date	Time
Vir	1 Jan 1937	01:46
Lib	3 Jan 1937	10:56
Sco	5 Jan 1937	22:58
Sag	8 Jan 1937	11:42
Cap	10 Jan 1937	22:52
Aqu	13 Jan 1937	07:24
Pis	15 Jan 1937	13:28
Ari	17 Jan 1937	17:48
Tau	19 Jan 1937	21:07
Gem	21 Jan 1937	23:53
Can	24 Jan 1937	02:38
Leo	26 Jan 1937	06:08
Vir	28 Jan 1937	11:31
Lib	30 Jan 1937	19:50
Sco	2 Feb 1937	07:11
Sag	4 Feb 1937	19:59
Cap	7 Feb 1937	07:33
Aqu	9 Feb 1937	15:59
Pis	11 Feb 1937	21:09
Ari	14 Feb 1937	00:12
Tau	16 Feb 1937	02:35
Gem	18 Feb 1937	05:22
Can	20 Feb 1937	09:04
Leo	22 Feb 1937	13:51
Vir	24 Feb 1937	20:05
Lib	27 Feb 1937	04:27
Sco	1 Mar 1937	15:23
Sag	4 Mar 1937	04:08
Cap	6 Mar 1937	16:22
Aqu	9 Mar 1937	01:34
Pis	11 Mar 1937	06:49
Ari	13 Mar 1937	08:59
Tau	15 Mar 1937	09:54
Gem	17 Mar 1937	11:19
Can	19 Mar 1937	14:26
Leo	21 Mar 1937	19:36
Vir	24 Mar 1937	02:44
Lib	26 Mar 1937	11:48
Sco	28 Mar 1937	22:51
Sag	31 Mar 1937	11:32
Cap	3 Apr 1937	00:16
Aqu	5 Apr 1937	10:37
Pis	7 Apr 1937	16:59
Ari	9 Apr 1937	19:28
Tau	11 Apr 1937	19:39
Gem	13 Apr 1937	19:34
Can	15 Apr 1937	21:03
Leo	18 Apr 1937	01:12
Vir	20 Apr 1937	08:16
Lib	22 Apr 1937	17:51
Sco	25 Apr 1937	05:21
Sag	27 Apr 1937	18:05
Cap	30 Apr 1937	06:56
Aqu	2 May 1937	18:08
Pis	5 May 1937	01:55
Ari	7 May 1937	05:47
Tau	9 May 1937	06:31
Gem	11 May 1937	05:56
Can	13 May 1937	06:00
Leo	15 May 1937	08:28
Vir	17 May 1937	14:20
Lib	19 May 1937	23:35
Sco	22 May 1937	11:18
Sag	25 May 1937	00:10
Cap	27 May 1937	12:53
Aqu	30 May 1937	00:12
Pis	1 Jun 1937	08:56
Ari	3 Jun 1937	14:21
Tau	5 Jun 1937	16:36
Gem	7 Jun 1937	16:45
Can	9 Jun 1937	16:31
Leo	11 Jun 1937	17:44
Vir	13 Jun 1937	22:02
Lib	16 Jun 1937	06:08
Sco	18 Jun 1937	17:31
Sag	21 Jun 1937	06:25
Cap	23 Jun 1937	18:58
Aqu	26 Jun 1937	05:54
Pis	28 Jun 1937	14:36
Ari	30 Jun 1937	20:49
Tau	3 Jul 1937	00:33
Gem	5 Jul 1937	02:15
Can	7 Jul 1937	02:53
Leo	9 Jul 1937	03:59
Vir	11 Jul 1937	07:16
Lib	13 Jul 1937	14:05
Sco	16 Jul 1937	00:37
Sag	18 Jul 1937	13:20
Cap	21 Jul 1937	01:50
Aqu	23 Jul 1937	12:19
Pis	25 Jul 1937	20:20
Ari	28 Jul 1937	02:14
Tau	30 Jul 1937	06:31
Gem	1 Aug 1937	09:29
Can	3 Aug 1937	11:34
Leo	5 Aug 1937	13:36
Vir	7 Aug 1937	16:54
Lib	9 Aug 1937	22:59
Sco	12 Aug 1937	08:37
Sag	14 Aug 1937	20:59
Cap	17 Aug 1937	09:37
Aqu	19 Aug 1937	20:04
Pis	22 Aug 1937	03:27
Ari	24 Aug 1937	08:23
Tau	26 Aug 1937	11:56
Gem	28 Aug 1937	15:01
Can	30 Aug 1937	18:03
Leo	1 Sep 1937	21:21
Vir	4 Sep 1937	01:35
Lib	6 Sep 1937	07:49
Sco	8 Sep 1937	17:00
Sag	11 Sep 1937	04:59
Cap	13 Sep 1937	17:51
Aqu	16 Sep 1937	04:51
Pis	18 Sep 1937	12:18
Ari	20 Sep 1937	16:30
Tau	22 Sep 1937	18:49
Gem	24 Sep 1937	20:46
Can	26 Sep 1937	23:25
Leo	29 Sep 1937	03:14
Vir	1 Oct 1937	08:29
Lib	3 Oct 1937	15:32
Sco	6 Oct 1937	00:56
Sag	8 Oct 1937	12:44
Cap	11 Oct 1937	01:46
Aqu	13 Oct 1937	13:36
Pis	15 Oct 1937	22:02
Ari	18 Oct 1937	02:31
Tau	20 Oct 1937	04:09
Gem	22 Oct 1937	04:40
Can	24 Oct 1937	05:46
Leo	26 Oct 1937	08:43
Vir	28 Oct 1937	14:02
Lib	30 Oct 1937	21:47
Sco	2 Nov 1937	07:48
Sag	4 Nov 1937	19:46
Cap	7 Nov 1937	08:50
Aqu	9 Nov 1937	21:18
Pis	12 Nov 1937	07:07
Ari	14 Nov 1937	12:58
Tau	16 Nov 1937	15:11
Gem	18 Nov 1937	15:10
Can	20 Nov 1937	14:48
Leo	22 Nov 1937	15:55
Vir	24 Nov 1937	19:56
Lib	27 Nov 1937	03:22
Sco	29 Nov 1937	13:47
Sag	2 Dec 1937	02:05
Cap	4 Dec 1937	15:07
Aqu	7 Dec 1937	03:40
Pis	9 Dec 1937	14:20
Ari	11 Dec 1937	21:53
Tau	14 Dec 1937	01:48
Gem	16 Dec 1937	02:42
Can	18 Dec 1937	02:03
Leo	20 Dec 1937	01:49
Vir	22 Dec 1937	03:58
Lib	24 Dec 1937	09:54
Sco	26 Dec 1937	19:45
Sag	29 Dec 1937	08:12
Cap	31 Dec 1937	21:17

1938

Aqu	3 Jan 1938	09:31
Pis	5 Jan 1938	20:06
Ari	8 Jan 1938	04:28
Tau	10 Jan 1938	10:05
Gem	12 Jan 1938	12:49
Can	14 Jan 1938	13:21
Leo	16 Jan 1938	13:09
Vir	18 Jan 1938	14:13
Lib	20 Jan 1938	18:27
Sco	23 Jan 1938	02:56
Sag	25 Jan 1938	14:52
Cap	28 Jan 1938	03:58
Aqu	30 Jan 1938	16:00

Pis	2 Feb 1938	01:58
Ari	4 Feb 1938	09:54
Tau	6 Feb 1938	15:58
Gem	8 Feb 1938	20:07
Can	10 Feb 1938	22:25
Leo	12 Feb 1938	23:33
Vir	15 Feb 1938	00:58
Lib	17 Feb 1938	04:28
Sco	19 Feb 1938	11:38
Sag	21 Feb 1938	22:34
Cap	24 Feb 1938	11:28
Aqu	26 Feb 1938	23:35

Pis	1 Mar 1938	09:13
Ari	3 Mar 1938	16:16
Tau	5 Mar 1938	21:29
Gem	8 Mar 1938	01:33
Can	10 Mar 1938	04:46
Leo	12 Mar 1938	07:23
Vir	14 Mar 1938	10:06
Lib	16 Mar 1938	14:09
Sco	18 Mar 1938	20:54
Sag	21 Mar 1938	07:01
Cap	23 Mar 1938	19:32
Aqu	26 Mar 1938	07:55
Pis	28 Mar 1938	17:51
Ari	31 Mar 1938	00:32

Tau	2 Apr 1938	04:42
Gem	4 Apr 1938	07:33
Can	6 Apr 1938	10:07
Leo	8 Apr 1938	13:04
Vir	10 Apr 1938	16:51
Lib	12 Apr 1938	22:03
Sco	15 Apr 1938	05:21
Sag	17 Apr 1938	15:20
Cap	20 Apr 1938	03:31
Aqu	22 Apr 1938	16:10
Pis	25 Apr 1938	02:52
Ari	27 Apr 1938	10:07
Tau	29 Apr 1938	14:01

Gem	1 May 1938	15:44
Can	3 May 1938	16:50
Leo	5 May 1938	18:42
Vir	7 May 1938	22:17
Lib	10 May 1938	04:06
Sco	12 May 1938	12:16
Sag	14 May 1938	22:41
Cap	17 May 1938	10:51
Aqu	19 May 1938	23:37
Pis	22 May 1938	11:07
Ari	24 May 1938	19:34
Tau	27 May 1938	00:15
Gem	29 May 1938	01:51
Can	31 May 1938	01:52

Leo	2 Jun 1938	02:09
Vir	4 Jun 1938	04:21
Lib	6 Jun 1938	09:36
Sco	8 Jun 1938	18:01
Sag	11 Jun 1938	04:57
Cap	13 Jun 1938	17:21
Aqu	16 Jun 1938	06:07
Pis	18 Jun 1938	18:02
Ari	21 Jun 1938	03:39
Tau	23 Jun 1938	09:48
Gem	25 Jun 1938	12:24
Can	27 Jun 1938	12:27
Leo	29 Jun 1938	11:46

Vir	1 Jul 1938	12:25
Lib	3 Jul 1938	16:09
Sco	5 Jul 1938	23:50
Sag	8 Jul 1938	10:46
Cap	10 Jul 1938	23:22
Aqu	13 Jul 1938	12:05
Pis	15 Jul 1938	23:55
Ari	18 Jul 1938	10:02
Tau	20 Jul 1938	17:31
Gem	22 Jul 1938	21:42
Can	24 Jul 1938	22:53
Leo	26 Jul 1938	22:26
Vir	28 Jul 1938	22:18
Lib	31 Jul 1938	00:36

Sco	2 Aug 1938	06:50
Sag	4 Aug 1938	17:02
Cap	7 Aug 1938	05:33
Aqu	9 Aug 1938	18:15
Pis	12 Aug 1938	05:45
Ari	14 Aug 1938	15:34
Tau	16 Aug 1938	23:24
Gem	19 Aug 1938	04:51
Can	21 Aug 1938	07:39
Leo	23 Aug 1938	08:26
Vir	25 Aug 1938	08:43
Lib	27 Aug 1938	10:27
Sco	29 Aug 1938	15:27

Sag	1 Sep 1938	00:29
Cap	3 Sep 1938	12:30
Aqu	6 Sep 1938	01:10
Pis	8 Sep 1938	12:28
Ari	10 Sep 1938	21:40
Tau	13 Sep 1938	04:54
Gem	15 Sep 1938	10:22
Can	17 Sep 1938	14:08
Leo	19 Sep 1938	16:26
Vir	21 Sep 1938	18:01
Lib	23 Sep 1938	20:19
Sco	26 Sep 1938	00:58
Sag	28 Sep 1938	09:03
Cap	30 Sep 1938	20:20

Aqu	3 Oct 1938	08:57
Pis	5 Oct 1938	20:26
Ari	8 Oct 1938	05:22
Tau	10 Oct 1938	11:42
Gem	12 Oct 1938	16:10
Can	14 Oct 1938	19:31
Leo	16 Oct 1938	22:19
Vir	19 Oct 1938	01:09
Lib	21 Oct 1938	04:43
Sco	23 Oct 1938	10:00
Sag	25 Oct 1938	17:54
Cap	28 Oct 1938	04:39
Aqu	30 Oct 1938	17:08

Pis	2 Nov 1938	05:09
Ari	4 Nov 1938	14:34
Tau	6 Nov 1938	20:40
Gem	9 Nov 1938	00:02
Can	11 Nov 1938	01:59
Leo	13 Nov 1938	03:50
Vir	15 Nov 1938	06:38
Lib	17 Nov 1938	11:04
Sco	19 Nov 1938	17:25
Sag	22 Nov 1938	01:57
Cap	24 Nov 1938	12:38
Aqu	27 Nov 1938	00:58
Pis	29 Nov 1938	13:29

Ari	2 Dec 1938	00:01
Tau	4 Dec 1938	07:00
Gem	6 Dec 1938	10:17
Can	8 Dec 1938	11:07
Leo	10 Dec 1938	11:18
Vir	12 Dec 1938	12:38
Lib	14 Dec 1938	16:27
Sco	16 Dec 1938	23:14
Sag	19 Dec 1938	08:31
Cap	21 Dec 1938	19:39
Aqu	24 Dec 1938	07:59
Pis	26 Dec 1938	20:40
Ari	29 Dec 1938	08:13
Tau	31 Dec 1938	16:47

1939

Sign	Date	Time
Gem	2 Jan 1939	21:18
Can	4 Jan 1939	22:19
Leo	6 Jan 1939	21:32
Vir	8 Jan 1939	21:09
Lib	10 Jan 1939	23:12
Sco	13 Jan 1939	04:54
Sag	15 Jan 1939	14:10
Cap	18 Jan 1939	01:44
Aqu	20 Jan 1939	14:15
Pis	23 Jan 1939	02:51
Ari	25 Jan 1939	14:41
Tau	28 Jan 1939	00:27
Gem	30 Jan 1939	06:50
Can	1 Feb 1939	09:21
Leo	3 Feb 1939	09:05
Vir	5 Feb 1939	08:02
Lib	7 Feb 1939	08:30
Sco	9 Feb 1939	12:23
Sag	11 Feb 1939	20:24
Cap	14 Feb 1939	07:41
Aqu	16 Feb 1939	20:22
Pis	19 Feb 1939	08:51
Ari	21 Feb 1939	20:23
Tau	24 Feb 1939	06:18
Gem	26 Feb 1939	13:46
Can	28 Feb 1939	18:06
Leo	2 Mar 1939	19:29
Vir	4 Mar 1939	19:16
Lib	6 Mar 1939	19:26
Sco	8 Mar 1939	22:01
Sag	11 Mar 1939	04:23
Cap	13 Mar 1939	14:36
Aqu	16 Mar 1939	03:01
Pis	18 Mar 1939	15:31
Ari	21 Mar 1939	02:40
Tau	23 Mar 1939	11:57
Gem	25 Mar 1939	19:14
Can	28 Mar 1939	00:18
Leo	30 Mar 1939	03:14
Vir	1 Apr 1939	04:38
Lib	3 Apr 1939	05:48
Sco	5 Apr 1939	08:22
Sag	7 Apr 1939	13:48
Cap	9 Apr 1939	22:47
Aqu	12 Apr 1939	10:33
Pis	14 Apr 1939	23:03
Ari	17 Apr 1939	10:12
Tau	19 Apr 1939	18:56
Gem	22 Apr 1939	01:15
Can	24 Apr 1939	05:43
Leo	26 Apr 1939	08:54
Vir	28 Apr 1939	11:26
Lib	30 Apr 1939	14:02

Sign	Date	Time
Sco	2 May 1939	17:36
Sag	4 May 1939	23:11
Cap	7 May 1939	07:33
Aqu	9 May 1939	18:40
Pis	12 May 1939	07:09
Ari	14 May 1939	18:40
Tau	17 May 1939	03:27
Gem	19 May 1939	09:05
Can	21 May 1939	12:22
Leo	23 May 1939	14:33
Vir	25 May 1939	16:50
Lib	27 May 1939	20:06
Sco	30 May 1939	00:47
Sag	1 Jun 1939	07:15
Cap	3 Jun 1939	15:50
Aqu	6 Jun 1939	02:40
Pis	8 Jun 1939	15:04
Ari	11 Jun 1939	03:09
Tau	13 Jun 1939	12:41
Gem	15 Jun 1939	18:32
Can	17 Jun 1939	21:05
Leo	19 Jun 1939	21:57
Vir	21 Jun 1939	22:56
Lib	24 Jun 1939	01:31
Sco	26 Jun 1939	06:25
Sag	28 Jun 1939	13:39
Cap	30 Jun 1939	22:54
Aqu	3 Jul 1939	09:54
Pis	5 Jul 1939	22:17
Ari	8 Jul 1939	10:49
Tau	10 Jul 1939	21:25
Gem	13 Jul 1939	04:19
Can	15 Jul 1939	07:15
Leo	17 Jul 1939	07:30
Vir	19 Jul 1939	07:07
Lib	21 Jul 1939	08:10
Sco	23 Jul 1939	12:05
Sag	25 Jul 1939	19:10
Cap	28 Jul 1939	04:50
Aqu	30 Jul 1939	16:15
Pis	2 Aug 1939	04:41
Ari	4 Aug 1939	17:22
Tau	7 Aug 1939	04:46
Gem	9 Aug 1939	13:04
Can	11 Aug 1939	17:20
Leo	13 Aug 1939	18:09
Vir	15 Aug 1939	17:19
Lib	17 Aug 1939	17:03
Sco	19 Aug 1939	19:20
Sag	22 Aug 1939	01:15
Cap	24 Aug 1939	10:34
Aqu	26 Aug 1939	22:09
Pis	29 Aug 1939	10:42
Ari	31 Aug 1939	23:14

Sign	Date	Time
Tau	3 Sep 1939	10:46
Gem	5 Sep 1939	20:01
Can	8 Sep 1939	01:50
Leo	10 Sep 1939	04:10
Vir	12 Sep 1939	04:08
Lib	14 Sep 1939	03:38
Sco	16 Sep 1939	04:43
Sag	18 Sep 1939	09:03
Cap	20 Sep 1939	17:11
Aqu	23 Sep 1939	04:24
Pis	25 Sep 1939	16:59
Ari	28 Sep 1939	05:22
Tau	30 Sep 1939	16:28
Gem	3 Oct 1939	01:37
Can	5 Oct 1939	08:15
Leo	7 Oct 1939	12:08
Vir	9 Oct 1939	13:45
Lib	11 Oct 1939	14:15
Sco	13 Oct 1939	15:18
Sag	15 Oct 1939	18:36
Cap	18 Oct 1939	01:23
Aqu	20 Oct 1939	11:40
Pis	23 Oct 1939	00:05
Ari	25 Oct 1939	12:27
Tau	27 Oct 1939	23:08
Gem	30 Oct 1939	07:30
Can	1 Nov 1939	13:40
Leo	3 Nov 1939	18:01
Vir	5 Nov 1939	20:56
Lib	7 Nov 1939	23:03
Sco	10 Nov 1939	01:14
Sag	12 Nov 1939	04:41
Cap	14 Nov 1939	10:43
Aqu	16 Nov 1939	20:00
Pis	19 Nov 1939	08:00
Ari	21 Nov 1939	20:35
Tau	24 Nov 1939	07:22
Gem	26 Nov 1939	15:08
Can	28 Nov 1939	20:10
Leo	30 Nov 1939	23:33
Vir	3 Dec 1939	02:23
Lib	5 Dec 1939	05:22
Sco	7 Dec 1939	08:57
Sag	9 Dec 1939	13:32
Cap	11 Dec 1939	19:51
Aqu	14 Dec 1939	04:42
Pis	16 Dec 1939	16:14
Ari	19 Dec 1939	05:02
Tau	21 Dec 1939	16:31
Gem	24 Dec 1939	00:35
Can	26 Dec 1939	05:02
Leo	28 Dec 1939	07:04
Vir	30 Dec 1939	08:29

1940

Sign	Date	Time	Sign	Date	Time	Sign	Date	Time
Lib	1 Jan 1940	10:44	**Pis**	1 May 1940	01:56	**Vir**	1 Sep 1940	12:55
Sco	3 Jan 1940	14:36	**Ari**	3 May 1940	14:51	**Lib**	3 Sep 1940	12:54
Sag	5 Jan 1940	20:12	**Tau**	6 May 1940	03:11	**Sco**	5 Sep 1940	13:17
Cap	8 Jan 1940	03:30	**Gem**	8 May 1940	13:32	**Sag**	7 Sep 1940	15:36
Aqu	10 Jan 1940	12:42	**Can**	10 May 1940	21:32	**Cap**	9 Sep 1940	20:46
Pis	13 Jan 1940	00:03	**Leo**	13 May 1940	03:22	**Aqu**	12 Sep 1940	04:51
Ari	15 Jan 1940	12:55	**Vir**	15 May 1940	07:17	**Pis**	14 Sep 1940	15:25
Tau	18 Jan 1940	01:14	**Lib**	17 May 1940	09:40	**Ari**	17 Sep 1940	03:43
Gem	20 Jan 1940	10:30	**Sco**	19 May 1940	11:11	**Tau**	19 Sep 1940	16:45
Can	22 Jan 1940	15:34	**Sag**	21 May 1940	13:00	**Gem**	22 Sep 1940	05:05
Leo	24 Jan 1940	17:10	**Cap**	23 May 1940	16:34	**Can**	24 Sep 1940	14:56
Vir	26 Jan 1940	17:12	**Aqu**	25 May 1940	23:19	**Leo**	26 Sep 1940	21:07
Lib	28 Jan 1940	17:43	**Pis**	28 May 1940	09:39	**Vir**	28 Sep 1940	23:40
Sco	30 Jan 1940	20:18	**Ari**	30 May 1940	22:18	**Lib**	30 Sep 1940	23:46
Sag	2 Feb 1940	01:36	**Tau**	2 Jun 1940	10:42	**Sco**	2 Oct 1940	23:12
Cap	4 Feb 1940	09:27	**Gem**	4 Jun 1940	20:48	**Sag**	4 Oct 1940	23:55
Aqu	6 Feb 1940	19:21	**Can**	7 Jun 1940	04:01	**Cap**	7 Oct 1940	03:29
Pis	9 Feb 1940	06:58	**Leo**	9 Jun 1940	09:00	**Aqu**	9 Oct 1940	10:45
Ari	11 Feb 1940	19:49	**Vir**	11 Jun 1940	12:40	**Pis**	11 Oct 1940	21:18
Tau	14 Feb 1940	08:35	**Lib**	13 Jun 1940	15:43	**Ari**	14 Oct 1940	09:50
Gem	16 Feb 1940	19:09	**Sco**	15 Jun 1940	18:31	**Tau**	16 Oct 1940	22:48
Can	19 Feb 1940	01:45	**Sag**	17 Jun 1940	21:34	**Gem**	19 Oct 1940	10:58
Leo	21 Feb 1940	04:18	**Cap**	20 Jun 1940	01:45	**Can**	21 Oct 1940	21:17
Vir	23 Feb 1940	04:11	**Aqu**	22 Jun 1940	08:15	**Leo**	24 Oct 1940	04:50
Lib	25 Feb 1940	03:29	**Pis**	24 Jun 1940	17:55	**Vir**	26 Oct 1940	09:08
Sco	27 Feb 1940	04:14	**Ari**	27 Jun 1940	06:12	**Lib**	28 Oct 1940	10:35
Sag	29 Feb 1940	07:55	**Tau**	29 Jun 1940	18:52	**Sco**	30 Oct 1940	10:24
Cap	2 Mar 1940	15:03	**Gem**	2 Jul 1940	05:14	**Sag**	1 Nov 1940	10:21
Aqu	5 Mar 1940	01:08	**Can**	4 Jul 1940	12:09	**Cap**	3 Nov 1940	12:23
Pis	7 Mar 1940	13:07	**Leo**	6 Jul 1940	16:11	**Aqu**	5 Nov 1940	18:03
Ari	10 Mar 1940	02:00	**Vir**	8 Jul 1940	18:44	**Pis**	8 Nov 1940	03:46
Tau	12 Mar 1940	14:43	**Lib**	10 Jul 1940	21:06	**Ari**	10 Nov 1940	16:13
Gem	15 Mar 1940	01:51	**Sco**	13 Jul 1940	00:07	**Tau**	13 Nov 1940	05:12
Can	17 Mar 1940	09:55	**Sag**	15 Jul 1940	04:04	**Gem**	15 Nov 1940	17:00
Leo	19 Mar 1940	14:13	**Cap**	17 Jul 1940	09:18	**Can**	18 Nov 1940	02:51
Vir	21 Mar 1940	15:19	**Aqu**	19 Jul 1940	16:22	**Leo**	20 Nov 1940	10:37
Lib	23 Mar 1940	14:47	**Pis**	22 Jul 1940	01:59	**Vir**	22 Nov 1940	16:10
Sco	25 Mar 1940	14:33	**Ari**	24 Jul 1940	14:01	**Lib**	24 Nov 1940	19:24
Sag	27 Mar 1940	16:31	**Tau**	27 Jul 1940	02:55	**Sco**	26 Nov 1940	20:44
Cap	29 Mar 1940	22:00	**Gem**	29 Jul 1940	14:02	**Sag**	28 Nov 1940	21:18
			Can	31 Jul 1940	21:31	**Cap**	30 Nov 1940	22:51
Aqu	1 Apr 1940	07:13	**Leo**	3 Aug 1940	01:19	**Aqu**	3 Dec 1940	03:13
Pis	3 Apr 1940	19:11	**Vir**	5 Aug 1940	02:50	**Pis**	5 Dec 1940	11:36
Ari	6 Apr 1940	08:09	**Lib**	7 Aug 1940	03:49	**Ari**	7 Dec 1940	23:26
Tau	8 Apr 1940	20:38	**Sco**	9 Aug 1940	05:45	**Tau**	10 Dec 1940	12:26
Gem	11 Apr 1940	07:31	**Sag**	11 Aug 1940	09:29	**Gem**	13 Dec 1940	00:06
Can	13 Apr 1940	16:03	**Cap**	13 Aug 1940	15:15	**Can**	15 Dec 1940	09:19
Leo	15 Apr 1940	21:42	**Aqu**	15 Aug 1940	23:08	**Leo**	17 Dec 1940	16:15
Vir	18 Apr 1940	00:33	**Pis**	18 Aug 1940	09:10	**Vir**	19 Dec 1940	21:34
Lib	20 Apr 1940	01:22	**Ari**	20 Aug 1940	21:14	**Lib**	22 Dec 1940	01:36
Sco	22 Apr 1940	01:33	**Tau**	23 Aug 1940	10:16	**Sco**	24 Dec 1940	04:29
Sag	24 Apr 1940	02:48	**Gem**	25 Aug 1940	22:12	**Sag**	26 Dec 1940	06:36
Cap	26 Apr 1940	06:49	**Can**	28 Aug 1940	06:53	**Cap**	28 Dec 1940	08:58
Aqu	28 Apr 1940	14:39	**Leo**	30 Aug 1940	11:29	**Aqu**	30 Dec 1940	13:09

Moon Signs

1941

Sign	Date	Time
Pis	1 Jan 1941	20:35
Ari	4 Jan 1941	07:34
Tau	6 Jan 1941	20:27
Gem	9 Jan 1941	08:26
Can	11 Jan 1941	17:33
Leo	13 Jan 1941	23:38
Vir	16 Jan 1941	03:45
Lib	18 Jan 1941	06:59
Sco	20 Jan 1941	10:03
Sag	22 Jan 1941	13:16
Cap	24 Jan 1941	17:01
Aqu	26 Jan 1941	22:06
Pis	29 Jan 1941	05:34
Ari	31 Jan 1941	16:02

Sign	Date	Time
Tau	3 Feb 1941	04:40
Gem	5 Feb 1941	17:09
Can	8 Feb 1941	02:56
Leo	10 Feb 1941	09:06
Vir	12 Feb 1941	12:20
Lib	14 Feb 1941	14:07
Sco	16 Feb 1941	15:52
Sag	18 Feb 1941	18:36
Cap	20 Feb 1941	22:54
Aqu	23 Feb 1941	05:01
Pis	25 Feb 1941	13:18
Ari	27 Feb 1941	23:54

Sign	Date	Time
Tau	2 Mar 1941	12:23
Gem	5 Mar 1941	01:11
Can	7 Mar 1941	12:02
Leo	9 Mar 1941	19:18
Vir	11 Mar 1941	22:50
Lib	13 Mar 1941	23:50
Sco	16 Mar 1941	00:03
Sag	18 Mar 1941	01:08
Cap	20 Mar 1941	04:25
Aqu	22 Mar 1941	10:34
Pis	24 Mar 1941	19:30
Ari	27 Mar 1941	06:39
Tau	29 Mar 1941	19:13

Sign	Date	Time
Gem	1 Apr 1941	08:06
Can	3 Apr 1941	19:42
Leo	6 Apr 1941	04:24
Vir	8 Apr 1941	09:19
Lib	10 Apr 1941	10:53
Sco	12 Apr 1941	10:31
Sag	14 Apr 1941	10:08
Cap	16 Apr 1941	11:39
Aqu	18 Apr 1941	16:31
Pis	21 Apr 1941	01:07
Ari	23 Apr 1941	12:34
Tau	26 Apr 1941	01:22
Gem	28 Apr 1941	14:10

Sign	Date	Time
Can	1 May 1941	01:55
Leo	3 May 1941	11:32
Vir	5 May 1941	18:05
Lib	7 May 1941	21:10
Sco	9 May 1941	21:32
Sag	11 May 1941	20:49
Cap	13 May 1941	21:04
Aqu	16 May 1941	00:16
Pis	18 May 1941	07:34
Ari	20 May 1941	18:34
Tau	23 May 1941	07:26
Gem	25 May 1941	20:09
Can	28 May 1941	07:36
Leo	30 May 1941	17:15

Sign	Date	Time
Vir	2 Jun 1941	00:37
Lib	4 Jun 1941	05:16
Sco	6 Jun 1941	07:13
Sag	8 Jun 1941	07:23
Cap	10 Jun 1941	07:31
Aqu	12 Jun 1941	09:42
Pis	14 Jun 1941	15:34
Ari	17 Jun 1941	01:30
Tau	19 Jun 1941	14:02
Gem	22 Jun 1941	02:43
Can	24 Jun 1941	13:50
Leo	26 Jun 1941	22:54
Vir	29 Jun 1941	06:02

Sign	Date	Time
Lib	1 Jul 1941	11:16
Sco	3 Jul 1941	14:33
Sag	5 Jul 1941	16:13
Cap	7 Jul 1941	17:20
Aqu	9 Jul 1941	19:36
Pis	12 Jul 1941	00:43
Ari	14 Jul 1941	09:35
Tau	16 Jul 1941	21:29
Gem	19 Jul 1941	10:09
Can	21 Jul 1941	21:14
Leo	24 Jul 1941	05:47
Vir	26 Jul 1941	12:02
Lib	28 Jul 1941	16:40
Sco	30 Jul 1941	20:08

Sign	Date	Time
Sag	1 Aug 1941	22:49
Cap	4 Aug 1941	01:17
Aqu	6 Aug 1941	04:32
Pis	8 Aug 1941	09:51
Ari	10 Aug 1941	18:12
Tau	13 Aug 1941	05:31
Gem	15 Aug 1941	18:09
Can	18 Aug 1941	05:37
Leo	20 Aug 1941	14:14
Vir	22 Aug 1941	19:52
Lib	24 Aug 1941	23:20
Sco	27 Aug 1941	01:48
Sag	29 Aug 1941	04:12
Cap	31 Aug 1941	07:17

Sign	Date	Time
Aqu	2 Sep 1941	11:39
Pis	4 Sep 1941	17:51
Ari	7 Sep 1941	02:29
Tau	9 Sep 1941	13:32
Gem	12 Sep 1941	02:05
Can	14 Sep 1941	14:08
Leo	16 Sep 1941	23:34
Vir	19 Sep 1941	05:28
Lib	21 Sep 1941	08:16
Sco	23 Sep 1941	09:23
Sag	25 Sep 1941	10:24
Cap	27 Sep 1941	12:45
Aqu	29 Sep 1941	17:16

Sign	Date	Time
Pis	2 Oct 1941	00:18
Ari	4 Oct 1941	09:37
Tau	6 Oct 1941	20:51
Gem	9 Oct 1941	09:22
Can	11 Oct 1941	21:52
Leo	14 Oct 1941	08:28
Vir	16 Oct 1941	15:34
Lib	18 Oct 1941	18:53
Sco	20 Oct 1941	19:25
Sag	22 Oct 1941	19:00
Cap	24 Oct 1941	19:40
Aqu	26 Oct 1941	23:03
Pis	29 Oct 1941	05:50
Ari	31 Oct 1941	15:38

Sign	Date	Time
Tau	3 Nov 1941	03:18
Gem	5 Nov 1941	15:51
Can	8 Nov 1941	04:25
Leo	10 Nov 1941	15:48
Vir	13 Nov 1941	00:27
Lib	15 Nov 1941	05:21
Sco	17 Nov 1941	06:39
Sag	19 Nov 1941	05:53
Cap	21 Nov 1941	05:11
Aqu	23 Nov 1941	06:46
Pis	25 Nov 1941	12:09
Ari	27 Nov 1941	21:26
Tau	30 Nov 1941	09:18

Sign	Date	Time
Gem	2 Dec 1941	21:59
Can	5 Dec 1941	10:21
Leo	7 Dec 1941	21:42
Vir	10 Dec 1941	07:11
Lib	12 Dec 1941	13:44
Sco	14 Dec 1941	16:50
Sag	16 Dec 1941	17:09
Cap	18 Dec 1941	16:26
Aqu	20 Dec 1941	16:53
Pis	22 Dec 1941	20:33
Ari	25 Dec 1941	04:24
Tau	27 Dec 1941	15:43
Gem	30 Dec 1941	04:26

Moon Signs

1942

Sign	Date	Time
Can	1 Jan 1942	16:41
Leo	4 Jan 1942	03:32
Vir	6 Jan 1942	12:41
Lib	8 Jan 1942	19:47
Sco	11 Jan 1942	00:22
Sag	13 Jan 1942	02:30
Cap	15 Jan 1942	03:06
Aqu	17 Jan 1942	03:52
Pis	19 Jan 1942	06:43
Ari	21 Jan 1942	13:09
Tau	23 Jan 1942	23:18
Gem	26 Jan 1942	11:43
Can	29 Jan 1942	00:02
Leo	31 Jan 1942	10:36

Sign	Date	Time
Vir	2 Feb 1942	18:57
Lib	5 Feb 1942	01:17
Sco	7 Feb 1942	05:55
Sag	9 Feb 1942	09:05
Cap	11 Feb 1942	11:18
Aqu	13 Feb 1942	13:27
Pis	15 Feb 1942	16:50
Ari	17 Feb 1942	22:47
Tau	20 Feb 1942	07:57
Gem	22 Feb 1942	19:46
Can	25 Feb 1942	08:14
Leo	27 Feb 1942	19:05

Sign	Date	Time
Vir	2 Mar 1942	03:04
Lib	4 Mar 1942	08:22
Sco	6 Mar 1942	11:49
Sag	8 Mar 1942	14:27
Cap	10 Mar 1942	17:08
Aqu	12 Mar 1942	20:30
Pis	15 Mar 1942	01:09
Ari	17 Mar 1942	07:40
Tau	19 Mar 1942	16:38
Gem	22 Mar 1942	04:00
Can	24 Mar 1942	16:32
Leo	27 Mar 1942	04:03
Vir	29 Mar 1942	12:35
Lib	31 Mar 1942	17:36

Sign	Date	Time
Sco	2 Apr 1942	19:53
Sag	4 Apr 1942	21:04
Cap	6 Apr 1942	22:42
Aqu	9 Apr 1942	01:56
Pis	11 Apr 1942	07:19
Ari	13 Apr 1942	14:49
Tau	16 Apr 1942	00:17
Gem	18 Apr 1942	11:36
Can	21 Apr 1942	00:09
Leo	23 Apr 1942	12:20
Vir	25 Apr 1942	22:00
Lib	28 Apr 1942	03:48
Sco	30 Apr 1942	05:58

Sign	Date	Time
Sag	2 May 1942	06:02
Cap	4 May 1942	06:04
Aqu	6 May 1942	07:56
Pis	8 May 1942	12:44
Ari	10 May 1942	20:31
Tau	13 May 1942	06:36
Gem	15 May 1942	18:14
Can	18 May 1942	06:48
Leo	20 May 1942	19:20
Vir	23 May 1942	06:06
Lib	25 May 1942	13:20
Sco	27 May 1942	16:30
Sag	29 May 1942	16:38
Cap	31 May 1942	15:43

Sign	Date	Time
Aqu	2 Jun 1942	15:59
Pis	4 Jun 1942	19:14
Ari	7 Jun 1942	02:11
Tau	9 Jun 1942	12:15
Gem	12 Jun 1942	00:11
Can	14 Jun 1942	12:49
Leo	17 Jun 1942	01:18
Vir	19 Jun 1942	12:32
Lib	21 Jun 1942	21:02
Sco	24 Jun 1942	01:48
Sag	26 Jun 1942	03:07
Cap	28 Jun 1942	02:29
Aqu	30 Jun 1942	02:01

Sign	Date	Time
Pis	2 Jul 1942	03:46
Ari	4 Jul 1942	09:11
Tau	6 Jul 1942	18:22
Gem	9 Jul 1942	06:09
Can	11 Jul 1942	18:51
Leo	14 Jul 1942	07:07
Vir	16 Jul 1942	18:08
Lib	19 Jul 1942	03:00
Sco	21 Jul 1942	09:00
Sag	23 Jul 1942	11:56
Cap	25 Jul 1942	12:37
Aqu	27 Jul 1942	12:37
Pis	29 Jul 1942	13:49
Ari	31 Jul 1942	17:54

Sign	Date	Time
Tau	3 Aug 1942	01:48
Gem	5 Aug 1942	12:54
Can	8 Aug 1942	01:29
Leo	10 Aug 1942	13:38
Vir	13 Aug 1942	00:08
Lib	15 Aug 1942	08:30
Sco	17 Aug 1942	14:36
Sag	19 Aug 1942	18:34
Cap	21 Aug 1942	20:45
Aqu	23 Aug 1942	22:07
Pis	25 Aug 1942	23:55
Ari	28 Aug 1942	03:39
Tau	30 Aug 1942	10:29

Sign	Date	Time
Gem	1 Sep 1942	20:40
Can	4 Sep 1942	08:59
Leo	6 Sep 1942	21:14
Vir	9 Sep 1942	07:30
Lib	11 Sep 1942	15:03
Sco	13 Sep 1942	20:17
Sag	15 Sep 1942	23:57
Cap	18 Sep 1942	02:47
Aqu	20 Sep 1942	05:26
Pis	22 Sep 1942	08:33
Ari	24 Sep 1942	12:57
Tau	26 Sep 1942	19:34
Gem	29 Sep 1942	05:04

Sign	Date	Time
Can	1 Oct 1942	17:02
Leo	4 Oct 1942	05:34
Vir	6 Oct 1942	16:12
Lib	8 Oct 1942	23:30
Sco	11 Oct 1942	03:45
Sag	13 Oct 1942	06:09
Cap	15 Oct 1942	08:13
Aqu	17 Oct 1942	11:01
Pis	19 Oct 1942	15:05
Ari	21 Oct 1942	20:36
Tau	24 Oct 1942	03:51
Gem	26 Oct 1942	13:18
Can	29 Oct 1942	00:59
Leo	31 Oct 1942	13:47

Sign	Date	Time
Vir	3 Nov 1942	01:17
Lib	5 Nov 1942	09:19
Sco	7 Nov 1942	13:25
Sag	9 Nov 1942	14:46
Cap	11 Nov 1942	15:17
Aqu	13 Nov 1942	16:48
Pis	15 Nov 1942	20:27
Ari	18 Nov 1942	02:30
Tau	20 Nov 1942	10:37
Gem	22 Nov 1942	20:34
Can	25 Nov 1942	08:16
Leo	27 Nov 1942	21:08
Vir	30 Nov 1942	09:28

Sign	Date	Time
Lib	2 Dec 1942	18:54
Sco	5 Dec 1942	00:04
Sag	7 Dec 1942	01:32
Cap	9 Dec 1942	01:06
Aqu	11 Dec 1942	00:57
Pis	13 Dec 1942	02:56
Ari	15 Dec 1942	08:04
Tau	17 Dec 1942	16:16
Gem	20 Dec 1942	02:45
Can	22 Dec 1942	14:45
Leo	25 Dec 1942	03:34
Vir	27 Dec 1942	16:09
Lib	30 Dec 1942	02:43

1943

Sign	Date	Time
Sco	1 Jan 1943	09:38
Sag	3 Jan 1943	12:31
Cap	5 Jan 1943	12:33
Aqu	7 Jan 1943	11:42
Pis	9 Jan 1943	12:03
Ari	11 Jan 1943	15:21
Tau	13 Jan 1943	22:22
Gem	16 Jan 1943	08:38
Can	18 Jan 1943	20:53
Leo	21 Jan 1943	09:43
Vir	23 Jan 1943	22:02
Lib	26 Jan 1943	08:46
Sco	28 Jan 1943	16:49
Sag	30 Jan 1943	21:32

Sign	Date	Time
Cap	1 Feb 1943	23:13
Aqu	3 Feb 1943	23:09
Pis	5 Feb 1943	23:08
Ari	8 Feb 1943	01:01
Tau	10 Feb 1943	06:16
Gem	12 Feb 1943	15:25
Can	15 Feb 1943	03:24
Leo	17 Feb 1943	16:17
Vir	20 Feb 1943	04:19
Lib	22 Feb 1943	14:28
Sco	24 Feb 1943	22:23
Sag	27 Feb 1943	03:58

Sign	Date	Time
Cap	1 Mar 1943	07:18
Aqu	3 Mar 1943	08:55
Pis	5 Mar 1943	09:54
Ari	7 Mar 1943	11:41
Tau	9 Mar 1943	15:53
Gem	11 Mar 1943	23:39
Can	14 Mar 1943	10:50
Leo	16 Mar 1943	23:40
Vir	19 Mar 1943	11:41
Lib	21 Mar 1943	21:19
Sco	24 Mar 1943	04:21
Sag	26 Mar 1943	09:22
Cap	28 Mar 1943	13:04
Aqu	30 Mar 1943	15:56

Sign	Date	Time
Pis	1 Apr 1943	18:26
Ari	3 Apr 1943	21:17
Tau	6 Apr 1943	01:38
Gem	8 Apr 1943	08:41
Can	10 Apr 1943	19:02
Leo	13 Apr 1943	07:39
Vir	15 Apr 1943	19:58
Lib	18 Apr 1943	05:40
Sco	20 Apr 1943	12:02
Sag	22 Apr 1943	15:55
Cap	24 Apr 1943	18:39
Aqu	26 Apr 1943	21:20
Pis	29 Apr 1943	00:35

Sign	Date	Time
Ari	1 May 1943	04:38
Tau	3 May 1943	09:57
Gem	5 May 1943	17:15
Can	8 May 1943	03:16
Leo	10 May 1943	15:38
Vir	13 May 1943	04:20
Lib	15 May 1943	14:42
Sco	17 May 1943	21:17
Sag	20 May 1943	00:31
Cap	22 May 1943	01:59
Aqu	24 May 1943	03:23
Pis	26 May 1943	05:57
Ari	28 May 1943	10:16
Tau	30 May 1943	16:24

Sign	Date	Time
Gem	2 Jun 1943	00:29
Can	4 Jun 1943	10:45
Leo	6 Jun 1943	23:02
Vir	9 Jun 1943	12:02
Lib	11 Jun 1943	23:20
Sco	14 Jun 1943	06:57
Sag	16 Jun 1943	10:34
Cap	18 Jun 1943	11:29
Aqu	20 Jun 1943	11:33
Pis	22 Jun 1943	12:36
Ari	24 Jun 1943	15:52
Tau	26 Jun 1943	21:52
Gem	29 Jun 1943	06:26

Sign	Date	Time
Can	1 Jul 1943	17:12
Leo	4 Jul 1943	05:38
Vir	6 Jul 1943	18:44
Lib	9 Jul 1943	06:43
Sco	11 Jul 1943	15:39
Sag	13 Jul 1943	20:35
Cap	15 Jul 1943	22:05
Aqu	17 Jul 1943	21:45
Pis	19 Jul 1943	21:30
Ari	21 Jul 1943	23:09
Tau	24 Jul 1943	03:52
Gem	26 Jul 1943	12:04
Can	28 Jul 1943	23:03
Leo	31 Jul 1943	11:42

Sign	Date	Time
Vir	3 Aug 1943	00:44
Lib	5 Aug 1943	12:50
Sco	7 Aug 1943	22:38
Sag	10 Aug 1943	05:07
Cap	12 Aug 1943	08:08
Aqu	14 Aug 1943	08:35
Pis	16 Aug 1943	08:06
Ari	18 Aug 1943	08:32
Tau	20 Aug 1943	11:40
Gem	22 Aug 1943	18:33
Can	25 Aug 1943	05:06
Leo	27 Aug 1943	17:48
Vir	30 Aug 1943	06:46

Sign	Date	Time
Lib	1 Sep 1943	18:32
Sco	4 Sep 1943	04:19
Sag	6 Sep 1943	11:37
Cap	8 Sep 1943	16:12
Aqu	10 Sep 1943	18:17
Pis	12 Sep 1943	18:45
Ari	14 Sep 1943	19:08
Tau	16 Sep 1943	21:14
Gem	19 Sep 1943	02:42
Can	21 Sep 1943	12:10
Leo	24 Sep 1943	00:33
Vir	26 Sep 1943	13:29
Lib	29 Sep 1943	00:55

Sign	Date	Time
Sco	1 Oct 1943	10:03
Sag	3 Oct 1943	17:02
Cap	5 Oct 1943	22:09
Aqu	8 Oct 1943	01:38
Pis	10 Oct 1943	03:43
Ari	12 Oct 1943	05:11
Tau	14 Oct 1943	07:25
Gem	16 Oct 1943	12:07
Can	18 Oct 1943	20:27
Leo	21 Oct 1943	08:11
Vir	23 Oct 1943	21:08
Lib	26 Oct 1943	08:36
Sco	28 Oct 1943	17:13
Sag	30 Oct 1943	23:13

Sign	Date	Time
Cap	2 Nov 1943	03:35
Aqu	4 Nov 1943	07:09
Pis	6 Nov 1943	10:15
Ari	8 Nov 1943	13:10
Tau	10 Nov 1943	16:32
Gem	12 Nov 1943	21:31
Can	15 Nov 1943	05:22
Leo	17 Nov 1943	16:27
Vir	20 Nov 1943	05:20
Lib	22 Nov 1943	17:17
Sco	25 Nov 1943	02:07
Sag	27 Nov 1943	07:33
Cap	29 Nov 1943	10:41

Sign	Date	Time
Aqu	1 Dec 1943	13:00
Pis	3 Dec 1943	15:35
Ari	5 Dec 1943	18:59
Tau	7 Dec 1943	23:30
Gem	10 Dec 1943	05:31
Can	12 Dec 1943	13:46
Leo	15 Dec 1943	00:36
Vir	17 Dec 1943	13:21
Lib	20 Dec 1943	01:54
Sco	22 Dec 1943	11:44
Sag	24 Dec 1943	17:43
Cap	26 Dec 1943	20:23
Aqu	28 Dec 1943	21:20
Pis	30 Dec 1943	22:17

1944

Sign	Date	Time
Ari	2 Jan 1944	00:34
Tau	4 Jan 1944	04:57
Gem	6 Jan 1944	11:44
Can	8 Jan 1944	20:47
Leo	11 Jan 1944	07:57
Vir	13 Jan 1944	20:37
Lib	16 Jan 1944	09:28
Sco	18 Jan 1944	20:26
Sag	21 Jan 1944	03:52
Cap	23 Jan 1944	07:25
Aqu	25 Jan 1944	08:08
Pis	27 Jan 1944	07:47
Ari	29 Jan 1944	08:14
Tau	31 Jan 1944	11:07
Gem	2 Feb 1944	17:16
Can	5 Feb 1944	02:39
Leo	7 Feb 1944	14:19
Vir	10 Feb 1944	03:07
Lib	12 Feb 1944	15:53
Sco	15 Feb 1944	03:23
Sag	17 Feb 1944	12:13
Cap	19 Feb 1944	17:32
Aqu	21 Feb 1944	19:26
Pis	23 Feb 1944	19:08
Ari	25 Feb 1944	18:30
Tau	27 Feb 1944	19:36
Gem	1 Mar 1944	00:06
Can	3 Mar 1944	08:38
Leo	5 Mar 1944	20:19
Vir	8 Mar 1944	09:17
Lib	10 Mar 1944	21:54
Sco	13 Mar 1944	09:11
Sag	15 Mar 1944	18:30
Cap	18 Mar 1944	01:11
Aqu	20 Mar 1944	04:54
Pis	22 Mar 1944	05:58
Ari	24 Mar 1944	05:41
Tau	26 Mar 1944	06:00
Gem	28 Mar 1944	08:58
Can	30 Mar 1944	15:59
Leo	2 Apr 1944	02:54
Vir	4 Apr 1944	15:48
Lib	7 Apr 1944	04:21
Sco	9 Apr 1944	15:10
Sag	12 Apr 1944	00:01
Cap	14 Apr 1944	06:55
Aqu	16 Apr 1944	11:44
Pis	18 Apr 1944	14:27
Ari	20 Apr 1944	15:35
Tau	22 Apr 1944	16:28
Gem	24 Apr 1944	18:58
Can	27 Apr 1944	00:49
Leo	29 Apr 1944	10:36
Vir	1 May 1944	23:03
Lib	4 May 1944	11:38
Sco	6 May 1944	22:16
Sag	9 May 1944	06:26
Cap	11 May 1944	12:31
Aqu	13 May 1944	17:09
Pis	15 May 1944	20:34
Ari	17 May 1944	23:02
Tau	20 May 1944	01:15
Gem	22 May 1944	04:26
Can	24 May 1944	10:04
Leo	26 May 1944	19:04
Vir	29 May 1944	06:58
Lib	31 May 1944	19:36
Sco	3 Jun 1944	06:31
Sag	5 Jun 1944	14:26
Cap	7 Jun 1944	19:40
Aqu	9 Jun 1944	23:11
Pis	12 Jun 1944	01:57
Ari	14 Jun 1944	04:40
Tau	16 Jun 1944	07:51
Gem	18 Jun 1944	12:11
Can	20 Jun 1944	18:27
Leo	23 Jun 1944	03:25
Vir	25 Jun 1944	14:57
Lib	28 Jun 1944	03:39
Sco	30 Jun 1944	15:09
Sag	2 Jul 1944	23:36
Cap	5 Jul 1944	04:40
Aqu	7 Jul 1944	07:13
Pis	9 Jul 1944	08:38
Ari	11 Jul 1944	10:18
Tau	13 Jul 1944	13:16
Gem	15 Jul 1944	18:10
Can	18 Jul 1944	01:21
Leo	20 Jul 1944	10:50
Vir	22 Jul 1944	22:24
Lib	25 Jul 1944	11:07
Sco	27 Jul 1944	23:15
Sag	30 Jul 1944	08:48
Cap	1 Aug 1944	14:40
Aqu	3 Aug 1944	17:09
Pis	5 Aug 1944	17:34
Ari	7 Aug 1944	17:42
Tau	9 Aug 1944	19:19
Gem	11 Aug 1944	23:38
Can	14 Aug 1944	07:03
Leo	16 Aug 1944	17:07
Vir	19 Aug 1944	05:00
Lib	21 Aug 1944	17:44
Sco	24 Aug 1944	06:12
Sag	26 Aug 1944	16:50
Cap	29 Aug 1944	00:10
Aqu	31 Aug 1944	03:42
Pis	2 Sep 1944	04:13
Ari	4 Sep 1944	03:27
Tau	6 Sep 1944	03:28
Gem	8 Sep 1944	06:13
Can	10 Sep 1944	12:47
Leo	12 Sep 1944	22:50
Vir	15 Sep 1944	11:00
Lib	17 Sep 1944	23:47
Sco	20 Sep 1944	12:10
Sag	22 Sep 1944	23:14
Cap	25 Sep 1944	07:54
Aqu	27 Sep 1944	13:08
Pis	29 Sep 1944	14:56
Ari	1 Oct 1944	14:29
Tau	3 Oct 1944	13:46
Gem	5 Oct 1944	14:59
Can	7 Oct 1944	19:56
Leo	10 Oct 1944	05:02
Vir	12 Oct 1944	17:04
Lib	15 Oct 1944	05:54
Sco	17 Oct 1944	18:02
Sag	20 Oct 1944	04:49
Cap	22 Oct 1944	13:47
Aqu	24 Oct 1944	20:17
Pis	26 Oct 1944	23:51
Ari	29 Oct 1944	00:52
Tau	31 Oct 1944	00:45
Gem	2 Nov 1944	01:28
Can	4 Nov 1944	05:03
Leo	6 Nov 1944	12:44
Vir	8 Nov 1944	23:58
Lib	11 Nov 1944	12:43
Sco	14 Nov 1944	00:46
Sag	16 Nov 1944	11:00
Cap	18 Nov 1944	19:19
Aqu	21 Nov 1944	01:45
Pis	23 Nov 1944	06:17
Ari	25 Nov 1944	08:55
Tau	27 Nov 1944	10:21
Gem	29 Nov 1944	11:55
Can	1 Dec 1944	15:16
Leo	3 Dec 1944	21:53
Vir	6 Dec 1944	08:03
Lib	8 Dec 1944	20:27
Sco	11 Dec 1944	08:40
Sag	13 Dec 1944	18:49
Cap	16 Dec 1944	02:20
Aqu	18 Dec 1944	07:43
Pis	20 Dec 1944	11:38
Ari	22 Dec 1944	14:41
Tau	24 Dec 1944	17:23
Gem	26 Dec 1944	20:25
Can	29 Dec 1944	00:44
Leo	31 Dec 1944	07:18

1945

Sign	Date	Time
Vir	2 Jan 1945	16:48
Lib	5 Jan 1945	04:43
Sco	7 Jan 1945	17:12
Sag	10 Jan 1945	03:54
Cap	12 Jan 1945	11:26
Aqu	14 Jan 1945	15:55
Pis	16 Jan 1945	18:26
Ari	18 Jan 1945	20:20
Tau	20 Jan 1945	22:47
Gem	23 Jan 1945	02:34
Can	25 Jan 1945	08:04
Leo	27 Jan 1945	15:32
Vir	30 Jan 1945	01:08

Sign	Date	Time
Lib	1 Feb 1945	12:45
Sco	4 Feb 1945	01:21
Sag	6 Feb 1945	12:56
Cap	8 Feb 1945	21:27
Aqu	11 Feb 1945	02:10
Pis	13 Feb 1945	03:51
Ari	15 Feb 1945	04:11
Tau	17 Feb 1945	05:04
Gem	19 Feb 1945	08:01
Can	21 Feb 1945	13:42
Leo	23 Feb 1945	21:58
Vir	26 Feb 1945	08:13
Lib	28 Feb 1945	19:56

Sign	Date	Time
Sco	3 Mar 1945	08:32
Sag	5 Mar 1945	20:43
Cap	8 Mar 1945	06:36
Aqu	10 Mar 1945	12:38
Pis	12 Mar 1945	14:48
Ari	14 Mar 1945	14:31
Tau	16 Mar 1945	13:54
Gem	18 Mar 1945	15:04
Can	20 Mar 1945	19:31
Leo	23 Mar 1945	03:31
Vir	25 Mar 1945	14:10
Lib	28 Mar 1945	02:14
Sco	30 Mar 1945	14:49

Sign	Date	Time
Sag	2 Apr 1945	03:06
Cap	4 Apr 1945	13:49
Aqu	6 Apr 1945	21:26
Pis	9 Apr 1945	01:08
Ari	11 Apr 1945	01:36
Tau	13 Apr 1945	00:39
Gem	15 Apr 1945	00:31
Can	17 Apr 1945	03:14
Leo	19 Apr 1945	09:52
Vir	21 Apr 1945	20:02
Lib	24 Apr 1945	08:14
Sco	26 Apr 1945	20:51
Sag	29 Apr 1945	08:55

Sign	Date	Time
Cap	1 May 1945	19:38
Aqu	4 May 1945	04:04
Pis	6 May 1945	09:19
Ari	8 May 1945	11:23
Tau	10 May 1945	11:23
Gem	12 May 1945	11:12
Can	14 May 1945	12:51
Leo	16 May 1945	17:56
Vir	19 May 1945	02:55
Lib	21 May 1945	14:42
Sco	24 May 1945	03:19
Sag	26 May 1945	15:10
Cap	29 May 1945	01:23
Aqu	31 May 1945	09:33

Sign	Date	Time
Pis	2 Jun 1945	15:24
Ari	4 Jun 1945	18:49
Tau	6 Jun 1945	20:22
Gem	8 Jun 1945	21:14
Can	10 Jun 1945	23:02
Leo	13 Jun 1945	03:20
Vir	15 Jun 1945	11:07
Lib	17 Jun 1945	22:05
Sco	20 Jun 1945	10:35
Sag	22 Jun 1945	22:25
Cap	25 Jun 1945	08:13
Aqu	27 Jun 1945	15:35
Pis	29 Jun 1945	20:50

Sign	Date	Time
Ari	2 Jul 1945	00:28
Tau	4 Jul 1945	03:03
Gem	6 Jul 1945	05:19
Can	8 Jul 1945	08:10
Leo	10 Jul 1945	12:43
Vir	12 Jul 1945	19:57
Lib	15 Jul 1945	06:12
Sco	17 Jul 1945	18:28
Sag	20 Jul 1945	06:35
Cap	22 Jul 1945	16:27
Aqu	24 Jul 1945	23:14
Pis	27 Jul 1945	03:25
Ari	29 Jul 1945	06:06
Tau	31 Jul 1945	08:28

Sign	Date	Time
Gem	2 Aug 1945	11:22
Can	4 Aug 1945	15:22
Leo	6 Aug 1945	20:52
Vir	9 Aug 1945	04:23
Lib	11 Aug 1945	14:21
Sco	14 Aug 1945	02:24
Sag	16 Aug 1945	14:55
Cap	19 Aug 1945	01:28
Aqu	21 Aug 1945	08:30
Pis	23 Aug 1945	12:03
Ari	25 Aug 1945	13:29
Tau	27 Aug 1945	14:33
Gem	29 Aug 1945	16:46
Can	31 Aug 1945	20:59

Sign	Date	Time
Leo	3 Sep 1945	03:19
Vir	5 Sep 1945	11:36
Lib	7 Sep 1945	21:48
Sco	10 Sep 1945	09:47
Sag	12 Sep 1945	22:36
Cap	15 Sep 1945	10:09
Aqu	17 Sep 1945	18:18
Pis	19 Sep 1945	22:16
Ari	21 Sep 1945	23:09
Tau	23 Sep 1945	22:53
Gem	25 Sep 1945	23:31
Can	28 Sep 1945	02:38
Leo	30 Sep 1945	08:46

Sign	Date	Time
Vir	2 Oct 1945	17:33
Lib	5 Oct 1945	04:16
Sco	7 Oct 1945	16:23
Sag	10 Oct 1945	05:16
Cap	12 Oct 1945	17:31
Aqu	15 Oct 1945	03:04
Pis	17 Oct 1945	08:32
Ari	19 Oct 1945	10:07
Tau	21 Oct 1945	09:29
Gem	23 Oct 1945	08:49
Can	25 Oct 1945	10:11
Leo	27 Oct 1945	14:55
Vir	29 Oct 1945	23:12

Sign	Date	Time
Lib	1 Nov 1945	10:07
Sco	3 Nov 1945	22:28
Sag	6 Nov 1945	11:17
Cap	8 Nov 1945	23:33
Aqu	11 Nov 1945	09:57
Pis	13 Nov 1945	17:03
Ari	15 Nov 1945	20:22
Tau	17 Nov 1945	20:46
Gem	19 Nov 1945	20:02
Can	21 Nov 1945	20:13
Leo	23 Nov 1945	23:12
Vir	26 Nov 1945	05:58
Lib	28 Nov 1945	16:18

Sign	Date	Time
Sco	1 Dec 1945	04:42
Sag	3 Dec 1945	17:29
Cap	6 Dec 1945	05:22
Aqu	8 Dec 1945	15:33
Pis	10 Dec 1945	23:18
Ari	13 Dec 1945	04:13
Tau	15 Dec 1945	06:28
Gem	17 Dec 1945	07:01
Can	19 Dec 1945	07:26
Leo	21 Dec 1945	09:30
Vir	23 Dec 1945	14:43
Lib	25 Dec 1945	23:45
Sco	28 Dec 1945	11:42
Sag	31 Dec 1945	00:31

1946

Cap	2 Jan 1946	12:09
Aqu	4 Jan 1946	21:36
Pis	7 Jan 1946	04:46
Ari	9 Jan 1946	09:54
Tau	11 Jan 1946	13:24
Gem	13 Jan 1946	15:41
Can	15 Jan 1946	17:31
Leo	17 Jan 1946	20:03
Vir	20 Jan 1946	00:40
Lib	22 Jan 1946	08:31
Sco	24 Jan 1946	19:39
Sag	27 Jan 1946	08:26
Cap	29 Jan 1946	20:16

Aqu	1 Feb 1946	05:22
Pis	3 Feb 1946	11:31
Ari	5 Feb 1946	15:37
Tau	7 Feb 1946	18:46
Gem	9 Feb 1946	21:44
Can	12 Feb 1946	00:58
Leo	14 Feb 1946	04:49
Vir	16 Feb 1946	10:03
Lib	18 Feb 1946	17:35
Sco	21 Feb 1946	04:04
Sag	23 Feb 1946	16:40
Cap	26 Feb 1946	05:00
Aqu	28 Feb 1946	14:32

Pis	2 Mar 1946	20:23
Ari	4 Mar 1946	23:22
Tau	7 Mar 1946	01:07
Gem	9 Mar 1946	03:11
Can	11 Mar 1946	06:28
Leo	13 Mar 1946	11:14
Vir	15 Mar 1946	17:31
Lib	18 Mar 1946	01:40
Sco	20 Mar 1946	12:04
Sag	23 Mar 1946	00:30
Cap	25 Mar 1946	13:16
Aqu	27 Mar 1946	23:48
Pis	30 Mar 1946	06:25

Ari	1 Apr 1946	09:15
Tau	3 Apr 1946	09:55
Gem	5 Apr 1946	10:25
Can	7 Apr 1946	12:21
Leo	9 Apr 1946	16:36
Vir	11 Apr 1946	23:20
Lib	14 Apr 1946	08:13
Sco	16 Apr 1946	19:02
Sag	19 Apr 1946	07:29
Cap	21 Apr 1946	20:27
Aqu	24 Apr 1946	07:55
Pis	26 Apr 1946	15:52
Ari	28 Apr 1946	19:44
Tau	30 Apr 1946	20:30

Gem	2 May 1946	20:03
Can	4 May 1946	20:22
Leo	6 May 1946	23:05
Vir	9 May 1946	04:56
Lib	11 May 1946	13:53
Sco	14 May 1946	01:08
Sag	16 May 1946	13:45
Cap	19 May 1946	02:40
Aqu	21 May 1946	14:29
Pis	23 May 1946	23:36
Ari	26 May 1946	05:03
Tau	28 May 1946	07:02
Gem	30 May 1946	06:53

Can	1 Jun 1946	06:28
Leo	3 Jun 1946	07:39
Vir	5 Jun 1946	11:57
Lib	7 Jun 1946	19:56
Sco	10 Jun 1946	07:04
Sag	12 Jun 1946	19:49
Cap	15 Jun 1946	08:38
Aqu	17 Jun 1946	20:14
Pis	20 Jun 1946	05:42
Ari	22 Jun 1946	12:17
Tau	24 Jun 1946	15:54
Gem	26 Jun 1946	17:06
Can	28 Jun 1946	17:09
Leo	30 Jun 1946	17:46

Vir	2 Jul 1946	20:45
Lib	5 Jul 1946	03:21
Sco	7 Jul 1946	13:41
Sag	10 Jul 1946	02:19
Cap	12 Jul 1946	15:04
Aqu	15 Jul 1946	02:15
Pis	17 Jul 1946	11:13
Ari	19 Jul 1946	17:58
Tau	21 Jul 1946	22:33
Gem	24 Jul 1946	01:17
Can	26 Jul 1946	02:43
Leo	28 Jul 1946	03:56
Vir	30 Jul 1946	06:32

Lib	1 Aug 1946	12:05
Sco	3 Aug 1946	21:22
Sag	6 Aug 1946	09:35
Cap	8 Aug 1946	22:22
Aqu	11 Aug 1946	09:22
Pis	13 Aug 1946	17:40
Ari	15 Aug 1946	23:35
Tau	18 Aug 1946	03:58
Gem	20 Aug 1946	07:21
Can	22 Aug 1946	10:05
Leo	24 Aug 1946	12:37
Vir	26 Aug 1946	15:53
Lib	28 Aug 1946	21:15
Sco	31 Aug 1946	05:48

Sag	2 Sep 1946	17:30
Cap	5 Sep 1946	06:23
Aqu	7 Sep 1946	17:40
Pis	10 Sep 1946	01:44
Ari	12 Sep 1946	06:48
Tau	14 Sep 1946	10:02
Gem	16 Sep 1946	12:45
Can	18 Sep 1946	15:41
Leo	20 Sep 1946	19:12
Vir	22 Sep 1946	23:37
Lib	25 Sep 1946	05:39
Sco	27 Sep 1946	14:12
Sag	30 Sep 1946	01:32

Cap	2 Oct 1946	14:28
Aqu	5 Oct 1946	02:25
Pis	7 Oct 1946	11:07
Ari	9 Oct 1946	16:03
Tau	11 Oct 1946	18:19
Gem	13 Oct 1946	19:36
Can	15 Oct 1946	21:22
Leo	18 Oct 1946	00:35
Vir	20 Oct 1946	05:34
Lib	22 Oct 1946	12:33
Sco	24 Oct 1946	21:40
Sag	27 Oct 1946	09:02
Cap	29 Oct 1946	21:58

Aqu	1 Nov 1946	10:34
Pis	3 Nov 1946	20:30
Ari	6 Nov 1946	02:26
Tau	8 Nov 1946	04:48
Gem	10 Nov 1946	05:06
Can	12 Nov 1946	05:15
Leo	14 Nov 1946	06:52
Vir	16 Nov 1946	11:05
Lib	18 Nov 1946	18:11
Sco	21 Nov 1946	03:57
Sag	23 Nov 1946	15:43
Cap	26 Nov 1946	04:38
Aqu	28 Nov 1946	17:28

Pis	1 Dec 1946	04:28
Ari	3 Dec 1946	12:03
Tau	5 Dec 1946	15:47
Gem	7 Dec 1946	16:29
Can	9 Dec 1946	15:49
Leo	11 Dec 1946	15:46
Vir	13 Dec 1946	18:08
Lib	16 Dec 1946	00:08
Sco	18 Dec 1946	09:43
Sag	20 Dec 1946	21:48
Cap	23 Dec 1946	10:49
Aqu	25 Dec 1946	23:28
Pis	28 Dec 1946	10:42
Ari	30 Dec 1946	19:29

1947

Tau	2 Jan 1947	01:04
Gem	4 Jan 1947	03:24
Can	6 Jan 1947	03:26
Leo	8 Jan 1947	02:52
Vir	10 Jan 1947	03:44
Lib	12 Jan 1947	07:54
Sco	14 Jan 1947	16:15
Sag	17 Jan 1947	04:02
Cap	19 Jan 1947	17:10
Aqu	22 Jan 1947	05:36
Pis	24 Jan 1947	16:22
Ari	27 Jan 1947	01:09
Tau	29 Jan 1947	07:44
Gem	31 Jan 1947	11:50

Can	2 Feb 1947	13:37
Leo	4 Feb 1947	14:00
Vir	6 Feb 1947	14:41
Lib	8 Feb 1947	17:38
Sco	11 Feb 1947	00:28
Sag	13 Feb 1947	11:15
Cap	16 Feb 1947	00:11
Aqu	18 Feb 1947	12:37
Pis	20 Feb 1947	22:56
Ari	23 Feb 1947	06:56
Tau	25 Feb 1947	13:06
Gem	27 Feb 1947	17:46

Can	1 Mar 1947	20:57
Leo	3 Mar 1947	22:59
Vir	6 Mar 1947	00:46
Lib	8 Mar 1947	03:50
Sco	10 Mar 1947	09:51
Sag	12 Mar 1947	19:33
Cap	15 Mar 1947	07:59
Aqu	17 Mar 1947	20:34
Pis	20 Mar 1947	06:56
Ari	22 Mar 1947	14:21
Tau	24 Mar 1947	19:28
Gem	26 Mar 1947	23:14
Can	29 Mar 1947	02:25
Leo	31 Mar 1947	05:21

Vir	2 Apr 1947	08:30
Lib	4 Apr 1947	12:39
Sco	6 Apr 1947	18:56
Sag	9 Apr 1947	04:12
Cap	11 Apr 1947	16:08
Aqu	14 Apr 1947	04:50
Pis	16 Apr 1947	15:45
Ari	18 Apr 1947	23:23
Tau	21 Apr 1947	03:54
Gem	23 Apr 1947	06:26
Can	25 Apr 1947	08:21
Leo	27 Apr 1947	10:43
Vir	29 Apr 1947	14:15

Lib	1 May 1947	19:23
Sco	4 May 1947	02:35
Sag	6 May 1947	12:09
Cap	8 May 1947	23:54
Aqu	11 May 1947	12:39
Pis	14 May 1947	00:18
Ari	16 May 1947	08:54
Tau	18 May 1947	13:49
Gem	20 May 1947	15:50
Can	22 May 1947	16:26
Leo	24 May 1947	17:17
Vir	26 May 1947	19:49
Lib	29 May 1947	00:54
Sco	31 May 1947	08:42

Sag	2 Jun 1947	18:53
Cap	5 Jun 1947	06:51
Aqu	7 Jun 1947	19:37
Pis	10 Jun 1947	07:46
Ari	12 Jun 1947	17:33
Tau	14 Jun 1947	23:43
Gem	17 Jun 1947	02:20
Can	19 Jun 1947	02:31
Leo	21 Jun 1947	02:06
Vir	23 Jun 1947	03:01
Lib	25 Jun 1947	06:50
Sco	27 Jun 1947	14:17
Sag	30 Jun 1947	00:46

Cap	2 Jul 1947	13:02
Aqu	5 Jul 1947	01:48
Pis	7 Jul 1947	14:01
Ari	10 Jul 1947	00:32
Tau	12 Jul 1947	08:10
Gem	14 Jul 1947	12:14
Can	16 Jul 1947	13:13
Leo	18 Jul 1947	12:33
Vir	20 Jul 1947	12:19
Lib	22 Jul 1947	14:33
Sco	24 Jul 1947	20:41
Sag	27 Jul 1947	06:39
Cap	29 Jul 1947	19:01

Aqu	1 Aug 1947	07:49
Pis	3 Aug 1947	19:48
Ari	6 Aug 1947	06:19
Tau	8 Aug 1947	14:41
Gem	10 Aug 1947	20:16
Can	12 Aug 1947	22:48
Leo	14 Aug 1947	23:05
Vir	16 Aug 1947	22:48
Lib	19 Aug 1947	00:04
Sco	21 Aug 1947	04:44
Sag	23 Aug 1947	13:34
Cap	26 Aug 1947	01:30
Aqu	28 Aug 1947	14:17
Pis	31 Aug 1947	02:02

Ari	2 Sep 1947	12:01
Tau	4 Sep 1947	20:09
Gem	7 Sep 1947	02:16
Can	9 Sep 1947	06:11
Leo	11 Sep 1947	08:02
Vir	13 Sep 1947	08:50
Lib	15 Sep 1947	10:16
Sco	17 Sep 1947	14:11
Sag	19 Sep 1947	21:50
Cap	22 Sep 1947	08:57
Aqu	24 Sep 1947	21:36
Pis	27 Sep 1947	09:23
Ari	29 Sep 1947	18:57

Tau	2 Oct 1947	02:14
Gem	4 Oct 1947	07:42
Can	6 Oct 1947	11:46
Leo	8 Oct 1947	14:40
Vir	10 Oct 1947	16:56
Lib	12 Oct 1947	19:31
Sco	14 Oct 1947	23:46
Sag	17 Oct 1947	06:52
Cap	19 Oct 1947	17:13
Aqu	22 Oct 1947	05:38
Pis	24 Oct 1947	17:45
Ari	27 Oct 1947	03:29
Tau	29 Oct 1947	10:14
Gem	31 Oct 1947	14:34

Can	2 Nov 1947	17:31
Leo	4 Nov 1947	20:03
Vir	6 Nov 1947	22:54
Lib	9 Nov 1947	02:42
Sco	11 Nov 1947	08:02
Sag	13 Nov 1947	15:33
Cap	16 Nov 1947	01:37
Aqu	18 Nov 1947	13:44
Pis	21 Nov 1947	02:15
Ari	23 Nov 1947	12:51
Tau	25 Nov 1947	20:04
Gem	27 Nov 1947	23:53
Can	30 Nov 1947	01:30

Leo	2 Dec 1947	02:30
Vir	4 Dec 1947	04:23
Lib	6 Dec 1947	08:13
Sco	8 Dec 1947	14:24
Sag	10 Dec 1947	22:49
Cap	13 Dec 1947	09:13
Aqu	15 Dec 1947	21:15
Pis	18 Dec 1947	09:58
Ari	20 Dec 1947	21:35
Tau	23 Dec 1947	06:10
Gem	25 Dec 1947	10:45
Can	27 Dec 1947	12:01
Leo	29 Dec 1947	11:41
Vir	31 Dec 1947	11:47

1948

Lib	2 Jan 1948	14:10
Sco	4 Jan 1948	19:51
Sag	7 Jan 1948	04:40
Cap	9 Jan 1948	15:40
Aqu	12 Jan 1948	03:53
Pis	14 Jan 1948	16:34
Ari	17 Jan 1948	04:42
Tau	19 Jan 1948	14:40
Gem	21 Jan 1948	20:59
Can	23 Jan 1948	23:21
Leo	25 Jan 1948	22:58
Vir	27 Jan 1948	21:56
Lib	29 Jan 1948	22:30
Sco	1 Feb 1948	02:28
Sag	3 Feb 1948	10:26
Cap	5 Feb 1948	21:29
Aqu	8 Feb 1948	09:58
Pis	10 Feb 1948	22:36
Ari	13 Feb 1948	10:36
Tau	15 Feb 1948	21:06
Gem	18 Feb 1948	04:54
Can	20 Feb 1948	09:07
Leo	22 Feb 1948	10:05
Vir	24 Feb 1948	09:21
Lib	26 Feb 1948	09:05
Sco	28 Feb 1948	11:24
Sag	1 Mar 1948	17:41
Cap	4 Mar 1948	03:50
Aqu	6 Mar 1948	16:13
Pis	9 Mar 1948	04:52
Ari	11 Mar 1948	16:32
Tau	14 Mar 1948	02:39
Gem	16 Mar 1948	10:43
Can	18 Mar 1948	16:12
Leo	20 Mar 1948	18:57
Vir	22 Mar 1948	19:41
Lib	24 Mar 1948	20:01
Sco	26 Mar 1948	21:50
Sag	29 Mar 1948	02:47
Cap	31 Mar 1948	11:34
Aqu	2 Apr 1948	23:18
Pis	5 Apr 1948	11:55
Ari	7 Apr 1948	23:26
Tau	10 Apr 1948	08:57
Gem	12 Apr 1948	16:19
Can	14 Apr 1948	21:40
Leo	17 Apr 1948	01:14
Vir	19 Apr 1948	03:29
Lib	21 Apr 1948	05:15
Sco	23 Apr 1948	07:49
Sag	25 Apr 1948	12:31
Cap	27 Apr 1948	20:21
Aqu	30 Apr 1948	07:15

Pis	2 May 1948	19:43
Ari	5 May 1948	07:27
Tau	7 May 1948	16:47
Gem	9 May 1948	23:18
Can	12 May 1948	03:37
Leo	14 May 1948	06:38
Vir	16 May 1948	09:13
Lib	18 May 1948	12:06
Sco	20 May 1948	15:55
Sag	22 May 1948	21:22
Cap	25 May 1948	05:07
Aqu	27 May 1948	15:30
Pis	30 May 1948	03:45
Ari	1 Jun 1948	15:53
Tau	4 Jun 1948	01:41
Gem	6 Jun 1948	08:05
Can	8 Jun 1948	11:27
Leo	10 Jun 1948	13:10
Vir	12 Jun 1948	14:48
Lib	14 Jun 1948	17:32
Sco	16 Jun 1948	22:03
Sag	19 Jun 1948	04:28
Cap	21 Jun 1948	12:50
Aqu	23 Jun 1948	23:15
Pis	26 Jun 1948	11:22
Ari	28 Jun 1948	23:54
Tau	1 Jul 1948	10:38
Gem	3 Jul 1948	17:47
Can	5 Jul 1948	21:05
Leo	7 Jul 1948	21:52
Vir	9 Jul 1948	22:03
Lib	11 Jul 1948	23:31
Sco	14 Jul 1948	03:28
Sag	16 Jul 1948	10:11
Cap	18 Jul 1948	19:13
Aqu	21 Jul 1948	06:02
Pis	23 Jul 1948	18:12
Ari	26 Jul 1948	06:56
Tau	28 Jul 1948	18:33
Gem	31 Jul 1948	02:59
Can	2 Aug 1948	07:19
Leo	4 Aug 1948	08:12
Vir	6 Aug 1948	07:32
Lib	8 Aug 1948	07:29
Sco	10 Aug 1948	09:57
Sag	12 Aug 1948	15:49
Cap	15 Aug 1948	00:51
Aqu	17 Aug 1948	12:02
Pis	20 Aug 1948	00:22
Ari	22 Aug 1948	13:04
Tau	25 Aug 1948	01:02
Gem	27 Aug 1948	10:38
Can	29 Aug 1948	16:32
Leo	31 Aug 1948	18:40

Vir	2 Sep 1948	18:19
Lib	4 Sep 1948	17:35
Sco	6 Sep 1948	18:33
Sag	8 Sep 1948	22:52
Cap	11 Sep 1948	06:56
Aqu	13 Sep 1948	17:58
Pis	16 Sep 1948	06:26
Ari	18 Sep 1948	19:01
Tau	21 Sep 1948	06:44
Gem	23 Sep 1948	16:39
Can	25 Sep 1948	23:44
Leo	28 Sep 1948	03:33
Vir	30 Sep 1948	04:39
Lib	2 Oct 1948	04:29
Sco	4 Oct 1948	04:58
Sag	6 Oct 1948	07:55
Cap	8 Oct 1948	14:31
Aqu	11 Oct 1948	00:42
Pis	13 Oct 1948	13:02
Ari	16 Oct 1948	01:35
Tau	18 Oct 1948	12:52
Gem	20 Oct 1948	22:13
Can	23 Oct 1948	05:20
Leo	25 Oct 1948	10:08
Vir	27 Oct 1948	12:52
Lib	29 Oct 1948	14:15
Sco	31 Oct 1948	15:31
Sag	2 Nov 1948	18:10
Cap	4 Nov 1948	23:40
Aqu	7 Nov 1948	08:41
Pis	9 Nov 1948	20:33
Ari	12 Nov 1948	09:11
Tau	14 Nov 1948	20:23
Gem	17 Nov 1948	05:01
Can	19 Nov 1948	11:09
Leo	21 Nov 1948	15:31
Vir	23 Nov 1948	18:47
Lib	25 Nov 1948	21:32
Sco	28 Nov 1948	00:18
Sag	30 Nov 1948	03:51
Cap	2 Dec 1948	09:16
Aqu	4 Dec 1948	17:31
Pis	7 Dec 1948	04:45
Ari	9 Dec 1948	17:29
Tau	12 Dec 1948	05:07
Gem	14 Dec 1948	13:42
Can	16 Dec 1948	19:00
Leo	18 Dec 1948	22:02
Vir	21 Dec 1948	00:18
Lib	23 Dec 1948	02:59
Sco	25 Dec 1948	06:38
Sag	27 Dec 1948	11:28
Cap	29 Dec 1948	17:46

1949

Sign	Date	Time
Aqu	1 Jan 1949	02:07
Pis	3 Jan 1949	12:58
Ari	6 Jan 1949	01:40
Tau	8 Jan 1949	14:01
Gem	10 Jan 1949	23:28
Can	13 Jan 1949	04:55
Leo	15 Jan 1949	07:06
Vir	17 Jan 1949	07:51
Lib	19 Jan 1949	09:03
Sco	21 Jan 1949	11:59
Sag	23 Jan 1949	17:08
Cap	26 Jan 1949	00:21
Aqu	28 Jan 1949	09:26
Pis	30 Jan 1949	20:26
Ari	2 Feb 1949	09:03
Tau	4 Feb 1949	21:56
Gem	7 Feb 1949	08:38
Can	9 Feb 1949	15:21
Leo	11 Feb 1949	18:00
Vir	13 Feb 1949	18:04
Lib	15 Feb 1949	17:43
Sco	17 Feb 1949	18:52
Sag	19 Feb 1949	22:50
Cap	22 Feb 1949	05:49
Aqu	24 Feb 1949	15:25
Pis	27 Feb 1949	02:53
Ari	1 Mar 1949	15:35
Tau	4 Mar 1949	04:32
Gem	6 Mar 1949	16:04
Can	9 Mar 1949	00:19
Leo	11 Mar 1949	04:32
Vir	13 Mar 1949	05:23
Lib	15 Mar 1949	04:39
Sco	17 Mar 1949	04:25
Sag	19 Mar 1949	06:30
Cap	21 Mar 1949	12:05
Aqu	23 Mar 1949	21:10
Pis	26 Mar 1949	08:49
Ari	28 Mar 1949	21:40
Tau	31 Mar 1949	10:28
Gem	2 Apr 1949	22:01
Can	5 Apr 1949	07:09
Leo	7 Apr 1949	12:57
Vir	9 Apr 1949	15:30
Lib	11 Apr 1949	15:46
Sco	13 Apr 1949	15:27
Sag	15 Apr 1949	16:23
Cap	17 Apr 1949	20:16
Aqu	20 Apr 1949	03:59
Pis	22 Apr 1949	15:07
Ari	25 Apr 1949	04:00
Tau	27 Apr 1949	16:40
Gem	30 Apr 1949	03:46
Can	2 May 1949	12:41
Leo	4 May 1949	19:10
Vir	6 May 1949	23:10
Lib	9 May 1949	01:05
Sco	11 May 1949	01:53
Sag	13 May 1949	02:57
Cap	15 May 1949	05:56
Aqu	17 May 1949	12:19
Pis	19 May 1949	22:26
Ari	22 May 1949	11:01
Tau	24 May 1949	23:40
Gem	27 May 1949	10:25
Can	29 May 1949	18:38
Leo	1 Jun 1949	00:35
Vir	3 Jun 1949	04:52
Lib	5 Jun 1949	07:56
Sco	7 Jun 1949	10:12
Sag	9 Jun 1949	12:23
Cap	11 Jun 1949	15:39
Aqu	13 Jun 1949	21:26
Pis	16 Jun 1949	06:38
Ari	18 Jun 1949	18:44
Tau	21 Jun 1949	07:29
Gem	23 Jun 1949	18:19
Can	26 Jun 1949	02:00
Leo	28 Jun 1949	07:00
Vir	30 Jun 1949	10:26
Lib	2 Jul 1949	13:21
Sco	4 Jul 1949	16:21
Sag	6 Jul 1949	19:44
Cap	9 Jul 1949	00:02
Aqu	11 Jul 1949	06:08
Pis	13 Jul 1949	15:01
Ari	16 Jul 1949	02:42
Tau	18 Jul 1949	15:35
Gem	21 Jul 1949	02:56
Can	23 Jul 1949	10:50
Leo	25 Jul 1949	15:17
Vir	27 Jul 1949	17:35
Lib	29 Jul 1949	19:19
Sco	31 Jul 1949	21:44
Sag	3 Aug 1949	01:25
Cap	5 Aug 1949	06:35
Aqu	7 Aug 1949	13:34
Pis	9 Aug 1949	22:46
Ari	12 Aug 1949	10:20
Tau	14 Aug 1949	23:17
Gem	17 Aug 1949	11:21
Can	19 Aug 1949	20:13
Leo	22 Aug 1949	01:06
Vir	24 Aug 1949	02:54
Lib	26 Aug 1949	03:23
Sco	28 Aug 1949	04:19
Sag	30 Aug 1949	07:00
Cap	1 Sep 1949	12:05
Aqu	3 Sep 1949	19:37
Pis	6 Sep 1949	05:26
Ari	8 Sep 1949	17:13
Tau	11 Sep 1949	06:11
Gem	13 Sep 1949	18:46
Can	16 Sep 1949	04:50
Leo	18 Sep 1949	11:02
Vir	20 Sep 1949	13:32
Lib	22 Sep 1949	13:41
Sco	24 Sep 1949	13:20
Sag	26 Sep 1949	14:21
Cap	28 Sep 1949	18:06
Aqu	1 Oct 1949	01:14
Pis	3 Oct 1949	11:20
Ari	5 Oct 1949	23:27
Tau	8 Oct 1949	12:26
Gem	11 Oct 1949	01:01
Can	13 Oct 1949	11:49
Leo	15 Oct 1949	19:34
Vir	17 Oct 1949	23:40
Lib	20 Oct 1949	00:46
Sco	22 Oct 1949	00:18
Sag	24 Oct 1949	00:08
Cap	26 Oct 1949	02:11
Aqu	28 Oct 1949	07:50
Pis	30 Oct 1949	17:21
Ari	2 Nov 1949	05:34
Tau	4 Nov 1949	18:36
Gem	7 Nov 1949	06:54
Can	9 Nov 1949	17:34
Leo	12 Nov 1949	01:59
Vir	14 Nov 1949	07:41
Lib	16 Nov 1949	10:34
Sco	18 Nov 1949	11:18
Sag	20 Nov 1949	11:15
Cap	22 Nov 1949	12:20
Aqu	24 Nov 1949	16:24
Pis	27 Nov 1949	00:36
Ari	29 Nov 1949	12:18
Tau	2 Dec 1949	01:21
Gem	4 Dec 1949	13:27
Can	6 Dec 1949	23:30
Leo	9 Dec 1949	07:27
Vir	11 Dec 1949	13:30
Lib	13 Dec 1949	17:44
Sco	15 Dec 1949	20:12
Sag	17 Dec 1949	21:31
Cap	19 Dec 1949	23:00
Aqu	22 Dec 1949	02:25
Pis	24 Dec 1949	09:20
Ari	26 Dec 1949	20:04
Tau	29 Dec 1949	08:57
Gem	31 Dec 1949	21:12

1950

Can 3 Jan 1950 06:55
Leo 5 Jan 1950 13:56
Vir 7 Jan 1950 19:05
Lib 9 Jan 1950 23:07
Sco 12 Jan 1950 02:27
Sag 14 Jan 1950 05:15
Cap 16 Jan 1950 08:06
Aqu 18 Jan 1950 12:07
Pis 20 Jan 1950 18:41
Ari 23 Jan 1950 04:37
Tau 25 Jan 1950 17:07
Gem 28 Jan 1950 05:42
Can 30 Jan 1950 15:49

Leo 1 Feb 1950 22:32
Vir 4 Feb 1950 02:35
Lib 6 Feb 1950 05:18
Sco 8 Feb 1950 07:50
Sag 10 Feb 1950 10:51
Cap 12 Feb 1950 14:44
Aqu 14 Feb 1950 19:57
Pis 17 Feb 1950 03:11
Ari 19 Feb 1950 13:01
Tau 22 Feb 1950 01:11
Gem 24 Feb 1950 14:02
Can 27 Feb 1950 01:01

Leo 1 Mar 1950 08:29
Vir 3 Mar 1950 12:23
Lib 5 Mar 1950 13:59
Sco 7 Mar 1950 14:55
Sag 9 Mar 1950 16:37
Cap 11 Mar 1950 20:07
Aqu 14 Mar 1950 01:52
Pis 16 Mar 1950 09:59
Ari 18 Mar 1950 20:21
Tau 21 Mar 1950 08:31
Gem 23 Mar 1950 21:27
Can 26 Mar 1950 09:15
Leo 28 Mar 1950 18:04
Vir 30 Mar 1950 22:59

Lib 2 Apr 1950 00:39
Sco 4 Apr 1950 00:35
Sag 6 Apr 1950 00:37
Cap 8 Apr 1950 02:30
Aqu 10 Apr 1950 07:24
Pis 12 Apr 1950 15:38
Ari 15 Apr 1950 02:31
Tau 17 Apr 1950 14:59
Gem 20 Apr 1950 03:53
Can 22 Apr 1950 16:01
Leo 25 Apr 1950 01:55
Vir 27 Apr 1950 08:28
Lib 29 Apr 1950 11:23

Sco 1 May 1950 11:36
Sag 3 May 1950 10:50
Cap 5 May 1950 11:09
Aqu 7 May 1950 14:23
Pis 9 May 1950 21:34
Ari 12 May 1950 08:18
Tau 14 May 1950 20:58
Gem 17 May 1950 09:51
Can 19 May 1950 21:49
Leo 22 May 1950 08:05
Vir 24 May 1950 15:49
Lib 26 May 1950 20:25
Sco 28 May 1950 21:59
Sag 30 May 1950 21:43

Cap 1 Jun 1950 21:27
Aqu 3 Jun 1950 23:19
Pis 6 Jun 1950 04:57
Ari 8 Jun 1950 14:44
Tau 11 Jun 1950 03:12
Gem 13 Jun 1950 16:04
Can 16 Jun 1950 03:44
Leo 18 Jun 1950 13:36
Vir 20 Jun 1950 21:30
Lib 23 Jun 1950 03:08
Sco 25 Jun 1950 06:18
Sag 27 Jun 1950 07:25
Cap 29 Jun 1950 07:48

Aqu 1 Jul 1950 09:20
Pis 3 Jul 1950 13:52
Ari 5 Jul 1950 22:25
Tau 8 Jul 1950 10:13
Gem 10 Jul 1950 23:01
Can 13 Jul 1950 10:32
Leo 15 Jul 1950 19:52
Vir 18 Jul 1950 03:05
Lib 20 Jul 1950 08:33
Sco 22 Jul 1950 12:26
Sag 24 Jul 1950 14:54
Cap 26 Jul 1950 16:39
Aqu 28 Jul 1950 18:55
Pis 30 Jul 1950 23:19

Ari 2 Aug 1950 07:03
Tau 4 Aug 1950 18:05
Gem 7 Aug 1950 06:43
Can 9 Aug 1950 18:26
Leo 12 Aug 1950 03:35
Vir 14 Aug 1950 10:02
Lib 16 Aug 1950 14:30
Sco 18 Aug 1950 17:48
Sag 20 Aug 1950 20:35
Cap 22 Aug 1950 23:23
Aqu 25 Aug 1950 02:53
Pis 27 Aug 1950 08:02
Ari 29 Aug 1950 15:45

Tau 1 Sep 1950 02:19
Gem 3 Sep 1950 14:45
Can 6 Sep 1950 02:53
Leo 8 Sep 1950 12:32
Vir 10 Sep 1950 18:54
Lib 12 Sep 1950 22:26
Sco 15 Sep 1950 00:26
Sag 17 Sep 1950 02:12
Cap 19 Sep 1950 04:48
Aqu 21 Sep 1950 09:00
Pis 23 Sep 1950 15:09
Ari 25 Sep 1950 23:32
Tau 28 Sep 1950 10:08
Gem 30 Sep 1950 22:26

Can 3 Oct 1950 10:58
Leo 5 Oct 1950 21:38
Vir 8 Oct 1950 04:52
Lib 10 Oct 1950 08:27
Sco 12 Oct 1950 09:30
Sag 14 Oct 1950 09:44
Cap 16 Oct 1950 10:55
Aqu 18 Oct 1950 14:27
Pis 20 Oct 1950 20:53
Ari 23 Oct 1950 05:58
Tau 25 Oct 1950 17:02
Gem 28 Oct 1950 05:22
Can 30 Oct 1950 18:03

Leo 2 Nov 1950 05:37
Vir 4 Nov 1950 14:19
Lib 6 Nov 1950 19:09
Sco 8 Nov 1950 20:28
Sag 10 Nov 1950 19:51
Cap 12 Nov 1950 19:25
Aqu 14 Nov 1950 21:15
Pis 17 Nov 1950 02:39
Ari 19 Nov 1950 11:40
Tau 21 Nov 1950 23:07
Gem 24 Nov 1950 11:38
Can 27 Nov 1950 00:12
Leo 29 Nov 1950 12:01

Vir 1 Dec 1950 21:52
Lib 4 Dec 1950 04:28
Sco 6 Dec 1950 07:18
Sag 8 Dec 1950 07:16
Cap 10 Dec 1950 06:16
Aqu 12 Dec 1950 06:34
Pis 14 Dec 1950 10:11
Ari 16 Dec 1950 17:58
Tau 19 Dec 1950 05:09
Gem 21 Dec 1950 17:49
Can 24 Dec 1950 06:17
Leo 26 Dec 1950 17:45
Vir 29 Dec 1950 03:40
Lib 31 Dec 1950 11:18

1951

Sco	2 Jan 1951	15:57
Sag	4 Jan 1951	17:37
Cap	6 Jan 1951	17:31
Aqu	8 Jan 1951	17:35
Pis	10 Jan 1951	19:56
Ari	13 Jan 1951	02:06
Tau	15 Jan 1951	12:11
Gem	18 Jan 1951	00:35
Can	20 Jan 1951	13:05
Leo	23 Jan 1951	00:11
Vir	25 Jan 1951	09:25
Lib	27 Jan 1951	16:45
Sco	29 Jan 1951	22:03
Sag	1 Feb 1951	01:15
Cap	3 Feb 1951	02:52
Aqu	5 Feb 1951	04:04
Pis	7 Feb 1951	06:29
Ari	9 Feb 1951	11:44
Tau	11 Feb 1951	20:33
Gem	14 Feb 1951	08:18
Can	16 Feb 1951	20:51
Leo	19 Feb 1951	08:00
Vir	21 Feb 1951	16:42
Lib	23 Feb 1951	23:00
Sco	26 Feb 1951	03:30
Sag	28 Feb 1951	06:49
Cap	2 Mar 1951	09:29
Aqu	4 Mar 1951	12:11
Pis	6 Mar 1951	15:46
Ari	8 Mar 1951	21:16
Tau	11 Mar 1951	05:32
Gem	13 Mar 1951	16:36
Can	16 Mar 1951	05:06
Leo	18 Mar 1951	16:44
Vir	21 Mar 1951	01:37
Lib	23 Mar 1951	07:20
Sco	25 Mar 1951	10:34
Sag	27 Mar 1951	12:40
Cap	29 Mar 1951	14:51
Aqu	31 Mar 1951	18:02
Pis	2 Apr 1951	22:45
Ari	5 Apr 1951	05:15
Tau	7 Apr 1951	13:52
Gem	10 Apr 1951	00:41
Can	12 Apr 1951	13:04
Leo	15 Apr 1951	01:17
Vir	17 Apr 1951	11:05
Lib	19 Apr 1951	17:13
Sco	21 Apr 1951	19:54
Sag	23 Apr 1951	20:39
Cap	25 Apr 1951	21:20
Aqu	27 Apr 1951	23:33
Pis	30 Apr 1951	04:13
Ari	2 May 1951	11:26
Tau	4 May 1951	20:46
Gem	7 May 1951	07:50
Can	9 May 1951	20:12
Leo	12 May 1951	08:49
Vir	14 May 1951	19:43
Lib	17 May 1951	03:03
Sco	19 May 1951	06:22
Sag	21 May 1951	06:43
Cap	23 May 1951	06:07
Aqu	25 May 1951	06:41
Pis	27 May 1951	10:06
Ari	29 May 1951	16:53
Tau	1 Jun 1951	02:33
Gem	3 Jun 1951	14:03
Can	6 Jun 1951	02:31
Leo	8 Jun 1951	15:11
Vir	11 Jun 1951	02:45
Lib	13 Jun 1951	11:29
Sco	15 Jun 1951	16:16
Sag	17 Jun 1951	17:25
Cap	19 Jun 1951	16:37
Aqu	21 Jun 1951	16:04
Pis	23 Jun 1951	17:49
Ari	25 Jun 1951	23:14
Tau	28 Jun 1951	08:17
Gem	30 Jun 1951	19:51
Can	3 Jul 1951	08:27
Leo	5 Jul 1951	21:00
Vir	8 Jul 1951	08:35
Lib	10 Jul 1951	18:04
Sco	13 Jul 1951	00:17
Sag	15 Jul 1951	03:02
Cap	17 Jul 1951	03:13
Aqu	19 Jul 1951	02:41
Pis	21 Jul 1951	03:29
Ari	23 Jul 1951	07:22
Tau	25 Jul 1951	15:07
Gem	28 Jul 1951	02:08
Can	30 Jul 1951	14:42
Leo	2 Aug 1951	03:07
Vir	4 Aug 1951	14:17
Lib	6 Aug 1951	23:33
Sco	9 Aug 1951	06:23
Sag	11 Aug 1951	10:30
Cap	13 Aug 1951	12:17
Aqu	15 Aug 1951	12:53
Pis	17 Aug 1951	13:53
Ari	19 Aug 1951	16:58
Tau	21 Aug 1951	23:28
Gem	24 Aug 1951	09:27
Can	26 Aug 1951	21:44
Leo	29 Aug 1951	10:09
Vir	31 Aug 1951	20:59
Lib	3 Sep 1951	05:32
Sco	5 Sep 1951	11:48
Sag	7 Sep 1951	16:10
Cap	9 Sep 1951	19:06
Aqu	11 Sep 1951	21:11
Pis	13 Sep 1951	23:22
Ari	16 Sep 1951	02:48
Tau	18 Sep 1951	08:42
Gem	20 Sep 1951	17:46
Can	23 Sep 1951	05:34
Leo	25 Sep 1951	18:07
Vir	28 Sep 1951	05:05
Lib	30 Sep 1951	13:07
Sco	2 Oct 1951	18:23
Sag	4 Oct 1951	21:47
Cap	7 Oct 1951	00:30
Aqu	9 Oct 1951	03:19
Pis	11 Oct 1951	06:46
Ari	13 Oct 1951	11:20
Tau	15 Oct 1951	17:37
Gem	18 Oct 1951	02:22
Can	20 Oct 1951	13:42
Leo	23 Oct 1951	02:24
Vir	25 Oct 1951	14:00
Lib	27 Oct 1951	22:23
Sco	30 Oct 1951	03:08
Sag	1 Nov 1951	05:19
Cap	3 Nov 1951	06:39
Aqu	5 Nov 1951	08:43
Pis	7 Nov 1951	12:23
Ari	9 Nov 1951	17:52
Tau	12 Nov 1951	01:07
Gem	14 Nov 1951	10:15
Can	16 Nov 1951	21:27
Leo	19 Nov 1951	10:11
Vir	21 Nov 1951	22:34
Lib	24 Nov 1951	08:07
Sco	26 Nov 1951	13:30
Sag	28 Nov 1951	15:19
Cap	30 Nov 1951	15:22
Aqu	2 Dec 1951	15:45
Pis	4 Dec 1951	18:07
Ari	6 Dec 1951	23:18
Tau	9 Dec 1951	07:04
Gem	11 Dec 1951	16:54
Can	14 Dec 1951	04:22
Leo	16 Dec 1951	17:04
Vir	19 Dec 1951	05:52
Lib	21 Dec 1951	16:40
Sco	23 Dec 1951	23:37
Sag	26 Dec 1951	02:25
Cap	28 Dec 1951	02:23
Aqu	30 Dec 1951	01:36

1952

Sign	Date	Time
Pis	1 Jan 1952	02:11
Ari	3 Jan 1952	05:41
Tau	5 Jan 1952	12:44
Gem	7 Jan 1952	22:42
Can	10 Jan 1952	10:34
Leo	12 Jan 1952	23:19
Vir	15 Jan 1952	12:00
Lib	17 Jan 1952	23:18
Sco	20 Jan 1952	07:43
Sag	22 Jan 1952	12:20
Cap	24 Jan 1952	13:38
Aqu	26 Jan 1952	13:06
Pis	28 Jan 1952	12:46
Ari	30 Jan 1952	14:33
Tau	1 Feb 1952	19:51
Gem	4 Feb 1952	04:55
Can	6 Feb 1952	16:44
Leo	9 Feb 1952	05:36
Vir	11 Feb 1952	18:01
Lib	14 Feb 1952	05:00
Sco	16 Feb 1952	13:44
Sag	18 Feb 1952	19:41
Cap	20 Feb 1952	22:48
Aqu	22 Feb 1952	23:48
Pis	25 Feb 1952	00:01
Ari	27 Feb 1952	01:12
Tau	29 Feb 1952	05:02
Gem	2 Mar 1952	12:37
Can	4 Mar 1952	23:41
Leo	7 Mar 1952	12:30
Vir	10 Mar 1952	00:50
Lib	12 Mar 1952	11:15
Sco	14 Mar 1952	19:20
Sag	17 Mar 1952	01:14
Cap	19 Mar 1952	05:19
Aqu	21 Mar 1952	07:54
Pis	23 Mar 1952	09:39
Ari	25 Mar 1952	11:35
Tau	27 Mar 1952	15:06
Gem	29 Mar 1952	21:36
Can	1 Apr 1952	07:39
Leo	3 Apr 1952	20:09
Vir	6 Apr 1952	08:39
Lib	8 Apr 1952	18:55
Sco	11 Apr 1952	02:12
Sag	13 Apr 1952	07:07
Cap	15 Apr 1952	10:41
Aqu	17 Apr 1952	13:43
Pis	19 Apr 1952	16:40
Ari	21 Apr 1952	19:56
Tau	24 Apr 1952	00:15
Gem	26 Apr 1952	06:40
Can	28 Apr 1952	16:06
Leo	1 May 1952	04:12
Vir	3 May 1952	16:57
Lib	6 May 1952	03:38
Sco	8 May 1952	10:47
Sag	10 May 1952	14:49
Cap	12 May 1952	17:08
Aqu	14 May 1952	19:14
Pis	16 May 1952	22:06
Ari	19 May 1952	02:07
Tau	21 May 1952	07:29
Gem	23 May 1952	14:37
Can	26 May 1952	00:06
Leo	28 May 1952	11:59
Vir	31 May 1952	00:56
Lib	2 Jun 1952	12:24
Sco	4 Jun 1952	20:18
Sag	7 Jun 1952	00:19
Cap	9 Jun 1952	01:46
Aqu	11 Jun 1952	02:27
Pis	13 Jun 1952	04:01
Ari	15 Jun 1952	07:29
Tau	17 Jun 1952	13:11
Gem	19 Jun 1952	21:04
Can	22 Jun 1952	07:04
Leo	24 Jun 1952	19:02
Vir	27 Jun 1952	08:06
Lib	29 Jun 1952	20:17
Sco	2 Jul 1952	05:25
Sag	4 Jul 1952	10:25
Cap	6 Jul 1952	12:01
Aqu	8 Jul 1952	11:54
Pis	10 Jul 1952	12:00
Ari	12 Jul 1952	13:57
Tau	14 Jul 1952	18:45
Gem	17 Jul 1952	02:38
Can	19 Jul 1952	13:05
Leo	22 Jul 1952	01:20
Vir	24 Jul 1952	14:24
Lib	27 Jul 1952	02:53
Sco	29 Jul 1952	13:03
Sag	31 Jul 1952	19:36
Cap	2 Aug 1952	22:26
Aqu	4 Aug 1952	22:40
Pis	6 Aug 1952	22:05
Ari	8 Aug 1952	22:34
Tau	11 Aug 1952	01:47
Gem	13 Aug 1952	08:37
Can	15 Aug 1952	18:52
Leo	18 Aug 1952	07:19
Vir	20 Aug 1952	20:22
Lib	23 Aug 1952	08:41
Sco	25 Aug 1952	19:10
Sag	28 Aug 1952	02:52
Cap	30 Aug 1952	07:23
Aqu	1 Sep 1952	09:02
Pis	3 Sep 1952	09:00
Ari	5 Sep 1952	08:57
Tau	7 Sep 1952	10:49
Gem	9 Sep 1952	16:07
Can	12 Sep 1952	01:25
Leo	14 Sep 1952	13:38
Vir	17 Sep 1952	02:41
Lib	19 Sep 1952	14:41
Sco	22 Sep 1952	00:42
Sag	24 Sep 1952	08:32
Cap	26 Sep 1952	14:05
Aqu	28 Sep 1952	17:24
Pis	30 Sep 1952	18:52
Ari	2 Oct 1952	19:34
Tau	4 Oct 1952	21:06
Gem	7 Oct 1952	01:16
Can	9 Oct 1952	09:17
Leo	11 Oct 1952	20:50
Vir	14 Oct 1952	09:50
Lib	16 Oct 1952	21:43
Sco	19 Oct 1952	07:09
Sag	21 Oct 1952	14:11
Cap	23 Oct 1952	19:28
Aqu	25 Oct 1952	23:27
Pis	28 Oct 1952	02:22
Ari	30 Oct 1952	04:34
Tau	1 Nov 1952	06:58
Gem	3 Nov 1952	11:03
Can	5 Nov 1952	18:12
Leo	8 Nov 1952	04:56
Vir	10 Nov 1952	17:47
Lib	13 Nov 1952	05:57
Sco	15 Nov 1952	15:17
Sag	17 Nov 1952	21:32
Cap	20 Nov 1952	01:39
Aqu	22 Nov 1952	04:51
Pis	24 Nov 1952	07:55
Ari	26 Nov 1952	11:09
Tau	28 Nov 1952	14:54
Gem	30 Nov 1952	19:53
Can	3 Dec 1952	03:09
Leo	5 Dec 1952	13:23
Vir	8 Dec 1952	01:57
Lib	10 Dec 1952	14:34
Sco	13 Dec 1952	00:37
Sag	15 Dec 1952	06:59
Cap	17 Dec 1952	10:16
Aqu	19 Dec 1952	12:02
Pis	21 Dec 1952	13:46
Ari	23 Dec 1952	16:30
Tau	25 Dec 1952	20:46
Gem	28 Dec 1952	02:48
Can	30 Dec 1952	10:54

1953

Sign	Date	Time
Leo	1 Jan 1953	21:17
Vir	4 Jan 1953	09:41
Lib	6 Jan 1953	22:36
Sco	9 Jan 1953	09:43
Sag	11 Jan 1953	17:14
Cap	13 Jan 1953	20:54
Aqu	15 Jan 1953	21:57
Pis	17 Jan 1953	22:07
Ari	19 Jan 1953	23:09
Tau	22 Jan 1953	02:21
Gem	24 Jan 1953	08:21
Can	26 Jan 1953	17:07
Leo	29 Jan 1953	04:06
Vir	31 Jan 1953	16:35
Lib	3 Feb 1953	05:31
Sco	5 Feb 1953	17:20
Sag	8 Feb 1953	02:19
Cap	10 Feb 1953	07:31
Aqu	12 Feb 1953	09:16
Pis	14 Feb 1953	08:58
Ari	16 Feb 1953	08:31
Tau	18 Feb 1953	09:52
Gem	20 Feb 1953	14:28
Can	22 Feb 1953	22:48
Leo	25 Feb 1953	10:06
Vir	27 Feb 1953	22:51
Lib	2 Mar 1953	11:41
Sco	4 Mar 1953	23:30
Sag	7 Mar 1953	09:19
Cap	9 Mar 1953	16:09
Aqu	11 Mar 1953	19:37
Pis	13 Mar 1953	20:16
Ari	15 Mar 1953	19:39
Tau	17 Mar 1953	19:45
Gem	19 Mar 1953	22:36
Can	22 Mar 1953	05:29
Leo	24 Mar 1953	16:14
Vir	27 Mar 1953	05:04
Lib	29 Mar 1953	17:51
Sco	1 Apr 1953	05:19
Sag	3 Apr 1953	14:58
Cap	5 Apr 1953	22:28
Aqu	8 Apr 1953	03:27
Pis	10 Apr 1953	05:49
Ari	12 Apr 1953	06:19
Tau	14 Apr 1953	06:31
Gem	16 Apr 1953	08:28
Can	18 Apr 1953	13:54
Leo	20 Apr 1953	23:28
Vir	23 Apr 1953	11:53
Lib	26 Apr 1953	00:40
Sco	28 Apr 1953	11:51
Sag	30 Apr 1953	20:52
Cap	3 May 1953	03:54
Aqu	5 May 1953	09:12
Pis	7 May 1953	12:46
Ari	9 May 1953	14:49
Tau	11 May 1953	16:12
Gem	13 May 1953	18:27
Can	15 May 1953	23:17
Leo	18 May 1953	07:47
Vir	20 May 1953	19:31
Lib	23 May 1953	08:16
Sco	25 May 1953	19:32
Sag	28 May 1953	04:08
Cap	30 May 1953	10:16
Aqu	1 Jun 1953	14:45
Pis	3 Jun 1953	18:12
Ari	5 Jun 1953	21:01
Tau	7 Jun 1953	23:41
Gem	10 Jun 1953	03:03
Can	12 Jun 1953	08:18
Leo	14 Jun 1953	16:27
Vir	17 Jun 1953	03:37
Lib	19 Jun 1953	16:16
Sco	22 Jun 1953	03:57
Sag	24 Jun 1953	12:46
Cap	26 Jun 1953	18:29
Aqu	28 Jun 1953	21:51
Pis	1 Jul 1953	00:08
Ari	3 Jul 1953	02:24
Tau	5 Jul 1953	05:23
Gem	7 Jul 1953	09:43
Can	9 Jul 1953	15:54
Leo	12 Jul 1953	00:29
Vir	14 Jul 1953	11:29
Lib	17 Jul 1953	00:04
Sco	19 Jul 1953	12:16
Sag	21 Jul 1953	21:58
Cap	24 Jul 1953	04:06
Aqu	26 Jul 1953	07:02
Pis	28 Jul 1953	08:07
Ari	30 Jul 1953	08:56
Tau	1 Aug 1953	10:58
Gem	3 Aug 1953	15:11
Can	5 Aug 1953	22:00
Leo	8 Aug 1953	07:16
Vir	10 Aug 1953	18:33
Lib	13 Aug 1953	07:08
Sco	15 Aug 1953	19:43
Sag	18 Aug 1953	06:30
Cap	20 Aug 1953	13:51
Aqu	22 Aug 1953	17:28
Pis	24 Aug 1953	18:12
Ari	26 Aug 1953	17:46
Tau	28 Aug 1953	18:10
Gem	30 Aug 1953	21:07
Can	2 Sep 1953	03:30
Leo	4 Sep 1953	13:05
Vir	7 Sep 1953	00:47
Lib	9 Sep 1953	13:27
Sco	12 Sep 1953	02:05
Sag	14 Sep 1953	13:31
Cap	16 Sep 1953	22:19
Aqu	19 Sep 1953	03:29
Pis	21 Sep 1953	05:06
Ari	23 Sep 1953	04:30
Tau	25 Sep 1953	03:45
Gem	27 Sep 1953	05:01
Can	29 Sep 1953	09:58
Leo	1 Oct 1953	18:54
Vir	4 Oct 1953	06:40
Lib	6 Oct 1953	19:28
Sco	9 Oct 1953	07:56
Sag	11 Oct 1953	19:19
Cap	14 Oct 1953	04:51
Aqu	16 Oct 1953	11:33
Pis	18 Oct 1953	14:54
Ari	20 Oct 1953	15:26
Tau	22 Oct 1953	14:47
Gem	24 Oct 1953	15:05
Can	26 Oct 1953	18:24
Leo	29 Oct 1953	01:56
Vir	31 Oct 1953	13:05
Lib	3 Nov 1953	01:51
Sco	5 Nov 1953	14:11
Sag	8 Nov 1953	01:06
Cap	10 Nov 1953	10:18
Aqu	12 Nov 1953	17:30
Pis	14 Nov 1953	22:16
Ari	17 Nov 1953	00:34
Tau	19 Nov 1953	01:15
Gem	21 Nov 1953	01:55
Can	23 Nov 1953	04:32
Leo	25 Nov 1953	10:42
Vir	27 Nov 1953	20:41
Lib	30 Nov 1953	09:05
Sco	2 Dec 1953	21:30
Sag	5 Dec 1953	08:08
Cap	7 Dec 1953	16:32
Aqu	9 Dec 1953	22:58
Pis	12 Dec 1953	03:46
Ari	14 Dec 1953	07:06
Tau	16 Dec 1953	09:22
Gem	18 Dec 1953	11:28
Can	20 Dec 1953	14:40
Leo	22 Dec 1953	20:23
Vir	25 Dec 1953	05:24
Lib	27 Dec 1953	17:11
Sco	30 Dec 1953	05:43

1954

Sag	1 Jan 1954	16:39
Cap	4 Jan 1954	00:44
Aqu	6 Jan 1954	06:09
Pis	8 Jan 1954	09:43
Ari	10 Jan 1954	12:27
Tau	12 Jan 1954	15:10
Gem	14 Jan 1954	18:29
Can	16 Jan 1954	23:01
Leo	19 Jan 1954	05:24
Vir	21 Jan 1954	14:14
Lib	24 Jan 1954	01:30
Sco	26 Jan 1954	14:03
Sag	29 Jan 1954	01:42
Cap	31 Jan 1954	10:25
Aqu	2 Feb 1954	15:37
Pis	4 Feb 1954	18:03
Ari	6 Feb 1954	19:14
Tau	8 Feb 1954	20:48
Gem	10 Feb 1954	23:55
Can	13 Feb 1954	05:10
Leo	15 Feb 1954	12:36
Vir	17 Feb 1954	22:01
Lib	20 Feb 1954	09:15
Sco	22 Feb 1954	21:43
Sag	25 Feb 1954	10:00
Cap	27 Feb 1954	19:57
Aqu	2 Mar 1954	02:06
Pis	4 Mar 1954	04:32
Ari	6 Mar 1954	04:40
Tau	8 Mar 1954	04:33
Gem	10 Mar 1954	06:06
Can	12 Mar 1954	10:38
Leo	14 Mar 1954	18:17
Vir	17 Mar 1954	04:21
Lib	19 Mar 1954	15:58
Sco	22 Mar 1954	04:26
Sag	24 Mar 1954	16:56
Cap	27 Mar 1954	03:54
Aqu	29 Mar 1954	11:36
Pis	31 Mar 1954	15:16
Ari	2 Apr 1954	15:40
Tau	4 Apr 1954	14:43
Gem	6 Apr 1954	14:41
Can	8 Apr 1954	17:29
Leo	11 Apr 1954	00:07
Vir	13 Apr 1954	10:03
Lib	15 Apr 1954	21:58
Sco	18 Apr 1954	10:32
Sag	20 Apr 1954	22:55
Cap	23 Apr 1954	10:10
Aqu	25 Apr 1954	19:02
Pis	28 Apr 1954	00:20
Ari	30 Apr 1954	02:08
Tau	2 May 1954	01:42
Gem	4 May 1954	01:07
Can	6 May 1954	02:31
Leo	8 May 1954	07:29
Vir	10 May 1954	16:23
Lib	13 May 1954	04:03
Sco	15 May 1954	16:42
Sag	18 May 1954	04:53
Cap	20 May 1954	15:49
Aqu	23 May 1954	00:47
Pis	25 May 1954	07:08
Ari	27 May 1954	10:31
Tau	29 May 1954	11:33
Gem	31 May 1954	11:41
Can	2 Jun 1954	12:47
Leo	4 Jun 1954	16:35
Vir	7 Jun 1954	00:07
Lib	9 Jun 1954	10:59
Sco	11 Jun 1954	23:29
Sag	14 Jun 1954	11:37
Cap	16 Jun 1954	22:04
Aqu	19 Jun 1954	06:26
Pis	21 Jun 1954	12:36
Ari	23 Jun 1954	16:43
Tau	25 Jun 1954	19:09
Gem	27 Jun 1954	20:42
Can	29 Jun 1954	22:36
Leo	2 Jul 1954	02:17
Vir	4 Jul 1954	08:57
Lib	6 Jul 1954	18:53
Sco	9 Jul 1954	07:04
Sag	11 Jul 1954	19:18
Cap	14 Jul 1954	05:40
Aqu	16 Jul 1954	13:18
Pis	18 Jul 1954	18:32
Ari	20 Jul 1954	22:07
Tau	23 Jul 1954	00:52
Gem	25 Jul 1954	03:30
Can	27 Jul 1954	06:41
Leo	29 Jul 1954	11:11
Vir	31 Jul 1954	17:50
Lib	3 Aug 1954	03:15
Sco	5 Aug 1954	15:03
Sag	8 Aug 1954	03:32
Cap	10 Aug 1954	14:19
Aqu	12 Aug 1954	21:53
Pis	15 Aug 1954	02:16
Ari	17 Aug 1954	04:37
Tau	19 Aug 1954	06:26
Gem	21 Aug 1954	08:56
Can	23 Aug 1954	12:50
Leo	25 Aug 1954	18:22
Vir	28 Aug 1954	01:44
Lib	30 Aug 1954	11:13
Sco	1 Sep 1954	22:49
Sag	4 Sep 1954	11:32
Cap	6 Sep 1954	23:09
Aqu	9 Sep 1954	07:30
Pis	11 Sep 1954	11:54
Ari	13 Sep 1954	13:22
Tau	15 Sep 1954	13:44
Gem	17 Sep 1954	14:55
Can	19 Sep 1954	18:13
Leo	22 Sep 1954	00:04
Vir	24 Sep 1954	08:11
Lib	26 Sep 1954	18:11
Sco	29 Sep 1954	05:52
Sag	1 Oct 1954	18:41
Cap	4 Oct 1954	07:04
Aqu	6 Oct 1954	16:45
Pis	8 Oct 1954	22:15
Ari	10 Oct 1954	23:57
Tau	12 Oct 1954	23:32
Gem	14 Oct 1954	23:11
Can	17 Oct 1954	00:51
Leo	19 Oct 1954	05:41
Vir	21 Oct 1954	13:45
Lib	24 Oct 1954	00:12
Sco	26 Oct 1954	12:11
Sag	29 Oct 1954	00:58
Cap	31 Oct 1954	13:35
Aqu	3 Nov 1954	00:21
Pis	5 Nov 1954	07:33
Ari	7 Nov 1954	10:41
Tau	9 Nov 1954	10:48
Gem	11 Nov 1954	09:51
Can	13 Nov 1954	10:00
Leo	15 Nov 1954	13:04
Vir	17 Nov 1954	19:53
Lib	20 Nov 1954	06:02
Sco	22 Nov 1954	18:13
Sag	25 Nov 1954	07:01
Cap	27 Nov 1954	19:24
Aqu	30 Nov 1954	06:19
Pis	2 Dec 1954	14:37
Ari	4 Dec 1954	19:34
Tau	6 Dec 1954	21:22
Gem	8 Dec 1954	21:16
Can	10 Dec 1954	21:07
Leo	12 Dec 1954	22:49
Vir	15 Dec 1954	03:54
Lib	17 Dec 1954	12:52
Sco	20 Dec 1954	00:44
Sag	22 Dec 1954	13:35
Cap	25 Dec 1954	01:40
Aqu	27 Dec 1954	12:00
Pis	29 Dec 1954	20:09

1955

Ari	1 Jan 1955	01:55
Tau	3 Jan 1955	05:24
Gem	5 Jan 1955	07:04
Can	7 Jan 1955	08:00
Leo	9 Jan 1955	09:42
Vir	11 Jan 1955	13:44
Lib	13 Jan 1955	21:16
Sco	16 Jan 1955	08:15
Sag	18 Jan 1955	21:01
Cap	21 Jan 1955	09:09
Aqu	23 Jan 1955	18:58
Pis	26 Jan 1955	02:10
Ari	28 Jan 1955	07:19
Tau	30 Jan 1955	11:06
Gem	1 Feb 1955	14:02
Can	3 Feb 1955	16:36
Leo	5 Feb 1955	19:29
Vir	7 Feb 1955	23:44
Lib	10 Feb 1955	06:33
Sco	12 Feb 1955	16:39
Sag	15 Feb 1955	05:07
Cap	17 Feb 1955	17:34
Aqu	20 Feb 1955	03:32
Pis	22 Feb 1955	10:08
Ari	24 Feb 1955	14:05
Tau	26 Feb 1955	16:46
Gem	28 Feb 1955	19:24
Can	2 Mar 1955	22:40
Leo	5 Mar 1955	02:49
Vir	7 Mar 1955	08:09
Lib	9 Mar 1955	15:20
Sco	12 Mar 1955	01:05
Sag	14 Mar 1955	13:13
Cap	17 Mar 1955	02:01
Aqu	19 Mar 1955	12:45
Pis	21 Mar 1955	19:44
Ari	23 Mar 1955	23:08
Tau	26 Mar 1955	00:31
Gem	28 Mar 1955	01:42
Can	30 Mar 1955	04:05
Leo	1 Apr 1955	08:21
Vir	3 Apr 1955	14:31
Lib	5 Apr 1955	22:34
Sco	8 Apr 1955	08:38
Sag	10 Apr 1955	20:42
Cap	13 Apr 1955	09:40
Aqu	15 Apr 1955	21:19
Pis	18 Apr 1955	05:28
Ari	20 Apr 1955	09:28
Tau	22 Apr 1955	10:29
Gem	24 Apr 1955	10:24
Can	26 Apr 1955	11:10
Leo	28 Apr 1955	14:09
Vir	30 Apr 1955	19:58
Lib	3 May 1955	04:26
Sco	5 May 1955	15:04
Sag	8 May 1955	03:19
Cap	10 May 1955	16:18
Aqu	13 May 1955	04:29
Pis	15 May 1955	13:52
Ari	17 May 1955	19:20
Tau	19 May 1955	21:11
Gem	21 May 1955	20:56
Can	23 May 1955	20:33
Leo	25 May 1955	21:54
Vir	28 May 1955	02:17
Lib	30 May 1955	10:08
Sco	1 Jun 1955	20:54
Sag	4 Jun 1955	09:24
Cap	6 Jun 1955	22:20
Aqu	9 Jun 1955	10:29
Pis	11 Jun 1955	20:31
Ari	14 Jun 1955	03:23
Tau	16 Jun 1955	06:50
Gem	18 Jun 1955	07:36
Can	20 Jun 1955	07:15
Leo	22 Jun 1955	07:37
Vir	24 Jun 1955	10:27
Lib	26 Jun 1955	16:56
Sco	29 Jun 1955	03:05
Sag	1 Jul 1955	15:34
Cap	4 Jul 1955	04:29
Aqu	6 Jul 1955	16:18
Pis	9 Jul 1955	02:08
Ari	11 Jul 1955	09:32
Tau	13 Jul 1955	14:19
Gem	15 Jul 1955	16:43
Can	17 Jul 1955	17:30
Leo	19 Jul 1955	18:03
Vir	21 Jul 1955	20:07
Lib	24 Jul 1955	01:17
Sco	26 Jul 1955	10:19
Sag	28 Jul 1955	22:24
Cap	31 Jul 1955	11:18
Aqu	2 Aug 1955	22:51
Pis	5 Aug 1955	08:03
Ari	7 Aug 1955	14:59
Tau	9 Aug 1955	20:03
Gem	11 Aug 1955	23:33
Can	14 Aug 1955	01:50
Leo	16 Aug 1955	03:34
Vir	18 Aug 1955	05:57
Lib	20 Aug 1955	10:35
Sco	22 Aug 1955	18:37
Sag	25 Aug 1955	06:03
Cap	27 Aug 1955	18:56
Aqu	30 Aug 1955	06:35
Pis	1 Sep 1955	15:22
Ari	3 Sep 1955	21:23
Tau	6 Sep 1955	01:36
Gem	8 Sep 1955	04:58
Can	10 Sep 1955	08:01
Leo	12 Sep 1955	11:02
Vir	14 Sep 1955	14:33
Lib	16 Sep 1955	19:35
Sco	19 Sep 1955	03:19
Sag	21 Sep 1955	14:12
Cap	24 Sep 1955	03:01
Aqu	26 Sep 1955	15:07
Pis	29 Sep 1955	00:11
Ari	1 Oct 1955	05:46
Tau	3 Oct 1955	08:51
Gem	5 Oct 1955	10:59
Can	7 Oct 1955	13:23
Leo	9 Oct 1955	16:41
Vir	11 Oct 1955	21:12
Lib	14 Oct 1955	03:14
Sco	16 Oct 1955	11:24
Sag	18 Oct 1955	22:08
Cap	21 Oct 1955	10:51
Aqu	23 Oct 1955	23:32
Pis	26 Oct 1955	09:36
Ari	28 Oct 1955	15:45
Tau	30 Oct 1955	18:30
Gem	1 Nov 1955	19:23
Can	3 Nov 1955	20:11
Leo	5 Nov 1955	22:21
Vir	8 Nov 1955	02:37
Lib	10 Nov 1955	09:16
Sco	12 Nov 1955	18:12
Sag	15 Nov 1955	05:17
Cap	17 Nov 1955	17:59
Aqu	20 Nov 1955	06:58
Pis	22 Nov 1955	18:10
Ari	25 Nov 1955	01:46
Tau	27 Nov 1955	05:27
Gem	29 Nov 1955	06:11
Can	1 Dec 1955	05:46
Leo	3 Dec 1955	06:07
Vir	5 Dec 1955	08:51
Lib	7 Dec 1955	14:49
Sco	10 Dec 1955	00:00
Sag	12 Dec 1955	11:34
Cap	15 Dec 1955	00:23
Aqu	17 Dec 1955	13:19
Pis	20 Dec 1955	01:01
Ari	22 Dec 1955	10:04
Tau	24 Dec 1955	15:32
Gem	26 Dec 1955	17:33
Can	28 Dec 1955	17:17
Leo	30 Dec 1955	16:36

1956

Vir	1 Jan 1956	17:31
Lib	3 Jan 1956	21:45
Sco	6 Jan 1956	06:00
Sag	8 Jan 1956	17:33
Cap	11 Jan 1956	06:34
Aqu	13 Jan 1956	19:19
Pis	16 Jan 1956	06:47
Ari	18 Jan 1956	16:17
Tau	20 Jan 1956	23:10
Gem	23 Jan 1956	03:05
Can	25 Jan 1956	04:19
Leo	27 Jan 1956	04:06
Vir	29 Jan 1956	04:18
Lib	31 Jan 1956	06:56
Sco	2 Feb 1956	13:34
Sag	5 Feb 1956	00:14
Cap	7 Feb 1956	13:08
Aqu	10 Feb 1956	01:52
Pis	12 Feb 1956	12:51
Ari	14 Feb 1956	21:48
Tau	17 Feb 1956	04:48
Gem	19 Feb 1956	09:50
Can	21 Feb 1956	12:49
Leo	23 Feb 1956	14:10
Vir	25 Feb 1956	15:05
Lib	27 Feb 1956	17:21
Sco	29 Feb 1956	22:46
Sag	3 Mar 1956	08:10
Cap	5 Mar 1956	20:33
Aqu	8 Mar 1956	09:19
Pis	10 Mar 1956	20:11
Ari	13 Mar 1956	04:26
Tau	15 Mar 1956	10:32
Gem	17 Mar 1956	15:11
Can	19 Mar 1956	18:47
Leo	21 Mar 1956	21:31
Vir	23 Mar 1956	23:53
Lib	26 Mar 1956	03:00
Sco	28 Mar 1956	08:19
Sag	30 Mar 1956	16:56
Cap	2 Apr 1956	04:38
Aqu	4 Apr 1956	17:24
Pis	7 Apr 1956	04:37
Ari	9 Apr 1956	12:45
Tau	11 Apr 1956	18:03
Gem	13 Apr 1956	21:30
Can	16 Apr 1956	00:15
Leo	18 Apr 1956	03:00
Vir	20 Apr 1956	06:17
Lib	22 Apr 1956	10:37
Sco	24 Apr 1956	16:45
Sag	27 Apr 1956	01:26
Cap	29 Apr 1956	12:45
Aqu	2 May 1956	01:27
Pis	4 May 1956	13:14
Ari	6 May 1956	22:04
Tau	9 May 1956	03:23
Gem	11 May 1956	06:00
Can	13 May 1956	07:21
Leo	15 May 1956	08:52
Vir	17 May 1956	11:40
Lib	19 May 1956	16:26
Sco	21 May 1956	23:27
Sag	24 May 1956	08:47
Cap	26 May 1956	20:11
Aqu	29 May 1956	08:51
Pis	31 May 1956	21:09
Ari	3 Jun 1956	07:04
Tau	5 Jun 1956	13:20
Gem	7 Jun 1956	16:09
Can	9 Jun 1956	16:42
Leo	11 Jun 1956	16:45
Vir	13 Jun 1956	18:03
Lib	15 Jun 1956	21:59
Sco	18 Jun 1956	05:03
Sag	20 Jun 1956	14:56
Cap	23 Jun 1956	02:43
Aqu	25 Jun 1956	15:25
Pis	28 Jun 1956	03:54
Ari	30 Jun 1956	14:42
Tau	2 Jul 1956	22:24
Gem	5 Jul 1956	02:25
Can	7 Jul 1956	03:19
Leo	9 Jul 1956	02:42
Vir	11 Jul 1956	02:35
Lib	13 Jul 1956	04:54
Sco	15 Jul 1956	10:58
Sag	17 Jul 1956	20:38
Cap	20 Jul 1956	08:41
Aqu	22 Jul 1956	21:28
Pis	25 Jul 1956	09:50
Ari	27 Jul 1956	20:53
Tau	30 Jul 1956	05:40
Gem	1 Aug 1956	11:15
Can	3 Aug 1956	13:31
Leo	5 Aug 1956	13:26
Vir	7 Aug 1956	12:50
Lib	9 Aug 1956	13:52
Sco	11 Aug 1956	18:20
Sag	14 Aug 1956	03:01
Cap	16 Aug 1956	14:48
Aqu	19 Aug 1956	03:37
Pis	21 Aug 1956	15:47
Ari	24 Aug 1956	02:29
Tau	26 Aug 1956	11:23
Gem	28 Aug 1956	17:59
Can	30 Aug 1956	21:50
Leo	1 Sep 1956	23:13
Vir	3 Sep 1956	23:20
Lib	6 Sep 1956	00:05
Sco	8 Sep 1956	03:27
Sag	10 Sep 1956	10:47
Cap	12 Sep 1956	21:46
Aqu	15 Sep 1956	10:28
Pis	17 Sep 1956	22:33
Ari	20 Sep 1956	08:47
Tau	22 Sep 1956	17:01
Gem	24 Sep 1956	23:24
Can	27 Sep 1956	03:59
Leo	29 Sep 1956	06:48
Vir	1 Oct 1956	08:24
Lib	3 Oct 1956	10:02
Sco	5 Oct 1956	13:20
Sag	7 Oct 1956	19:46
Cap	10 Oct 1956	05:48
Aqu	12 Oct 1956	18:09
Pis	15 Oct 1956	06:24
Ari	17 Oct 1956	16:35
Tau	20 Oct 1956	00:06
Gem	22 Oct 1956	05:28
Can	24 Oct 1956	09:23
Leo	26 Oct 1956	12:27
Vir	28 Oct 1956	15:09
Lib	30 Oct 1956	18:10
Sco	1 Nov 1956	22:25
Sag	4 Nov 1956	04:56
Cap	6 Nov 1956	14:25
Aqu	9 Nov 1956	02:19
Pis	11 Nov 1956	14:50
Ari	14 Nov 1956	01:35
Tau	16 Nov 1956	09:11
Gem	18 Nov 1956	13:44
Can	20 Nov 1956	16:17
Leo	22 Nov 1956	18:10
Vir	24 Nov 1956	20:32
Lib	27 Nov 1956	00:11
Sco	29 Nov 1956	05:34
Sag	1 Dec 1956	12:59
Cap	3 Dec 1956	22:37
Aqu	6 Dec 1956	10:16
Pis	8 Dec 1956	22:56
Ari	11 Dec 1956	10:36
Tau	13 Dec 1956	19:15
Gem	16 Dec 1956	00:05
Can	18 Dec 1956	01:51
Leo	20 Dec 1956	02:11
Vir	22 Dec 1956	02:56
Lib	24 Dec 1956	05:39
Sco	26 Dec 1956	11:09
Sag	28 Dec 1956	19:20
Cap	31 Dec 1956	05:37

1957

Aqu 2 Jan 1957 17:25
Pis 5 Jan 1957 06:04
Ari 7 Jan 1957 18:22
Tau 10 Jan 1957 04:26
Gem 12 Jan 1957 10:42
Can 14 Jan 1957 13:04
Leo 16 Jan 1957 12:50
Vir 18 Jan 1957 12:04
Lib 20 Jan 1957 12:56
Sco 22 Jan 1957 17:03
Sag 25 Jan 1957 00:53
Cap 27 Jan 1957 11:33
Aqu 29 Jan 1957 23:42

Pis 1 Feb 1957 12:20
Ari 4 Feb 1957 00:41
Tau 6 Feb 1957 11:36
Gem 8 Feb 1957 19:34
Can 10 Feb 1957 23:37
Leo 13 Feb 1957 00:17
Vir 14 Feb 1957 23:17
Lib 16 Feb 1957 22:51
Sco 19 Feb 1957 01:07
Sag 21 Feb 1957 07:23
Cap 23 Feb 1957 17:27
Aqu 26 Feb 1957 05:43
Pis 28 Feb 1957 18:25

Ari 3 Mar 1957 06:30
Tau 5 Mar 1957 17:20
Gem 8 Mar 1957 02:02
Can 10 Mar 1957 07:44
Leo 12 Mar 1957 10:10
Vir 14 Mar 1957 10:19
Lib 16 Mar 1957 09:59
Sco 18 Mar 1957 11:16
Sag 20 Mar 1957 15:54
Cap 23 Mar 1957 00:35
Aqu 25 Mar 1957 12:17
Pis 28 Mar 1957 00:59
Ari 30 Mar 1957 12:54

Tau 1 Apr 1957 23:10
Gem 4 Apr 1957 07:30
Can 6 Apr 1957 13:36
Leo 8 Apr 1957 17:24
Vir 10 Apr 1957 19:13
Lib 12 Apr 1957 20:08
Sco 14 Apr 1957 21:46
Sag 17 Apr 1957 01:44
Cap 19 Apr 1957 09:09
Aqu 21 Apr 1957 19:53
Pis 24 Apr 1957 08:22
Ari 26 Apr 1957 20:21
Tau 29 Apr 1957 06:17

Gem 1 May 1957 13:46
Can 3 May 1957 19:08
Leo 5 May 1957 22:53
Vir 8 May 1957 01:36
Lib 10 May 1957 03:57
Sco 12 May 1957 06:48
Sag 14 May 1957 11:14
Cap 16 May 1957 18:13
Aqu 19 May 1957 04:12
Pis 21 May 1957 16:20
Ari 24 May 1957 04:33
Tau 26 May 1957 14:42
Gem 28 May 1957 21:46
Can 31 May 1957 02:05

Leo 2 Jun 1957 04:45
Vir 4 Jun 1957 06:59
Lib 6 Jun 1957 09:46
Sco 8 Jun 1957 13:41
Sag 10 Jun 1957 19:09
Cap 13 Jun 1957 02:37
Aqu 15 Jun 1957 12:24
Pis 18 Jun 1957 00:15
Ari 20 Jun 1957 12:45
Tau 22 Jun 1957 23:37
Gem 25 Jun 1957 07:06
Can 27 Jun 1957 11:00
Leo 29 Jun 1957 12:30

Vir 1 Jul 1957 13:24
Lib 3 Jul 1957 15:16
Sco 5 Jul 1957 19:10
Sag 8 Jul 1957 01:21
Cap 10 Jul 1957 09:35
Aqu 12 Jul 1957 19:43
Pis 15 Jul 1957 07:32
Ari 17 Jul 1957 20:14
Tau 20 Jul 1957 07:57
Gem 22 Jul 1957 16:33
Can 24 Jul 1957 21:04
Leo 26 Jul 1957 22:16
Vir 28 Jul 1957 21:59
Lib 30 Jul 1957 22:21

Sco 2 Aug 1957 01:01
Sag 4 Aug 1957 06:47
Cap 6 Aug 1957 15:23
Aqu 9 Aug 1957 02:02
Pis 11 Aug 1957 14:02
Ari 14 Aug 1957 02:46
Tau 16 Aug 1957 15:00
Gem 19 Aug 1957 00:50
Can 21 Aug 1957 06:48
Leo 23 Aug 1957 08:50
Vir 25 Aug 1957 08:25
Lib 27 Aug 1957 07:42
Sco 29 Aug 1957 08:46
Sag 31 Aug 1957 13:08

Cap 2 Sep 1957 21:06
Aqu 5 Sep 1957 07:50
Pis 7 Sep 1957 20:04
Ari 10 Sep 1957 08:44
Tau 12 Sep 1957 20:57
Gem 15 Sep 1957 07:25
Can 17 Sep 1957 14:48
Leo 19 Sep 1957 18:30
Vir 21 Sep 1957 19:11
Lib 23 Sep 1957 18:32
Sco 25 Sep 1957 18:40
Sag 27 Sep 1957 21:28
Cap 30 Sep 1957 04:00

Aqu 2 Oct 1957 14:04
Pis 5 Oct 1957 02:17
Ari 7 Oct 1957 14:56
Tau 10 Oct 1957 02:47
Gem 12 Oct 1957 13:00
Can 14 Oct 1957 20:53
Leo 17 Oct 1957 01:58
Vir 19 Oct 1957 04:23
Lib 21 Oct 1957 05:03
Sco 23 Oct 1957 05:31
Sag 25 Oct 1957 07:33
Cap 27 Oct 1957 12:42
Aqu 29 Oct 1957 21:33

Pis 1 Nov 1957 09:18
Ari 3 Nov 1957 21:59
Tau 6 Nov 1957 09:37
Gem 8 Nov 1957 19:08
Can 11 Nov 1957 02:23
Leo 13 Nov 1957 07:36
Vir 15 Nov 1957 11:06
Lib 17 Nov 1957 13:25
Sco 19 Nov 1957 15:17
Sag 21 Nov 1957 17:51
Cap 23 Nov 1957 22:30
Aqu 26 Nov 1957 06:16
Pis 28 Nov 1957 17:16

Ari 1 Dec 1957 05:56
Tau 3 Dec 1957 17:47
Gem 6 Dec 1957 02:59
Can 8 Dec 1957 09:15
Leo 10 Dec 1957 13:22
Vir 12 Dec 1957 16:28
Lib 14 Dec 1957 19:22
Sco 16 Dec 1957 22:35
Sag 19 Dec 1957 02:31
Cap 21 Dec 1957 07:47
Aqu 23 Dec 1957 15:19
Pis 26 Dec 1957 01:41
Ari 28 Dec 1957 14:12
Tau 31 Dec 1957 02:36

1958

Sign	Date	Time
Gem	2 Jan 1958	12:20
Can	4 Jan 1958	18:21
Leo	6 Jan 1958	21:21
Vir	8 Jan 1958	22:59
Lib	11 Jan 1958	00:52
Sco	13 Jan 1958	04:02
Sag	15 Jan 1958	08:50
Cap	17 Jan 1958	15:13
Aqu	19 Jan 1958	23:23
Pis	22 Jan 1958	09:42
Ari	24 Jan 1958	22:03
Tau	27 Jan 1958	10:56
Gem	29 Jan 1958	21:46

Sign	Date	Time
Can	1 Feb 1958	04:40
Leo	3 Feb 1958	07:37
Vir	5 Feb 1958	08:10
Lib	7 Feb 1958	08:23
Sco	9 Feb 1958	10:04
Sag	11 Feb 1958	14:12
Cap	13 Feb 1958	20:55
Aqu	16 Feb 1958	05:51
Pis	18 Feb 1958	16:39
Ari	21 Feb 1958	05:01
Tau	23 Feb 1958	18:04
Gem	26 Feb 1958	05:52
Can	28 Feb 1958	14:15

Sign	Date	Time
Leo	2 Mar 1958	18:26
Vir	4 Mar 1958	19:14
Lib	6 Mar 1958	18:35
Sco	8 Mar 1958	18:34
Sag	10 Mar 1958	20:57
Cap	13 Mar 1958	02:37
Aqu	15 Mar 1958	11:28
Pis	17 Mar 1958	22:41
Ari	20 Mar 1958	11:17
Tau	23 Mar 1958	00:15
Gem	25 Mar 1958	12:18
Can	27 Mar 1958	21:51
Leo	30 Mar 1958	03:44

Sign	Date	Time
Vir	1 Apr 1958	06:01
Lib	3 Apr 1958	05:53
Sco	5 Apr 1958	05:16
Sag	7 Apr 1958	06:06
Cap	9 Apr 1958	10:01
Aqu	11 Apr 1958	17:41
Pis	14 Apr 1958	04:38
Ari	16 Apr 1958	17:22
Tau	19 Apr 1958	06:16
Gem	21 Apr 1958	18:03
Can	24 Apr 1958	03:45
Leo	26 Apr 1958	10:42
Vir	28 Apr 1958	14:39
Lib	30 Apr 1958	16:06

Sign	Date	Time
Sco	2 May 1958	16:14
Sag	4 May 1958	16:43
Cap	6 May 1958	19:21
Aqu	9 May 1958	01:30
Pis	11 May 1958	11:27
Ari	13 May 1958	23:57
Tau	16 May 1958	12:49
Gem	19 May 1958	00:13
Can	21 May 1958	09:22
Leo	23 May 1958	16:14
Vir	25 May 1958	20:59
Lib	27 May 1958	23:54
Sco	30 May 1958	01:33

Sign	Date	Time
Sag	1 Jun 1958	02:53
Cap	3 Jun 1958	05:22
Aqu	5 Jun 1958	10:34
Pis	7 Jun 1958	19:23
Ari	10 Jun 1958	07:20
Tau	12 Jun 1958	20:12
Gem	15 Jun 1958	07:30
Can	17 Jun 1958	16:03
Leo	19 Jun 1958	22:03
Vir	22 Jun 1958	02:21
Lib	24 Jun 1958	05:42
Sco	26 Jun 1958	08:30
Sag	28 Jun 1958	11:11
Cap	30 Jun 1958	14:32

Sign	Date	Time
Aqu	2 Jul 1958	19:45
Pis	5 Jul 1958	03:57
Ari	7 Jul 1958	15:18
Tau	10 Jul 1958	04:09
Gem	12 Jul 1958	15:46
Can	15 Jul 1958	00:14
Leo	17 Jul 1958	05:30
Vir	19 Jul 1958	08:41
Lib	21 Jul 1958	11:11
Sco	23 Jul 1958	13:57
Sag	25 Jul 1958	17:25
Cap	27 Jul 1958	21:53
Aqu	30 Jul 1958	03:52

Sign	Date	Time
Pis	1 Aug 1958	12:12
Ari	3 Aug 1958	23:14
Tau	6 Aug 1958	12:04
Gem	9 Aug 1958	00:15
Can	11 Aug 1958	09:24
Leo	13 Aug 1958	14:42
Vir	15 Aug 1958	17:06
Lib	17 Aug 1958	18:16
Sco	19 Aug 1958	19:49
Sag	21 Aug 1958	22:48
Cap	24 Aug 1958	03:38
Aqu	26 Aug 1958	10:28
Pis	28 Aug 1958	19:25
Ari	31 Aug 1958	06:35

Sign	Date	Time
Tau	2 Sep 1958	19:23
Gem	5 Sep 1958	08:06
Can	7 Sep 1958	18:22
Leo	10 Sep 1958	00:40
Vir	12 Sep 1958	03:18
Lib	14 Sep 1958	03:44
Sco	16 Sep 1958	03:49
Sag	18 Sep 1958	05:16
Cap	20 Sep 1958	09:13
Aqu	22 Sep 1958	16:03
Pis	25 Sep 1958	01:33
Ari	27 Sep 1958	13:07
Tau	30 Sep 1958	01:58

Sign	Date	Time
Gem	2 Oct 1958	14:50
Can	5 Oct 1958	01:59
Leo	7 Oct 1958	09:49
Vir	9 Oct 1958	13:48
Lib	11 Oct 1958	14:43
Sco	13 Oct 1958	14:11
Sag	15 Oct 1958	14:09
Cap	17 Oct 1958	16:23
Aqu	19 Oct 1958	22:05
Pis	22 Oct 1958	07:20
Ari	24 Oct 1958	19:10
Tau	27 Oct 1958	08:07
Gem	29 Oct 1958	20:49

Sign	Date	Time
Can	1 Nov 1958	08:08
Leo	3 Nov 1958	17:02
Vir	5 Nov 1958	22:44
Lib	8 Nov 1958	01:15
Sco	10 Nov 1958	01:29
Sag	12 Nov 1958	01:03
Cap	14 Nov 1958	01:55
Aqu	16 Nov 1958	05:52
Pis	18 Nov 1958	13:57
Ari	21 Nov 1958	01:28
Tau	23 Nov 1958	14:30
Gem	26 Nov 1958	03:00
Can	28 Nov 1958	13:50
Leo	30 Nov 1958	22:40

Sign	Date	Time
Vir	3 Dec 1958	05:17
Lib	5 Dec 1958	09:30
Sco	7 Dec 1958	11:27
Sag	9 Dec 1958	12:01
Cap	11 Dec 1958	12:47
Aqu	13 Dec 1958	15:38
Pis	15 Dec 1958	22:13
Ari	18 Dec 1958	08:45
Tau	20 Dec 1958	21:37
Gem	23 Dec 1958	10:08
Can	25 Dec 1958	20:32
Leo	28 Dec 1958	04:33
Vir	30 Dec 1958	10:40

Moon Signs

1959

Lib	1 Jan 1959	15:20
Sco	3 Jan 1959	18:41
Sag	5 Jan 1959	20:55
Cap	7 Jan 1959	22:50
Aqu	10 Jan 1959	01:52
Pis	12 Jan 1959	07:40
Ari	14 Jan 1959	17:09
Tau	17 Jan 1959	05:32
Gem	19 Jan 1959	18:15
Can	22 Jan 1959	04:46
Leo	24 Jan 1959	12:12
Vir	26 Jan 1959	17:13
Lib	28 Jan 1959	20:53
Sco	31 Jan 1959	00:05

Sag	2 Feb 1959	03:10
Cap	4 Feb 1959	06:28
Aqu	6 Feb 1959	10:41
Pis	8 Feb 1959	16:50
Ari	11 Feb 1959	01:55
Tau	13 Feb 1959	13:47
Gem	16 Feb 1959	02:39
Can	18 Feb 1959	13:49
Leo	20 Feb 1959	21:36
Vir	23 Feb 1959	02:05
Lib	25 Feb 1959	04:28
Sco	27 Feb 1959	06:14

Sag	1 Mar 1959	08:33
Cap	3 Mar 1959	12:06
Aqu	5 Mar 1959	17:16
Pis	8 Mar 1959	00:26
Ari	10 Mar 1959	09:54
Tau	12 Mar 1959	21:37
Gem	15 Mar 1959	10:30
Can	17 Mar 1959	22:26
Leo	20 Mar 1959	07:22
Vir	22 Mar 1959	12:26
Lib	24 Mar 1959	14:26
Sco	26 Mar 1959	14:53
Sag	28 Mar 1959	15:31
Cap	30 Mar 1959	17:48

Aqu	1 Apr 1959	22:42
Pis	4 Apr 1959	06:23
Ari	6 Apr 1959	16:32
Tau	9 Apr 1959	04:31
Gem	11 Apr 1959	17:24
Can	14 Apr 1959	05:47
Leo	16 Apr 1959	15:54
Vir	18 Apr 1959	22:26
Lib	21 Apr 1959	01:17
Sco	23 Apr 1959	01:33
Sag	25 Apr 1959	00:59
Cap	27 Apr 1959	01:33
Aqu	29 Apr 1959	04:55

Pis	1 May 1959	11:59
Ari	3 May 1959	22:19
Tau	6 May 1959	10:39
Gem	8 May 1959	23:34
Can	11 May 1959	11:56
Leo	13 May 1959	22:39
Vir	16 May 1959	06:37
Lib	18 May 1959	11:05
Sco	20 May 1959	12:23
Sag	22 May 1959	11:50
Cap	24 May 1959	11:24
Aqu	26 May 1959	13:10
Pis	28 May 1959	18:42
Ari	31 May 1959	04:18

Tau	2 Jun 1959	16:37
Gem	5 Jun 1959	05:35
Can	7 Jun 1959	17:43
Leo	10 Jun 1959	04:18
Vir	12 Jun 1959	12:49
Lib	14 Jun 1959	18:41
Sco	16 Jun 1959	21:37
Sag	18 Jun 1959	22:13
Cap	20 Jun 1959	22:01
Aqu	22 Jun 1959	23:01
Pis	25 Jun 1959	03:10
Ari	27 Jun 1959	11:28
Tau	29 Jun 1959	23:11

Gem	2 Jul 1959	12:05
Can	5 Jul 1959	00:02
Leo	7 Jul 1959	10:07
Vir	9 Jul 1959	18:15
Lib	12 Jul 1959	00:25
Sco	14 Jul 1959	04:32
Sag	16 Jul 1959	06:41
Cap	18 Jul 1959	07:41
Aqu	20 Jul 1959	09:05
Pis	22 Jul 1959	12:42
Ari	24 Jul 1959	19:54
Tau	27 Jul 1959	06:43
Gem	29 Jul 1959	19:23

Can	1 Aug 1959	07:23
Leo	3 Aug 1959	17:09
Vir	6 Aug 1959	00:29
Lib	8 Aug 1959	05:56
Sco	10 Aug 1959	09:59
Sag	12 Aug 1959	12:57
Cap	14 Aug 1959	15:18
Aqu	16 Aug 1959	17:53
Pis	18 Aug 1959	22:00
Ari	21 Aug 1959	04:52
Tau	23 Aug 1959	14:58
Gem	26 Aug 1959	03:18
Can	28 Aug 1959	15:33
Leo	31 Aug 1959	01:32

Vir	2 Sep 1959	08:30
Lib	4 Sep 1959	12:55
Sco	6 Sep 1959	15:52
Sag	8 Sep 1959	18:20
Cap	10 Sep 1959	21:04
Aqu	13 Sep 1959	00:43
Pis	15 Sep 1959	05:54
Ari	17 Sep 1959	13:16
Tau	19 Sep 1959	23:13
Gem	22 Sep 1959	11:16
Can	24 Sep 1959	23:48
Leo	27 Sep 1959	10:35
Vir	29 Sep 1959	18:03

Lib	1 Oct 1959	22:07
Sco	3 Oct 1959	23:53
Sag	6 Oct 1959	00:54
Cap	8 Oct 1959	02:39
Aqu	10 Oct 1959	06:12
Pis	12 Oct 1959	12:06
Ari	14 Oct 1959	20:20
Tau	17 Oct 1959	06:39
Gem	19 Oct 1959	18:39
Can	22 Oct 1959	07:22
Leo	24 Oct 1959	19:03
Vir	27 Oct 1959	03:47
Lib	29 Oct 1959	08:40
Sco	31 Oct 1959	10:13

Sag	2 Nov 1959	10:01
Cap	4 Nov 1959	10:05
Aqu	6 Nov 1959	12:14
Pis	8 Nov 1959	17:35
Ari	11 Nov 1959	02:10
Tau	13 Nov 1959	13:04
Gem	16 Nov 1959	01:16
Can	18 Nov 1959	13:56
Leo	21 Nov 1959	02:03
Vir	23 Nov 1959	12:06
Lib	25 Nov 1959	18:40
Sco	27 Nov 1959	21:20
Sag	29 Nov 1959	21:11

Cap	1 Dec 1959	20:11
Aqu	3 Dec 1959	20:35
Pis	6 Dec 1959	00:17
Ari	8 Dec 1959	07:59
Tau	10 Dec 1959	18:55
Gem	13 Dec 1959	07:23
Can	15 Dec 1959	20:00
Leo	18 Dec 1959	07:57
Vir	20 Dec 1959	18:29
Lib	23 Dec 1959	02:27
Sco	25 Dec 1959	07:00
Sag	27 Dec 1959	08:14
Cap	29 Dec 1959	07:37
Aqu	31 Dec 1959	07:15

1960

Pis	2 Jan 1960	09:19
Ari	4 Jan 1960	15:22
Tau	7 Jan 1960	01:22
Gem	9 Jan 1960	13:44
Can	12 Jan 1960	02:22
Leo	14 Jan 1960	13:58
Vir	17 Jan 1960	00:02
Lib	19 Jan 1960	08:13
Sco	21 Jan 1960	13:58
Sag	23 Jan 1960	17:02
Cap	25 Jan 1960	17:59
Aqu	27 Jan 1960	18:18
Pis	29 Jan 1960	19:57

Ari	1 Feb 1960	00:40
Tau	3 Feb 1960	09:16
Gem	5 Feb 1960	20:58
Can	8 Feb 1960	09:36
Leo	10 Feb 1960	21:07
Vir	13 Feb 1960	06:34
Lib	15 Feb 1960	13:54
Sco	17 Feb 1960	19:23
Sag	19 Feb 1960	23:10
Cap	22 Feb 1960	01:38
Aqu	24 Feb 1960	03:32
Pis	26 Feb 1960	06:03
Ari	28 Feb 1960	10:38

Tau	1 Mar 1960	18:18
Gem	4 Mar 1960	05:07
Can	6 Mar 1960	17:36
Leo	9 Mar 1960	05:24
Vir	11 Mar 1960	14:46
Lib	13 Mar 1960	21:18
Sco	16 Mar 1960	01:36
Sag	18 Mar 1960	04:37
Cap	20 Mar 1960	07:14
Aqu	22 Mar 1960	10:10
Pis	24 Mar 1960	14:02
Ari	26 Mar 1960	19:29
Tau	29 Mar 1960	03:13
Gem	31 Mar 1960	13:32

Can	3 Apr 1960	01:45
Leo	5 Apr 1960	14:00
Vir	8 Apr 1960	00:00
Lib	10 Apr 1960	06:35
Sco	12 Apr 1960	10:00
Sag	14 Apr 1960	11:37
Cap	16 Apr 1960	13:01
Aqu	18 Apr 1960	15:32
Pis	20 Apr 1960	19:55
Ari	23 Apr 1960	02:23
Tau	25 Apr 1960	10:50
Gem	27 Apr 1960	21:16
Can	30 Apr 1960	09:22

Leo	2 May 1960	21:58
Vir	5 May 1960	08:57
Lib	7 May 1960	16:29
Sco	9 May 1960	20:05
Sag	11 May 1960	20:54
Cap	13 May 1960	20:50
Aqu	15 May 1960	21:51
Pis	18 May 1960	01:24
Ari	20 May 1960	07:55
Tau	22 May 1960	16:59
Gem	25 May 1960	03:54
Can	27 May 1960	16:06
Leo	30 May 1960	04:50

Vir	1 Jun 1960	16:37
Lib	4 Jun 1960	01:29
Sco	6 Jun 1960	06:19
Sag	8 Jun 1960	07:30
Cap	10 Jun 1960	06:47
Aqu	12 Jun 1960	06:22
Pis	14 Jun 1960	08:18
Ari	16 Jun 1960	13:43
Tau	18 Jun 1960	22:33
Gem	21 Jun 1960	09:46
Can	23 Jun 1960	22:09
Leo	26 Jun 1960	10:51
Vir	28 Jun 1960	22:51

Lib	1 Jul 1960	08:45
Sco	3 Jul 1960	15:07
Sag	5 Jul 1960	17:42
Cap	7 Jul 1960	17:33
Aqu	9 Jul 1960	16:43
Pis	11 Jul 1960	17:19
Ari	13 Jul 1960	21:08
Tau	16 Jul 1960	04:48
Gem	18 Jul 1960	15:40
Can	21 Jul 1960	04:08
Leo	23 Jul 1960	16:45
Vir	26 Jul 1960	04:31
Lib	28 Jul 1960	14:32
Sco	30 Jul 1960	21:53

Sag	2 Aug 1960	02:02
Cap	4 Aug 1960	03:24
Aqu	6 Aug 1960	03:20
Pis	8 Aug 1960	03:42
Ari	10 Aug 1960	06:21
Tau	12 Aug 1960	12:36
Gem	14 Aug 1960	22:29
Can	17 Aug 1960	10:42
Leo	19 Aug 1960	23:17
Vir	22 Aug 1960	10:40
Lib	24 Aug 1960	20:08
Sco	27 Aug 1960	03:22
Sag	29 Aug 1960	08:18
Cap	31 Aug 1960	11:07

Aqu	2 Sep 1960	12:34
Pis	4 Sep 1960	13:51
Ari	6 Sep 1960	16:26
Tau	8 Sep 1960	21:45
Gem	11 Sep 1960	06:30
Can	13 Sep 1960	18:10
Leo	16 Sep 1960	06:46
Vir	18 Sep 1960	18:06
Lib	21 Sep 1960	02:57
Sco	23 Sep 1960	09:16
Sag	25 Sep 1960	13:41
Cap	27 Sep 1960	16:53
Aqu	29 Sep 1960	19:32

Pis	1 Oct 1960	22:14
Ari	4 Oct 1960	01:46
Tau	6 Oct 1960	07:08
Gem	8 Oct 1960	15:16
Can	11 Oct 1960	02:18
Leo	13 Oct 1960	14:54
Vir	16 Oct 1960	02:39
Lib	18 Oct 1960	11:30
Sco	20 Oct 1960	17:05
Sag	22 Oct 1960	20:15
Cap	24 Oct 1960	22:28
Aqu	27 Oct 1960	00:57
Pis	29 Oct 1960	04:26
Ari	31 Oct 1960	09:11

Tau	2 Nov 1960	15:27
Gem	4 Nov 1960	23:44
Can	7 Nov 1960	10:26
Leo	9 Nov 1960	22:59
Vir	12 Nov 1960	11:22
Lib	14 Nov 1960	21:06
Sco	17 Nov 1960	02:51
Sag	19 Nov 1960	05:16
Cap	21 Nov 1960	06:01
Aqu	23 Nov 1960	07:04
Pis	25 Nov 1960	09:49
Ari	27 Nov 1960	14:51
Tau	29 Nov 1960	21:59

Gem	2 Dec 1960	07:00
Can	4 Dec 1960	17:51
Leo	7 Dec 1960	06:20
Vir	9 Dec 1960	19:12
Lib	12 Dec 1960	06:09
Sco	14 Dec 1960	13:11
Sag	16 Dec 1960	16:05
Cap	18 Dec 1960	16:15
Aqu	20 Dec 1960	15:48
Pis	22 Dec 1960	16:47
Ari	24 Dec 1960	20:34
Tau	27 Dec 1960	03:30
Gem	29 Dec 1960	13:01

Moon Signs

1961

Can	1 Jan 1961	00:21
Leo	3 Jan 1961	12:53
Vir	6 Jan 1961	01:47
Lib	8 Jan 1961	13:29
Sco	10 Jan 1961	22:07
Sag	13 Jan 1961	02:38
Cap	15 Jan 1961	03:40
Aqu	17 Jan 1961	02:55
Pis	19 Jan 1961	02:32
Ari	21 Jan 1961	04:26
Tau	23 Jan 1961	09:52
Gem	25 Jan 1961	18:49
Can	28 Jan 1961	06:21
Leo	30 Jan 1961	19:04
Vir	2 Feb 1961	07:47
Lib	4 Feb 1961	19:26
Sco	7 Feb 1961	04:50
Sag	9 Feb 1961	10:59
Cap	11 Feb 1961	13:49
Aqu	13 Feb 1961	14:13
Pis	15 Feb 1961	13:52
Ari	17 Feb 1961	14:41
Tau	19 Feb 1961	18:20
Gem	22 Feb 1961	01:52
Can	24 Feb 1961	12:48
Leo	27 Feb 1961	01:34
Vir	1 Mar 1961	14:11
Lib	4 Mar 1961	01:20
Sco	6 Mar 1961	10:22
Sag	8 Mar 1961	17:03
Cap	10 Mar 1961	21:17
Aqu	12 Mar 1961	23:28
Pis	15 Mar 1961	00:25
Ari	17 Mar 1961	01:32
Tau	19 Mar 1961	04:25
Gem	21 Mar 1961	10:32
Can	23 Mar 1961	20:22
Leo	26 Mar 1961	08:48
Vir	28 Mar 1961	21:28
Lib	31 Mar 1961	08:20
Sco	2 Apr 1961	16:35
Sag	4 Apr 1961	22:32
Cap	7 Apr 1961	02:51
Aqu	9 Apr 1961	06:02
Pis	11 Apr 1961	08:31
Ari	13 Apr 1961	10:55
Tau	15 Apr 1961	14:17
Gem	17 Apr 1961	19:55
Can	20 Apr 1961	04:49
Leo	22 Apr 1961	16:42
Vir	25 Apr 1961	05:30
Lib	27 Apr 1961	16:33
Sco	30 Apr 1961	00:25

Sag	2 May 1961	05:24
Cap	4 May 1961	08:39
Aqu	6 May 1961	11:23
Pis	8 May 1961	14:22
Ari	10 May 1961	17:55
Tau	12 May 1961	22:25
Gem	15 May 1961	04:34
Can	17 May 1961	13:17
Leo	20 May 1961	00:44
Vir	22 May 1961	13:37
Lib	25 May 1961	01:16
Sco	27 May 1961	09:33
Sag	29 May 1961	14:09
Cap	31 May 1961	16:19
Aqu	2 Jun 1961	17:44
Pis	4 Jun 1961	19:50
Ari	6 Jun 1961	23:23
Tau	9 Jun 1961	04:37
Gem	11 Jun 1961	11:40
Can	13 Jun 1961	20:49
Leo	16 Jun 1961	08:15
Vir	18 Jun 1961	21:11
Lib	21 Jun 1961	09:30
Sco	23 Jun 1961	18:50
Sag	26 Jun 1961	00:03
Cap	28 Jun 1961	01:58
Aqu	30 Jun 1961	02:17
Pis	2 Jul 1961	02:52
Ari	4 Jul 1961	05:11
Tau	6 Jul 1961	10:01
Gem	8 Jul 1961	17:26
Can	11 Jul 1961	03:13
Leo	13 Jul 1961	14:56
Vir	16 Jul 1961	03:54
Lib	18 Jul 1961	16:37
Sco	21 Jul 1961	03:03
Sag	23 Jul 1961	09:40
Cap	25 Jul 1961	12:27
Aqu	27 Jul 1961	12:40
Pis	29 Jul 1961	12:13
Ari	31 Jul 1961	12:56
Tau	2 Aug 1961	16:19
Gem	4 Aug 1961	23:04
Can	7 Aug 1961	08:56
Leo	9 Aug 1961	20:59
Vir	12 Aug 1961	09:59
Lib	14 Aug 1961	22:42
Sco	17 Aug 1961	09:43
Sag	19 Aug 1961	17:43
Cap	21 Aug 1961	22:05
Aqu	23 Aug 1961	23:24
Pis	25 Aug 1961	23:02
Ari	27 Aug 1961	22:49
Tau	30 Aug 1961	00:37

Gem	1 Sep 1961	05:52
Can	3 Sep 1961	15:00
Leo	6 Sep 1961	03:00
Vir	8 Sep 1961	16:04
Lib	11 Sep 1961	04:32
Sco	13 Sep 1961	15:21
Sag	15 Sep 1961	23:53
Cap	18 Sep 1961	05:41
Aqu	20 Sep 1961	08:42
Pis	22 Sep 1961	09:35
Ari	24 Sep 1961	09:39
Tau	26 Sep 1961	10:42
Gem	28 Sep 1961	14:32
Can	30 Sep 1961	22:19
Leo	3 Oct 1961	09:43
Vir	5 Oct 1961	22:44
Lib	8 Oct 1961	11:02
Sco	10 Oct 1961	21:18
Sag	13 Oct 1961	05:20
Cap	15 Oct 1961	11:22
Aqu	17 Oct 1961	15:36
Pis	19 Oct 1961	18:09
Ari	21 Oct 1961	19:35
Tau	23 Oct 1961	21:06
Gem	26 Oct 1961	00:25
Can	28 Oct 1961	07:02
Leo	30 Oct 1961	17:29
Vir	2 Nov 1961	06:16
Lib	4 Nov 1961	18:41
Sco	7 Nov 1961	04:39
Sag	9 Nov 1961	11:49
Cap	11 Nov 1961	16:58
Aqu	13 Nov 1961	20:58
Pis	16 Nov 1961	00:17
Ari	18 Nov 1961	03:09
Tau	20 Nov 1961	06:02
Gem	22 Nov 1961	09:59
Can	24 Nov 1961	16:20
Leo	27 Nov 1961	02:01
Vir	29 Nov 1961	14:24
Lib	2 Dec 1961	03:06
Sco	4 Dec 1961	13:28
Sag	6 Dec 1961	20:23
Cap	9 Dec 1961	00:29
Aqu	11 Dec 1961	03:10
Pis	13 Dec 1961	05:41
Ari	15 Dec 1961	08:43
Tau	17 Dec 1961	12:38
Gem	19 Dec 1961	17:47
Can	22 Dec 1961	00:50
Leo	24 Dec 1961	10:25
Vir	26 Dec 1961	22:29
Lib	29 Dec 1961	11:25
Sco	31 Dec 1961	22:40

1962

Sign	Date	Time
Sag	3 Jan 1962	06:22
Cap	5 Jan 1962	10:22
Aqu	7 Jan 1962	11:59
Pis	9 Jan 1962	12:53
Ari	11 Jan 1962	14:34
Tau	13 Jan 1962	18:00
Gem	15 Jan 1962	23:42
Can	18 Jan 1962	07:39
Leo	20 Jan 1962	17:49
Vir	23 Jan 1962	05:53
Lib	25 Jan 1962	18:51
Sco	28 Jan 1962	06:53
Sag	30 Jan 1962	15:58

Sign	Date	Time
Cap	1 Feb 1962	21:08
Aqu	3 Feb 1962	22:55
Pis	5 Feb 1962	22:52
Ari	7 Feb 1962	22:50
Tau	10 Feb 1962	00:35
Gem	12 Feb 1962	05:18
Can	14 Feb 1962	13:20
Leo	17 Feb 1962	00:03
Vir	19 Feb 1962	12:26
Lib	22 Feb 1962	01:21
Sco	24 Feb 1962	13:35
Sag	26 Feb 1962	23:44

Sign	Date	Time
Cap	1 Mar 1962	06:37
Aqu	3 Mar 1962	09:50
Pis	5 Mar 1962	10:15
Ari	7 Mar 1962	09:31
Tau	9 Mar 1962	09:40
Gem	11 Mar 1962	12:36
Can	13 Mar 1962	19:25
Leo	16 Mar 1962	05:55
Vir	18 Mar 1962	18:32
Lib	21 Mar 1962	07:27
Sco	23 Mar 1962	19:27
Sag	26 Mar 1962	05:48
Cap	28 Mar 1962	13:44
Aqu	30 Mar 1962	18:42

Sign	Date	Time
Pis	1 Apr 1962	20:41
Ari	3 Apr 1962	20:40
Tau	5 Apr 1962	20:25
Gem	7 Apr 1962	22:00
Can	10 Apr 1962	03:12
Leo	12 Apr 1962	12:36
Vir	15 Apr 1962	00:56
Lib	17 Apr 1962	13:52
Sco	20 Apr 1962	01:35
Sag	22 Apr 1962	11:25
Cap	24 Apr 1962	19:19
Aqu	27 Apr 1962	01:06
Pis	29 Apr 1962	04:39

Sign	Date	Time
Ari	1 May 1962	06:11
Tau	3 May 1962	06:48
Gem	5 May 1962	08:16
Can	7 May 1962	12:28
Leo	9 May 1962	20:35
Vir	12 May 1962	08:10
Lib	14 May 1962	21:01
Sco	17 May 1962	08:41
Sag	19 May 1962	18:02
Cap	22 May 1962	01:07
Aqu	24 May 1962	06:30
Pis	26 May 1962	10:28
Ari	28 May 1962	13:14
Tau	30 May 1962	15:16

Sign	Date	Time
Gem	1 Jun 1962	17:40
Can	3 Jun 1962	21:57
Leo	6 Jun 1962	05:22
Vir	8 Jun 1962	16:11
Lib	11 Jun 1962	04:50
Sco	13 Jun 1962	16:44
Sag	16 Jun 1962	02:02
Cap	18 Jun 1962	08:28
Aqu	20 Jun 1962	12:48
Pis	22 Jun 1962	15:58
Ari	24 Jun 1962	18:42
Tau	26 Jun 1962	21:34
Gem	29 Jun 1962	01:09

Sign	Date	Time
Can	1 Jul 1962	06:18
Leo	3 Jul 1962	13:55
Vir	6 Jul 1962	00:22
Lib	8 Jul 1962	12:47
Sco	11 Jul 1962	01:04
Sag	13 Jul 1962	10:58
Cap	15 Jul 1962	17:31
Aqu	17 Jul 1962	21:06
Pis	19 Jul 1962	22:59
Ari	22 Jul 1962	00:33
Tau	24 Jul 1962	02:56
Gem	26 Jul 1962	06:56
Can	28 Jul 1962	13:00
Leo	30 Jul 1962	21:20

Sign	Date	Time
Vir	2 Aug 1962	07:57
Lib	4 Aug 1962	20:17
Sco	7 Aug 1962	08:54
Sag	9 Aug 1962	19:47
Cap	12 Aug 1962	03:16
Aqu	14 Aug 1962	07:06
Pis	16 Aug 1962	08:16
Ari	18 Aug 1962	08:25
Tau	20 Aug 1962	09:20
Gem	22 Aug 1962	12:28
Can	24 Aug 1962	18:33
Leo	27 Aug 1962	03:29
Vir	29 Aug 1962	14:35

Sign	Date	Time
Lib	1 Sep 1962	03:00
Sco	3 Sep 1962	15:45
Sag	6 Sep 1962	03:24
Cap	8 Sep 1962	12:17
Aqu	10 Sep 1962	17:25
Pis	12 Sep 1962	19:01
Ari	14 Sep 1962	18:32
Tau	16 Sep 1962	18:00
Gem	18 Sep 1962	19:28
Can	21 Sep 1962	00:26
Leo	23 Sep 1962	09:07
Vir	25 Sep 1962	20:30
Lib	28 Sep 1962	09:07
Sco	30 Sep 1962	21:47

Sign	Date	Time
Sag	3 Oct 1962	09:38
Cap	5 Oct 1962	19:33
Aqu	8 Oct 1962	02:19
Pis	10 Oct 1962	05:28
Ari	12 Oct 1962	05:40
Tau	14 Oct 1962	04:43
Gem	16 Oct 1962	04:50
Can	18 Oct 1962	08:04
Leo	20 Oct 1962	15:30
Vir	23 Oct 1962	02:30
Lib	25 Oct 1962	15:13
Sco	28 Oct 1962	03:47
Sag	30 Oct 1962	15:18

Sign	Date	Time
Cap	2 Nov 1962	01:16
Aqu	4 Nov 1962	09:00
Pis	6 Nov 1962	13:50
Ari	8 Nov 1962	15:44
Tau	10 Nov 1962	15:44
Gem	12 Nov 1962	15:43
Can	14 Nov 1962	17:48
Leo	16 Nov 1962	23:40
Vir	19 Nov 1962	09:33
Lib	21 Nov 1962	21:57
Sco	24 Nov 1962	10:32
Sag	26 Nov 1962	21:42
Cap	29 Nov 1962	06:59

Sign	Date	Time
Aqu	1 Dec 1962	14:24
Pis	3 Dec 1962	19:52
Ari	5 Dec 1962	23:15
Tau	8 Dec 1962	00:58
Gem	10 Dec 1962	02:07
Can	12 Dec 1962	04:21
Leo	14 Dec 1962	09:20
Vir	16 Dec 1962	17:58
Lib	19 Dec 1962	05:40
Sco	21 Dec 1962	18:17
Sag	24 Dec 1962	05:31
Cap	26 Dec 1962	14:17
Aqu	28 Dec 1962	20:41
Pis	31 Dec 1962	01:19

Moon Signs

1963

Sign	Date	Time
Ari	2 Jan 1963	04:47
Tau	4 Jan 1963	07:32
Gem	6 Jan 1963	10:13
Can	8 Jan 1963	13:41
Leo	10 Jan 1963	19:00
Vir	13 Jan 1963	03:07
Lib	15 Jan 1963	14:04
Sco	18 Jan 1963	02:34
Sag	20 Jan 1963	14:19
Cap	22 Jan 1963	23:21
Aqu	25 Jan 1963	05:13
Pis	27 Jan 1963	08:34
Ari	29 Jan 1963	10:43
Tau	31 Jan 1963	12:54

Sign	Date	Time
Gem	2 Feb 1963	16:02
Can	4 Feb 1963	20:40
Leo	7 Feb 1963	03:05
Vir	9 Feb 1963	11:36
Lib	11 Feb 1963	22:18
Sco	14 Feb 1963	10:38
Sag	16 Feb 1963	22:55
Cap	19 Feb 1963	08:58
Aqu	21 Feb 1963	15:22
Pis	23 Feb 1963	18:16
Ari	25 Feb 1963	19:04
Tau	27 Feb 1963	19:38

Sign	Date	Time
Gem	1 Mar 1963	21:39
Can	4 Mar 1963	02:08
Leo	6 Mar 1963	09:14
Vir	8 Mar 1963	18:33
Lib	11 Mar 1963	05:34
Sco	13 Mar 1963	17:50
Sag	16 Mar 1963	06:26
Cap	18 Mar 1963	17:33
Aqu	21 Mar 1963	01:19
Pis	23 Mar 1963	05:03
Ari	25 Mar 1963	05:36
Tau	27 Mar 1963	04:56
Gem	29 Mar 1963	05:12
Can	31 Mar 1963	08:13

Sign	Date	Time
Leo	2 Apr 1963	14:45
Vir	5 Apr 1963	00:20
Lib	7 Apr 1963	11:49
Sco	10 Apr 1963	00:13
Sag	12 Apr 1963	12:47
Cap	15 Apr 1963	00:25
Aqu	17 Apr 1963	09:32
Pis	19 Apr 1963	14:51
Ari	21 Apr 1963	16:28
Tau	23 Apr 1963	15:50
Gem	25 Apr 1963	15:06
Can	27 Apr 1963	16:27
Leo	29 Apr 1963	21:25

Sign	Date	Time
Vir	2 May 1963	06:12
Lib	4 May 1963	17:41
Sco	7 May 1963	06:15
Sag	9 May 1963	18:41
Cap	12 May 1963	06:12
Aqu	14 May 1963	15:50
Pis	16 May 1963	22:30
Ari	19 May 1963	01:46
Tau	21 May 1963	02:20
Gem	23 May 1963	01:53
Can	25 May 1963	02:29
Leo	27 May 1963	05:58
Vir	29 May 1963	13:22

Sign	Date	Time
Lib	1 Jun 1963	00:08
Sco	3 Jun 1963	12:37
Sag	6 Jun 1963	00:59
Cap	8 Jun 1963	12:05
Aqu	10 Jun 1963	21:20
Pis	13 Jun 1963	04:19
Ari	15 Jun 1963	08:45
Tau	17 Jun 1963	10:53
Gem	19 Jun 1963	11:43
Can	21 Jun 1963	12:46
Leo	23 Jun 1963	15:44
Vir	25 Jun 1963	21:56
Lib	28 Jun 1963	07:40
Sco	30 Jun 1963	19:47

Sign	Date	Time
Sag	3 Jul 1963	08:10
Cap	5 Jul 1963	19:02
Aqu	8 Jul 1963	03:35
Pis	10 Jul 1963	09:51
Ari	12 Jul 1963	14:15
Tau	14 Jul 1963	17:14
Gem	16 Jul 1963	19:26
Can	18 Jul 1963	21:44
Leo	21 Jul 1963	01:15
Vir	23 Jul 1963	07:06
Lib	25 Jul 1963	16:02
Sco	28 Jul 1963	03:37
Sag	30 Jul 1963	16:07

Sign	Date	Time
Cap	2 Aug 1963	03:11
Aqu	4 Aug 1963	11:23
Pis	6 Aug 1963	16:44
Ari	8 Aug 1963	20:05
Tau	10 Aug 1963	22:37
Gem	13 Aug 1963	01:15
Can	15 Aug 1963	04:38
Leo	17 Aug 1963	09:16
Vir	19 Aug 1963	15:40
Lib	22 Aug 1963	00:25
Sco	24 Aug 1963	11:38
Sag	27 Aug 1963	00:14
Cap	29 Aug 1963	11:55
Aqu	31 Aug 1963	20:35

Sign	Date	Time
Pis	3 Sep 1963	01:35
Ari	5 Sep 1963	03:51
Tau	7 Sep 1963	05:01
Gem	9 Sep 1963	06:45
Can	11 Sep 1963	10:07
Leo	13 Sep 1963	15:29
Vir	15 Sep 1963	22:47
Lib	18 Sep 1963	07:59
Sco	20 Sep 1963	19:10
Sag	23 Sep 1963	07:49
Cap	25 Sep 1963	20:14
Aqu	28 Sep 1963	06:02
Pis	30 Sep 1963	11:44

Sign	Date	Time
Ari	2 Oct 1963	13:46
Tau	4 Oct 1963	13:49
Gem	6 Oct 1963	13:58
Can	8 Oct 1963	16:00
Leo	10 Oct 1963	20:54
Vir	13 Oct 1963	04:33
Lib	15 Oct 1963	14:23
Sco	18 Oct 1963	01:52
Sag	20 Oct 1963	14:31
Cap	23 Oct 1963	03:19
Aqu	25 Oct 1963	14:18
Pis	27 Oct 1963	21:34
Ari	30 Oct 1963	00:38

Sign	Date	Time
Tau	1 Nov 1963	00:41
Gem	2 Nov 1963	23:48
Can	5 Nov 1963	00:08
Leo	7 Nov 1963	03:24
Vir	9 Nov 1963	10:14
Lib	11 Nov 1963	20:07
Sco	14 Nov 1963	07:56
Sag	16 Nov 1963	20:38
Cap	19 Nov 1963	09:21
Aqu	21 Nov 1963	20:49
Pis	24 Nov 1963	05:31
Ari	26 Nov 1963	10:23
Tau	28 Nov 1963	11:47
Gem	30 Nov 1963	11:14

Sign	Date	Time
Can	2 Dec 1963	10:45
Leo	4 Dec 1963	12:20
Vir	6 Dec 1963	17:25
Lib	9 Dec 1963	02:21
Sco	11 Dec 1963	14:03
Sag	14 Dec 1963	02:52
Cap	16 Dec 1963	15:20
Aqu	19 Dec 1963	02:27
Pis	21 Dec 1963	11:26
Ari	23 Dec 1963	17:40
Tau	25 Dec 1963	20:56
Gem	27 Dec 1963	21:57
Can	29 Dec 1963	22:06
Leo	31 Dec 1963	23:09

Moon Signs

1964

Sign	Date	Time
Vir	3 Jan 1964	02:48
Lib	5 Jan 1964	10:10
Sco	7 Jan 1964	21:03
Sag	10 Jan 1964	09:48
Cap	12 Jan 1964	22:12
Aqu	15 Jan 1964	08:46
Pis	17 Jan 1964	17:03
Ari	19 Jan 1964	23:09
Tau	22 Jan 1964	03:22
Gem	24 Jan 1964	06:04
Can	26 Jan 1964	07:50
Leo	28 Jan 1964	09:45
Vir	30 Jan 1964	13:09
Lib	1 Feb 1964	19:24
Sco	4 Feb 1964	05:12
Sag	6 Feb 1964	17:34
Cap	9 Feb 1964	06:10
Aqu	11 Feb 1964	16:38
Pis	14 Feb 1964	00:07
Ari	16 Feb 1964	05:09
Tau	18 Feb 1964	08:44
Gem	20 Feb 1964	11:47
Can	22 Feb 1964	14:48
Leo	24 Feb 1964	18:10
Vir	26 Feb 1964	22:30
Lib	29 Feb 1964	04:45
Sco	2 Mar 1964	13:54
Sag	5 Mar 1964	01:46
Cap	7 Mar 1964	14:34
Aqu	10 Mar 1964	01:33
Pis	12 Mar 1964	09:03
Ari	14 Mar 1964	13:13
Tau	16 Mar 1964	15:29
Gem	18 Mar 1964	17:25
Can	20 Mar 1964	20:11
Leo	23 Mar 1964	00:14
Vir	25 Mar 1964	05:41
Lib	27 Mar 1964	12:47
Sco	29 Mar 1964	22:03
Sag	1 Apr 1964	09:40
Cap	3 Apr 1964	22:35
Aqu	6 Apr 1964	10:22
Pis	8 Apr 1964	18:45
Ari	10 Apr 1964	23:06
Tau	13 Apr 1964	00:35
Gem	15 Apr 1964	01:05
Can	17 Apr 1964	02:23
Leo	19 Apr 1964	05:39
Vir	21 Apr 1964	11:17
Lib	23 Apr 1964	19:07
Sco	26 Apr 1964	05:00
Sag	28 Apr 1964	16:45

Sign	Date	Time
Cap	1 May 1964	05:41
Aqu	3 May 1964	18:05
Pis	6 May 1964	03:41
Ari	8 May 1964	09:13
Tau	10 May 1964	11:07
Gem	12 May 1964	11:00
Can	14 May 1964	10:53
Leo	16 May 1964	12:31
Vir	18 May 1964	17:02
Lib	21 May 1964	00:41
Sco	23 May 1964	10:57
Sag	25 May 1964	23:02
Cap	28 May 1964	11:59
Aqu	31 May 1964	00:31
Pis	2 Jun 1964	10:59
Ari	4 Jun 1964	18:02
Tau	6 Jun 1964	21:18
Gem	8 Jun 1964	21:48
Can	10 Jun 1964	21:16
Leo	12 Jun 1964	21:35
Vir	15 Jun 1964	00:28
Lib	17 Jun 1964	06:53
Sco	19 Jun 1964	16:48
Sag	22 Jun 1964	05:02
Cap	24 Jun 1964	18:01
Aqu	27 Jun 1964	06:20
Pis	29 Jun 1964	16:55
Ari	2 Jul 1964	00:50
Tau	4 Jul 1964	05:41
Gem	6 Jul 1964	07:41
Can	8 Jul 1964	07:56
Leo	10 Jul 1964	08:00
Vir	12 Jul 1964	09:44
Lib	14 Jul 1964	14:41
Sco	16 Jul 1964	23:32
Sag	19 Jul 1964	11:27
Cap	22 Jul 1964	00:25
Aqu	24 Jul 1964	12:29
Pis	26 Jul 1964	22:34
Ari	29 Jul 1964	06:24
Tau	31 Jul 1964	11:59
Gem	2 Aug 1964	15:27
Can	4 Aug 1964	17:12
Leo	6 Aug 1964	18:10
Vir	8 Aug 1964	19:49
Lib	10 Aug 1964	23:52
Sco	13 Aug 1964	07:31
Sag	15 Aug 1964	18:43
Cap	18 Aug 1964	07:37
Aqu	20 Aug 1964	19:38
Pis	23 Aug 1964	05:12
Ari	25 Aug 1964	12:13
Tau	27 Aug 1964	17:22
Gem	29 Aug 1964	21:15

Sign	Date	Time
Can	1 Sep 1964	00:12
Leo	3 Sep 1964	02:35
Vir	5 Sep 1964	05:11
Lib	7 Sep 1964	09:19
Sco	9 Sep 1964	16:19
Sag	12 Sep 1964	02:47
Cap	14 Sep 1964	15:29
Aqu	17 Sep 1964	03:46
Pis	19 Sep 1964	13:20
Ari	21 Sep 1964	19:42
Tau	23 Sep 1964	23:44
Gem	26 Sep 1964	02:45
Can	28 Sep 1964	05:38
Leo	30 Sep 1964	08:52
Vir	2 Oct 1964	12:42
Lib	4 Oct 1964	17:43
Sco	7 Oct 1964	00:57
Sag	9 Oct 1964	11:02
Cap	11 Oct 1964	23:31
Aqu	14 Oct 1964	12:14
Pis	16 Oct 1964	22:30
Ari	19 Oct 1964	05:03
Tau	21 Oct 1964	08:23
Gem	23 Oct 1964	10:02
Can	25 Oct 1964	11:37
Leo	27 Oct 1964	14:13
Vir	29 Oct 1964	18:24
Lib	1 Nov 1964	00:24
Sco	3 Nov 1964	08:24
Sag	5 Nov 1964	18:42
Cap	8 Nov 1964	07:04
Aqu	10 Nov 1964	20:07
Pis	13 Nov 1964	07:27
Ari	15 Nov 1964	15:08
Tau	17 Nov 1964	18:56
Gem	19 Nov 1964	19:57
Can	21 Nov 1964	20:03
Leo	23 Nov 1964	20:58
Vir	26 Nov 1964	00:03
Lib	28 Nov 1964	05:53
Sco	30 Nov 1964	14:30
Sag	3 Dec 1964	01:23
Cap	5 Dec 1964	13:52
Aqu	8 Dec 1964	02:56
Pis	10 Dec 1964	14:58
Ari	13 Dec 1964	00:10
Tau	15 Dec 1964	05:31
Gem	17 Dec 1964	07:20
Can	19 Dec 1964	07:01
Leo	21 Dec 1964	06:30
Vir	23 Dec 1964	07:41
Lib	25 Dec 1964	12:05
Sco	27 Dec 1964	20:11
Sag	30 Dec 1964	07:20

Moon Signs

1965

Cap 1 Jan 1965 20:05
Aqu 4 Jan 1965 09:03
Pis 6 Jan 1965 21:05
Ari 9 Jan 1965 07:07
Tau 11 Jan 1965 14:08
Gem 13 Jan 1965 17:47
Can 15 Jan 1965 18:34
Leo 17 Jan 1965 17:56
Vir 19 Jan 1965 17:54
Lib 21 Jan 1965 20:28
Sco 24 Jan 1965 03:01
Sag 26 Jan 1965 13:32
Cap 29 Jan 1965 02:20
Aqu 31 Jan 1965 15:16

Pis 3 Feb 1965 02:54
Ari 5 Feb 1965 12:42
Tau 7 Feb 1965 20:22
Gem 10 Feb 1965 01:34
Can 12 Feb 1965 04:12
Leo 14 Feb 1965 04:53
Vir 16 Feb 1965 05:04
Lib 18 Feb 1965 06:44
Sco 20 Feb 1965 11:46
Sag 22 Feb 1965 20:57
Cap 25 Feb 1965 09:16
Aqu 27 Feb 1965 22:13

Pis 2 Mar 1965 09:37
Ari 4 Mar 1965 18:44
Tau 7 Mar 1965 01:48
Gem 9 Mar 1965 07:13
Can 11 Mar 1965 11:01
Leo 13 Mar 1965 13:22
Vir 15 Mar 1965 14:55
Lib 17 Mar 1965 17:03
Sco 19 Mar 1965 21:32
Sag 22 Mar 1965 05:36
Cap 24 Mar 1965 17:06
Aqu 27 Mar 1965 05:58
Pis 29 Mar 1965 17:31

Ari 1 Apr 1965 02:17
Tau 3 Apr 1965 08:27
Gem 5 Apr 1965 12:53
Can 7 Apr 1965 16:23
Leo 9 Apr 1965 19:22
Vir 11 Apr 1965 22:14
Lib 14 Apr 1965 01:38
Sco 16 Apr 1965 06:41
Sag 18 Apr 1965 14:31
Cap 21 Apr 1965 01:23
Aqu 23 Apr 1965 14:03
Pis 26 Apr 1965 02:00
Ari 28 Apr 1965 11:10
Tau 30 Apr 1965 17:02

Gem 2 May 1965 20:25
Can 4 May 1965 22:38
Leo 7 May 1965 00:49
Vir 9 May 1965 03:46
Lib 11 May 1965 08:04
Sco 13 May 1965 14:09
Sag 15 May 1965 22:31
Cap 18 May 1965 09:19
Aqu 20 May 1965 21:49
Pis 23 May 1965 10:13
Ari 25 May 1965 20:17
Tau 28 May 1965 02:46
Gem 30 May 1965 05:58

Can 1 Jun 1965 07:04
Leo 3 Jun 1965 07:46
Vir 5 Jun 1965 09:33
Lib 7 Jun 1965 13:29
Sco 9 Jun 1965 20:03
Sag 12 Jun 1965 05:09
Cap 14 Jun 1965 16:20
Aqu 17 Jun 1965 04:50
Pis 19 Jun 1965 17:28
Ari 22 Jun 1965 04:28
Tau 24 Jun 1965 12:14
Gem 26 Jun 1965 16:17
Can 28 Jun 1965 17:19
Leo 30 Jun 1965 16:58

Vir 2 Jul 1965 17:10
Lib 4 Jul 1965 19:42
Sco 7 Jul 1965 01:38
Sag 9 Jul 1965 10:53
Cap 11 Jul 1965 22:28
Aqu 14 Jul 1965 11:07
Pis 16 Jul 1965 23:43
Ari 19 Jul 1965 11:11
Tau 21 Jul 1965 20:12
Gem 24 Jul 1965 01:46
Can 26 Jul 1965 03:51
Leo 28 Jul 1965 03:36
Vir 30 Jul 1965 02:54

Lib 1 Aug 1965 03:54
Sco 3 Aug 1965 08:20
Sag 5 Aug 1965 16:48
Cap 8 Aug 1965 04:21
Aqu 10 Aug 1965 17:08
Pis 13 Aug 1965 05:36
Ari 15 Aug 1965 16:56
Tau 18 Aug 1965 02:26
Gem 20 Aug 1965 09:19
Can 22 Aug 1965 13:02
Leo 24 Aug 1965 14:00
Vir 26 Aug 1965 13:35
Lib 28 Aug 1965 13:52
Sco 30 Aug 1965 16:53

Sag 2 Sep 1965 00:00
Cap 4 Sep 1965 10:51
Aqu 6 Sep 1965 23:32
Pis 9 Sep 1965 11:55
Ari 11 Sep 1965 22:48
Tau 14 Sep 1965 07:55
Gem 16 Sep 1965 15:05
Can 18 Sep 1965 19:59
Leo 20 Sep 1965 22:33
Vir 22 Sep 1965 23:29
Lib 25 Sep 1965 00:15
Sco 27 Sep 1965 02:47
Sag 29 Sep 1965 08:42

Cap 1 Oct 1965 18:28
Aqu 4 Oct 1965 06:47
Pis 6 Oct 1965 19:13
Ari 9 Oct 1965 05:53
Tau 11 Oct 1965 14:15
Gem 13 Oct 1965 20:38
Can 16 Oct 1965 01:25
Leo 18 Oct 1965 04:50
Vir 20 Oct 1965 07:12
Lib 22 Oct 1965 09:20
Sco 24 Oct 1965 12:31
Sag 26 Oct 1965 18:08
Cap 29 Oct 1965 03:05
Aqu 31 Oct 1965 14:49

Pis 3 Nov 1965 03:21
Ari 5 Nov 1965 14:20
Tau 7 Nov 1965 22:28
Gem 10 Nov 1965 03:53
Can 12 Nov 1965 07:28
Leo 14 Nov 1965 10:13
Vir 16 Nov 1965 12:54
Lib 18 Nov 1965 16:09
Sco 20 Nov 1965 20:36
Sag 23 Nov 1965 02:56
Cap 25 Nov 1965 11:45
Aqu 27 Nov 1965 23:03
Pis 30 Nov 1965 11:38

Ari 2 Dec 1965 23:21
Tau 5 Dec 1965 08:09
Gem 7 Dec 1965 13:25
Can 9 Dec 1965 15:56
Leo 11 Dec 1965 17:07
Vir 13 Dec 1965 18:35
Lib 15 Dec 1965 21:33
Sco 18 Dec 1965 02:40
Sag 20 Dec 1965 10:01
Cap 22 Dec 1965 19:26
Aqu 25 Dec 1965 06:43
Pis 27 Dec 1965 19:16
Ari 30 Dec 1965 07:38

1966

Tau 1 Jan 1966 17:45
Gem 4 Jan 1966 00:04
Can 6 Jan 1966 02:38
Leo 8 Jan 1966 02:49
Vir 10 Jan 1966 02:34
Lib 12 Jan 1966 03:53
Sco 14 Jan 1966 08:08
Sag 16 Jan 1966 15:39
Cap 19 Jan 1966 01:44
Aqu 21 Jan 1966 13:25
Pis 24 Jan 1966 01:57
Ari 26 Jan 1966 14:32
Tau 29 Jan 1966 01:41
Gem 31 Jan 1966 09:41

Can 2 Feb 1966 13:39
Leo 4 Feb 1966 14:12
Vir 6 Feb 1966 13:11
Lib 8 Feb 1966 12:51
Sco 10 Feb 1966 15:15
Sag 12 Feb 1966 21:33
Cap 15 Feb 1966 07:25
Aqu 17 Feb 1966 19:25
Pis 20 Feb 1966 08:04
Ari 22 Feb 1966 20:29
Tau 25 Feb 1966 07:52
Gem 27 Feb 1966 17:01

Can 1 Mar 1966 22:46
Leo 4 Mar 1966 00:54
Vir 6 Mar 1966 00:35
Lib 7 Mar 1966 23:48
Sco 10 Mar 1966 00:47
Sag 12 Mar 1966 05:18
Cap 14 Mar 1966 13:55
Aqu 17 Mar 1966 01:34
Pis 19 Mar 1966 14:17
Ari 22 Mar 1966 02:32
Tau 24 Mar 1966 13:30
Gem 26 Mar 1966 22:40
Can 29 Mar 1966 05:22
Leo 31 Mar 1966 09:10

Vir 2 Apr 1966 10:29
Lib 4 Apr 1966 10:39
Sco 6 Apr 1966 11:30
Sag 8 Apr 1966 14:54
Cap 10 Apr 1966 22:02
Aqu 13 Apr 1966 08:41
Pis 15 Apr 1966 21:12
Ari 18 Apr 1966 09:25
Tau 20 Apr 1966 19:59
Gem 23 Apr 1966 04:26
Can 25 Apr 1966 10:46
Leo 27 Apr 1966 15:08
Vir 29 Apr 1966 17:48

Lib 1 May 1966 19:30
Sco 3 May 1966 21:23
Sag 6 May 1966 00:52
Cap 8 May 1966 07:12
Aqu 10 May 1966 16:51
Pis 13 May 1966 04:54
Ari 15 May 1966 17:14
Tau 18 May 1966 03:47
Gem 20 May 1966 11:38
Can 22 May 1966 16:59
Leo 24 May 1966 20:36
Vir 26 May 1966 23:21
Lib 29 May 1966 01:59
Sco 31 May 1966 05:10

Sag 2 Jun 1966 09:38
Cap 4 Jun 1966 16:09
Aqu 7 Jun 1966 01:20
Pis 9 Jun 1966 12:56
Ari 12 Jun 1966 01:25
Tau 14 Jun 1966 12:27
Gem 16 Jun 1966 20:24
Can 19 Jun 1966 01:03
Leo 21 Jun 1966 03:28
Vir 23 Jun 1966 05:07
Lib 25 Jun 1966 07:22
Sco 27 Jun 1966 11:03
Sag 29 Jun 1966 16:30

Cap 1 Jul 1966 23:51
Aqu 4 Jul 1966 09:14
Pis 6 Jul 1966 20:39
Ari 9 Jul 1966 09:15
Tau 11 Jul 1966 21:02
Gem 14 Jul 1966 05:50
Can 16 Jul 1966 10:42
Leo 18 Jul 1966 12:26
Vir 20 Jul 1966 12:46
Lib 22 Jul 1966 13:38
Sco 24 Jul 1966 16:31
Sag 26 Jul 1966 22:04
Cap 29 Jul 1966 06:03
Aqu 31 Jul 1966 16:01

Pis 3 Aug 1966 03:35
Ari 5 Aug 1966 16:14
Tau 8 Aug 1966 04:36
Gem 10 Aug 1966 14:36
Can 12 Aug 1966 20:39
Leo 14 Aug 1966 22:48
Vir 16 Aug 1966 22:34
Lib 18 Aug 1966 22:05
Sco 20 Aug 1966 23:24
Sag 23 Aug 1966 03:51
Cap 25 Aug 1966 11:37
Aqu 27 Aug 1966 21:55
Pis 30 Aug 1966 09:47

Ari 1 Sep 1966 22:26
Tau 4 Sep 1966 10:58
Gem 6 Sep 1966 21:50
Can 9 Sep 1966 05:25
Leo 11 Sep 1966 08:59
Vir 13 Sep 1966 09:24
Lib 15 Sep 1966 08:32
Sco 17 Sep 1966 08:34
Sag 19 Sep 1966 11:22
Cap 21 Sep 1966 17:52
Aqu 24 Sep 1966 03:47
Pis 26 Sep 1966 15:48
Ari 29 Sep 1966 04:28

Tau 1 Oct 1966 16:46
Gem 4 Oct 1966 03:42
Can 6 Oct 1966 12:10
Leo 8 Oct 1966 17:23
Vir 10 Oct 1966 19:25
Lib 12 Oct 1966 19:28
Sco 14 Oct 1966 19:20
Sag 16 Oct 1966 20:59
Cap 19 Oct 1966 01:56
Aqu 21 Oct 1966 10:41
Pis 23 Oct 1966 22:20
Ari 26 Oct 1966 11:02
Tau 28 Oct 1966 23:04
Gem 31 Oct 1966 09:26

Can 2 Nov 1966 17:42
Leo 4 Nov 1966 23:34
Vir 7 Nov 1966 03:08
Lib 9 Nov 1966 04:53
Sco 11 Nov 1966 05:52
Sag 13 Nov 1966 07:35
Cap 15 Nov 1966 11:37
Aqu 17 Nov 1966 19:03
Pis 20 Nov 1966 05:52
Ari 22 Nov 1966 18:30
Tau 25 Nov 1966 06:36
Gem 27 Nov 1966 16:29
Can 29 Nov 1966 23:48

Leo 2 Dec 1966 05:00
Vir 4 Dec 1966 08:47
Lib 6 Dec 1966 11:42
Sco 8 Dec 1966 14:17
Sag 10 Dec 1966 17:12
Cap 12 Dec 1966 21:30
Aqu 15 Dec 1966 04:19
Pis 17 Dec 1966 14:17
Ari 20 Dec 1966 02:38
Tau 22 Dec 1966 15:06
Gem 25 Dec 1966 01:12
Can 27 Dec 1966 07:57
Leo 29 Dec 1966 11:56
Vir 31 Dec 1966 14:32

Moon Signs

1967

Lib	2 Jan 1967	17:03
Sco	4 Jan 1967	20:15
Sag	7 Jan 1967	00:27
Cap	9 Jan 1967	05:52
Aqu	11 Jan 1967	13:05
Pis	13 Jan 1967	22:44
Ari	16 Jan 1967	10:47
Tau	18 Jan 1967	23:38
Gem	21 Jan 1967	10:36
Can	23 Jan 1967	17:50
Leo	25 Jan 1967	21:19
Vir	27 Jan 1967	22:35
Lib	29 Jan 1967	23:32

Sco	1 Feb 1967	01:44
Sag	3 Feb 1967	05:55
Cap	5 Feb 1967	12:10
Aqu	7 Feb 1967	20:16
Pis	10 Feb 1967	06:18
Ari	12 Feb 1967	18:16
Tau	15 Feb 1967	07:18
Gem	17 Feb 1967	19:14
Can	20 Feb 1967	03:46
Leo	22 Feb 1967	08:03
Vir	24 Feb 1967	09:03
Lib	26 Feb 1967	08:44
Sco	28 Feb 1967	09:09

Sag	2 Mar 1967	11:53
Cap	4 Mar 1967	17:34
Aqu	7 Mar 1967	02:03
Pis	9 Mar 1967	12:41
Ari	12 Mar 1967	00:52
Tau	14 Mar 1967	13:53
Gem	17 Mar 1967	02:17
Can	19 Mar 1967	12:07
Leo	21 Mar 1967	18:03
Vir	23 Mar 1967	20:07
Lib	25 Mar 1967	19:49
Sco	27 Mar 1967	19:10
Sag	29 Mar 1967	20:08

Cap	1 Apr 1967	00:11
Aqu	3 Apr 1967	07:48
Pis	5 Apr 1967	18:28
Ari	8 Apr 1967	06:56
Tau	10 Apr 1967	19:55
Gem	13 Apr 1967	08:13
Can	15 Apr 1967	18:35
Leo	18 Apr 1967	01:52
Vir	20 Apr 1967	05:41
Lib	22 Apr 1967	06:40
Sco	24 Apr 1967	06:18
Sag	26 Apr 1967	06:26
Cap	28 Apr 1967	08:54
Aqu	30 Apr 1967	14:57

Pis	3 May 1967	00:47
Ari	5 May 1967	13:09
Tau	8 May 1967	02:08
Gem	10 May 1967	14:07
Can	13 May 1967	00:09
Leo	15 May 1967	07:47
Vir	17 May 1967	12:50
Lib	19 May 1967	15:29
Sco	21 May 1967	16:29
Sag	23 May 1967	17:05
Cap	25 May 1967	18:57
Aqu	27 May 1967	23:44
Pis	30 May 1967	08:18

Ari	1 Jun 1967	20:06
Tau	4 Jun 1967	09:03
Gem	6 Jun 1967	20:50
Can	9 Jun 1967	06:17
Leo	11 Jun 1967	13:17
Vir	13 Jun 1967	18:23
Lib	15 Jun 1967	21:57
Sco	18 Jun 1967	00:24
Sag	20 Jun 1967	02:19
Cap	22 Jun 1967	04:46
Aqu	24 Jun 1967	09:11
Pis	26 Jun 1967	16:49
Ari	29 Jun 1967	03:52

Tau	1 Jul 1967	16:42
Gem	4 Jul 1967	04:37
Can	6 Jul 1967	13:46
Leo	8 Jul 1967	19:57
Vir	11 Jul 1967	00:06
Lib	13 Jul 1967	03:19
Sco	15 Jul 1967	06:17
Sag	17 Jul 1967	09:21
Cap	19 Jul 1967	12:59
Aqu	21 Jul 1967	17:59
Pis	24 Jul 1967	01:28
Ari	26 Jul 1967	12:00
Tau	29 Jul 1967	00:39
Gem	31 Jul 1967	12:59

Can	2 Aug 1967	22:30
Leo	5 Aug 1967	04:25
Vir	7 Aug 1967	07:35
Lib	9 Aug 1967	09:34
Sco	11 Aug 1967	11:43
Sag	13 Aug 1967	14:52
Cap	15 Aug 1967	19:17
Aqu	18 Aug 1967	01:17
Pis	20 Aug 1967	09:18
Ari	22 Aug 1967	19:47
Tau	25 Aug 1967	08:20
Gem	27 Aug 1967	21:07
Can	30 Aug 1967	07:33

Leo	1 Sep 1967	14:06
Vir	3 Sep 1967	17:06
Lib	5 Sep 1967	18:02
Sco	7 Sep 1967	18:43
Sag	9 Sep 1967	20:39
Cap	12 Sep 1967	00:43
Aqu	14 Sep 1967	07:08
Pis	16 Sep 1967	15:53
Ari	19 Sep 1967	02:46
Tau	21 Sep 1967	15:20
Gem	24 Sep 1967	04:20
Can	26 Sep 1967	15:44
Leo	28 Sep 1967	23:39

Vir	1 Oct 1967	03:37
Lib	3 Oct 1967	04:33
Sco	5 Oct 1967	04:13
Sag	7 Oct 1967	04:31
Cap	9 Oct 1967	07:03
Aqu	11 Oct 1967	12:46
Pis	13 Oct 1967	21:38
Ari	16 Oct 1967	08:57
Tau	18 Oct 1967	21:40
Gem	21 Oct 1967	10:37
Can	23 Oct 1967	22:25
Leo	26 Oct 1967	07:39
Vir	28 Oct 1967	13:17
Lib	30 Oct 1967	15:30

Sco	1 Nov 1967	15:25
Sag	3 Nov 1967	14:51
Cap	5 Nov 1967	15:44
Aqu	7 Nov 1967	19:45
Pis	10 Nov 1967	03:42
Ari	12 Nov 1967	14:58
Tau	15 Nov 1967	03:51
Gem	17 Nov 1967	16:39
Can	20 Nov 1967	04:12
Leo	22 Nov 1967	13:45
Vir	24 Nov 1967	20:44
Lib	27 Nov 1967	00:46
Sco	29 Nov 1967	02:12

Sag	1 Dec 1967	02:09
Cap	3 Dec 1967	02:25
Aqu	5 Dec 1967	04:56
Pis	7 Dec 1967	11:20
Ari	9 Dec 1967	21:43
Tau	12 Dec 1967	10:31
Gem	14 Dec 1967	23:17
Can	17 Dec 1967	10:21
Leo	19 Dec 1967	19:20
Vir	22 Dec 1967	02:20
Lib	24 Dec 1967	07:26
Sco	26 Dec 1967	10:35
Sag	28 Dec 1967	12:08
Cap	30 Dec 1967	13:11

1968

Sign	Date	Time
Aqu	1 Jan 1968	15:24
Pis	3 Jan 1968	20:36
Ari	6 Jan 1968	05:45
Tau	8 Jan 1968	18:02
Gem	11 Jan 1968	06:53
Can	13 Jan 1968	17:53
Leo	16 Jan 1968	02:08
Vir	18 Jan 1968	08:10
Lib	20 Jan 1968	12:46
Sco	22 Jan 1968	16:27
Sag	24 Jan 1968	19:23
Cap	26 Jan 1968	21:56
Aqu	29 Jan 1968	01:06
Pis	31 Jan 1968	06:15
Ari	2 Feb 1968	14:40
Tau	5 Feb 1968	02:15
Gem	7 Feb 1968	15:08
Can	10 Feb 1968	02:33
Leo	12 Feb 1968	10:48
Vir	14 Feb 1968	16:01
Lib	16 Feb 1968	19:20
Sco	18 Feb 1968	21:59
Sag	21 Feb 1968	00:47
Cap	23 Feb 1968	04:11
Aqu	25 Feb 1968	08:36
Pis	27 Feb 1968	14:42
Ari	29 Feb 1968	23:15
Tau	3 Mar 1968	10:27
Gem	5 Mar 1968	23:16
Can	8 Mar 1968	11:20
Leo	10 Mar 1968	20:26
Vir	13 Mar 1968	01:50
Lib	15 Mar 1968	04:22
Sco	17 Mar 1968	05:32
Sag	19 Mar 1968	06:53
Cap	21 Mar 1968	09:34
Aqu	23 Mar 1968	14:16
Pis	25 Mar 1968	21:15
Ari	28 Mar 1968	06:31
Tau	30 Mar 1968	17:54
Gem	2 Apr 1968	06:39
Can	4 Apr 1968	19:12
Leo	7 Apr 1968	05:27
Vir	9 Apr 1968	12:02
Lib	11 Apr 1968	14:59
Sco	13 Apr 1968	15:31
Sag	15 Apr 1968	15:23
Cap	17 Apr 1968	16:22
Aqu	19 Apr 1968	19:57
Pis	22 Apr 1968	02:46
Ari	24 Apr 1968	12:32
Tau	27 Apr 1968	00:22
Gem	29 Apr 1968	13:10

Sign	Date	Time
Can	2 May 1968	01:48
Leo	4 May 1968	12:52
Vir	6 May 1968	20:56
Lib	9 May 1968	01:19
Sco	11 May 1968	02:28
Sag	13 May 1968	01:53
Cap	15 May 1968	01:31
Aqu	17 May 1968	03:22
Pis	19 May 1968	08:53
Ari	21 May 1968	18:14
Tau	24 May 1968	06:15
Gem	26 May 1968	19:11
Can	29 May 1968	07:42
Leo	31 May 1968	18:52
Vir	3 Jun 1968	03:51
Lib	5 Jun 1968	09:47
Sco	7 Jun 1968	12:28
Sag	9 Jun 1968	12:41
Cap	11 Jun 1968	12:05
Aqu	13 Jun 1968	12:47
Pis	15 Jun 1968	16:42
Ari	18 Jun 1968	00:50
Tau	20 Jun 1968	12:25
Gem	23 Jun 1968	01:21
Can	25 Jun 1968	13:42
Leo	28 Jun 1968	00:29
Vir	30 Jun 1968	09:25
Lib	2 Jul 1968	16:09
Sco	4 Jul 1968	20:19
Sag	6 Jul 1968	22:03
Cap	8 Jul 1968	22:23
Aqu	10 Jul 1968	23:04
Pis	13 Jul 1968	02:04
Ari	15 Jul 1968	08:52
Tau	17 Jul 1968	19:30
Gem	20 Jul 1968	08:12
Can	22 Jul 1968	20:30
Leo	25 Jul 1968	06:54
Vir	27 Jul 1968	15:09
Lib	29 Jul 1968	21:31
Sco	1 Aug 1968	02:10
Sag	3 Aug 1968	05:10
Cap	5 Aug 1968	06:57
Aqu	7 Aug 1968	08:37
Pis	9 Aug 1968	11:46
Ari	11 Aug 1968	17:53
Tau	14 Aug 1968	03:36
Gem	16 Aug 1968	15:50
Can	19 Aug 1968	04:14
Leo	21 Aug 1968	14:39
Vir	23 Aug 1968	22:20
Lib	26 Aug 1968	03:44
Sco	28 Aug 1968	07:37
Sag	30 Aug 1968	10:40

Sign	Date	Time
Cap	1 Sep 1968	13:21
Aqu	3 Sep 1968	16:19
Pis	5 Sep 1968	20:27
Ari	8 Sep 1968	02:49
Tau	10 Sep 1968	12:06
Gem	12 Sep 1968	23:54
Can	15 Sep 1968	12:27
Leo	17 Sep 1968	23:24
Vir	20 Sep 1968	07:14
Lib	22 Sep 1968	11:58
Sco	24 Sep 1968	14:38
Sag	26 Sep 1968	16:30
Cap	28 Sep 1968	18:44
Aqu	30 Sep 1968	22:11
Pis	3 Oct 1968	03:21
Ari	5 Oct 1968	10:35
Tau	7 Oct 1968	20:06
Gem	10 Oct 1968	07:43
Can	12 Oct 1968	20:23
Leo	15 Oct 1968	08:07
Vir	17 Oct 1968	16:57
Lib	19 Oct 1968	22:03
Sco	22 Oct 1968	00:04
Sag	24 Oct 1968	00:32
Cap	26 Oct 1968	01:14
Aqu	28 Oct 1968	03:43
Pis	30 Oct 1968	08:54
Ari	1 Nov 1968	16:50
Tau	4 Nov 1968	03:01
Gem	6 Nov 1968	14:47
Can	9 Nov 1968	03:26
Leo	11 Nov 1968	15:44
Vir	14 Nov 1968	01:53
Lib	16 Nov 1968	08:25
Sco	18 Nov 1968	11:04
Sag	20 Nov 1968	11:03
Cap	22 Nov 1968	10:20
Aqu	24 Nov 1968	11:03
Pis	26 Nov 1968	14:53
Ari	28 Nov 1968	22:26
Tau	1 Dec 1968	08:57
Gem	3 Dec 1968	21:05
Can	6 Dec 1968	09:43
Leo	8 Dec 1968	22:02
Vir	11 Dec 1968	08:58
Lib	13 Dec 1968	17:08
Sco	15 Dec 1968	21:30
Sag	17 Dec 1968	22:26
Cap	19 Dec 1968	21:32
Aqu	21 Dec 1968	21:00
Pis	23 Dec 1968	23:02
Ari	26 Dec 1968	05:02
Tau	28 Dec 1968	14:57
Gem	31 Dec 1968	03:10

1969

Can	2 Jan 1969	15:52
Leo	5 Jan 1969	03:54
Vir	7 Jan 1969	14:41
Lib	9 Jan 1969	23:31
Sco	12 Jan 1969	05:31
Sag	14 Jan 1969	08:17
Cap	16 Jan 1969	08:38
Aqu	18 Jan 1969	08:16
Pis	20 Jan 1969	09:21
Ari	22 Jan 1969	13:44
Tau	24 Jan 1969	22:13
Gem	27 Jan 1969	09:53
Can	29 Jan 1969	22:35
Leo	1 Feb 1969	10:28
Vir	3 Feb 1969	20:40
Lib	6 Feb 1969	04:59
Sco	8 Feb 1969	11:17
Sag	10 Feb 1969	15:22
Cap	12 Feb 1969	17:28
Aqu	14 Feb 1969	18:30
Pis	16 Feb 1969	20:03
Ari	18 Feb 1969	23:49
Tau	21 Feb 1969	07:02
Gem	23 Feb 1969	17:41
Can	26 Feb 1969	06:11
Leo	28 Feb 1969	18:11
Vir	3 Mar 1969	04:06
Lib	5 Mar 1969	11:32
Sco	7 Mar 1969	16:55
Sag	9 Mar 1969	20:47
Cap	11 Mar 1969	23:39
Aqu	14 Mar 1969	02:09
Pis	16 Mar 1969	05:03
Ari	18 Mar 1969	09:27
Tau	20 Mar 1969	16:20
Gem	23 Mar 1969	02:12
Can	25 Mar 1969	14:18
Leo	28 Mar 1969	02:36
Vir	30 Mar 1969	12:52
Lib	1 Apr 1969	20:02
Sco	4 Apr 1969	00:21
Sag	6 Apr 1969	02:56
Cap	8 Apr 1969	05:04
Aqu	10 Apr 1969	07:46
Pis	12 Apr 1969	11:41
Ari	14 Apr 1969	17:13
Tau	17 Apr 1969	00:43
Gem	19 Apr 1969	10:28
Can	21 Apr 1969	22:17
Leo	24 Apr 1969	10:50
Vir	26 Apr 1969	21:55
Lib	29 Apr 1969	05:43
Sco	1 May 1969	09:48
Sag	3 May 1969	11:18
Cap	5 May 1969	11:56
Aqu	7 May 1969	13:28
Pis	9 May 1969	17:04
Ari	11 May 1969	23:09
Tau	14 May 1969	07:28
Gem	16 May 1969	17:41
Can	19 May 1969	05:30
Leo	21 May 1969	18:12
Vir	24 May 1969	06:06
Lib	26 May 1969	15:06
Sco	28 May 1969	20:04
Sag	30 May 1969	21:29
Cap	1 Jun 1969	21:06
Aqu	3 Jun 1969	21:04
Pis	5 Jun 1969	23:14
Ari	8 Jun 1969	04:37
Tau	10 Jun 1969	13:06
Gem	12 Jun 1969	23:48
Can	15 Jun 1969	11:52
Leo	18 Jun 1969	00:34
Vir	20 Jun 1969	12:52
Lib	22 Jun 1969	23:02
Sco	25 Jun 1969	05:30
Sag	27 Jun 1969	07:59
Cap	29 Jun 1969	07:44
Aqu	1 Jul 1969	06:49
Pis	3 Jul 1969	07:26
Ari	5 Jul 1969	11:17
Tau	7 Jul 1969	18:53
Gem	10 Jul 1969	05:31
Can	12 Jul 1969	17:47
Leo	15 Jul 1969	06:28
Vir	17 Jul 1969	18:41
Lib	20 Jul 1969	05:19
Sco	22 Jul 1969	13:02
Sag	24 Jul 1969	17:10
Cap	26 Jul 1969	18:09
Aqu	28 Jul 1969	17:34
Pis	30 Jul 1969	17:30
Ari	1 Aug 1969	19:55
Tau	4 Aug 1969	02:03
Gem	6 Aug 1969	11:50
Can	8 Aug 1969	23:57
Leo	11 Aug 1969	12:38
Vir	14 Aug 1969	00:32
Lib	16 Aug 1969	10:50
Sco	18 Aug 1969	18:53
Sag	21 Aug 1969	00:10
Cap	23 Aug 1969	02:47
Aqu	25 Aug 1969	03:35
Pis	27 Aug 1969	04:03
Ari	29 Aug 1969	05:57
Tau	31 Aug 1969	10:51
Gem	2 Sep 1969	19:23
Can	5 Sep 1969	06:56
Leo	7 Sep 1969	19:35
Vir	10 Sep 1969	07:20
Lib	12 Sep 1969	17:01
Sco	15 Sep 1969	00:24
Sag	17 Sep 1969	05:41
Cap	19 Sep 1969	09:13
Aqu	21 Sep 1969	11:30
Pis	23 Sep 1969	13:22
Ari	25 Sep 1969	15:55
Tau	27 Sep 1969	20:29
Gem	30 Sep 1969	04:06
Can	2 Oct 1969	14:52
Leo	5 Oct 1969	03:24
Vir	7 Oct 1969	15:20
Lib	10 Oct 1969	00:47
Sco	12 Oct 1969	07:18
Sag	14 Oct 1969	11:32
Cap	16 Oct 1969	14:35
Aqu	18 Oct 1969	17:20
Pis	20 Oct 1969	20:25
Ari	23 Oct 1969	00:17
Tau	25 Oct 1969	05:32
Gem	27 Oct 1969	13:01
Can	29 Oct 1969	23:13
Leo	1 Nov 1969	11:34
Vir	3 Nov 1969	23:59
Lib	6 Nov 1969	09:57
Sco	8 Nov 1969	16:16
Sag	10 Nov 1969	19:29
Cap	12 Nov 1969	21:08
Aqu	14 Nov 1969	22:53
Pis	17 Nov 1969	01:52
Ari	19 Nov 1969	06:31
Tau	21 Nov 1969	12:52
Gem	23 Nov 1969	20:59
Can	26 Nov 1969	07:10
Leo	28 Nov 1969	19:21
Vir	1 Dec 1969	08:13
Lib	3 Dec 1969	19:16
Sco	6 Dec 1969	02:28
Sag	8 Dec 1969	05:42
Cap	10 Dec 1969	06:20
Aqu	12 Dec 1969	06:27
Pis	14 Dec 1969	07:56
Ari	16 Dec 1969	11:56
Tau	18 Dec 1969	18:35
Gem	21 Dec 1969	03:28
Can	23 Dec 1969	14:08
Leo	26 Dec 1969	02:21
Vir	28 Dec 1969	15:19
Lib	31 Dec 1969	03:17

1970

Sign	Date	Time
Sco	2 Jan 1970	12:01
Sag	4 Jan 1970	16:32
Cap	6 Jan 1970	17:29
Aqu	8 Jan 1970	16:47
Pis	10 Jan 1970	16:36
Ari	12 Jan 1970	18:48
Tau	15 Jan 1970	00:21
Gem	17 Jan 1970	09:07
Can	19 Jan 1970	20:13
Leo	22 Jan 1970	08:40
Vir	24 Jan 1970	21:32
Lib	27 Jan 1970	09:41
Sco	29 Jan 1970	19:33
Sag	1 Feb 1970	01:48
Cap	3 Feb 1970	04:20
Aqu	5 Feb 1970	04:19
Pis	7 Feb 1970	03:37
Ari	9 Feb 1970	04:17
Tau	11 Feb 1970	07:59
Gem	13 Feb 1970	15:29
Can	16 Feb 1970	02:17
Leo	18 Feb 1970	14:53
Vir	21 Feb 1970	03:41
Lib	23 Feb 1970	15:29
Sco	26 Feb 1970	01:22
Sag	28 Feb 1970	08:37
Cap	2 Mar 1970	12:53
Aqu	4 Mar 1970	14:33
Pis	6 Mar 1970	14:48
Ari	8 Mar 1970	15:16
Tau	10 Mar 1970	17:43
Gem	12 Mar 1970	23:38
Can	15 Mar 1970	09:19
Leo	17 Mar 1970	21:39
Vir	20 Mar 1970	10:29
Lib	22 Mar 1970	21:56
Sco	25 Mar 1970	07:09
Sag	27 Mar 1970	14:05
Cap	29 Mar 1970	18:59
Aqu	31 Mar 1970	22:07
Pis	3 Apr 1970	00:00
Ari	5 Apr 1970	01:32
Tau	7 Apr 1970	04:02
Gem	9 Apr 1970	09:02
Can	11 Apr 1970	17:33
Leo	14 Apr 1970	05:15
Vir	16 Apr 1970	18:06
Lib	19 Apr 1970	05:34
Sco	21 Apr 1970	14:14
Sag	23 Apr 1970	20:14
Cap	26 Apr 1970	00:25
Aqu	28 Apr 1970	03:42
Pis	30 Apr 1970	06:37

Sign	Date	Time
Ari	2 May 1970	09:32
Tau	4 May 1970	13:05
Gem	6 May 1970	18:17
Can	9 May 1970	02:17
Leo	11 May 1970	13:22
Vir	14 May 1970	02:10
Lib	16 May 1970	14:01
Sco	18 May 1970	22:48
Sag	21 May 1970	04:10
Cap	23 May 1970	07:12
Aqu	25 May 1970	09:25
Pis	27 May 1970	11:59
Ari	29 May 1970	15:27
Tau	31 May 1970	20:03
Gem	3 Jun 1970	02:10
Can	5 Jun 1970	10:26
Leo	7 Jun 1970	21:17
Vir	10 Jun 1970	10:02
Lib	12 Jun 1970	22:27
Sco	15 Jun 1970	08:00
Sag	17 Jun 1970	13:37
Cap	19 Jun 1970	16:04
Aqu	21 Jun 1970	17:00
Pis	23 Jun 1970	18:11
Ari	25 Jun 1970	20:52
Tau	28 Jun 1970	01:35
Gem	30 Jun 1970	08:24
Can	2 Jul 1970	17:21
Leo	5 Jul 1970	04:26
Vir	7 Jul 1970	17:11
Lib	10 Jul 1970	06:02
Sco	12 Jul 1970	16:40
Sag	14 Jul 1970	23:24
Cap	17 Jul 1970	02:18
Aqu	19 Jul 1970	02:44
Pis	21 Jul 1970	02:37
Ari	23 Jul 1970	03:43
Tau	25 Jul 1970	07:18
Gem	27 Jul 1970	13:53
Can	29 Jul 1970	23:14
Leo	1 Aug 1970	10:44
Vir	3 Aug 1970	23:34
Lib	6 Aug 1970	12:32
Sco	8 Aug 1970	23:55
Sag	11 Aug 1970	08:06
Cap	13 Aug 1970	12:23
Aqu	15 Aug 1970	13:30
Pis	17 Aug 1970	13:01
Ari	19 Aug 1970	12:51
Tau	21 Aug 1970	14:47
Gem	23 Aug 1970	20:04
Can	26 Aug 1970	04:58
Leo	28 Aug 1970	16:38
Vir	31 Aug 1970	05:36

Sign	Date	Time
Lib	2 Sep 1970	18:25
Sco	5 Sep 1970	05:54
Sag	7 Sep 1970	14:57
Cap	9 Sep 1970	20:50
Aqu	11 Sep 1970	23:32
Pis	13 Sep 1970	23:56
Ari	15 Sep 1970	23:35
Tau	18 Sep 1970	00:22
Gem	20 Sep 1970	04:02
Can	22 Sep 1970	11:42
Leo	24 Sep 1970	22:55
Vir	27 Sep 1970	11:53
Lib	30 Sep 1970	00:32
Sco	2 Oct 1970	11:34
Sag	4 Oct 1970	20:30
Cap	7 Oct 1970	03:09
Aqu	9 Oct 1970	07:25
Pis	11 Oct 1970	09:29
Ari	13 Oct 1970	10:12
Tau	15 Oct 1970	11:00
Gem	17 Oct 1970	13:44
Can	19 Oct 1970	19:59
Leo	22 Oct 1970	06:12
Vir	24 Oct 1970	18:57
Lib	27 Oct 1970	07:36
Sco	29 Oct 1970	18:14
Sag	1 Nov 1970	02:23
Cap	3 Nov 1970	08:32
Aqu	5 Nov 1970	13:10
Pis	7 Nov 1970	16:32
Ari	9 Nov 1970	18:51
Tau	11 Nov 1970	20:50
Gem	13 Nov 1970	23:49
Can	16 Nov 1970	05:23
Leo	18 Nov 1970	14:36
Vir	21 Nov 1970	02:50
Lib	23 Nov 1970	15:38
Sco	26 Nov 1970	02:23
Sag	28 Nov 1970	10:01
Cap	30 Nov 1970	15:05
Aqu	2 Dec 1970	18:44
Pis	4 Dec 1970	21:55
Ari	7 Dec 1970	01:03
Tau	9 Dec 1970	04:24
Gem	11 Dec 1970	08:33
Can	13 Dec 1970	14:33
Leo	15 Dec 1970	23:22
Vir	18 Dec 1970	11:05
Lib	21 Dec 1970	00:00
Sco	23 Dec 1970	11:25
Sag	25 Dec 1970	19:27
Cap	28 Dec 1970	00:00
Aqu	30 Dec 1970	02:23

1971

Pis	1 Jan 1971	04:08
Ari	3 Jan 1971	06:26
Tau	5 Jan 1971	10:00
Gem	7 Jan 1971	15:09
Can	9 Jan 1971	22:09
Leo	12 Jan 1971	07:24
Vir	14 Jan 1971	18:57
Lib	17 Jan 1971	07:53
Sco	19 Jan 1971	20:03
Sag	22 Jan 1971	05:15
Cap	24 Jan 1971	10:31
Aqu	26 Jan 1971	12:35
Pis	28 Jan 1971	13:01
Ari	30 Jan 1971	13:36
Tau	1 Feb 1971	15:49
Gem	3 Feb 1971	20:35
Can	6 Feb 1971	04:07
Leo	8 Feb 1971	14:06
Vir	11 Feb 1971	01:58
Lib	13 Feb 1971	14:50
Sco	16 Feb 1971	03:21
Sag	18 Feb 1971	13:44
Cap	20 Feb 1971	20:36
Aqu	22 Feb 1971	23:41
Pis	25 Feb 1971	00:04
Ari	26 Feb 1971	23:30
Tau	28 Feb 1971	23:55
Gem	3 Mar 1971	03:02
Can	5 Mar 1971	09:48
Leo	7 Mar 1971	19:55
Vir	10 Mar 1971	08:10
Lib	12 Mar 1971	21:05
Sco	15 Mar 1971	09:30
Sag	17 Mar 1971	20:22
Cap	20 Mar 1971	04:36
Aqu	22 Mar 1971	09:27
Pis	24 Mar 1971	11:06
Ari	26 Mar 1971	10:45
Tau	28 Mar 1971	10:16
Gem	30 Mar 1971	11:45
Can	1 Apr 1971	16:51
Leo	4 Apr 1971	02:06
Vir	6 Apr 1971	14:16
Lib	9 Apr 1971	03:16
Sco	11 Apr 1971	15:27
Sag	14 Apr 1971	02:02
Cap	16 Apr 1971	10:37
Aqu	18 Apr 1971	16:45
Pis	20 Apr 1971	20:07
Ari	22 Apr 1971	21:08
Tau	24 Apr 1971	21:07
Gem	26 Apr 1971	21:59
Can	29 Apr 1971	01:45
Leo	1 May 1971	09:35
Vir	3 May 1971	21:03
Lib	6 May 1971	09:59
Sco	8 May 1971	22:02
Sag	11 May 1971	08:07
Cap	13 May 1971	16:08
Aqu	15 May 1971	22:19
Pis	18 May 1971	02:39
Ari	20 May 1971	05:11
Tau	22 May 1971	06:31
Gem	24 May 1971	08:01
Can	26 May 1971	11:27
Leo	28 May 1971	18:16
Vir	31 May 1971	04:48
Lib	2 Jun 1971	17:26
Sco	5 Jun 1971	05:36
Sag	7 Jun 1971	15:27
Cap	9 Jun 1971	22:44
Aqu	12 Jun 1971	04:02
Pis	14 Jun 1971	08:01
Ari	16 Jun 1971	11:05
Tau	18 Jun 1971	13:39
Gem	20 Jun 1971	16:24
Can	22 Jun 1971	20:30
Leo	25 Jun 1971	03:13
Vir	27 Jun 1971	13:07
Lib	30 Jun 1971	01:22
Sco	2 Jul 1971	13:45
Sag	4 Jul 1971	23:58
Cap	7 Jul 1971	07:03
Aqu	9 Jul 1971	11:26
Pis	11 Jul 1971	14:14
Ari	13 Jul 1971	16:32
Tau	15 Jul 1971	19:10
Gem	17 Jul 1971	22:47
Can	20 Jul 1971	03:57
Leo	22 Jul 1971	11:17
Vir	24 Jul 1971	21:10
Lib	27 Jul 1971	09:12
Sco	29 Jul 1971	21:50
Sag	1 Aug 1971	08:49
Cap	3 Aug 1971	16:31
Aqu	5 Aug 1971	20:46
Pis	7 Aug 1971	22:34
Ari	9 Aug 1971	23:27
Tau	12 Aug 1971	00:56
Gem	14 Aug 1971	04:11
Can	16 Aug 1971	09:50
Leo	18 Aug 1971	17:57
Vir	21 Aug 1971	04:19
Lib	23 Aug 1971	16:23
Sco	26 Aug 1971	05:09
Sag	28 Aug 1971	16:56
Cap	31 Aug 1971	01:53
Aqu	2 Sep 1971	07:03
Pis	4 Sep 1971	08:50
Ari	6 Sep 1971	08:43
Tau	8 Sep 1971	08:38
Gem	10 Sep 1971	10:26
Can	12 Sep 1971	15:22
Leo	14 Sep 1971	23:38
Vir	17 Sep 1971	10:29
Lib	19 Sep 1971	22:47
Sco	22 Sep 1971	11:32
Sag	24 Sep 1971	23:42
Cap	27 Sep 1971	09:51
Aqu	29 Sep 1971	16:38
Pis	1 Oct 1971	19:36
Ari	3 Oct 1971	19:40
Tau	5 Oct 1971	18:42
Gem	7 Oct 1971	18:53
Can	9 Oct 1971	22:12
Leo	12 Oct 1971	05:31
Vir	14 Oct 1971	16:16
Lib	17 Oct 1971	04:47
Sco	19 Oct 1971	17:30
Sag	22 Oct 1971	05:31
Cap	24 Oct 1971	16:04
Aqu	27 Oct 1971	00:10
Pis	29 Oct 1971	04:56
Ari	31 Oct 1971	06:26
Tau	2 Nov 1971	05:55
Gem	4 Nov 1971	05:27
Can	6 Nov 1971	07:15
Leo	8 Nov 1971	12:58
Vir	10 Nov 1971	22:45
Lib	13 Nov 1971	11:05
Sco	15 Nov 1971	23:49
Sag	18 Nov 1971	11:29
Cap	20 Nov 1971	21:36
Aqu	23 Nov 1971	05:52
Pis	25 Nov 1971	11:46
Ari	27 Nov 1971	15:03
Tau	29 Nov 1971	16:08
Gem	1 Dec 1971	16:25
Can	3 Dec 1971	17:51
Leo	5 Dec 1971	22:18
Vir	8 Dec 1971	06:41
Lib	10 Dec 1971	18:19
Sco	13 Dec 1971	07:01
Sag	15 Dec 1971	18:37
Cap	18 Dec 1971	04:07
Aqu	20 Dec 1971	11:32
Pis	22 Dec 1971	17:10
Ari	24 Dec 1971	21:09
Tau	26 Dec 1971	23:44
Gem	29 Dec 1971	01:38
Can	31 Dec 1971	04:02

1972

Leo	2 Jan 1972	08:22
Vir	4 Jan 1972	15:51
Lib	7 Jan 1972	02:33
Sco	9 Jan 1972	15:03
Sag	12 Jan 1972	02:57
Cap	14 Jan 1972	12:25
Aqu	16 Jan 1972	19:03
Pis	18 Jan 1972	23:27
Ari	21 Jan 1972	02:35
Tau	23 Jan 1972	05:17
Gem	25 Jan 1972	08:14
Can	27 Jan 1972	12:02
Leo	29 Jan 1972	17:21

Vir	1 Feb 1972	00:56
Lib	3 Feb 1972	11:07
Sco	5 Feb 1972	23:18
Sag	8 Feb 1972	11:37
Cap	10 Feb 1972	21:49
Aqu	13 Feb 1972	04:36
Pis	15 Feb 1972	08:10
Ari	17 Feb 1972	09:50
Tau	19 Feb 1972	11:12
Gem	21 Feb 1972	13:36
Can	23 Feb 1972	17:52
Leo	26 Feb 1972	00:15
Vir	28 Feb 1972	08:39

Lib	1 Mar 1972	19:00
Sco	4 Mar 1972	07:00
Sag	6 Mar 1972	19:36
Cap	9 Mar 1972	06:49
Aqu	11 Mar 1972	14:41
Pis	13 Mar 1972	18:39
Ari	15 Mar 1972	19:37
Tau	17 Mar 1972	19:28
Gem	19 Mar 1972	20:13
Can	21 Mar 1972	23:27
Leo	24 Mar 1972	05:46
Vir	26 Mar 1972	14:48
Lib	29 Mar 1972	01:42
Sco	31 Mar 1972	13:49

Sag	3 Apr 1972	02:27
Cap	5 Apr 1972	14:20
Aqu	7 Apr 1972	23:36
Pis	10 Apr 1972	04:57
Ari	12 Apr 1972	06:32
Tau	14 Apr 1972	05:54
Gem	16 Apr 1972	05:17
Can	18 Apr 1972	06:46
Leo	20 Apr 1972	11:48
Vir	22 Apr 1972	20:25
Lib	25 Apr 1972	07:34
Sco	27 Apr 1972	19:56
Sag	30 Apr 1972	08:30

Cap	2 May 1972	20:28
Aqu	5 May 1972	06:35
Pis	7 May 1972	13:26
Ari	9 May 1972	16:34
Tau	11 May 1972	16:47
Gem	13 May 1972	15:57
Can	15 May 1972	16:16
Leo	17 May 1972	19:38
Vir	20 May 1972	02:57
Lib	22 May 1972	13:37
Sco	25 May 1972	02:01
Sag	27 May 1972	14:33
Cap	30 May 1972	02:12

Aqu	1 Jun 1972	12:14
Pis	3 Jun 1972	19:51
Ari	6 Jun 1972	00:26
Tau	8 Jun 1972	02:14
Gem	10 Jun 1972	02:24
Can	12 Jun 1972	02:45
Leo	14 Jun 1972	05:10
Vir	16 Jun 1972	11:04
Lib	18 Jun 1972	20:39
Sco	21 Jun 1972	08:43
Sag	23 Jun 1972	21:14
Cap	26 Jun 1972	08:36
Aqu	28 Jun 1972	18:02

Pis	1 Jul 1972	01:18
Ari	3 Jul 1972	06:22
Tau	5 Jul 1972	09:24
Gem	7 Jul 1972	11:04
Can	9 Jul 1972	12:30
Leo	11 Jul 1972	15:06
Vir	13 Jul 1972	20:17
Lib	16 Jul 1972	04:49
Sco	18 Jul 1972	16:15
Sag	21 Jul 1972	04:46
Cap	23 Jul 1972	16:10
Aqu	26 Jul 1972	01:06
Pis	28 Jul 1972	07:28
Ari	30 Jul 1972	11:50

Tau	1 Aug 1972	14:57
Gem	3 Aug 1972	17:33
Can	5 Aug 1972	20:18
Leo	7 Aug 1972	23:57
Vir	10 Aug 1972	05:23
Lib	12 Aug 1972	13:28
Sco	15 Aug 1972	00:20
Sag	17 Aug 1972	12:49
Cap	20 Aug 1972	00:37
Aqu	22 Aug 1972	09:42
Pis	24 Aug 1972	15:28
Ari	26 Aug 1972	18:40
Tau	28 Aug 1972	20:43
Gem	30 Aug 1972	22:56

Can	2 Sep 1972	02:12
Leo	4 Sep 1972	06:54
Vir	6 Sep 1972	13:16
Lib	8 Sep 1972	21:37
Sco	11 Sep 1972	08:16
Sag	13 Sep 1972	20:42
Cap	16 Sep 1972	09:07
Aqu	18 Sep 1972	19:04
Pis	21 Sep 1972	01:07
Ari	23 Sep 1972	03:44
Tau	25 Sep 1972	04:27
Gem	27 Sep 1972	05:14
Can	29 Sep 1972	07:39

Leo	1 Oct 1972	12:26
Vir	3 Oct 1972	19:31
Lib	6 Oct 1972	04:35
Sco	8 Oct 1972	15:27
Sag	11 Oct 1972	03:52
Cap	13 Oct 1972	16:43
Aqu	16 Oct 1972	03:50
Pis	18 Oct 1972	11:11
Ari	20 Oct 1972	14:21
Tau	22 Oct 1972	14:37
Gem	24 Oct 1972	14:03
Can	26 Oct 1972	14:45
Leo	28 Oct 1972	18:14
Vir	31 Oct 1972	01:00

Lib	2 Nov 1972	10:27
Sco	4 Nov 1972	21:46
Sag	7 Nov 1972	10:16
Cap	9 Nov 1972	23:10
Aqu	12 Nov 1972	11:01
Pis	14 Nov 1972	19:55
Ari	17 Nov 1972	00:42
Tau	19 Nov 1972	01:52
Gem	21 Nov 1972	01:05
Can	23 Nov 1972	00:32
Leo	25 Nov 1972	02:13
Vir	27 Nov 1972	07:25
Lib	29 Nov 1972	16:15

Sco	2 Dec 1972	03:42
Sag	4 Dec 1972	16:22
Cap	7 Dec 1972	05:06
Aqu	9 Dec 1972	16:53
Pis	12 Dec 1972	02:31
Ari	14 Dec 1972	08:58
Tau	16 Dec 1972	11:58
Gem	18 Dec 1972	12:24
Can	20 Dec 1972	11:57
Leo	22 Dec 1972	12:35
Vir	24 Dec 1972	16:03
Lib	26 Dec 1972	23:23
Sco	29 Dec 1972	10:11
Sag	31 Dec 1972	22:51

1973

Cap	3 Jan 1973	11:30
Aqu	5 Jan 1973	22:46
Pis	8 Jan 1973	08:02
Ari	10 Jan 1973	14:57
Tau	12 Jan 1973	19:24
Gem	14 Jan 1973	21:40
Can	16 Jan 1973	22:38
Leo	18 Jan 1973	23:41
Vir	21 Jan 1973	02:24
Lib	23 Jan 1973	08:17
Sco	25 Jan 1973	17:52
Sag	28 Jan 1973	06:10
Cap	30 Jan 1973	18:54
Aqu	2 Feb 1973	05:55
Pis	4 Feb 1973	14:21
Ari	6 Feb 1973	20:28
Tau	9 Feb 1973	00:53
Gem	11 Feb 1973	04:10
Can	13 Feb 1973	06:44
Leo	15 Feb 1973	09:12
Vir	17 Feb 1973	12:32
Lib	19 Feb 1973	17:58
Sco	22 Feb 1973	02:36
Sag	24 Feb 1973	14:15
Cap	27 Feb 1973	03:03
Aqu	1 Mar 1973	14:21
Pis	3 Mar 1973	22:30
Ari	6 Mar 1973	03:36
Tau	8 Mar 1973	06:50
Gem	10 Mar 1973	09:31
Can	12 Mar 1973	12:29
Leo	14 Mar 1973	16:08
Vir	16 Mar 1973	20:42
Lib	19 Mar 1973	02:49
Sco	21 Mar 1973	11:16
Sag	23 Mar 1973	22:27
Cap	26 Mar 1973	11:15
Aqu	28 Mar 1973	23:11
Pis	31 Mar 1973	07:54
Ari	2 Apr 1973	12:47
Tau	4 Apr 1973	14:58
Gem	6 Apr 1973	16:12
Can	8 Apr 1973	18:04
Leo	10 Apr 1973	21:32
Vir	13 Apr 1973	02:47
Lib	15 Apr 1973	09:50
Sco	17 Apr 1973	18:51
Sag	20 Apr 1973	06:02
Cap	22 Apr 1973	18:49
Aqu	25 Apr 1973	07:20
Pis	27 Apr 1973	17:09
Ari	29 Apr 1973	22:52
Tau	2 May 1973	01:01
Gem	4 May 1973	01:16
Can	6 May 1973	01:35
Leo	8 May 1973	03:37
Vir	10 May 1973	08:13
Lib	12 May 1973	15:31
Sco	15 May 1973	01:10
Sag	17 May 1973	12:42
Cap	20 May 1973	01:30
Aqu	22 May 1973	14:17
Pis	25 May 1973	01:04
Ari	27 May 1973	08:13
Tau	29 May 1973	11:26
Gem	31 May 1973	11:52
Can	2 Jun 1973	11:21
Leo	4 Jun 1973	11:50
Vir	6 Jun 1973	14:52
Lib	8 Jun 1973	21:16
Sco	11 Jun 1973	06:52
Sag	13 Jun 1973	18:43
Cap	16 Jun 1973	07:37
Aqu	18 Jun 1973	20:18
Pis	21 Jun 1973	07:28
Ari	23 Jun 1973	15:48
Tau	25 Jun 1973	20:36
Gem	27 Jun 1973	22:17
Can	29 Jun 1973	22:08
Leo	1 Jul 1973	21:56
Vir	3 Jul 1973	23:32
Lib	6 Jul 1973	04:24
Sco	8 Jul 1973	13:06
Sag	11 Jul 1973	00:48
Cap	13 Jul 1973	13:45
Aqu	16 Jul 1973	02:14
Pis	18 Jul 1973	13:06
Ari	20 Jul 1973	21:43
Tau	23 Jul 1973	03:40
Gem	25 Jul 1973	06:58
Can	27 Jul 1973	08:10
Leo	29 Jul 1973	08:29
Vir	31 Jul 1973	09:35
Lib	2 Aug 1973	13:14
Sco	4 Aug 1973	20:36
Sag	7 Aug 1973	07:37
Cap	9 Aug 1973	20:29
Aqu	12 Aug 1973	08:52
Pis	14 Aug 1973	19:14
Ari	17 Aug 1973	03:15
Tau	19 Aug 1973	09:13
Gem	21 Aug 1973	13:26
Can	23 Aug 1973	16:07
Leo	25 Aug 1973	17:49
Vir	27 Aug 1973	19:33
Lib	29 Aug 1973	22:53
Sco	1 Sep 1973	05:18
Sag	3 Sep 1973	15:25
Cap	6 Sep 1973	04:01
Aqu	8 Sep 1973	16:30
Pis	11 Sep 1973	02:39
Ari	13 Sep 1973	09:55
Tau	15 Sep 1973	14:58
Gem	17 Sep 1973	18:48
Can	19 Sep 1973	22:01
Leo	22 Sep 1973	00:56
Vir	24 Sep 1973	03:59
Lib	26 Sep 1973	08:01
Sco	28 Sep 1973	14:19
Sag	30 Sep 1973	23:48
Cap	3 Oct 1973	12:02
Aqu	6 Oct 1973	00:48
Pis	8 Oct 1973	11:22
Ari	10 Oct 1973	18:29
Tau	12 Oct 1973	22:35
Gem	15 Oct 1973	01:08
Can	17 Oct 1973	03:29
Leo	19 Oct 1973	06:25
Vir	21 Oct 1973	10:19
Lib	23 Oct 1973	15:28
Sco	25 Oct 1973	22:28
Sag	28 Oct 1973	07:58
Cap	30 Oct 1973	19:57
Aqu	2 Nov 1973	08:58
Pis	4 Nov 1973	20:25
Ari	7 Nov 1973	04:18
Tau	9 Nov 1973	08:25
Gem	11 Nov 1973	09:59
Can	13 Nov 1973	10:47
Leo	15 Nov 1973	12:21
Vir	17 Nov 1973	15:41
Lib	19 Nov 1973	21:16
Sco	22 Nov 1973	05:07
Sag	24 Nov 1973	15:11
Cap	27 Nov 1973	03:13
Aqu	29 Nov 1973	16:17
Pis	2 Dec 1973	04:31
Ari	4 Dec 1973	13:49
Tau	6 Dec 1973	19:08
Gem	8 Dec 1973	20:57
Can	10 Dec 1973	20:52
Leo	12 Dec 1973	20:45
Vir	14 Dec 1973	22:22
Lib	17 Dec 1973	02:54
Sco	19 Dec 1973	10:45
Sag	21 Dec 1973	21:20
Cap	24 Dec 1973	09:41
Aqu	26 Dec 1973	22:43
Pis	29 Dec 1973	11:09
Ari	31 Dec 1973	21:33

1974

Sign	Date	Time
Tau	3 Jan 1974	04:37
Gem	5 Jan 1974	07:59
Can	7 Jan 1974	08:28
Leo	9 Jan 1974	07:42
Vir	11 Jan 1974	07:42
Lib	13 Jan 1974	10:23
Sco	15 Jan 1974	16:54
Sag	18 Jan 1974	03:13
Cap	20 Jan 1974	15:48
Aqu	23 Jan 1974	04:50
Pis	25 Jan 1974	17:00
Ari	28 Jan 1974	03:31
Tau	30 Jan 1974	11:40
Gem	1 Feb 1974	16:53
Can	3 Feb 1974	19:05
Leo	5 Feb 1974	19:11
Vir	7 Feb 1974	18:52
Lib	9 Feb 1974	20:11
Sco	12 Feb 1974	00:59
Sag	14 Feb 1974	10:02
Cap	16 Feb 1974	22:16
Aqu	19 Feb 1974	11:21
Pis	21 Feb 1974	23:15
Ari	24 Feb 1974	09:12
Tau	26 Feb 1974	17:11
Gem	28 Feb 1974	23:09
Can	3 Mar 1974	02:59
Leo	5 Mar 1974	04:49
Vir	7 Mar 1974	05:33
Lib	9 Mar 1974	06:52
Sco	11 Mar 1974	10:41
Sag	13 Mar 1974	18:20
Cap	16 Mar 1974	05:41
Aqu	18 Mar 1974	18:38
Pis	21 Mar 1974	06:33
Ari	23 Mar 1974	16:02
Tau	25 Mar 1974	23:09
Gem	28 Mar 1974	04:33
Can	30 Mar 1974	08:39
Leo	1 Apr 1974	11:40
Vir	3 Apr 1974	13:56
Lib	5 Apr 1974	16:23
Sco	7 Apr 1974	20:26
Sag	10 Apr 1974	03:28
Cap	12 Apr 1974	13:57
Aqu	15 Apr 1974	02:34
Pis	17 Apr 1974	14:43
Ari	20 Apr 1974	00:19
Tau	22 Apr 1974	06:53
Gem	24 Apr 1974	11:10
Can	26 Apr 1974	14:17
Leo	28 Apr 1974	17:03
Vir	30 Apr 1974	20:00
Lib	2 May 1974	23:39
Sco	5 May 1974	04:43
Sag	7 May 1974	12:06
Cap	9 May 1974	22:15
Aqu	12 May 1974	10:34
Pis	14 May 1974	23:02
Ari	17 May 1974	09:18
Tau	19 May 1974	16:09
Gem	21 May 1974	19:53
Can	23 May 1974	21:45
Leo	25 May 1974	23:12
Vir	28 May 1974	01:26
Lib	30 May 1974	05:16
Sco	1 Jun 1974	11:11
Sag	3 Jun 1974	19:22
Cap	6 Jun 1974	05:48
Aqu	8 Jun 1974	18:02
Pis	11 Jun 1974	06:43
Ari	13 Jun 1974	17:52
Tau	16 Jun 1974	01:45
Gem	18 Jun 1974	05:59
Can	20 Jun 1974	07:21
Leo	22 Jun 1974	07:30
Vir	24 Jun 1974	08:11
Lib	26 Jun 1974	10:58
Sco	28 Jun 1974	16:40
Sag	1 Jul 1974	01:21
Cap	3 Jul 1974	12:19
Aqu	6 Jul 1974	00:41
Pis	8 Jul 1974	13:25
Ari	11 Jul 1974	01:10
Tau	13 Jul 1974	10:20
Gem	15 Jul 1974	15:53
Can	17 Jul 1974	17:56
Leo	19 Jul 1974	17:43
Vir	21 Jul 1974	17:10
Lib	23 Jul 1974	18:19
Sco	25 Jul 1974	22:47
Sag	28 Jul 1974	07:00
Cap	30 Jul 1974	18:11
Aqu	2 Aug 1974	06:46
Pis	4 Aug 1974	19:26
Ari	7 Aug 1974	07:15
Tau	9 Aug 1974	17:12
Gem	12 Aug 1974	00:13
Can	14 Aug 1974	03:48
Leo	16 Aug 1974	04:26
Vir	18 Aug 1974	03:42
Lib	20 Aug 1974	03:45
Sco	22 Aug 1974	06:37
Sag	24 Aug 1974	13:35
Cap	27 Aug 1974	00:15
Aqu	29 Aug 1974	12:52
Pis	1 Sep 1974	01:29
Ari	3 Sep 1974	12:57
Tau	5 Sep 1974	22:50
Gem	8 Sep 1974	06:36
Can	10 Sep 1974	11:38
Leo	12 Sep 1974	13:53
Vir	14 Sep 1974	14:12
Lib	16 Sep 1974	14:17
Sco	18 Sep 1974	16:14
Sag	20 Sep 1974	21:48
Cap	23 Sep 1974	07:22
Aqu	25 Sep 1974	19:38
Pis	28 Sep 1974	08:14
Ari	30 Sep 1974	19:25
Tau	3 Oct 1974	04:39
Gem	5 Oct 1974	12:00
Can	7 Oct 1974	17:30
Leo	9 Oct 1974	21:02
Vir	11 Oct 1974	22:55
Lib	14 Oct 1974	00:11
Sco	16 Oct 1974	02:24
Sag	18 Oct 1974	07:15
Cap	20 Oct 1974	15:45
Aqu	23 Oct 1974	03:20
Pis	25 Oct 1974	15:56
Ari	28 Oct 1974	03:13
Tau	30 Oct 1974	11:59
Gem	1 Nov 1974	18:23
Can	3 Nov 1974	23:00
Leo	6 Nov 1974	02:30
Vir	8 Nov 1974	05:18
Lib	10 Nov 1974	07:59
Sco	12 Nov 1974	11:24
Sag	14 Nov 1974	16:39
Cap	17 Nov 1974	00:43
Aqu	19 Nov 1974	11:39
Pis	22 Nov 1974	00:11
Ari	24 Nov 1974	11:58
Tau	26 Nov 1974	21:04
Gem	29 Nov 1974	02:57
Can	1 Dec 1974	06:21
Leo	3 Dec 1974	08:31
Vir	5 Dec 1974	10:40
Lib	7 Dec 1974	13:43
Sco	9 Dec 1974	18:13
Sag	12 Dec 1974	00:35
Cap	14 Dec 1974	09:04
Aqu	16 Dec 1974	19:48
Pis	19 Dec 1974	08:12
Ari	21 Dec 1974	20:35
Tau	24 Dec 1974	06:44
Gem	26 Dec 1974	13:14
Can	28 Dec 1974	16:15
Leo	30 Dec 1974	17:05

1975

Vir	1 Jan 1975	17:33
Lib	3 Jan 1975	19:22
Sco	5 Jan 1975	23:40
Sag	8 Jan 1975	06:39
Cap	10 Jan 1975	15:58
Aqu	13 Jan 1975	03:03
Pis	15 Jan 1975	15:23
Ari	18 Jan 1975	04:03
Tau	20 Jan 1975	15:20
Gem	22 Jan 1975	23:21
Can	25 Jan 1975	03:19
Leo	27 Jan 1975	04:00
Vir	29 Jan 1975	03:14
Lib	31 Jan 1975	03:14

Sco	2 Feb 1975	05:53
Sag	4 Feb 1975	12:11
Cap	6 Feb 1975	21:43
Aqu	9 Feb 1975	09:17
Pis	11 Feb 1975	21:45
Ari	14 Feb 1975	10:22
Tau	16 Feb 1975	22:08
Gem	19 Feb 1975	07:34
Can	21 Feb 1975	13:17
Leo	23 Feb 1975	15:12
Vir	25 Feb 1975	14:36
Lib	27 Feb 1975	13:39

Sco	1 Mar 1975	14:35
Sag	3 Mar 1975	19:06
Cap	6 Mar 1975	03:40
Aqu	8 Mar 1975	15:10
Pis	11 Mar 1975	03:49
Ari	13 Mar 1975	16:18
Tau	16 Mar 1975	03:52
Gem	18 Mar 1975	13:42
Can	20 Mar 1975	20:47
Leo	23 Mar 1975	00:30
Vir	25 Mar 1975	01:20
Lib	27 Mar 1975	00:51
Sco	29 Mar 1975	01:09
Sag	31 Mar 1975	04:10

Cap	2 Apr 1975	11:09
Aqu	4 Apr 1975	21:45
Pis	7 Apr 1975	10:17
Ari	9 Apr 1975	22:43
Tau	12 Apr 1975	09:53
Gem	14 Apr 1975	19:14
Can	17 Apr 1975	02:26
Leo	19 Apr 1975	07:14
Vir	21 Apr 1975	09:42
Lib	23 Apr 1975	10:41
Sco	25 Apr 1975	11:40
Sag	27 Apr 1975	14:21
Cap	29 Apr 1975	20:09

Aqu	2 May 1975	05:33
Pis	4 May 1975	17:34
Ari	7 May 1975	06:02
Tau	9 May 1975	17:03
Gem	12 May 1975	01:43
Can	14 May 1975	08:07
Leo	16 May 1975	12:38
Vir	18 May 1975	15:45
Lib	20 May 1975	18:05
Sco	22 May 1975	20:26
Sag	24 May 1975	23:52
Cap	27 May 1975	05:31
Aqu	29 May 1975	14:10

Pis	1 Jun 1975	01:32
Ari	3 Jun 1975	14:01
Tau	6 Jun 1975	01:17
Gem	8 Jun 1975	09:48
Can	10 Jun 1975	15:21
Leo	12 Jun 1975	18:45
Vir	14 Jun 1975	21:10
Lib	16 Jun 1975	23:41
Sco	19 Jun 1975	02:59
Sag	21 Jun 1975	07:35
Cap	23 Jun 1975	13:56
Aqu	25 Jun 1975	22:33
Pis	28 Jun 1975	09:33
Ari	30 Jun 1975	22:02

Tau	3 Jul 1975	09:53
Gem	5 Jul 1975	18:58
Can	8 Jul 1975	00:22
Leo	10 Jul 1975	02:49
Vir	12 Jul 1975	03:55
Lib	14 Jul 1975	05:21
Sco	16 Jul 1975	08:23
Sag	18 Jul 1975	13:32
Cap	20 Jul 1975	20:46
Aqu	23 Jul 1975	05:56
Pis	25 Jul 1975	16:58
Ari	28 Jul 1975	05:27
Tau	30 Jul 1975	17:53

Gem	2 Aug 1975	04:01
Can	4 Aug 1975	10:15
Leo	6 Aug 1975	12:42
Vir	8 Aug 1975	12:53
Lib	10 Aug 1975	12:51
Sco	12 Aug 1975	14:30
Sag	14 Aug 1975	18:59
Cap	17 Aug 1975	02:25
Aqu	19 Aug 1975	12:09
Pis	21 Aug 1975	23:32
Ari	24 Aug 1975	12:02
Tau	27 Aug 1975	00:44
Gem	29 Aug 1975	11:52
Can	31 Aug 1975	19:34

Leo	2 Sep 1975	23:06
Vir	4 Sep 1975	23:28
Lib	6 Sep 1975	22:38
Sco	8 Sep 1975	22:46
Sag	11 Sep 1975	01:42
Cap	13 Sep 1975	08:12
Aqu	15 Sep 1975	17:51
Pis	18 Sep 1975	05:32
Ari	20 Sep 1975	18:07
Tau	23 Sep 1975	06:43
Gem	25 Sep 1975	18:13
Can	28 Sep 1975	03:06
Leo	30 Sep 1975	08:19

Vir	2 Oct 1975	10:02
Lib	4 Oct 1975	09:38
Sco	6 Oct 1975	09:09
Sag	8 Oct 1975	10:36
Cap	10 Oct 1975	15:30
Aqu	13 Oct 1975	00:10
Pis	15 Oct 1975	11:40
Ari	18 Oct 1975	00:20
Tau	20 Oct 1975	12:43
Gem	22 Oct 1975	23:50
Can	25 Oct 1975	08:56
Leo	27 Oct 1975	15:19
Vir	29 Oct 1975	18:46
Lib	31 Oct 1975	19:55

Sco	2 Nov 1975	20:07
Sag	4 Nov 1975	21:10
Cap	7 Nov 1975	00:46
Aqu	9 Nov 1975	08:00
Pis	11 Nov 1975	18:42
Ari	14 Nov 1975	07:17
Tau	16 Nov 1975	19:37
Gem	19 Nov 1975	06:14
Can	21 Nov 1975	14:35
Leo	23 Nov 1975	20:47
Vir	26 Nov 1975	01:04
Lib	28 Nov 1975	03:47
Sco	30 Nov 1975	05:36

Sag	2 Dec 1975	07:33
Cap	4 Dec 1975	10:59
Aqu	6 Dec 1975	17:12
Pis	9 Dec 1975	02:52
Ari	11 Dec 1975	15:06
Tau	14 Dec 1975	03:38
Gem	16 Dec 1975	14:11
Can	18 Dec 1975	21:48
Leo	21 Dec 1975	02:53
Vir	23 Dec 1975	06:27
Lib	25 Dec 1975	09:27
Sco	27 Dec 1975	12:28
Sag	29 Dec 1975	15:53
Cap	31 Dec 1975	20:17

1976

Sign	Date	Time
Aqu	3 Jan 1976	02:33
Pis	5 Jan 1976	11:36
Ari	7 Jan 1976	23:21
Tau	10 Jan 1976	12:09
Gem	12 Jan 1976	23:18
Can	15 Jan 1976	07:00
Leo	17 Jan 1976	11:14
Vir	19 Jan 1976	13:25
Lib	21 Jan 1976	15:11
Sco	23 Jan 1976	17:48
Sag	25 Jan 1976	21:51
Cap	28 Jan 1976	03:24
Aqu	30 Jan 1976	10:34

Sign	Date	Time
Pis	1 Feb 1976	19:47
Ari	4 Feb 1976	07:17
Tau	6 Feb 1976	20:13
Gem	9 Feb 1976	08:15
Can	11 Feb 1976	16:58
Leo	13 Feb 1976	21:31
Vir	15 Feb 1976	22:58
Lib	17 Feb 1976	23:14
Sco	20 Feb 1976	00:14
Sag	22 Feb 1976	03:19
Cap	24 Feb 1976	08:54
Aqu	26 Feb 1976	16:48
Pis	29 Feb 1976	02:42

Sign	Date	Time
Ari	2 Mar 1976	14:22
Tau	5 Mar 1976	03:18
Gem	7 Mar 1976	15:55
Can	10 Mar 1976	01:57
Leo	12 Mar 1976	07:54
Vir	14 Mar 1976	09:57
Lib	16 Mar 1976	09:44
Sco	18 Mar 1976	09:18
Sag	20 Mar 1976	10:35
Cap	22 Mar 1976	14:49
Aqu	24 Mar 1976	22:20
Pis	27 Mar 1976	08:34
Ari	29 Mar 1976	20:37

Sign	Date	Time
Tau	1 Apr 1976	09:33
Gem	3 Apr 1976	22:15
Can	6 Apr 1976	09:05
Leo	8 Apr 1976	16:36
Vir	10 Apr 1976	20:15
Lib	12 Apr 1976	20:53
Sco	14 Apr 1976	20:14
Sag	16 Apr 1976	20:15
Cap	18 Apr 1976	22:44
Aqu	21 Apr 1976	04:48
Pis	23 Apr 1976	14:28
Ari	26 Apr 1976	02:37
Tau	28 Apr 1976	15:37

Sign	Date	Time
Gem	1 May 1976	04:04
Can	3 May 1976	14:52
Leo	5 May 1976	23:08
Vir	8 May 1976	04:20
Lib	10 May 1976	06:39
Sco	12 May 1976	07:02
Sag	14 May 1976	07:04
Cap	16 May 1976	08:32
Aqu	18 May 1976	13:03
Pis	20 May 1976	21:27
Ari	23 May 1976	09:07
Tau	25 May 1976	22:06
Gem	28 May 1976	10:21
Can	30 May 1976	20:38

Sign	Date	Time
Leo	2 Jun 1976	04:37
Vir	4 Jun 1976	10:20
Lib	6 Jun 1976	13:59
Sco	8 Jun 1976	15:58
Sag	10 Jun 1976	17:06
Cap	12 Jun 1976	18:45
Aqu	14 Jun 1976	22:32
Pis	17 Jun 1976	05:43
Ari	19 Jun 1976	16:32
Tau	22 Jun 1976	05:21
Gem	24 Jun 1976	17:36
Can	27 Jun 1976	03:28
Leo	29 Jun 1976	10:39

Sign	Date	Time
Vir	1 Jul 1976	15:46
Lib	3 Jul 1976	19:34
Sco	5 Jul 1976	22:33
Sag	8 Jul 1976	01:05
Cap	10 Jul 1976	03:49
Aqu	12 Jul 1976	07:53
Pis	14 Jul 1976	14:37
Ari	17 Jul 1976	00:40
Tau	19 Jul 1976	13:11
Gem	22 Jul 1976	01:40
Can	24 Jul 1976	11:38
Leo	26 Jul 1976	18:18
Vir	28 Jul 1976	22:23
Lib	31 Jul 1976	01:13

Sign	Date	Time
Sco	2 Aug 1976	03:55
Sag	4 Aug 1976	07:03
Cap	6 Aug 1976	10:55
Aqu	8 Aug 1976	15:57
Pis	10 Aug 1976	23:01
Ari	13 Aug 1976	08:49
Tau	15 Aug 1976	21:05
Gem	18 Aug 1976	09:53
Can	20 Aug 1976	20:33
Leo	23 Aug 1976	03:30
Vir	25 Aug 1976	07:03
Lib	27 Aug 1976	08:41
Sco	29 Aug 1976	10:05
Sag	31 Aug 1976	12:29

Sign	Date	Time
Cap	2 Sep 1976	16:29
Aqu	4 Sep 1976	22:20
Pis	7 Sep 1976	06:11
Ari	9 Sep 1976	16:18
Tau	12 Sep 1976	04:30
Gem	14 Sep 1976	17:32
Can	17 Sep 1976	05:06
Leo	19 Sep 1976	13:09
Vir	21 Sep 1976	17:15
Lib	23 Sep 1976	18:27
Sco	25 Sep 1976	18:33
Sag	27 Sep 1976	19:21
Cap	29 Sep 1976	22:14

Sign	Date	Time
Aqu	2 Oct 1976	03:50
Pis	4 Oct 1976	12:10
Ari	6 Oct 1976	22:50
Tau	9 Oct 1976	11:11
Gem	12 Oct 1976	00:14
Can	14 Oct 1976	12:23
Leo	16 Oct 1976	21:48
Vir	19 Oct 1976	03:23
Lib	21 Oct 1976	05:26
Sco	23 Oct 1976	05:16
Sag	25 Oct 1976	04:49
Cap	27 Oct 1976	05:55
Aqu	29 Oct 1976	10:06
Pis	31 Oct 1976	17:53

Sign	Date	Time
Ari	3 Nov 1976	04:46
Tau	5 Nov 1976	17:23
Gem	8 Nov 1976	06:21
Can	10 Nov 1976	18:27
Leo	13 Nov 1976	04:36
Vir	15 Nov 1976	11:45
Lib	17 Nov 1976	15:33
Sco	19 Nov 1976	16:31
Sag	21 Nov 1976	16:03
Cap	23 Nov 1976	16:04
Aqu	25 Nov 1976	18:30
Pis	28 Nov 1976	00:48
Ari	30 Nov 1976	11:02

Sign	Date	Time
Tau	2 Dec 1976	23:41
Gem	5 Dec 1976	12:38
Can	8 Dec 1976	00:20
Leo	10 Dec 1976	10:11
Vir	12 Dec 1976	17:55
Lib	14 Dec 1976	23:12
Sco	17 Dec 1976	02:00
Sag	19 Dec 1976	02:53
Cap	21 Dec 1976	03:12
Aqu	23 Dec 1976	04:48
Pis	25 Dec 1976	09:37
Ari	27 Dec 1976	18:32
Tau	30 Dec 1976	06:43

Moon Signs

1977

Sign	Date	Time
Gem	1 Jan 1977	19:42
Can	4 Jan 1977	07:12
Leo	6 Jan 1977	16:20
Vir	8 Jan 1977	23:22
Lib	11 Jan 1977	04:47
Sco	13 Jan 1977	08:44
Sag	15 Jan 1977	11:17
Cap	17 Jan 1977	13:02
Aqu	19 Jan 1977	15:12
Pis	21 Jan 1977	19:30
Ari	24 Jan 1977	03:20
Tau	26 Jan 1977	14:41
Gem	29 Jan 1977	03:37
Can	31 Jan 1977	15:19
Leo	3 Feb 1977	00:10
Vir	5 Feb 1977	06:17
Lib	7 Feb 1977	10:35
Sco	9 Feb 1977	14:04
Sag	11 Feb 1977	17:11
Cap	13 Feb 1977	20:14
Aqu	15 Feb 1977	23:45
Pis	18 Feb 1977	04:45
Ari	20 Feb 1977	12:23
Tau	22 Feb 1977	23:07
Gem	25 Feb 1977	11:50
Can	28 Feb 1977	00:01
Leo	2 Mar 1977	09:24
Vir	4 Mar 1977	15:18
Lib	6 Mar 1977	18:34
Sco	8 Mar 1977	20:36
Sag	10 Mar 1977	22:42
Cap	13 Mar 1977	01:40
Aqu	15 Mar 1977	05:59
Pis	17 Mar 1977	12:06
Ari	19 Mar 1977	20:23
Tau	22 Mar 1977	07:05
Gem	24 Mar 1977	19:38
Can	27 Mar 1977	08:16
Leo	29 Mar 1977	18:40
Vir	1 Apr 1977	01:23
Lib	3 Apr 1977	04:38
Sco	5 Apr 1977	05:39
Sag	7 Apr 1977	06:08
Cap	9 Apr 1977	07:40
Aqu	11 Apr 1977	11:24
Pis	13 Apr 1977	17:49
Ari	16 Apr 1977	02:52
Tau	18 Apr 1977	14:02
Gem	21 Apr 1977	02:37
Can	23 Apr 1977	15:24
Leo	26 Apr 1977	02:42
Vir	28 Apr 1977	10:50
Lib	30 Apr 1977	15:11
Sco	2 May 1977	16:23
Sag	4 May 1977	15:58
Cap	6 May 1977	15:54
Aqu	8 May 1977	17:59
Pis	10 May 1977	23:30
Ari	13 May 1977	08:30
Tau	15 May 1977	20:04
Gem	18 May 1977	08:50
Can	20 May 1977	21:35
Leo	23 May 1977	09:12
Vir	25 May 1977	18:30
Lib	28 May 1977	00:27
Sco	30 May 1977	02:55
Sag	1 Jun 1977	02:53
Cap	3 Jun 1977	02:07
Aqu	5 Jun 1977	02:44
Pis	7 Jun 1977	06:35
Ari	9 Jun 1977	14:35
Tau	12 Jun 1977	01:57
Gem	14 Jun 1977	14:49
Can	17 Jun 1977	03:28
Leo	19 Jun 1977	14:53
Vir	22 Jun 1977	00:28
Lib	24 Jun 1977	07:34
Sco	26 Jun 1977	11:40
Sag	28 Jun 1977	13:01
Cap	30 Jun 1977	12:48
Aqu	2 Jul 1977	12:57
Pis	4 Jul 1977	15:32
Ari	6 Jul 1977	22:04
Tau	9 Jul 1977	08:33
Gem	11 Jul 1977	21:15
Can	14 Jul 1977	09:49
Leo	16 Jul 1977	20:51
Vir	19 Jul 1977	05:58
Lib	21 Jul 1977	13:08
Sco	23 Jul 1977	18:13
Sag	25 Jul 1977	21:03
Cap	27 Jul 1977	22:14
Aqu	29 Jul 1977	23:05
Pis	1 Aug 1977	01:24
Ari	3 Aug 1977	06:54
Tau	5 Aug 1977	16:18
Gem	8 Aug 1977	04:29
Can	10 Aug 1977	17:04
Leo	13 Aug 1977	03:56
Vir	15 Aug 1977	12:25
Lib	17 Aug 1977	18:48
Sco	19 Aug 1977	23:34
Sag	22 Aug 1977	03:02
Cap	24 Aug 1977	05:30
Aqu	26 Aug 1977	07:41
Pis	28 Aug 1977	10:47
Ari	30 Aug 1977	16:12
Tau	2 Sep 1977	00:52
Gem	4 Sep 1977	12:27
Can	7 Sep 1977	01:02
Leo	9 Sep 1977	12:12
Vir	11 Sep 1977	20:33
Lib	14 Sep 1977	02:06
Sco	16 Sep 1977	05:45
Sag	18 Sep 1977	08:28
Cap	20 Sep 1977	11:04
Aqu	22 Sep 1977	14:12
Pis	24 Sep 1977	18:30
Ari	27 Sep 1977	00:41
Tau	29 Sep 1977	09:22
Gem	1 Oct 1977	20:33
Can	4 Oct 1977	09:08
Leo	6 Oct 1977	20:57
Vir	9 Oct 1977	05:58
Lib	11 Oct 1977	11:28
Sco	13 Oct 1977	14:10
Sag	15 Oct 1977	15:27
Cap	17 Oct 1977	16:50
Aqu	19 Oct 1977	19:36
Pis	22 Oct 1977	00:27
Ari	24 Oct 1977	07:34
Tau	26 Oct 1977	16:53
Gem	29 Oct 1977	04:08
Can	31 Oct 1977	16:40
Leo	3 Nov 1977	05:03
Vir	5 Nov 1977	15:15
Lib	7 Nov 1977	21:49
Sco	10 Nov 1977	00:40
Sag	12 Nov 1977	01:03
Cap	14 Nov 1977	00:51
Aqu	16 Nov 1977	02:00
Pis	18 Nov 1977	05:58
Ari	20 Nov 1977	13:13
Tau	22 Nov 1977	23:09
Gem	25 Nov 1977	10:48
Can	27 Nov 1977	23:20
Leo	30 Nov 1977	11:52
Vir	2 Dec 1977	23:04
Lib	5 Dec 1977	07:17
Sco	7 Dec 1977	11:31
Sag	9 Dec 1977	12:20
Cap	11 Dec 1977	11:26
Aqu	13 Dec 1977	11:00
Pis	15 Dec 1977	13:10
Ari	17 Dec 1977	19:11
Tau	20 Dec 1977	04:54
Gem	22 Dec 1977	16:51
Can	25 Dec 1977	05:29
Leo	27 Dec 1977	17:51
Vir	30 Dec 1977	05:13

1978

Lib	1 Jan 1978	14:30
Sco	3 Jan 1978	20:34
Sag	5 Jan 1978	23:02
Cap	7 Jan 1978	22:54
Aqu	9 Jan 1978	22:05
Pis	11 Jan 1978	22:51
Ari	14 Jan 1978	03:05
Tau	16 Jan 1978	11:31
Gem	18 Jan 1978	23:06
Can	21 Jan 1978	11:50
Leo	24 Jan 1978	00:01
Vir	26 Jan 1978	10:55
Lib	28 Jan 1978	20:07
Sco	31 Jan 1978	03:02
Sag	2 Feb 1978	07:13
Cap	4 Feb 1978	08:49
Aqu	6 Feb 1978	09:04
Pis	8 Feb 1978	09:48
Ari	10 Feb 1978	12:57
Tau	12 Feb 1978	19:51
Gem	15 Feb 1978	06:24
Can	17 Feb 1978	18:55
Leo	20 Feb 1978	07:09
Vir	22 Feb 1978	17:39
Lib	25 Feb 1978	02:02
Sco	27 Feb 1978	08:27
Sag	1 Mar 1978	13:01
Cap	3 Mar 1978	15:57
Aqu	5 Mar 1978	17:50
Pis	7 Mar 1978	19:46
Ari	9 Mar 1978	23:09
Tau	12 Mar 1978	05:18
Gem	14 Mar 1978	14:48
Can	17 Mar 1978	02:49
Leo	19 Mar 1978	15:11
Vir	22 Mar 1978	01:48
Lib	24 Mar 1978	09:40
Sco	26 Mar 1978	15:00
Sag	28 Mar 1978	18:37
Cap	30 Mar 1978	21:23
Aqu	2 Apr 1978	00:05
Pis	4 Apr 1978	03:20
Ari	6 Apr 1978	07:51
Tau	8 Apr 1978	14:22
Gem	10 Apr 1978	23:28
Can	13 Apr 1978	10:59
Leo	15 Apr 1978	23:30
Vir	18 Apr 1978	10:42
Lib	20 Apr 1978	18:52
Sco	22 Apr 1978	23:37
Sag	25 Apr 1978	01:59
Cap	27 Apr 1978	03:27
Aqu	29 Apr 1978	05:27
Pis	1 May 1978	09:00
Ari	3 May 1978	14:27
Tau	5 May 1978	21:52
Gem	8 May 1978	07:18
Can	10 May 1978	18:41
Leo	13 May 1978	07:16
Vir	15 May 1978	19:14
Lib	18 May 1978	04:23
Sco	20 May 1978	09:37
Sag	22 May 1978	11:30
Cap	24 May 1978	11:41
Aqu	26 May 1978	12:10
Pis	28 May 1978	14:37
Ari	30 May 1978	19:52
Tau	2 Jun 1978	03:50
Gem	4 Jun 1978	13:53
Can	7 Jun 1978	01:30
Leo	9 Jun 1978	14:07
Vir	12 Jun 1978	02:34
Lib	14 Jun 1978	12:54
Sco	16 Jun 1978	19:27
Sag	18 Jun 1978	21:59
Cap	20 Jun 1978	21:51
Aqu	22 Jun 1978	21:08
Pis	24 Jun 1978	21:57
Ari	27 Jun 1978	01:54
Tau	29 Jun 1978	09:21
Gem	1 Jul 1978	19:37
Can	4 Jul 1978	07:33
Leo	6 Jul 1978	20:12
Vir	9 Jul 1978	08:44
Lib	11 Jul 1978	19:47
Sco	14 Jul 1978	03:45
Sag	16 Jul 1978	07:48
Cap	18 Jul 1978	08:32
Aqu	20 Jul 1978	07:41
Pis	22 Jul 1978	07:26
Ari	24 Jul 1978	09:47
Tau	26 Jul 1978	15:51
Gem	29 Jul 1978	01:31
Can	31 Jul 1978	13:28
Leo	3 Aug 1978	02:10
Vir	5 Aug 1978	14:28
Lib	8 Aug 1978	01:29
Sco	10 Aug 1978	10:10
Sag	12 Aug 1978	15:41
Cap	14 Aug 1978	18:02
Aqu	16 Aug 1978	18:14
Pis	18 Aug 1978	18:04
Ari	20 Aug 1978	19:29
Tau	23 Aug 1978	00:07
Gem	25 Aug 1978	08:31
Can	27 Aug 1978	19:59
Leo	30 Aug 1978	08:39
Vir	1 Sep 1978	20:45
Lib	4 Sep 1978	07:15
Sco	6 Sep 1978	15:37
Sag	8 Sep 1978	21:38
Cap	11 Sep 1978	01:18
Aqu	13 Sep 1978	03:08
Pis	15 Sep 1978	04:09
Ari	17 Sep 1978	05:49
Tau	19 Sep 1978	09:43
Gem	21 Sep 1978	16:56
Can	24 Sep 1978	03:31
Leo	26 Sep 1978	16:01
Vir	29 Sep 1978	04:10
Lib	1 Oct 1978	14:15
Sco	3 Oct 1978	21:47
Sag	6 Oct 1978	03:05
Cap	8 Oct 1978	06:52
Aqu	10 Oct 1978	09:42
Pis	12 Oct 1978	12:12
Ari	14 Oct 1978	15:06
Tau	16 Oct 1978	19:22
Gem	19 Oct 1978	02:06
Can	21 Oct 1978	11:53
Leo	24 Oct 1978	00:03
Vir	26 Oct 1978	12:30
Lib	28 Oct 1978	22:49
Sco	31 Oct 1978	05:52
Sag	2 Nov 1978	10:02
Cap	4 Nov 1978	12:40
Aqu	6 Nov 1978	15:03
Pis	8 Nov 1978	18:05
Ari	10 Nov 1978	22:11
Tau	13 Nov 1978	03:35
Gem	15 Nov 1978	10:45
Can	17 Nov 1978	20:16
Leo	20 Nov 1978	08:08
Vir	22 Nov 1978	20:56
Lib	25 Nov 1978	08:06
Sco	27 Nov 1978	15:37
Sag	29 Nov 1978	19:22
Cap	1 Dec 1978	20:43
Aqu	3 Dec 1978	21:35
Pis	5 Dec 1978	23:36
Ari	8 Dec 1978	03:39
Tau	10 Dec 1978	09:50
Gem	12 Dec 1978	17:54
Can	15 Dec 1978	03:49
Leo	17 Dec 1978	15:37
Vir	20 Dec 1978	04:33
Lib	22 Dec 1978	16:39
Sco	25 Dec 1978	01:30
Sag	27 Dec 1978	06:07
Cap	29 Dec 1978	07:15
Aqu	31 Dec 1978	06:52

1979

Pis	2 Jan 1979	07:07
Ari	4 Jan 1979	09:41
Tau	6 Jan 1979	15:17
Gem	8 Jan 1979	23:42
Can	11 Jan 1979	10:14
Leo	13 Jan 1979	22:16
Vir	16 Jan 1979	11:09
Lib	18 Jan 1979	23:39
Sco	21 Jan 1979	09:49
Sag	23 Jan 1979	16:06
Cap	25 Jan 1979	18:27
Aqu	27 Jan 1979	18:11
Pis	29 Jan 1979	17:25
Ari	31 Jan 1979	18:11

Tau	2 Feb 1979	22:03
Gem	5 Feb 1979	05:32
Can	7 Feb 1979	16:05
Leo	10 Feb 1979	04:25
Vir	12 Feb 1979	17:17
Lib	15 Feb 1979	05:36
Sco	17 Feb 1979	16:11
Sag	19 Feb 1979	23:49
Cap	22 Feb 1979	03:59
Aqu	24 Feb 1979	05:11
Pis	26 Feb 1979	04:51
Ari	28 Feb 1979	04:54

Tau	2 Mar 1979	07:09
Gem	4 Mar 1979	12:59
Can	6 Mar 1979	22:34
Leo	9 Mar 1979	10:47
Vir	11 Mar 1979	23:41
Lib	14 Mar 1979	11:40
Sco	16 Mar 1979	21:48
Sag	19 Mar 1979	05:37
Cap	21 Mar 1979	10:55
Aqu	23 Mar 1979	13:50
Pis	25 Mar 1979	15:04
Ari	27 Mar 1979	15:47
Tau	29 Mar 1979	17:36
Gem	31 Mar 1979	22:09

Can	3 Apr 1979	06:23
Leo	5 Apr 1979	17:57
Vir	8 Apr 1979	06:51
Lib	10 Apr 1979	18:44
Sco	13 Apr 1979	04:14
Sag	15 Apr 1979	11:16
Cap	17 Apr 1979	16:22
Aqu	19 Apr 1979	20:01
Pis	21 Apr 1979	22:40
Ari	24 Apr 1979	00:51
Tau	26 Apr 1979	03:27
Gem	28 Apr 1979	07:48
Can	30 Apr 1979	15:11

Leo	3 May 1979	01:56
Vir	5 May 1979	14:40
Lib	8 May 1979	02:46
Sco	10 May 1979	12:08
Sag	12 May 1979	18:24
Cap	14 May 1979	22:24
Aqu	17 May 1979	01:25
Pis	19 May 1979	04:18
Ari	21 May 1979	07:29
Tau	23 May 1979	11:20
Gem	25 May 1979	16:27
Can	27 May 1979	23:51
Leo	30 May 1979	10:08

Vir	1 Jun 1979	22:40
Lib	4 Jun 1979	11:10
Sco	6 Jun 1979	21:03
Sag	9 Jun 1979	03:13
Cap	11 Jun 1979	06:23
Aqu	13 Jun 1979	08:05
Pis	15 Jun 1979	09:56
Ari	17 Jun 1979	12:52
Tau	19 Jun 1979	17:17
Gem	21 Jun 1979	23:22
Can	24 Jun 1979	07:24
Leo	26 Jun 1979	17:46
Vir	29 Jun 1979	06:13

Lib	1 Jul 1979	19:07
Sco	4 Jul 1979	05:57
Sag	6 Jul 1979	12:54
Cap	8 Jul 1979	16:06
Aqu	10 Jul 1979	16:58
Pis	12 Jul 1979	17:22
Ari	14 Jul 1979	18:57
Tau	16 Jul 1979	22:43
Gem	19 Jul 1979	04:59
Can	21 Jul 1979	13:40
Leo	24 Jul 1979	00:30
Vir	26 Jul 1979	13:01
Lib	29 Jul 1979	02:05
Sco	31 Jul 1979	13:45

Sag	2 Aug 1979	22:04
Cap	5 Aug 1979	02:21
Aqu	7 Aug 1979	03:27
Pis	9 Aug 1979	03:05
Ari	11 Aug 1979	03:10
Tau	13 Aug 1979	05:21
Gem	15 Aug 1979	10:42
Can	17 Aug 1979	19:17
Leo	20 Aug 1979	06:28
Vir	22 Aug 1979	19:11
Lib	25 Aug 1979	08:13
Sco	27 Aug 1979	20:11
Sag	30 Aug 1979	05:38

Cap	1 Sep 1979	11:31
Aqu	3 Sep 1979	13:57
Pis	5 Sep 1979	14:02
Ari	7 Sep 1979	13:29
Tau	9 Sep 1979	14:13
Gem	11 Sep 1979	17:53
Can	14 Sep 1979	01:27
Leo	16 Sep 1979	12:25
Vir	19 Sep 1979	01:15
Lib	21 Sep 1979	14:10
Sco	24 Sep 1979	01:53
Sag	26 Sep 1979	11:34
Cap	28 Sep 1979	18:39
Aqu	30 Sep 1979	22:47

Pis	3 Oct 1979	00:22
Ari	5 Oct 1979	00:27
Tau	7 Oct 1979	00:45
Gem	9 Oct 1979	03:07
Can	11 Oct 1979	09:09
Leo	13 Oct 1979	19:11
Vir	16 Oct 1979	07:50
Lib	18 Oct 1979	20:43
Sco	21 Oct 1979	08:01
Sag	23 Oct 1979	17:08
Cap	26 Oct 1979	00:10
Aqu	28 Oct 1979	05:16
Pis	30 Oct 1979	08:28

Ari	1 Nov 1979	10:08
Tau	3 Nov 1979	11:16
Gem	5 Nov 1979	13:26
Can	7 Nov 1979	18:23
Leo	10 Nov 1979	03:14
Vir	12 Nov 1979	15:20
Lib	15 Nov 1979	04:15
Sco	17 Nov 1979	15:28
Sag	19 Nov 1979	23:55
Cap	22 Nov 1979	06:01
Aqu	24 Nov 1979	10:35
Pis	26 Nov 1979	14:16
Ari	28 Nov 1979	17:16
Tau	30 Nov 1979	19:54

Gem	2 Dec 1979	23:02
Can	5 Dec 1979	04:01
Leo	7 Dec 1979	12:09
Vir	9 Dec 1979	23:32
Lib	12 Dec 1979	12:28
Sco	15 Dec 1979	00:06
Sag	17 Dec 1979	08:35
Cap	19 Dec 1979	13:53
Aqu	21 Dec 1979	17:12
Pis	23 Dec 1979	19:49
Ari	25 Dec 1979	22:40
Tau	28 Dec 1979	02:07
Gem	30 Dec 1979	06:31

1980

Can 1 Jan 1980 12:29
Leo 3 Jan 1980 20:47
Vir 6 Jan 1980 07:48
Lib 8 Jan 1980 20:37
Sco 11 Jan 1980 08:54
Sag 13 Jan 1980 18:16
Cap 15 Jan 1980 23:49
Aqu 18 Jan 1980 02:23
Pis 20 Jan 1980 03:32
Ari 22 Jan 1980 04:51
Tau 24 Jan 1980 07:31
Gem 26 Jan 1980 12:11
Can 28 Jan 1980 19:02
Leo 31 Jan 1980 04:08

Vir 2 Feb 1980 15:21
Lib 5 Feb 1980 04:04
Sco 7 Feb 1980 16:45
Sag 10 Feb 1980 03:18
Cap 12 Feb 1980 10:10
Aqu 14 Feb 1980 13:18
Pis 16 Feb 1980 13:53
Ari 18 Feb 1980 13:42
Tau 20 Feb 1980 14:35
Gem 22 Feb 1980 17:57
Can 25 Feb 1980 00:35
Leo 27 Feb 1980 10:10
Vir 29 Feb 1980 21:53

Lib 3 Mar 1980 10:39
Sco 5 Mar 1980 23:21
Sag 8 Mar 1980 10:37
Cap 10 Mar 1980 19:01
Aqu 12 Mar 1980 23:43
Pis 15 Mar 1980 01:09
Ari 17 Mar 1980 00:40
Tau 19 Mar 1980 00:13
Gem 21 Mar 1980 01:48
Can 23 Mar 1980 06:55
Leo 25 Mar 1980 15:58
Vir 28 Mar 1980 03:51
Lib 30 Mar 1980 16:48

Sco 2 Apr 1980 05:20
Sag 4 Apr 1980 16:33
Cap 7 Apr 1980 01:41
Aqu 9 Apr 1980 07:58
Pis 11 Apr 1980 11:05
Ari 13 Apr 1980 11:39
Tau 15 Apr 1980 11:10
Gem 17 Apr 1980 11:42
Can 19 Apr 1980 15:12
Leo 21 Apr 1980 22:52
Vir 24 Apr 1980 10:12
Lib 26 Apr 1980 23:08
Sco 29 Apr 1980 11:33

Sag 1 May 1980 22:20
Cap 4 May 1980 07:13
Aqu 6 May 1980 14:02
Pis 8 May 1980 18:33
Ari 10 May 1980 20:43
Tau 12 May 1980 21:23
Gem 14 May 1980 22:08
Can 17 May 1980 00:53
Leo 19 May 1980 07:14
Vir 21 May 1980 17:32
Lib 24 May 1980 06:10
Sco 26 May 1980 18:36
Sag 29 May 1980 05:04
Cap 31 May 1980 13:13

Aqu 2 Jun 1980 19:28
Pis 5 Jun 1980 00:08
Ari 7 Jun 1980 03:22
Tau 9 Jun 1980 05:29
Gem 11 Jun 1980 07:22
Can 13 Jun 1980 10:30
Leo 15 Jun 1980 16:22
Vir 18 Jun 1980 01:47
Lib 20 Jun 1980 13:55
Sco 23 Jun 1980 02:25
Sag 25 Jun 1980 13:00
Cap 27 Jun 1980 20:45
Aqu 30 Jun 1980 02:02

Pis 2 Jul 1980 05:48
Ari 4 Jul 1980 08:45
Tau 6 Jul 1980 11:30
Gem 8 Jul 1980 14:33
Can 10 Jul 1980 18:44
Leo 13 Jul 1980 01:03
Vir 15 Jul 1980 10:11
Lib 17 Jul 1980 21:54
Sco 20 Jul 1980 10:32
Sag 22 Jul 1980 21:41
Cap 25 Jul 1980 05:44
Aqu 27 Jul 1980 10:33
Pis 29 Jul 1980 13:10
Ari 31 Jul 1980 14:52

Tau 2 Aug 1980 16:54
Gem 4 Aug 1980 20:09
Can 7 Aug 1980 01:12
Leo 9 Aug 1980 08:23
Vir 11 Aug 1980 17:54
Lib 14 Aug 1980 05:31
Sco 16 Aug 1980 18:14
Sag 19 Aug 1980 06:07
Cap 21 Aug 1980 15:10
Aqu 23 Aug 1980 20:31
Pis 25 Aug 1980 22:42
Ari 27 Aug 1980 23:10
Tau 29 Aug 1980 23:41

Gem 1 Sep 1980 01:50
Can 3 Sep 1980 06:39
Leo 5 Sep 1980 14:22
Vir 8 Sep 1980 00:30
Lib 10 Sep 1980 12:22
Sco 13 Sep 1980 01:05
Sag 15 Sep 1980 13:26
Cap 17 Sep 1980 23:43
Aqu 20 Sep 1980 06:29
Pis 22 Sep 1980 09:25
Ari 24 Sep 1980 09:36
Tau 26 Sep 1980 08:53
Gem 28 Sep 1980 09:21
Can 30 Sep 1980 12:47

Leo 2 Oct 1980 19:57
Vir 5 Oct 1980 06:18
Lib 7 Oct 1980 18:29
Sco 10 Oct 1980 07:14
Sag 12 Oct 1980 19:36
Cap 15 Oct 1980 06:36
Aqu 17 Oct 1980 14:51
Pis 19 Oct 1980 19:30
Ari 21 Oct 1980 20:41
Tau 23 Oct 1980 19:55
Gem 25 Oct 1980 19:16
Can 27 Oct 1980 21:00
Leo 30 Oct 1980 02:39

Vir 1 Nov 1980 12:19
Lib 4 Nov 1980 00:31
Sco 6 Nov 1980 13:18
Sag 9 Nov 1980 01:24
Cap 11 Nov 1980 12:14
Aqu 13 Nov 1980 21:08
Pis 16 Nov 1980 03:19
Ari 18 Nov 1980 06:21
Tau 20 Nov 1980 06:50
Gem 22 Nov 1980 06:26
Can 24 Nov 1980 07:18
Leo 26 Nov 1980 11:24
Vir 28 Nov 1980 19:37

Lib 1 Dec 1980 07:12
Sco 3 Dec 1980 19:59
Sag 6 Dec 1980 07:56
Cap 8 Dec 1980 18:11
Aqu 11 Dec 1980 02:34
Pis 13 Dec 1980 09:02
Ari 15 Dec 1980 13:19
Tau 17 Dec 1980 15:35
Gem 19 Dec 1980 16:39
Can 21 Dec 1980 18:02
Leo 23 Dec 1980 21:34
Vir 26 Dec 1980 04:32
Lib 28 Dec 1980 15:04
Sco 31 Dec 1980 03:35

Moon Signs

1981

Sag	2 Jan 1981	15:40
Cap	5 Jan 1981	01:39
Aqu	7 Jan 1981	09:11
Pis	9 Jan 1981	14:41
Ari	11 Jan 1981	18:43
Tau	13 Jan 1981	21:44
Gem	16 Jan 1981	00:16
Can	18 Jan 1981	03:07
Leo	20 Jan 1981	07:20
Vir	22 Jan 1981	14:02
Lib	24 Jan 1981	23:45
Sco	27 Jan 1981	11:48
Sag	30 Jan 1981	00:10
Cap	1 Feb 1981	10:35
Aqu	3 Feb 1981	17:54
Pis	5 Feb 1981	22:20
Ari	8 Feb 1981	01:00
Tau	10 Feb 1981	03:10
Gem	12 Feb 1981	05:50
Can	14 Feb 1981	09:42
Leo	16 Feb 1981	15:10
Vir	18 Feb 1981	22:34
Lib	21 Feb 1981	08:12
Sco	23 Feb 1981	19:54
Sag	26 Feb 1981	08:28
Cap	28 Feb 1981	19:45
Aqu	3 Mar 1981	03:49
Pis	5 Mar 1981	08:11
Ari	7 Mar 1981	09:47
Tau	9 Mar 1981	10:22
Gem	11 Mar 1981	11:42
Can	13 Mar 1981	15:05
Leo	15 Mar 1981	21:02
Vir	18 Mar 1981	05:19
Lib	20 Mar 1981	15:30
Sco	23 Mar 1981	03:13
Sag	25 Mar 1981	15:50
Cap	28 Mar 1981	03:51
Aqu	30 Mar 1981	13:13
Pis	1 Apr 1981	18:40
Ari	3 Apr 1981	20:24
Tau	5 Apr 1981	20:03
Gem	7 Apr 1981	19:47
Can	9 Apr 1981	21:34
Leo	12 Apr 1981	02:37
Vir	14 Apr 1981	10:56
Lib	16 Apr 1981	21:37
Sco	19 Apr 1981	09:38
Sag	21 Apr 1981	22:14
Cap	24 Apr 1981	10:30
Aqu	26 Apr 1981	20:55
Pis	29 Apr 1981	03:55
Ari	1 May 1981	06:56
Tau	3 May 1981	06:58
Gem	5 May 1981	06:00
Can	7 May 1981	06:17
Leo	9 May 1981	09:41
Vir	11 May 1981	16:55
Lib	14 May 1981	03:24
Sco	16 May 1981	15:37
Sag	19 May 1981	04:13
Cap	21 May 1981	16:19
Aqu	24 May 1981	02:59
Pis	26 May 1981	11:03
Ari	28 May 1981	15:42
Tau	30 May 1981	17:09
Gem	1 Jun 1981	16:47
Can	3 Jun 1981	16:38
Leo	5 Jun 1981	18:42
Vir	8 Jun 1981	00:26
Lib	10 Jun 1981	09:55
Sco	12 Jun 1981	21:54
Sag	15 Jun 1981	10:30
Cap	17 Jun 1981	22:20
Aqu	20 Jun 1981	08:35
Pis	22 Jun 1981	16:43
Ari	24 Jun 1981	22:16
Tau	27 Jun 1981	01:15
Gem	29 Jun 1981	02:20
Can	1 Jul 1981	02:56
Leo	3 Jul 1981	04:47
Vir	5 Jul 1981	09:26
Lib	7 Jul 1981	17:41
Sco	10 Jul 1981	05:01
Sag	12 Jul 1981	17:34
Cap	15 Jul 1981	05:18
Aqu	17 Jul 1981	15:00
Pis	19 Jul 1981	22:24
Ari	22 Jul 1981	03:42
Tau	24 Jul 1981	07:17
Gem	26 Jul 1981	09:41
Can	28 Jul 1981	11:40
Leo	30 Jul 1981	14:20
Vir	1 Aug 1981	18:54
Lib	4 Aug 1981	02:24
Sco	6 Aug 1981	12:58
Sag	9 Aug 1981	01:21
Cap	11 Aug 1981	13:19
Aqu	13 Aug 1981	22:54
Pis	16 Aug 1981	05:33
Ari	18 Aug 1981	09:48
Tau	20 Aug 1981	12:42
Gem	22 Aug 1981	15:17
Can	24 Aug 1981	18:16
Leo	26 Aug 1981	22:09
Vir	29 Aug 1981	03:31
Lib	31 Aug 1981	11:03
Sco	2 Sep 1981	21:10
Sag	5 Sep 1981	09:23
Cap	7 Sep 1981	21:47
Aqu	10 Sep 1981	07:57
Pis	12 Sep 1981	14:32
Ari	14 Sep 1981	17:54
Tau	16 Sep 1981	19:29
Gem	18 Sep 1981	20:58
Can	20 Sep 1981	23:39
Leo	23 Sep 1981	04:08
Vir	25 Sep 1981	10:28
Lib	27 Sep 1981	18:39
Sco	30 Sep 1981	04:52
Sag	2 Oct 1981	16:59
Cap	5 Oct 1981	05:48
Aqu	7 Oct 1981	17:00
Pis	10 Oct 1981	00:30
Ari	12 Oct 1981	03:59
Tau	14 Oct 1981	04:42
Gem	16 Oct 1981	04:41
Can	18 Oct 1981	05:51
Leo	20 Oct 1981	09:34
Vir	22 Oct 1981	16:04
Lib	25 Oct 1981	00:56
Sco	27 Oct 1981	11:37
Sag	29 Oct 1981	23:47
Cap	1 Nov 1981	12:44
Aqu	4 Nov 1981	00:48
Pis	6 Nov 1981	09:50
Ari	8 Nov 1981	14:36
Tau	10 Nov 1981	15:43
Gem	12 Nov 1981	14:59
Can	14 Nov 1981	14:36
Leo	16 Nov 1981	16:32
Vir	18 Nov 1981	21:53
Lib	21 Nov 1981	06:32
Sco	23 Nov 1981	17:36
Sag	26 Nov 1981	05:59
Cap	28 Nov 1981	18:51
Aqu	1 Dec 1981	07:08
Pis	3 Dec 1981	17:14
Ari	5 Dec 1981	23:46
Tau	8 Dec 1981	02:29
Gem	10 Dec 1981	02:29
Can	12 Dec 1981	01:40
Leo	14 Dec 1981	02:08
Vir	16 Dec 1981	05:37
Lib	18 Dec 1981	12:58
Sco	20 Dec 1981	23:38
Sag	23 Dec 1981	12:10
Cap	26 Dec 1981	00:58
Aqu	28 Dec 1981	12:52
Pis	30 Dec 1981	22:59

1982

Ari	2 Jan 1982	06:32
Tau	4 Jan 1982	11:00
Gem	6 Jan 1982	12:47
Can	8 Jan 1982	13:00
Leo	10 Jan 1982	13:21
Vir	12 Jan 1982	15:37
Lib	14 Jan 1982	21:17
Sco	17 Jan 1982	06:45
Sag	19 Jan 1982	18:59
Cap	22 Jan 1982	07:49
Aqu	24 Jan 1982	19:24
Pis	27 Jan 1982	04:48
Ari	29 Jan 1982	11:57
Tau	31 Jan 1982	17:02

Gem	2 Feb 1982	20:19
Can	4 Feb 1982	22:17
Leo	6 Feb 1982	23:49
Vir	9 Feb 1982	02:15
Lib	11 Feb 1982	07:01
Sco	13 Feb 1982	15:15
Sag	16 Feb 1982	02:44
Cap	18 Feb 1982	15:35
Aqu	21 Feb 1982	03:13
Pis	23 Feb 1982	12:07
Ari	25 Feb 1982	18:16
Tau	27 Feb 1982	22:30

Gem	2 Mar 1982	01:49
Can	4 Mar 1982	04:47
Leo	6 Mar 1982	07:49
Vir	8 Mar 1982	11:27
Lib	10 Mar 1982	16:33
Sco	13 Mar 1982	00:17
Sag	15 Mar 1982	11:03
Cap	17 Mar 1982	23:46
Aqu	20 Mar 1982	11:51
Pis	22 Mar 1982	20:59
Ari	25 Mar 1982	02:35
Tau	27 Mar 1982	05:38
Gem	29 Mar 1982	07:43
Can	31 Mar 1982	10:08

Leo	2 Apr 1982	13:36
Vir	4 Apr 1982	18:17
Lib	7 Apr 1982	00:26
Sco	9 Apr 1982	08:32
Sag	11 Apr 1982	19:06
Cap	14 Apr 1982	07:40
Aqu	16 Apr 1982	20:16
Pis	19 Apr 1982	06:18
Ari	21 Apr 1982	12:21
Tau	23 Apr 1982	14:57
Gem	25 Apr 1982	15:47
Can	27 Apr 1982	16:43
Leo	29 Apr 1982	19:08

Vir	1 May 1982	23:45
Lib	4 May 1982	06:32
Sco	6 May 1982	15:23
Sag	9 May 1982	02:16
Cap	11 May 1982	14:49
Aqu	14 May 1982	03:43
Pis	16 May 1982	14:44
Ari	18 May 1982	22:02
Tau	21 May 1982	01:20
Gem	23 May 1982	01:53
Can	25 May 1982	01:38
Leo	27 May 1982	02:27
Vir	29 May 1982	05:42
Lib	31 May 1982	12:02

Sco	2 Jun 1982	21:11
Sag	5 Jun 1982	08:31
Cap	7 Jun 1982	21:11
Aqu	10 Jun 1982	10:06
Pis	12 Jun 1982	21:42
Ari	15 Jun 1982	06:19
Tau	17 Jun 1982	11:04
Gem	19 Jun 1982	12:32
Can	21 Jun 1982	12:12
Leo	23 Jun 1982	11:57
Vir	25 Jun 1982	13:36
Lib	27 Jun 1982	18:29
Sco	30 Jun 1982	03:01

Sag	2 Jul 1982	14:25
Cap	5 Jul 1982	03:14
Aqu	7 Jul 1982	16:02
Pis	10 Jul 1982	03:34
Ari	12 Jul 1982	12:47
Tau	14 Jul 1982	18:59
Gem	16 Jul 1982	22:01
Can	18 Jul 1982	22:44
Leo	20 Jul 1982	22:35
Vir	22 Jul 1982	23:20
Lib	25 Jul 1982	02:45
Sco	27 Jul 1982	09:58
Sag	29 Jul 1982	20:47

Cap	1 Aug 1982	09:35
Aqu	3 Aug 1982	22:16
Pis	6 Aug 1982	09:22
Ari	8 Aug 1982	18:19
Tau	11 Aug 1982	00:58
Gem	13 Aug 1982	05:21
Can	15 Aug 1982	07:39
Leo	17 Aug 1982	08:39
Vir	19 Aug 1982	09:39
Lib	21 Aug 1982	12:22
Sco	23 Aug 1982	18:20
Sag	26 Aug 1982	04:10
Cap	28 Aug 1982	16:41
Aqu	31 Aug 1982	05:22

Pis	2 Sep 1982	16:09
Ari	5 Sep 1982	00:22
Tau	7 Sep 1982	06:26
Gem	9 Sep 1982	10:56
Can	11 Sep 1982	14:17
Leo	13 Sep 1982	16:45
Vir	15 Sep 1982	18:56
Lib	17 Sep 1982	22:03
Sco	20 Sep 1982	03:32
Sag	22 Sep 1982	12:30
Cap	25 Sep 1982	00:30
Aqu	27 Sep 1982	13:20
Pis	30 Sep 1982	00:16

Ari	2 Oct 1982	08:04
Tau	4 Oct 1982	13:07
Gem	6 Oct 1982	16:38
Can	8 Oct 1982	19:38
Leo	10 Oct 1982	22:43
Vir	13 Oct 1982	02:08
Lib	15 Oct 1982	06:22
Sco	17 Oct 1982	12:20
Sag	19 Oct 1982	21:02
Cap	22 Oct 1982	08:37
Aqu	24 Oct 1982	21:34
Pis	27 Oct 1982	09:10
Ari	29 Oct 1982	17:24
Tau	31 Oct 1982	22:02

Gem	3 Nov 1982	00:21
Can	5 Nov 1982	01:58
Leo	7 Nov 1982	04:09
Vir	9 Nov 1982	07:39
Lib	11 Nov 1982	12:45
Sco	13 Nov 1982	19:41
Sag	16 Nov 1982	04:51
Cap	18 Nov 1982	16:20
Aqu	21 Nov 1982	05:19
Pis	23 Nov 1982	17:41
Ari	26 Nov 1982	03:05
Tau	28 Nov 1982	08:30
Gem	30 Nov 1982	10:34

Can	2 Dec 1982	10:57
Leo	4 Dec 1982	11:26
Vir	6 Dec 1982	13:32
Lib	8 Dec 1982	18:10
Sco	11 Dec 1982	01:34
Sag	13 Dec 1982	11:26
Cap	15 Dec 1982	23:14
Aqu	18 Dec 1982	12:11
Pis	21 Dec 1982	00:54
Ari	23 Dec 1982	11:32
Tau	25 Dec 1982	18:36
Gem	27 Dec 1982	21:47
Can	29 Dec 1982	22:11
Leo	31 Dec 1982	21:32

1983

Sign	Date	Time
Vir	2 Jan 1983	21:49
Lib	5 Jan 1983	00:45
Sco	7 Jan 1983	07:16
Sag	9 Jan 1983	17:13
Cap	12 Jan 1983	05:25
Aqu	14 Jan 1983	18:25
Pis	17 Jan 1983	07:01
Ari	19 Jan 1983	18:07
Tau	22 Jan 1983	02:34
Gem	24 Jan 1983	07:38
Can	26 Jan 1983	09:27
Leo	28 Jan 1983	09:09
Vir	30 Jan 1983	08:34

Sign	Date	Time
Lib	1 Feb 1983	09:47
Sco	3 Feb 1983	14:32
Sag	5 Feb 1983	23:29
Cap	8 Feb 1983	11:33
Aqu	11 Feb 1983	00:39
Pis	13 Feb 1983	13:00
Ari	15 Feb 1983	23:44
Tau	18 Feb 1983	08:29
Gem	20 Feb 1983	14:50
Can	22 Feb 1983	18:30
Leo	24 Feb 1983	19:45
Vir	26 Feb 1983	19:48
Lib	28 Feb 1983	20:30

Sign	Date	Time
Sco	2 Mar 1983	23:51
Sag	5 Mar 1983	07:14
Cap	7 Mar 1983	18:28
Aqu	10 Mar 1983	07:29
Pis	12 Mar 1983	19:46
Ari	15 Mar 1983	05:59
Tau	17 Mar 1983	14:03
Gem	19 Mar 1983	20:18
Can	22 Mar 1983	00:51
Leo	24 Mar 1983	03:42
Vir	26 Mar 1983	05:17
Lib	28 Mar 1983	06:48
Sco	30 Mar 1983	09:57

Sign	Date	Time
Sag	1 Apr 1983	16:19
Cap	4 Apr 1983	02:29
Aqu	6 Apr 1983	15:05
Pis	9 Apr 1983	03:29
Ari	11 Apr 1983	13:35
Tau	13 Apr 1983	20:57
Gem	16 Apr 1983	02:13
Can	18 Apr 1983	06:13
Leo	20 Apr 1983	09:25
Vir	22 Apr 1983	12:11
Lib	24 Apr 1983	15:03
Sco	26 Apr 1983	19:04
Sag	29 Apr 1983	01:28

Sign	Date	Time
Cap	1 May 1983	11:01
Aqu	3 May 1983	23:08
Pis	6 May 1983	11:42
Ari	8 May 1983	22:14
Tau	11 May 1983	05:35
Gem	13 May 1983	10:02
Can	15 May 1983	12:47
Leo	17 May 1983	15:00
Vir	19 May 1983	17:36
Lib	21 May 1983	21:11
Sco	24 May 1983	02:17
Sag	26 May 1983	09:27
Cap	28 May 1983	19:06
Aqu	31 May 1983	06:59

Sign	Date	Time
Pis	2 Jun 1983	19:40
Ari	5 Jun 1983	06:58
Tau	7 Jun 1983	15:03
Gem	9 Jun 1983	19:36
Can	11 Jun 1983	21:31
Leo	13 Jun 1983	22:21
Vir	15 Jun 1983	23:38
Lib	18 Jun 1983	02:36
Sco	20 Jun 1983	07:59
Sag	22 Jun 1983	15:55
Cap	25 Jun 1983	02:08
Aqu	27 Jun 1983	14:06
Pis	30 Jun 1983	02:50

Sign	Date	Time
Ari	2 Jul 1983	14:46
Tau	5 Jul 1983	00:03
Gem	7 Jul 1983	05:40
Can	9 Jul 1983	07:49
Leo	11 Jul 1983	07:53
Vir	13 Jul 1983	07:42
Lib	15 Jul 1983	09:10
Sco	17 Jul 1983	13:38
Sag	19 Jul 1983	21:31
Cap	22 Jul 1983	08:10
Aqu	24 Jul 1983	20:26
Pis	27 Jul 1983	09:10
Ari	29 Jul 1983	21:19

Sign	Date	Time
Tau	1 Aug 1983	07:35
Gem	3 Aug 1983	14:41
Can	5 Aug 1983	18:08
Leo	7 Aug 1983	18:36
Vir	9 Aug 1983	17:48
Lib	11 Aug 1983	17:50
Sco	13 Aug 1983	20:44
Sag	16 Aug 1983	03:33
Cap	18 Aug 1983	13:59
Aqu	21 Aug 1983	02:25
Pis	23 Aug 1983	15:08
Ari	26 Aug 1983	03:07
Tau	28 Aug 1983	13:36
Gem	30 Aug 1983	21:47

Sign	Date	Time
Can	2 Sep 1983	02:51
Leo	4 Sep 1983	04:46
Vir	6 Sep 1983	04:35
Lib	8 Sep 1983	04:13
Sco	10 Sep 1983	05:48
Sag	12 Sep 1983	11:08
Cap	14 Sep 1983	20:33
Aqu	17 Sep 1983	08:44
Pis	19 Sep 1983	21:28
Ari	22 Sep 1983	09:09
Tau	24 Sep 1983	19:11
Gem	27 Sep 1983	03:23
Can	29 Sep 1983	09:23

Sign	Date	Time
Leo	1 Oct 1983	12:52
Vir	3 Oct 1983	14:14
Lib	5 Oct 1983	14:41
Sco	7 Oct 1983	16:05
Sag	9 Oct 1983	20:20
Cap	12 Oct 1983	04:30
Aqu	14 Oct 1983	15:59
Pis	17 Oct 1983	04:40
Ari	19 Oct 1983	16:17
Tau	22 Oct 1983	01:46
Gem	24 Oct 1983	09:08
Can	26 Oct 1983	14:45
Leo	28 Oct 1983	18:49
Vir	30 Oct 1983	21:31

Sign	Date	Time
Lib	1 Nov 1983	23:30
Sco	4 Nov 1983	01:53
Sag	6 Nov 1983	06:08
Cap	8 Nov 1983	13:31
Aqu	11 Nov 1983	00:10
Pis	13 Nov 1983	12:39
Ari	16 Nov 1983	00:35
Tau	18 Nov 1983	10:04
Gem	20 Nov 1983	16:44
Can	22 Nov 1983	21:09
Leo	25 Nov 1983	00:18
Vir	27 Nov 1983	03:01
Lib	29 Nov 1983	05:56

Sign	Date	Time
Sco	1 Dec 1983	09:40
Sag	3 Dec 1983	14:56
Cap	5 Dec 1983	22:28
Aqu	8 Dec 1983	08:39
Pis	10 Dec 1983	20:52
Ari	13 Dec 1983	09:15
Tau	15 Dec 1983	19:31
Gem	18 Dec 1983	02:22
Can	20 Dec 1983	06:01
Leo	22 Dec 1983	07:43
Vir	24 Dec 1983	09:01
Lib	26 Dec 1983	11:18
Sco	28 Dec 1983	15:26
Sag	30 Dec 1983	21:43

1984

Cap	2 Jan 1984	06:06
Aqu	4 Jan 1984	16:30
Pis	7 Jan 1984	04:33
Ari	9 Jan 1984	17:14
Tau	12 Jan 1984	04:35
Gem	14 Jan 1984	12:38
Can	16 Jan 1984	16:46
Leo	18 Jan 1984	17:48
Vir	20 Jan 1984	17:34
Lib	22 Jan 1984	18:06
Sco	24 Jan 1984	21:04
Sag	27 Jan 1984	03:12
Cap	29 Jan 1984	12:12
Aqu	31 Jan 1984	23:10

Pis	3 Feb 1984	11:21
Ari	6 Feb 1984	00:02
Tau	8 Feb 1984	12:03
Gem	10 Feb 1984	21:37
Can	13 Feb 1984	03:18
Leo	15 Feb 1984	05:08
Vir	17 Feb 1984	04:31
Lib	19 Feb 1984	03:39
Sco	21 Feb 1984	04:44
Sag	23 Feb 1984	09:22
Cap	25 Feb 1984	17:49
Aqu	28 Feb 1984	05:01

Pis	1 Mar 1984	17:28
Ari	4 Mar 1984	06:06
Tau	6 Mar 1984	18:08
Gem	9 Mar 1984	04:28
Can	11 Mar 1984	11:46
Leo	13 Mar 1984	15:19
Vir	15 Mar 1984	15:45
Lib	17 Mar 1984	14:51
Sco	19 Mar 1984	14:49
Sag	21 Mar 1984	17:40
Cap	24 Mar 1984	00:36
Aqu	26 Mar 1984	11:08
Pis	28 Mar 1984	23:36
Ari	31 Mar 1984	12:12

Tau	2 Apr 1984	23:54
Gem	5 Apr 1984	10:03
Can	7 Apr 1984	17:58
Leo	9 Apr 1984	22:59
Vir	12 Apr 1984	01:09
Lib	14 Apr 1984	01:28
Sco	16 Apr 1984	01:41
Sag	18 Apr 1984	03:43
Cap	20 Apr 1984	09:10
Aqu	22 Apr 1984	18:26
Pis	25 Apr 1984	06:25
Ari	27 Apr 1984	19:01
Tau	30 Apr 1984	06:29

Gem	2 May 1984	16:00
Can	4 May 1984	23:24
Leo	7 May 1984	04:42
Vir	9 May 1984	08:00
Lib	11 May 1984	09:53
Sco	13 May 1984	11:21
Sag	15 May 1984	13:50
Cap	17 May 1984	18:42
Aqu	20 May 1984	02:55
Pis	22 May 1984	14:08
Ari	25 May 1984	02:38
Tau	27 May 1984	14:12
Gem	29 May 1984	23:21

Can	1 Jun 1984	05:53
Leo	3 Jun 1984	10:17
Vir	5 Jun 1984	13:26
Lib	7 Jun 1984	16:02
Sco	9 Jun 1984	18:47
Sag	11 Jun 1984	22:26
Cap	14 Jun 1984	03:47
Aqu	16 Jun 1984	11:41
Pis	18 Jun 1984	22:17
Ari	21 Jun 1984	10:39
Tau	23 Jun 1984	22:36
Gem	26 Jun 1984	08:02
Can	28 Jun 1984	14:07
Leo	30 Jun 1984	17:29

Vir	2 Jul 1984	19:27
Lib	4 Jul 1984	21:26
Sco	7 Jul 1984	00:28
Sag	9 Jul 1984	05:02
Cap	11 Jul 1984	11:22
Aqu	13 Jul 1984	19:41
Pis	16 Jul 1984	06:09
Ari	18 Jul 1984	18:25
Tau	21 Jul 1984	06:51
Gem	23 Jul 1984	17:09
Can	25 Jul 1984	23:42
Leo	28 Jul 1984	02:40
Vir	30 Jul 1984	03:28

Lib	1 Aug 1984	04:02
Sco	3 Aug 1984	06:03
Sag	5 Aug 1984	10:29
Cap	7 Aug 1984	17:24
Aqu	10 Aug 1984	02:25
Pis	12 Aug 1984	13:12
Ari	15 Aug 1984	01:27
Tau	17 Aug 1984	14:12
Gem	20 Aug 1984	01:29
Can	22 Aug 1984	09:18
Leo	24 Aug 1984	12:58
Vir	26 Aug 1984	13:31
Lib	28 Aug 1984	12:56
Sco	30 Aug 1984	13:23

Sag	1 Sep 1984	16:29
Cap	3 Sep 1984	22:55
Aqu	6 Sep 1984	08:11
Pis	8 Sep 1984	19:24
Ari	11 Sep 1984	07:46
Tau	13 Sep 1984	20:32
Gem	16 Sep 1984	08:24
Can	18 Sep 1984	17:35
Leo	20 Sep 1984	22:46
Vir	23 Sep 1984	00:17
Lib	24 Sep 1984	23:40
Sco	26 Sep 1984	23:04
Sag	29 Sep 1984	00:32

Cap	1 Oct 1984	05:27
Aqu	3 Oct 1984	14:03
Pis	6 Oct 1984	01:19
Ari	8 Oct 1984	13:50
Tau	11 Oct 1984	02:27
Gem	13 Oct 1984	14:12
Can	15 Oct 1984	23:58
Leo	18 Oct 1984	06:40
Vir	20 Oct 1984	09:54
Lib	22 Oct 1984	10:30
Sco	24 Oct 1984	10:07
Sag	26 Oct 1984	10:43
Cap	28 Oct 1984	14:05
Aqu	30 Oct 1984	21:13

Pis	2 Nov 1984	07:49
Ari	4 Nov 1984	20:19
Tau	7 Nov 1984	08:52
Gem	9 Nov 1984	20:09
Can	12 Nov 1984	05:30
Leo	14 Nov 1984	12:32
Vir	16 Nov 1984	17:06
Lib	18 Nov 1984	19:28
Sco	20 Nov 1984	20:30
Sag	22 Nov 1984	21:34
Cap	25 Nov 1984	00:18
Aqu	27 Nov 1984	06:05
Pis	29 Nov 1984	15:33

Ari	2 Dec 1984	03:41
Tau	4 Dec 1984	16:19
Gem	7 Dec 1984	03:22
Can	9 Dec 1984	11:55
Leo	11 Dec 1984	18:07
Vir	13 Dec 1984	22:34
Lib	16 Dec 1984	01:50
Sco	18 Dec 1984	04:26
Sag	20 Dec 1984	06:58
Cap	22 Dec 1984	10:21
Aqu	24 Dec 1984	15:47
Pis	27 Dec 1984	00:18
Ari	29 Dec 1984	11:49

Moon Signs

1985

Tau 1 Jan 1985 00:35
Gem 3 Jan 1985 11:58
Can 5 Jan 1985 20:16
Leo 8 Jan 1985 01:26
Vir 10 Jan 1985 04:39
Lib 12 Jan 1985 07:13
Sco 14 Jan 1985 10:07
Sag 16 Jan 1985 13:47
Cap 18 Jan 1985 18:28
Aqu 21 Jan 1985 00:38
Pis 23 Jan 1985 09:02
Ari 25 Jan 1985 20:05
Tau 28 Jan 1985 08:52
Gem 30 Jan 1985 20:59

Can 2 Feb 1985 05:58
Leo 4 Feb 1985 11:00
Vir 6 Feb 1985 13:08
Lib 8 Feb 1985 14:10
Sco 10 Feb 1985 15:48
Sag 12 Feb 1985 19:08
Cap 15 Feb 1985 00:27
Aqu 17 Feb 1985 07:35
Pis 19 Feb 1985 16:37
Ari 22 Feb 1985 03:42
Tau 24 Feb 1985 16:26
Gem 27 Feb 1985 05:10

Can 1 Mar 1985 15:22
Leo 3 Mar 1985 21:26
Vir 5 Mar 1985 23:41
Lib 7 Mar 1985 23:46
Sco 9 Mar 1985 23:47
Sag 12 Mar 1985 01:29
Cap 14 Mar 1985 05:54
Aqu 16 Mar 1985 13:11
Pis 18 Mar 1985 22:50
Ari 21 Mar 1985 10:19
Tau 23 Mar 1985 23:05
Gem 26 Mar 1985 12:00
Can 28 Mar 1985 23:11
Leo 31 Mar 1985 06:50

Vir 2 Apr 1985 10:23
Lib 4 Apr 1985 10:52
Sco 6 Apr 1985 10:10
Sag 8 Apr 1985 10:18
Cap 10 Apr 1985 12:57
Aqu 12 Apr 1985 19:03
Pis 15 Apr 1985 04:30
Ari 17 Apr 1985 16:17
Tau 20 Apr 1985 05:11
Gem 22 Apr 1985 17:59
Can 25 Apr 1985 05:25
Leo 27 Apr 1985 14:08
Vir 29 Apr 1985 19:23

Lib 1 May 1985 21:20
Sco 3 May 1985 21:16
Sag 5 May 1985 20:55
Cap 7 May 1985 22:12
Aqu 10 May 1985 02:38
Pis 12 May 1985 10:56
Ari 14 May 1985 22:25
Tau 17 May 1985 11:22
Gem 19 May 1985 23:59
Can 22 May 1985 11:03
Leo 24 May 1985 19:52
Vir 27 May 1985 02:05
Lib 29 May 1985 05:39
Sco 31 May 1985 07:06

Sag 2 Jun 1985 07:32
Cap 4 Jun 1985 08:33
Aqu 6 Jun 1985 11:52
Pis 8 Jun 1985 18:46
Ari 11 Jun 1985 05:23
Tau 13 Jun 1985 18:10
Gem 16 Jun 1985 06:44
Can 18 Jun 1985 17:21
Leo 21 Jun 1985 01:30
Vir 23 Jun 1985 07:31
Lib 25 Jun 1985 11:46
Sco 27 Jun 1985 14:36
Sag 29 Jun 1985 16:29

Cap 1 Jul 1985 18:21
Aqu 3 Jul 1985 21:36
Pis 6 Jul 1985 03:40
Ari 8 Jul 1985 13:20
Tau 11 Jul 1985 01:43
Gem 13 Jul 1985 14:22
Can 16 Jul 1985 00:52
Leo 18 Jul 1985 08:24
Vir 20 Jul 1985 13:28
Lib 22 Jul 1985 17:09
Sco 24 Jul 1985 20:15
Sag 26 Jul 1985 23:12
Cap 29 Jul 1985 02:20
Aqu 31 Jul 1985 06:25

Pis 2 Aug 1985 12:34
Ari 4 Aug 1985 21:43
Tau 7 Aug 1985 09:40
Gem 9 Aug 1985 22:30
Can 12 Aug 1985 09:26
Leo 14 Aug 1985 16:56
Vir 16 Aug 1985 21:13
Lib 18 Aug 1985 23:43
Sco 21 Aug 1985 01:50
Sag 23 Aug 1985 04:35
Cap 25 Aug 1985 08:24
Aqu 27 Aug 1985 13:31
Pis 29 Aug 1985 20:24

Ari 1 Sep 1985 05:41
Tau 3 Sep 1985 17:27
Gem 6 Sep 1985 06:26
Can 8 Sep 1985 18:09
Leo 11 Sep 1985 02:25
Vir 13 Sep 1985 06:51
Lib 15 Sep 1985 08:32
Sco 17 Sep 1985 09:16
Sag 19 Sep 1985 10:40
Cap 21 Sep 1985 13:49
Aqu 23 Sep 1985 19:11
Pis 26 Sep 1985 02:50
Ari 28 Sep 1985 12:42

Tau 1 Oct 1985 00:34
Gem 3 Oct 1985 13:35
Can 6 Oct 1985 01:57
Leo 8 Oct 1985 11:31
Vir 10 Oct 1985 17:08
Lib 12 Oct 1985 19:11
Sco 14 Oct 1985 19:12
Sag 16 Oct 1985 19:05
Cap 18 Oct 1985 20:35
Aqu 21 Oct 1985 00:55
Pis 23 Oct 1985 08:27
Ari 25 Oct 1985 18:47
Tau 28 Oct 1985 06:58
Gem 30 Oct 1985 19:58

Can 2 Nov 1985 08:30
Leo 4 Nov 1985 19:02
Vir 7 Nov 1985 02:16
Lib 9 Nov 1985 05:51
Sco 11 Nov 1985 06:30
Sag 13 Nov 1985 05:51
Cap 15 Nov 1985 05:52
Aqu 17 Nov 1985 08:25
Pis 19 Nov 1985 14:43
Ari 22 Nov 1985 00:42
Tau 24 Nov 1985 13:06
Gem 27 Nov 1985 02:07
Can 29 Nov 1985 14:22

Leo 2 Dec 1985 00:58
Vir 4 Dec 1985 09:12
Lib 6 Dec 1985 14:32
Sco 8 Dec 1985 16:55
Sag 10 Dec 1985 17:12
Cap 12 Dec 1985 16:59
Aqu 14 Dec 1985 18:14
Pis 16 Dec 1985 22:51
Ari 19 Dec 1985 07:36
Tau 21 Dec 1985 19:40
Gem 24 Dec 1985 08:44
Can 26 Dec 1985 20:43
Leo 29 Dec 1985 06:43
Vir 31 Dec 1985 14:42

Moon Signs

1986

Sign	Date	Time
Lib	2 Jan 1986	20:44
Sco	5 Jan 1986	00:43
Sag	7 Jan 1986	02:46
Cap	9 Jan 1986	03:41
Aqu	11 Jan 1986	05:01
Pis	13 Jan 1986	08:39
Ari	15 Jan 1986	16:03
Tau	18 Jan 1986	03:13
Gem	20 Jan 1986	16:11
Can	23 Jan 1986	04:13
Leo	25 Jan 1986	13:46
Vir	27 Jan 1986	20:50
Lib	30 Jan 1986	02:09

Sign	Date	Time
Sco	1 Feb 1986	06:18
Sag	3 Feb 1986	09:30
Cap	5 Feb 1986	12:01
Aqu	7 Feb 1986	14:35
Pis	9 Feb 1986	18:32
Ari	12 Feb 1986	01:21
Tau	14 Feb 1986	11:38
Gem	17 Feb 1986	00:16
Can	19 Feb 1986	12:37
Leo	21 Feb 1986	22:23
Vir	24 Feb 1986	04:57
Lib	26 Feb 1986	09:06
Sco	28 Feb 1986	12:05

Sign	Date	Time
Sag	2 Mar 1986	14:51
Cap	4 Mar 1986	17:55
Aqu	6 Mar 1986	21:42
Pis	9 Mar 1986	02:48
Ari	11 Mar 1986	10:03
Tau	13 Mar 1986	20:03
Gem	16 Mar 1986	08:22
Can	18 Mar 1986	21:03
Leo	21 Mar 1986	07:37
Vir	23 Mar 1986	14:38
Lib	25 Mar 1986	18:22
Sco	27 Mar 1986	20:04
Sag	29 Mar 1986	21:20
Cap	31 Mar 1986	23:25

Sign	Date	Time
Aqu	3 Apr 1986	03:11
Pis	5 Apr 1986	09:03
Ari	7 Apr 1986	17:11
Tau	10 Apr 1986	03:36
Gem	12 Apr 1986	15:50
Can	15 Apr 1986	04:41
Leo	17 Apr 1986	16:08
Vir	20 Apr 1986	00:22
Lib	22 Apr 1986	04:49
Sco	24 Apr 1986	06:15
Sag	26 Apr 1986	06:15
Cap	28 Apr 1986	06:40
Aqu	30 Apr 1986	09:06

Sign	Date	Time
Pis	2 May 1986	14:30
Ari	4 May 1986	23:01
Tau	7 May 1986	09:58
Gem	9 May 1986	22:25
Can	12 May 1986	11:17
Leo	14 May 1986	23:14
Vir	17 May 1986	08:43
Lib	19 May 1986	14:39
Sco	21 May 1986	17:01
Sag	23 May 1986	16:56
Cap	25 May 1986	16:14
Aqu	27 May 1986	16:59
Pis	29 May 1986	20:55

Sign	Date	Time
Ari	1 Jun 1986	04:42
Tau	3 Jun 1986	15:45
Gem	6 Jun 1986	04:26
Can	8 Jun 1986	17:15
Leo	11 Jun 1986	05:10
Vir	13 Jun 1986	15:17
Lib	15 Jun 1986	22:36
Sco	18 Jun 1986	02:34
Sag	20 Jun 1986	03:34
Cap	22 Jun 1986	02:59
Aqu	24 Jun 1986	02:50
Pis	26 Jun 1986	05:12
Ari	28 Jun 1986	11:35
Tau	30 Jun 1986	21:54

Sign	Date	Time
Gem	3 Jul 1986	10:31
Can	5 Jul 1986	23:18
Leo	8 Jul 1986	10:54
Vir	10 Jul 1986	20:49
Lib	13 Jul 1986	04:39
Sco	15 Jul 1986	09:57
Sag	17 Jul 1986	12:33
Cap	19 Jul 1986	13:09
Aqu	21 Jul 1986	13:17
Pis	23 Jul 1986	14:59
Ari	25 Jul 1986	20:02
Tau	28 Jul 1986	05:11
Gem	30 Jul 1986	17:18

Sign	Date	Time
Can	2 Aug 1986	06:03
Leo	4 Aug 1986	17:26
Vir	7 Aug 1986	02:43
Lib	9 Aug 1986	10:03
Sco	11 Aug 1986	15:35
Sag	13 Aug 1986	19:16
Cap	15 Aug 1986	21:21
Aqu	17 Aug 1986	22:44
Pis	20 Aug 1986	00:52
Ari	22 Aug 1986	05:27
Tau	24 Aug 1986	13:37
Gem	27 Aug 1986	01:00
Can	29 Aug 1986	13:39

Sign	Date	Time
Leo	1 Sep 1986	01:07
Vir	3 Sep 1986	10:04
Lib	5 Sep 1986	16:32
Sco	7 Sep 1986	21:11
Sag	10 Sep 1986	00:39
Cap	12 Sep 1986	03:27
Aqu	14 Sep 1986	06:06
Pis	16 Sep 1986	09:27
Ari	18 Sep 1986	14:34
Tau	20 Sep 1986	22:26
Gem	23 Sep 1986	09:13
Can	25 Sep 1986	21:44
Leo	28 Sep 1986	09:38
Vir	30 Sep 1986	18:56

Sign	Date	Time
Lib	3 Oct 1986	01:01
Sco	5 Oct 1986	04:34
Sag	7 Oct 1986	06:47
Cap	9 Oct 1986	08:52
Aqu	11 Oct 1986	11:45
Pis	13 Oct 1986	16:03
Ari	15 Oct 1986	22:13
Tau	18 Oct 1986	06:35
Gem	20 Oct 1986	17:15
Can	23 Oct 1986	05:37
Leo	25 Oct 1986	18:02
Vir	28 Oct 1986	04:19
Lib	30 Oct 1986	11:02

Sign	Date	Time
Sco	1 Nov 1986	14:18
Sag	3 Nov 1986	15:18
Cap	5 Nov 1986	15:48
Aqu	7 Nov 1986	17:28
Pis	9 Nov 1986	21:30
Ari	12 Nov 1986	04:14
Tau	14 Nov 1986	13:24
Gem	17 Nov 1986	00:26
Can	19 Nov 1986	12:45
Leo	22 Nov 1986	01:24
Vir	24 Nov 1986	12:44
Lib	26 Nov 1986	20:57
Sco	29 Nov 1986	01:11

Sign	Date	Time
Sag	1 Dec 1986	02:07
Cap	3 Dec 1986	01:28
Aqu	5 Dec 1986	01:23
Pis	7 Dec 1986	03:48
Ari	9 Dec 1986	09:49
Tau	11 Dec 1986	19:10
Gem	14 Dec 1986	06:41
Can	16 Dec 1986	19:09
Leo	19 Dec 1986	07:43
Vir	21 Dec 1986	19:30
Lib	24 Dec 1986	05:04
Sco	26 Dec 1986	11:04
Sag	28 Dec 1986	13:18
Cap	30 Dec 1986	12:53

Moon Signs

1987

Aqu 1 Jan 1987 11:54
Pis 3 Jan 1987 12:37
Ari 5 Jan 1987 16:51
Tau 8 Jan 1987 01:13
Gem 10 Jan 1987 12:39
Can 13 Jan 1987 01:18
Leo 15 Jan 1987 13:44
Vir 18 Jan 1987 01:14
Lib 20 Jan 1987 11:08
Sco 22 Jan 1987 18:30
Sag 24 Jan 1987 22:34
Cap 26 Jan 1987 23:41
Aqu 28 Jan 1987 23:16
Pis 30 Jan 1987 23:25

Ari 2 Feb 1987 02:10
Tau 4 Feb 1987 08:53
Gem 6 Feb 1987 19:23
Can 9 Feb 1987 07:54
Leo 11 Feb 1987 20:20
Vir 14 Feb 1987 07:25
Lib 16 Feb 1987 16:44
Sco 19 Feb 1987 00:03
Sag 21 Feb 1987 05:08
Cap 23 Feb 1987 07:56
Aqu 25 Feb 1987 09:08
Pis 27 Feb 1987 10:07

Ari 1 Mar 1987 12:37
Tau 3 Mar 1987 18:11
Gem 6 Mar 1987 03:26
Can 8 Mar 1987 15:24
Leo 11 Mar 1987 03:53
Vir 13 Mar 1987 14:54
Lib 15 Mar 1987 23:33
Sco 18 Mar 1987 05:56
Sag 20 Mar 1987 10:31
Cap 22 Mar 1987 13:47
Aqu 24 Mar 1987 16:17
Pis 26 Mar 1987 18:45
Ari 28 Mar 1987 22:12
Tau 31 Mar 1987 03:46

Gem 2 Apr 1987 12:17
Can 4 Apr 1987 23:33
Leo 7 Apr 1987 12:03
Vir 9 Apr 1987 23:26
Lib 12 Apr 1987 08:04
Sco 14 Apr 1987 13:39
Sag 16 Apr 1987 17:00
Cap 18 Apr 1987 19:20
Aqu 20 Apr 1987 21:45
Pis 23 Apr 1987 01:02
Ari 25 Apr 1987 05:40
Tau 27 Apr 1987 12:06
Gem 29 Apr 1987 20:43

Can 2 May 1987 07:39
Leo 4 May 1987 20:06
Vir 7 May 1987 08:06
Lib 9 May 1987 17:28
Sco 11 May 1987 23:07
Sag 14 May 1987 01:40
Cap 16 May 1987 02:36
Aqu 18 May 1987 03:42
Pis 20 May 1987 06:23
Ari 22 May 1987 11:23
Tau 24 May 1987 18:38
Gem 27 May 1987 03:55
Can 29 May 1987 14:59

Leo 1 Jun 1987 03:25
Vir 3 Jun 1987 15:55
Lib 6 Jun 1987 02:22
Sco 8 Jun 1987 09:04
Sag 10 Jun 1987 11:51
Cap 12 Jun 1987 12:04
Aqu 14 Jun 1987 11:45
Pis 16 Jun 1987 12:55
Ari 18 Jun 1987 16:56
Tau 21 Jun 1987 00:09
Gem 23 Jun 1987 09:54
Can 25 Jun 1987 21:22
Leo 28 Jun 1987 09:51
Vir 30 Jun 1987 22:33

Lib 3 Jul 1987 09:53
Sco 5 Jul 1987 18:02
Sag 7 Jul 1987 22:03
Cap 9 Jul 1987 22:42
Aqu 11 Jul 1987 21:49
Pis 13 Jul 1987 21:36
Ari 16 Jul 1987 00:01
Tau 18 Jul 1987 06:04
Gem 20 Jul 1987 15:32
Can 23 Jul 1987 03:13
Leo 25 Jul 1987 15:49
Vir 28 Jul 1987 04:25
Lib 30 Jul 1987 15:58

Sco 2 Aug 1987 01:07
Sag 4 Aug 1987 06:46
Cap 6 Aug 1987 08:50
Aqu 8 Aug 1987 08:36
Pis 10 Aug 1987 08:01
Ari 12 Aug 1987 09:10
Tau 14 Aug 1987 13:39
Gem 16 Aug 1987 21:59
Can 19 Aug 1987 09:19
Leo 21 Aug 1987 21:57
Vir 24 Aug 1987 10:22
Lib 26 Aug 1987 21:35
Sco 29 Aug 1987 06:48
Sag 31 Aug 1987 13:22

Cap 2 Sep 1987 17:03
Aqu 4 Sep 1987 18:21
Pis 6 Sep 1987 18:36
Ari 8 Sep 1987 19:34
Tau 10 Sep 1987 22:58
Gem 13 Sep 1987 05:54
Can 15 Sep 1987 16:22
Leo 18 Sep 1987 04:50
Vir 20 Sep 1987 17:12
Lib 23 Sep 1987 03:57
Sco 25 Sep 1987 12:29
Sag 27 Sep 1987 18:48
Cap 29 Sep 1987 23:07

Aqu 2 Oct 1987 01:50
Pis 4 Oct 1987 03:39
Ari 6 Oct 1987 05:34
Tau 8 Oct 1987 08:58
Gem 10 Oct 1987 15:04
Can 13 Oct 1987 00:31
Leo 15 Oct 1987 12:34
Vir 18 Oct 1987 01:05
Lib 20 Oct 1987 11:48
Sco 22 Oct 1987 19:40
Sag 25 Oct 1987 00:56
Cap 27 Oct 1987 04:32
Aqu 29 Oct 1987 07:26
Pis 31 Oct 1987 10:19

Ari 2 Nov 1987 13:40
Tau 4 Nov 1987 18:02
Gem 7 Nov 1987 00:16
Can 9 Nov 1987 09:10
Leo 11 Nov 1987 20:45
Vir 14 Nov 1987 09:28
Lib 16 Nov 1987 20:47
Sco 19 Nov 1987 04:46
Sag 21 Nov 1987 09:15
Cap 23 Nov 1987 11:31
Aqu 25 Nov 1987 13:12
Pis 27 Nov 1987 15:40
Ari 29 Nov 1987 19:36

Tau 2 Dec 1987 01:06
Gem 4 Dec 1987 08:13
Can 6 Dec 1987 17:20
Leo 9 Dec 1987 04:40
Vir 11 Dec 1987 17:30
Lib 14 Dec 1987 05:39
Sco 16 Dec 1987 14:39
Sag 18 Dec 1987 19:32
Cap 20 Dec 1987 21:07
Aqu 22 Dec 1987 21:20
Pis 24 Dec 1987 22:10
Ari 27 Dec 1987 01:06
Tau 29 Dec 1987 06:36
Gem 31 Dec 1987 14:29

Moon Signs

1988

Sign	Date	Time
Can	3 Jan 1988	00:17
Leo	5 Jan 1988	11:47
Vir	8 Jan 1988	00:35
Lib	10 Jan 1988	13:16
Sco	12 Jan 1988	23:37
Sag	15 Jan 1988	05:58
Cap	17 Jan 1988	08:14
Aqu	19 Jan 1988	08:01
Pis	21 Jan 1988	07:26
Ari	23 Jan 1988	08:31
Tau	25 Jan 1988	12:37
Gem	27 Jan 1988	20:02
Can	30 Jan 1988	06:11

Sign	Date	Time
Leo	1 Feb 1988	18:06
Vir	4 Feb 1988	06:54
Lib	6 Feb 1988	19:35
Sco	9 Feb 1988	06:41
Sag	11 Feb 1988	14:34
Cap	13 Feb 1988	18:36
Aqu	15 Feb 1988	19:24
Pis	17 Feb 1988	18:43
Ari	19 Feb 1988	18:35
Tau	21 Feb 1988	20:51
Gem	24 Feb 1988	02:43
Can	26 Feb 1988	12:12
Leo	29 Feb 1988	00:12

Sign	Date	Time
Vir	2 Mar 1988	13:06
Lib	5 Mar 1988	01:31
Sco	7 Mar 1988	12:26
Sag	9 Mar 1988	20:57
Cap	12 Mar 1988	02:30
Aqu	14 Mar 1988	05:07
Pis	16 Mar 1988	05:41
Ari	18 Mar 1988	05:45
Tau	20 Mar 1988	07:05
Gem	22 Mar 1988	11:22
Can	24 Mar 1988	19:27
Leo	27 Mar 1988	06:53
Vir	29 Mar 1988	19:48

Sign	Date	Time
Lib	1 Apr 1988	08:04
Sco	3 Apr 1988	18:25
Sag	6 Apr 1988	02:27
Cap	8 Apr 1988	08:18
Aqu	10 Apr 1988	12:09
Pis	12 Apr 1988	14:23
Ari	14 Apr 1988	15:46
Tau	16 Apr 1988	17:31
Gem	18 Apr 1988	21:11
Can	21 Apr 1988	04:05
Leo	23 Apr 1988	14:34
Vir	26 Apr 1988	03:15
Lib	28 Apr 1988	15:36

Sign	Date	Time
Sco	1 May 1988	01:38
Sag	3 May 1988	08:51
Cap	5 May 1988	13:53
Aqu	7 May 1988	17:36
Pis	9 May 1988	20:38
Ari	11 May 1988	23:23
Tau	14 May 1988	02:22
Gem	16 May 1988	06:31
Can	18 May 1988	13:06
Leo	20 May 1988	22:52
Vir	23 May 1988	11:12
Lib	25 May 1988	23:48
Sco	28 May 1988	10:05
Sag	30 May 1988	16:56

Sign	Date	Time
Cap	1 Jun 1988	20:57
Aqu	3 Jun 1988	23:33
Pis	6 Jun 1988	02:00
Ari	8 Jun 1988	05:03
Tau	10 Jun 1988	09:02
Gem	12 Jun 1988	14:15
Can	14 Jun 1988	21:19
Leo	17 Jun 1988	06:57
Vir	19 Jun 1988	19:03
Lib	22 Jun 1988	07:57
Sco	24 Jun 1988	18:58
Sag	27 Jun 1988	02:16
Cap	29 Jun 1988	05:59

Sign	Date	Time
Aqu	1 Jul 1988	07:29
Pis	3 Jul 1988	08:33
Ari	5 Jul 1988	10:37
Tau	7 Jul 1988	14:27
Gem	9 Jul 1988	20:16
Can	12 Jul 1988	04:08
Leo	14 Jul 1988	14:11
Vir	17 Jul 1988	02:17
Lib	19 Jul 1988	15:21
Sco	22 Jul 1988	03:12
Sag	24 Jul 1988	11:40
Cap	26 Jul 1988	16:06
Aqu	28 Jul 1988	17:24
Pis	30 Jul 1988	17:23

Sign	Date	Time
Ari	1 Aug 1988	17:53
Tau	3 Aug 1988	20:24
Gem	6 Aug 1988	01:43
Can	8 Aug 1988	09:53
Leo	10 Aug 1988	20:26
Vir	13 Aug 1988	08:45
Lib	15 Aug 1988	21:51
Sco	18 Aug 1988	10:10
Sag	20 Aug 1988	19:53
Cap	23 Aug 1988	01:47
Aqu	25 Aug 1988	04:04
Pis	27 Aug 1988	04:01
Ari	29 Aug 1988	03:29
Tau	31 Aug 1988	04:23

Sign	Date	Time
Gem	2 Sep 1988	08:12
Can	4 Sep 1988	15:37
Leo	7 Sep 1988	02:15
Vir	9 Sep 1988	14:48
Lib	12 Sep 1988	03:51
Sco	14 Sep 1988	16:06
Sag	17 Sep 1988	02:24
Cap	19 Sep 1988	09:43
Aqu	21 Sep 1988	13:41
Pis	23 Sep 1988	14:50
Ari	25 Sep 1988	14:29
Tau	27 Sep 1988	14:29
Gem	29 Sep 1988	16:43

Sign	Date	Time
Can	1 Oct 1988	22:40
Leo	4 Oct 1988	08:31
Vir	6 Oct 1988	21:01
Lib	9 Oct 1988	10:03
Sco	11 Oct 1988	21:57
Sag	14 Oct 1988	07:57
Cap	16 Oct 1988	15:44
Aqu	18 Oct 1988	21:04
Pis	20 Oct 1988	23:57
Ari	23 Oct 1988	00:58
Tau	25 Oct 1988	01:22
Gem	27 Oct 1988	02:56
Can	29 Oct 1988	07:28
Leo	31 Oct 1988	16:04

Sign	Date	Time
Vir	3 Nov 1988	04:01
Lib	5 Nov 1988	17:03
Sco	8 Nov 1988	04:46
Sag	10 Nov 1988	14:05
Cap	12 Nov 1988	21:11
Aqu	15 Nov 1988	02:36
Pis	17 Nov 1988	06:33
Ari	19 Nov 1988	09:12
Tau	21 Nov 1988	11:02
Gem	23 Nov 1988	13:12
Can	25 Nov 1988	17:19
Leo	28 Nov 1988	00:53
Vir	30 Nov 1988	12:00

Sign	Date	Time
Lib	3 Dec 1988	00:55
Sco	5 Dec 1988	12:50
Sag	7 Dec 1988	21:54
Cap	10 Dec 1988	04:06
Aqu	12 Dec 1988	08:25
Pis	14 Dec 1988	11:53
Ari	16 Dec 1988	15:03
Tau	18 Dec 1988	18:11
Gem	20 Dec 1988	21:43
Can	23 Dec 1988	02:35
Leo	25 Dec 1988	09:58
Vir	27 Dec 1988	20:27
Lib	30 Dec 1988	09:09

Moon Signs

1989

Sco	1 Jan 1989	21:33
Sag	4 Jan 1989	07:11
Cap	6 Jan 1989	13:12
Aqu	8 Jan 1989	16:30
Pis	10 Jan 1989	18:30
Ari	12 Jan 1989	20:36
Tau	14 Jan 1989	23:36
Gem	17 Jan 1989	03:57
Can	19 Jan 1989	09:57
Leo	21 Jan 1989	18:02
Vir	24 Jan 1989	04:32
Lib	26 Jan 1989	17:01
Sco	29 Jan 1989	05:48
Sag	31 Jan 1989	16:29

Cap	2 Feb 1989	23:28
Aqu	5 Feb 1989	02:50
Pis	7 Feb 1989	03:52
Ari	9 Feb 1989	04:18
Tau	11 Feb 1989	05:45
Gem	13 Feb 1989	09:23
Can	15 Feb 1989	15:40
Leo	18 Feb 1989	00:33
Vir	20 Feb 1989	11:34
Lib	23 Feb 1989	00:05
Sco	25 Feb 1989	12:56
Sag	28 Feb 1989	00:28

Cap	2 Mar 1989	08:56
Aqu	4 Mar 1989	13:35
Pis	6 Mar 1989	14:58
Ari	8 Mar 1989	14:36
Tau	10 Mar 1989	14:26
Gem	12 Mar 1989	16:17
Can	14 Mar 1989	21:28
Leo	17 Mar 1989	06:13
Vir	19 Mar 1989	17:39
Lib	22 Mar 1989	06:24
Sco	24 Mar 1989	19:10
Sag	27 Mar 1989	06:53
Cap	29 Mar 1989	16:24
Aqu	31 Mar 1989	22:43

Pis	3 Apr 1989	01:36
Ari	5 Apr 1989	01:50
Tau	7 Apr 1989	01:08
Gem	9 Apr 1989	01:32
Can	11 Apr 1989	04:58
Leo	13 Apr 1989	12:32
Vir	15 Apr 1989	23:40
Lib	18 Apr 1989	12:31
Sco	21 Apr 1989	01:12
Sag	23 Apr 1989	12:37
Cap	25 Apr 1989	22:14
Aqu	28 Apr 1989	05:32
Pis	30 Apr 1989	10:02

Ari	2 May 1989	11:50
Tau	4 May 1989	11:55
Gem	6 May 1989	12:04
Can	8 May 1989	14:21
Leo	10 May 1989	20:23
Vir	13 May 1989	06:30
Lib	15 May 1989	19:07
Sco	18 May 1989	07:47
Sag	20 May 1989	18:51
Cap	23 May 1989	03:53
Aqu	25 May 1989	11:00
Pis	27 May 1989	16:13
Ari	29 May 1989	19:25
Tau	31 May 1989	20:59

Gem	2 Jun 1989	22:03
Can	5 Jun 1989	00:18
Leo	7 Jun 1989	05:28
Vir	9 Jun 1989	14:30
Lib	12 Jun 1989	02:31
Sco	14 Jun 1989	15:11
Sag	17 Jun 1989	02:11
Cap	19 Jun 1989	10:41
Aqu	21 Jun 1989	16:56
Pis	23 Jun 1989	21:36
Ari	26 Jun 1989	01:06
Tau	28 Jun 1989	03:45
Gem	30 Jun 1989	06:08

Can	2 Jul 1989	09:19
Leo	4 Jul 1989	14:38
Vir	6 Jul 1989	23:05
Lib	9 Jul 1989	10:30
Sco	11 Jul 1989	23:09
Sag	14 Jul 1989	10:30
Cap	16 Jul 1989	19:01
Aqu	19 Jul 1989	00:34
Pis	21 Jul 1989	04:06
Ari	23 Jul 1989	06:40
Tau	25 Jul 1989	09:10
Gem	27 Jul 1989	12:15
Can	29 Jul 1989	16:32
Leo	31 Jul 1989	22:42

Vir	3 Aug 1989	07:19
Lib	5 Aug 1989	18:28
Sco	8 Aug 1989	07:05
Sag	10 Aug 1989	19:02
Cap	13 Aug 1989	04:16
Aqu	15 Aug 1989	09:58
Pis	17 Aug 1989	12:45
Ari	19 Aug 1989	13:59
Tau	21 Aug 1989	15:11
Gem	23 Aug 1989	17:39
Can	25 Aug 1989	22:14
Leo	28 Aug 1989	05:12
Vir	30 Aug 1989	14:30

Lib	2 Sep 1989	01:48
Sco	4 Sep 1989	14:23
Sag	7 Sep 1989	02:50
Cap	9 Sep 1989	13:12
Aqu	11 Sep 1989	20:01
Pis	13 Sep 1989	23:06
Ari	15 Sep 1989	23:38
Tau	17 Sep 1989	23:23
Gem	20 Sep 1989	00:17
Can	22 Sep 1989	03:51
Leo	24 Sep 1989	10:45
Vir	26 Sep 1989	20:32
Lib	29 Sep 1989	08:15

Sco	1 Oct 1989	20:53
Sag	4 Oct 1989	09:29
Cap	6 Oct 1989	20:44
Aqu	9 Oct 1989	05:06
Pis	11 Oct 1989	09:36
Ari	13 Oct 1989	10:40
Tau	15 Oct 1989	09:52
Gem	17 Oct 1989	09:20
Can	19 Oct 1989	11:10
Leo	21 Oct 1989	16:48
Vir	24 Oct 1989	02:16
Lib	26 Oct 1989	14:11
Sco	29 Oct 1989	02:56
Sag	31 Oct 1989	15:22

Cap	3 Nov 1989	02:46
Aqu	5 Nov 1989	12:08
Pis	7 Nov 1989	18:24
Ari	9 Nov 1989	21:07
Tau	11 Nov 1989	21:09
Gem	13 Nov 1989	20:19
Can	15 Nov 1989	20:52
Leo	18 Nov 1989	00:47
Vir	20 Nov 1989	08:55
Lib	22 Nov 1989	20:25
Sco	25 Nov 1989	09:13
Sag	27 Nov 1989	21:29
Cap	30 Nov 1989	08:26

Aqu	2 Dec 1989	17:42
Pis	5 Dec 1989	00:47
Ari	7 Dec 1989	05:11
Tau	9 Dec 1989	06:58
Gem	11 Dec 1989	07:15
Can	13 Dec 1989	07:49
Leo	15 Dec 1989	10:42
Vir	17 Dec 1989	17:19
Lib	20 Dec 1989	03:46
Sco	22 Dec 1989	16:18
Sag	25 Dec 1989	04:37
Cap	27 Dec 1989	15:10
Aqu	29 Dec 1989	23:37

1990

Pis	1 Jan 1990	06:10
Ari	3 Jan 1990	10:56
Tau	5 Jan 1990	14:03
Gem	7 Jan 1990	16:01
Can	9 Jan 1990	17:52
Leo	11 Jan 1990	21:03
Vir	14 Jan 1990	02:58
Lib	16 Jan 1990	12:18
Sco	19 Jan 1990	00:16
Sag	21 Jan 1990	12:43
Cap	23 Jan 1990	23:26
Aqu	26 Jan 1990	07:24
Pis	28 Jan 1990	12:50
Ari	30 Jan 1990	16:34
Tau	1 Feb 1990	19:27
Gem	3 Feb 1990	22:12
Can	6 Feb 1990	01:27
Leo	8 Feb 1990	05:51
Vir	10 Feb 1990	12:14
Lib	12 Feb 1990	21:10
Sco	15 Feb 1990	08:34
Sag	17 Feb 1990	21:07
Cap	20 Feb 1990	08:29
Aqu	22 Feb 1990	16:52
Pis	24 Feb 1990	21:48
Ari	27 Feb 1990	00:16
Tau	1 Mar 1990	01:43
Gem	3 Mar 1990	03:38
Can	5 Mar 1990	07:02
Leo	7 Mar 1990	12:25
Vir	9 Mar 1990	19:47
Lib	12 Mar 1990	05:09
Sco	14 Mar 1990	16:25
Sag	17 Mar 1990	04:56
Cap	19 Mar 1990	17:01
Aqu	22 Mar 1990	02:30
Pis	24 Mar 1990	08:08
Ari	26 Mar 1990	10:15
Tau	28 Mar 1990	10:26
Gem	30 Mar 1990	10:43
Can	1 Apr 1990	12:51
Leo	3 Apr 1990	17:50
Vir	6 Apr 1990	01:42
Lib	8 Apr 1990	11:45
Sco	10 Apr 1990	23:18
Sag	13 Apr 1990	11:48
Cap	16 Apr 1990	00:14
Aqu	18 Apr 1990	10:51
Pis	20 Apr 1990	17:57
Ari	22 Apr 1990	20:57
Tau	24 Apr 1990	21:02
Gem	26 Apr 1990	20:12
Can	28 Apr 1990	20:40

Leo	1 May 1990	00:10
Vir	3 May 1990	07:18
Lib	5 May 1990	17:28
Sco	8 May 1990	05:22
Sag	10 May 1990	17:56
Cap	13 May 1990	06:21
Aqu	15 May 1990	17:30
Pis	18 May 1990	01:52
Ari	20 May 1990	06:31
Tau	22 May 1990	07:42
Gem	24 May 1990	07:00
Can	26 May 1990	06:34
Leo	28 May 1990	08:30
Vir	30 May 1990	14:09
Lib	1 Jun 1990	23:31
Sco	4 Jun 1990	11:22
Sag	6 Jun 1990	23:59
Cap	9 Jun 1990	12:11
Aqu	11 Jun 1990	23:08
Pis	14 Jun 1990	07:59
Ari	16 Jun 1990	13:54
Tau	18 Jun 1990	16:42
Gem	20 Jun 1990	17:14
Can	22 Jun 1990	17:09
Leo	24 Jun 1990	18:25
Vir	26 Jun 1990	22:43
Lib	29 Jun 1990	06:47
Sco	1 Jul 1990	18:01
Sag	4 Jul 1990	06:35
Cap	6 Jul 1990	18:39
Aqu	9 Jul 1990	05:06
Pis	11 Jul 1990	13:28
Ari	13 Jul 1990	19:36
Tau	15 Jul 1990	23:28
Gem	18 Jul 1990	01:31
Can	20 Jul 1990	02:44
Leo	22 Jul 1990	04:29
Vir	24 Jul 1990	08:18
Lib	26 Jul 1990	15:19
Sco	29 Jul 1990	01:39
Sag	31 Jul 1990	14:00
Cap	3 Aug 1990	02:08
Aqu	5 Aug 1990	12:18
Pis	7 Aug 1990	19:54
Ari	10 Aug 1990	01:12
Tau	12 Aug 1990	04:54
Gem	14 Aug 1990	07:41
Can	16 Aug 1990	10:12
Leo	18 Aug 1990	13:11
Vir	20 Aug 1990	17:33
Lib	23 Aug 1990	00:18
Sco	25 Aug 1990	09:57
Sag	27 Aug 1990	21:57
Cap	30 Aug 1990	10:22

Aqu	1 Sep 1990	20:50
Pis	4 Sep 1990	04:05
Ari	6 Sep 1990	08:22
Tau	8 Sep 1990	10:55
Gem	10 Sep 1990	13:05
Can	12 Sep 1990	15:53
Leo	14 Sep 1990	19:52
Vir	17 Sep 1990	01:19
Lib	19 Sep 1990	08:34
Sco	21 Sep 1990	18:06
Sag	24 Sep 1990	05:52
Cap	26 Sep 1990	18:36
Aqu	29 Sep 1990	05:53
Pis	1 Oct 1990	13:41
Ari	3 Oct 1990	17:41
Tau	5 Oct 1990	19:06
Gem	7 Oct 1990	19:47
Can	9 Oct 1990	21:30
Leo	12 Oct 1990	01:17
Vir	14 Oct 1990	07:21
Lib	16 Oct 1990	15:27
Sco	19 Oct 1990	01:24
Sag	21 Oct 1990	13:09
Cap	24 Oct 1990	02:02
Aqu	26 Oct 1990	14:13
Pis	28 Oct 1990	23:20
Ari	31 Oct 1990	04:13
Tau	2 Nov 1990	05:31
Gem	4 Nov 1990	05:06
Can	6 Nov 1990	05:07
Leo	8 Nov 1990	07:24
Vir	10 Nov 1990	12:49
Lib	12 Nov 1990	21:09
Sco	15 Nov 1990	07:39
Sag	17 Nov 1990	19:39
Cap	20 Nov 1990	08:31
Aqu	22 Nov 1990	21:06
Pis	25 Nov 1990	07:31
Ari	27 Nov 1990	14:05
Tau	29 Nov 1990	16:37
Gem	1 Dec 1990	16:22
Can	3 Dec 1990	15:28
Leo	5 Dec 1990	16:00
Vir	7 Dec 1990	19:39
Lib	10 Dec 1990	03:01
Sco	12 Dec 1990	13:28
Sag	15 Dec 1990	01:44
Cap	17 Dec 1990	14:34
Aqu	20 Dec 1990	02:59
Pis	22 Dec 1990	13:47
Ari	24 Dec 1990	21:44
Tau	27 Dec 1990	02:08
Gem	29 Dec 1990	03:25
Can	31 Dec 1990	03:02

Moon Signs

1991

Leo	2 Jan 1991	02:55
Vir	4 Jan 1991	04:57
Lib	6 Jan 1991	10:34
Sco	8 Jan 1991	19:59
Sag	11 Jan 1991	08:06
Cap	13 Jan 1991	21:00
Aqu	16 Jan 1991	09:04
Pis	18 Jan 1991	19:23
Ari	21 Jan 1991	03:27
Tau	23 Jan 1991	09:00
Gem	25 Jan 1991	12:06
Can	27 Jan 1991	13:23
Leo	29 Jan 1991	14:04
Vir	31 Jan 1991	15:44

Lib	2 Feb 1991	20:03
Sco	5 Feb 1991	04:02
Sag	7 Feb 1991	15:23
Cap	10 Feb 1991	04:16
Aqu	12 Feb 1991	16:16
Pis	15 Feb 1991	01:58
Ari	17 Feb 1991	09:11
Tau	19 Feb 1991	14:24
Gem	21 Feb 1991	18:10
Can	23 Feb 1991	20:56
Leo	25 Feb 1991	23:13
Vir	28 Feb 1991	01:51

Lib	2 Mar 1991	06:03
Sco	4 Mar 1991	13:09
Sag	6 Mar 1991	23:36
Cap	9 Mar 1991	12:14
Aqu	12 Mar 1991	00:30
Pis	14 Mar 1991	10:10
Ari	16 Mar 1991	16:37
Tau	18 Mar 1991	20:40
Gem	20 Mar 1991	23:37
Can	23 Mar 1991	02:27
Leo	25 Mar 1991	05:43
Vir	27 Mar 1991	09:41
Lib	29 Mar 1991	14:50
Sco	31 Mar 1991	22:02

Sag	3 Apr 1991	07:59
Cap	5 Apr 1991	20:20
Aqu	8 Apr 1991	08:59
Pis	10 Apr 1991	19:17
Ari	13 Apr 1991	01:48
Tau	15 Apr 1991	05:05
Gem	17 Apr 1991	06:41
Can	19 Apr 1991	08:18
Leo	21 Apr 1991	11:05
Vir	23 Apr 1991	15:30
Lib	25 Apr 1991	21:37
Sco	28 Apr 1991	05:34
Sag	30 Apr 1991	15:42

Cap	3 May 1991	03:55
Aqu	5 May 1991	16:51
Pis	8 May 1991	04:03
Ari	10 May 1991	11:33
Tau	12 May 1991	15:07
Gem	14 May 1991	16:02
Can	16 May 1991	16:14
Leo	18 May 1991	17:30
Vir	20 May 1991	21:01
Lib	23 May 1991	03:08
Sco	25 May 1991	11:42
Sag	27 May 1991	22:22
Cap	30 May 1991	10:41

Aqu	1 Jun 1991	23:41
Pis	4 Jun 1991	11:35
Ari	6 Jun 1991	20:24
Tau	9 Jun 1991	01:11
Gem	11 Jun 1991	02:36
Can	13 Jun 1991	02:17
Leo	15 Jun 1991	02:11
Vir	17 Jun 1991	04:03
Lib	19 Jun 1991	09:02
Sco	21 Jun 1991	17:19
Sag	24 Jun 1991	04:16
Cap	26 Jun 1991	16:49
Aqu	29 Jun 1991	05:47

Pis	1 Jul 1991	17:51
Ari	4 Jul 1991	03:33
Tau	6 Jul 1991	09:51
Gem	8 Jul 1991	12:41
Can	10 Jul 1991	13:02
Leo	12 Jul 1991	12:35
Vir	14 Jul 1991	13:13
Lib	16 Jul 1991	16:35
Sco	18 Jul 1991	23:42
Sag	21 Jul 1991	10:17
Cap	23 Jul 1991	22:55
Aqu	26 Jul 1991	11:49
Pis	28 Jul 1991	23:34
Ari	31 Jul 1991	09:19

Tau	2 Aug 1991	16:31
Gem	4 Aug 1991	20:54
Can	6 Aug 1991	22:46
Leo	8 Aug 1991	23:09
Vir	10 Aug 1991	23:35
Lib	13 Aug 1991	01:53
Sco	15 Aug 1991	07:34
Sag	17 Aug 1991	17:11
Cap	20 Aug 1991	05:34
Aqu	22 Aug 1991	18:27
Pis	25 Aug 1991	05:51
Ari	27 Aug 1991	15:00
Tau	29 Aug 1991	21:59

Gem	1 Sep 1991	03:02
Can	3 Sep 1991	06:19
Leo	5 Sep 1991	08:13
Vir	7 Sep 1991	09:35
Lib	9 Sep 1991	11:52
Sco	11 Sep 1991	16:43
Sag	14 Sep 1991	01:15
Cap	16 Sep 1991	13:04
Aqu	19 Sep 1991	01:57
Pis	21 Sep 1991	13:19
Ari	23 Sep 1991	21:55
Tau	26 Sep 1991	03:59
Gem	28 Sep 1991	08:25
Can	30 Sep 1991	11:58

Leo	2 Oct 1991	14:58
Vir	4 Oct 1991	17:45
Lib	6 Oct 1991	21:01
Sco	9 Oct 1991	02:01
Sag	11 Oct 1991	09:59
Cap	13 Oct 1991	21:10
Aqu	16 Oct 1991	10:04
Pis	18 Oct 1991	21:52
Ari	21 Oct 1991	06:33
Tau	23 Oct 1991	11:54
Gem	25 Oct 1991	15:08
Can	27 Oct 1991	17:37
Leo	29 Oct 1991	20:20
Vir	31 Oct 1991	23:47

Lib	3 Nov 1991	04:13
Sco	5 Nov 1991	10:09
Sag	7 Nov 1991	18:21
Cap	10 Nov 1991	05:16
Aqu	12 Nov 1991	18:06
Pis	15 Nov 1991	06:33
Ari	17 Nov 1991	16:07
Tau	19 Nov 1991	21:48
Gem	22 Nov 1991	00:22
Can	24 Nov 1991	01:25
Leo	26 Nov 1991	02:38
Vir	28 Nov 1991	05:12
Lib	30 Nov 1991	09:47

Sco	2 Dec 1991	16:33
Sag	5 Dec 1991	01:33
Cap	7 Dec 1991	12:41
Aqu	10 Dec 1991	01:26
Pis	12 Dec 1991	14:18
Ari	15 Dec 1991	01:05
Tau	17 Dec 1991	08:09
Gem	19 Dec 1991	11:20
Can	21 Dec 1991	11:54
Leo	23 Dec 1991	11:39
Vir	25 Dec 1991	12:25
Lib	27 Dec 1991	15:38
Sco	29 Dec 1991	22:04

Moon Signs

1992

Sag	1 Jan 1992	07:30
Cap	3 Jan 1992	19:09
Aqu	6 Jan 1992	07:59
Pis	8 Jan 1992	20:52
Ari	11 Jan 1992	08:22
Tau	13 Jan 1992	17:00
Gem	15 Jan 1992	21:53
Can	17 Jan 1992	23:25
Leo	19 Jan 1992	22:56
Vir	21 Jan 1992	22:23
Lib	23 Jan 1992	23:44
Sco	26 Jan 1992	04:33
Sag	28 Jan 1992	13:21
Cap	31 Jan 1992	01:08
Aqu	2 Feb 1992	14:09
Pis	5 Feb 1992	02:50
Ari	7 Feb 1992	14:14
Tau	9 Feb 1992	23:35
Gem	12 Feb 1992	06:08
Can	14 Feb 1992	09:30
Leo	16 Feb 1992	10:14
Vir	18 Feb 1992	09:47
Lib	20 Feb 1992	10:05
Sco	22 Feb 1992	13:13
Sag	24 Feb 1992	20:27
Cap	27 Feb 1992	07:34
Aqu	29 Feb 1992	20:34
Pis	3 Mar 1992	09:10
Ari	5 Mar 1992	20:06
Tau	8 Mar 1992	05:05
Gem	10 Mar 1992	12:03
Can	12 Mar 1992	16:49
Leo	14 Mar 1992	19:20
Vir	16 Mar 1992	20:13
Lib	18 Mar 1992	20:55
Sco	20 Mar 1992	23:21
Sag	23 Mar 1992	05:13
Cap	25 Mar 1992	15:09
Aqu	28 Mar 1992	03:45
Pis	30 Mar 1992	16:23
Ari	2 Apr 1992	03:03
Tau	4 Apr 1992	11:17
Gem	6 Apr 1992	17:33
Can	8 Apr 1992	22:18
Leo	11 Apr 1992	01:46
Vir	13 Apr 1992	04:09
Lib	15 Apr 1992	06:10
Sco	17 Apr 1992	09:10
Sag	19 Apr 1992	14:41
Cap	21 Apr 1992	23:41
Aqu	24 Apr 1992	11:39
Pis	27 Apr 1992	00:19
Ari	29 Apr 1992	11:12
Tau	1 May 1992	19:09
Gem	4 May 1992	00:28
Can	6 May 1992	04:09
Leo	8 May 1992	07:07
Vir	10 May 1992	09:56
Lib	12 May 1992	13:05
Sco	14 May 1992	17:15
Sag	16 May 1992	23:23
Cap	19 May 1992	08:13
Aqu	21 May 1992	19:44
Pis	24 May 1992	08:25
Ari	26 May 1992	19:52
Tau	29 May 1992	04:15
Gem	31 May 1992	09:18
Can	2 Jun 1992	11:57
Leo	4 Jun 1992	13:35
Vir	6 Jun 1992	15:28
Lib	8 Jun 1992	18:33
Sco	10 Jun 1992	23:27
Sag	13 Jun 1992	06:29
Cap	15 Jun 1992	15:50
Aqu	18 Jun 1992	03:19
Pis	20 Jun 1992	16:00
Ari	23 Jun 1992	04:03
Tau	25 Jun 1992	13:27
Gem	27 Jun 1992	19:13
Can	29 Jun 1992	21:41
Leo	1 Jul 1992	22:15
Vir	3 Jul 1992	22:38
Lib	6 Jul 1992	00:28
Sco	8 Jul 1992	04:54
Sag	10 Jul 1992	12:18
Cap	12 Jul 1992	22:16
Aqu	15 Jul 1992	10:03
Pis	17 Jul 1992	22:44
Ari	20 Jul 1992	11:07
Tau	22 Jul 1992	21:35
Gem	25 Jul 1992	04:44
Can	27 Jul 1992	08:08
Leo	29 Jul 1992	08:39
Vir	31 Jul 1992	08:01
Lib	2 Aug 1992	08:18
Sco	4 Aug 1992	11:17
Sag	6 Aug 1992	17:57
Cap	9 Aug 1992	04:01
Aqu	11 Aug 1992	16:07
Pis	14 Aug 1992	04:51
Ari	16 Aug 1992	17:11
Tau	19 Aug 1992	04:09
Gem	21 Aug 1992	12:35
Can	23 Aug 1992	17:36
Leo	25 Aug 1992	19:15
Vir	27 Aug 1992	18:46
Lib	29 Aug 1992	18:11
Sco	31 Aug 1992	19:39
Sag	3 Sep 1992	00:52
Cap	5 Sep 1992	10:07
Aqu	7 Sep 1992	22:08
Pis	10 Sep 1992	10:56
Ari	12 Sep 1992	23:02
Tau	15 Sep 1992	09:47
Gem	17 Sep 1992	18:40
Can	20 Sep 1992	00:58
Leo	22 Sep 1992	04:18
Vir	24 Sep 1992	05:08
Lib	26 Sep 1992	04:55
Sco	28 Sep 1992	05:44
Sag	30 Sep 1992	09:35
Cap	2 Oct 1992	17:29
Aqu	5 Oct 1992	04:53
Pis	7 Oct 1992	17:37
Ari	10 Oct 1992	05:36
Tau	12 Oct 1992	15:48
Gem	15 Oct 1992	00:08
Can	17 Oct 1992	06:36
Leo	19 Oct 1992	11:00
Vir	21 Oct 1992	13:27
Lib	23 Oct 1992	14:39
Sco	25 Oct 1992	16:05
Sag	27 Oct 1992	19:29
Cap	30 Oct 1992	02:19
Aqu	1 Nov 1992	12:44
Pis	4 Nov 1992	01:12
Ari	6 Nov 1992	13:19
Tau	8 Nov 1992	23:18
Gem	11 Nov 1992	06:49
Can	13 Nov 1992	12:18
Leo	15 Nov 1992	16:23
Vir	17 Nov 1992	19:28
Lib	19 Nov 1992	22:03
Sco	22 Nov 1992	00:52
Sag	24 Nov 1992	05:01
Cap	26 Nov 1992	11:39
Aqu	28 Nov 1992	21:20
Pis	1 Dec 1992	09:23
Ari	3 Dec 1992	21:48
Tau	6 Dec 1992	08:16
Gem	8 Dec 1992	15:36
Can	10 Dec 1992	20:05
Leo	12 Dec 1992	22:47
Vir	15 Dec 1992	00:56
Lib	17 Dec 1992	03:33
Sco	19 Dec 1992	07:20
Sag	21 Dec 1992	12:43
Cap	23 Dec 1992	20:05
Aqu	26 Dec 1992	05:43
Pis	28 Dec 1992	17:28
Ari	31 Dec 1992	06:07

Moon Signs

1993

Tau	2 Jan 1993	17:30
Gem	5 Jan 1993	01:41
Can	7 Jan 1993	06:10
Leo	9 Jan 1993	07:49
Vir	11 Jan 1993	08:21
Lib	13 Jan 1993	09:31
Sco	15 Jan 1993	12:43
Sag	17 Jan 1993	18:31
Cap	20 Jan 1993	02:47
Aqu	22 Jan 1993	13:01
Pis	25 Jan 1993	00:48
Ari	27 Jan 1993	13:28
Tau	30 Jan 1993	01:36
Gem	1 Feb 1993	11:13
Can	3 Feb 1993	16:56
Leo	5 Feb 1993	18:51
Vir	7 Feb 1993	18:29
Lib	9 Feb 1993	17:58
Sco	11 Feb 1993	19:24
Sag	14 Feb 1993	00:09
Cap	16 Feb 1993	08:21
Aqu	18 Feb 1993	19:05
Pis	21 Feb 1993	07:12
Ari	23 Feb 1993	19:50
Tau	26 Feb 1993	08:11
Gem	28 Feb 1993	18:52
Can	3 Mar 1993	02:15
Vir	7 Mar 1993	05:52
Lib	9 Mar 1993	04:46
Sco	11 Mar 1993	04:40
Sag	13 Mar 1993	07:34
Cap	15 Mar 1993	14:29
Aqu	18 Mar 1993	00:53
Pis	20 Mar 1993	13:11
Ari	23 Mar 1993	01:51
Tau	25 Mar 1993	13:59
Gem	28 Mar 1993	00:47
Can	30 Mar 1993	09:13
Leo	1 Apr 1993	14:20
Vir	3 Apr 1993	16:10
Lib	5 Apr 1993	15:54
Sco	7 Apr 1993	15:32
Sag	9 Apr 1993	17:10
Cap	11 Apr 1993	22:25
Aqu	14 Apr 1993	07:36
Pis	16 Apr 1993	19:33
Ari	19 Apr 1993	08:14
Tau	21 Apr 1993	20:07
Gem	24 Apr 1993	06:27
Can	26 Apr 1993	14:45
Leo	28 Apr 1993	20:39
Vir	30 Apr 1993	23:59

Lib	3 May 1993	01:19
Sco	5 May 1993	01:57
Sag	7 May 1993	03:35
Cap	9 May 1993	07:51
Aqu	11 May 1993	15:44
Pis	14 May 1993	02:51
Ari	16 May 1993	15:24
Tau	19 May 1993	03:16
Gem	21 May 1993	13:06
Can	23 May 1993	20:38
Leo	26 May 1993	02:02
Vir	28 May 1993	05:46
Lib	30 May 1993	08:18
Sco	1 Jun 1993	10:23
Sag	3 Jun 1993	13:02
Cap	5 Jun 1993	17:26
Aqu	8 Jun 1993	00:40
Pis	10 Jun 1993	10:57
Ari	12 Jun 1993	23:14
Tau	15 Jun 1993	11:18
Gem	17 Jun 1993	21:11
Can	20 Jun 1993	04:05
Leo	22 Jun 1993	08:26
Vir	24 Jun 1993	11:18
Lib	26 Jun 1993	13:46
Sco	28 Jun 1993	16:37
Sag	30 Jun 1993	20:28
Cap	3 Jul 1993	01:49
Aqu	5 Jul 1993	09:15
Pis	7 Jul 1993	19:10
Ari	10 Jul 1993	07:11
Tau	12 Jul 1993	19:37
Gem	15 Jul 1993	06:06
Can	17 Jul 1993	13:06
Leo	19 Jul 1993	16:47
Vir	21 Jul 1993	18:24
Lib	23 Jul 1993	19:40
Sco	25 Jul 1993	22:01
Sag	28 Jul 1993	02:13
Cap	30 Jul 1993	08:27
Aqu	1 Aug 1993	16:37
Pis	4 Aug 1993	02:44
Ari	6 Aug 1993	14:39
Tau	9 Aug 1993	03:22
Gem	11 Aug 1993	14:46
Can	13 Aug 1993	22:45
Leo	16 Aug 1993	02:42
Vir	18 Aug 1993	03:40
Lib	20 Aug 1993	03:35
Sco	22 Aug 1993	04:28
Sag	24 Aug 1993	07:46
Cap	26 Aug 1993	13:58
Aqu	28 Aug 1993	22:42
Pis	31 Aug 1993	09:19

Ari	2 Sep 1993	21:21
Tau	5 Sep 1993	10:09
Gem	7 Sep 1993	22:15
Can	10 Sep 1993	07:36
Leo	12 Sep 1993	12:50
Vir	14 Sep 1993	14:19
Lib	16 Sep 1993	13:44
Sco	18 Sep 1993	13:15
Sag	20 Sep 1993	14:54
Cap	22 Sep 1993	19:54
Aqu	25 Sep 1993	04:19
Pis	27 Sep 1993	15:13
Ari	30 Sep 1993	03:29
Tau	2 Oct 1993	16:13
Gem	5 Oct 1993	04:26
Can	7 Oct 1993	14:41
Leo	9 Oct 1993	21:32
Vir	12 Oct 1993	00:34
Lib	14 Oct 1993	00:47
Sco	16 Oct 1993	00:01
Sag	18 Oct 1993	00:24
Cap	20 Oct 1993	03:43
Aqu	22 Oct 1993	10:50
Pis	24 Oct 1993	21:18
Ari	27 Oct 1993	09:39
Tau	29 Oct 1993	22:20
Gem	1 Nov 1993	10:12
Can	3 Nov 1993	20:24
Leo	6 Nov 1993	04:06
Vir	8 Nov 1993	08:46
Lib	10 Nov 1993	10:41
Sco	12 Nov 1993	10:59
Sag	14 Nov 1993	11:21
Cap	16 Nov 1993	13:35
Aqu	18 Nov 1993	19:08
Pis	21 Nov 1993	04:28
Ari	23 Nov 1993	16:30
Tau	26 Nov 1993	05:14
Gem	28 Nov 1993	16:47
Can	1 Dec 1993	02:16
Leo	3 Dec 1993	09:32
Vir	5 Dec 1993	14:42
Lib	7 Dec 1993	18:03
Sco	9 Dec 1993	20:04
Sag	11 Dec 1993	21:39
Cap	14 Dec 1993	00:07
Aqu	16 Dec 1993	04:52
Pis	18 Dec 1993	13:00
Ari	21 Dec 1993	00:19
Tau	23 Dec 1993	13:04
Gem	26 Dec 1993	00:45
Can	28 Dec 1993	09:45
Leo	30 Dec 1993	15:59

Moon Signs

1994

Vir	1 Jan 1994	20:14
Lib	3 Jan 1994	23:31
Sco	6 Jan 1994	02:29
Sag	8 Jan 1994	05:34
Cap	10 Jan 1994	09:16
Aqu	12 Jan 1994	14:26
Pis	14 Jan 1994	22:04
Ari	17 Jan 1994	08:42
Tau	19 Jan 1994	21:22
Gem	22 Jan 1994	09:34
Can	24 Jan 1994	18:55
Leo	27 Jan 1994	00:37
Vir	29 Jan 1994	03:38
Lib	31 Jan 1994	05:34
Sco	2 Feb 1994	07:49
Sag	4 Feb 1994	11:15
Cap	6 Feb 1994	16:02
Aqu	8 Feb 1994	22:17
Pis	11 Feb 1994	06:23
Ari	13 Feb 1994	16:49
Tau	16 Feb 1994	05:20
Gem	18 Feb 1994	18:05
Can	21 Feb 1994	04:27
Leo	23 Feb 1994	10:46
Vir	25 Feb 1994	13:26
Lib	27 Feb 1994	14:06
Sco	1 Mar 1994	14:43
Sag	3 Mar 1994	16:54
Cap	5 Mar 1994	21:25
Aqu	8 Mar 1994	04:15
Pis	10 Mar 1994	13:10
Ari	12 Mar 1994	23:59
Tau	15 Mar 1994	12:27
Gem	18 Mar 1994	01:28
Can	20 Mar 1994	12:52
Leo	22 Mar 1994	20:38
Vir	25 Mar 1994	00:12
Lib	27 Mar 1994	00:46
Sco	29 Mar 1994	00:15
Sag	31 Mar 1994	00:42
Cap	2 Apr 1994	03:38
Aqu	4 Apr 1994	09:46
Pis	6 Apr 1994	18:51
Ari	9 Apr 1994	06:09
Tau	11 Apr 1994	18:47
Gem	14 Apr 1994	07:47
Can	16 Apr 1994	19:40
Leo	19 Apr 1994	04:44
Vir	21 Apr 1994	09:57
Lib	23 Apr 1994	11:39
Sco	25 Apr 1994	11:18
Sag	27 Apr 1994	10:49
Cap	29 Apr 1994	12:06
Aqu	1 May 1994	16:35
Pis	4 May 1994	00:48
Ari	6 May 1994	12:02
Tau	9 May 1994	00:50
Gem	11 May 1994	13:43
Can	14 May 1994	01:26
Leo	16 May 1994	10:57
Vir	18 May 1994	17:30
Lib	20 May 1994	20:54
Sco	22 May 1994	21:50
Sag	24 May 1994	21:43
Cap	26 May 1994	22:18
Aqu	29 May 1994	01:20
Pis	31 May 1994	08:04
Ari	2 Jun 1994	18:31
Tau	5 Jun 1994	07:14
Gem	7 Jun 1994	20:03
Can	10 Jun 1994	07:21
Leo	12 Jun 1994	16:28
Vir	14 Jun 1994	23:15
Lib	17 Jun 1994	03:47
Sco	19 Jun 1994	06:20
Sag	21 Jun 1994	07:32
Cap	23 Jun 1994	08:37
Aqu	25 Jun 1994	11:10
Pis	27 Jun 1994	16:44
Ari	30 Jun 1994	02:07
Tau	2 Jul 1994	14:23
Gem	5 Jul 1994	03:12
Can	7 Jul 1994	14:17
Leo	9 Jul 1994	22:42
Vir	12 Jul 1994	04:48
Lib	14 Jul 1994	09:14
Sco	16 Jul 1994	12:34
Sag	18 Jul 1994	15:09
Cap	20 Jul 1994	17:30
Aqu	22 Jul 1994	20:39
Pis	25 Jul 1994	01:57
Ari	27 Jul 1994	10:31
Tau	29 Jul 1994	22:13
Gem	1 Aug 1994	11:04
Can	3 Aug 1994	22:21
Leo	6 Aug 1994	06:31
Vir	8 Aug 1994	11:41
Lib	10 Aug 1994	15:06
Sco	12 Aug 1994	17:56
Sag	14 Aug 1994	20:53
Cap	17 Aug 1994	00:18
Aqu	19 Aug 1994	04:34
Pis	21 Aug 1994	10:28
Ari	23 Aug 1994	18:55
Tau	26 Aug 1994	06:13
Gem	28 Aug 1994	19:07
Can	31 Aug 1994	07:00
Leo	2 Sep 1994	15:36
Vir	4 Sep 1994	20:33
Lib	6 Sep 1994	22:56
Sco	9 Sep 1994	00:26
Sag	11 Sep 1994	02:25
Cap	13 Sep 1994	05:44
Aqu	15 Sep 1994	10:43
Pis	17 Sep 1994	17:31
Ari	20 Sep 1994	02:30
Tau	22 Sep 1994	13:48
Gem	25 Sep 1994	02:41
Can	27 Sep 1994	15:11
Leo	30 Sep 1994	00:54
Vir	2 Oct 1994	06:39
Lib	4 Oct 1994	08:55
Sco	6 Oct 1994	09:22
Sag	8 Oct 1994	09:47
Cap	10 Oct 1994	11:45
Aqu	12 Oct 1994	16:10
Pis	14 Oct 1994	23:19
Ari	17 Oct 1994	08:56
Tau	19 Oct 1994	20:34
Gem	22 Oct 1994	09:27
Can	24 Oct 1994	22:15
Leo	27 Oct 1994	09:04
Vir	29 Oct 1994	16:20
Lib	31 Oct 1994	19:45
Sco	2 Nov 1994	20:19
Sag	4 Nov 1994	19:46
Cap	6 Nov 1994	20:02
Aqu	8 Nov 1994	22:49
Pis	11 Nov 1994	05:04
Ari	13 Nov 1994	14:44
Tau	16 Nov 1994	02:44
Gem	18 Nov 1994	15:41
Can	21 Nov 1994	04:21
Leo	23 Nov 1994	15:32
Vir	26 Nov 1994	00:07
Lib	28 Nov 1994	05:22
Sco	30 Nov 1994	07:21
Sag	2 Dec 1994	07:13
Cap	4 Dec 1994	06:42
Aqu	6 Dec 1994	07:52
Pis	8 Dec 1994	12:25
Ari	10 Dec 1994	21:04
Tau	13 Dec 1994	08:56
Gem	15 Dec 1994	21:59
Can	18 Dec 1994	10:24
Leo	20 Dec 1994	21:12
Vir	23 Dec 1994	06:01
Lib	25 Dec 1994	12:26
Sco	27 Dec 1994	16:17
Sag	29 Dec 1994	17:45
Cap	31 Dec 1994	17:57

Moon Signs

1995

Sign	Date	Time
Aqu	2 Jan 1995	18:39
Pis	4 Jan 1995	21:50
Ari	7 Jan 1995	04:57
Tau	9 Jan 1995	15:58
Gem	12 Jan 1995	04:57
Can	14 Jan 1995	17:20
Leo	17 Jan 1995	03:36
Vir	19 Jan 1995	11:39
Lib	21 Jan 1995	17:53
Sco	23 Jan 1995	22:31
Sag	26 Jan 1995	01:36
Cap	28 Jan 1995	03:26
Aqu	30 Jan 1995	05:03

Sign	Date	Time
Pis	1 Feb 1995	08:06
Ari	3 Feb 1995	14:13
Tau	6 Feb 1995	00:09
Gem	8 Feb 1995	12:43
Can	11 Feb 1995	01:16
Leo	13 Feb 1995	11:30
Vir	15 Feb 1995	18:51
Lib	18 Feb 1995	00:00
Sco	20 Feb 1995	03:55
Sag	22 Feb 1995	07:12
Cap	24 Feb 1995	10:10
Aqu	26 Feb 1995	13:14
Pis	28 Feb 1995	17:16

Sign	Date	Time
Ari	2 Mar 1995	23:31
Tau	5 Mar 1995	08:51
Gem	7 Mar 1995	20:55
Can	10 Mar 1995	09:40
Leo	12 Mar 1995	20:27
Vir	15 Mar 1995	03:54
Lib	17 Mar 1995	08:17
Sco	19 Mar 1995	10:52
Sag	21 Mar 1995	12:57
Cap	23 Mar 1995	15:31
Aqu	25 Mar 1995	19:09
Pis	28 Mar 1995	00:18
Ari	30 Mar 1995	07:26

Sign	Date	Time
Tau	1 Apr 1995	16:58
Gem	4 Apr 1995	04:49
Can	6 Apr 1995	17:40
Leo	9 Apr 1995	05:15
Vir	11 Apr 1995	13:37
Lib	13 Apr 1995	18:20
Sco	15 Apr 1995	20:12
Sag	17 Apr 1995	20:51
Cap	19 Apr 1995	21:54
Aqu	22 Apr 1995	00:39
Pis	24 Apr 1995	05:50
Ari	26 Apr 1995	13:41
Tau	28 Apr 1995	23:53

Sign	Date	Time
Gem	1 May 1995	11:53
Can	4 May 1995	00:44
Leo	6 May 1995	12:54
Vir	8 May 1995	22:32
Lib	11 May 1995	04:29
Sco	13 May 1995	06:53
Sag	15 May 1995	06:58
Cap	17 May 1995	06:35
Aqu	19 May 1995	07:40
Pis	21 May 1995	11:41
Ari	23 May 1995	19:13
Tau	26 May 1995	05:46
Gem	28 May 1995	18:07
Can	31 May 1995	06:59

Sign	Date	Time
Leo	2 Jun 1995	19:17
Vir	5 Jun 1995	05:46
Lib	7 Jun 1995	13:11
Sco	9 Jun 1995	17:03
Sag	11 Jun 1995	17:49
Cap	13 Jun 1995	17:05
Aqu	15 Jun 1995	16:52
Pis	17 Jun 1995	19:13
Ari	20 Jun 1995	01:30
Tau	22 Jun 1995	11:36
Gem	25 Jun 1995	00:02
Can	27 Jun 1995	12:56
Leo	30 Jun 1995	01:01

Sign	Date	Time
Vir	2 Jul 1995	11:35
Lib	4 Jul 1995	19:54
Sco	7 Jul 1995	01:17
Sag	9 Jul 1995	03:37
Cap	11 Jul 1995	03:43
Aqu	13 Jul 1995	03:21
Pis	15 Jul 1995	04:37
Ari	17 Jul 1995	09:24
Tau	19 Jul 1995	18:20
Gem	22 Jul 1995	06:23
Can	24 Jul 1995	19:16
Leo	27 Jul 1995	07:06
Vir	29 Jul 1995	17:12

Sign	Date	Time
Lib	1 Aug 1995	01:23
Sco	3 Aug 1995	07:29
Sag	5 Aug 1995	11:13
Cap	7 Aug 1995	12:51
Aqu	9 Aug 1995	13:28
Pis	11 Aug 1995	14:47
Ari	13 Aug 1995	18:41
Tau	16 Aug 1995	02:26
Gem	18 Aug 1995	13:40
Can	21 Aug 1995	02:23
Leo	23 Aug 1995	14:12
Vir	25 Aug 1995	23:50
Lib	28 Aug 1995	07:15
Sco	30 Aug 1995	12:50

Sign	Date	Time
Sag	1 Sep 1995	16:56
Cap	3 Sep 1995	19:44
Aqu	5 Sep 1995	21:47
Pis	8 Sep 1995	00:09
Ari	10 Sep 1995	04:14
Tau	12 Sep 1995	11:22
Gem	14 Sep 1995	21:48
Can	17 Sep 1995	10:15
Leo	19 Sep 1995	22:19
Vir	22 Sep 1995	08:01
Lib	24 Sep 1995	14:49
Sco	26 Sep 1995	19:20
Sag	28 Sep 1995	22:30

Sign	Date	Time
Cap	1 Oct 1995	01:10
Aqu	3 Oct 1995	03:59
Pis	5 Oct 1995	07:35
Ari	7 Oct 1995	12:42
Tau	9 Oct 1995	20:05
Gem	12 Oct 1995	06:09
Can	14 Oct 1995	18:20
Leo	17 Oct 1995	06:46
Vir	19 Oct 1995	17:11
Lib	22 Oct 1995	00:14
Sco	24 Oct 1995	04:06
Sag	26 Oct 1995	05:56
Cap	28 Oct 1995	07:15
Aqu	30 Oct 1995	09:24

Sign	Date	Time
Pis	1 Nov 1995	13:18
Ari	3 Nov 1995	19:21
Tau	6 Nov 1995	03:35
Gem	8 Nov 1995	13:55
Can	11 Nov 1995	01:57
Leo	13 Nov 1995	14:37
Vir	16 Nov 1995	02:01
Lib	18 Nov 1995	10:16
Sco	20 Nov 1995	14:39
Sag	22 Nov 1995	15:56
Cap	24 Nov 1995	15:48
Aqu	26 Nov 1995	16:15
Pis	28 Nov 1995	18:59

Sign	Date	Time
Ari	1 Dec 1995	00:52
Tau	3 Dec 1995	09:40
Gem	5 Dec 1995	20:34
Can	8 Dec 1995	08:44
Leo	10 Dec 1995	21:24
Vir	13 Dec 1995	09:26
Lib	15 Dec 1995	19:08
Sco	18 Dec 1995	01:05
Sag	20 Dec 1995	03:12
Cap	22 Dec 1995	02:46
Aqu	24 Dec 1995	01:52
Pis	26 Dec 1995	02:46
Ari	28 Dec 1995	07:06
Tau	30 Dec 1995	15:21

Moon Signs

1996

Gem	2 Jan 1996	02:29
Can	4 Jan 1996	14:56
Leo	7 Jan 1996	03:30
Vir	9 Jan 1996	15:29
Lib	12 Jan 1996	01:54
Sco	14 Jan 1996	09:29
Sag	16 Jan 1996	13:23
Cap	18 Jan 1996	14:06
Aqu	20 Jan 1996	13:14
Pis	22 Jan 1996	13:03
Ari	24 Jan 1996	15:37
Tau	26 Jan 1996	22:17
Gem	29 Jan 1996	08:42
Can	31 Jan 1996	21:10

Leo	3 Feb 1996	09:45
Vir	5 Feb 1996	21:22
Lib	8 Feb 1996	07:29
Sco	10 Feb 1996	15:34
Sag	12 Feb 1996	20:57
Cap	14 Feb 1996	23:28
Aqu	16 Feb 1996	23:59
Pis	19 Feb 1996	00:09
Ari	21 Feb 1996	01:59
Tau	23 Feb 1996	07:08
Gem	25 Feb 1996	16:14
Can	28 Feb 1996	04:10

Leo	1 Mar 1996	16:47
Vir	4 Mar 1996	04:12
Lib	6 Mar 1996	13:39
Sco	8 Mar 1996	21:04
Sag	11 Mar 1996	02:31
Cap	13 Mar 1996	06:07
Aqu	15 Mar 1996	08:15
Pis	17 Mar 1996	09:50
Ari	19 Mar 1996	12:16
Tau	21 Mar 1996	16:59
Gem	24 Mar 1996	01:00
Can	26 Mar 1996	12:06
Leo	29 Mar 1996	00:36
Vir	31 Mar 1996	12:13

Lib	2 Apr 1996	21:25
Sco	5 Apr 1996	03:56
Sag	7 Apr 1996	08:21
Cap	9 Apr 1996	11:29
Aqu	11 Apr 1996	14:09
Pis	13 Apr 1996	16:59
Ari	15 Apr 1996	20:43
Tau	18 Apr 1996	02:06
Gem	20 Apr 1996	09:54
Can	22 Apr 1996	20:25
Leo	25 Apr 1996	08:44
Vir	27 Apr 1996	20:48
Lib	30 Apr 1996	06:26

Sco	2 May 1996	12:41
Sag	4 May 1996	16:04
Cap	6 May 1996	17:53
Aqu	8 May 1996	19:39
Pis	10 May 1996	22:29
Ari	13 May 1996	03:00
Tau	15 May 1996	09:24
Gem	17 May 1996	17:47
Can	20 May 1996	04:16
Leo	22 May 1996	16:28
Vir	25 May 1996	04:58
Lib	27 May 1996	15:32
Sco	29 May 1996	22:29

Sag	1 Jun 1996	01:41
Cap	3 Jun 1996	02:28
Aqu	5 Jun 1996	02:45
Pis	7 Jun 1996	04:19
Ari	9 Jun 1996	08:23
Tau	11 Jun 1996	15:11
Gem	14 Jun 1996	00:16
Can	16 Jun 1996	11:08
Leo	18 Jun 1996	23:21
Vir	21 Jun 1996	12:06
Lib	23 Jun 1996	23:36
Sco	26 Jun 1996	07:52
Sag	28 Jun 1996	11:59
Cap	30 Jun 1996	12:46

Aqu	2 Jul 1996	12:05
Pis	4 Jul 1996	12:07
Ari	6 Jul 1996	14:42
Tau	8 Jul 1996	20:44
Gem	11 Jul 1996	05:52
Can	13 Jul 1996	17:08
Leo	16 Jul 1996	05:31
Vir	18 Jul 1996	18:16
Lib	21 Jul 1996	06:13
Sco	23 Jul 1996	15:42
Sag	25 Jul 1996	21:22
Cap	27 Jul 1996	23:16
Aqu	29 Jul 1996	22:47
Pis	31 Jul 1996	22:01

Ari	2 Aug 1996	23:06
Tau	5 Aug 1996	03:34
Gem	7 Aug 1996	11:49
Can	9 Aug 1996	22:57
Leo	12 Aug 1996	11:29
Vir	15 Aug 1996	00:07
Lib	17 Aug 1996	11:54
Sco	19 Aug 1996	21:49
Sag	22 Aug 1996	04:47
Cap	24 Aug 1996	08:21
Aqu	26 Aug 1996	09:10
Pis	28 Aug 1996	08:49
Ari	30 Aug 1996	09:15

Tau	1 Sep 1996	12:21
Gem	3 Sep 1996	19:08
Can	6 Sep 1996	05:29
Leo	8 Sep 1996	17:54
Vir	11 Sep 1996	06:28
Lib	13 Sep 1996	17:51
Sco	16 Sep 1996	03:19
Sag	18 Sep 1996	10:29
Cap	20 Sep 1996	15:11
Aqu	22 Sep 1996	17:39
Pis	24 Sep 1996	18:43
Ari	26 Sep 1996	19:45
Tau	28 Sep 1996	22:24

Gem	1 Oct 1996	04:02
Can	3 Oct 1996	13:15
Leo	6 Oct 1996	01:11
Vir	8 Oct 1996	13:48
Lib	11 Oct 1996	00:59
Sco	13 Oct 1996	09:44
Sag	15 Oct 1996	16:06
Cap	17 Oct 1996	20:36
Aqu	19 Oct 1996	23:50
Pis	22 Oct 1996	02:22
Ari	24 Oct 1996	04:50
Tau	26 Oct 1996	08:11
Gem	28 Oct 1996	13:35
Can	30 Oct 1996	21:57

Leo	2 Nov 1996	09:16
Vir	4 Nov 1996	21:56
Lib	7 Nov 1996	09:27
Sco	9 Nov 1996	18:01
Sag	11 Nov 1996	23:25
Cap	14 Nov 1996	02:43
Aqu	16 Nov 1996	05:14
Pis	18 Nov 1996	08:00
Ari	20 Nov 1996	11:34
Tau	22 Nov 1996	16:12
Gem	24 Nov 1996	22:20
Can	27 Nov 1996	06:37
Leo	29 Nov 1996	17:29

Vir	2 Dec 1996	06:10
Lib	4 Dec 1996	18:23
Sco	7 Dec 1996	03:37
Sag	9 Dec 1996	08:57
Cap	11 Dec 1996	11:13
Aqu	13 Dec 1996	12:14
Pis	15 Dec 1996	13:44
Ari	17 Dec 1996	16:55
Tau	19 Dec 1996	22:10
Gem	22 Dec 1996	05:17
Can	24 Dec 1996	14:14
Leo	27 Dec 1996	01:09
Vir	29 Dec 1996	13:44

Moon Signs

1997

Sign	Date	Time
Lib	1 Jan 1997	02:31
Sco	3 Jan 1997	13:00
Sag	5 Jan 1997	19:26
Cap	7 Jan 1997	21:53
Aqu	9 Jan 1997	21:59
Pis	11 Jan 1997	21:51
Ari	13 Jan 1997	23:22
Tau	16 Jan 1997	03:40
Gem	18 Jan 1997	10:53
Can	20 Jan 1997	20:28
Leo	23 Jan 1997	07:50
Vir	25 Jan 1997	20:26
Lib	28 Jan 1997	09:20
Sco	30 Jan 1997	20:47
Sag	2 Feb 1997	04:50
Cap	4 Feb 1997	08:43
Aqu	6 Feb 1997	09:20
Pis	8 Feb 1997	08:33
Ari	10 Feb 1997	08:29
Tau	12 Feb 1997	10:57
Gem	14 Feb 1997	16:53
Can	17 Feb 1997	02:13
Leo	19 Feb 1997	13:52
Vir	22 Feb 1997	02:38
Lib	24 Feb 1997	15:22
Sco	27 Feb 1997	02:55
Sag	1 Mar 1997	11:59
Cap	3 Mar 1997	17:38
Aqu	5 Mar 1997	19:53
Pis	7 Mar 1997	19:56
Ari	9 Mar 1997	19:32
Tau	11 Mar 1997	20:38
Gem	14 Mar 1997	00:49
Can	16 Mar 1997	08:51
Leo	18 Mar 1997	20:08
Vir	21 Mar 1997	08:59
Lib	23 Mar 1997	21:34
Sco	26 Mar 1997	08:41
Sag	28 Mar 1997	17:39
Cap	31 Mar 1997	00:05
Aqu	2 Apr 1997	03:58
Pis	4 Apr 1997	05:42
Ari	6 Apr 1997	06:19
Tau	8 Apr 1997	07:20
Gem	10 Apr 1997	10:29
Can	12 Apr 1997	17:03
Leo	15 Apr 1997	03:22
Vir	17 Apr 1997	16:00
Lib	20 Apr 1997	04:35
Sco	22 Apr 1997	15:18
Sag	24 Apr 1997	23:30
Cap	27 Apr 1997	05:32
Aqu	29 Apr 1997	09:49

Sign	Date	Time
Pis	1 May 1997	12:49
Ari	3 May 1997	14:59
Tau	5 May 1997	17:04
Gem	7 May 1997	20:21
Can	10 May 1997	02:13
Leo	12 May 1997	11:33
Vir	14 May 1997	23:43
Lib	17 May 1997	12:26
Sco	19 May 1997	23:10
Sag	22 May 1997	06:50
Cap	24 May 1997	11:50
Aqu	26 May 1997	15:19
Pis	28 May 1997	18:17
Ari	30 May 1997	21:17
Tau	2 Jun 1997	00:39
Gem	4 Jun 1997	04:54
Can	6 Jun 1997	11:02
Leo	8 Jun 1997	19:58
Vir	11 Jun 1997	07:43
Lib	13 Jun 1997	20:35
Sco	16 Jun 1997	07:50
Sag	18 Jun 1997	15:38
Cap	20 Jun 1997	20:01
Aqu	22 Jun 1997	22:20
Pis	25 Jun 1997	00:09
Ari	27 Jun 1997	02:38
Tau	29 Jun 1997	06:23
Gem	1 Jul 1997	11:35
Can	3 Jul 1997	18:32
Leo	6 Jul 1997	03:45
Vir	8 Jul 1997	15:21
Lib	11 Jul 1997	04:20
Sco	13 Jul 1997	16:20
Sag	16 Jul 1997	01:01
Cap	18 Jul 1997	05:45
Aqu	20 Jul 1997	07:28
Pis	22 Jul 1997	07:59
Ari	24 Jul 1997	09:03
Tau	26 Jul 1997	11:54
Gem	28 Jul 1997	17:04
Can	31 Jul 1997	00:38
Leo	2 Aug 1997	10:27
Vir	4 Aug 1997	22:15
Lib	7 Aug 1997	11:16
Sco	9 Aug 1997	23:49
Sag	12 Aug 1997	09:43
Cap	14 Aug 1997	15:41
Aqu	16 Aug 1997	17:58
Pis	18 Aug 1997	18:00
Ari	20 Aug 1997	17:44
Tau	22 Aug 1997	18:57
Gem	24 Aug 1997	22:57
Can	27 Aug 1997	06:10
Leo	29 Aug 1997	16:19

Sign	Date	Time
Vir	1 Sep 1997	04:27
Lib	3 Sep 1997	17:29
Sco	6 Sep 1997	06:09
Sag	8 Sep 1997	16:53
Cap	11 Sep 1997	00:21
Aqu	13 Sep 1997	04:09
Pis	15 Sep 1997	04:58
Ari	17 Sep 1997	04:24
Tau	19 Sep 1997	04:21
Gem	21 Sep 1997	06:38
Can	23 Sep 1997	12:34
Leo	25 Sep 1997	22:13
Vir	28 Sep 1997	10:27
Lib	30 Sep 1997	23:32
Sco	3 Oct 1997	11:56
Sag	5 Oct 1997	22:41
Cap	8 Oct 1997	07:03
Aqu	10 Oct 1997	12:27
Pis	12 Oct 1997	14:58
Ari	14 Oct 1997	15:24
Tau	16 Oct 1997	15:16
Gem	18 Oct 1997	16:26
Can	20 Oct 1997	20:46
Leo	23 Oct 1997	05:10
Vir	25 Oct 1997	16:59
Lib	28 Oct 1997	06:04
Sco	30 Oct 1997	18:15
Sag	2 Nov 1997	04:26
Cap	4 Nov 1997	12:30
Aqu	6 Nov 1997	18:33
Pis	8 Nov 1997	22:33
Ari	11 Nov 1997	00:43
Tau	13 Nov 1997	01:45
Gem	15 Nov 1997	03:05
Can	17 Nov 1997	06:32
Leo	19 Nov 1997	13:38
Vir	22 Nov 1997	00:33
Lib	24 Nov 1997	13:29
Sco	27 Nov 1997	01:42
Sag	29 Nov 1997	11:27
Cap	1 Dec 1997	18:38
Aqu	3 Dec 1997	23:57
Pis	6 Dec 1997	04:06
Ari	8 Dec 1997	07:23
Tau	10 Dec 1997	09:59
Gem	12 Dec 1997	12:35
Can	14 Dec 1997	16:25
Leo	16 Dec 1997	22:58
Vir	19 Dec 1997	09:00
Lib	21 Dec 1997	21:34
Sco	24 Dec 1997	10:06
Sag	26 Dec 1997	20:06
Cap	29 Dec 1997	02:47
Aqu	31 Dec 1997	06:58

Moon Signs

1998

Pis	2 Jan 1998	09:55
Ari	4 Jan 1998	12:43
Tau	6 Jan 1998	15:52
Gem	8 Jan 1998	19:42
Can	11 Jan 1998	00:43
Leo	13 Jan 1998	07:45
Vir	15 Jan 1998	17:31
Lib	18 Jan 1998	05:44
Sco	20 Jan 1998	18:34
Sag	23 Jan 1998	05:24
Cap	25 Jan 1998	12:37
Aqu	27 Jan 1998	16:26
Pis	29 Jan 1998	18:08
Ari	31 Jan 1998	19:20

Tau	2 Feb 1998	21:25
Gem	5 Feb 1998	01:09
Can	7 Feb 1998	06:57
Leo	9 Feb 1998	14:57
Vir	12 Feb 1998	01:09
Lib	14 Feb 1998	13:17
Sco	17 Feb 1998	02:12
Sag	19 Feb 1998	13:54
Cap	21 Feb 1998	22:28
Aqu	24 Feb 1998	03:09
Pis	26 Feb 1998	04:41
Ari	28 Feb 1998	04:41

Tau	2 Mar 1998	05:00
Gem	4 Mar 1998	07:14
Can	6 Mar 1998	12:27
Leo	8 Mar 1998	20:45
Vir	11 Mar 1998	07:35
Lib	13 Mar 1998	19:57
Sco	16 Mar 1998	08:50
Sag	18 Mar 1998	20:55
Cap	21 Mar 1998	06:42
Aqu	23 Mar 1998	12:59
Pis	25 Mar 1998	15:41
Ari	27 Mar 1998	15:48
Tau	29 Mar 1998	15:06
Gem	31 Mar 1998	15:38

Can	2 Apr 1998	19:09
Leo	5 Apr 1998	02:36
Vir	7 Apr 1998	13:25
Lib	10 Apr 1998	02:04
Sco	12 Apr 1998	14:55
Sag	15 Apr 1998	02:51
Cap	17 Apr 1998	13:03
Aqu	19 Apr 1998	20:40
Pis	22 Apr 1998	01:04
Ari	24 Apr 1998	02:29
Tau	26 Apr 1998	02:08
Gem	28 Apr 1998	01:56
Can	30 Apr 1998	03:57

Leo	2 May 1998	09:50
Vir	4 May 1998	19:46
Lib	7 May 1998	08:18
Sco	9 May 1998	21:09
Sag	12 May 1998	08:47
Cap	14 May 1998	18:38
Aqu	17 May 1998	02:29
Pis	19 May 1998	08:02
Ari	21 May 1998	11:04
Tau	23 May 1998	12:05
Gem	25 May 1998	12:25
Can	27 May 1998	13:59
Leo	29 May 1998	18:37

Vir	1 Jun 1998	03:21
Lib	3 Jun 1998	15:16
Sco	6 Jun 1998	04:05
Sag	8 Jun 1998	15:33
Cap	11 Jun 1998	00:49
Aqu	13 Jun 1998	08:02
Pis	15 Jun 1998	13:30
Ari	17 Jun 1998	17:22
Tau	19 Jun 1998	19:47
Gem	21 Jun 1998	21:26
Can	23 Jun 1998	23:39
Leo	26 Jun 1998	04:04
Vir	28 Jun 1998	11:55
Lib	30 Jun 1998	23:04

Sco	3 Jul 1998	11:44
Sag	5 Jul 1998	23:22
Cap	8 Jul 1998	08:26
Aqu	10 Jul 1998	14:51
Pis	12 Jul 1998	19:21
Ari	14 Jul 1998	22:44
Tau	17 Jul 1998	01:33
Gem	19 Jul 1998	04:17
Can	21 Jul 1998	07:42
Leo	23 Jul 1998	12:49
Vir	25 Jul 1998	20:34
Lib	28 Jul 1998	07:14
Sco	30 Jul 1998	19:44

Sag	2 Aug 1998	07:47
Cap	4 Aug 1998	17:17
Aqu	6 Aug 1998	23:29
Pis	9 Aug 1998	03:03
Ari	11 Aug 1998	05:10
Tau	13 Aug 1998	07:04
Gem	15 Aug 1998	09:46
Can	17 Aug 1998	13:55
Leo	19 Aug 1998	20:00
Vir	22 Aug 1998	04:21
Lib	24 Aug 1998	15:02
Sco	27 Aug 1998	03:25
Sag	29 Aug 1998	15:54

Cap	1 Sep 1998	02:21
Aqu	3 Sep 1998	09:19
Pis	5 Sep 1998	12:46
Ari	7 Sep 1998	13:51
Tau	9 Sep 1998	14:16
Gem	11 Sep 1998	15:40
Can	13 Sep 1998	19:20
Leo	16 Sep 1998	01:48
Vir	18 Sep 1998	10:52
Lib	20 Sep 1998	21:57
Sco	23 Sep 1998	10:21
Sag	25 Sep 1998	23:03
Cap	28 Sep 1998	10:28
Aqu	30 Sep 1998	18:52

Pis	2 Oct 1998	23:21
Ari	5 Oct 1998	00:30
Tau	6 Oct 1998	23:57
Gem	8 Oct 1998	23:44
Can	11 Oct 1998	01:49
Leo	13 Oct 1998	07:25
Vir	15 Oct 1998	16:32
Lib	18 Oct 1998	04:02
Sco	20 Oct 1998	16:36
Sag	23 Oct 1998	05:15
Cap	25 Oct 1998	17:04
Aqu	28 Oct 1998	02:42
Pis	30 Oct 1998	08:56

Ari	1 Nov 1998	11:25
Tau	3 Nov 1998	11:11
Gem	5 Nov 1998	10:11
Can	7 Nov 1998	10:40
Leo	9 Nov 1998	14:33
Vir	11 Nov 1998	22:37
Lib	14 Nov 1998	09:57
Sco	16 Nov 1998	22:40
Sag	19 Nov 1998	11:11
Cap	21 Nov 1998	22:44
Aqu	24 Nov 1998	08:42
Pis	26 Nov 1998	16:13
Ari	28 Nov 1998	20:32
Tau	30 Nov 1998	21:51

Gem	2 Dec 1998	21:29
Can	4 Dec 1998	21:28
Leo	6 Dec 1998	23:56
Vir	9 Dec 1998	06:21
Lib	11 Dec 1998	16:43
Sco	14 Dec 1998	05:16
Sag	16 Dec 1998	17:47
Cap	19 Dec 1998	04:54
Aqu	21 Dec 1998	14:15
Pis	23 Dec 1998	21:44
Ari	26 Dec 1998	03:02
Tau	28 Dec 1998	06:04
Gem	30 Dec 1998	07:21

Moon Signs

1999

Can	1 Jan 1999	08:15
Leo	3 Jan 1999	10:31
Vir	5 Jan 1999	15:49
Lib	8 Jan 1999	00:53
Sco	10 Jan 1999	12:48
Sag	13 Jan 1999	01:22
Cap	15 Jan 1999	12:27
Aqu	17 Jan 1999	21:10
Pis	20 Jan 1999	03:39
Ari	22 Jan 1999	08:24
Tau	24 Jan 1999	11:51
Gem	26 Jan 1999	14:28
Can	28 Jan 1999	16:56
Leo	30 Jan 1999	20:15

Vir	2 Feb 1999	01:37
Lib	4 Feb 1999	09:56
Sco	6 Feb 1999	21:06
Sag	9 Feb 1999	09:37
Cap	11 Feb 1999	21:08
Aqu	14 Feb 1999	05:56
Pis	16 Feb 1999	11:38
Ari	18 Feb 1999	15:05
Tau	20 Feb 1999	17:28
Gem	22 Feb 1999	19:53
Can	24 Feb 1999	23:08
Leo	27 Feb 1999	03:44

Vir	1 Mar 1999	10:04
Lib	3 Mar 1999	18:34
Sco	6 Mar 1999	05:21
Sag	8 Mar 1999	17:45
Cap	11 Mar 1999	05:53
Aqu	13 Mar 1999	15:30
Pis	15 Mar 1999	21:28
Ari	18 Mar 1999	00:11
Tau	20 Mar 1999	01:08
Gem	22 Mar 1999	02:05
Can	24 Mar 1999	04:33
Leo	26 Mar 1999	09:22
Vir	28 Mar 1999	16:34
Lib	31 Mar 1999	01:49

Sco	2 Apr 1999	12:48
Sag	5 Apr 1999	01:07
Cap	7 Apr 1999	13:38
Aqu	10 Apr 1999	00:22
Pis	12 Apr 1999	07:33
Ari	14 Apr 1999	10:44
Tau	16 Apr 1999	11:06
Gem	18 Apr 1999	10:39
Can	20 Apr 1999	11:28
Leo	22 Apr 1999	15:06
Vir	24 Apr 1999	22:04
Lib	27 Apr 1999	07:46
Sco	29 Apr 1999	19:12

Sag	2 May 1999	07:35
Cap	4 May 1999	20:11
Aqu	7 May 1999	07:39
Pis	9 May 1999	16:14
Ari	11 May 1999	20:51
Tau	13 May 1999	21:55
Gem	15 May 1999	21:07
Can	17 May 1999	20:39
Leo	19 May 1999	22:38
Vir	22 May 1999	04:15
Lib	24 May 1999	13:29
Sco	27 May 1999	01:04
Sag	29 May 1999	13:36

Cap	1 Jun 1999	02:04
Aqu	3 Jun 1999	13:35
Pis	5 Jun 1999	22:58
Ari	8 Jun 1999	05:07
Tau	10 Jun 1999	07:42
Gem	12 Jun 1999	07:47
Can	14 Jun 1999	07:13
Leo	16 Jun 1999	08:07
Vir	18 Jun 1999	12:13
Lib	20 Jun 1999	20:10
Sco	23 Jun 1999	07:17
Sag	25 Jun 1999	19:50
Cap	28 Jun 1999	08:11
Aqu	30 Jun 1999	19:18

Pis	3 Jul 1999	04:33
Ari	5 Jul 1999	11:19
Tau	7 Jul 1999	15:20
Gem	9 Jul 1999	16:59
Can	11 Jul 1999	17:26
Leo	13 Jul 1999	18:25
Vir	15 Jul 1999	21:39
Lib	18 Jul 1999	04:19
Sco	20 Jul 1999	14:30
Sag	23 Jul 1999	02:47
Cap	25 Jul 1999	15:07
Aqu	28 Jul 1999	01:53
Pis	30 Jul 1999	10:26

Ari	1 Aug 1999	16:46
Tau	3 Aug 1999	21:07
Gem	5 Aug 1999	23:56
Can	8 Aug 1999	01:52
Leo	10 Aug 1999	03:55
Vir	12 Aug 1999	07:21
Lib	14 Aug 1999	13:24
Sco	16 Aug 1999	22:40
Sag	19 Aug 1999	10:31
Cap	21 Aug 1999	22:58
Aqu	24 Aug 1999	09:47
Pis	26 Aug 1999	17:49
Ari	28 Aug 1999	23:07
Tau	31 Aug 1999	02:39

Gem	2 Sep 1999	05:24
Can	4 Sep 1999	08:09
Leo	6 Sep 1999	11:28
Vir	8 Sep 1999	15:56
Lib	10 Sep 1999	22:16
Sco	13 Sep 1999	07:08
Sag	15 Sep 1999	18:34
Cap	18 Sep 1999	07:12
Aqu	20 Sep 1999	18:37
Pis	23 Sep 1999	02:49
Ari	25 Sep 1999	07:32
Tau	27 Sep 1999	09:49
Gem	29 Sep 1999	11:20

Can	1 Oct 1999	13:31
Leo	3 Oct 1999	17:12
Vir	5 Oct 1999	22:39
Lib	8 Oct 1999	05:51
Sco	10 Oct 1999	15:01
Sag	13 Oct 1999	02:18
Cap	15 Oct 1999	15:02
Aqu	18 Oct 1999	03:15
Pis	20 Oct 1999	12:30
Ari	22 Oct 1999	17:40
Tau	24 Oct 1999	19:24
Gem	26 Oct 1999	19:33
Can	28 Oct 1999	20:09
Leo	30 Oct 1999	22:47

Vir	2 Nov 1999	04:07
Lib	4 Nov 1999	11:56
Sco	6 Nov 1999	21:45
Sag	9 Nov 1999	09:14
Cap	11 Nov 1999	21:59
Aqu	14 Nov 1999	10:44
Pis	16 Nov 1999	21:18
Ari	19 Nov 1999	03:55
Tau	21 Nov 1999	06:25
Gem	23 Nov 1999	06:13
Can	25 Nov 1999	05:28
Leo	27 Nov 1999	06:18
Vir	29 Nov 1999	10:11

Lib	1 Dec 1999	17:29
Sco	4 Dec 1999	03:35
Sag	6 Dec 1999	15:27
Cap	9 Dec 1999	04:12
Aqu	11 Dec 1999	16:57
Pis	14 Dec 1999	04:16
Ari	16 Dec 1999	12:28
Tau	18 Dec 1999	16:44
Gem	20 Dec 1999	17:38
Can	22 Dec 1999	16:51
Leo	24 Dec 1999	16:31
Vir	26 Dec 1999	18:33
Lib	29 Dec 1999	00:15
Sco	31 Dec 1999	09:36

Moon Signs

2000

Sign	Date	Time
Sag	2 Jan 2000	22:31
Cap	5 Jan 2000	11:23
Aqu	7 Jan 2000	23:51
Pis	10 Jan 2000	10:57
Ari	12 Jan 2000	19:47
Tau	15 Jan 2000	01:36
Gem	17 Jan 2000	04:23
Can	19 Jan 2000	05:00
Leo	21 Jan 2000	04:57
Vir	23 Jan 2000	06:06
Lib	25 Jan 2000	10:09
Sco	27 Jan 2000	18:00
Sag	30 Jan 2000	05:17
Cap	1 Feb 2000	18:09
Aqu	4 Feb 2000	06:30
Pis	6 Feb 2000	17:01
Ari	9 Feb 2000	01:16
Tau	11 Feb 2000	07:19
Gem	13 Feb 2000	11:21
Can	15 Feb 2000	13:44
Leo	17 Feb 2000	15:10
Vir	19 Feb 2000	16:53
Lib	21 Feb 2000	20:21
Sco	24 Feb 2000	02:58
Sag	26 Feb 2000	13:10
Cap	29 Feb 2000	01:44
Aqu	2 Mar 2000	14:13
Pis	5 Mar 2000	00:28
Ari	7 Mar 2000	07:53
Tau	9 Mar 2000	12:59
Gem	11 Mar 2000	16:45
Can	13 Mar 2000	19:50
Leo	15 Mar 2000	22:42
Vir	18 Mar 2000	01:48
Lib	20 Mar 2000	05:56
Sco	22 Mar 2000	12:18
Sag	24 Mar 2000	21:43
Cap	27 Mar 2000	09:50
Aqu	29 Mar 2000	22:33
Pis	1 Apr 2000	09:10
Ari	3 Apr 2000	16:20
Tau	5 Apr 2000	20:27
Gem	7 Apr 2000	22:57
Can	10 Apr 2000	01:15
Leo	12 Apr 2000	04:15
Vir	14 Apr 2000	08:18
Lib	16 Apr 2000	13:35
Sco	18 Apr 2000	20:35
Sag	21 Apr 2000	05:57
Cap	23 Apr 2000	17:46
Aqu	26 Apr 2000	06:41
Pis	28 Apr 2000	18:05
Ari	1 May 2000	01:52
Tau	3 May 2000	05:53
Gem	5 May 2000	07:22
Can	7 May 2000	08:13
Leo	9 May 2000	10:01
Vir	11 May 2000	13:41
Lib	13 May 2000	19:27
Sco	16 May 2000	03:16
Sag	18 May 2000	13:09
Cap	21 May 2000	01:00
Aqu	23 May 2000	13:59
Pis	26 May 2000	02:05
Ari	28 May 2000	11:05
Tau	30 May 2000	16:00
Gem	1 Jun 2000	17:33
Can	3 Jun 2000	17:29
Leo	5 Jun 2000	17:45
Vir	7 Jun 2000	19:57
Lib	10 Jun 2000	00:59
Sco	12 Jun 2000	08:55
Sag	14 Jun 2000	19:17
Cap	17 Jun 2000	07:26
Aqu	19 Jun 2000	20:25
Pis	22 Jun 2000	08:50
Ari	24 Jun 2000	18:54
Tau	27 Jun 2000	01:16
Gem	29 Jun 2000	03:58
Can	1 Jul 2000	04:08
Leo	3 Jul 2000	03:37
Vir	5 Jul 2000	04:19
Lib	7 Jul 2000	07:46
Sco	9 Jul 2000	14:48
Sag	12 Jul 2000	01:05
Cap	14 Jul 2000	13:27
Aqu	17 Jul 2000	02:25
Pis	19 Jul 2000	14:42
Ari	22 Jul 2000	01:07
Tau	24 Jul 2000	08:42
Gem	26 Jul 2000	12:59
Can	28 Jul 2000	14:28
Leo	30 Jul 2000	14:22
Vir	1 Aug 2000	14:27
Lib	3 Aug 2000	16:31
Sco	5 Aug 2000	22:05
Sag	8 Aug 2000	07:30
Cap	10 Aug 2000	19:43
Aqu	13 Aug 2000	08:42
Pis	15 Aug 2000	20:40
Ari	18 Aug 2000	06:42
Tau	20 Aug 2000	14:29
Gem	22 Aug 2000	19:53
Can	24 Aug 2000	22:58
Leo	27 Aug 2000	00:16
Vir	29 Aug 2000	00:54
Lib	31 Aug 2000	02:33
Sco	2 Sep 2000	06:55
Sag	4 Sep 2000	15:08
Cap	7 Sep 2000	02:46
Aqu	9 Sep 2000	15:43
Pis	12 Sep 2000	03:33
Ari	14 Sep 2000	12:58
Tau	16 Sep 2000	20:04
Gem	19 Sep 2000	01:21
Can	21 Sep 2000	05:15
Leo	23 Sep 2000	07:59
Vir	25 Sep 2000	10:01
Lib	27 Sep 2000	12:21
Sco	29 Sep 2000	16:29
Sag	1 Oct 2000	23:50
Cap	4 Oct 2000	10:42
Aqu	6 Oct 2000	23:32
Pis	9 Oct 2000	11:34
Ari	11 Oct 2000	20:49
Tau	14 Oct 2000	03:04
Gem	16 Oct 2000	07:17
Can	18 Oct 2000	10:36
Leo	20 Oct 2000	13:41
Vir	22 Oct 2000	16:51
Lib	24 Oct 2000	20:29
Sco	27 Oct 2000	01:23
Sag	29 Oct 2000	08:40
Cap	31 Oct 2000	19:01
Aqu	3 Nov 2000	07:39
Pis	5 Nov 2000	20:11
Ari	8 Nov 2000	06:01
Tau	10 Nov 2000	12:10
Gem	12 Nov 2000	15:26
Can	14 Nov 2000	17:50
Leo	16 Nov 2000	19:18
Vir	18 Nov 2000	22:15
Lib	21 Nov 2000	02:34
Sco	23 Nov 2000	08:32
Sag	25 Nov 2000	16:32
Cap	28 Nov 2000	02:56
Aqu	30 Nov 2000	15:25
Pis	3 Dec 2000	04:21
Ari	5 Dec 2000	15:15
Tau	7 Dec 2000	22:24
Gem	10 Dec 2000	01:49
Can	12 Dec 2000	02:47
Leo	14 Dec 2000	03:08
Vir	16 Dec 2000	04:29
Lib	18 Dec 2000	08:00
Sco	20 Dec 2000	14:11
Sag	22 Dec 2000	22:57
Cap	25 Dec 2000	09:53
Aqu	27 Dec 2000	22:24
Pis	30 Dec 2000	11:25